BUT FOR BIRMINGHAM

THE LOCAL

AND NATIONAL

MOVEMENTS

IN THE CIVIL

RIGHTS

STRUGGLE

Glenn T. Eskew

But for

THE

UNIVERSITY

OF NORTH

CAROLINA

PRESS

CHAPEL HILL

AND LONDON

Birmingham

Designed by April Leidig-Higgins

Set in Electra by Keystone Typesetting, Inc.

The paper in this book meets the guidelines for permanence and durability of the Committee on Production Guidelines for Book Longevity of the Council on Library Resources.

Library of Congress Cataloging-in-Publication Data

Eskew, Glenn T.   But for Birmingham : the local and national movements in the civil rights struggle / by Glenn T. Eskew.

p. cm.   Based on the author's thesis (Ph.D.)— University of Georgia, 1993. Includes bibliographical references (p.   ) and index.

ISBN 0-8078-2363-5 (cloth: alk. paper)

ISBN 0-8078-4667-8 (pbk.: alk. paper)

1. Civil rights movements—Alabama—Birmingham—History—20th century. 2. Afro-Americans—Civil rights—Alabama—Birmingham—History—20th century. 3. Civil rights movements—United States—History—20th century. 4. Afro-Americans—Civil rights—History—20th century. 5. Birmingham (Ala.)—Race relations. I. Title.

F334.B69N435   1997   97-5092

323.1'196073'0761781—dc21   CIP

01 00 99 98 97   5 4 3 2 1

Portions of this work appeared previously, in somewhat different form, as "The Freedom Ride Riot and Political Reform in Birmingham, 1961–1963," *The Alabama Review* 49, no. 3 (July 1996): 181–220, © 1996 The University of Alabama Press, and "Bombingham: Black Protest in Postwar Birmingham," *The Historian* 59, no. 2 (Winter 1997): 371–90, and are reprinted here with permission.

For my mother and father

CONTENTS

ILLUSTRATIONS

ACKNOWLEDGMENTS

While attending the National Endowment for the Humanities (NEH) Summer Institute on Teaching the History of the Southern Civil Rights Movement, I presented some of the ideas in this manuscript to my associates and received a warning from Vincent Harding about engaging in revisionist history. The professor knows well, for he speaks from experience: his own magisterial *There Is a River* once revised how scholars saw "The Black Struggle for Freedom in America." His new book, *Hope and History: Why We Must Share the Story of the Movement*, continues that earlier analysis. By nature, Harding's history is one of continuous struggle that glosses over discontinuities, levels differences, and reduces abstractions to generalities like a flooding river that has escaped its banks. Harding was concerned that my "revisionist" history of the movement might sacrifice the activist history he favored for "scholarly objectivity." Harding was right. This study strips away the romanticism surrounding the movement to tell the story of actual events as they happened. It considers the role of ideology in explaining how some African Americans accommodated segregation whereas others rebelled against the social structure. Instead of finding one long continuous struggle, this study notes discontinuity in black protest. Neither does it allow sympathy for the struggle to cloud critical analysis of the period. The effort here is to address the history of the movement in all its complexity.

Harding's work set the tone of the NEH Summer Institute, and although this study differs in its approach, it greatly benefited from the experience. The excellent faculty headed by Patricia Sullivan, Julian Bond, John Dittmer, Kathleen Cleaver, Waldo Martin, and Vincent Harding presented engaging lectures and directed lively discussions on the black freedom struggle. The W. E. B. Du Bois Institute at Harvard University hosted the five-week affair on the Cambridge campus in June and July 1995. The kind staff at Blackside, Inc., of Boston—in particular, Judy Richardson and Ceasar McDowell—supplemented the curriculum with showings of segments from the excellent television series, *Eyes on the Prize*. Special lectures by Gerald Gill, Eric Foner, Adam Fairclough, August Meier, and John Bracey, and guest appearances by George Stoney, Dorothy Burnham, Bob Zellner, Johnnie Carr, and James and Esther Jackson made the sessions remarkable. Spirited debates with participants Phyllis Boanes, David Chappell, Michael Hanchard, Stephen Messer, Chris Metress, Bill Moore, Keith Osajima, Brian Sullivan, Bob Van Dyke, Harry McKinley Williams, Sarah Willie, Peter Lau, and Larissa Smith added to the learning experience; although none of them are responsible for the analysis that follows, their comments underscored the need for a revisionist analysis of the civil rights movement.

Since joining the history faculty at Georgia State University in Atlanta in 1993, I have received only support and encouragement for my work. Department head Timothy J. Crimmins and graduate coordinator John M. Matthews have been most helpful, as have Charles Steffen, Diane Willen, Cynthia Schwenk, Mohammed Ali-Hassan, Hugh Hudson, Gary Fink, Jacqueline Rouse, and Cliff Kuhn. Special assistance was provided by Carolyn Whithers, Elizabeth Adams, Deirdre Welton, and the staff of Pullen Library. Georgia State kindly paid for the numerous photographs that are reproduced in this book.

With the new job came new teaching responsibilities that delayed the rewriting of the manuscript. Yet through it all, the good people of the University of North Carolina (UNC) Press gave me wide berth to work out the problems as I saw best. I hope the final result rewards them for their patience. In particular, David Perry has been most understanding, but also have his colleagues Lewis Bateman, Ron Maner, Stevie Champion, Myra Royal, Elizabeth Gray, and Elaine Maisner.

In addition to the two readers for the UNC Press, numerous scholars and specialists have read the manuscript—or parts of it—and offered helpful criticisms including Elizabeth Jacoway, Robin D. G. Kelley, Robert J. Norrell, Judith Stein, Merl Reed, J. Mills Thornton III, Dan Carter, and Alan Draper. I deeply appreciate their comments and assistance.

This book began life as my doctoral dissertation at the University of Georgia. Peculiar circumstances in the last half of the 1980s produced an unusually positive climate for academic growth in the history department in Athens. A promising mix of enlightened professors, enthusiastic graduate students, and benign administrators created a community of ideas that nurtured young scholars intrigued by southern history. A core group of faculty members—Numan V. Bartley, Joseph Berrigan, Jean Friedman, Eugene Genovese, William F. Holmes, John C. Inscoe, Hubert McAlexander, William S. McFeely, Robert Pratt, Emory Thomas, and Bennett H. Wall—provoked, encouraged, directed, and sustained thought on the South. They placed the region in a broad context without slighting its complex history or reducing its people to stereotypes. A select group of graduate students eagerly responded to the exciting instruction offered by the faculty in southern history. Friendships developed as theses were argued and books discussed in the spirit of constructive, scholarly debate. Camaraderie marked these special years in the department headed by Lester Stephens. The outstanding *Georgia Historical Quarterly* edited by Inscoe, Thomas G. Dyer, and Sheree H. Dendy set the standard of excellence. Access to the Southern Historical Association through Holmes, Gloria Davis, and Catheryn Tyson demonstrated the promise of the profession. This study is a product of that environment in Athens, and, though I am responsible for any errors, its strengths are directly attributable to the university's remarkable graduate program in southern history.

First and foremost my major professor, Bud Bartley, has skillfully assisted this project, which began as a thesis under his direction in 1987. His third and final doctoral student, I am honored to have worked with him. As with the other two students, James C. Cobb and Randall L. Patton, I count his influence as having been the greatest on my graduate career. I appreciate the work of my reading committee, Holmes, McFeely, Pratt, and Thomas, each of whom taught me more by their professional behavior, in social settings and in the classroom, than I can ever repay. A special thanks also go to Nash Boney, Tom Ganschow, Linda Piper, Ron Rader, Carl Vipperman, Earl Ziemke, and the late Phinizy Spalding of Georgia, and Leah Rawls Atkins, Wayne Flynt, Robert J. Jakeman, and Elizabeth Pickering of Auburn University. I am fortunate that Andrew Manis recommended my 1987 thesis to David J. Garrow, who decided to include it in his edited series, *Martin Luther King, Jr. and the Civil Rights Movement*, in 1989. Ralph Carlson published it in its entirety as the leading work in Volume 8, *Birmingham, Alabama, 1956–1963: The Black Struggle for Civil Rights*.

The Albert Einstein Institution selected my proposal for a fellowship in 1991–92 and renewed it in 1992–93, which enabled me to concentrate on the research and writing of this study. Located in Cambridge, Massachusetts, the Einstein Institution is a nonprofit organization that supports work on the strategic use of nonviolent sanctions in problems of political violence. I am in debt to the thought-provoking scholarship of Gene Sharp and appreciate the encouragement and support of Ronald M. McCarthy. Every serious researcher should receive an opportunity to work under the auspices of such a foundation. The experience was both beneficial and pleasant.

Funding from the Einstein Institution facilitated research at the John Fitzgerald Kennedy Presidential Library and the Mugar Library at Boston University. Maria and John Anthony welcomed me on my research trip up north. The excellent staff of the University of Georgia Libraries, from Inter-Library Loan to Special Collections, always responded with quick service. The brunt of the research was in the Birmingham Public Library. The staff in Southern History and the Department of Archives and Manuscripts made my work a joy. Several cheerful ladies, Yvonne Crumpler, Anne Knight, Diane Gregg, Francine Cooper, Elizabeth Wilauer, and Delores Jones, assisted me in many ways, as did archivist Dr. Marvin Y. Whiting, Don Veasey, Jim Murray, and Jim Baggett. On my periodic visits, Dr. Whiting listened to my ideas and directed me to the proper sources. A word of praise is needed for the two sainted librarians, Jessie Ham and Margaret Miller, who headed Southern History for forty years, clipped local newspapers for the vertical files, and organized the wealth of materials in the Tutwiler Collection.

Friends have supported me throughout the undertaking. My comrades Patton, Brian S. Wills, and Jonathan Bryant have discussed the issues presented in these pages over countless hours in our LeConte Hall office, drinking beers at O'Malley's, or at social gatherings in my living room. Other compatriots Wally and Robin Warren, Jennifer Lund Smith, Stanley Deaton, Andrew Chancey, Carolyn and Lewis Bashaw, Bob Mayer, Mary Gambrell Rolinson, LeeAnn Grabavoy, Chris Phillips, and Russ Duncan added to my learning experience, as did John Eglin, David Negus, and Michael Lignos. Kevin Pittard and his wife, Michele Gillespie, offered valuable criticism of the 1987 thesis. In Birmingham, people who contributed to this study in some form include Beverly Braswell, Chris King, Jim Shoemaker, Faith Benner, and Jane McRay. Lunches with my aunt, Margie McIntosh, or a trio of college buddies, Alec Harvey, Anthony Cicio, and Rob McLaughlin, broke the monotony of archival work.

The love of family members has supported me throughout the writing of this book. My sister, Becky E. Carter, and her family in Aiken, South Carolina, gave me needed refuge on several occasions, as did my brother, John R. Eskew, who allowed me to escape to New Orleans. My wife, Pamela Hall, and I were dating while I wrote the dissertation. Little did she know at the time how long the process of publication would take. To my parents I owe the greatest debt. Over the years they offered me shelter on research trips home, helped me out when necessary, and provided advice while allowing me to pursue my own objectives. As a result, I never worried for I could depend on them come what may. This volume is thus respectfully dedicated to Robert L. and Martha Bonner Eskew.

BUT FOR BIRMINGHAM

But for Birmingham,
we would not be here today.
—F. L. Shuttlesworth

Stalemate

ivil order collapsed in Birmingham, Alabama, when Bull Connor's fire hoses and police dogs failed to control the thousands of African American activists and schoolchildren who converged on the downtown business district shortly after noon on May 7, 1963. Singing freedom songs, parading with picket signs, kneeling in prayer, black folk swarmed down the streets and sidewalks through the heart of Birmingham at the height of the day. A sea of dark faces produced wave upon wave of jubilant integrationists whose light-spirited singing drowned out the chimes playing "Dixie" from the Protective Life Building. The gloved white women who normally met under the clock at Loveman's Department Store had stayed home because of the "troubles" downtown, an outcome that, coupled with the yearlong black boycott of white-owned businesses, increased the anxiety of apoplectic merchants; yet this day, those women might have seen their maids marching toward them. For white people, it appeared that Armageddon had arrived; the black masses knew it as Jubilee Day: the fear had gone. Shouts of joy blended with once sinister sirens as protesters passed patrolmen unmolested. Outmaneuvered, outmanned, the jails full, the police could do nothing. As the executives of the city's leading industries adjourned an emergency meeting and exited the chamber of commerce boardroom into the bedlam below, Birmingham's crisis became clear: the city suffered from an impasse among its disparate interests.[1]

For five weeks the Southern Christian Leadership Conference (SCLC), under the direction of the Reverend Dr. Martin Luther King Jr., had conducted protests against racial discrimination in the industrial city. King and the SCLC arrived at the behest of the Reverend Fred L. Shuttlesworth and the Alabama Christian Movement for Human Rights (ACMHR), Birmingham's indigenous civil rights movement that had struggled against segregation since 1956. National civil rights activists targeted intransigent Birmingham because of the strength of its local movement. Shuttlesworth hoped King's prestige would generate enough pressure to force the "white power structure," the movement's name for the local corporate executives and civic leaders who managed the city's political economy, to dismantle institutionalized racial discrimination. King wanted to improve his tarnished reputation as a national civil rights leader. Movement leaders organized demonstrations to attract national attention to the racial problems of the strife-torn town in order to pressure white businessmen into supporting desegregation. In response to the provocation, Commissioner of Public Safety T. Eugene "Bull" Connor provided made-to-order legal violence that, when packaged by the media as footage, photo, and story line, shocked a disbelieving nation and embarrassed a presidency that touted the American consensus of freedom and democracy.

Since April 3, 1963, scattered stories on the Birmingham campaign briefly appeared in the back pages of the nation's press. Connor's use of police dogs on April 7 warranted sensational coverage, but the superficial accounts faded quickly from view. Undeterred, activists marched on, with King being arrested on April 12. The incarceration of the prominent integrationist renewed interest in the Birmingham demonstrations, but the fits and starts of the movement reflected the inability of its leadership to manufacture the "creative tension" it believed necessary to bring to a head the pressures fighting for and against race reform.

Finally on May 2, 1963, movement organizers shifted strategy by allowing schoolchildren to march in the protests. Silently filing out of Sixteenth Street Baptist Church in rows of two, the serious youngsters burst into cheerful song once placed under arrest. Tuned to the "Old Gray Mare," they playfully taunted policemen: "I ain't scared of your jail 'cause I want

5

As a result of economic stagnation, the skyline of Birmingham changed little between 1952, when this photograph was taken, and 1963, when civil rights demonstrations brought the city to the nation's attention and forced a resolution of the country's growing racial crisis. General Photograph Collection, BPLDAM.

my freedom."[2] *Time* magazine captured the image of "the little Negro girl splendid in a newly starched dress" looking at the armed officers and calling to her friend: "Hurry, up, Lucille. If you stay behind, you won't get arrested with our group."[3] A six-year-old girl joined the seven hundred African Americans jailed that day.

Flustered by the movement's use of schoolchildren, Bull Connor fortified his defenses around Kelly Ingram Park in anticipation of renewed protests on Friday, May 3. As the singing students stepped out of the sanctuary on Sixteenth Street and crossed the expanse of the park, Connor's slickered-down firemen, standing tall in their black boots, loosed their swivel-mounted pressure hoses on the youngsters. Streams of water ripped through the line of demonstrators, spinning students down the pavement with a force strong enough to shatter windshields and strip off tree bark. Teenagers lay in the gutters, bleeding. The African American onlookers who had gathered on the fringes of the scene angrily responded to the display of brute force, throwing rocks and bricks at the white men in uniform.

Ordering out the canine corps, Bull Connor waved forward a group of white spectators: "Let those people come to the corner, sergeant. I want 'em to see the dogs work. Look at those niggers run."[4] Snapping at the end of their leashes, the German shepherds lunged at their black victims, burying their snarling teeth in the stomachs of bystanders too slow to get out of the way. Swinging billy clubs, policemen beat back the black crowd. It took five white-capped cops with ties tightly clipped to their white shirts to restrain one large black woman. She sprawled on the cement beneath the officers, one of whom pressed his knee into her neck, nightstick at the ready. The day's arrests brought the total to 1,200 behind bars.

Pictures in Saturday morning's paper sickened President John F. Kennedy, who sent his envoy, Burke Marshall, assistant attorney general for civil rights, to Birmingham to convince King to stop the demonstrations. An enthusiastic Governor George C. Wallace wired the city commission his desire to join in the defense of segregation. Although the weekend brought a decline in the size of demonstrations, it did not reduce tensions in the polarized city. A visibly restrained Bull Connor arrested the school-children who marched on Monday, May 6. The movement had filled the jail, so the commissioner commandeered the stockade at the state fair grounds as a holding pen for the protesters. Arriving in school buses, students packed it, too. Exhausted firemen and policemen, having stretched their resources to the limit, braced for the morrow.

Before darkness fell, different interest groups gathered around the city to discuss the day's events and organize for Tuesday. Many met enthusiastically, others joined in desperation, but all realized that the demonstrations had reached a climax. Birmingham stood at the breaking point. Something had to give to dislodge the logjam created by the convergence of forces struggling over race reform. For years, different segments of the city's population had sought conflicting goals, and their irreconcilable differences clashed in the streets of Birmingham.

Although members of the Alabama Christian Movement for Human Rights had met on every Monday night since 1956, this Monday, May 6, 1963, seemed different. Not only had the mass meeting attracted so many African Americans that St. James Baptist Church reached capacity hours before the service, with the spillover crowds filling nearby Thirgood and St. Luke's, but also the activists at last heard their charismatic local leaders and Martin Luther King inform them that their protracted struggle had reached its end. For seven dangerous years Shuttlesworth and his stalwart assistants—the Reverends Edward Gardner, Charles Billups, Nelson Smith, and Calvin and Abraham Woods—had pressed the indigenous movement's demands: desegregation of public accommodations and equal employment opportunity. Whereas previously the National Association for the Advancement of Colored People (NAACP) had directed protest through petitions and lawsuits, Shuttlesworth's use of direct action signaled a clear break with the traditional Negro leadership class.

The movement's objectives called for the "upgrading and hiring of Negroes on a nondiscriminatory basis throughout the industrial community of Birmingham" as well as desegregation and biracial communication.[5] How to address these goals proved the crux of the crisis. Although white people viewed the movement's demands as revolutionary, the movement proposed no revolution. The activists' requests for Negro policemen and bus drivers revealed the central desire for access to "whites only" jobs in Birmingham. By ending discrimination in the marketplace, movement members sought full integration into the existing system as consumers and commodified labor—hence the struggle to remove the race wage that paid black workers less by limiting them to inferior positions in the city's economy and to dismantle the segregated social structure that propped up the unequal system.

MANUFACTURING and the metal industries characterized metropolitan Birmingham in 1960. The census reported a total population of 634,864 for Jefferson County and 340,887 for the city of Birmingham, with 205,620 white and 135,113 black people living in the urban core. Whereas more than 65 percent of the county's population was white, 40 percent of the city's population was black. Nearly one-half of the whites employed in the metropolitan area worked as craftsmen, foremen, and operatives while nearly one-half of the black employed worked as operatives and laborers. Professionals comprised only one-seventh of the total, with nearly one-third of them white engineers. Most black professionals were schoolteachers. A growing service-consumer sector claimed more than one-third of the metropolitan economy, with women filling a majority of the clerical, sales, and service worker jobs. Much of the growth occurred in the suburbs surrounding Birmingham. Five-sixths of the people residing in the urban core also worked there, but only one-third of the suburbanites commuted to jobs in the city proper; the rest worked in the metropolitan suburbs, with a majority of men employed in mining and manufacturing and a majority of women in the burgeoning service economy.[6] As in other cities, Birmingham's urban and suburban neighborhoods reflected class differences.

Scattered about the town, black communities characterized Negro income levels. The poorest of the poor in Birmingham were black and lived on the city's southside. With an average annual income of $1,500, black laborers and maids rented houses from absentee landlords in an area that stretched from Green Springs Highway in the west to Thirty-second Street in the east. During the 1960s and 1970s urban renewal projects cleared the "blight" from Southside as the University of Alabama in Birmingham expanded its campus. A more traditional Negro neighborhood, the Tittusville community near Elyton, housed average African American families with a median income of $3,627. Slightly more than half owned their homes situated to the southwest of the old Alice blast furnace. The area included slum properties soon to be razed for a housing project and a development known as Honeysuckle Hill. Across town, the black middle class lived in the College Hills and north Smithfield section of Graymont, a formerly white community on the northern fringe of Birmingham-Southern College. With a median income of $5,281, a majority of families owned their homes. Though few laborers lived here, tradesmen, teachers, and other black professionals resided on "Dynamite Hill." Indeed, educators earned an annual median income of $6,545, on average $1,500 more than other black professionals, a reflection of the forced parity in wages for black and white teachers in the state's educational system. The city disfranchised the overwhelming majority of African Americans, and many of Birmingham's few black voters cast ballots in the Graymont Armory near Legion Field, Precinct 9, Box 1. Birmingham's black community enjoyed its own popular culture arising out of its neighborhood churches and juke joints, and the segregated cinemas, night clubs, and beer dives on Fourth Avenue and along Eighteenth Street in the black business district.[7]

Members of Birmingham's black and white semiskilled and unskilled working class lived in racially mixed areas such as North Birmingham, where foremen and operatives in the manufacturing and metal industries earned a median family income of $4,947. Nearly an equal number of people rented their homes as owned them in this nonunion industrial neighborhood near the American Cast Iron Pipe Company (ACIPCO). As with other noncraft workers, many black and white people in the community were disfranchised and a majority of those who could vote consistently opposed racial demagogues. The same was true of the Italian and black foundry workers in the western part of Birmingham. Segregated by ethnicity and race in Ensley, these operatives and laborers worked for the Tennessee Coal, Iron, and Railroad Company (TCI). Two-thirds owned homes while earning a median family income of $4,367. Largely disfranchised, the few registered Italian and black semiskilled and unskilled workers tended to support liberal candidates.[8]

Many of Birmingham's steelworkers, craftsmen, and other members of the lower middle class who worked in "whites only" jobs were registered to vote. They consistently supported conservative politicians pledged to defend segregation. In the white sections of Ensley, almost all the steelworkers made an average family wage of $6,600 and owned their homes. Only 4 of the 11,298 residents in the neighborhood were African American. A similar situation existed in East Lake, where of the combined 12,841 residents, only 2 were black people. Earning a median family income of $6,103, most of the white men were clerks, craftsmen, or salesmen while the women were homemakers or held clerical jobs. They owned their homes and many had graduated from high school.[9]

Most of Birmingham's middle class and upper middle class lived outside the municipal limits in southern Jefferson County. The old silk stocking district of Highland and Forest Parks continued to house Birmingham's in-town affluent with an annual median family income of $7,237. Here, city professionals and managers lived in comfortable houses built into the slope of Red Mountain. Along Redmont and Cliff Roads, the very red rock of the mountain's crest provided a foundation for the mansions of the millionaires. On an ore crag overlooking the city and surrounded by fiery sumac that flickered in the fall wind like flames stood the cast iron statue of Vulcan, god of fire and metal working. Bubbling below in Jones Valley were the blast furnaces of Birmingham. Over the mountain on the rolling hills to the south in Shades Valley were the bedroom suburbs of Homewood, Mountain Brook, and Vestavia Hills. Dogwood-shaded lush coves provided a naturally cool escape from the hot pavement and soot-filled skies of Birmingham. The three separate municipalities had a combined population of 48,685, of which only 2,504 were African Americans, almost all of whom lived in the old Rosedale and Oxford mining communities of Homewood. Here resided Birmingham's professional and managerial workers. The average median family income in 1960 was $10,668. A majority of adults had attended college. While the men worked the women stayed home. Most voted for Republicans and conservative Democrats. Unlike in other southern cities such as Atlanta, which had annexed Buckhead and other suburbs in 1952, Birmingham's middle class remained in privately incorporated municipalities. Corporate transplants sent to run absentee-owned industries in Birmingham moved into Homewood, Mountain Brook, and Vestavia Hills where more than one-third of the residents had been born in a different state. In contrast, only one out of fifteen had moved from out of state to the industrial suburb of Fairfield. Nearly three-fourths of the over-the-mountain neighborhoods had developed during the past decade, a reflection of the growing service-consumer economy.[10]

Most of the Big Mules—the colloquial name given to the handful of chief executives and attorneys who managed the iron and steel industries, the insurance companies, the utilities, and the banks—lived in Mountain Brook, the eighth wealthiest city in the nation in 1960 with a median family income of $14,689. Owners as well as managers of capital built brick estates along the edge of Birmingham's principal country clubs. Here, leading members of the chamber of commerce moved within elite circles in exclusive societies that operated outside the jurisdiction of city officials. Social registers mirrored the interlocking directorates that united Birmingham's corporations. Through private understanding, influential men determined local policy that conformed to the agenda of the absentee-owned corporations.[11]

As a company town of the U.S. Steel Corporation, Birmingham's iron and steel industry was controlled from corporate boardrooms in New York City and Pittsburgh where decisions were made that affected the district: decisions that protected racial discrimination in the marketplace. Industrialists derived their profits from the low price of labor, which set the South apart from the North and kept Birmingham's workforce tied to the plantation and the separate regional labor market. The use of a discriminatory race wage kept the working class divided along racial lines, with white workers earning more than black workers but both below the national scale. As an outpost in the colonial economy, Birmingham's industrial sector produced raw, unfinished materials using cheap, unskilled labor. Dominated by the iron and steel interests, the chamber of commerce articulated Birmingham's strategic policy, which conformed to the desires of U.S. Steel. No alternative group effectively challenged this rule, although the labor movement, black activists, progressives, and the lower middle class competed over nonstrategic policy, the day-to-day issues addressed through local politics. Birmingham's outside-owned industrial base, its lack of indigenous capital, and its heretofore absence of reform-minded businessmen hindered change.[12]

When George R. Leighton derided Birmingham as the "City of Perpetual Promise" in *Harper's Magazine,* he struck an exposed nerve. Nearly everyone, from the initial capitalists who had boosted Birmingham in the 1870s to the city commissioners in the 1960s, believed that the district held unlimited potential in untapped mineral wealth. What concerned people was how to participate in the inevitable industrial prosperity, not when that promise might be fulfilled. By questioning the latter, Leighton audaciously ridiculed Birmingham's civic religion, a faith held by all except the high priests of the Tennessee Coal, Iron, and Railroad Company who knew they lied when leading the liturgy of "growth." U.S. Steel bought TCI in 1907 to prevent the promise from ever being fulfilled. It never was.[13]

With most of the white middle class living over the mountain and thus unable to vote in municipal elections, and with most black people and noncraft white workers disfranchised, Birmingham's white lower middle class, the craftsmen and steelworkers, policemen and other municipal employees, shopkeepers and clerks, comprised a majority of the registered electorate in Birmingham. Out of a total urban population of 340,887, Birmingham had approximately 80,000 registrants of which half voted in 1961. Only 10 percent of the county's black population had successfully registered. Unskilled and semiskilled white workers faired little better. The peculiar political composition reinforced resistance to race reform as the white lower middle class returned to office candidates pledged to uphold segregation. Rooted in the evangelical community and institutionalized by city hall, an overarching concern with morality, Americanism, and white supremacy characterized Birmingham's civic philosophy. Through Protestant "patriotic" movements such as the True Americans and the Ku Klux Klan, various Masonic orders and federated women's clubs, the lower middle class influenced the day-to-day affairs of the larger society. Birmingham earned distinction as a city of churchgoers because of the excessive number of sanctuaries and the high rate of attendance at services and Sunday school. Prohibition and blue laws had once limited social opportunities in the fundamentalist town. Birmingham expressed a petite bourgeois mentality that had developed naturally over time.[14]

Throughout most of Birmingham's history, the interests of the industrial and financial elite and the lower middle class coalesced in a defense of racial discrimination. Although white workers held the better-paying jobs in the district, they struggled against the threat of a seemingly endless supply of cheap black labor. During unionization drives, corporations often favored black strikebreakers in a bid to upset the local labor market by playing the races against each other. With the collapse of industrial paternalism during the 1920s and 1930s, an opportunity for structural change in the system occurred. Labor leaders and liberal politicians promoted biracial unions and a politicized working class to achieve industrial democracy. With New Deal support, the broadly conceived movement gained strength among black and white people in Birmingham. Recognizing the threat, the Big Mules responded to the class-based biracial challenge by reforming the Bourbon system. The neo-Bourbons strengthened the colonial economy and reinforced the race wage. The postwar shift from economic liberalism to racial liberalism ended the biracial reform movement as it left behind an abstract concern over black civil rights. The neo-Bourbons consolidated their hold over regional politics through the Dixiecrat movement and massive resistance. Once again industries reserved the better-paying jobs for white workers. As *Time* magazine recognized in 1958, Birmingham's white community had nothing to gain from desegregation except competition with black workers over a limited number of low-wage jobs. Thus white workers viewed "desegregation less as an abstract threat to be fended off by lawyers than as a specific, bread-and-butter threat to jobs, promotions, family security."[15]

Sanctioned by the corporate structure, extralegal vigilante violence and legal police brutality maintained the status quo in race relations. The more than fifty unsolved racial bombings in the postwar period and the white mob attacks against integrationists such as Shuttlesworth and the Freedom Riders buttressed Bull Connor's official use of police brutality to defend racial norms. As long as the city's political economy rested on racial discrimination, legal and extralegal violence resisted challenges to segregation. Thus when civil rights activists took to the streets in the spring of 1963 to break the stalemate in race relations, Birmingham, unlike other southern cities, refused to negotiate. Bull Connor's brutal attempt to suppress the protests logically evolved from Birmingham's industrial heritage with its peculiar socioeconomic and political composition.

Yet several white men had recognized the need to address the movement's demands. During May attorney David Vann, whose clients included area merchants, discussed the black boycott of white businesses with civil rights leaders. He was assisted by Burke Marshall who acted as an intermediary, ferrying messages to white and black groups in a bid to open biracial communication. Marshall sought a local solution to the racial problem that excluded federal intervention. Fearing Connor and a white backlash but watching the black boycott bankrupt their businesses, several Birmingham merchants accepted an agreement worked out by Vann, Marshall, and movement leaders to desegregate their facilities but only if the city's white industrial leadership announced its support of the negotiated accord.

Working within a small circle of service-consumer economy spokesmen, local real estate executive Sidney W. Smyer promoted Marshall's compromise in order to end the demonstrations. Smyer had realized the need for race reform after Birmingham received negative publicity following the vigilante violence that greeted the Freedom Riders in 1961. With young lawyers, small businessmen, and liberal reformers, Smyer orchestrated a change in city government to ease racial tensions in Birmingham. In doing so he challenged the civic leadership of the iron and steel interests that defended the race wage and segregation. A split in the white power structure developed between those people willing to concede desegregation and those who refused to integrate. In the spring of 1963, the civil rights demonstrations exacerbated the division. Smyer advocated adjustments with the black community to prevent further erosion of Birmingham's national reputation. He so advised the Senior Citizens Committee, an unofficial group he created while president of the chamber of commerce, which represented seventy businesses employing 80 percent of the district's workforce. The Senior Citizens Committee was composed of Big Mules and was in essence what movement leaders called the white power structure. Birmingham's middle class remained silent during the disturbances, tacitly following the lead of the corporate elite. Smyer and his allies had much in common with the metropolitan business leadership in other southern cities that had led coalitions of reluctant reformers to acquiesce to demands for integration. With economic progress the goal, they sacrificed segregation for pecuniary gain.

Atlanta epitomized the transition by distancing itself from the rest of the Deep South, becoming the "city too busy to hate." Corporate intervention directed Atlanta's shift into the modern era as the service-consumer sector emerged in the postwar years. Unlike many other southern cities, Atlanta enjoyed a distinctive political economy that to a great degree local boosters controlled. Fully diversified, with transportation, financial, wholesale, and manufacturing sectors in nearly equal doses, Atlanta had experienced "healthy" development throughout the early decades of the century. Indigenous capital symbolized by Coca-Cola determined strategic policy locally, policy that promoted economic expansion at all costs. On the eve of World War II, Atlanta appeared poised for greatness. With federal dollars providing the stimulus, the corporate structure embarked on a course of phenomenal growth: Only the issue of race threatened to cloud the horizon. Determined that Atlanta would not undergo a Little Rock experience, Coca-Cola's Robert W. Woodruff led an informal coalition of progressive white businessmen that assisted Mayors William B. Hartsfield and Ivan Allen Jr. in making token race reforms. Members of the traditional Negro leadership class, including A. T. Walden of Atlanta Life Insurance, restauranteur John Wesley Dobbs, and the Reverend Martin Luther King Sr., quietly negotiated with the white power structure. Commentary favorable to desegregation by Atlanta *Constitution* editor Ralph McGill set the tone of white guilt and racial responsibility that characterized Atlanta's civic mentality. Consequently, the city weathered the civil rights movement relatively untouched by the storms that battered other southern cities. Atlanta thus epitomized the southern transition in positive race relations and provided a role model for progressive leadership in the region.[16]

Smyer in Birmingham and Woodruff in Atlanta were responding to the regional manifestation of the civil rights movement. With the collapse of industrial paternalism and the rise of the service-consumer economy in the South, African Americans organized indigenous civil rights groups to agitate for full integration into the American system. The new local movements joined a long-suffering national movement for race reform headquartered in the North. During the late 1950s and early 1960s the two distinct protest efforts coalesced, one approaching reform from the local level and the other from the national level. Together they advocated black demands for assimilation into the system.

It is increasingly clear that changes in the South's political economy contributed to the collapse of the old racial order.[17] It is also apparent that the struggle to create a new racial order in the region involved forces on the local and national levels. To understand the civil rights struggle, one must understand the intersection of the local and national movements. Historians have analyzed the civil rights struggle from the top down and the bottom up. Recent studies have offered a synthesis of the two approaches, but most have obscured the origins of the movement within a cloud of relativism that borders on ahistoricism as scholars search deeper into the past to find continuities in black protest.[18] Supporting discontinuity instead, this study analyzes ideology and argues that the civil rights movement began when local black activists in the South organized new indigenous protest groups in the 1950s and 1960s that demanded immediate and equal access to the system.[19] Headed by "race men," or, as King called them, "New Negroes," the local movements marked a departure in black protest as the new leaders appealed to a mass base by refusing to accommodate Jim Crow.[20] These local organizations aligned with a national movement that had been fighting for southern race reform for decades from its power base in the North. The two distinctive movements appealed to the federal government for relief through the courts, the halls of Congress, and the chief executive's office. The interplay of these forces combined with the resistance of southern white people marked the emergence of the civil rights movement.

In black communities across the South, indigenous protest groups rose up demanding equal access to the system. Whether or not instigated or supported externally, local people themselves mobilized for change. Charismatic leaders expressed the local concerns for civil rights. They modified the institutional framework of the black church and the shared religious culture of the black community to create a new movement culture. Aldon Morris has described the protest groups as "movement centers," with names such as the Montgomery Improvement Association, the Alabama Christian Movement for Human Rights, and the Albany Movement. When local people asked national civil rights organizations for assistance, the dynamics of indigenous protest changed with the intervention of professional activists. Organizations such as the Fellowship of Reconciliation (FOR), the Congress of Racial Equality (CORE), the Student Nonviolent Coordinating Committee (SNCC), the NAACP, and the SCLC sent staff members and resources to assist local civil rights demonstrations. Specialists brought into the community techniques, strategies, and access to other national institutions. Suddenly the isolated local movement was linked to the larger world of the national movement.[21]

The NAACP epitomized the national civil rights movement. Founded in 1909 by northern neoabolitionists, the NAACP set as its agenda the reformation of southern race relations. From its headquarters in New York City, the NAACP campaigned against lynch law, conducted voter registration drives, and supported legal challenges to the separate-but-equal ruling of *Plessy v. Ferguson* in its bid to gain first-class citizenship. In southern cities, the black elite not in sympathy with Booker T. Washington's accommodationist National Negro Business League chartered NAACP branches and supported the organization through contributions. Yet the objectives of

15

the national movement did not always resonate on the local level. The distance between the NAACP headquarters in New York City and the local chapters could also be measured in racial attitude. In Birmingham and elsewhere, the traditional Negro leadership class endorsed NAACP policies in principle but in action accommodated Jim Crow when such a position suited local interests. The national movement thus remained an external force with its own objectives that occasionally gained support from local leaders. Both parties benefited from the affiliation, but neither willingly surrendered sovereignty.[22]

Usually elitist, local NAACP chapters appealed to the traditional Negro leadership class while claiming to represent the interests of the black masses. Only during the popular front initiatives of the 1930s did the NAACP attract a mass-based following. Likewise, the plethora of black citizenship groups and voting rights clubs that organized in the 1940s and 1950s reserved membership for the black elite while voicing concern that the educated among the black masses register to vote. Common black folk had their own institutions such as the black locals of segregated unions and the southern chapters of the Universal Negro Improvement Association, but it was in the churches that the black masses felt most at home. It is little wonder, then, that preachers led the mass-based civil rights movement.[23]

For decades, black protest from the classes and the masses had followed a process of petitioning white leaders for ameliorating reforms that maintained the segregated social structure. With the civil rights struggle of the 1950s and 1960s, however, new indigenous groups championed the national movement's goals. Yet the bureaucracy of the NAACP and the stodgy and elitist nature of its local branches inhibited an aggressive response by the local NAACP leadership. Class conflict developed as the black elite defended its position in society while admitting that it did not control the black masses it claimed to represent. Unwilling to wait on the traditional Negro leadership class, the preachers in the new mass-based local movements filled the void by creating their own national movement, the SCLC.

The SCLC brought the black masses and the traditional Negro leadership class together in what appeared to be common cause for civil rights. White people viewed as monolithic the black community, which in actuality was deeply splintered by class divisions that had hindered protest movements in the past. During the 1960s contemporary black scholars routinely described the "black masses" and the elite Negro "classes." The most scathing critique came from the pen of the Howard University sociologist E. Franklin Frazier. In his seminal *Black Bourgeoisie*, Frazier castigated the traditional Negro leadership class for its disdain of the black masses. Other observers such as Louis E. Lomax and Daniel C. Thompson found similar class divisions. Nonetheless, many scholars continue to posit the arcane notion that the black community was united in its outlook and belief.[24] During the civil rights movement, the SCLC played a central role in establishing the authority of the traditional Negro leadership class over the black masses. This aspect of the civil rights story has yet to be told.

Often the national movement acted as a liaison between the local movement and the federal government. The involvement of the federal government in civil rights protests proved definitive, for only Washington had the power to restructure southern race relations through Supreme Court decisions, executive interventions, and legislative acts. The 1954 *Brown v. Board of Education* ruling was the legal precedent that announced the inevitability of desegregation. Yet the president's policy of federalism, which left race reform and the protection of civil rights workers in the hands of local authorities, and the stranglehold in Congress exercised by southern legislators underscored the difficulty of altering race relations from the top down. Nonetheless, with the push for reform from below came changes in the system from above, a direct result of the intersection of the local and national movements and the federal government in the civil rights struggle.

The SCLC brought these forces together in the streets of Birmingham, where mass protest forced the president of the United States to propose sweeping legislation that, when passed as the Civil Rights Act of 1964, ended the stalemate in national race relations by opening the system to African Americans. The pages that follow offer an analysis of this struggle.

17

CHAPTER ONE

The National Movement

B irmingham transformed the Southern Christian Leadership Conference. Civil rights activists had organized the SCLC in the aftermath of the Montgomery bus boycott as a national movement to coordinate the efforts of local protest groups. They selected the charismatic spokesman of the Montgomery Improvement Association (MIA), the Reverend Dr. Martin Luther King Jr., as president. From 1957 until 1961 the SCLC drifted without much purpose, proposing voter registration drives and offering belated assistance to student activists following the sit-ins and the Freedom Rides. With corporate foundation grants that funded the Citizenship Education Program (CEP) and the Voter Education Project (VEP), the SCLC conducted workshops to register black voters. The NAACP viewed the fledgling civil rights organization as a threat to its interests. Radical black youths thought the SCLC lacked initiative. In 1961 the Albany Movement offered the SCLC an opportunity to return to the direct action strategy that had succeeded in Montgomery. Yet, unlike the simplicity of the bus boycott, the SCLC found the movement in southwestern Georgia more complex for a variety of reasons. With the inability of the SCLC to make substantial gains in Albany, critics questioned the effectiveness of the organization. Thus on the eve of the Spring 1963 demonstrations in Birmingham, the SCLC had little to show for six years of protest work. The success of the Birmingham campaign changed all that.

Although many people date the beginning of the civil rights movement with the Montgomery bus boycott of 1955–56, a similar boycott had occurred just two years before in Baton Rouge, Louisiana. The Reverend T. J. Jemison, a charismatic minister and newcomer to the city, headed an indigenous protest effort centered in the black church. He combined activist congregations with middle-class civic groups to form an umbrella organization that coordinated a boycott of city buses. During June 1953 Baton Rouge's black community stayed off the buses until the city agreed to provide black patrons with better—yet still segregated—seating arrangements. The conservative nature of the demands reflected the transitional period in postwar black protest when black leaders advocated increased public services within the confines of Jim Crow. Jemison scheduled mass meetings to mobilize the black community behind the boycott. Modeled on church services, the meetings unified the participants, reinforced the community's resolve, kept African Americans abreast of the boycott, and raised revenues for the protest. Indeed, Baton Rouge—with its charismatic leadership style, organizational structure, and moral tenor—reflected an evolving movement culture in the South centered in the black church.[1]

Events in Montgomery, Alabama, brought the emerging reform movement to the nation's attention. For months, black civic groups headed by Jo Ann Robinson and E. D. Nixon had planned a boycott of city buses in order to achieve more equitable seating and courteous treatment on public transportation. When Rosa Parks refused to surrender her bus seat to a white patron on December 1, 1955, and was arrested for violating the city's segregation ordinance, Robinson and Nixon asked her to serve as a focal point for the protest. As Robinson printed leaflets announcing a one-day boycott of the buses, Nixon contacted the Reverend Ralph Abernathy and other ministers to enlist the black church in the December 5 event. Most African Americans stayed off the buses that morning, and that afternoon the civic leaders and ministers organized the MIA as an umbrella group and named the Reverend Dr. Martin Luther King Jr. as president.[2]

Black Montgomery embraced the boycott. Packed mass meetings demonstrated the new movement culture as charismatic leaders led the congregation of civil rights activists in singing, praying, and planning. The umbrella organizational structure of the MIA successfully brought other-wise divided elements of the black community together in common cause. Black middle-class groups such as the Women's Political Council, the Progressive Democratic Association, and the Citizens' Steering Commit-tee joined with the Interdenominational Ministerial Alliance in coordinat-ing the boycott. The black masses of maids and laborers participated by attending mass meetings, staying off the buses, and walking to work or riding in car pools created by the MIA and operated by black professionals and their wives who owned cars. Even some white women assisted the bus boycott by driving their employees to and from domestic duties.[3]

The African American unity surprised Montgomery's white power struc-ture, which tried to sow dissent in the movement by emphasizing class divisions within the black community. Yet when given the opportunity, the white officials failed to exploit divisions among the black leaders of the boycott. Feeling upstaged by King, E. D. Nixon began to distance himself from the protest. The Reverend U. J. Fields, the secretary of the MIA, resigned in June 1956, claiming that King and others in the organization's leadership had "misused" funds for personal gain. A week passed in which MIA officials ultimately resolved the conflict by having King return from a vacation in California and appear with Fields at a mass meeting. The criticism from within the MIA actually strengthened the determination of the members, who increasingly articulated a rhetoric of nonviolence.[4]

The MIA borrowed strategy from the Baton Rouge bus boycott and received assistance from the national movement. King and Abernathy re-membered the previous protest and contacted Jemison for advice. Conse-quently, during the Montgomery bus boycott the MIA adopted the car pool strategy used in Baton Rouge. Likewise, when word of the Montgomery boycott reached national civil rights groups, professional activists departed for Alabama. The FOR sent the white Reverend Glenn Smiley and the War Resister's League sent the black Bayard Rustin to Montgomery. Both organizations advocated nonviolence and Christian pacifism. Both Rustin and Smiley hoped King would become a black Gandhi who could lead a nonviolent movement for race reform in the South. To achieve this end, they and others from the national movement systematically coached King and trained local volunteers in the techniques of nonviolence as the indige-nous movement adapted the protest philosophy to suit its needs. Many white people attributed the organized racial conflict to the involvement of these external advisers and the NAACP.[5]

In response to the bus boycott and the simultaneous effort by Autherine

Lucy to desegregate the University of Alabama, state authorities targeted the NAACP in a campaign of massive resistance. For three years NAACP attorney Arthur Shores and Autherine Lucy, a Birmingham resident and graduate of Miles College, had waged a legal fight to gain admission to the state's flagship institution. In January 1956 the board of trustees bowed to the authority of federal court rulings and admitted the first African American to the university. Lucy attended classes the first week in February, but mob violence by white students and Ku Klux Klansmen provided the pretext with which the board expelled her. Alabama governor James E. Folsom attributed her actions to the NAACP and "professional outside agitators." Alabama attorney general John Patterson also blamed the desegregation attempt as well as the Montgomery bus boycott on the NAACP. He requested a temporary restraining order against the NAACP for failing to register under state law as a foreign corporation. The state circuit court issued the injunction, and rather than surrender membership lists and other information, the NAACP obeyed the court order. The legal attack effectively banned the NAACP from Alabama for eight years. Yet the defiance of state authorities and the white people who joined the ever popular citizens councils actually stiffened the resolve of the black activists.[6]

As in Baton Rouge, the Montgomery movement initially sought to ameliorate racial customs within the Jim Crow social structure. At the initial mass meeting, black Montgomery opted to stay off the buses until the city met the MIA's demands of first come, first seated within segregated sections on the bus, the hiring of black bus drivers for the routes through black sections of town, and the courteous treatment of black patrons by white bus drivers. Unlike Baton Rouge, however, the intransigence of Montgomery's white officials and the violence of white vigilantes led the MIA to alter its moderate demands and challenge the color line directly. The Montgomery bus boycott thus reflected the evolution of postwar black protest from a request for improved but segregated public services to a demand for equal access to the system.

White vigilante violence convinced the MIA to seek redress through the federal courts while the state courts assisted the white power structure in its efforts to suppress the boycott. In response to the dynamite bombing of King's house on January 30, 1956, the MIA approved attorney Fred Gray's plan to challenge the constitutionality of Montgomery's segregated seating ordinance. Filed in federal court on February 1, *Browder v. Gayle* ultimately shifted MIA strategy away from a reliance on negotiations with white city officials to an anticipated favorable ruling from the federal

courts. Using the grand jury, however, Montgomery's white power structure indicted the black leaders of the movement under Alabama's antiboycott law. Officials arrested, tried, and convicted King, but the MIA
appealed the verdict. The city petitioned the state court for a temporary
injunction that halted the MIA's car pool. Yet in light of *Brown* and other
recent decisions, the federal district court found Montgomery's segregated
seating ordinance unconstitutional. City officials appealed the ruling to the
U.S. Supreme Court, which upheld the lower court decision in *Browder
v. Gayle* on November 13, 1956. Once official notification of the ruling
reached Montgomery on December 21 and the buses were desegregated,
the MIA called off the boycott. King, Abernathy, and Smiley boarded a bus
for the first time in a year and sat up front in the formerly white section.
Three weeks later, six bombs targeted movement leaders as white vigilantes
resisted the court-ordered racial change.[7]

A national media increasingly interested in southern race relations identified King as a new leader in black America. The January 7, 1957, issue of
Time magazine featured King on the cover and included a glowing account of his activities in Montgomery. Earlier white media coverage of the
bus boycott had been limited, although black newspapers had devoted a
great deal of attention to the protest. Nonetheless, the mainstream media
increasingly played a central role in the movement by broadcasting nationally what previously had been ignored as a local story. No longer did
white violence against civil rights activists escape unnoticed. The growth of
television in the late 1950s and early 1960s expanded the coverage of the
movement. The more sensational an event, the more likely the national
coverage. The inverse was also true. Thus the media enabled the movement to present its demands for racial equality to a national audience
through sound bites and film clips. In time, the movement developed a
postmodern appearance as activists staged protests for the journalists and
television crews, proving "the medium is the message," as argued by Marshall McLuhan. Not only did Americans feel outrage when witnessing
simulated racial brutality via the television, but so did an international
audience. In an age of consensus politics and Cold War braggadocio,
abuses of American democracy made hot film footage and front-page
reading at home and abroad. With American markets expanding throughout the world, Washington was becoming more sensitive to southern race
relations.[8]

Coverage of the Montgomery bus boycott in the black press encouraged
the formation of local movements in other southern cities as black minis-

ters led an indigenous protest for civil rights reform. The lengthy struggle against bus segregation in New Orleans was typical. The first protest occurred in January 1956, and demonstrations periodically resumed until complete desegregation resulted in 1958. The Reverend A. L. Davis headed the New Orleans movement, which derived strength from students. In May 1956 students provoked a bus boycott in Tallahassee, Florida, that evolved into a mass movement led by the Reverend C. K. Steele. The next month the Reverend Fred L. Shuttlesworth formed the Alabama Christian Movement for Human Rights in Birmingham. Davis, Steele, and Shuttlesworth had watched Jemison's earlier protest in Baton Rouge and had witnessed the organizational meetings of the MIA. They borrowed strategy from these earlier boycotts. Yet as "movement centers," the protests in New Orleans, Tallahassee, and Birmingham remained locally inspired and controlled.[9]

To capitalize on the Montgomery bus boycott, northern activists assisted southern black preachers in organizing a new national movement that could unite the emerging local movement and counterbalance a passive NAACP in the South. Rustin and Smiley separately proposed to King the creation of a regional umbrella organization to assist indigenous groups in a nonviolent direct action struggle for civil rights. The two pacifists competed over strategy, with Smiley suggesting an integrated approach that would appeal to black and white activists in the South and Rustin recommending an all-black approach that would emphasize the organic nature of the protest. During 1956 and 1957 the Fellowship of Reconciliation held several meetings in Atlanta at which it conducted seminars on nonviolence. Despite the efforts of Smiley and the FOR, the black preachers followed Rustin's plans for a new national movement.[10]

The impetus behind the SCLC came from In Friendship, a group of northern activists formed in early 1956 by Rustin, Ella Baker, and Stanley Levison. Rustin was raised by Quaker grandparents in Pennsylvania, a heritage that encouraged his activism in the Young Communist League, the March on Washington movement, the FOR, and the War Resister's League. He supplemented his abilities as a teacher of nonviolence by using his enormous skills as a writer to compose position papers and to ghost essays for King and the movement. Baker was a black native of North Carolina who had lived in New York City for many years before returning to the postwar South as the NAACP director of branches. Through this position she developed valuable contacts among the traditional Negro leadership class in the region, and she learned organizational skills while

conducting NAACP membership drives. Levison was a white Jewish businessman from the city whose background as an activist and lawyer put him
in touch with powerful people in New York's left-wing community. While
his alleged communist sympathies fueled federal criticism of the movement, his dedication to social change, his legal expertise, and his abilities as
a fund-raiser contributed greatly to the cause. These three individuals directed the SCLC as advisers and staff members during the organization's
early years. Baker ultimately quit over the chauvinism of the black ministers, but Levison and Rustin continued to influence the SCLC throughout
King's life. The talents of the three members of In Friendship comple-
mented one another and the charismatic leadership of King.[11]

To make the initiative appear indigenous, Rustin consulted King on how
best to organize the black preachers. When forming In Friendship, Rustin,
Baker, and Levison had asked A. Philip Randolph to chair the group because of his reputation within the national movement. As the head of the
Brotherhood of Sleeping Car Porters and the March on Washington movement, Randolph had demonstrated a deep concern over the well-being of
black workers. Although he took a less-than-active role in organizing the
SCLC, he stressed the need for the organization to appear spontaneous
and independent. One evening in December 1956 Rustin, Baker, and
Levison gathered in New York City and debated strategy late into the night,
drafting lists of activist black leaders in the South who could issue the call
for a conference on civil rights and nonviolent protest. Rustin telephoned
the Reverend C. K. Steele of Tallahassee to see if he would make an
announcement for such a meeting, but Steele declined to act without
King's assistance. In the end, Rustin convinced King, Steele, Jemison, and
Shuttlesworth to issue the call jointly on January 3, 1957. The night before
the meeting convened, Rustin and Baker completed seven "working papers" that set the agenda for the gathering.[12]

About sixty black leaders attended the Atlanta conference on January
10–11, 1957, as Rustin, Baker, and Shuttlesworth led the discussions on the
"working papers." Church bombings in Montgomery had forced King,
Abernathy, and several other participants to return briefly to Alabama,
although they made it back to Atlanta in time to endorse the meeting's
resolutions. Rustin believed it imperative that the momentum from Montgomery be maintained, so he promoted the new organization as a vehicle
that could generate and sustain protests elsewhere in the South. The working papers proposed various forms of direct action that the black masses
could undertake. Although more militant than any previous NAACP strat-

egy in the South, the papers focused on bus boycotts and voting rights campaigns that would stress nonviolence. Reflecting this strategy, the group adopted the cumbersome name, the Southern Negro Leaders' Conference on Transportation and Nonviolent Integration, chose King as acting chairman, and sent telegrams to Washington demanding that the Eisenhower administration meet with black leaders to discuss southern compliance with the *Brown* decision. The meeting adjourned with the understanding that the temporary group would reconvene during the next month.[13]

Nearly one hundred black activists gathered in New Orleans on February 14, 1957, to formally elect King president of the new organization that they renamed the Southern Leadership Conference. Not until the August 1957 meeting would the word *Christian* be added, making the permanent title, the Southern Christian Leadership Conference. The constitution of the SCLC stated its purpose as "achieving full citizenship rights, equality, and the integration of the Negro in all aspects of American life." As an umbrella organization, the SCLC recognized the importance of cultivating associations with "other bodies whose aims and methods are closely akin to the aims and the methods of the SCLC," although it declined individual memberships in order to prevent unwanted comparisons to the NAACP. In New Orleans, King reported to the conference that the Eisenhower administration had refused the Atlanta entreaties to meet with representatives of the national movement. In response, the SCLC announced a pilgrimage whereby the ministers would go to Washington anyway and pray for a change of heart among those in the federal government. The Prayer Pilgrimage for Freedom to be held in the spring of 1957 would signify the arrival of the SCLC on the scene of the national movement.[14]

In March 1957 King joined Rustin, Randolph, and Roy Wilkins of the NAACP in a planning session for the pilgrimage to Washington, which was set for May 17, the third anniversary of the *Brown* decision. Although willing to participate in the demonstration in order to condemn the southern massive resistance that had shut down its state branches in Alabama and Louisiana, the NAACP worried about the challenge posed by the SCLC and its charismatic leader. The organizations also conflicted over protest strategy, for Wilkins disapproved of the direct action espoused by the SCLC, and King acknowledged as important only the legal work of the NAACP. Earlier King had criticized the NAACP for not giving the proceeds it raised off the Montgomery bus boycott to the MIA, although Wilkins had made sure to finance the *Browder v. Gayle* case. Thus, from the outset an uneasy competition existed between the NAACP and the SCLC.[15]

Wilkins and King cochaired the Prayer Pilgrimage for Freedom with Randolph, but the members of In Friendship—Rustin, Baker, and Levison—did the work behind the scenes. All of the prominent black leaders and celebrities of the day participated in the May 17, 1957, event, including Jackie Robinson, Harry Belafonte, Adam Clayton Powell, and Mahalia Jackson. Ella Baker publicized the pilgrimage, which drew a disappointingly small crowd to the base of the Lincoln Memorial. Levison and Rustin advised King on what to say, but in his characteristically brilliant way, the black minister developed his own speech around the phrase, "Give Us the Ballot." Although King's message echoed the legislation before Congress that would later pass as the watered-down Civil Rights Act of 1957, it also reflected the concern of the traditional Negro leadership class over winning the right to vote. In contrast to King's focus on the ballot, a militant Shuttlesworth reminded the audience that "a new voice is arising all over now—the voice of the church of a living and ruling God, unafraid, uncompromising, and unceasing. Led by her ministers, she cries out that all men are brothers and that justice and mercy must flow as the waters." Yet Shuttlesworth remained in the shadow of King, who received accolades for his 27 address. With the Prayer Pilgrimage for Freedom, King and the SCLC moved to the forefront of the national movement.[16]

Rather than follow the uncompromising radicalism of Shuttlesworth, the SCLC chose King's conservative call for the ballot in part because there were no bus boycotts to support. Indeed, the absence of direct action protests for civil rights on the local level in the South made it difficult for the SCLC to do what it had set out to do. As an umbrella organization, the SCLC had intended to assist its affiliated chapters in local protests. The nature of the assistance was never fully articulated, but the idea was to conduct workshops in nonviolent direct action. Yet instead of prolonged boycotts as in Montgomery, the indigenous movements in other southern cities such as Birmingham and Atlanta had staged one-day protests to trigger arrests and arrange court cases that could then be used to challenge the color line. With no protests to support, the SCLC searched for a reason for being. Picking up on King's call for the ballot, Levison, Baker, and Rustin fixated on voter registration drives.[17]

By centering on the ballot and not direct action protests or boycotts, the SCLC attracted unwanted comparisons to the NAACP. In Friendship had proposed for the SCLC a voter registration drive that it called the Crusade for Citizenship. In Atlanta on October 18, 1957, King explained to the SCLC executive board meeting that the SCLC's role was to coordinate "work with local agencies and especially the NAACP where it is now functioning" so that together all could work to register black voters. Yet it was apparent that the SCLC had no problem undertaking the activities once seen as the standard work of the NAACP in the Deep South, especially in the states that had outlawed the organization. Although according to King, Wilkins had "expressed joy that southern leadership had at last developed," the executive secretary of the NAACP soon rued the day that the indigenous movement had ever materialized. In response to King's announcement of a crusade, Wilkins outlined an NAACP-sponsored voter registration drive in the South that did not include the participation of the SCLC. Despite the competition, neither effort proved successful.[18]

As the SCLC's first major initiative, Baker launched the Crusade for Citizenship in 1958. To staff the voter registration drive, the conference had at first employed Rustin but realized his homosexuality would hinder his usefulness to the southern movement. The SCLC offered the position of executive director to the black educator Lucius Holsey Pitts, who declined. Finally, at the urging of Rustin, Levison, and King, Baker agreed to move to Atlanta and set up an office for the crusade but also for the SCLC. Her previous work with the NAACP had brought her in contact with indigenous leaders across the South whom she could now contact on behalf of the SCLC. Indeed, much of her earlier work had concerned voter registration campaigns, so she was familiar with the process of organizing workshops. Although Baker chafed at the SCLC's method of charismatic leadership and its informal administrative practices, she nonetheless approved of its limited voting rights strategy. Not until late 1959 did Baker advocate radical direct action. Thus, the early conservatism of the SCLC reflected Baker's own predisposition. The SCLC's top-down approach to the crusade also revealed the failure of Montgomery to generate a groundswell of popular southern black support for the civil rights struggle.[19]

The Crusade for Citizenship set the tone of the SCLC's activities from its beginnings in 1958 until the student sit-ins of 1960 shocked the organization out of its lethargy. Delays had caused the crusade to be postponed from its original kick-off date of January 20, 1958, to February 12, Abraham Lincoln's birthday. On that day, the SCLC planned mass meetings in some twenty southern cities to dramatize the grassroots support for the regional campaign. Thirteen thousand people attended the meetings on what turned out to be one of the coldest nights of the century for much of the South. King addressed a rally in Miami, Florida, calling on America to give black citizens the vote. Although SCLC members spoke at many of the mass meetings, these followers made little effort to organize local campaigns. Consequently, several weeks later the Crusade for Citizenship had registered few new black voters. Yet Baker pressed on, encouraging the local leaders to inform her of any progress and planning voting clinics for the Spring 1958 meeting of the SCLC.[20]

The agenda of the Clarksdale, Mississippi, meeting revealed the confusion over purpose that plagued the SCLC during its early years as it acted as if it were the NAACP. Although the conference ostensibly taught nonviolent direct action techniques, the May 29, 1958, meeting consisted of workshops to train activists how to teach volunteers how to register to vote. Not only did the SCLC sound like the NAACP, but also many of the delegates in attendance were officials of their local NAACP branches. Of the 190 people present, 130 were Mississippians, and of these, Dr. Aaron Henry, Amzie Moore, and Medgar Evers were top officials in that state's NAACP. The other key participants had been active NAACP members in Alabama and Louisiana before massive resistance shut down those operations. Indeed, seven of the twelve members of the SCLC administrative committee were from these two states. In true NAACP fashion, the SCLC awarded citations to those individuals who had conducted successful campaigns whether for the SCLC or for the NAACP. At Baker's urging, the former head of the recently suppressed Birmingham branch of the NAACP, W. C. Patton, conducted the principal workshop. He "emphasized the necessity of organizing on the precinct, street and block level; and that concentrated effort must be made to both increase registration and then get out the vote afterwards." Patton's analysis promoted grassroots organizing as used by the NAACP in its membership drives. Yet the SCLC had been set up as a top-down organization designed to assist indigenous movements by providing expert advice and tactical help. The SCLC had neither the staff nor the resources to build indigenous movements block by block from the bottom up. Nonetheless, such organizing was exactly what Baker had spent her time doing for the NAACP, and she carried that strategy with her into the SCLC.[21]

More in keeping with the SCLC's role as a member of the national movement was King's telegram to Dwight D. Eisenhower criticizing the president for refusing to meet with black leaders. This time, the Eisenhower administration responded to the request for a conference. On June 23, 1958, King joined Randolph, Wilkins, and Lester B. Granger of the National Urban League in a discussion with the president. The black leaders urged Eisenhower to enforce federal law in the South. They left the

White House content that they had delivered their message. The equal billing for King increased the prestige of the SCLC within the national movement, although the meeting accomplished little else.[22]

To run the SCLC office and to assist the Crusade for Citizenship, the SCLC hired the Reverend Dr. John L. Tilley as its first executive director. Baker had recommended Tilley to Levison out of the apparently mistaken belief that Tilley had been responsible for a successful voter registration drive in Baltimore, Maryland. Tilley's first act at the SCLC was to assist Baker with the Clarksdale meeting, after which he was to follow up on the crusade. To adequately prepare the SCLC's citizenship workshops, Tilley wrote the southern secretaries of state requesting the various requirements each state had for registering voters. King had promised to double the black electorate by the 1960 presidential election, so there was a need to mobilize across the South. Tilley epitomized the SCLC's new initiative. He wrote supporters, "As Christian leaders, charged with the responsibility of helping to bring abundant life to our constituencies and others, we can find no more direct and quick route to full citizenship than the full and proper use of the ballot." Despite Tilley's efforts, the SCLC failed to generate mass support for the crusade. Only $50,000 of the projected $200,000 had been raised, mostly from northern and union sources, and copies of King's account of the Montgomery bus boycott, *Stride Toward Freedom*, had been selling so poorly that Tilley surrendered the responsibilities of marketing to Baker.[23]

At the Norfolk meeting of the SCLC in October 1958, Tilley and Baker stressed the use of "psychology" to mobilize the black masses behind the movement. The SCLC attempted to overcome debilitating problems by acknowledging class conflict within the black community and by confronting competition with other civil rights groups. The objective of the meeting was to "build and strengthen bonds between the masses and the professionals in the Negro community." As one participant remarked, "There are those who feel that an almost perfect combination is formed when we join the legal competency of the NAACP with the nonviolent philosophy and the Christian emphasis of the SCLC." Despite the rhetoric, the NAACP still viewed the conference as a threat, and the black masses generally ignored the initiatives of both organizations.[24]

By the Norfolk meeting it was evident that the SCLC had been largely ineffectual, although most of its members blamed the executive director for the organization's faults. Shortly after the conference, Tilley wrote the pastors who had participated with requests for the names of churches that might want to join the SCLC. In addition to preaching at his home church in Baltimore, Tilley was asked by King to conduct a voter registration drive in Atlanta and to arrange a conference on "nonviolence and social action." Indigenous movements occasionally wrote the SCLC for help. Tilley responded to the requests for assistance with a clear explanation of SCLC objectives, a confession that suggested the problems of the organization were not all of his own making. "Our special concern is to work with interested citizens in various communities in the attempt to increase the voter-registration of Negroes and to develop a keener sense of the value of the vote for improving the status of our racial group generally." In response to a request for help, Tilley explained: "Should you wish our services, we shall be glad to work with you in the voter-registration drive, and could make available to you the services of myself or a member of our staff who has had experience in such drives, to work with you for a week or two, or longer if necessary. There will be no charge for such service. However, should you wish to cover or contribute to the cost of travel and living, incidental to such service, such would be appreciated." Tilley's almost pathetic response sounded less like an offer of assistance than a desperate bid for involvement. Indeed, the organization was looking for opportunities to get involved in order to justify its existence. The SCLC had sent Baker to Shreveport, Louisiana, to assist in a similar campaign, but her efforts and Tilley's letters were not markedly increasing SCLC activities or revenues. On his return from a tour of India, where he had studied *satyagraha* on the invitation of the Gandhi Fund, King confronted the SCLC's lackluster performance by firing Tilley. Again Baker filled the void as acting executive director.[25]

Having found little popular support to build on, the SCLC discovered that its most important asset was King himself, and so the organization promoted a "cult of personality" to capitalize on his popularity. Southern black people regularly turned out to see and hear the black Moses of the Montgomery bus boycott, whether or not they were also willing to join him in nonviolent direct action. Northern black and white people willingly contributed money to support King's work in the SCLC. Tensions developed in the Atlanta headquarters as Baker's dislike for male charismatic leadership increased and as legitimating activities declined. Although not a sham organization, the conference nonetheless suffered from a positive image that lacked substance. King's many absences increased as he spent an inordinate amount of time traveling on behalf of the SCLC. As its president, King made the final decisions on policy, but his subordinates often determined the daily routine.[26]

King brought with him into the Southern Christian Leadership Conference the prejudices of the traditional Negro leadership class. Born into a prominent African American family, educated at Morehouse College and up North, and groomed for a public life of service, King had received the best training Atlanta's black elite could offer. Not only were his father and his grandfather pillars of the traditional Negro leadership class in that city, but also it was expected that he too would join the ranks of elite black leaders. His pastorate of Montgomery's prestigious Dexter Avenue Baptist Church signified a stepping stone along the way to an existence of segregated privilege shared by a minority within the black community. That the bus boycott awoke King to the problems faced by the masses of African Americans is credit to his character, yet that protest alone did not succeed in altering the middle-class outlook of the minister. Many times King's instincts told him to support the direct action of the movement's militants, but instead he followed the advice of his father and the other more conservative members of the traditional Negro leadership class and hindered protest. Only after years of internal struggle did King finally resolve the "conservative militant" conflict and transcend the class biases that had imbued his upbringing. Indeed, in the early years of the civil rights movement, King's loyalties remained with the black elite; consequently, he played a central role in the struggle of the traditional Negro leadership class for control over the awakened black masses.[27]

In contrast, the "race men" who organized the indigenous movement on the local level often clashed with members of the traditional Negro leadership class. Many of the movement's militants arose out of the black masses and felt no loyalty to the black elite. As race men, they thrived off the class conflict within the black community. Indeed, Shuttlesworth and the local movement he led in Birmingham, the ACMHR, never attracted the support of the traditional Negro leadership class. Instead, he pitched the movement to the responsible members of the black masses who saw desegregation as the ticket to a better world. As a board member of the SCLC, Shuttlesworth encouraged the organization to adopt a more activist approach to race reform. As an indigenous leader, Shuttlesworth promoted the interests of the local movement over those of the conference. As he wrote King on the eve of the sit-ins, "When the flowery speeches have been made, we still have the hard job of getting down and helping people," warning that the SCLC "must move now, or else [be] hard put in the not too distant future, to justify our existence." The militant Shuttlesworth emphasized, "the times are far too critical for us to get good solid ideas on what should be done in certain situations, and then take too long a time to put these ideas into action." Shuttlesworth's entreaties fell on deaf ears.[28]

Throughout 1959 the SCLC drifted without much purpose. As acting executive director, Baker tried to limit the organization to clear goals, but her efforts amounted to little more than proposals for voter registration projects. She recommended that the SCLC join the Highlander Folk School and Septima O. Clark in running an adult education program that, through the training of teachers, would increase the number of black voters in the South. The Citizenship Education Program would not get under way until the summer of 1961. More in keeping with the purpose for which the SCLC had formed were the two workshops it supported on nonviolent direct action. Sixty-five black and white people attended the First South-wide Institute on Nonviolent Resistance to Segregation held for two days on the campus of Spelman College in July 1959, and more than a thousand people attended a mass meeting and institute on nonviolence in Jackson, Mississippi, organized by the Reverend James Lawson. Yet such programs were exceptions. For the most part, the SCLC promoted voter registration campaigns in Mobile, Montgomery, and Birmingham by sending out "several thousand pieces of mimeographed material."[29]

Picking up on Shuttlesworth's frustrations, Baker asked the SCLC board of directors at the Columbia, South Carolina, meeting in September 1959 two rhetorical questions: "Have we been so busy doing the things that had to be done that we have failed to [do] what *should* be done?" and "Have we really come to grips with what it takes to do the job for which the conference was organized; and are we willing to pay the price?" She then recommended that the SCLC stop holding so many meetings and start seriously evaluating its program. Although not abandoning her focus on the franchise, Baker nonetheless recognized the need for nonviolent direct action.[30]

Yet King remained committed to the ballot, as his response to Baker made clear: "Since one of the basic concerns of SCLC at the present time is that of increasing the number of Negro registered voters, we must seek to use every resource at our disposal to make this possible. Honesty impels us to admit that we have not really scratched the surface in this area." King identified the problem as a lack of "any genuine cooperation and coordination between national and local organizations working to increase the vote." As a leader in the national movement, King called on "persons directing voting campaigns in southern communities" to join the SCLC.[31]

King acknowledged Baker's concerns and voiced some of his own. He appointed a committee to develop a program for 1960 that would help the SCLC "keep a sense of direction and meet the many challenges ahead." Perhaps most important, he agreed to leave Montgomery and the MIA and return to Atlanta as associate pastor at Ebenezer Baptist Church and work directly out of the SCLC office. The only reference King made to direct action involved the hint of nonviolent protests at airport terminals where segregation remained enforced despite court rulings on interstate travel. King called for the removal of the "whites only" signs. He suggested that while the NAACP could handle the "legal phase" of the challenge, the SCLC could handle the "extra-legal" phase. "Maybe through the power of moral persuasion we will be able to save many dollars which would be necessary to fight this battle in the courts." King's cryptic comment revealed a latent desire for mass direct action using nonviolent methods. The target betrayed his elitism, but the failure to act nonetheless reflected the fomentation of this protest strategy. In time, King would realize that the value of nonviolent direct action resided not in its financial savings but in its potential for sensational media coverage. This would occur during the Birmingham demonstrations of 1963, when the SCLC dropped its concern for moral persuasion and adopted the strategy of nonviolent coercion. The last of ten resolutions ratified by the conference during the Columbia meeting reaffirmed "the principle of social change through nonviolent direct action." In 1959 the question remained how to implement that protest strategy.[32]

Continuing her critique, Baker circulated a memo on October 23, 1959, entitled "SCLC as a Crusade," in which she defined the purpose of the organization and discussed future areas of action. Baker described the SCLC as "a service agency through which autonomous bodies can achieve coordinated action and share their experiences and resources." Unlike the NAACP, the SCLC did not solicit individual memberships nor did it establish local branches. Instead, it sought "to supplement rather than duplicate the work of existing organizations." Yet the rest of the memo suggested that Baker knew that so far the SCLC had acted as if it were the NAACP, for she strongly advocated a departure in SCLC policy. Baker realized that the "SCLC must offer, basically, a different 'brand of goods,'" that fills unmet needs of the people. At the same time, it must provide for a sense of achievement and recognition for many people, particularly local leadership." Baker wanted the Crusade for Citizenship to become a grassroots crusade led by indigenous activists. She suggested different ways of recruiting activists and encouraged the SCLC to join FOR in "a program for developing action teams in nonviolent direct action." Yet despite the rhetoric and the desire for something new, Baker returned to the theme of the franchise: "The suggested projects would not prevent SCLC from continuing its program of workshops and voter registration assistance where possible; but would add to the leavening influence of our efforts and help generate more of a crusade by putting more people in motion."[33]

King echoed Baker's memo in his October 27, 1959, recommendations to the special committee evaluating the SCLC. To put rumors at rest, he emphasized "that instead of halting its activities the conference is actually expanding its activities." King called on Wilkins and the NAACP to stop sowing "seeds of dissention" and to join the SCLC in another voter registration drive. Winning the franchise remained the central goal of King, and he encouraged the conference to "select some few cities where intensified voting drives can be conducted without any resistance from state or local authorities." Having simplified the process, King then caught the contra- **35** diction and stressed that the SCLC would only "assist in [the] setting up [of] such drives. Since we are a service agency we would naturally seek to work through and coordinate the activities of already existing groups." King authorized Baker to coordinate the initiative, and she immediately contacted members of Birmingham's traditional Negro leadership class about arranging a registration drive there. She neglected to inform Shuttlesworth, although she consulted the millionaire A. G. Gaston and the Reverend J. L. Ware, both members of the black elite who had opposed the dynamics of the indigenous movement. Having failed to involve the charismatic Shuttlesworth and the ACMHR, the campaign amounted to naught.[34]

In concluding his comment, King hearkened back to the criticisms of Baker and Shuttlesworth. King noted, "while the voting drive still holds a significant place in our total program, we must not neglect other important areas. Therefore, I recommend that we begin thinking of some of the other areas that should gain our immediate attention." Three months later, in January 1960, Baker wrote the SCLC board of directors of the need for "exhaustive thinking" on the role of the Southern Christian Leadership Conference in the civil rights struggle. Within a matter of weeks, the time for thinking had passed as black students began the sit-ins and thus stole the initiative for direct action out from under the SCLC.[35]

The spontaneous decision by four young black men to sit down at the whites-only lunch counter and request service from the F. W. Woolworth store in Greensboro, North Carolina, on February 1, 1960, triggered a regional protest by black college students that reflected the rise of the new ideology of racial equality that rejected white paternalism. Whereas the bus boycotts had relied on passive forms of resistance, the sit-in movement signified the widespread adoption of nonviolent direct action by black youths across the South. Unlike many members of the traditional Negro leadership class who willingly negotiated with white leaders and accommodated Jim Crow, the students refused to compromise their demands for immediate access to the system.[36]

The black student protest surprised the national movement as much as it surprised the rest of the nation. By coincidence, Shuttlesworth was guest preaching in High Point, North Carolina, during the initial sit-ins, and his host "carried me by where these people were going to sit-in. . . . I called back to Atlanta and told Ella [Baker] what was going on. I said, 'this is the thing. You must tell Martin [King] that we must get with this, and really this can shake up the world.'" Baker informed her superiors at the SCLC, but she also notified activists on black college campuses. She asked them, "What are you all going to do? It is time to move." To assist the students, the SCLC and CORE dispatched advisers to the sit-ins to train them in nonviolence as the NAACP offered them legal help. The national movement scrambled to exploit and control the dynamic initiative.[37]

The SCLC and CORE sponsored the formation of the Student Nonviolent Coordinating Committee in April 1960 and provided valuable financial assistance to the students. After the initial sit-ins, the formerly personal and unplanned protests took on structural forms with leaders selected who notified white officials of demands for desegregation. Baker encouraged the students to form an independent national umbrella organization that could tie the various indigenous youth groups into a network for the purpose of sharing legal and financial resources. She arranged for the student leaders to gather at Shaw University in Raleigh, North Carolina, on April 15, 1960. There the black students organized SNCC. They followed Baker's advice and remained a student-led group independent of the SCLC and CORE, although the SNCC leaders quickly joined the ranks of the national movement.[38]

For most of 1960 the SCLC was in a state of disarray as it underwent major administrative changes while living off the momentum of the sit-ins by organizing workshops on nonviolence. Baker had scheduled her departure for the end of June 1960, and King was negotiating with the Reverend

Wyatt Tee Walker of the SCLC affiliate in Petersburg, Virginia, to come on board as the new executive director. During the Shaw meeting of SNCC, Baker had not hidden her dislike for King's charismatic style of leadership, for she encouraged the students to adopt a decentralized and democratic approach that promoted the leadership of local people. In contrast, after the meeting the SCLC reinforced its top-down approach while continuing to debate its purpose. King's special committee reported in May 1960 on the "future program" of the conference. Responding to the sit-ins, the report made "clear that SCLC provides spiritual, dynamic and nonviolent philosophy to [the] student movement." This was to be achieved through "nonviolent institutions" held in Petersburg, Raleigh, Orangeburg, Atlanta, Tuskegee, and Nashville. The old focus on the franchise was given a new name, "mass action registration," with voting clinics set for Shreveport, Birmingham, and Memphis. The first two locations were cities that the SCLC had mined before with limited success. In short, the sit-ins had enabled it to teach the methods of nonviolence but the organization had failed to follow up or join in the direct action, instead remaining shackled to the limited strategy of voter registration drives.[39]

As the SCLC's new executive director, Wyatt Tee Walker, built a fire under the moribund organization. The charismatic minister brought with him to the conference the same male chauvinism and ego that Baker had found so offensive in King. Consequently, the two men got along quite well. Walker had pastored the historic Gillfield Baptist Church in Petersburg. As a "race man," he had embraced the emerging indigenous movement. He staged a protest for the desegregation of the city library in June 1959, but opposition by the traditional Negro leadership class in the local chapter of the NAACP thwarted his efforts. In response, Walker organized the Petersburg Improvement Association and continued his civil rights activities. During the SCLC's meeting in Norfolk in 1958, King had considered Walker as a replacement for Tilley. In May 1960 King arranged for Walker to meet with Levison and Rustin in order to get their input. They approved, and King offered Walker the job. He accepted the position, notified his congregation in Virginia, and prepared to assume his new duties by August 1960. Rather arrogantly, Walker described himself as an "organization man" who had the "administrative skills and the characteristics of a son of a bitch who didn't care about being loved to get it done—I didn't give a damn about whether people liked me, but I knew I could do the job." What he lacked in tact, he made up for in determination. Walker brought with him from Petersburg two assistants who joined the SCLC's staff, Dorothy Cotton as secretary and James R. Wood as director of public relations. Together, the three set out to remake the conference.[40]

In his first two months as executive director, Walker restructured the SCLC's administration, reviewed its program of activities, and increased its revenues. He reported to the SCLC board of directors assembled in Shreveport on October 11, 1960, that the work had been both "fruitful and frustrating" in that much had been accomplished but much remained to be done. Walker stated that he had doubled the staff of the conference and in the process established "clear-cut lines of responsibility" and put in place "a definite chain of command." This was to end confusion over whether its decisions were made in Atlanta or New York City. In a dig at Baker, Walker informed the board that he would not "belabor" members with the "minute details as to when I report to work, and how long I take for lunch, or how many memoranda have been sent out." His fellow black Baptist ministers understood that he would run the SCLC's office just as they ran their churches, autocratically and on faith.[41]

In evaluating the SCLC's program of action, Walker admitted problems but blamed others. He claimed that one of the three institutes on non-violence had resulted in a direct action protest against segregation. Yet his efforts to promote "mass action registration" with "stand-ins" at southern courthouses had failed miserably. Walker attributed the low turnout to a "blackout" in the press, and he specifically identified the black-owned *Birmingham World* for neglecting the civil rights initiative. Walker also acknowledged that "voter registration" offered the area of "least drama and attraction and perhaps the greatest apathy." Instead, he agreed with King's concern that the SCLC "do something creative this year." So that there would be no doubt, Walker emphasized: "We make no apology for being a nonviolent, mass direct-action organization, and that we give absolute support to the student movement. Our philosophy turns on 400 persons being arrested and remaining in jail rather than to be costly by requiring 400 bail bond fees [*sic*]." His rhetoric—largely borrowed from SNCC—would change with his understanding of movement strategy.[42]

It was with money matters that Walker made his lasting contribution to the Southern Christian Leadership Conference. In his report, Walker emphasized that he was "centralizing our finances in the home office" and "establishing a system of budget controls." To increase revenues, he solicited donations, but he reported that only 5 percent of the 10,000 appeals mailed out since his arrival had netted a contribution to the SCLC. Nonetheless, with Levison, Walker would perfect this method of fund-raising.[43]

Several factors had forced the SCLC to redesign its system of bookkeeping. In early 1960 the Reverend U. J. Fields had told a grand jury in Montgomery that King's income was higher in 1958 and 1959 than reported on his state income tax returns. Responding to Alabama's tax officials, King had already agreed to pay back taxes. Nonetheless, he was forced to testify, and although a white grand jury ultimately exonerated the civil rights leader, the episode pointed to the need for better records management. Donations to the SCLC were routinely scribbled down by hand in spiral notebooks. There existed no organized method of posting receipts. Churches paid the $25 affiliation fee; individuals sent in $5 and $10 contributions, and if they were lucky, they received a letter of acknowledgment. In the early years of the conference, the money trickled in and there was little complaint about the inefficient bookkeeping. A hostile article in *Jet* magazine in late 1959 suggested that the SCLC had raised only $25,000 over its first three years of existence, a ridiculously low figure but one that hinted at the small budgets of the organization.[44]

Levison prepared King's defense on the charges of tax fraud by creating a fund-raising committee and by constructing a list of proven contributors to the SCLC who could be solicited for future donations. The King Defense Committee financed a libelous newspaper ad that resulted in the landmark U.S. Supreme Court decision of *Sullivan v. New York Times*. Over the course of the case, Shuttlesworth had his car impounded by the state of Alabama for payment of the judgment awarded to the "libeled" Montgomery city commissioners. Nevertheless, the direct mail strategy markedly increased donations to the SCLC. By August 1961, some 12,000 donors on a growing list had given the conference $80,000 at an administrative cost of only $10,000.[45] With an appeal from King following each new civil rights outrage regardless of SCLC involvement, the possibilities were virtually endless. Freedom rallies also raised money for the SCLC. In October 1960 one such mass meeting in Shreveport took in $481.59 and a rally in Cleveland, Ohio, netted $1,445.92. The rallies featured speeches by civil rights veterans and appearances by black celebrities; although they were occasional events, they generated much-needed income for the SCLC.[46]

To keep track of all the checks, bills, and loose change that entered the SCLC office, Walker introduced a "monthly budget summary" that listed anticipated and actual income and disbursements. To elaborate on expenditures, he maintained a "monthly statement of accounting." By 1962 the conference was posting weekly budget summaries. As treasurer of the SCLC, Ralph Abernathy approved of Walker's new bookkeeping. In the six months following Walker's arrival in Atlanta, the conference raised almost $200,000. In November 1960 it received $13,841.06 but spent only $8,171.05. Between November and April 1961 it took in donations totaling $69,425.19 and spent $54,958.42. The substantial increase in income can be attributed to Levison's efforts, for of the money raised during the six-month period, $30,980 came from direct mail sources. A third of the income paid SCLC salaries, with the rest going toward operating expenses such as legal fees, life insurance policies, telephone bills, and traveling costs. As the income increased and the budget expanded, SCLC operations increased and expanded.[47]

The new ability of the SCLC to account for its finances enabled the organization to attract large grants from charitable organizations. In the fall of 1960 massive resistance in Tennessee forced Highlander Folk School to move its Citizenship Education Program to Liberty County, Georgia. With a $40,000 grant from the Marshall Field Foundation and the use of an old school owned by the American Missionary Association and the United Church of Christ, the SCLC set up the CEP in Dorchester and hired Septima Clark from Highlander to run the school. She would receive assistance from Dorothy Cotton. The Reverend Andrew Young, a congregational minister and an employee of the National Council of Churches who hailed from a prominent mulatto family in New Orleans, administered the grant for the Field Foundation while working more closely with King and the SCLC. The school resumed classes in July 1961. The SCLC sent adult pupils for a week's training in basic arithmetic, literacy, leadership skills, and voting rights. With the CEP, the conference could finally point to a concrete example of its work. As long as the books balanced, the Field Foundation promised financial assistance. For the first time, the SCLC approached stability.[48]

In 1962 the national movement joined the Justice Department in Washington, the Southern Regional Council (SRC) in Atlanta, and the Field and Taconic Foundations in New York City in replicating Dorchester's successful CEP by creating the Voter Education Project. The goal was to register black voters for the Democratic Party. The SCLC eagerly supported the initiative, which financed voter registration drives led by indigenous leaders across the South. In part a response to the Freedom Rides, the Kennedy administration used the VEP to shift the recent turn toward direct action back to the struggle for the franchise. Preferring biracial negotiations to racial conflict, the SRC agreed to share its tax-exempt status with the VEP. The wealthy corporate philanthropist Stephen R. Currier, whose fortune from the air-conditioning industry financed the Taconic Foundation, saw the VEP as America's road to progress. With the VEP's initial foundation funding at $162,000, the SCLC, NAACP, CORE, National Urban League, and SNCC saw it as a valuable resource for their own civil rights initiatives. Yet SNCC had split over its decision to participate in VEP, for some students saw voting rights as a distraction designed to defuse the militancy of direct action. Ella Baker favored the VEP and convinced SNCC to support both voting rights and direct action. For the Southern Christian Leadership Conference, the VEP was a dream come true, although sloppy bookkeeping would compromise the funding the SCLC received in 1963.[49]

The Freedom Rides of 1961 reinvigorated the waning sit-in movement, reinforced the decided shift toward nonviolent direct action, and further involved the federal government in the struggle. Similar to CORE's 1947 Journey of Reconciliation, the Freedom Ride tested the Supreme Court's decision of *Boynton v. Virginia*, which had desegregated lunch counters and rest rooms in interstate travel. In the Upper South, the activists met 41 little resistance, but in Alabama, the Ku Klux Klan firebombed one bus in Anniston and beat the integrationists in Birmingham. Again the SCLC had not anticipated the civil rights protest, although local movements such as the ACMHR in Birmingham had been directly notified of the challenge by CORE and had responded with needed resources. Shaken by the extent of vigilante violence, CORE halted the Freedom Ride, yet SNCC members in Nashville and Atlanta determined that the protest should go on.[50]

Newly inaugurated President John F. Kennedy attempted to limit the negative international reaction to the racial violence by compromising the Freedom Ride. Working behind the scenes, Attorney General Robert Kennedy struck an agreement with Alabama and Mississippi officials that ended the Klan brutality but did not protect the constitutional rights of the integrationists. The Kennedy administration implemented a policy of "federalism" that left the enforcement of civil rights up to local officials. Authorities in Jackson, Mississippi, quietly arrested the activists, quickly arraigned and convicted them, and sent them off to jail. Extending to the Freedom Rides the jail-in strategy developed during the January 1961 sit-in at Rock Hill, South Carolina, SNCC activists refused to post bond and served their prison sentences, thus demonstrating their commitment to nonviolence. The Freedom Rides underscored the Kennedy administration's reluctance to support national civil rights reform and the national media's preoccupation with sensationalism. The protest proved less successful in achieving desegregation.[51]

The Freedom Rides reiterated the point that the students had taken the initiative for direct action away from the Southern Christian Leadership Conference. Following the May 1961 riots, the SCLC assisted SNCC and CORE with the protests, raised money off the controversy, and engaged in rhetorical threats, but did little else. Indeed, in some ways King spoke on behalf of people he did not represent. He acquiesced in the Kennedy administration's efforts to halt the protest. When the students continued the Freedom Ride anyway, King did not participate despite being asked to do so. Instead, the SCLC concentrated on the CEP and the new VEP to promote voter registration drives. But administrative problems were a distraction. A personality clash between Walker and the public relations director James R. Wood forced King to ask for Wood's resignation. Erratic budgets hurt long-range planning as the SCLC lived hand to mouth. With anticipated budgets requiring $5,884 per month, it took in $8,479 in January 1961 and spent $8,299 (some $2,415 over budget), for a net gain of $179; but in February 1961, it took in only $2,476 but spent $7,590, for a net loss of $5,114. Typical of the inconsistencies in income, such roller-coaster revenues required creative financing. Controversy dogged the organization. A conflict erupted between the conference and the conservative black National Baptist Convention over the use of direct action, an ironic situation given the SCLC's actual experience with the protest method. The students who were responsible criticized the SCLC for keeping the money it raised off the excitement surrounding the Freedom Rides rather than giving a fair share of the proceeds to SNCC. As a spokesman for the national movement, King attracted media attention and received financial support, but the movement had moved beyond SCLC voter registration drives and rhetorical nonviolence to the substantial direct action campaigns of SNCC and CORE. King confronted a harsh reality: either join the students or justify the continued existence of the SCLC.[52]

The sensational protests of outside agitators struck southern communities like lightning, sparking the creation of local movements that coalesced with the national movement in the struggle for race reform. In October 1961 outside agitators Charles Sherrod and Cordell Reagon opened a SNCC office in Albany and began mobilizing the black community behind civil rights reform. While they faced opposition from members of the traditional Negro leadership class such as the local officials in the NAACP and the administration at all-black Albany State College, Sherrod and Reagon found their message well received by "race men" in Albany, the black working class, and the local student population. To control the growing protest, the black middle class joined the students, laborers, and outside agitators in creating the Albany Movement as an umbrella organization that united SNCC with NAACP and several religious and civic groups. For the first time since the Montgomery bus boycott, much of the black community mobilized behind the indigenous movement. Formed on November 17, 1961, the Albany Movement elected Dr. William Anderson as president, Slater King as vice president, and Marion Page as secretary. The white power structure had ignored previous complaints filed as a petition by Anderson and other activists who wanted to start biracial discussions. This simple request for civil communication became the basis of demands made by the Albany Movement.[53]

The black rebellion against segregation grew. On November 22, 1961, five members of SNCC sat down at the white lunch counter in Albany's Trailways bus station to test the Interstate Commerce Commission's recent ruling in support of desegregation. Local police arrested the protesters. The Albany Movement responded by holding mass meetings and marches on city hall. The arrival and immediate arrest of several Freedom Riders on December 10 escalated racial tensions in the southwestern Georgia town. On December 13, an additional 267 black students were arrested. As Anderson recalled: "The Albany Movement was totally unplanned and unrehearsed. We had no strategies. There were no major planning sessions. It was a spontaneous movement that had its impetus from the people and their desires for change. We were not prepared for the arrest of hundreds of people. There was little cash, most of which went for car pooling and for relief of those who lost their jobs because of their participation in the movement. There were no provisions to get people out of jail or to provide legal services." Given this lack of order, the movement defaulted to a strategy of filling the jail. Albany police chief Laurie Pritchett responded to the Gandhian tactic by politely arresting the protesters and locking them up in nearby county and city jails so that his facility remained virtually empty. By December 15 he had incarcerated more than 500 people this way.[54]

Anderson decided that the Albany Movement needed the expert assistance of the SCLC, so he invited King to join the demonstrations. Emotions were running high. The local leader was responding to the harassment of white vigilantes and state troopers sent by Georgia governor Ernest Vandiver. Anderson also felt responsible for the jailed protesters who could

43

not post bail bond. He turned to the SCLC to help solve the problem. Not everyone in the Albany Movement approved of his decision. Sherrod, Reagon, and others in SNCC as well as indigenous leaders Marion Page and Slater King opposed the intervention of the SCLC.[55]

King arrived in town and spoke at a mass meeting on December 15, 1961, promising to demonstrate the next day. His message electrified the 1,000 African Americans assembled in Shiloh Baptist Church: "Don't get weary. We will wear them down with our capacity to suffer." On the afternoon of December 16 King, Abernathy, and Anderson headed a march of more than 250 black activists. Pritchett arrested all of the demonstrators. With King's participation, the Southern Christian Leadership Conference officially joined the Albany Movement.[56]

At first it appeared that the Albany Movement could solve the SCLC's chronic problems. A year before King had ordered Walker to find "something creative" for it to do in 1961, and, no thanks to Walker, the conference had stumbled into just such an activity. Indeed, by engaging in direct action in Albany, the SCLC finally went about the business it had been set up to do: coordinating direct action protests and nonviolent resistance to segregation. At that time Walker and others in the organization such as Andrew Young hesitated to join the protest, but, as Walker later explained, King "could not say at Dr. Anderson's invitation that it won't work into my schedule, or I can't come, because nonviolent struggle is what Dr. King was about."[57]

Tensions between SNCC and the SCLC increased after King's arrival in Albany. Although distrustful of Walker, some SNCC volunteers ridiculed King, derisively calling him "De Lawd" for miraculously appearing at their campaigns, stealing their thunder, and assuming to speak for the movement. With King in jail, Sherrod, Slater King, Marion Page, and others in SNCC knew "that federal and public opinion would pressure the city's white leaders." They also feared that once Albany's white power structure began to give, "at the first sign of weakness, Martin's lieutenants would engineer a settlement that could be construed in the national press as an exclusive SCLC victory but that the locals would find thoroughly inadequate." On learning of the truce that secured King's release from prison, a student in SNCC said, "You curse first, then I will."[58]

Rather than helping the movement, King's brief stay in jail actually hurt the campaign. In keeping with Pritchett's plan to farm out arrested demonstrators to neighboring county facilities, King was sent to Sumter County and locked up in the Americus jail. King informed a reporter of his commitment to civil disobedience: "I will not accept bond. If convicted I will refuse to pay the fine. I expect to spend Christmas in jail. I hope thousands will join me." Behind the scenes, however, King's attorney, the black Atlanta lawyer Donald Hollowell, joined Pritchett and Albany mayor Asa Kelley in secret negotiations to get the civil rights leader released. An understanding was quickly reached. In return for a cessation of civil rights demonstrations, the city agreed to waive the cash bonds (but not drop the charges) and release the arrested activists, conform to the desegregation ruling of the Interstate Commerce Commission, and initiate biracial negotiations sixty days later. Yet there was no formal statement to be signed, for Pritchett and Albany's white power structure refused to publicly acknowledge the negotiations. Despite opposition from within the Albany Movement, Hollowell and King convinced Anderson and Page to accept the truce. In the place of a written agreement, the SCLC offered a formal statement that expressed the particulars that the parties had agreed to verbally. Once out on bond, however, King brushed off criticisms with the observation that he did not "want to stand in the way of meaningful negotiations."[59]

Theories abound as to why King bailed out of Albany. The first most widely accepted view was voiced by David L. Lewis in his 1970 account, *King: A Critical Biography*. Lewis suggested that the Albany truce was arranged by black community leaders to get King and the SCLC out of town. "In order not to be committed to a compromise authored by Martin and Anderson, the community, with its vanity and jealousy, made a pact with the city that was confused and ulteriorly motivated. It was decided to compel the jailed leaders to accept bond by arranging an inconclusive truce whose terms would expire after Martin and the SCLC personalities had returned to Atlanta." As if to endorse this interpretation, Lewis quotes King later explaining: "I'm sorry I was bailed out. I didn't understand at the time what was happening. We thought that the victory had been won. When we got out, we discovered it was all a hoax." Lewis's account functions as an apologia for King.[60]

Most of the interpretations that attribute King's release to a divided black community lay the blame on the students. Wyatt Tee Walker expanded on the black conspiracy theory by getting in his licks on SNCC. He told an interviewer in 1967 that "we [SCLC] should have won Albany and we could have won Albany but for the anxiety and the ambition of a Charlie Jones and the bitterness of an Ella Baker." Taylor Branch quotes Charles Jones and Cordell Reagon of SNCC claiming to have "orchestrated the Albany negotiations toward precisely the result that followed: King's removal from Albany, bearing the onus of a weak settlement." Adam Fairclough adds a different scenario: the Albany Movement was near a settlement with the white power structure before King's arrival. The involvement of the SCLC in the protest hardened the resistance of white negotiators. Therefore, to recoup ground lost, black leaders accepted a truce that ended the protests and removed King from the picture in return for vague promises of reform.[61]

Several scholars note humanitarian concerns to explain the SCLC's weak agreement. Fairclough argues that King accepted bail in order to get Anderson—who was allegedly on the verge of a nervous breakdown—out of jail. Branch repeats the theory, suggesting that during a prison visit King told Walker: "Wyatt, you've got to get us out of here," adding that "Andy's not going to make it." Other scholars have also questioned Anderson's mental state. However, in his "Reflections" on the Albany Movement, Anderson says nothing about mental instability as triggering the truce. Gaining the release of the seven hundred other protesters locked behind bars topped the concerns of some local leaders. David Garrow identifies Marion Page as supporting the truce in order to secure the freedom of the demonstrators. Garrow also identifies Page as an unwitting and naive informant who regularly notified police chief Laurie Pritchett about movement strategy. Yet Garrow does not suggest that perhaps Page supported the negotiated truce as the best way to end the protests, an outcome that Pritchett wanted.[62]

Despite his promise to stay until Christmas, King himself wanted out of jail, so he arranged for his assistants to spring him from prison. Walker's quote to Branch makes this clear. King's attorney, Hollowell, found Page and his attorney, C. B. King, willing to go along with a truce. The agreement was favored by Pritchett, for it secured the release of King. Andrew Young confirms these motivations when he confessed that the SCLC went into Albany half-cocked. King "got put in jail, with no plan, no thought of what we were going to do." Forced to think about it, the conference bailed King out after two days. The first time, King ended his incarceration, but neither he nor his assistants anticipated the negative response that his action would receive.[63]

Swift in its critique of affairs in Albany, the national media roundly denounced King as a failure and the Albany Movement as a defeat. Having been slow to pick up on SNCC's protest, the major newspapers and news magazines had followed the Albany Movement after King's arrival on the scene. The journalists were eager for a resolution and pounced on the announcement of the truce. The *New York Herald Tribune* headlined its coverage with the banner, "A Major Defeat for Martin Luther King." *Newsweek* asked, "Who Won What?" Commenting on King's failure to remain in jail until Christmas, *Time* questioned his commitment to the moral struggle. It was not until after his arrest and incarceration that King realized the blunder he had committed by getting involved in a movement for which he was unprepared. By getting released from jail, King had committed an even bigger blunder.[64]

In a journalistic study written in 1962 that is otherwise sympathetic and somewhat flattering to King, Louis E. Lomax criticized the integrationist for his actions in Albany. In *The Negro Revolt*, Lomax identified King's decision to leave jail in December as the real telling point on his leadership: "Then Martin Luther King changed his mind. He had promised that he would stay in jail until a change came; he invited others to come and spend Christmas in jail with him. Had he stuck to this, as Gandhi would have done, Albany would have been desegregated. But Martin came out on bond." Lomax acknowledged that only King could "tell the true story" of what happened in Albany, although others also knew the truth. "Knowing Martin as I do," Lomax wrote, "I doubt he will ever part his lips. When I unearthed the truth and asked him to confirm it, his only reply was, 'If you print it I will not be nonviolent with you!' And then he smiled." Lomax drew some conclusions from King's actions: "The next town he visits to inspire those who are ready to suffer for their rights he will find people saying, 'Remember Albany.' And there will be the old, ugly self-criticism Southern Negroes used to level at each other when Martin and I were young boys in Georgia. I can see and hear it now: 'Lord, child,' some big mouth will say when Martin comes to his town. 'We got to watch our nigger leaders. They'll lead you into trouble with the white folks and then run off and leave you like he did them people in Albany.'" By suggesting a sellout, Lomax hoped that his warning to King would prepare the SCLC for "the crucial encounter [that] lies not far ahead."[65]

With the collapse of the truce in January 1962 following the refusal of the white power structure to acknowledge the December truce, SNCC initiated new protests against segregation in all of its manifestations. Sit-ins occurred at the bus station and downtown drugstores. Activists picketed white merchants who had refused to desegregate and hire black clerks. Demonstrators marched on city hall. Yet with no clearly defined target, the widespread protests proved ineffectual. The demonstrations had revealed that previous racial customs of accommodation were in a state of collapse. The dramatic growth of the city's black population—it having doubled over the past decade—had strained the old racial paternalism to the breaking point. SNCC found that many black people responded to the new ideology of racial equality and Freedom Now because they were no longer tied to the white community. Yet SNCC also found resistance from Albany's traditional Negro leadership class, which had vested interests in the stability of the segregated social structure.[66]

King's return to Albany on July 10, 1962, for sentencing in connection with his December arrest reinvigorated the local movement. At first some of King's lieutenants questioned the wisdom of resuming the protests, but in time Wyatt Tee Walker of the SCLC joined Charlie Jones of SNCC in coordinating the offensive. Students staged kneel-ins at area churches, read-ins at the library, and swim-ins at the pool. The judge offered King the choice of a $178 fine or forty-five days at hard labor. King chose the latter, as did his comrade Ralph Abernathy. The two men had prepared to serve their time. The Albany Movement held mass meetings and protest marches. Attendance ran high at the meetings but low at the marches, which required volunteers to face arrest and jail. Race relations worsened in Albany as black bystanders taunted police. Black youths pelted patrol cars with rocks. Attempting to restore order and stop the counterproductive violence, movement leaders struggled to control the actions of the black underclass, which—although uninvited—had joined in the protest. Tensions mounted as the movement recaptured some of the spirit and determination that had marked the protest during the previous fall.[67]

King's second sojourn in jail was as short as his first, although this time not by his own choosing. Two days into the sentence King and Abernathy were brought before Pritchett, who explained that their fine had been paid in cash by a black man and that they were free to go. A stunned King contested the turn of events but could do nothing except leave the jail. Again Pritchett had bested the Albany Movement, this time by borrowing a play out of King's own book. Bailing King and Abernathy out of jail compromised their moral standing and slowed the momentum of the movement. It was December all over again. While King complained about the "conniving tactics" of his opponents, others speculated as to the identity of the mysterious bondsman who apparently acted on the behalf of Mayor Kelley. The strategy worked but only in the short term, and not as well as the legal suppression that followed.[68]

48

Having stymied King's prison protest, Albany officials used the courts to halt the demonstrations. On July 20, 1962, Mayor Kelley convinced Judge Robert J. Elliott of the federal court to issue a temporary injunction against King, Abernathy, Anderson, and others in the Albany Movement, enjoining them from leading mass marches. King angrily complained to the Kennedy administration, which had appointed Judge Elliott, but Burke Marshall, Attorney General Robert Kennedy's special assistant on civil rights, informed the integrationist that he had to obey the ruling until an appeals court had overturned the injunction. Having condemned southern governments for ignoring federal court rulings on desegregation, the SCLC felt that it could not commit the same sin. Scholars have since suggested that this decision led to the collapse of the campaign. Despite SNCC's objections, the Albany Movement obeyed the injunction while the SCLC mounted an appeal. The demonstrations stalled. On July 25 federal judge Elbert P. Tuttle lifted the temporary injunction. That night, following the arrest of activists during a protest march, black bystanders again joined in the demonstration, this time throwing brickbats and bottles at the law enforcement officers. A sarcastic Pritchett queried reporters, "Did you see them nonviolent rocks?"[69]

A frustrated King wondered what to do next. The Albany Movement's efforts to engage the white power structure in biracial discussions had failed. The black boycott of white-owned businesses was holding, but the strategy had taken longer than expected to be effective. Scrambling for something, King announced yet another voter registration drive as a way of expanding the protest. Finally, on July 27, 1962, King held a prayer meeting at city hall and was arrested for disturbing the peace. He opted for a return to jail in a desperate bid to force Albany's white power structure to grant concessions to the Albany Movement. King lost the gamble.[70]

With King in jail, a domineering Walker bossed the Albany Movement. Having committed the SCLC's "total resources" to the campaign, he imperiously ordered others around. Some indigenous leaders and SNCC workers responded to Walker's arrogance by making clear their opposition to the hostile takeover. A student in SNCC complained to the black journalist Louis E. Lomax: "We did the spadework for this thing. Why didn't Walker stay the hell in Atlanta, send us more money, let us have Martin to speak and walk with the marchers! If he had done that we could have won. No, he had to come running into town like an Alexander who has stopped crying because he's just found a new world to conquer." Or as an indigenous leader asked: "Why can't these national organizations understand that this is a local movement?" The man obviously saw the campaign as a local concern, but the SCLC now saw Albany as an opportunity.[71]

For two weeks King sat behind bars as Walker and others in the Southern Christian Leadership Conference attempted to breathe life into the dying campaign. To compound the problems of infighting among the professional civil rights activists, fewer local people volunteered for the protests. The indigenous leaders had long since lost control of their movement. The December 1961 truce had yet to be honored by city officials, who had refused to hold biracial discussions or entertain movement requests until after the "outside agitators" had departed.

Efforts to commit the Justice Department had failed miserably as the Kennedys, studiously avoiding the controversy in public, quietly worked behind the scenes to arrange a truce that did not require any specific action on their part. When asked about Albany at a press conference, President Kennedy responded as if to reinforce the Justice Department's policy of federalism. He questioned why the United States could negotiate with the Soviets but the "city council of Albany will not sit down with the citizens of Albany, who may be Negroes." The comment cheered the movement but also reflected the hands-off approach to civil rights advocated by the chief executive. On August 10, 1962, King was tried on charges stemming from his July 27 arrest, convicted, and released on a suspended sentence for time served. Again a free man, King left for Atlanta.[72]

The movement was in retreat. Although King was gone, the white power structure refused to conduct discussions with Page, Anderson, and other locals in the Albany Movement, claiming that the issues were before the courts. In response to the stonewalling, King returned to Albany and threatened to resume protests. But the local leaders had had enough. The stalemate had worn them out. Massive resistance had triumphed. Anderson announced a moratorium on demonstrations, explaining that the Albany Movement was concentrating its efforts on voter registration drives. To save face, the SCLC offered to conduct citizenship schools. Again a dejected King returned to Atlanta. This time the campaign was over for good. It had ended in a devastating defeat.[73]

Withdrawing to Atlanta, the SCLC regrouped. For the first time, the organization had committed all of its resources to a direct action campaign. It had done what it was set up to do but the effort had proven unsuccessful. Despite the jailing of 1,200 black volunteers, the movement had wrestled not one concession out of the white power structure. The two dozen SCLC and SNCC workers in Albany had succeeded in organizing the local community behind the protest, but the inability to win any tangible victory made the local activists question their commitment and participation. Defeat had delivered a double blow.[74]

The Albany Movement had not helped SCLC finances, either. John A. Ricks has estimated that the organization spent $10,000 in Albany. In doing the books for the period July 12 to August 15, Walker registered donations worth $2,500 to offset expenditures of $2,508.36, leaving the SCLC $8.36 in the red for the campaign. An analysis of the SCLC statements of income and disbursements for the same period finds an additional expense of $2,500 earmarked for Albany. National headlines did not necessarily generate revenues, either, as the conference discovered its income fluctuating over July and August. The week of King's second incarceration, on July 10, saw the SCLC take in $5,625.50. The next week following his surprise release, income fell to $3,335.74. During the SCLC's negotiations the week of July 23–27, income rose to $5,639.06. The week after King's third incarceration, income dramatically dropped to $1,354.21. During King's second week in jail, income increased to $6,181.29. Following his final release on August 10, income again declined to $1,555.12. As the Albany Movement collapsed, the SCLC's income rose to its highest level, topping out at $9,994.92. The next two weeks again saw a decline, with $881.46 posted for August 31 and $2,710.41 posted for September 7, 1962. The highs and lows reflected the sporadic nature of direct mail solicitations and the emotional responses of supporters. The figures also included funds for the VEP that were being laundered through the SCLC's regular account.[75]

In assessing the Albany campaign, Wyatt Tee Walker lost none of his arrogance. At the annual meeting held in Birmingham in September 1962, he reported to the SCLC board of directors: "Albany was a proving ground for SCLC. I try to say this as modestly as possible, but I believe SCLC came of age in Albany. We demonstrated that we have an organization that in a moment of national crisis has the personnel, the resources, the program, and the know-how to do a job with Madison Avenue efficiency and yet with the grass-roots touch. It must be said that Albany presented a great challenge that SCLC as a team was able to meet." Although Walker acknowledged that "at the moment, the apparent decisive victory has not come," he nonetheless believed that "the unapparent critical enemy has been defeated," for the SCLC was "able to demonstrate—to the world . . . the complete moral indefensibility of the segregated system."[76]

Media assessment of the Albany Movement reached a very different conclusion from that of Walker's, as journalists praised Chief Pritchett for maintaining order while under racial duress. Perhaps the most complimentary was *Time* magazine, which said that Pritchett had "dealt unemotionally and with dignity with the Negroes" while keeping "them from turning the town inside out." His actions avoided a "bloody battleground." Although "tough," Pritchett had also "won the respect of both sides in the Albany dispute," *Time* reported. The magazine did not mention that all the while Pritchett defended the segregated social structure and successfully hid the brutality so often used to keep it in place. In contrast to Pritchett stood a compromised King. "Too much success has drained him of the captivating fervor that made him famous," *Time* suggested. Even among his followers who had "expected that King's mere presence in town would bring 'freedom here and now,'" there was a reluctance "to 'put on your walking shoes' and continue the Gandhian protest marches." As journalism professor Richard Lentz concluded in his analysis of *Time*'s coverage in Albany, "King was The Loser—a failure at nonviolence, rejected by his own people, swallowed up by success, unable even (the final indignity) to remain in jail as a martyr. Cool, tough, affable Laurie Pritchett was the winner, gaining the respect of his enemies, certainly King's, while enforcing the law with an even hand." *Time*'s image of King after Albany was a far cry from that of the man who had triumphed in Montgomery and been featured on the cover of the magazine five years before.[77]

As the Southern Christian Leadership Conference survived off the public image of its leader, the negative press following the Albany campaign boded ill for the future of the organization. To rebuild his seriously damaged reputation, King needed a new opportunity. The Reverend Shuttlesworth recognized the vulnerability of King and the SCLC, so he encouraged them to come to Birmingham to assist the local movement in its struggle for race reform. Although hesitant at first, King realized that he had no alternative but to go to Birmingham. Indeed, but for Birmingham, the SCLC might never have known a success.

CHAPTER TWO

Bombingham

T he dynamite blast that shattered the house of Sam Matthews on August 18, 1947, marked the first in a series of racially motivated bombings brought on by the postwar transformation of Birmingham, Alabama. Although racial attacks occurred in other southern cities, the frequency and number—some fifty dynamitings between 1947 and 1965—made Birmingham an exception and gave rise to the sobriquet "Bombingham." At first, the victims of the bombings were African Americans who had responded to a postwar shortage of adequate black housing by moving onto the fringes of white neighborhoods. In time, civil rights integrationists became the targets of the attacks. White vigilantes saw their acts of terrorism as a defense of white supremacy. African Americans responded to the dynamitings by defending black property rights. The traditional Negro leadership class had sought a solution within the confines of Jim Crow, but the failure of white political leaders to address the housing shortage drove black home owners to challenge the color line through a legal battle over Birmingham's unconstitutional racial zoning ordinance. An analysis of residential bombings in postwar Birmingham reveals the evolution of black protest from a request for separate but equal public services to a demand for an end to segregation.[1]

Two decades of depression and world war had given way to a postwar boom that allowed residents to focus on domestic needs; yet for black families wanting to leave congested neighborhoods, the shortage of houses and land for expansion in "Negro" areas created a desperate situation. Birmingham enforced illegal zoning laws that restricted black access to housing. The adoption of a general zoning code in 1915 and its revision into a comprehensive zoning ordinance in 1926 initiated a process of prohibiting African Americans from living in certain areas of Birmingham, a spatial manifestation of white supremacy. Despite the U.S. Supreme Court's 1917 decision against residential segregation, the author of the Birmingham ordinance confidently explained in 1933 that the zoning had been "quite acceptable to both races since adoption." In the postwar period, however, an acute lack of housing altered the black middle class's accommodation to the zoning arrangement in Birmingham. A group of black property owners who had been denied access to their new houses or land because of the racial zoning ordinance appealed to the NAACP for assistance in early 1946. The black attorney for the local NAACP branch, Arthur Shores, took on the fight.[2]

The highly contested area of North Smithfield in the Graymont subdivision of Birmingham became a battleground over the city's zoning ordinance. The lower-status white section of North Smithfield—an older residential neighborhood near Legion Field approximately five blocks square—was surrounded on three sides by the black section anchored around the Smithfield Court Housing Project for Negroes. The case of Alice P. Allen illustrated the transition of North Smithfield's white area to black. Mrs. Allen was an employee at Colored Methodist Episcopal (CME) Church–affiliated Miles College. In 1946 she had bought a house on Eleventh Avenue with the understanding that the tract was properly zoned "Negro." The realtor had listed the house in the newspaper for sale to white people but after finding no takers sold it to Mrs. Allen. White neighbors pressured her not to move in, and vigilantes broke out the windows. The city refused to allow her to occupy the house, so she rented it to

North Smithfield. The shaded areas on the map refer to houses owned by African Americans and the Smithfield Court Housing Project for Negroes. Center Street divided the races, with white people living to the west. As black people moved across the street, vigilantes bombed their houses, giving the neighborhood the nickname "Dynamite Hill." Police Surveillance Files, BPLDAM.

white people and hired Arthur Shores to file suit against Birmingham's zoning law. Rather than defend the ordinance at that time, the city rezoned the lot in question and allowed her to move into the house. Prospective black neighbors up the street were less fortunate.[3]

Forty-three-year-old Sam Matthews, a black drill operator at Ishkooda Ore Mines, in 1946 bought a lot for a new house on the outskirts of North Smithfield on the edge of the black community of East Thomas from a white realtor, William R. Coleman. In anticipation of the land being rezoned "Negro," Coleman had purchased nearly fifty lots for resale to black home builders. He had checked with the city commission, city engineer, and zoning commission to confirm his understanding that the land would be rezoned. He then sold the property to Matthews and several others. Before the commission acted, however, members of the Graymont and College Hill Civic Association protested the rezoning. White people living in the area feared not only a perceived decline in property values but also the possible integration of school districts if black people moved into the neighborhood. Coleman attended a meeting of the neighborhood group in the McCoy Memorial Church where angry white members confronted the developer. J. E. Monteith sat in the audience that night and later accosted the real estate agent. Monteith asked Coleman if he intended to sell any other lots to African Americans. When Coleman said yes, Monteith responded: "We ain't going to stand for that at all. . . . You sold that lot down there to that negro knowing it was zoned for white people." As Coleman turned to leave, Monteith seethed: "You'd better get going now. If you don't we are going to wait on you." Coleman swore out a "breach of the peace" warrant against Monteith.[4]

Believing the land properly zoned "Negro," Matthews applied for and received a building permit from H. E. Hagood, the city building inspector, after which he constructed a six-room frame house at 120 Eleventh Court North. Once it was completed, Matthews returned to Hagood seeking an occupancy permit. When the inspector denied the request, Matthews contacted Shores, who filed a suit against Birmingham's zoning law. Members of the black community contributed to the legal costs, with churches taking up money to finance the case. On July 31, 1947, Judge Clarence Mullins of the U.S. district court ruled the ordinance unconstitutional. Night riders painted a skull-and-crossbones threat on the house to warn Matthews not to move in. Then on August 18 around 10:45 P.M. vigilantes detonated six sticks of dynamite in the living room of the vacant house, destroying the structure. By this time Matthews had tried to rent or sell the house to white people but had found no takers because of its close proximity to other black-owned houses. With the blast demolishing his uninsured $3,700 investment, Matthews wanted to drop the "whole thing and hoped that he would never have to go into court."[5]

Police did not bother to investigate the bombing until after Shores and Matthews had filed a report of the crime the next morning. Detectives delayed taking statements for several days. The all-around resistance reflected the police department's support for the white-sanctioned vigilante violence. One suspect, J. E. Monteith, worked in the plant department of the Southern Bell Company and lived a block and a half from Matthews's house. He told officers that the explosion woke him up but that he rolled over and returned to sleep. A longtime resident of his community, Monteith explained that "he was not in favor of solving the case." The court dropped the "breach of the peace" charge against him. Likewise, detectives closed the Matthews case after their investigation "failed to reveal sufficient evidence to make an arrest." For three decades similar words appeared at the bottom of Birmingham Police Department case reports on unsolved bombings in the city.[6]

Angela Y. Davis was a young black girl growing up on "the hill" when the dynamitings began. In 1948 her parents had moved out of the Smithfield Court Housing Project for Negroes and into a large white gabled house on the "colored" side of Center Street. She remembered the Monteiths as "an elderly couple across the street" on the "white" side who "sat on their porch all the time, their eyes heavy with belligerence." As Angela grew older and as more black children moved to "the hill," she joined them in summertime games of hide-and-seek that quickly developed into challenges "to go up on the Montees' porch" and ring the doorbell. "The old woman or old man came out, trying to figure out what was going on. When they finally caught on to our game, even though they could seldom find us, they stood on the porch screaming, 'You little niggers better leave us alone!'"[7]

In addition to William R. Coleman and the white Coleman-Kendrick Real Estate Company, the black Hollins and Shores Real Estate Company, headed by Arthur Shores, aggressively bought houses formerly owned by white people for resale to black people in the North Smithfield area. Shores's firm negotiated the sale of the Eleventh Avenue, West, house of B. S. Brown, a white man, to African Americans Johnnie and Emily Madison in October 1948. Brown assured the anxious couple that "there would be no objection to Negroes in this neighborhood." Madison closed the deal on February 1, 1949, and began repairing and redecorating the house. He

57

On the night of March 25, 1949, a house recently purchased by African Methodist Episcopal Church bishop S. L. Green was destroyed by a dynamite bomb planted by white vigilantes. He had recently purchased the structure from a white widow who had decided that the neighborhood was "going colored." Police Surveillance Files, BPLDAM.

worked for the Tennessee Coal, Iron, and Railroad Company and his wife for the Bankhead Hotel. The couple bought new furniture for their home. Visiting the house after dark one night, the Madisons discovered a pile of old window shades burning in the backyard. Emily Madison said: "Johnnie, I don't like this. Why would anyone set this on fire?" The next week, on March 24, 1949, Johnnie Madison worked on the house until 10:30 P.M. Two hours later vigilantes placed dynamite under the floor of a rear bedroom on the corner of the house and lit the fuse. The explosion—one of three that night—demolished the structure. Similar blasts destroyed two other houses just up the street, both recently purchased by Bishop S. L. Green of the African Methodist Episcopal (AME) Church.[8]

The chancellor at AME-affiliated Daniel Payne College in Birmingham, Green had acquired one house from a white family through the Thornton Real Estate Company. Shores assisted Green with the insurance and legal matters concerning the transfer of property. Shortly thereafter

Green bought the adjoining house and land from Amie Thomas, a white woman. Previously, several real estate agents had asked if they could list her property for sale, having advised her that the neighborhood "was going colored." For forty years she had lived in the house with her husband, "had raised a family there and expected to be carried to the cemetery from that particular home." Once black people began buying the surrounding property she decided to sell, and when Bishop Green expressed an interest she negotiated directly with him. At the time of the bombing, Green had yet to occupy the house.[9]

The three blasts in March 1949 occurred just over the hill from the explosion that destroyed the Matthews house in July 1947. The Graymont–College Hills Civic Association demanded that the city commission enforce the zoning laws and stop the transition of the neighborhood from white to black. Association members Monteith, John J. Gould, and Sam L. Chesnut were questioned by detectives but revealed nothing to officers. All had been contacted by Coleman, Shores, and other realtors about selling their houses. An employee of the post office, Gould had lived in his house for forty-five years and "had never had any trouble with any Negroes" until the last year, when they had been moving into his immediate neighborhood. Chesnut felt the same way. Having lived in North Smithfield since 1908, he refused to leave, turning down one outlandish offer for his house by asking the inquiring man whom he intended to sell to. To the realtor's "it doesn't matter, does it?" Chesnut had replied, "It does to me."[10]

On the night of the bombing, Chesnut said he was called back to work as paymaster at the Alabama Power Company. From 11:00 P.M. to 1:00 A.M.—the hours of vigilante action, with the bombings at 12:30 A.M.—he reportedly attended to his business and then checked out. Although company watchmen confirmed that Chesnut had been at the plant, officials could not verify what he was doing. Neither could Chesnut recall a suspicious incident that, according to his white neighbor C. E. Henderson, had happened the day before. Henderson said he had received a call from an unidentified man who explained that he "was familiar with the situation that the neighborhood was having with the negroes." Several minutes later the caller drove up the alley in a black car and stopped where Henderson and Chesnut were talking in the back yard. Again the man refused to identify himself, but he asked Henderson to get in the car and show him the houses bought by Negroes in areas zoned "white." Henderson complied, and Chesnut denied ever seeing the man or the car. The afternoon before the bombings Henderson received another call notifying him that someone was "going to burn some wood on the hill that night." Apparently the vigilantes notified members of the white community in advance of their actions.[11]

Two black women renting a house from Shores on Center Street recalled a "good deal of activity" that night as cars circled the hill after dark. The women reported that between eleven and midnight two black automobiles containing white men parked bumper to bumper across the street from the house. Then mysteriously they drove away. Moments after the explosions, a black cab driver turned the corner and startled another parked car that took off at great speed. The cabbie gave police a car tag number, but nothing came of the report, apparently because the police were assisting the vigilantes. The Reverend O. C. Bickerstaff of the AME Church witnessed a police car with its parking lights on, poised as if guarding the intersection of Tenth Avenue and Center Street minutes after and just blocks from the explosions. Bickerstaff testified that as he drove past the patrol car, "another police car came by the first and blinked its lights." Rumors circulated about police involvement in the bombings.[12]

As detectives ended their unsuccessful investigation and white ministers collected donations from middle-class churches to rebuild the bombed houses, white vigilantes threatened black people wanting to move into the disputed area of North Smithfield. On May 21, 1949, William German, a black insurance salesman from Florida, was warned not to occupy the house he had bought at 1100 Center Street North. Robert E. Chambliss, a city employee who identified himself as a Klansman, stopped German, pointed to the shattered remains of Bishop Green's property, and said: "If you move in, that is liable to happen to you." Willie German listened to Chambliss and vacated the premises. Mayor W. Cooper Green suspended Chambliss—who worked in the city's auto repair shop—for ten days because of his comments. Robert E. "Dynamite Bob" Chambliss would later be convicted for the bombing of the Sixteenth Street Baptist Church that killed four black girls in September 1963.[13]

To limit black access to housing and thus halt the bombings, the city commissioners proposed the creation of a buffer zone that would separate the black and white neighborhoods of Smithfield. Arthur Shores demanded an opportunity to speak against the city commission's proposal, and at the May 1949 hearing he denounced the plan by detailing the unconstitutionality of the buffer idea.

On July 1, 1949, the Reverend Milton Curry Jr. put his furniture in the house at 1100 Center Street North. Birmingham building inspector H. E.

Hagood refused to issue an occupancy permit, but Shores advised Curry to stand firm, for "he was within his rights in moving into the house and was willing and determined to remain there." Nevertheless, Curry rented the house to another black man, B. W. Henderson.[14] Again vigilantes struck. On July 28, 1949, Henderson carried to Shores's legal office a bomb that had failed to go off. He found the three sticks of dynamite wrapped in a newspaper near the chimney of his house. Having no faith in the local police force, Shores immediately contacted the Federal Bureau of Investigation (FBI). U.S. district attorney John D. Hill had sent the FBI to Birmingham on May 31, 1949, to investigate the unsolved bombings. Reflecting the federal agency's defense of the racial status quo, a duplicitous FBI agent informed Shores that "this evidence did not fit in with their theory and for him to turn it over to the municipal police." Reluctantly, Shores turned the unexploded bomb over to the Birmingham Police Department.[15]

As the only practicing black attorney in Alabama for nearly twenty years, Shores had anticipated the lack of cooperation from the local police, but he had expected more from the federal government. A native of Birmingham, Arthur Davis Shores was born on September 25, 1904. He attended Parker High School and worked his way through Talladega College, graduating in 1927. While employed as principal at Dunbar High School in Bessemer, he completed through correspondence the LL.B. degree from the University of Kansas. Shores opened his law practice in 1937 and won his first of many NAACP-supported cases in July 1939, when he prosecuted a white Birmingham officer charged with police brutality against a black man. The personnel board suspended the patrolman for thirty days. When the Jefferson County Board of Registrars refused to enfranchise African Americans seeking the vote in a drive that summer, Shores filed suit against the board and appealed unsuccessfully when he lost in the lower courts. In 1941 he defended a black man demoted by the railroad because of his race. Shores and Charles Hamilton Houston of the NAACP Legal Defense and Educational Fund, Inc., argued the case, *Steele v. Louisville and Nashville Railroad Company et al.*, before the U.S. Supreme Court in 1944. The court's ruling prohibited discrimination against nonunion workers, in this case predominantly black employees. Like other lone black attorneys elsewhere in the South, Shores represented the legal interests of the NAACP on the local level. His law practice, real estate interests, and directorship of a black-owned bank placed him among the elite of Birmingham's black middle class. Short and stocky, above the crisp suit and polished attire a warm face often smiled, slightly turning up the tips of a distinctive mustache. His controlled posture underscored a shrewd mind and determined will. His measured approach to Birmingham's crisis in black housing contrasted sharply with the illogical antics of the city's white politicians.[16]

During the first week of August 1949, the Birmingham City Commission confronted the shortage of housing by discussing the racial zoning ordinance. Commissioner of Public Improvements James W. "Jimmy" Morgan called the city's zoning ordinance unconstitutional because of its requirement for racial separation. The next week, Commissioner of Public Safety T. Eugene "Bull" Connor surprised Morgan and Mayor W. Cooper Green with a new ordinance, 709-F, designed to circumvent the previous problem of racial zoning. Connor bragged that "the best legal minds in the state" had prepared the measure and given it to him that morning. The new law put police power behind the enforcement of residential segregation by making it a misdemeanor for whites to move into black or blacks to move into white areas "generally and historically recognized at the time" as racially specific neighborhoods. Connor later confessed that his mentor, former state senator and TCI attorney James A. Simpson, had written the ordinance.[17]

As Simpson explained in a letter to City Attorney James H. Willis, the new ordinance had nothing to do with zoning and everything to do with the separate-but-equal logic behind other segregation laws. Simpson drafted the measure to ward off "amalgamation." He argued: "If you let the situation disintegrate and negroes continue to infiltrate white areas and whites infiltrate negro areas so that your lines of demarcation become broken down, you are in for disorders and bloodshed and our ancient and excellent plan of life here in Alabama is gone." Simpson offered the city free legal advice on the matter.[18]

In announcing the new ordinance, Bull Connor accused Arthur Shores of creating the zoning conflict in North Smithfield: "It is impossible to compromise with Shores who is putting money above his race." Connor passionately added: "I tell you we're going to have bloodshed in this town as sure as you're sitting here. The white people are not going to stand for it." What these white people would not tolerate according to Connor was the selling of houses to black people. The police commissioner promised, "Pass this law and the first one who moves in, white or Negro, I guarantee you Connor's men will put him in the jug." Connor believed that the new ordinance would survive the Supreme Court and that his legal friends would "take it there at no charge if necessary."[19]

Circumventing Birmingham's unconstitutional racial zoning ordinance

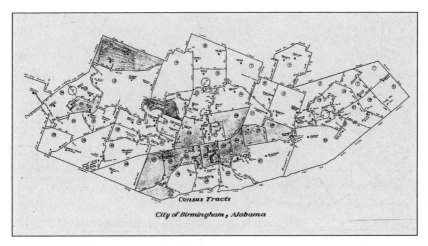

The city's predominantly black neighborhoods. Birmingham enforced unconstitutional racial zoning laws that relegated black people to the areas highlighted on this map. Cooper Green Papers, BPLDAM.

did not solve the shortage of adequate black housing, as Commissioner Morgan recognized by asking: "Where are those Negroes going to live and build? Almost fifty percent of our people are colored. So much of our area is zoned for white." Morgan spoke a simple truth. The *Birmingham World*, which had commended Morgan for his "courageous" stand when he called the zoning law unconstitutional the week before, otherwise chastised the commissioners for their insensitivity. The newspaper charged: "Negro citizens are bottled in the slums and restricted to the blighted areas . . . [they] . . . are zoned near the railroad tracks, near the over-flowing creeks, near the shops." In housing, as in everything else in Birmingham, black people suffered severe discrimination.[20]

According to the 1940 U.S. Census, African Americans occupied 29,477 of the 71,798 dwellings within Birmingham's city limits. Of these, less than one-sixth were owner-occupied. Nearly a third had no indoor toilet. More than two-thirds of Birmingham's black population lived in "blighted" areas zoned for commercial use. A decade later the census reported that African Americans occupied only 33,448 of the 95,512 dwellings within the city limits. Although the number of owner-occupied units had doubled to nearly one out of every three, the gain of 6,172 dwellings was offset by the relative lack of growth in black housing during the 1940s as opposed to the dramatic increase in white housing. In addition, the city's population increased from 158,622 white and 108,961 black people in 1940 to 195,922 white and 130,025 black people in 1950. The question quickly became, where were all these new black people supposed to live in Birmingham?[21]

Although African Americans earned more in Birmingham than elsewhere in the region as a result of the industrial demand for semiskilled labor, they lived in the poorest quality housing of any metropolitan area in the Southeast. With the city's origins as a collection of company towns came a housing legacy of shoddy construction and overcrowding. Speculators bought tracts of marginal land and crammed them full of "nigger houses," a cheap investment that reaped a rich reward by exploiting a captive black workforce dependent on segregated rental housing. More often than not, realtors built the shotgun-type dwellings out of unseasoned pine with tar paper roofs. Similar to a shoe box—one room deep and two to four rooms long—the short side faced the street, which, with the front and back doors opened, enabled one to fire a gun through the structure. The widespread use of this typical sharecropper's cabin reflected the urban adaptation of rural race relations.[22]

Whereas an overwhelming majority of Birmingham's black citizens rented houses, they did so for lack of any alternative, and those who owned struggled to keep their property. Living in a company town, or "project house" as it was called in Birmingham, carried a stigma that many African Americans struggled to overcome by saving money in the hope of buying their own home. The desire to get out from under the corporation and live in "independent" housing explained why so many black people accepted dwellings of a lesser quality than that of the company or rental house. Typical black residential communities in Birmingham, such as Tuxedo Junction, consisted of both rental and owner-occupied dwellings. Property owners protested when slum clearance threatened this area of Ensley made famous by Birmingham native Erskine Hawkins's jazz tune of the same name. The words of Ellen Dorsey, a resident and home owner since 1924, captured the atmosphere of Tuxedo Junction, for it was "Our little Negro town, where we can be off to ourselves, and we want to remain." Interspersed among the 1,710 mostly rental properties were 292 owner-occupied dwellings. A slum area, 1,385 of the dilapidated houses lacked private baths. A majority of the residents earned less than $2,000 a year as semiskilled and unskilled laborers in Birmingham's industries or as maids. Most were married.[23]

The press debate over slum clearance in Tuxedo highlighted the horrible conditions in the blighted area—the lack of screens and indoor toilets—to justify bulldozing and building the proposed 500-unit Tuxedo Court

Housing Project for Negroes. Unlike the paternalistic whites who saw the project as a way of removing a health hazard while improving the lives of some "colored citizens," African Americans opposed the destruction of their property. Julia Simmons, a "poor widow woman with no one to do anything for me," wrote the city commission in the hope of keeping her house: "I worked and got this place so I would have some place to live when I got disable [sic] to work and I am about at that stage now so I am putting it in your hands[;] please do what you can for me." Although stalled by federal budget cuts, the city ultimately razed her neighborhood and built the Tuxedo Court Housing Project for Negroes in 1957.[24]

Not only did public housing replace renter- and owner-occupied slum dwellings without regard for those displaced, but also it sheltered a growing number of the black working poor and unskilled unemployed. J. C. de Holl headed the Housing Authority of the Birmingham District, chartered in 1935, and he directed the construction of the city's first housing project, Smithfield Court for Negroes, authorized by Franklin D. Roosevelt, financed with federal funds, and built with labor from the Project Works Administration. With the U.S. Housing Act of 1937, the city built three more projects, the white Elyton Village and Central City and the black Southtown. A separate housing development, Eastwood Village, existed for veterans and servicemen. Even in housing the segregated projects revealed discrimination in Birmingham, for the authority operated 1,774 white units as opposed to 992 black units. In general, black and not white people were displaced by slum clearance.[25]

Not until the Housing Act of 1949 did the city develop plans for new projects, using Title 1 to condemn property through slum clearance. As with company housing, public housing carried the stigma of living in the "projects," something few people—black or white—wanted. Yet statistics from the annual reports of the Housing Authority of the Birmingham District suggest that white residents experienced greater economic opportunity and thus used public housing as temporary shelter (as envisioned by its designers) because of the high turnover rate in white vacancies, while less mobility suggests that black residents experienced less economic opportunity and hence increasingly became permanent dwellers in public housing. Job discrimination in favor of whites and the declining need for black unskilled labor contributed to the problem. Thus while whites moved through the system, blacks moved into the system. In time, second- and third-generation black families found little chance of escaping the inner-city poverty of public housing.[26]

Public housing absorbed only a fraction of those African Americans forced to move through slum clearance. Using Title 1 of the Housing Act of 1949, the city selected three major Negro residential neighborhoods for future projects: Tittusville, Tuxedo Junction, and Avondale. Black tenant families lived in 90 percent of the housing on these combined sites—an area covering 272 acres. In Tuxedo and Avondale, the proposed projects would displace 7,600 residents, almost all of them poor black people. The twelve and a half blocks of southside, out of which urban renewal would create the medical complex of the University of Alabama in Birmingham, claimed the dwellings of 523 black and 92 white families. The city made no provisions for these displaced people other than to offer them a number on the waiting list for public housing if any vacancies were to arise. Thus through slum clearance and urban renewal projects, the city increased the number of African Americans seeking adequate housing, a need unfulfilled by public housing.[27]

Most African Americans lived in congested neighborhoods surrounded by white residences that precluded expansion. The controversy over North Smithfield began as a natural outgrowth of overcrowding when black people living nearby sought access to the area as white people moved to the suburbs. The African Americans bought the old housing stock in a logical progression of their segregated neighborhood. They had no alternative, as the city zoned only three small areas "Negro" residential that could accommodate less than one-third of Birmingham's black population. These in-town neighborhoods housed Birmingham's black middle class of professionals, with on average 90 percent of the houses owner-occupied. The residents maintained their dwellings and paid property taxes. Nevertheless, the city neglected the neighborhoods by not paving roads, putting in street lights, or extending public transportation to the area. Although contractors developed black subdivisions such as Honeysuckle Hill, the white builders failed to recognize the purchasing power of some African Americans by building small, inexpensive houses that few middle-class black people wanted. Consequently, the black elite moved into North Smithfield and the formerly white middle-class area of Graymont where substantial houses, street lights, and paved roads already existed. The other two-thirds of black Birmingham lived in congested industrial areas or flood plains that lacked basic public services. Consistent with racial zoning ordinances, these black neighborhoods developed as industrial suburbs or satellite communities. Unlike Atlanta and most southern cities prior to 1970, Birmingham had a substantial black suburban population.[28]

The postwar shortage of black housing resulted from a lack of land properly although unconstitutionally zoned "Negro" for the expansion of black neighborhoods. While Commissioner Morgan attempted to address the problem, Bull Connor made it a point to care less about the needs of the city's black citizens, perhaps out of a desire to see Birmingham's black population decrease. Connor found an ally in the zoning board, which resisted adding new land to black communities and which rezoned as "white" some land already owned by African Americans. As a result, many black neighborhoods were decreasing in size, a problem exacerbated by slum clearance and urban renewal. During 1948 and 1949 alone, African Americans lost 1,200 dwellings, with little provision made for new structures as public housing units absorbed only a fraction of those displaced. An expanding business district aggravated the situation. The increasing urban population, severe postwar shortage of adequate housing, and baby boom combined to create a crisis in black housing.[29]

Desperate to escape the congested ghetto, African Americans readily bought white-owned houses, although generally in areas they believed had been rezoned "Negro." In their bid for adequate housing they challenged the color line. They bought property on the edges of formerly white neighborhoods near black communities. As white people moved out, black people moved in, usually block by block in an orderly manner. The transition afforded the unscrupulous an opportunity to buy low and sell high, but occasionally both races profited. Having acquired adequate housing, these new black home owners defended their rights in property from attacks by white vigilantes.[30]

Three nights after the city commission adopted Simpson's ordinance to authorize the police department to enforce racial zoning, explosions rocked the city, but this time, as the blasts lit up the night sky, the black community fought back. Around 10:00 P.M. on August 12, 1949, B. W. Henderson, the black man living at 1100 Center Street North foiled one bombing attempt when a white man who had stepped out of a car realized that "the Negroes are watching us." The vigilante climbed back in and the car drove off, but Henderson followed, trying to get down the tag number. The suspicious car met two others near the Smithfield Court Housing Project as Henderson returned home to warn his friends of the threat. Neighbors and ministers joined family members on the porch of the Reverend E. B. DeYampert's house in a show of strength. Several were armed. Around midnight, a black Buick slowly drove down Center Street, coming to a complete stop in front of DeYampert's house. The front passenger door

67

opened and the car light turned on, revealing several white men inside the vehicle. After a passenger threw something at the house, shots were fired at the car by those gathered on the porch. Once the charge ignited, sound and smoke filled the front yard. Seconds later, another explosion occurred at Henderson's house two doors away. Neither bomb reached its target, but both blew huge craters in the yard. The percussions knocked the windows out of both buildings. As the vigilantes drove off into the night, hundreds of outraged African Americans swarmed over "Dynamite Hill."[31]

When the blast occurred, five-year-old Angela Davis was washing out the white shoelaces for her Sunday shoes in preparation for church the next morning. Suddenly, "an explosion a hundred times louder than the loudest, most frightening thunderclap I had ever heard shook our house. Medicine bottles fell off the shelves, shattering all around me. The floor seemed to slip away from my feet as I raced into the kitchen and my frightened mother's arms." Outside, "crowds of angry Black people came up the hill and stood on 'our' side, staring at the bombed-out ruins of the Deyaberts' [sic] house. Far into the night they spoke of death, of white hatred, death, white people, and more death. But of their own fear they said nothing. Apparently it did not exist, for Black families continued to move in. The bombings were such a constant response that soon our neighborhood became known as Dynamite Hill."[32]

The local chapter of the NAACP fired off a telegram to Mayor Green demanding "day and night police protection for the Negro home dwellers in Smithfield." The NAACP reminded the commissioners that detectives had yet to solve any of the six bombings. Commissioner Morgan released a statement to the newspapers expressing his regret and reiterating "that some land should be made available to our colored citizens to construct homes." In protest of the bombings, two thousand African Americans gathered on the lawn at the Smithfield Court Housing Project on August 17, 1949. Various black middle-class organizations sponsored the mass meeting to vent community frustrations. The audience adopted resolutions that criticized Bull Connor's comment that he could not "protect the lives and property" of African Americans who lived in the disputed area and condemned the city commission's "questionable and illegal means to ram down the throats of law abiding citizens the unconstitutional compromise zoning plan of an opposing group."[33]

The black protest crowd at Smithfield Court praised the courage of Arthur Shores and identified him as representing the "combined thinking of Negro leadership and fellowship" in Birmingham. Shores emerged as a spokesman for desegregation. Yet, along with his peers in the traditional Negro leadership class, Shores also accommodated Jim Crow paternalism when accommodation suited his interests. The willingness of black leaders such as Shores to negotiate and compromise with white leaders reflected their ability to broker agreements within the confines of segregation. Such racial diplomacy in the city was set forth first by the Reverend Dr. William Rufus Pettiford as the new century began.[34]

THROUGH RACIAL UPLIFT and self-segregation, Pettiford articulated the ideology of the traditional Negro leadership class in Birmingham. He pastored the socially prominent Sixteenth Street Baptist Church, the city's oldest black congregation, and he headed the Alabama Penny Savings Bank, a black institution. Pettiford joined other black businessmen in advocating economic self-help and racial solidarity while accepting an accommodationist ideology articulated best by Booker T. Washington. In 1899 Pettiford headed a black delegation that petitioned the city to finance a Negro industrial school. He succeeded in part by convincing the white school board president of the need for what later became Parker High School. Pettiford demonstrated the practice of petitioning white leaders for public services while accepting Jim Crow, a pragmatic choice between discrimination and outright exclusion simultaneously made by black leaders in other southern cities. Birmingham's traditional Negro leadership class followed this pattern of protest through the activities of the NAACP and other organizations.[35]

Although small, the local black elite articulated a class consciousness comparable to that of the city's white elite. Birmingham had few Negro colleges, as opposed to other southern metropolises such as Atlanta and Nashville, a fact that contributed to the limited number of university-educated African Americans living in the area. Only two schools, Miles College of the CME Church and Daniel Payne College of the AME Church, operated in Birmingham; nevertheless, both provided cultural and political leadership within the black community. A handful of black businessmen catering to a Negro clientele had organized a chapter of the National Negro Business League, but it folded for lack of support. Lawyers, doctors, and dentists operated out of offices in the Pythian Temple on Eighteenth Street and the Colored Masonic Temple on Fourth Avenue North. Both buildings demarcated the black business district and provided settings for social activities. Greek fraternities, such as Alpha Phi Alpha and

Omega Psi Phi, and women's groups, such as Periclean Club, Imperial Club and Links, Inc., offered outlets for the black bourgeoisie, and this class comprised the core membership of the NAACP. As a result, many African Americans viewed the organization as elitist. The NAACP's penchant for bureaucracy and its inactivity on behalf of Birmingham's common black folk further alienated the black working class.[36]

During the early years of the Great Depression, Communist Party (CP) operatives moved into Birmingham to organize the black masses. Although opposed by the NAACP, the CP quickly spread as a grassroots movement among the black working poor and unemployed. The efforts of the International Labor Defense (ILD) on behalf of the Scottsboro Boys and the initial failure of the NAACP to participate in this case contributed to the popularity of the CP and thus provided a mass-based challenge to the traditional Negro leadership class in Birmingham. In addition, the depression limited black involvement in the NAACP, which saw its local membership decline to an all-time low of only six paid members in 1931. To reverse the decline, the national NAACP endorsed the ILD in order to gain mass support. In contrast, the CP's decision to foster a popular front among its members, the black middle class, and white liberals had the effect of curtailing independent leadership from the black working class. When the ILD disbanded in 1937, the CP encouraged its activists to join the NAACP, whose roster likewise expanded to 750, the largest number since the 1920s. By the 1940s thousands of African Americans belonged to the Birmingham branch.[37]

In the aftermath of World War II, black activists working within a biracial popular front attempted to revive the liberal reform movement of the 1930s. In Birmingham, the Southern Negro Youth Congress (SNYC), an organization for the black masses that had ties to the NAACP and the CP, directed a voting rights campaign for returning veterans. In late January 1946 about one hundred black servicemen in uniform marched in double file formation to the Jefferson County Courthouse to present their discharge papers and register to vote. County officials rejected a majority of the applicants for failing to adequately "interpret the U.S. Constitution," a favorite trick used by white authorities to prevent black enfranchisement in Alabama. Louis E. Burnham of the SNYC and the Reverends J. L. Ware and John W. Goodgame created a Citizens Veterans' Committee to file an appeal in circuit court on behalf of the failed registrants and to gain support from the Veterans Administration for job training and other benefits available under the G.I. Bill of Rights.[38]

Responding to the SNYC-led initiative, Emory O. Jackson, editor of the black biweekly *Birmingham World* and secretary of the local NAACP chapter, began a campaign to finance the legal fight for the black veteran vote. Like all good newspaper editors, Jackson could be obstinate. Born in Buena Vista, Georgia, in 1908, Emory Overton Jackson moved with his parents to the Enon Ridge neighborhood of Birmingham in 1919. He matriculated at Morehouse College in Atlanta and there exhibited a sensitivity to discrimination. Working on the *Maroon Tiger*, the undergraduate Jackson protested the "Faculty Men" and "Boys" labeling of campus rest room facilities and succeeded in convincing the administration at the prestigious college to drop the designations. Graduating from Morehouse in 1932, Jackson accepted a teaching post, first in Dothan, Alabama, and then at Westfield High, in Jefferson County, where he taught Robert E. Johnson who later edited *Jet* magazine. The *Birmingham World* hired Jackson as managing editor in 1943 after he completed service in World War II. In his column "The Tip Off," Jackson demonstrated a crusading spirit akin to that of the old-fashioned newspaper editor. Despite his numerous associations— memberships in many of the Negro civic and fraternal organizations in the city—he remained an independent voice within the black community. His brusque style alienated other members of the traditional Negro leadership class, and, regardless of their views, he consistently demanded an end to Jim Crow and full civil rights for African Americans.[39]

After police shot to death black ex-Marine Timothy Hood for allegedly moving the color bar that maintained segregated seating on the streetcar and for fighting with the conductor, twelve hundred African Americans marched in protest. Publicity on behalf of the veterans' campaign appeared in the *World*, with guest editorials telling the former servicemen that "this battle is not to be waged with bullets, it is to be waged with ballots." In his "Tip Off" column, Jackson warned of the difficulties applicants faced and gave the correct answers to questions asked by registrars. Nonetheless, the veterans' registration effort stalled. This earlier movement for civil rights collapsed when local white resistance combined with national red-baiting, as when Bull Connor shut down the SNYC during a political rally for Henry Wallace in 1948. The black veterans' movement never achieved its potential in Birmingham, and Jackson never recovered from the lost opportunity.[40]

Membership in the local NAACP declined rapidly with the collapse of the popular front and the increase in racial hostility expressed by Dixiecrats and other white people. Participation in the Birmingham branch dropped from more than 7,000 in 1947, to 6,614 members in 1948, 2,444 in 1949,

1,907 in 1950, and 1,554 in 1951. Infighting among factions within the local chapter hindered a registration drive designed to halt the downturn. Assisted by the national office, the membership campaign revealed the inner workings of the Birmingham branch.[41]

A rift developed between Jackson and local NAACP branch leadership. A majority of the executive committee that determined local strategy had decided to hold a "Miss NAACP Contest" to attract new interest in the organization. As branch secretary, Jackson opposed the plan to award monetary prizes to the beauty pageant contestants as inconsistent with NAACP policy. The rift became public during the NAACP membership drive headed by committee chairman and funeral home operator W. E. Shortridge. Shortridge authorized the brothers of Alpha Phi Alpha fraternity to conduct the membership drive, and Jackson—an Omega—denounced the plan as elitist. In the pages of the *World*, Jackson called on "the humble people to have a showdown with its high leadership." He accused Shortridge and others of supporting activities antithetical to NAACP policy, in particular participating in a private effort to pressure the city for a "Negro" golf course. Finally, in April 1952 a disgusted Jackson resigned as secretary of the Birmingham branch of the NAACP. He referred to "a shocking and disgraceful departure from NAACP principles" and declared: "The Branch no longer represents the crusading spirit which brought me to it several years ago. It has allowed certain members to corrupt its program and to advocate courses of action and procedures which are in contradiction, hostility, and opposition to the methods, philosophy and aims of the NAACP."[42]

Although no longer an official in the local branch, Jackson remained a member of the national organization, and the *World* continued to publish information about NAACP activities. Nonetheless, Jackson had lost the crusading spirit. As he wrote a friend during Autherine Lucy's desegregation attempt at the University of Alabama, "When the 'Lucy Case' is settled one way or the other I plan to remove myself from the front-line scene. All of my life has been spent in the interest of the other fellow. I want to be able to read, relax, and retire. Retirement is merely a withdrawl [*sic*] from battle, not a cessation from earning a living."[43]

A lack of interest within the black community and the inept leadership of president W. C. Patton limited the effectiveness of the NAACP's Birmingham branch. Despite "Miss NAACP Contests," the local organization continued to deteriorate. While the traditional Negro leadership class dominated the NAACP through the service of Patton, the Reverend Ware, and attorneys Shores, Peter Hall, and Orzell Billingsley, other more activist members such as Mrs. Lucinda B. Robey, W. E. Shortridge, and later the Reverend Fred L. Shuttlesworth struggled to generate interest in the NAACP among the black masses.[44]

Limited in mass appeal, the NAACP provided the only organized and consistent black protest in Birmingham during the postwar years. The association defended black property rights by condemning the racial bombings and police brutality, adopting resolutions against the building of a sewage treatment plant in a black neighborhood, and filing suit to stop slum clearance projects that targeted black-owned homes. Quick to pass a petition in protest of any white provocation, the local branch proved equally willing to negotiate with white leaders behind closed doors. Such conferences occasionally produced results that contradicted the national organization's stated goals. The Freedom Train incident of 1947 demonstrated the inconsistency in objectives between the local and national organizations.[45]

In a bid to bolster patriotic feelings during the emerging Cold War, the U.S. government entrusted its most valuable documents—the Declaration of Independence, the Constitution, the Bill of Rights, the Emancipation Proclamation—to the American Heritage Foundation for a train tour of the forty-eight states in the fall of 1947. Planners picked Birmingham as a stop, and local people prepared for the public display. When national organizers balked at the decision to segregate viewers in Memphis, Birmingham officials scrambled to cover up similar arrangements. Dr. Ernest W. Taggart of the NAACP and other Negro leaders had compromised with city commissioners on a Jim Crow strategy that would allow Bull Connor to enforce the city's segregation laws during the viewing of the national treasures. Apparently NAACP executive director Walter White got wind of the idea and decided to make hay out of southern discrimination, for the national office pressured the American Heritage Foundation to cancel the Birmingham stop unless total integration occurred. The local branch quickly altered its prior agreement and parroted national policy. Defending segregation, Birmingham's leaders canceled the stop and thus prevented citizens from seeing the documents that attested to their liberties. The Freedom Train incident demonstrated the duplicity of the traditional Negro leadership class. As the African American steelworker Hosea Hudson recalled about the NAACP but in a different context: "They still didn't want to rock the boat, make they good [white] friends mad. The [black] leadership was still trying to make deals."[46]

More often than not, the traditional Negro leadership class quietly worked with white leaders to achieve its goals without the interference of the NAACP. Following in the footsteps of Pettiford, the black businessman A. G. Gaston usually wrote city commissioners requesting minor favors, and they generally responded in the affirmative. An only child born in Demopolis in 1892 and initially raised by his landowning grandparents—his father having died while working on the railroad—Arthur George Gaston moved to Birmingham in his early teens to live with his mother, who cooked for the Lovemans, a prominent family that operated the city's premier department store. When Art's mother decided the young boy needed an education, she enrolled him in the Tuggle Institute, located in Birmingham's elite black neighborhood on Enon Ridge in the hills northwest of the city. Gaston's inspiration and role model was Booker T. Washington. The first book Gaston read and one he thumbed often was the president of Tuskegee Institute's autobiography *Up From Slavery*. He took its message of individual initiative to heart. While serving in the army in France during World War I, Gaston sent $15 of his pay home each month to finance the purchase of a house—the first of many lots he bought. After the war he took a job at one of TCI's mills. A year later, finding himself stuck in the same menial position, he searched for a way out. Remembering that as a merchant A. B. Loveman had once peddled goods door-to-door, Gaston began selling his mother's box lunches to his fellow crewmen. This successful business venture led him to the one that would amass his first fortune: selling burial insurance to industrial workers. Gaston had found his niche. The Booker T. Washington Burial Society grew steadily into the centerpiece of a constellation of black enterprises that included funeral homes, radio stations, real estate, a cemetery, bank, school, and motel. By 1990 his corporate worth topped $35 million and made him one of the wealthiest black men in America. He died in 1996 at the age of 103. Occasionally the accommodationist Gaston defended the racial status quo, as when he called on Bull Connor to enforce segregated zoning.[47]

The struggle to convince the city commission to construct a Negro golf course epitomized the strategy of patient negotiations for segregated services used by the traditional Negro leadership class. Representing the black bourgeoisie in the Magic City Golf Club, Dr. E. W. Taggart petitioned the city park and recreation board to buy land near the Negro neighborhood of Powderly Heights for the proposed facility. The sportsmen had an important ally in that Mayor Green supported their request. As he explained to Charles W. Hall of the Birmingham Country Club, "We feel we must go ahead on the proposition before it is too late and the courts rule that they can play on the white golf course." Green compared the project to the recently designed facility at Vestavia Hills Country Club, and he saw the undertaking through to completion. In appreciation of his hard work, the black elite joined the city in naming the nine holes the Coopergreen Park and Golf Course.[48]

As in the negotiations for the "Negro" golf course, an increased demand for Jim Crow public services led to a rise in black activism. In the postwar years, municipal leaders authorized a general increase in government-sponsored programs and public utilities to meet the needs of urban expansion. Black protest emerged as a rejection of continued exclusion and as a desire for access to the new public services within the context of separate but equal. With the civil rights movement this activism developed into a black demand for equal access as consumers and equal opportunity for jobs.

From its founding, Birmingham's park and recreation facilities inadequately met the needs of its black and white population. When developers laid out the city, they set aside only three small areas a few blocks long for public use: Capitol (renamed Woodrow Wilson and then Charles Linn) Park, East (renamed Marconi) Park, and West (renamed Kelly Ingram) Park. Progressive Mayor George B. Ward increased the acreage under city control, but the random expansion remained slow and marked by discrimination. Birmingham spent less per capita on parks and recreation than any other major southern city.[49]

A political consciousness among the black masses developed around the issue of public parks. Groups such as the Interdenominational Recreational Council of 1941 organized petitions requesting that the city commission construct "proper parks, playgrounds and recreational centers" in order "to decrease and possibly eliminate entirely juvenile delinquency." Using the black church as its base, the Interdenominational Recreational Council collected hundreds of signatures involving everyday people in the protest. Adopting similar methods, Negro neighborhood associations such as the South Elyton Civic League, the Enon Ridge Civic League, and the Civic League of Zion City corresponded with city commissioners requesting recreational facilities and other Jim Crow neighborhood improvements.[50]

Although aware of the needs of its black citizens, the city continued to treat the requests paternalistically, giving little thought to the opinions or desires of the black community. When Emory O. Jackson headed a movement to rename the Colored Memorial Park on the southside after Julius Ellsberry, a black man killed at Pearl Harbor and the first casualty from Birmingham in World War II, just as the white Kelly Ingram was the first victim of World War I and had a park named after him, the city commission not only refused to entertain the request, but also Mayor Green accused Jackson of doing "more harm to the negro park cause here than anything that has happened . . . in the last ten years." Despite not acknowledging the hero, the city continued to create segregated parks throughout the 1950s and early 1960s, in some instances merely redefining as "Negro" formerly "white" facilities.[51]

The issue of Jim Crow library services compared to that of the parks. Again, Birmingham woefully neglected the needs of its black and white patrons. Although white citizens constructed a magnificent central facility in the latter 1920s, the system of branch libraries—several of them financed through the Carnegie Foundation—remained inadequate. In response to a subscription drive by African Americans, officials located a "Negro" library, the Booker T. Washington branch, in the Colored Masonic Temple in 1918 and added a smaller collection at Slossfield in 1940.[52]

The need for a central "Negro" library became more pressing during a debate over a bond issue in 1953. Library officials believed that in order "to preserve our Southern tradition of segregation, it is essential that the facilities provided for Negro citizens immediately be made more nearly on the same level as those provided the white citizens." Members of the traditional Negro leadership class responded to the plans within the context of accommodation. The Reverend Luke Beard, pastor of the Sixteenth Street Baptist Church, wrote to thank the board for taking this "great step forward in the general progress of Birmingham." The local NAACP commended the city commission for placing African Americans on an advisory committee to the library board and hoped that "in the not too distant future" black citizens would serve on the board itself. When the city considered the construction of a new building for the "white" branch in Ensley, the Negro Ensley Civic League petitioned the city to convert the old facility into a "Negro" branch. Thus as with the parks, so too with the libraries, a rising black demand for Jim Crow municipal facilities and the federal threat of desegregation convinced Birmingham to provide more—albeit unequal— public services to the black community at the same time it increased operations for white citizens.[53]

Unlike Atlanta, where an expanding black electorate convinced city officials to increase public services to the black community, Birmingham's black community wielded no political influence. Only 456 of the more than 28,000 registered voters in Jefferson County in 1935 were black. Holding the franchise became a sign of status within Birmingham's black community. In 1938 Hosea Hudson and several other radicals organized the

Right To Vote Club to get the black masses registered. The effort immediately clashed with the traditional Negro leadership class's control over the
Negro ballot.[54]

Hudson recalled a meeting with the elitist Jefferson County Negro
Democratic League, directed by conservatives D. L. White and Henry
Harris, at which they attempted to convince the democratic Right To Vote
Club to merge with their organization. According to Hudson, white city
leaders responded to Communist Party agitation in 1933 by supporting the
incorporation of the Jefferson County Negro Democratic League under
the leadership of White and Harris and working out an arrangement with
the Jefferson County Board of Registrars that approved Negro voters recommended by the league. As White explained to the upstart Hudson, the
white registrars had told the Negro conservatives: "We only going qualify
those that you all will recommend, send down or bring down. Your friends,
we'll qualify them. But don't send everybody down. Don't bring no common nigras, and don't bring over fifty a year."[55]

The Right To Vote Club remained independent of the traditional Negro
leadership class and succeeded in getting many of its members registered
before disbanding in 1940. Anywhere from 878 to 3,000 African Americans
were registered by 1940. Just over a decade later, in 1952, the number had
inched up to 3,650. The repeal of the cumulative feature on the state poll
tax in December 1953 greatly expanded the electorate. The Southern Regional Council estimated that the number of black voters increased in
Birmingham to approximately 5,250 by 1954. This figure rose by 1956 to
5,400, approximately 4.4 percent of the black voting age population in Jefferson County. It would double to 11,900 by 1960. The board of registrars reputedly maintained an arrangement with the traditional Negro leadership
class and continued to approve select members of the black elite, especially
schoolteachers, such as future mayor Richard Arrington, whom the board
automatically excused from the standard discriminatory questions.[56]

Reflecting its conservatism and bureaucratic tendencies, Birmingham's
traditional Negro leadership class formed two local groups that addressed
the issue of voter qualification and participation in the political system.
The Jefferson County Progressive Democratic Council endorsed candidates for office as the "oldest partisan political organization among Negroes
in Birmingham." Attorney Arthur D. Shores served as president. Similar to
other groups across the state, the Jefferson County Progressive Democratic
Council worked to register black voters. An effort to assist such groups culminated in the 1951 formation of the Alabama State Coordinating Council

for Registration and Voting, headed by W. C. Patton. Through its voter education program the council sponsored speakers at meetings designed to inculcate values of good citizenship within the black community. Both the Jefferson County Progressive Democratic Council and the Alabama State Coordinating Association for Registration and Voting appealed to an elite group of Negro citizens and never took root among the African American masses. Consequently, the organizations achieved little, although both attracted white opposition as did the activities of the NAACP.[57]

Although willing to compromise on other black requests for segregated municipal services, with the housing crisis the city stood firm in its refusal to provide more land zoned "Negro," as demonstrated in the Monk case. Like so many other black people who moved into the disputed area of North Smithfield, Mary Means Monk had attempted to work out the zoning problem with the authorities according to Jim Crow custom. She purchased a vacant lot at 950 Center Street in June 1949. City building inspector H. E. Hagood delayed granting a building permit because of Commissioner Morgan's absence but encouraged her to clear off the land and start construction. When Morgan returned, he explained that the zoning committee had discussed the situation and had failed to act but that she should continue working on the house. Monk's contractor laid the foundation but stopped building when he needed the approval of the city inspector before putting in the plumbing. She returned to Morgan, who told her to get Shores to call him, for "he would direct him in some way that he probably could get the city to give a building permit" to Monk. Shores filed suit against the city, demanding permission to complete the house.[58]

City attorney Willis defended residential segregation in Birmingham by citing the new ordinance that put police power behind zoning enforcement, which therefore prohibited Monk from erecting a house in an area "generally and historically recognized . . . for occupancy by members of the white race." On September 28, 1949, Shores amended Monk's case to include fourteen other people as well as A. G. Gaston's Booker T. Washington Insurance Company, which owned forty-seven lots in the area. Shores filed the class action suit against the city of Birmingham, calling the racial zoning ordinances unconstitutional. Recognizing the likelihood of just such a ruling, Willis began to backslide. He met with the Graymont–College Hills Civic Association in a futile attempt to convince the white residents to allow the rezoning of some land along Center Street to "Negro" in order to have the case dismissed and thus protect racial zoning in the rest of the city. The association discussed Willis's plan at its November 1, 1949, meeting and voted "100 percent against any change of the Center Street zoning line." Furthermore, the members adopted a resolution requesting that the city hire additional counsel to defend the ordinances in court.[59]

Responding to its white constituency's desire for a legal battle, the city commission obtained the assistance of Klansman, Dixiecrat, and all-around race baiter Horace C. Wilkinson. Bull Connor's prediction that the "best legal minds in the state" would defend the racial zoning ordinances for free proved false, for the city commission secured Wilkinson's services by paying a fee of $5,000 plus an additional $1,000 for local legal assistance. On November 14, 1949, Wilkinson informed Willis that the $1,500 allotted for research in Washington, D.C., would have to be increased to $2,500. For a city government renowned for its frugality, paying such exorbitant legal fees for what was generally recognized as a lost cause suggested racial politics. The city commission financed the Monk case as a symbolic gesture to assure the shopkeepers, steelworkers, plant managers, clerks, firemen, and other members of Birmingham's white lower middle class that segregation would be upheld.[60]

When *City of Birmingham v. Monk* reached federal court on December 13, 1949, Judge Clarence Mullins forcefully declared as unconstitutional Birmingham's racial zoning ordinances. Wilkinson filed an appeal in January 1950. Not everyone agreed with the city commission's decision to continue the case. The broker George B. Alexander defended Judge Mullins's ruling but blamed the problem on "people of the ilk and breed of the negro lawyer, Arthur Shores." Others were more forthright. Mrs. R. D. DeLaure wrote Mayor Green to say that the Ku Klux Klan "ought to get Shores." Although vigilantes avoided the attorney, they were far from silent.[61]

Having elite white "friends" did not protect Dr. and Mrs. Joel A. Boykin from the bombers who dynamited their new house on April 13, 1950. Back in 1948 Boykin, a black dentist, had drafted plans for a $10,000 house and office to be constructed on a "white" buffer lot he owned in a block otherwise zoned "Negro." Previous efforts to build on city-approved land had failed, so Boykin appealed to the zoning board of adjustment to get the tract rezoned. Ten white neighbors protested his application at the hearing, and the board turned down the request. Boykin contacted his white attorney, the prominent realtor Sidney W. Smyer, who interceded on his behalf. Despite Smyer's pleading, the zoning board stood firm. Nevertheless, Boykin hired a black contractor and built the structure on Twelfth Terrace North, some five blocks from Smithfield.[62]

The explosion at the Boykin house rattled black and white residents of this western section of Birmingham, all of whom agreed that "what happened shouldn't have occurred." Right after the blast, a black neighbor, Lubirta Jones, ran outside to rescue her little dog, Lady, as pieces of rock rained down. She told a reporter: "We are colored and have lived in our house here for almost two years. We'd like to keep living here in peace." Fellow black dentist Dr. J. J. Thompson expressed little sympathy: "Those folks were warned before they started that house. And I know from experience that when a Negro gets a warning, he'd better heed it." In 1921 Thompson had ignored three warnings to leave a neighborhood, so vigilantes burned to the ground his house, garage, barn, and chicken coop. The white neighbors across the street from Boykin had listed their house for sale but found no white takers, although several black families expressed an interest. An elderly white woman who lived nearby, Mrs. Jack Guest, explained that she had no complaints about her African American neighbors and added, "It was a mighty nice house they blew up."[63]

Vigilantes struck another house ten days later. Night riders destroyed the two-story frame structure at 1100 Center Street in North Smithfield shortly after eight o'clock on April 22, 1950, when a dynamite bomb exploded, caving in the front porch, splintering timbers, and shattering windows. Three people, including a three-month-old baby, miraculously emerged from the debris. Down the street when the explosion occurred, the owner raced to the rubble of his house: "Isn't it a shame?" a hysterical Henderson asked a reporter. "It's awful. It's ridiculous that this could happen in a civilized country. I should have known it, because I was down to Dr. Boykin's after they blew up his house." Then Henderson recalled: "Just last Monday, a group of white fellows walked by and gave this house the eye. I watched them from the window and heard one of them say, 'This one will be next.'"[64]

The April 1950 spate of bombings finally elicited a response from the local press. The *Birmingham News*, in a strongly worded and reproachful editorial, spoke to the vigilantes: "The men who performed the deed are cowards. They must be found. The city's police declare they are active in trying to find the criminals. In other previous bombings not one arrest has ever been made." After returning to an earlier argument that deplored the threat to property, the *News* concluded, "The time has come when action is demanded and when excuses no longer will satisfy anyone." Likewise, the *Birmingham Age-Herald* criticized the inaction of the police department and called for state and federal forces to help "apprehend these law violators." The *Birmingham Post* offered a five-hundred-dollar reward for information leading to the arrest of the perpetrators. "The bombings have got to stop," the newspaper implored.[65]

Amid the society news and announcements of corporate transfers printed in the *Shades Valley Sun*, the column of the anonymous "Button Gwinnett" condemned the dynamiting and demanded the "preservation of law and order." Recognizing Smithfield as "properly a place for Negroes," the opinion called for a "voluntary agreement between the races for demarcation of the sections of the city where they are to live" as the best way to maintain "reasonable lines of separation." Using a pseudonym, Charles F. Zukoski wrote the column for the weekly that serviced the affluent enclaves of Homewood, Mountain Brook, and Vestavia Hills. He hoped to impress Birmingham's elite who lived over the mountain.[66]

Through his position at the First National Bank, Zukoski had assisted the Big Mules in their reform of the Bourbon system during the 1930s and 1940s, but after World War II he saw the confrontational aspects of the states' rights and Dixiecrat movement as derailing the corporate reforms he promoted. Correspondingly, the Button Gwinnett columns enabled Zukoski to articulate the emerging opinions of a racial liberal in the postwar era. As he wrote in October 1948, "Change is inevitable and will either be an orderly and self-imposed one or a violent and destructive assault from without." He struggled to convince others of the need for orderly change. Zukoski never wavered from his conservative demand for Negro civil rights, but he consistently denied writing the columns for the *Sun* because he believed that his supervisors at the bank would view the ideas as "radical if not downright heresy." After numerous complaints, First National demanded that Zukoski either stop writing the opinions or resign. The Button Gwinnett series ceased after December 12, 1957. Nevertheless, Zukoski's outspoken support for race reform persuaded the bank to offer him early retirement in June 1962. Espousing a northeastern establishment approach to solving problems, Zukoski and his Button Gwinnett columns presented an alternative voice for hidebound Birmingham.[67]

Despite assurances from police chief C. Floyd Eddins that "We're going to keep right on top of this thing until we find out who did it," law enforcement officers made little headway in their investigation of Birmingham's eighth unsolved racial bombing. Police did question Robert E. Chambliss about the explosion but "uncovered no new leads." Fired by the city after his 1949 indictment by a grand jury for "flogging while masked," Klansman Chambliss was tried and acquitted of the charge in March 1950. Governor

James E. Folsom sent two state investigators to assist the four city detectives and three sheriff's deputies already probing the explosions.[68]

In October 1950 the U.S. court of appeals heard Horace Wilkinson's defense of Birmingham's racial zoning ordinances. Thurgood Marshall of the NAACP's Legal Defense and Educational Fund, Inc., joined Arthur Shores and Peter A. Hall in presenting Monk's case. On December 19, 1950, the Fifth Circuit upheld Judge Mullins's lower court ruling in *City of Birmingham v. Monk*. The decision found zoning ordinances 1604, 1605, and 709-F in violation of the Fourteenth Amendment and enjoined Birmingham from enforcing them. On December 20 the city complied with the court's ruling and allowed Mary Monk to occupy her home. The next evening, vigilantes dynamited the house.[69]

The bombing followed the pattern of those that had preceded it. Believing her ordeal over, Monk had moved into the house located at 950 Center Street North in Smithfield. A friend helping her clean the kitchen witnessed two suspicious men standing at the back of the lot staring at the house. Uneasy and afraid that bombers might strike, she left on the outside light on the night of December 21. Around 10:30 P.M., as Monk turned down the bed in the front room, she heard a thud on the screen porch. Fearing the worst, she turned and ran, reaching the hallway when the charge ignited. The blast nearly reduced her house to rubble. Black neighbors saw speeding cars leaving the scene. During the police interrogation that followed, detectives tried to bait Monk by inquiring whether she thought the "communist" NAACP or those "people up in Washington" should meddle in Birmingham's racial affairs. Probably in all honesty, she replied, "The city should work it out . . . the people in Birmingham ought to work it out themselves, since they are the ones that live here."[70]

Monk spoke from the perspective of a black schoolteacher seeking adequate housing. Indeed, her case symbolized the struggle of Birmingham's black middle class reluctantly forcing an issue—the unconstitutionality of the city's racial zoning laws—because of the obstinacy of city commissioners who refused to approve new land for black neighborhoods. The resistance of white people had escalated the crisis in black housing into a conflict over segregation. The decision of Monk, Shores, and Gaston to fight a legal challenge to Birmingham's segregated zoning ordinance reflected a transitional period in black protest that occurred in the years preceding the civil rights movement. Originally a defense of black property rights, the postwar protest evolved from a request for segregated municipal services to a demand for desegregation. With the emergence of the Alabama Christian Movement for Human Rights led by the Reverend Fred L. Shuttlesworth, the transition in black protest was completed, for the new organization used nonviolent direct action to achieve integration. When Shuttlesworth survived the dynamiting of his own house in 1956, his reputation as a charismatic civil rights activist increased tenfold.

After the Monk bombing, the racially motivated vigilante violence continued. Supporting the status quo in race relations, the police department scuttled its investigations while the fire department stood by and watched firebombed buildings burn down. One student of Birmingham's racial zoning troubles concluded in 1951 that Bull Connor and the police department were "part of this violent scheme to prevent Negroes from enjoying those rights and privileges granted them by the Constitution of the United States." The testimony of a city detective corroborated his theory. Angela Davis claimed that "Connor would announce on the radio that a 'nigger family' had moved in on the white side of the street. His prediction 'There will be bloodshed tonight' would be followed by a bombing. So common were the bombings on Dynamite Hill that the horror of them diminished." Yet the effect of the terrorism was extensive. As the years passed and hostilities increased, outside opinion of Birmingham deteriorated. The unsolved bombings earned Birmingham the sobriquet "Bombingham" and an international reputation as a city plagued by racial turmoil.[71]

CHAPTER THREE

Bull's Birmingham

Years before the spring demonstrations of 1963, T. Eugene "Bull" Connor symbolized Birmingham. The popular commissioner of public safety had consistently won reelection since 1937 as a union-busting, segregating defender of public virtue. He received the electoral support of the white lower middle class that dominated local politics. Like his constituency, Connor felt threatened by the postwar changes occurring in Birmingham. Although the outcome of a series of police scandals persuaded him not to seek a fifth term in 1953, he responded to the emerging civil rights movement by riding the rising discontent of a frustrated lower-status white electorate back into office in 1957. His power base eroded, Connor nonetheless promised to resist the black demand for an end to racial discrimination in the marketplace.

In 1950 annual income by race underscored racial discrimination in employment, as black people in metropolitan Birmingham earned on average $1,087 to the $2,274 made by white people. In broad measure, the marketplace divided labor into two general areas: "whites only" jobs and "nigger work." A middle ground of sorts existed among the nearly 12,000 semiskilled black and white operatives. Although professionals existed in both races, they served segregated societies. Of the more than 9,000 employed professionals, fewer than 1,000 were African Americans, of which the overwhelming majority were schoolteachers and preachers. White people held almost all the management, sales, clerical, crafts, and supervisory and better operative jobs. As the mudsills of the colonial economy, African Americans worked as charwomen, janitors, maids, and laborers.[1]

Black and white workers earned an income commensurate with the status and skill required for the job. Black women occupied the bottom of the scale as domestics, with a median income of $538. Black laborers averaged slightly better with $1,725. Black and white operatives averaged $2,203. White professionals and managers topped the scale, earning around $4,000 annually. White steelworkers holding positions as foremen made $4,032. Craftsmen averaged $3,000. Other "whites only" jobs paid comparable wages: railroad workers made $3,217; bus drivers, $3,250; policemen, $2,932. To protect their earnings white civil servants, steelworkers, craftsmen, and operatives prohibited African Americans from holding skilled positions. Through municipal policies, corporate management, and union rules, they fashioned job security around the barrier of race.[2]

Birmingham's stunted electorate—the white lower middle class with its allies among the Big Mules—chose its own to manage city affairs. As a consequence, the municipal government defended the segregated social structure that protected "whites only" jobs. The 1950 census listed 212,520 citizens over the age of twenty-one living in Birmingham, with 134,052 of these white and 78,468 black people. In 1953 only 60,000 to 65,000 of the possible 212,520 residents were registered to vote in city elections. Yet only a third of those qualified actually voted in municipal elections, with approximately 22,000 casting ballots in the 1953 commission race. Thus out of a total voting age population of 212,520, approximately 22,000 or roughly 10 percent participated in Birmingham's elections of 1953. Some 3,650 black citizens made the qualified voting list in 1952. Veteran newspaper reporter Irving Beiman believed that 15,000 members of organized labor could vote in 1947, and they were mainly members of the American Federation of Labor (AFL). The Congress of Industrial Organizations (CIO) protested its inability to register semiskilled and unskilled workers in 1954. The problem centered around the operations of the Jefferson County Board of Registrars.[3]

Through a battery of unconstitutional questions, including the interpretative requirements of the Boswell amendment, Birmingham's registrars kept the populace disfranchised. As chairman of the board, H. A. Thompson controlled voter registration in the city. First appointed in 1947, "Mr. Gus," a seventy-year-old man described by the *Birmingham News* as a "strong Dixiecrat plumper," served as chairman until 1955; during that time he fought to prevent what he called the "mass registration of all persons over the age of 21 years, regardless of the qualifications now required under the laws of the State of Alabama." In his courthouse office by eight every morning, Mr. Gus worked to restrict the electorate by opposing poll tax reform and other democratic measures designed to enlarge the voting pool in Birmingham, something that he feared "would result in a social and economic calamity in Alabama."[4]

Three major neighborhoods—East Lake, Woodlawn, and West End— occupied a strategic place in city politics, casting from a quarter to a third of the vote in 1957. An analysis of the census tracts for East Lake, Woodlawn, and West End revealed that 33,635 black and white citizens over the age of twenty-five lived there, with a total of 8,600 nonwhites in the area. A rough estimate suggests that around 25,000 whites from East Lake, Woodlawn, and West End could vote, and a third of them did, when in the city as a whole only one out of ten participated in elections.[5]

Historically streetcar suburbs linked to the central business district and outlying industrial areas, the communities of East Lake, Woodlawn, and West End housed the city's white-collar clerks, insurance and real estate agents, bookkeepers, and small businessmen as well as the highly skilled industrial craftsmen, carpenters, machinists, and railroad workers. Municipal employees and civil servants from politicians, secretaries, and schoolteachers to policemen and firemen also lived in these neighborhoods, as did a few doctors, lawyers, and ministers. Founded around the turn of the century, all three developed distinctive communities centered around their respective churches, schools, and businesses. Typical of the lot was West End.

The subdivision of West End formed when a streetcar line tied Jefferson County's original settlement of Elyton to Birmingham. The residents— some new to the city, some from Elyton—developed a "strong communal feeling." In traditional southern fashion, social life organized around the churches as Baptists, Methodists, and Presbyterians attended each other's services. In 1915 the major denominations constructed West End Tabernacle as an open-air pavilion, which in the summer sheltered Sunday night services, revivals, and other affairs of the evangelical community. Neighborhood congregations sliced watermelons and shared ice cream socials. Children played under the oaks in West End Park. Small businesses stretched along Tuscaloosa Avenue selling hardware and groceries and "Co'colas" in the drugstores. The American Cafe served up home cooking to residents who stopped by on their way walking to the streetcar or the park or the church or while out shopping. They greeted each other by name, talking on the front porch for hours. Unpretentious, neighborly, and comfortable, West End offered its average inhabitants the best of community life.[6]

Success spoiled the idyllic picture as postwar change forever altered West End. The community bonds that had led residents to share with each other during the Great Depression snapped as servicemen returned from war and moved into new suburbs elsewhere in Birmingham. The middle class moved over the mountain to Homewood and Mountain Brook, while the lower middle and working class expanded into white suburbs along a northern curve that extended from Trussville in the east, through Center Point, Gardendale, Fultondale, Pleasant Grove, and Hueytown in the west. At the same time, housing stock in the urban center deteriorated. Repairs, postponed by depression and war, awaited owners who often decided to sell rather than renovate. Buses replaced the streetcars, but the automobile proved the real nemesis as individuals exercised their independence from public transportation. Soon the shops on Tuscaloosa Avenue suffered competition from strip malls that opened on the edge of the neighborhood. Losing its more prosperous residents, experiencing economic decline among its shopkeepers, and witnessing the fragmentation of its once active social life, West End grappled with urban change.[7]

On the surface it appeared that West End held its own between 1940 and 1970 as a white neighborhood of managers, operatives, craftsmen, and clerical workers. Census data from 1940, 1950, 1960, and 1970 for Tract 40, the West End area, demonstrated a median education of eleven years with around 40 percent high school graduates. Just over a third of the residents at any given time were age twenty-four or younger in this community of families. An established neighborhood, most of the structures were built before 1919, although development in the 1920s nearly doubled the number of dwellings. The depression halted construction, which briefly resumed in the 1940s before slowing for good. Five-sixths of the area's housing in 1970 had been constructed before 1949.[8]

Demographic shifts underlay this apparent continuity as West End experienced dramatic change. Growth characterized the 1940s as the population increased over the decade by nearly a thousand people, but after 1950 a decline set in. Wages reflected the postwar prosperity, and a housing shortage inflated property values. Yet statistics revealed trends that transformed

West End over the three decades. The more prosperous members of the community left, with the less fortunate taking their place. One-fourth of West End's residents had relocated into the neighborhood (most from elsewhere in Birmingham) during the 1940s. The number increased to one-third during the 1950s and one-half during the 1960s, suggesting a lack of cohesion in the community. Because the number of dwellings declined over the same period, the transition suggests those moving in replaced previous residents who had moved out.

Likewise, shifts in the workforce exhibited the transformation of the community. The number of women entering the labor market increased proportionally to the overall population of the tract as the number of employed men declined, revealing an increase in female-headed households. Women in the service industries showed a marked rise over the four decades as clerical workers and professionals held steady. Change among male breadwinners highlighted the overall transition. Whereas most of West End's men worked as professionals, managers, clerks and salesmen, craftsmen, and operatives in 1940 and 1950, fewer held the same positions in the 1960s and 1970s. In addition, the number of employed men declined by nearly one-half over the thirty-year period.

Instead of increasing, property values, once adjusted for inflation, decreased. Although family income appeared constant, in reality, an erosion occurred, for fewer women stayed home as housewives, and the increase in two-income families failed to offset the effects of inflation. Thus a decline in wages, property values, population, and employment status, plus an increase in female workers, demonstrated demographic shifts in West End—a transformation made all the more apparent by the great number of people moving out of or into the neighborhood. The sense of community once shared in the West End Tabernacle diminished in the postwar era. Unsettled by the upheaval and the decline in their standard of living, residents who remained sought to protect their community, striking out at the most obvious elements of change in defense of an increasingly archaic racial status quo.

Nowhere else was the desire for control more readily apparent than in the operations of the police department, and no one epitomized the anxieties of the white lower middle class better than the police commissioner, Bull Connor. Born on July 11, 1897, in Selma, Alabama, Theophilus Eugene Connor moved to Birmingham in 1922. His father had worked as a train dispatcher, and from him Connor learned how to operate a telegraph. Briefly employed by the railroad, the *Birmingham News*, and the private

89

security force at the Tennessee Coal, Iron, and Railroad Company, Connor stumbled into a part-time job interpreting wire reports to re-create baseball games for matinee audiences. Later he called the Birmingham Barons games for local radio. An instant hit, Connor gained the nickname "Bull" because of his gruff voice, a mistaken comparison to a local newspaper columnist, and his ability to "shoot the bull" while describing games over the radio. Thanks to his popularity, Connor in 1934 won a seat in the state house of representatives, where he fought for whatever his mentor, James A. Simpson, supported in the state senate. "Me and Jim," Connor fondly said to preface his remarks on pending legislation. In 1937 Connor entered the race for the Birmingham City Commission at the urging of Simpson, who hoped to remove a renegade faction from city hall. Successful with his borrowed platform of civil service reform, Connor led in the runoff, followed by James W. "Jimmy" Morgan, who also joined the three-man commission under the mayoralship of Jimmie Jones. As a product of the white lower middle class, Connor epitomized its values and protected its interests while accepting the broad directives of the Big Mules.[9]

90   Throughout his life, James Alexander Simpson protected the privileged and defended absentee-owned corporations in Birmingham through his law practice and through his association with Bull Connor. The young son of an idealistic Union veteran, Simpson experienced a happy childhood in a socialist commune; yet the failure of the Ruskin Colony and the resulting deprivations suffered by his family set him on a conservative course. After attending Vanderbilt University he moved to Birmingham, formed the law firm Lange, Simpson and Brantley in 1919, and married an heiress of the Woodward Iron Company. The tragic loss of his wife during childbirth in 1921 apparently led Simpson to withdraw into his legal career. "Infatuated is he with the law," read a journalist's description of Simpson, adding that his "approach to anything is purely legal" and that he "dismisses levity." With age, Simpson found less to laugh at. An insider among the Big Mules and a legal retainer for several of the city's major corporations including TCI and the *Birmingham News*, Simpson promoted the interests of the industrial and financial elite from his position as legislator, having been elected to the state house in 1927. His platform consistently supported no new taxes and civil service reform. When he ran for state senate in 1935, reporters recognized Simpson's immense power in Montgomery, saying he wielded "tremendous influence in shaping the course of legislation and political affairs in this state." He served three terms as senator from Jefferson County, but he lost two elections for the U.S. Senate—in 1944 and 1946—despite run-

ning rabidly racist campaigns. Birmingham reporter Irving Beiman identified Simpson as the "principal spokesman" for the Big Mules. Through Bull Connor, Simpson implemented the agenda of Birmingham's iron and steel interests.[10]

Before Connor earned a reputation for racial brutality maintaining segregation, he was known for violently preventing the unionization of Birmingham's heavy industries. The two issues were related. Popular front liberals Virginia and Clifford Durr recalled that Connor had directed the "steel police" at TCI. It was here that he took lessons in law and order before his election to the city commission. During the organizational drives of the 1930s, Connor routinely held unionists "in jail incommunicado for months at a time. A lot of them just disappeared. Nobody knows where they went, just died or killed or thrown in the river, or something," the Durrs charged. When the Southern Conference for Human Welfare convened in Birmingham in November 1938, delegates participated in an integrated setting for nearly twenty-four hours before Bull Connor forcibly segregated the proceedings. The delay was significant, for the city commission had initially welcomed the white and black New Deal liberals and labor leaders who gathered to discuss the region's ills. To hinder the biracial unionization drives of the United Mine Workers and other unions in the district, the Big Mules had convinced Connor to enforce the segregation ordinances. For the rest of his political career, Connor carefully separated black from white in order to hinder working-class solidarity. Labor counselor Jerome Cooper recalled that when Phillip Murray of the U.S. Steelworkers of America spoke before an integrated audience, Connor ordered police to racially divide the crowd with rope. "Three burly white steelworkers cut the rope down" and repeated the action after police retied the barrier. As Connor understood, segregation reinforced the race wage in Birmingham.[11]

As commissioner of public safety, Connor saw himself protecting the morals of society, which he did by enforcing city ordinances that concerned everything from liquor licenses to segregated seating. His speciality was race relations, but he periodically routed gambling rings, closed down disorderly houses, and bottled up bootleggers. Though Connor invested the vice squad—a crack team of patrolmen who peered into windows looking for perverts—to assist him in the fight against lewd and indecent behavior, often he acted alone, the sole arbiter of public good taste. In his quest for wholesome family entertainment, Bull banned movies that he deemed deviant. In one celebrated case in 1941 involving the showing of *French Girls' Club*, he violated a court injunction and spent forty-eight hours in jail. Worried about the welfare of youngsters, Connor yanked fifty-two comic book titles from the newsstands in 1948. Though such acts earned headlines and won the hearts of moral crusaders, his overriding concern remained race, and for Connor that meant using the police force to control the black community.[12]

Over the years the all-white Birmingham Police Department had developed a well-deserved reputation for brutality, especially against African Americans. In the eyes of local law enforcement, black people were inferior beings, singular manifestations of a monolithic mass. From the police commissioner down to the patrolman on the beat, institutionalized racism influenced the daily operations of the Birmingham Police Department. Officers regularly beat black suspects in an exercise of authority to show who ruled the streets. If reported—a rare event—offending officers received a light reprimand, if any at all. Time and again, fatalities occurred; coroners ruled "justifiable homicide." A prejudiced court system wherein judges called black defendants "niggers" concluded the dispensation of white man's law. Police brutality like vigilante bombings represented manifestations of community-sanctioned violence in defense of racial norms.[13]

Citing the "shameful record of violence visited upon Negroes of Birmingham, Alabama by that city's Police Department," the NAACP, at its annual convention held in Atlanta in July 1951, called on the Civil Rights Division of the U.S. Department of Justice to investigate police brutality in Birmingham. Another resolution petitioned the U.S. Steel Corporation to use its influence in city hall to stop the violence. The NAACP's action followed requests from local chapter members and "relatives of some of the victims of police bullets." Emory O. Jackson, editor of the *Birmingham World* and executive secretary of the association's Birmingham branch, charged that the police killed a black person "after every liberal Federal Court decision." Bull Connor "welcomed" the investigation, hoping "they will subpoena Emory Jackson because of some questions we'd like to ask him under oath since he seems to be so interested in seeing an investigation made." The new police chief who had replaced the late C. Floyd Eddins, Marcus Hancock, acknowledged, "We don't fear the results of any investigation," probably because he knew it would amount to nothing.[14]

Whereas reports of excessive use of force against white people often received publicity, press coverage of police brutality against black people appeared less frequently. Occasionally officers roughed up white suspects during an arrest, especially if those accused had been drinking. Policemen pistol-whipped Vernon Grant, a twenty-two-year-old white man, on September 15, 1951, after he allegedly took them on a high-speed chase. Held in jail for vagrancy, police charged him with drunk driving, carrying a concealed weapon, and resisting arrest. Grant contested the official account of events. He claimed that after officers hit him he broke away and ran, at which point the policemen fired their revolvers over his head, ran after him, and knocked him to the ground, kicking him severely. Grant last saw his wallet, identification, and eighty-seven dollars in cash when he surrendered them to authorities. During the trial, recorder's court judge Oliver B. Hall dropped the vagrancy and concealed weapon (a scout knife in the glove box) charges but fined Grant for the other violations. Grant's complaint about the excessive use of force in his arrest was one of at least eight made in September 1951.[15]

In addition to white men, Birmingham police officers were accused of beating white women, teenagers, and the handicapped. As Horace C. Wilkinson explained in a letter to the *Birmingham News*, police occasionally mistook a "spastic for a drunk." Although he found this "inexcusable," the archsegregationist believed that "the man who gets drunk and makes a general nuisance of himself deserves a good beating." Calling the criticism of law enforcement unfair, Wilkinson concluded: "There is no justification for continually harping on a police officer for protecting himself and resenting insults by whipping a prisoner who deserves every lick he receives." Chief Hancock agreed with Wilkinson and consistently exonerated officers accused of wrongdoing.[16]

The circumstances surrounding the fatal shooting by police of a black man on June 14, 1953, demonstrated the institutionalization of police brutality against African Americans in Birmingham. According to a press release from the police department quoted at length in the city's newspapers, an officer killed David "Little Buddy" Garrett for resisting arrest. Around 3:00 A.M. Garrett apparently ran into a patrol wagon driven by Officer R. G. Lutrell. The policeman informed the thirty-year-old black coal miner that he was under arrest. Allegedly drunk, Garrett shouted, "Damned if you're going to arrest me," and took off running. Lutrell gave chase, following Garrett up an alley. He fired a warning shot into the ground and commanded the suspect to surrender. Cornered, Garrett reputedly turned on Lutrell, hit him, and hollered, "You ain't gonna take me to jail." The officer struck back, knocking him to the ground. As he rose, Garrett allegedly took out a switchblade and, drawing back, prepared to strike Lutrell saying, "I said I wasn't going to jail. I'll kill you." Again Lutrell fired his revolver, the bullets ripping open Garrett's guts, tearing into his arm, and turning down

93

into his body. Stumbling, Garrett collapsed on the pavement near Fifth Avenue South, only two blocks from his house. Coroner Joe L. Hilderbrand ruled the shooting a "justifiable homicide." The press accepted the official report down to the highly questionable reconstructed dialogue. To add weight to the image of Garrett as dangerous and worthy of death, detectives claimed to have had an outstanding warrant for his arrest on charges of assault with intent to kill. As if by routine, the newspapers, police department, and city government processed the legal lynching of Little Buddy Garrett.[17]

Police brutality against African Americans often appeared in the press in roundabout ways. During a court trial, the testimony of Leroy McCray, a Negro witness, revealed the torture methods used by Bull Connor's policemen. Attorneys Albert Boutwell and Abraham Berkowitz represented another black man, Thad Donald, in an arson trial in November 1951 and called McCray to the witness stand, for he had been arrested with Donald that January night. The lawyers just wanted McCray's forced confession thrown out. McCray claimed that during an interrogation, officers forced him to drop his pants, then for forty-five minutes they beat him repeatedly across the buttocks with a hose. In a search of the jail, the attorneys found a cable in the room just as described by McCray. For five days Birmingham police had subjected McCray and Donald to protracted questioning, never once charging the black men with a crime or offering them bond. As Officer G. L. Pattie admitted on the stand, "We keep them 'til we've completed our investigation."[18]

Many black people developed their perceptions of the Birmingham Police Department from personal contact. As related to her white boss, the experience of Bessie Baxter Ammons, a janitress at the "Colored" Smithfield Court Housing Project, reflected the climate of fear under which black folk lived in Birmingham. Before the sun cracked through a gray dawn on January 20, 1951, the fifty-year-old charwoman walked to work. A police car pulled up to her and a uniformed officer reputedly called out, "Gal, where are you going? Come here!!" Having done nothing to provoke the encounter, the black woman responded, "Not me. For what? I'm going to work." The cop replied, "I say, come here!!" And with that he jumped out of the patrol car, flashed a light in her face, and drew his gun. "You mean you aint going to put your black ass in this car?" Bessie Ammons said, "No I aint going to get in that car."[19]

When asked to produce identification, she showed her keys to the Smithfield Court office and responded, "If you don't believe that I work there, you can come on down there and see." Releasing his prey, the unidentified policeman admonished: "Whenever you go anywhere you had better have some kind of identification on you. I ought to put your black ass in jail for vagrancy." Emboldened, the black woman retorted, "I got a job." But the cop snapped back: "Whenever any policeman tells you to get in the car, you had better do it. I mean what I say. I'm the law. Get on down the street." Bessie Ammons knew better than to get in the car, where in all likelihood she would be beaten, sexually molested, raped, or, worst of all, taken to the city jail. For good reason, Birmingham's black people feared the city jail. Prisoners were beaten and sometimes died behind bars. The notorious facility even had its own song, "Birmingham Jail."

Occasionally criticism of the police department surfaced, as when prominent people made public their views on the violence. The wife of Mayor Cooper Green spoke against police brutality in the fall of 1951, when she reported witnessing officers manhandle a prisoner. The comment led Charles W. McGehee of radio station WTNB to write in support of her action. He called the police department "a political vehicle and a small-time gestapo for Bull Connor." A man from the industrial suburb of Pratt City wondered how citizens could "condemn foreign brutality and permit it here." Other people in Birmingham called for the firing of police chief Hancock. In commenting on the violence, the press recommended restraint. The front-page *News* column "From Where I Stand" by Vulcan (a.k.a. Walling Keith) encouraged policemen to accept "oral abuse from drunks and irate citizens" without losing their tempers. The *Post-Herald* blamed the brutality on "inadequate training." Chief Hancock responded to the charges by asking citizens to report such infractions.[20]

Several systemic problems ensured that the Birmingham Police Department attracted the less-than-qualified applicant. Low wages—$236.25 a month in January 1951, less than the average railroad worker or truck driver—and a rule against holding outside jobs contributed to a high turnover rate among officers. In 1951 the police department lost more than one-fourth of its employees through resignations, dismissals, and retirements. Poor training also contributed to the problem, with nearly half of the 364 officers in October 1951 having served on the force for less than two years. Under the watchful eye of Bull Connor and the instruction of Lieutenant E. T. Rouse, Birmingham educated policemen at its training school. As an introduction to the legal structure, graduates listened to recorder's court judge Oliver B. Hall while feasting on "T-bone steaks and trimmings" in the dining room of the Fraternal Order of Police (FOP) before receiving their diplomas. The FOP acted as a union of sorts, looking out for the interests of its members.[21]

Many policemen formerly had served in the military, an inconvenience during the early months of the Korean conflict when the Alabama National Guard called up the reserves, obligating its members to resign from the force. During the same period, the city discharged other policemen for "misrepresentation on their job applications," "conduct unbecoming an officer," and "disobedience of orders." Most often policemen received a lighter sentence, as when the department caught Officer J. M. Ivy asleep in the patrol car while on his beat in Wylam and gave him a five-day suspension, or when Detectives J. T. Howell and R. R. Chambers got a fifteen-day suspension for slipping away while on duty without permission. The lack of professionalism, inferior quality of the applicant, and unattractiveness of the work and wages contributed to the city's inability to retain decent law enforcement personnel.[22]

The police department had problems with corruption, as many of its members participated in policy rackets, protection schemes, bootlegging, and burglary rings. Former police chief James Parsons estimated that 45 percent of the force received payoffs, 45 percent would have accepted them if offered, and only 10 percent steadfastly refused to be bought off. One anonymous letter, which explained, "I cant sign this. I dont want Mr. Connors thugs to shoot me," claimed that "the Birmingham police are working the negro sections as hard as the policy man, for protection money." Whereas some cops on the beat accepted bribes to ignore illegal liquor, prostitution, and gambling, others used their badge and uniform to intimidate citizens. Some criminals found it easier to operate while on the side of the law. A night watchman making his rounds came upon a sergeant and six policemen allegedly attempting to open the safe at the Blue Diamond Company. He observed one officer trying to pry open the door with a crowbar. Discovered, the policemen explained that they had stumbled across an attempted burglary. The department's October 1953 internal investigation cleared the officers of wrongdoing. In November 1953 detectives charged two policemen with grand larceny following a break-in at the Duke Brothers Furniture Company. Neither officer had served more than two years. The following summer, authorities broke a burglary ring run by twenty-three policemen who had stolen $50,000 during forty-one crimes. Also in October 1953 a traffic cop had committed armed robbery when he held up a filling station. With the criminals dressed in blue, the Birmingham Police Department's reputation suffered.[23]

The corruption and police brutality contributed to a series of scandals that rocked the department for more than two years and brought down a handful of officers, two police chiefs, and the commissioner of public safety. A raid on a bordello began the row. Complaining to Captain Charles L. Pierce, Paul Locascio, the unhappy neighbor of Thelma Ward, charged the forty-five-year-old madam with operating a disorderly house at 912 Thirteenth Street South. The ambitious Detective Henry Darnell informed Locascio that Ward would be found "not guilty." After police chief Marcus Hancock confessed to visiting the abode but finding nothing awry, the recorder's court cleared the known prostitute of the charge on December 5, 1951. In a police hearing that followed to investigate the conduct of Darnell, the detective exclaimed, "They're out to give me the ax and I'm going to unload." Although he failed to elaborate at that time, later testimony revealed that Chief Hancock had demanded $100 a month from Ward in protection money. In addition, Ward swore she had once broken her foot while visiting Hancock at his fish camp retreat. Furious over Darnell's testimony and Hancock's actions, Bull Connor excoriated the police chief, threatening to fire him if he did not resign. Connor placed Hancock and Darnell on sick leave. On December 20, 1951, Hancock asked for a physical disability retirement. The next evening Detective Darnell disclosed an adulterous Bull Connor with his secretary in the Tutwiler Hotel.[24]

Caught in his own web of hypocrisy, the commissioner of public safety and his brunette secretary, the tall thirty-four-year-old former Wave, Miss Christina Brown, were charged with "joint occupancy of a room with a female (male) person, and having sexual intercourse with a person other than his wife (her husband)," an ordinance proposed by Connor several years before. Proclaiming his innocence, Connor described the incident as a trap resulting from the feud in the police department. Darnell later testified that he acted on an anonymous tip out of "self-protection" because Connor had wanted him fired ever since a "Vulcan" column suggested him as a possible candidate for the position of police commissioner. Apparently Connor met Brown in Room 706 of the Tutwiler after Captain Pierce got him the room key during a Christmas cocktail party in the hotel ballroom on December 21, 1951. Accompanied by *Birmingham Post-Herald* reporter Billy Mobley and several others, Darnell banged on the door for twenty-three minutes before it opened, revealing Connor and Brown fully dressed in overcoats and hats. Chagrined, the police commissioner begged Darnell not to press charges. Connor pleaded: "Think of me Henry. You

97

Detective Henry Darnell (left) confronts Bull Connor shortly after catching the commissioner of public safety in the act of adultery. The resulting scandal revealed a corrupt Connor's capricious nature and kept him from running for reelection in 1953. BPLDAM.

are crucifying me. You're ruining me politically." He asked him to consider his "poor, sick wife." Darnell called in his superior officer, Captain C. E. "Bud" Huey, for assistance, but Huey was one of Connor's favorites, and he alleged that he "saw no violation" and therefore kept Connor's name off the docket. Five days later, Darnell filed charges against the two after a "gentlemen's agreement" with Connor fell through.[25]

Sordid details emerged during the sensational trial attended by capacity crowds as Assistant City Attorney J. Edmund Odum constructed the prosecution's case of moral turpitude. The city dropped its plan to add twenty-seven other counts of morals violations after heated protests by Connor's attorney John Foster. Testifying in court on January 6, 1952, Darnell explained: "Just like thousands of others, I'm fed up to here (moving his hands to his neck) with Mr. Connor and his actions. If judgment day were called for killers, murderers, thieves, sinners and hypocrites, and they all were resurrected tomorrow, Mr. Connor would be underneath all of them." On the first day of the trial Darnell discovered five sticks of dynamite under the seat of his car with a fuse attached to the exhaust pipe. Pointing to Connor, Darnell told the judge, "There's only one man in this whole wide world who would like to see me dead." The defense accused Darnell of seeking revenge, referring to the "gentlemen's agreement"— where Darnell told Connor, "Commissioner, I'm sorry this had to happen, but I am willing to forget it if you will leave me alone"—as an act of blackmail. Recorder's court judge Ralph E. Parker convicted Connor on the charges and sentenced him to a 180-day suspended sentence and a $100 fine.[26]

Gambling on a jury trial, attorney John Foster filed Connor's appeal in circuit court as outrage over the scandal spread. Testimony during the proceedings convinced the Jefferson County Circuit Court Grand Jury to launch an investigation into Connor's operations as commissioner of public safety, a post he refused to vacate despite his conviction. In response to the ruling, Connor accused Judge Parker of seeking revenge because Connor had opposed Parker's appointment to the bench. When Assistant City Attorney J. Edmund Odum independently investigated conditions within the police department, his superior James H. Willis accused him of insubordination. The "Odum Report" contained many of the rank-and-file complaints voiced by the Fraternal Order of Police. In response, the city commission—with Connor's participation—fired Odum. Connor rewarded Captain Pierce, who had testified on his behalf, by making him the new police chief, filling the position vacated by Hancock.[27]

The *Birmingham News* demanded Connor's resignation. The newspaper argued, "Mr. Connor cannot do the kind of job that is needed in his high office. Conditions within his department cannot be what they should be so long as he continues in office." City employees surreptitiously initiated a recall petition. Mayor Cooper Green and Commissioner Jimmy Morgan requested that the Jefferson County Personnel Board look into the charges against Bull Connor and the operations of the Department of Public Safety. Morgan specifically recommended that the commission employ an outsider to conduct the investigation. Because the personnel board had the power to subpoena witnesses and command records, it presented the logical place for such an undertaking; yet the independent body refused to touch the political scandal. Green sided with Connor in killing Morgan's suggestion for the use of a "foreign expert." In the end, the city commission drafted a Citizens' Committee to conduct the inquiry. Composed of investment banker Mervyn H. Sterne, retired industrialist H. A. Berg, and attorneys Greye Tate and R. Dupont Thompson, the Citizens'

Committee carried the imprimatur of the white power structure but otherwise exercised no real power. It listened to dozens of witnesses for thirteen days before completing its investigation on February 6, 1952.[28]

Throughout the early winter of 1952 the Jefferson County Grand Jury heard testimony from more than one hundred witnesses concerning Connor and the Department of Public Safety. In a scathing report issued on February 7, 1952, the grand jury called for Connor's impeachment. Broad in scope, the conclusions criticized the operations of the police department, noting the existence of "graft and corruption," the deplorable conditions in the city jail, extensive mistrust among officers, and the fraternizing among gamblers and prostitutes by patrolmen. The grand jury saved its harshest commentary for Connor. With precision, it described the police commissioner as "a 'hard task master,' explosive, vindictive against those employees under his authority who disagree with him, given to jumping at conclusions, dictatorial, immoral, autocratic, and a failure as an executive in his relationship with his subordinates." Furthermore, the jury found: "Connor does not seek or heed advice or information from his staff; he brow-beats his subordinates with whom he does not agree. He orders his subordinates what to do without clear statements of his policies and with little or no idea of his objectives; he has been found to usurp the duties of his officers in an attempt, personally, to do the jobs of his lowest subordinates; he listens to no advice and learns neither from his friends, his enemies nor experience; he cracks the whip of authority but uses no persuasion, logic or reason, if any he has." Damningly incisive, the evaluation captured Connor's character. Ruling him incompetent and unfit to hold office, the grand jury indicted Bull Connor on fifteen counts—among them, adultery, sexually harassing and assaulting another female employee, sending city prisoners to work for private individuals including himself and the Federation of Women's Clubs, other acts of malfeasance, and malicious interference in the operations of the fire department. Still Connor refused to resign.[29]

The Citizens' Committee issued its report on February 19, 1952. Though not as caustic as the grand jury findings, the report nevertheless criticized Connor and the running of the police department. On the one hand complimenting Connor's handling of organized crime and gambling, the report found the commissioner of public safety "deficient in executive ability," lacking an "objective outlook," and having a "frequently imperious" manner. Accusing Connor of favoritism, the Citizens' Committee identified cases of reprisal in the operations of his department: "Commissioner Connor's mind seems to turn to punishment for shortcomings and derelictions in duty, rather than to prevention, instruction and admonition." In other matters the report recommended the hiring of Negro policemen and new uniforms to change the image of the force but no pay raise. It whitewashed the charges of police brutality and the unsolved bombings. As the newspapers noted, the committee wavered in its treatment of Connor, leaving it up to the impeachment proceedings and recall effort to determine his future. One committee member, retired Woodward Iron executive H. A. Berg, issued a minority report that added his belief that Connor had "destroyed his future usefulness as head of the Police Department." Both the *Birmingham News* and *Post-Herald* renewed demands for Connor's resignation. The police commissioner released a statement saying he agreed "in the main" with the Citizens' Committee report, although Connor accused Berg of attacking him because of traffic violations in 1937 and 1938. Defending Berg, fellow committeeman Mervyn H. Sterne referred to Connor's "silly blast" as "typical of actions which caused the Citizens' Committee to conclude that Commissioner Connor is prone to take sudden impulsive and erratic action, without mature consideration, and that his mind seems to turn to punishment and reprisal." Despite the committee's negative evaluation, Connor remained in office.[30]

Although Bull Connor survived an impeachment trial begun in March 1952, his April appeal in circuit court failed to reverse the earlier conviction on charges of moral turpitude. Nevertheless, the police commissioner went after the detective who caught him with his secretary in the Tutwiler: he had Chief Charles L. Pierce fire Henry Darnell. City commissioner James W. Morgan demanded a public hearing in Darnell's case that ultimately reinstated the detective. In July 1952 Connor's protégé, Captain C. E. Huey, who had received premature advancement and other favored treatment in his grooming for the position of chief even though he had falsified his job application in connection with a burglary charge in 1931, resigned from the force after leading the highway patrol on a chase while off duty that ended when he wrecked into and killed a forty-seven-year-old schoolmarm. At a police hearing in October, a "little black book" kept by Huey and containing alleged violations made by Darnell and other detectives found its way before the Jefferson County Civil Service Personnel Board. Director Ray Mullins listened to Darnell and the four other detectives as they appealed low efficiency ratings assigned them since their falling out with Bull Connor. Acting under Connor's orders, Chief Pierce fired the five detectives on October 6, 1952. During the course of the hearing, Darnell testified that he had "conspired" with Pierce to discredit former Chief

Hancock in order to replace him with Pierce. Other detectives said they had paid Pierce cash for favors. In response to the accusations, Pierce requested suspension without pay pending the completion of an investigation. The city commission returned E. H. Brown to acting chief and reinstated the five detectives. Within a month of having been demoted to detective, Pierce shot a man during an arrest; the killing was ruled justifiable homicide. Meanwhile, Connor kept up his persecution of the five detectives.[31]

During the January 29, 1953, hearing on charges that the five detectives had attempted to blackmail Pierce into raising their efficiency scores, personnel board chairman Howard Yielding—an ally of Bull Connor's who had testified on his behalf during the failed impeachment hearings the year before—refused to excuse himself despite having announced his opinion of the defendants' guilt to the press. Connor acted as sole prosecutor at the hearing. Not surprisingly, the personnel board ruled against the officers, firing Darnell and demoting the other four from the rank of detective to patrolman. Darnell turned in his badge after eighteen years of service. Following continued harassment, one of the demoted detectives resigned in February 1953 with the statement: "During the last year, I have, undoubtedly, incurred the ill feeling of Commissioner Connor. He is apparently determined to try to cause my dismissal for no reason other than his personal feelings."[32]

Indeed, Bull Connor demonstrated the accuracy of the grand jury findings and the Citizens' Committee report by seeking reprisals against Darnell and the other detectives. Vindictive, this former champion of civil service reform flagrantly used favoritism to advance the obsequious and punish the disloyal. The police scandal revealed Connor's extensive reach beyond his own bailiwick and demonstrated the inability or unwillingness of city institutions such as the personnel board to challenge his authority. The police commissioner ignored repeated calls for his resignation and completed his term, leaving office in November 1953 after deciding not to run for reelection. In the end, Bull Connor had weathered a series of storms that would have swamped a less audacious man. Brazen to the core, he would return to power in 1957. Until then, he operated a filling station near his Woodlawn home, ever a presence in local politics.

The election of Robert E. Lindbergh as commissioner of public safety in 1953 presented an opportunity for change in Birmingham. Unlike other Sun Belt cities that experienced G.I. revolts that ushered in reformist politicians in the postwar period, Birmingham retained its old leadership, reflecting the stagnant character of the city's business class. A decent man, Lindbergh entered office with the goal of reforming the police department. He selected retired army colonel Paul L. Singer to reorganize the department during a one-year appointment as director of police. While Singer demonstrated his enthusiasm by cracking down on gambling and prostitution, he also initiated substantial reforms within the department that clarified the chain of command, increased supervision, and improved the workload and salaries of officers. Singer lifted a gag rule instituted by Connor that had prevented patrolmen from talking with the press and withheld arrest records and crime reports from the public. He restructured the examination process of advancement to reduce the potential for abuse. In response to Singer's shake-up, Commissioner Lindbergh began "pep talks" to strengthen morale among patrolmen and initiated training under the FBI. In general, Lindbergh and Singer's reforms attempted to improve the daily operations of the force while making it more democratic.[33]

Despite their best efforts, the problems in the police department proved insurmountable, especially regarding race relations. When Dr. J. King Chandler III, the black president of Daniel Payne College, complained of police brutality, Colonel Singer outlined his measures to reorganize and retrain officers. Singer blamed low wages for keeping the city from hiring the personnel it desired. In response to brutality, he authorized "psycho metric tests" on recruits to "reveal any anti-social psychological tendency such as sadism" before approving employment. He informed "Mr. Chandler" that he would not tolerate an officer insulting "any Negro citizen by calling him 'nigger' or 'boy,'" and he promised a "reprimand" and "disciplinary action" if such offenses continued. Not only the content but also the tone of the letter denoted a major change in the leadership of the police department. The other two city commissioners, however, failed to support fully Lindbergh's reforms.[34]

A particularly outrageous example of police brutality in late December 1954 presented a moment of truth when Birmingham's political leadership could have moved in a positive direction in race relations but opted instead to defend the white lower-middle-class status quo formerly identified with Bull Connor. Police arrested Charles Patrick, a black man, following a conflict over a downtown parking place with a white woman, Mrs. J. W. Siniard, whose husband was a policeman. On hearing of the incident, Officer Jim Siniard and his partner left their assigned beat, went to the jail, and received admittance to see the prisoner whereupon they mercilessly beat him behind bars. When Lindbergh learned of the beating, he immediately launched an investigation. After the accused changed their initial denials and confessed to the brutality, the police commissioner and his chief of police, G. L. Pattie, fired the two officers. Citing their record on the force, Mayor Morgan and Commissioner Wade Bradley reinstated the veteran patrolmen, giving them thirty-day suspensions instead. By not backing up Lindbergh, the other two commissioners in effect compromised his authority. Their actions ended an opportunity to improve race relations in Birmingham by sanctioning police brutality.[35]

Many people in Birmingham deplored the city commission's refusal to sustain the ruling of the police commissioner and his police chief. In a letter to Mayor Morgan, whom she had previously held in "high esteem," Mrs. A. S. Davis wrote that she "believed" him to be a "Christian," but after his reinstatement of the officers she "felt a terrible let down" and wondered if she had known him "at all." Informing Morgan of the public opinion expressed about the beating on the local radio program "The People Speak," Mrs. J. E. Hall reported four to one telephone calls against reinstatement. She explained, "I felt myself growing prouder every minute at the justice and lack of prejudice of those southern people on that broadcast." The Young Men's Business Club (YMBC) denounced the police brutality and the lack of safety for prisoners in jail while commending Lindbergh and Pattie. Attorney Jerome A. Cooper praised the "dignity, honesty and fairness" of the police department reformers. The Birmingham News labeled the thirty-day suspension "inadequate" and questioned whether the city wanted "this attitude of mind enforcing our laws." Recognizing the real issue, the News concluded: "Does not this relatively light reproof involve danger that other officers, under the plea of personal strain, might yield to impulses to beat prisoners?" Indeed it did, reaffirming police brutality against African Americans as official policy in Birmingham.[36]

Angered by the beating, the black community rallied around the issue of police brutality. Under the leadership of the NAACP, a mass meeting held in the Sixteenth Street Baptist Church on January 16, 1955, adopted a resolution that deplored the violence, denounced Morgan and Bradley, and commended Lindbergh and Pattie. Linking brutality to a lack of black policemen, the NAACP urged the city to hire "Negroes in the Police Department" in order to "immeasurably strengthen the department and increase the confidence of Negroes in their City Government." For several years the issue of Negro policemen had generated protest within the black community. The Birmingham World called on the city to hire black policemen. The Birmingham News did likewise, noting that Talladega employed

Negro officers, "why not Birmingham?" The *News* sent its crack reporter, Irving Beiman, to observe black law enforcement in Atlanta, where, since 1948, African American officers could arrest other black people while patrolling black neighborhoods. Beiman returned to Birmingham and published a series of glowing features on the subject. The Jefferson County Coordinating Council of Social Forces (JCCCSF), a progressive group of citizens in the city that included Charles F. Zukoski, investigated the issue of Negro police and drafted a favorable report in 1952. It concluded that eighty-two southern cities employed black policemen and that of the metropolises only Birmingham refused to do so. A survey of thirty southern cities revealed positive responses to the use of Negro policemen. Some people interviewed in Birmingham supported the proposal. Whereas Bull Connor had refused to consider the idea, Bob Lindbergh proved more receptive; nevertheless, the city commission failed to adopt the measure despite repeated appeals by black and white leaders.[37]

Professional baseball provided another opportunity whereby Birmingham's city commission attempted to dismantle the more extreme examples of segregation and move the city toward progressive race relations. When it appeared that the Birmingham Barons baseball team might make the Dixie Series in the fall of 1953, the city commission announced its intention to amend the city code that prohibited blacks and whites from playing sports together. Two years before, Bull Connor had the commission adopt the law in response to the rise of integrated professional sports. Only Memphis joined Birmingham in banning black athletes from playing with whites. Applauding the commission's reform effort, the *Post-Herald* argued that to have acted otherwise "would have done the city untold injury by branding it before the world as a backward and benighted community." The play-off victory of Nashville over Birmingham prevented the Barons from representing the Southern Association against the winner in the integrated Texas League, so the commission dropped the issue temporarily.[38]

In February 1954 Morgan and Lindbergh revised the ordinance to allow integrated professional sports in Birmingham. Progressive elements in the city again praised the decision. The Young Men's Business Club passed a resolution commending the action, as did the Methodist Ministers' Association. A superintendent of the Birmingham Baptist Association encouraged church leaders to support the city commission. But not everyone approved. Attorney Hugh Lock Sr., a crusty throwback to the Democratic bolt of 1928 and the Dixiecrat movement, initiated a petition drive to force a referendum on the issue. After receiving the necessary five thousand signatures, the commission scheduled the required election on the revised ordinance. Held on June 1, 1954, the outcome represented a referendum on the *Brown* decision. Birmingham voted three-to-one to retain segregation. The city's brush with moderation went down in flames, and a disgusted Mayor Morgan left for his vacation retreat in Florida.[39]

Birmingham's political leaders had attempted to steer the troubled city on a course of racial moderation. Since the *Brown v. Board of Education* decision of May 17, 1954, had declared segregated schools unconstitutional, southern reactionaries had launched a campaign of massive resistance to prevent the enforcement of the court decree. Yet Alabama avoided the initial hysterical response to *Brown* that marked reactions in other southern states. While Virginia's Governor Harry F. Byrd resurrected interposition as the strategy of massive resistance, Alabama's Governor Gordon Persons warned against "half-baked" plans concocted to address the ruling. In anticipation of an unfavorable decision on segregation, Persons in 1953 had appointed a legislative committee under the leadership of Albert Boutwell to propose a way around the court by keeping Alabama's schools open and segregated. Having replaced James A. Simpson as Jefferson County's state senator, Boutwell proved himself equally as reactionary.[40]

Birmingham's press offered varied comment following *Brown*. Whereas the *News* regretted the decision and defended states' rights, the *Post-Herald* called for "slow, deliberate thinking before acting." Only the African American *Birmingham World* championed the ruling. A public opinion poll conducted by the *Post-Herald* found a generous mix of those who approved, reluctantly accepted, or disapproved of the *Brown* decision, but in general apathy characterized the initial response of Birmingham's black and white communities. The attempted firebombing of black dentist Dr. John W. Nixon's new house a week after *Brown* announced the response of extreme white supremacists.[41]

Shortly after the *Brown* decision, Alabama voters reelected James E. Folsom governor. Back in office, the neopopulist encouraged racial moderation and rallied his hill county legislators in opposition to the segregationist measures proposed by the neo-Bourbons. Throughout 1955 the Folsom administration defeated reactionary legislation and kept Alabama on a steadier keel than other Deep South states. But sanity slipped away as events and time conspired against this last effort at racial moderation. The unfolding Montgomery bus boycott and Autherine Lucy's aborted attempt to desegregate the University of Alabama generated a climate of hostility to race reform as white supremacists organized citizens' councils throughout the state. By 1956 Folsom could no longer hold back the voices of extremism. A special session called to revise the archaic constitution of 1901 instead passed an interposition measure and other segregationist legislation. In April 1956 Folsom, out of political expediency, signed his first anti-integration law, Boutwell's "freedom of choice" amendment, which established a legal loophole to avoid school desegregation. According to the law, guardians could choose to send their children to either all-white, all-black, or mixed schools, but, as Boutwell noted, "It does not provide for any freedom of choice for a Negro child to attend a white school or a white child to attend a Negro school." Folsom's final effort to counter the fire-eaters failed when he lost a bid for state Democratic national committee-man to a little-known candidate of the citizens' council. That May, the electorate voted three-to-one against Folsom. Alabama's capitulation to racism was complete. Hardly anyone resisted massive resistance in 1957. By the state's gubernatorial race of 1958, an ambitious former Folsom aide, George C. Wallace, lost to John Patterson when he was "out-niggered" in the campaign. No longer would Alabamians entertain a moderate approach to race relations.[42]

107

Members of the white power structure and the lower middle class organized Birmingham's massive resistance to *Brown*. Foreshadowing the citizens' council movement, the American States' Rights Association (ASRA) incorporated in April 1954, when six hundred white supremacists, including, according to the *News*, "a substantial number of prominent and wealthy people," met in Birmingham. Headed by Olin H. Horton, a personnel manager in an insurance company, the ASRA organized to "maintain segregation . . . fight the FEPC [Fair Employment Practices Commission] . . . keep Communist propaganda out of our schools . . . [and] . . . preserve states' rights." Other members included Black Belt state senators Sam Engelhardt Jr. and Walter C. Givhan. The ASRA quickly became the first important white supremacy group in Alabama. It ran quarter-page display ads in daily and weekly newspapers and sponsored broadcasts by fiery Asa E. "Ace" Carter over WILD radio to disseminate its message. The ASRA protested favorable comments about the United Nations (UN) published in the handbook of the Girl Scouts of America, and it pressured the school board to fire a teacher accused of spreading "subversive" UN material in the classroom. The activists also banned books from the library. By November 1954 the ASRA boasted a mailing list of five thousand names.[43]

Within a year, the ASRA and its chief propagandist, Ace Carter, had joined with attorney and archsegregationist Hugh Locke Sr. and druggist

John H. Whitley to organize in the industrial suburb of Tarrant City the Birmingham district's first citizens' council. More than five hundred people, including many women, attended the initial meeting that marked the tenth citizens' council formed in Alabama, the previous ones having appeared in the Black Belt. Like a house fire, the movement quickly consumed Birmingham. Growing black activism fanned the flames. By January 1956 a newly created Eastern Section Citizens' Council assembled in the ballroom of Cascade Plunge, a popular recreational facility in East Lake. In one week in February 1956, citizens' councils formed in West End, Fairfield, and Ensley. The next week saw the incorporation of the Roebuck and Homewood Citizens' Councils. By March about sixty chapters had met in Alabama. Membership was open to white men and women over the age of eighteen who believed in segregation and paid yearly dues of three dollars.[44]

In the Birmingham district, unionists provided an important segment of citizens' council membership. In several ways, massive resistance reflected the postwar character of trade unionism in the area. Racial discrimination at TCI found expression through the citizens' council chapters organized by steelworkers in Ensley and the industrial suburbs of Fairfield and Bessemer. Craftsmen from East Lake and Tarrant City took the indigenous protest movement one step further by withdrawing from the AFL-CIO over national policies on race and organizing the segregationist Southern Crafts, Inc., in July 1956. With management's blessings, the nearly all-white workforce at the Hayes Aircraft Corporation joined the renegade union movement. A leader in the aerospace industry, Hayes received most of its contract work from the federal government. Without the support of the AFL-CIO, however, the segregationist Southern Crafts collapsed when its independent leadership failed to win wage concessions from Hayes. Nonetheless, the workforce remained active in massive resistance through the citizens' councils and the Ku Klux Klan.[45]

Leaders in the citizens' council movement used the meetings to inform supporters about the threat of integration. Occasionally councillors planned "creative" programs, as when Whitley of Tarrant City played a recording of an NAACP speaker to "give further proof to our members of that organization's aims," but normally speakers like Givhan of Dallas County or Engelhardt of Macon County or firebrand Ace Carter addressed the audience. Perhaps typical was the February meeting where, criticizing the NAACP for registering black voters, former commissioner Bull Connor eloquently warned the Central Park Citizens' Council, "If you don't regis-

108

ter and vote they are going to outvote you, and where are you." Through the ballot, white people could "beat the NAACP so fast it won't be funny." Connor hoped they would vote for him in his upcoming race for the city commission seat vacated by Wade Bradley. He failed to win despite running a racist campaign in which he called his opponent, James T. "Jabo" Waggoner, the choice of the NAACP. Waggoner linked Connor to the extremism of Ace Carter and said that, although a segregationist, he opposed any race-baiting that created turmoil. The election turned, not on the race issue, but on the office of commissioner of public improvements, a position Waggoner had trained for and one viewed unsuitable for Bull Connor.[46]

In addition to the council movement, massive resistance found expression in Birmingham through a protest group of Methodist laymen. Meeting on December 14, 1954, in the ornate Spanish baroque sanctuary of the socially prominent Highlands Methodist Church on the southside of Birmingham, some 250 laymen and ministers listened to the church's pastor, the Reverend Dr. Guy McGowan, the Reverend Dr. Stanley Frazer of St. James Methodist Church in Montgomery, and local realtor and attorney Sidney W. Smyer outline plans to prevent the desegregation of the Methodist church. Credited with doing much of the "spadework" that set up the organization later named the Association of Methodist Ministers and Laymen was Olin H. Horton, president of the ASRA. The laymen's association formed to combat the Council of Methodist Bishops' resolution supporting the *Brown* decision. The churchgoers feared that their national bishops would force the integration of the 3-million-member white Southeast Jurisdiction of the church with the 300,000-member Negro Central Jurisdiction.[47]

Only sixteen years before, the Methodist Episcopal Church, South, had merged with the northern branch, becoming the United Methodist Church, in a ceremony held in Birmingham's Municipal Auditorium. The Protestant denomination had split over slavery in 1844, and reunification occurred in 1938 in part with the understanding that the South's distinctly organized black and white jurisdictions would remain separate. Now the issue of canonical desegregation raised new questions of secession. The lay leaders put these rumors to rest, explaining that the group would fight within the church structure. Smyer declared, "I will warn you again and again that there are going to be times when we are going to have to stand up and fight for our convictions." Mrs. Joe Sargent, of Trinity Methodist Church in Homewood, who headed the women's auxiliary, added that

Once a Dixiecrat and leader in the state's massive resistance movement, Sidney W. Smyer Sr. converted to racial moderation in the wake of negative publicity following Birmingham's brutal reception of the Freedom Riders. His business interests in the Birmingham Realty Company made him a "Big Mule." Portrait Collection, BPLDAM.

after the women "find out what we stand for they'll put the fire under the men." The laymen's association stood for massive resistance, and these concerned Methodists elected Smyer president of their white supremacy organization.[48]

Sid Smyer hailed from a powerful and notable extended family. Although born on May 30, 1897, in Cherokee County near Gadsden, Alabama, Sidney William Smyer moved with his family to Birmingham shortly before the turn of the century. He grew up on his father's dairy farm next to the state fair grounds and attended West End Elementary and Birmingham High School. In the summertime he peddled vegetables—suffering the "indignity" of being mistaken for a "dago" because most truck farmers in the city were Italian—and he worked in the steel mills to earn college tuition. After receiving a law degree from the University of Alabama and serving in World War I, Smyer returned to Birmingham as an attorney associated with his older brother, Shuford Brandon Smyer, and uncles Edgar Jones Smyer and Rufus Brandon Smyer. During the 1898–1910 Greater Birmingham annexation drive, E. J. Smyer had failed in his effort to exempt from taxes for fifty years all industrial property in the city. Only U.S. Steel achieved that distinction. Sid inherited his uncle's sense of fiscal responsibility. The Smyer clan built their mansions on a crest of Shades Mountain overlooking the yet-to-be-developed suburbs of Homewood and Mountain Brook near Vestavia, the famed temple home of their neighbor, former mayor George B. Ward. Sid later occupied one of these houses. Both uncles were charter members of Highlands Methodist Church. Sid would charter Canterbury Methodist in Mountain Brook. All lived into their eighties.[49]

Snopesian in outlook, Smyer epitomized the business conservative's philosophy of the bottom line. Yet he cultivated an unassuming, good-ole-boy air of rural intelligence. This contradiction could distract and disarm his opponents. The young Rotarian gained political notice when he helped launch the Alabama Economy League in 1932. Smyer joined in the fight for civil service, leading the opposition to Governor Bibb Graves in the state house after his election in 1934. He won a second term in 1938 and pushed through much of Governor Frank Dixon's neo-Bourbon platform. Passionate about efficiency, Smyer crusaded against and defeated in 1938 a greatly needed $11 million bond issue to expand municipal services in Birmingham. Throughout his tenure on Goat Hill, the future Dixiecrat consistently touted the interests of the Big Mule–Black Belt coalition.[50]

During his second year in the legislature, Smyer was appointed general counsel to the board of directors of the Birmingham Realty Company. He became vice president in 1942, president in 1953, and chairman of the board in 1967, when his son, Sidney W. Smyer Jr., became the president. The successor to the Elyton Land Company, which had founded Birmingham in 1871, Birmingham Realty controlled most of the land from Red Mountain north, including the residential suburb of Norwood and between Sixth Street to the west and Thirty-sixth Street to the east—basically the entire downtown of Birmingham—as well as other tracts of land in Jefferson County. Conservative management kept the property under tight control, rarely, if ever, selling property. When Smyer became president he altered Birmingham Realty's policies, unloading some holdings, developing others, in general using the company's assets to generate profits. During his fourteen-year tenure as president, the firm saw an increase from $343,000 to $1,243,000 in gross rental income and constructed forty new buildings for lease to local and national tenants. Unlike the Big Mules, who remained mired in the colonial economy, Smyer understood economic growth as the key to the postwar boom. To direct the development of the service economy, he became a charter member of the Jefferson County Planning Commission in 1947. His relentless work at regional planning led to the nickname "Mr. Zoning." Later in life he opposed a "short-sighted" effort to reduce Birmingham's already low property taxes because the national concerns that rented 70 percent of the Birmingham Realty Company's holdings wanted the essential public services paid for by ad valorem taxes. With his brother Shuford the director and his uncle the president of the Title Guarantee Loan and Trust Company and himself in charge of Birmingham Realty, the Smyer family dominated the city's real estate market.[51]

In addition to the Smyers, several other prominent families belonged to Highlands Methodist—the center of massive resistance in the church—including two state legislators, Lawrence Dumas and Tram Sessions; Ruth Lawson Hanson, the wife of the *Birmingham News* publisher; and industrialists Richard J. Stockham and Darius A. Thomas. Whereas the congregation endorsed the laymen's association by having its minister actively involved, other church leaders disapproved. The Birmingham Methodist Ministers Association renounced the movement, which they believed would "encourage prejudice and hatred" and could be "used by chronic agitators to stir up dissension and strife." Smyer denied that the laymen intended to create "racial tension"; rather, he maintained, they were concerned with reports that the May 1956 General Conference of the Methodist Church would adopt resolutions calling racial discrimination and enforced segregation un-Christian and evil. To counter the threat, Smyer proposed the election of prosegregation delegates to the General Conference. Other church problems concerned the laymen, including the issue of social engineering. At a May 1955 gathering in the Tutwiler Hotel, three hundred ministers and laymen from Alabama, northwestern Florida, and Mississippi heard Frazer describe church publications that promoted racial integration through "a sort of brain-washing." Wanting to distribute his own propaganda, Smyer criticized the editor of the state Methodist organ, the *Alabama Christian Advocate*, for refusing to publish the prosegregation material of the laymen's association.[52]

The Methodist massive resistance movement lost its struggle with the national denomination when the delegates to the 1956 General Conference adopted the nondiscriminatory clauses. By this time Smyer had dropped out of the laymen's association. Apparently he reevaluated his racial beliefs and began the process of sacrificing white supremacy for pecuniary gain. Others held fast to their principles, and Highlands remained the clearinghouse of Methodist massive resistance. In September 1958 the church sponsored a prosegregation rally where lieutenant governor nominate Albert Boutwell renewed the cry for states' rights. Church members Larry Dumas, now state senator from Jefferson County, and house member Tram Sessions joined other legislators from Birmingham in the program.[53]

The following spring saw Highlands at it again, as white supremacists organized the Methodist Laymen's Union, headed by the Birmingham judge and Sunday school teacher, Whit Windham. The new group had a decided Black Belt tone to its composition. As its official statement *A Pronouncement* made clear, the laymen intended to prevent the integration of the church. More than 1,800 Methodists attended the proceedings, filling the huge sanctuary and its basement to overflowing. Richard Stockham, a valve manufacturer, and Cooper Green, the former mayor and vice president of the Alabama Power Company, were among those selected as committee chairmen. A lone seminarian arose to denounce the racism of *A Pronouncement* and was shouted down. Laymen tailed the student, Thomas Reeves, back to Methodist-supported Birmingham-Southern College and then led an entourage of fifteen horn-honking cars around the campus. These Christians convinced Reeves's congregation to bar him from its pulpit. The Methodist Laymen's Union next went after the Reverend Robert Hughes, of Birmingham, who served as executive secretary of the Alabama Council on Human Relations, a moderate group connected

to the Southern Regional Council. For this act of brotherly love, the laymen succeeded in sending Hughes to Africa by getting him reassigned as a
missionary. Citing the laymen's association, the New York Times identified
Birmingham as the center of "racism in Protestant church groups," a distinction that embarrassed church leaders. When in July 1959 Larry Dumas
proposed legislation that would allow Protestant churches threatened with
integration to break out of their national denominations while retaining
church property, many Methodists felt that the laymen's association had
gone too far. Nevertheless, massive resistance remained a factor in church
politics as the Methodist laymen's associations joined the Ku Klux Klan
and the citizens' councils in a defense of white supremacy.[54]

No one articulated the rhetoric of massive resistance or expressed the
perversion of petite bourgeois republicanism better than Asa Earl "Ace"
Carter. The charismatic Carter grew up on a dairy farm in the small community of Oxford outside Anniston in nearby Calhoun County. Stationed
in the Pacific during World War II, Carter participated in such navy mis-
sions as the battle of Leyte Gulf and the invasion of Okinawa. He used the
G.I. Bill to study journalism at the University of Colorado after which he
worked as a radio announcer in Denver. He then held several broadcast
positions before moving in 1953 to Birmingham's WILD. A year later the
American States' Rights Association sponsored Carter's racist commen-
taries carried by radio over twenty stations across the state. The anti-Semitic
nature of his diatribes led to a boycott of WILD and the ultimate cancella-
tion of the program in 1955, an act that fed his paranoia. This extremism
contributed to the split in Alabama's citizens' council movement, for the
neo-Bourbon bigotry of Black Belt senators Sam Engelhardt Jr. and Walter
C. Givhan repudiated the hatred of Jews articulated by Carter. In response
to his dismissal, Carter incorporated the renegade North Alabama Citizens'
Council in 1956.[55]

Carter created his own faction of the Klan—the original Ku Klux Klan of
the Confederacy—as a paramilitary vigilante group that dressed in gray.
He believed that "BE-BOP PROMOTES COMMUNISM," and he denounced rock 'n' roll for its "morally degenerating influence on white
teenagers." On April 10, 1956, members of his Klan climbed on stage and
assaulted Nat "King" Cole during a performance in Birmingham attended
by 4,000 white youth. When two of his Klan followers questioned his
management of finances, Carter shot them with the revolver he always
carried. Attempted murder charges were later dropped. The following year
his Klansmen castrated a black man selected at random.[56]

114

Six members of the white supremacist splinter group kidnapped Judge Edward Aaron near the industrial suburb of Tarrant City and castrated him in a bizarre initiation rite on September 2, 1957. Even by Birmingham standards, the event proved particularly gruesome. On Labor Day afternoon, Klan officers met at the home of Jesse Mabry—one of several citizens' council members convicted of attacking Nat "King" Cole—to select an assistant to exalted cyclops Joe P. Pritchett. The group chose Bart A. Floyd. The meeting broke up as the six men piled into two cars to "pick up a Negro to scare hell out of." Seeing Aaron walking with his girlfriend near Zion City, the Klansmen screeched to a halt, grabbed the thirty-four-year-old black painter, and threw him into the backseat. Arriving at the secret lair in Chalkville, Floyd pulled the hapless man from the vehicle, hollered "make like a dog," and led him crawling into the cinder block hideout. Once inside, cyclops Pritchett asked Aaron if he knew the Reverend Fred L. Shuttlesworth, the local integration leader. Aaron answered no. Pritchett then asked if he wanted to die or lose his genitals, to which the African American responded neither, but then chose emasculation. Although Aaron informed his captors that he did not belong to the civil rights movement, the Klansmen told him to "tell Negro leaders the same thing would happen to them if they attempted to enroll Negro children in white schools." The robed sextet then forced him to strip from below the waist and lie on the dirt floor. After Pritchett kicked him in the face, another night rider hit him in the head with a wrench. Turning to Floyd—who was to prove himself "worthy" to be the cyclops's assistant—Pritchett said, "do your duty." Taking out a razor, Floyd reached between Aaron's legs and "proceeded to cut." Dousing the victim with turpentine to aggravate his wound (but which probably saved his life), Floyd held aloft his blade and boasted, "I have a souvenir." The Klansmen gathered up Aaron, tossed him in the trunk, and later dumped him out near Springdale, where police officers found the mutilated man near death from loss of blood. In time, Birmingham juries convicted four of the six Klansmen for the act of mayhem and sentenced them to twenty years in the state prison. The parole board appointed by Governor George C. Wallace commuted the terms in 1963.[57]

Carter's magazine, *The Southerner*, combined "scientific" racial evidence to document Negro "inferiority" with McCarthyesque exposés on communist infiltration of America, investigative pieces designed to intimidate local efforts at racial moderation and features on Confederate heroes. The magazine consolidated much of the material that Carter previously had distributed by leaflet through the American States' Rights Association.

One can see in the literature the confused efforts of concerned individuals who, though warped by white supremacy, struggled to control their lives and their community. The ASRA memos and *Southerner* articles criticized the transition of Birmingham's neighborhoods caused by the building of suburbs, defended traditional education that emphasized local and national history, and worked to halt the trend toward "internationalism." But mostly the material listed racial statistics on venereal disease and illegitimate births and warned of inevitable mongrelization. Himself a filling station owner, Carter understood the fears and aspirations of the lower middle class, and in an age of social change and declining economic independence his twisted traditional values—those of America, Christianity, and white supremacy—found their final flourish in this tragically disoriented movement.[58]

Running as white supremacist par excellence, Carter lost to fellow service station operator and white lower-middle-class leader Bull Connor in the 1957 municipal race that returned the former police commissioner to office. Carter placed a distant fifth out of five in the Democratic primary election for lieutenant governor in 1958. He then jumped on the George C. Wallace bandwagon, working to elect the cocky fighting judge from Barbour County governor in 1962. As speechwriter, Carter penned Wallace's most famous words: "Segregation now. Segregation tomorrow. Segregation forever." Breaking with Wallace in 1970 over what he perceived to be the governor's growing liberalism, Carter ran against his former boss in that year, only to suffer a humiliating defeat. He then disappeared.[59]

Resurfacing in Abilene, Texas, in 1972 under the alias Forrest Carter, he wrote in 1973 *The Rebel Outlaw: Josey Wales*, better known as the 1976 movie starring Clint Eastwood. This story of an unreconstructed rebel in the postwar West hounded by the government presented Carter's fantasy of his own past and the defeated republican virtues he championed. As Forrest, Carter fabricated a new life, claiming to be a Cherokee named Little Tree who was orphaned at age five, self-educated, and a cowboy. Several other books, including the 1976 *Education of Little Tree* and 1980 *Cry Geronimo*, became best-sellers and earned Carter a reputation as an activist for Native American causes, which he supported liberally through his royalties. Occasionally the old hatred seethed out from underneath the facade, especially when he had been drinking. Though alcohol might have routed the demons, it bloated his face and on one drunken day in 1979 it led his son to punch him. Carter fell, struck a countertop, and choked to death. No family members attended his funeral.[60]

Ace Carter's failure to legitimate racial extremism relegated his brand of white supremacy to an underground movement while demonstrating the general decency of the white lower middle class. Similar to the vigilantes who dynamited houses, Ace Carter acted on his beliefs; yet the majority of Birmingham's white electorate was not so extreme. At the movement's height in the spring of 1956, Carter directed seventy-three citizens' councils with a combined membership of more than 50,000 statewide and a local membership in the thousands. But his rhetoric grew too harsh. Carter's call for the resignation of University of Alabama president O. C. Charmichael and the impeachment of Governor Folsom over the Autherine Lucy affair alienated many supporters. After the March 1956 split, Engelhardt and Givhan of the reorganized Alabama Association of Citizens' Councils denounced those members of Carter's splinter group as "demagogic rabble rousers" and "prisoners of hate." Once in the mainstream of massive resistance, Carter found himself increasingly on the fringe, shunned by the state's "respectable" segregationists. In April 1956 Engelhardt began raiding Carter's citizens' council units in Birmingham. Within a week the Eastern Section Citizens' Council—which claimed 2,200 members—broke away from Carter's movement, and his trusted assistant who ran the Roebuck Citizens' Council resigned. The record crowds quit going to hear Ace. To complete the takeover of Birmingham's citizens' councils, the Black Belt leaders grouped the old North Alabama units under the rubric, the Ninth Congressional District, in order to tie the movement back to state politics. By the second anniversary of *Brown*, Carter had lost as the citizens' councils of Alabama finished "weeding out the undesirable, radical elements from all places of authority in our state councils." In a show of unity, the Jefferson County legislative delegation headed by state senator Albert Boutwell joined members of the city commission—except Mayor Morgan—and other politicians in a citizens' council rally commemorating Black Monday. Bull Connor and Jabo Waggoner also attended the affair.[61]

When sixty or so of Carter's following picketed a rock concert in Birmingham on May 20, 1956—some carrying placards printed with "Ask Your Preacher about Jungle Music"—twelve teenage boys protested their demonstration outside Municipal Auditorium. With signs reading "Rock and Roll Is Here to Stay," the young men embarrassingly rebuffed the North Alabama Citizens' Council. In early June the *Montgomery Advertiser* targeted Carter, calling him a "loathsome fuhrer." Carter sued for defamation. Further humiliation for Carter occurred over his association with John Kasper. A professional agitator and Carter's apprentice, the clean-cut

Columbia University graduate from New Jersey joined his mentor in stirring up racial hatred during the desegregation of schools in Clinton, Tennessee. Six months later it was revealed that an unrepentant Kasper, while living in Greenwich Village, had danced the Shango with his black girlfriend in mixed social settings. Discredited, Carter and Kasper found their invitations to speaking engagements given to other white supremacists.[62]

The 1957 race for commissioner of public safety brought to a head the forces of reaction and reform in Birmingham. Three of the five candidates in the first primary represented clear segments of the city's population. Incumbent Robert E. Lindbergh ran for reelection on his record as a moderate, Bull Connor sought to return to office as a staunch segregationist, and extremist Ace Carter wanted to stop what he saw as the "communist-inspired integration and federal power control drive." Lindbergh won the most votes with 14,528, followed by Connor with 11,938. Carter polled 1,675 and the other two candidates claimed 3,117. Although he attracted little support, Carter took some of the white lower-status vote from Bull Connor. Ace pulled his largest support from East Lake, Woodlawn, and West End, placing a distant third with his best showing of 44 ballots in one box in Central Park. As a fringe candidate, Carter stood on the outskirts of respectable politics in Birmingham. Although he held similar beliefs, Bull Connor proved more palatable to the electorate.[63]

City officials scheduled a runoff for June 4, 1957, to determine who Birmingham's police commissioner would be: Bull Connor or Bob Lindbergh. During the month leading up to the election, voters witnessed a campaign dominated by the race issue. Since Connor had left office in disgrace in 1953, he had unsuccessfully sought election as sheriff of Jefferson County in 1954 and commissioner of public improvements in 1956, with former state senator Jim Simpson directing his campaign strategy. A natural on the citizens' council circuit, Bull delivered prosegregation speeches across the state and around Birmingham. In 1956 he supported Ace Carter's fight against bebop and Nat "King" Cole. In the June 1957 primary runoff, Connor would garner the votes of Ace's supporters. Again Simpson assisted Connor's campaign. Bull Connor called Lindbergh soft on segregation and ran on his own record as a racial extremist. The incumbent stood by his past four years in office as a racial moderate who upheld the city's segregation laws but clearly worked for race reform. The *Birmingham News* endorsed Lindbergh but fell silent in the days before the election.[64]

One hundred and three votes altered the course of Birmingham's history as Bull Connor won reelection as commissioner of public safety with 15,891 to the 15,788 polled by Lindbergh. Around 45 percent of the city's qualified voting list of 70,000 (a large turnout that surprised pollsters) had determined the outcome of the election. The white lower middle class provided Bull's margin of victory. Connor carried East Lake, Woodlawn, and West End. Whereas Connor attracted the vote of white steelworkers living near TCI in Ensley, Precinct 45, Box 3A with 428 to 225, 3B with 278 to 153, 4A with 383 to 258, and 5A with 449 to 283, Lindbergh won the working-class vote from the Italian and black neighborhoods, Precinct 45, Boxes 1A with 398 to 153 and 2A with 272 to 183. Other noncraft working-class votes pulled by Lindbergh included the nonunion ACIPCO district, Precinct 42, Box 1A with 348 to 261 and the Stockham Valve Company district, Precinct 10, Box 12A with 289 to 237. Much of Lindbergh's support came from the affluent southside, with the Highland Avenue boxes showing two-to-one support for the incumbent. The one district identified as predominantly black, the Graymont Armory at Legion Field, Precinct 9, Box 1A, cast 464 ballots for Lindbergh to the 111 for Connor.[65]

Connor interpreted his victory as a clear signal to defend segregation. Yet the margin of only 103 votes in a hotly contested campaign also revealed that many in the electorate favored a moderate approach to race relations. Comprised of the affluent and educated, portions of the noncraft working class and the black community, this heterogeneous segment of the populace would play an important role in the business community's reform movement of the early 1960s. Lindbergh's inability to win reelection underscored Birmingham's failure to carry out the positive race reforms he had proposed during his four-year term. With Bull Connor back in office, Birmingham prepared for a showdown with the civil rights movement.

CHAPTER FOUR

The Local Movement

The formation of the Alabama Christian Movement for Human Rights in 1956 marked a clear departure from traditional black protest in Birmingham and foreshadowed the nonviolent direct action tactics of the student sit-ins and Freedom Rides. Heretofore, the traditional Negro leadership class had petitioned and patiently negotiated with white officials in an often vain attempt to secure the barest of public services. Generally directed by the NAACP, black protest occurred as a symbolic gesture against segregation. Under the leadership of the Reverend Fred L. Shuttlesworth, the Alabama Christian Movement for Human Rights cast aside vocal protestations and rhetorical resolutions for dangerous physical contact with the white power structure. Though retaining the legalistic strategy of the NAACP, the ACMHR added an urgency evidenced by confrontational protest. The advent of nonviolent direct action radically altered race relations in Birmingham. One man stood out as the leader of the new black protest: the Reverend Fred L. Shuttlesworth.

Born in the agricultural community of Mount Meigs near the state capital in Montgomery County on March 18, 1922, Fred Lee moved at age three to the Birmingham district when his mother, Alberta, married Tom Shuttlesworth, an unemployed miner suffering from silicosis. During the depression the family lived on welfare while residing in the black section of Oxmoor, a mining community on the edge of Red Mountain southwest of the city. Young Fred sold Birmingham newspapers to earn enough money to buy a bicycle on which he traveled into town and to school. A darling of his teachers at the Wenonah School and Rosedale High, the bright student returned their attention with adoration. He recalled how they taught him to analyze things, a lesson he later applied to southern politicians: "pay attention to what they do; not what they say." Preachers provided the other role models for the impressionable lad. After graduating valedictorian of the class of 1940, Shuttlesworth worked as a handyman in a doctor's office, where he met a young nursing student named Ruby L. Keeler. They married in October 1941. A richly dark man, Shuttlesworth stood a trim five-foot-nine, weighed 150 pounds, and sported a mustache. During World War II he held several jobs while seeking advanced technical training. In 1943 he moved his family to Mobile, having gained employment in the defense industry at Brookley Field Air Force Base.[1]

Since childhood, Shuttlesworth had attended Methodist services—his mother belonged to St. Matthews African Methodist Episcopal Church—but one night in Mobile he visited a Baptist congregation and found the worship spiritually "invigorating." He soon joined the denomination. Not long afterward, Shuttlesworth felt moved by God to preach the gospel. The deacons at Corinthian Baptist Church granted him a license. When not driving a truck at Brookley Field, building his family a house, or praying with other Christians, he assiduously studied the Bible. Soon Shuttlesworth started classes at Cedar Grove Seminary in nearby Pritchard. There white missionaries provided by the Southern Baptist Convention encouraged him to attend Selma University. The motivated young man applied to the small Baptist school, received admission, and moved his family to Dallas County in 1948. That summer he pastored two rural churches before answering a call from the black First Baptist Church of Selma. He taught in the county public schools while completing his A.B. degree from Selma University in 1951; then he attended Alabama State College in Montgomery, earning a B.S. degree in 1952.[2]

The strong-willed minister who was given to dictatorial control clashed with his deacons at First Baptist. Shuttlesworth's problems at the oldest black Baptist church in Dallas County revealed important personality traits. As he was wont to do, Shuttlesworth viewed his opposition as "evil" and the work of the devil. His fight with the deacons bothered him greatly and affected his ability to work and rest. While traveling to the National Baptist Convention in 1952, a distressed and sleepless Shuttlesworth stuck his head out the door of the fast-moving train at 2:00 A.M. and, feeling the wind cut his eyes dry, called out to God: "If the Bible is true then all have to suffer and I'm willing, but fix me so I won't worry so much. I'm willing to sacrifice my family and everything because this load is too heavy." The moment proved a turning point in the minister's life, for he believed that what "seemed like the weight of the train" fell from his shoulders as God lifted his burden. Relieved, Shuttlesworth returned to his seat and slept. Henceforth, he "never worried" while making decisions based on what "the Lord" told him to do.[3] Others would view his religious convictions as arrogance.

With this new resolve, Shuttlesworth bypassed his deacons and appealed directly to his congregation. When one elder advised him that since he pastored First Baptist he was now a "Big Nigger" and should "quit associating" with "little fellows," Shuttlesworth spurned the member's elitism by responding, "God must have loved little Niggers; he made so many of them." Unable to tolerate his deacons any longer, Shuttlesworth resigned his position at First Baptist in December 1952. He spent the next four months as an increasingly popular guest preacher before receiving a call from Bethel Baptist Church in Birmingham. Accepting the offer in March 1953, he returned to his former home. Selma had prepared Shuttlesworth for future tribulations in Birmingham. In connection with civil rights persecution he later admitted, "The train experience was one that let me know that he [God] wasn't going to forsake me when I was right."[4]

Shuttlesworth's perceived encounters with God fed his authoritarian nature. He applied his moral self-righteousness to a growing belief in the need for race reform. Confrontations with white foremen while working in Mobile presaged his rebellion against the segregated social structure. After moving back to Birmingham he joined the local branch of the NAACP and quickly became an activist in that ossified chapter. Passing a newspaper stand near the post office in May 1954, a headline caught his eye: "Supreme Court Outlaws Segregation." As Shuttlesworth read about the *Brown* decision, he realized, "This means that we have the same right everybody else has and I am going to give my attention to it." For the first time in his life, he "felt like a man." But black Birmingham failed to respond to the ruling, in part because it lacked a civic organization that captured "the interests of a large number of Negroes." The city's traditional Negro leadership class proved unable—or unwilling—to "grasp the significance" of the *Brown* decision, for the ruling did little to alter black protest in Birmingham.[5]

Impatient with the lack of reform, Shuttlesworth decided to strike out at the inactivity of black preachers in the Baptist Ministers Conference, which was headed by the Reverend J. L. Ware. In 1955 he latched onto the issue of Negro policemen. When the Baptist Ministers Conference refused to endorse a petition he sponsored calling on the city to hire black officers, Shuttlesworth sidestepped the body, getting seventy-seven preachers to sign the resolution. During a meeting with the city commission he presented the petition but "learned right then that a white man smiles like he means 'yes' but he means 'hell no.'" Although sympathetic to the cause of Negro policemen, having also been encouraged to hire them by the biracial Jefferson County Coordinating Council of Social Forces, Mayor Jimmy Morgan and Police Commissioner Robert Lindbergh hesitated to act because of public opposition from their lower-status white electorate. Shuttlesworth pressed on, gathering favorable information from other southern cities that employed black patrolmen and collecting 4,500 black and 119 white signatures on additional petitions. After receiving the new evidence, the city commission promised to act within ten days. During the interim, the Emmett Till lynching heightened racial tensions and Morgan decided to table the request indefinitely. Instead of concurring, hat in hand, with the mayor's decision, a blunt Shuttlesworth told Morgan: "Emmett Till's death had nothing to do with Negro police. You are telling us that you won't give them to us; we'll have to fight to get them."[6]

The black community recognized Shuttlesworth's bold stand. The NAACP elected him membership chairman in an effort to boost morale. Shuttlesworth had addressed a NAACP gathering of black Birmingham at an Emancipation Day celebration, at which he argued that the inactivity of the city's traditional Negro leadership class should end because the *Brown* decision authorized African Americans to demand their full rights of citizenship. As chairman, he attempted to turn the NAACP into a grassroots movement, but the court injunction against the organization in May 1956 dashed this dream. A state of "helplessness and hopelessness" descended on black Birmingham. Demoralized people contacted the minister asking what could be done about the situation. Early on the morning of June 2, 1956, a distraught Shuttlesworth again felt the presence of God, this time telling him, "They are trying to kill hope, but you can't kill people's hope." He awoke with the scripture "You shall know the truth and the truth shall make you free" echoing in his head. He interpreted this to mean that the "people had to know the truth, that the state was saying to them you cannot be free and you cannot even fight to be free." The experience left him with the impression that he should form a new protest group.[7]

The next day, while talking with several members of the outlawed NAACP's executive board, Shuttlesworth proposed a "mass meeting to see if Negroes wanted to organize a fight for their own rights." He convinced four other pastors—Reverends N. H. Smith Jr., T. L. Lane, G. B. Pruitt, and R. L. Alford—to join in the call. They announced the rally in the press and over the radio, scheduling the event for June 5, 1956, at Sardis Baptist Church.[8]

The small group of activist preachers immediately met opposition from several fronts within the black community. One old minister announced that God told him that Shuttlesworth should cancel the mass meeting. Shuttlesworth retorted: "Is that so? Now just when did the Lord start sending my messages through you? You go back and tell the Lord that the meeting is on, and the only way I'll call it off is if he comes down here and tells me Himself." During a strategy session held on June 4, 1956, in the Smith and Gaston Funeral Home, other ministers advised against the undertaking. They labeled Shuttlesworth and the other activists "hotheaded" and discouraged the plan. Nevertheless, the fire-eaters drafted a series of resolutions for adoption the next night at the mass meeting, foremost among them, the name of the new organization: the Alabama Christian Movement for Human Rights. A "Declaration of Principles" described the group's patriotic and Christian philosophy while setting forth its civil rights objectives.[9]

More than a thousand people packed Reverend Alford's Sardis Baptist Church as prayer and hymn singing started the June 5, 1956, mass meeting. Evoking the tenor of a tent revival, the congregation fell under the sway of the charismatic Shuttlesworth, who adroitly worked the pent-up emotions and aspirations into a communal outcry for equality. "Our citizens are restive under the dismal yoke of segregation. . . . Aren't you," he called out to a resounding "Yes!" from the audience. "These are dark days when men would like to kill hope . . . dark days. But hope is not dead. Hope is alive here tonight." The crowd cheered in agreement. "The Negro citizens of Birmingham are crying for leadership to better their condition," Shuttlesworth recognized, "the only thing we are interested in is uniting our people

No photograph captures the charisma of the Reverend Fred L. Shuttlesworth better than this one, taken by civil rights activist Danny Lyon during the funeral of the four black girls killed in the bombing of Sixteenth Street Baptist Church. An inspirational speaker, Shuttlesworth also led by example. Danny Lyon.

in seeing that the laws of our land are upheld according to the Constitution of the United States." Shifting the rhetoric to the risk involved, he acknowledged: "The Citizens' Councils won't like this. But then, I don't like a lot of things they do." The activist wiped his brow as the temperature in the pulpit neared ninety degrees. He asked the congregation, "Would you be willing tonight for a white man to sit down beside you?" The gathering roared its approval. "Then you believe in integration."[10]

Having worked the crowd to a fever pitch, Shuttlesworth introduced the Reverend N. H. Smith Jr., who proposed the ACMHR's "Declaration of Principles." The audience adopted the measures by standing ovation. Representatives from the Baptist Ministers Conference voiced their opposition. Shuttlesworth relinquished the floor to the prominent Reverend M. W. Witt, who argued against the movement, as did the Reverend G. W. Mc-Murray, who said: "We should think sanely of what we are doing. Birmingham is too over-organized now." Shuttlesworth dismissed the other Negro groups as ineffective. Preventing the crowd from shouting down this opposition, he asked it to vote again on the decision to form the ACMHR. Twice more the congregation acclaimed its assent, then it elected Shuttlesworth president, Alford first vice president, Smith secretary, and W. E.

Shortridge treasurer of the new civil rights organization. Emphasizing the seriousness of the undertaking, Shuttlesworth stressed the need for money to finance court challenges to segregation. "This is not the time for Uncle Toms," he declared, "We must pledge all we have . . . including our moral support and loyalty." Then the mass meeting adjourned until the following Monday night, when it reconvened at Reverend Smith's New Pilgrim Baptist Church. For the next decade and a half, the ACMHR met every Monday, known within the black community as "mass night" or "movement night." Members adopted the slogan "the movement is moving," and black Birmingham braced for active civil rights protest.[11]

An editorial in the *Birmingham World* on the morning of the mass meeting supported the new initiative, but the traditional Negro leadership class opposed it. Emory Jackson hoped that the white "attack on the NAACP" would "awaken more of the leadership of the Negro group," for he believed "the fight for freedom in Alabama" would "continue either with or without the NAACP." Shuttlesworth represented an answer to Jackson's call, but many other former NAACP members refused to participate in the new organization. Powerful forces in Birmingham's black community opposed the activism of the ACMHR. In addition to Reverends Witt and McMurray, the president of the influential Baptist Ministers Conference, Ware, denounced the new protest group. He joined other Negro conservatives in forming the Jefferson County Betterment Association to counter the ACMHR, which they viewed as "too militant for its own good." Many in the defunct NAACP concurred with Ware and refused to support the ACMHR, including past president of the local branch W. C. Patton, Dr. John Nixon, insurance salesman John Drew, and attorneys Arthur D. Shores and Orzell Billingsley Jr. Aware of the feelings of the traditional Negro leadership class, Shuttlesworth remarked, "Many of the upper class persons who worked in the NAACP are professional people who seem to feel that it is almost taboo to align actively with us." Some schoolteachers contributed financially, and some, such as principal Lucinda B. Robey, assumed active roles in the movement; but most declined to join the ACMHR, and almost no doctors or dentists affiliated. Reflecting its composition, the ACMHR consciously attracted "the lower class."[12]

Socioeconomically, members of the ACMHR fit into an amorphous black lower middle class somewhere between the working class and the black elite, as they fared slightly better financially than the average person in Birmingham's black community. Perhaps an equal number of men and women belonged to the ACMHR, and though more women may have regularly attended the mass meetings, more men were regularly arrested during protests. More than 70 percent were over age thirty, and most headed stable and small nuclear families. Only a third held unskilled jobs, with 15 percent in skilled and professional positions. All aspired to the middle class. These folk had little patience with those who exhibited "scandalizing Negro morals" such as "bobtailed and bossy women," those who drank liquor or used switchblade knives and .45s "as a badge of American manhood." Indeed, through the civil rights movement ACMHR members sought to end job discrimination and thus enter the system and achieve the American Dream. While not of the black bourgeoisie, members of the civil rights movement such as Shuttlesworth nonetheless expressed bourgeois values.[13]

At first, the ACMHR followed the lead of the NAACP by drafting resolutions, passing petitions, and attempting to negotiate with the white power structure. As several former officers of the Birmingham branch associated with the ACMHR, the fledgling organization adopted the legalistic strategy of the NAACP. The Montgomery Improvement Association offered another role model for the ACMHR. Shuttlesworth's Baptist connections had introduced him to the Reverends Dr. Martin Luther King Jr. and Ralph David Abernathy before the bus boycott began in the state capital, and he had witnessed the incorporation of the MIA at its organizational mass meeting in December 1955. Nevertheless, although Shuttlesworth consciously mirrored the movement in Montgomery, the ACMHR remained quite distinct, in part because it lacked the support of other civil rights organizations in Birmingham. The MIA attracted a wide range of black groups under its umbrella structure; in Birmingham, the ACMHR stood alone.[14]

From its inception, the ACMHR set out to achieve two major goals: an end to discrimination in accommodations and equal access to employment. Persistent in its demands, the ACMHR only varied its strategy over time. Similar to the movements in Montgomery and Tallahassee, the Birmingham movement initially used bourgeois reform methods. After its first mass meeting, the ACMHR followed the MIA and appointed a transportation committee that petitioned the Birmingham Transit Company to institute a "first come, first seated" policy on city buses. The bus company and city commission ignored the request. Mayor Morgan dismissed the chance of a bus boycott with the paternalistic observation, "I do not think our colored people here are going to unite in anything of that type." Two weeks later, Shuttlesworth sent a follow-up letter that referred to the federal

128

injunction against bus segregation that Montgomery officials had appealed to the U.S. Supreme Court by asking how Birmingham would respond to the justices' decision. He added that African Americans were "deeply concerned about receiving a more just and equitable share of this City's economy, both in better jobs and better opportunities." To the delight and praise of the citizens' councils, white leaders in Birmingham answered the requests by promising to enforce segregated seating on city buses.[15]

The issue of equal employment opportunities proved central to the overall goal of the ACMHR. The movement not only sought to end discrimination in accommodations, such as achieving integrated seating on buses, but it also wanted the city to hire Negro bus drivers. As citizens and taxpayers, ACMHR members desired employment in the better-paying civil service jobs, positions reserved for "whites only." The new demand for service sector employment reflected the black community's refusal to be left behind as the Birmingham district "modernized." The decline in unskilled positions in industry limited opportunities for the city's growing African American population and made the need for economic reform more pressing. Thus the changing nature of Birmingham's role in the world economy also influenced black activism by encouraging a desire for equitable commodification.[16]

True to the activist nature of the new organization, instead of drafting more petitions Shuttlesworth recruited two African American volunteers to take the city's civil service examination for positions as policemen. On August 20, 1956, accompanied by Shuttlesworth, the two black men—George Johnson and Clyde Jones—went to city hall, where Ray Mullins, director of personnel, refused to administer the test because it stipulated "whites only." Shuttlesworth called the action discriminatory and said, "We feel that if our people have the qualifications then this office should recognize them as applicants for the job." Mullins claimed to have no authority over the matter and referred the minister to the city commission, which had set the job requirements. Two days later, the Englander Company fired Jones for his "extracurricular activity." Jones and Johnson again attempted to take the examination on August 27, 1956, and Mullins again denied the request. The ACMHR then filed suit against the personnel board for failing to accept Negro applications, and officials held a secret meeting at which they deleted the "whites only" qualification.[17]

The successful conclusion of the Montgomery bus boycott led Shuttlesworth and the ACMHR to mount a direct action challenge to segregated seating on Birmingham's buses. After hesitating for the first two months of the protest, the Montgomery Improvement Association in February 1956 finally filed an integration suit to desegregate public transportation. As the case wound through federal court, black folk in the state capital developed alternatives to riding the bus. In November, the U.S. Supreme Court affirmed a lower court ruling that declared segregated seating unconstitutional. The MIA continued its boycott until, on December 20, 1956, official notice of the decision reached Montgomery when U.S. marshals served the injunctions that prohibited the city from enforcing segregated seating.[18]

In response to events in Montgomery, Shuttlesworth and the Reverend N. H. Smith Jr. wrote the Birmingham Transit Company and city officials requesting compliance with the court order by December 26, 1956. If the city commission failed to repeal the segregation ordinance at its scheduled meeting on that day, then the ACMHR "would ride the buses in a desegregated fashion anyway." Such a bold stand threatened a confrontation with the white power structure and signaled a clear departure from the passive black protests of petitions and boycotts.[19]

Social custom had always segregated seating on Birmingham's streetcars until an ordinance authorized the city to enforce the practice. During World War II incidents of African Americans breaking the custom occurred with some frequency, prompting Police Commissioner Bull Connor to install "color boards" between black and white sections. The Birmingham Electric Company, which operated the transit system, conducted a survey that recorded "complaints and incidents involving [the] race question" and documented black transgressions of the social order that ranged from "fighting between trainman and Negro" to "Negro nurse with white child in white section." The most serious confrontations involved the drawing of guns on black people by bus operators authorized to act as surrogate police officers. Birmingham's armed drivers shot at least two African Americans during the war. The report revealed how some people dealt with discrimination on a daily basis. The transportation department concluded that "younger Negroes" provoked the "racial disturbances"; yet, as the armed services and defense industries absorbed more black citizens, a decline in confrontations occurred. Bull Connor cited a "tense" racial situation after the war and requested that military police stationed in the city remain on call. Nevertheless, the incidents continued to diminish.[20]

When Shuttlesworth presented an ultimatum to the city commission to either desegregate seating or face a direct action challenge by the members of the ACMHR, he acted rashly considering Birmingham's history of brutally enforcing segregation. He also established himself as the prime target for vigilante violence. Emphasizing law and order, the *Birmingham News* cautioned: "It would be helpful, in our view, if action were not pressed at this time to end bus segregation at once here in Birmingham. But apparently action to that end is going to be pressed." Indeed, Shuttlesworth intended to use the inaction of the city commission as a "signal for bus riders to seat themselves in accordance with the nonsegregation decision of the United States Supreme Court."[21]

Earlier in the month, Shuttlesworth had attended the week-long Institute on Nonviolence and Social Change sponsored by the MIA in Montgomery. There he discussed bus boycotts and nonviolent sanctions with the Reverends Theodore J. Jemison of Baton Rouge, Joseph E. Lowery of Mobile, and C. K. Steele of Tallahassee, as well as other civil rights activists. Under the direction of Martin Luther King and the MIA staff, the institute's program prepared movement members for the nonviolent integration of Montgomery's transit system. Shuttlesworth absorbed the proceedings, then returned to Birmingham and applied the strategies. Approximately 1,500 African Americans attended a Christmas Eve mass meeting at New Hope Baptist Church, where Shuttlesworth instructed the audience on how to peacefully integrate Birmingham's buses. He urged the volunteers "to be courteous and not to strike back" if attacked. The ACMHR distributed leaflets similar to those used by the movements in Tallahassee and Montgomery. Shuttlesworth informed the crowd that after the city commission meeting on December 26, 1956, the executive board of the ACMHR would meet "to plan specifically what we will do." The minister explained to an Associated Press reporter, "We hope we won't have to do anything but ride," adding, "We are pledging ourselves here and now to nonviolence."[22]

During his Christmas sermon Shuttlesworth told his congregation, "If it takes being killed to get integration, I'll do just that thing for God is with me all the way." Pastors get little rest on holy days, and on the night of December 25, 1956, a tired Reverend Shuttlesworth stretched out on his bed while talking with a church deacon and thinking about the next day's scheduled challenge to bus segregation. At 9:40 vigilantes lobbed six sticks of dynamite at the minister's northside home in Collegeville. Apparently the missile grazed a chain-link fence that separated the frame parsonage from the church. This chance deflection prevented the bomb from rolling underneath the center of the one-story, five-room house; instead, it stopped squarely beneath the side room containing the two men talking. The force from the explosion threw Shuttlesworth into the air and destroyed the frame and box springs, but the mattress apparently protected him from the blast. The deacon did not fare so well, for he received injuries, as did two of the Shuttlesworth children.[23]

The strength of the single explosion tore kitchen appliances from the walls of a back room. The blast knocked the foundations out from under the front porch, which collapsed as the roof caved in. Violent shock waves shattered the windows of Bethel Baptist Church next door and carried debris over three houses to a vacant lot down the street. The blast blew a hole through the basement of the brick church. After the explosion, Mrs. Ruby Shuttlesworth found herself in the middle of the destroyed home surrounded by "smoke and dust." Yet she saw the lights on the family Christmas tree sparkling beneath the clutter. Neighbors poured out of their houses on hearing the familiar, frightening sound. A crowd of more than five hundred had gathered around the shell of the structure by the time emergency crews arrived. The fire department set up spotlights to assist officers in sifting through the rubble, for the extensive damage hindered the search for survivors. Several men attempted to hold back the police, but Shuttlesworth's appearance restrained their actions.[24]

As Shuttlesworth emerged from under the rubble that Christmas night, he interpreted his survival as a sign that God had chosen him to direct the civil rights struggle in Birmingham. "The Lord has protected me, I'm not injured," he said. "He's all right," lifted a woman's voice from among the five hundred onlookers assembled around the smoking ruins, "and he's going to be all right." Someone else called out, "God saved the Reverend to lead the movement."[25] That simple belief in divine providence became a tenet of faith among ACMHR members.

In the exceptional documentary *Eyes on the Prize*, Shuttlesworth recalled the bombing by referring to the legal and extralegal defense of Birmingham's status quo in race relations: "I walked out from this, instead of running away from the blast, running away from the klansmen, I said to the klansmen police that came . . . he said, 'Reverend, if I were you, I'd get out of town fast I could.' I said, 'Officer, you're not me. You go back and tell your klan brethren if God could keep me through this then I'm here for the duration.' I think that's what gave people the feeling that I wouldn't run, I didn't run and that God had to be there."[26] Indeed, the explosion galvanized the ACMHR into the civil rights movement in Birmingham; nevertheless, the twin engines of vigilante violence and police brutality—community sanctioned to prevent race reform—continued to operate unabated.

THE LOCAL MOVEMENT

A dynamite blast damaged Bethel Baptist Church a second time on December 15, 1962, again blowing out the stained glass windows and causing structural damage. The light-colored brick visible above the windows marks the repairs made after the first dynamite attack on the structure Christmas night in 1956, when the Reverend Fred L. Shuttlesworth was pastor of the congregation and leader of the movement to desegregate the city's buses. *Birmingham Post-Herald*, BPLDAM.

On the morning after the blast, 150 stone-faced sentinels of the citizens' councils silently stared as Mayor Jimmy Morgan rapped the city commission meeting to order. Organized over the past tumultuous year, the citizens' councils now witnessed the materialization of their darkest fear: active black protest in Birmingham. Months before, various councils complained that the city commission had failed to adequately enforce segregation on the city buses. Now African Americans threatened to ignore the ordinance altogether. These white men intended to prevent any black demand for desegregation—but no one raised that issue during the tense seven-minute meeting. A severe Morgan repeated, "Do we have anything else to come before the commission this morning?" Hearing no response

THE LOCAL MOVEMENT

he adjourned the session as disappointed but relieved councillors vowed to return the next week. A delegation from the ACMHR arrived twenty minutes late and expressed surprise at having missed the commissioners.[27]

Simultaneously gathered in the Smith and Gaston Funeral Home, anxious ACMHR activists awaited word on the commission meeting. The nearly two hundred in attendance gave Shuttlesworth a standing ovation when he entered the room. "The fight is on," he exclaimed, "we had announced before that we would ride the buses." Referring to his brush with death the previous night, Shuttlesworth declared that "violence will not have any effect." He then struck the wellspring of his faith as a civil rights revolutionary: "One reason I was sure that God wanted them unsegregated is because I came through this alive. That bomb had my name on it, but God erased it off." His resolve found accord among the other fanatical Christians who comprised the men and women of the ACMHR. "When I went to the meeting the next morning Rev. Shuttlesworth was the first thing I saw. And I knowed as how their house was blowed up, and I couldn't figure out how he was there. And I said then, that I'm going into it. And I went into it on that day," testified Rosa Walker. She recalled: "I was frightened but I figured we needed help to get us more jobs and better education. And we had the man here to help us."[28]

Capitalizing on the element of surprise, Shuttlesworth misled city officials into thinking the bus challenge would occur the day after the commission meeting. Instead, the charismatic leader marched his followers out of the funeral home and onto the transit system that morning. For over an hour, some 250 African Americans rode in the white section of Birmingham's buses unmolested by the police. If white people reacted at all, they merely showed curiosity. No incidents of violence transpired. Once aware of the confrontation, Birmingham policemen arrested 21 ACMHR members for violating the city's segregated seating ordinance. Articulating this new philosophy of direct action, Shuttlesworth later recalled: "We say we're going to ride and we ride. We do what we say for a change. So we rode the buses and over 250 people [sic] got arrested I guess, enjoying desegregated riding."[29]

Shuttlesworth's refusal to tolerate second-class citizenship any longer reflected an ideology of individualism that demanded an immediate end to segregation in all its forms and presaged the 1960 direct action of the four black students in Greensboro, North Carolina.[30] In response to the Supreme Court ruling, African Americans rode desegregated buses in Montgomery, and in Tallahassee they ignored the "color boards" and sat where they pleased. Mobile's transit system simply gave up on trying to separate the races.

On December 26, 1956, the morning edition of the *Birmingham World* praised the developments, asserted that "the old law is dead," and encouraged the city to "move immediately into the new reality." Instead, Birmingham doggedly defended the past as Police Commissioner Robert Lindbergh echoed the Alabama Public Service Commission in nullifying the court decision. Reactionary as ever, Birmingham's white officialdom refused to consider dismantling segregation. To emphasize the point, on January 3, 1957, Judge Ralph E. Parker of the recorder's court summarily convicted the twenty-one African Americans arrested during the direct action challenge. The ACMHR filed an appeal.[31]

In March 1957 a case concerning interstate travel convinced Shuttlesworth to again confront the establishment in a direct action challenge to segregation. Previously, police had arrested two prominent Birmingham African Americans for refusing to move to the "colored" section of the Terminal Station while waiting for their train to Milwaukee on December 22, 1956. The ACMHR decided to sponsor Carl and Alexinia Baldwin's legal fight. On March 5, 1957, U.S. district court judge Seybourn H. Lynne dismissed the suit. He argued that denying Negroes the use of the main waiting room did not "compel" them to "occupy waiting rooms designated 'colored.'" The next day an exasperated Shuttlesworth announced that he would test the integration of the train station.[32]

Radio stations broadcast the minister's intentions, notifying the citizens' councils of the challenge. When Shuttlesworth and his wife Ruby arrived at the beautiful Spanish baroque structure, a white mob greeted them. Robert E. Chambliss and other Klansmen pushed them away from the front entrance. The Shuttlesworths turned to a side door and, once inside the spacious marble lobby, bought tickets to Atlanta. Lamar Weaver, a Presbyterian lay minister, white steelworker, and unionist, warmly shook the hands of the Shuttlesworths and sat down with them as they waited for their train. A few minutes later patrolmen approached, checked their tickets, and asked Weaver to leave since he had no travel plans. Angry white men followed Weaver after he exited the building. The crowd called him "nigger lover," threw rocks and bricks at his car—breaking the windows— and attempted to turn it over before he drove away. The police deliberately allowed the vigilante violence to occur by not protecting Weaver, who subsequently moved to Cincinnati, Ohio, but officers did prevent the mob from reaching the Shuttlesworths. Once safely in Atlanta, the daring civil rights leader commended Commissioner Lindbergh as a "man of high morals" and noted that "since they [Birmingham policemen] didn't arrest us for traveling unsegregated, it would look bad if they would arrest anybody in the future. They should take the segregated signs down." Despite Shuttlesworth's successful venture, Birmingham remained wedded to racial discrimination.[33]

Referring to the mob scene at the Terminal Station, the city commission reaffirmed segregation as "necessary for the avoidance of friction, enmity and violence between the races." The commission acted in advance of the trial of the twenty-one African Americans charged with violating the city's segregation ordinance in the December 1956 bus challenge. Judge Ralph Parker listened to testimony on the morning of March 18, 1957, as the city attorney argued that "the threat of desegregation" created a dangerous climate that, if not curtailed, could force the white community to "explode into anonymous and unpreventable acts of violent resentment." Representing the ACMHR, attorney Arthur Shores held that segregated seating violated the Fourteenth Amendment to the U.S. Constitution. Three days later, Parker found the twenty-one protesters guilty and ordered them to pay fines of $50 plus court costs. Declaring the Fourteenth Amendment "null and void," the judge explained that Congress had "pulled a fast one" by not ratifying the amendment in a "valid, constitutional process." The ACMHR filed an appeal and asked the U.S. district court to rule the ordinance unconstitutional and restrain the city from enforcing segregation.[34]

By the June 1957 anniversary of its founding, the ACMHR celebrated its triumph as the premier civil rights organization in Birmingham. Within the black community, the group's favorable reputation derived from Shuttlesworth's willingness to confront the white power structure, as evidenced by the transition to direct action clearly made in the bus challenge of 1956. In recognition of its first year, the ACMHR selected the theme "Christian Emphasis on Freedom and Race Relations" and invited the Reverend C. K. Steele, leader of Tallahassee's successful bus boycott, to address the audience. Shuttlesworth had joined Steele and Martin Luther King in issuing the call that led to the formation of the Southern Christian Leadership Conference in February 1957. The SCLC acted as a regional umbrella organization that assisted and coordinated the efforts of affiliates such as the ACMHR. Thus the past year found the Birmingham movement linked to the larger civil rights struggle.[35]

Indeed, the Christmas bombing of his house thrust Shuttlesworth into the limelight as a leading integrationist. In May 1957 he accompanied other

"Southern Freedom Fighters" at the Prayer Pilgrimage in Washington D.C. Shuttlesworth's comments confirmed his—and the ACMHR's—abiding belief in an American system compromised by racial discrimination. "Is the great American ideal of fair play, equality and justice which even now holds Communism at bay in the four quarters of the earth to fall or fade from view when challenging the internal enemy of Segregation and 2nd class citizens?" [sic] he asked. In other addresses, the civil rights activist returned to this theme of hypocrisy by pointing out the inconsistencies in the ideology when compared to the reality in the region: "This hour in history calls for the elimination of the double standards of justice in the South, for the uncommitted 1/3 of the world's population is looking into our affairs. They are seeing bad things." Although critical of U.S. foreign policy—in particular, the arms race with the Soviets and the country's treatment of people of color around the world—Shuttlesworth nonetheless defended the American consensus, the same dream held by those in his movement.[36]

The religious conviction that God would enable them to defeat segregation and gain first-class citizenship differentiated ACMHR members from the rest of Birmingham's black community. The ministers who formed the ACMHR determined to create a "Christian movement" as opposed to an "organization" such as the NAACP, reasoning that "you can outlaw an organization, but not a movement, and this would be a moving force forward. It would be a movement to actively fight and attack segregation on every front." The religious nature of the movement consciously set the ACMHR apart from the NAACP and signified a new type of leadership and followers. As Adam Fairclough observed, the preachers moved "into the vanguard of black protest in the South." Yet this Christian activism was less an awakening than a renewal. In Birmingham the black church had traditionally played one of two roles: either defender of the status quo or advocate of change.[37]

An evangelical ethos pervaded the South's culture and dominated life in Birmingham even though it ran at odds with the modern industrial urban environment. For years industrialists had kept black preachers on their payrolls, constructed churches for mill village employees, and promoted a fundamentalist view of individual salvation with its concomitant belief in social Darwinian damnation. Successful Negro ministers in the Birmingham district echoed these beliefs. The Reverends Luke Beard at Sixteenth Street Baptist Church and John W. Goodgame at Sixth Avenue Baptist Church accommodated the prevailing ideology by opposing unionization, the Communist Party, and other black radical grassroots movements to alter race relations. The white elite identified these black bourgeois preachers as the Negro leaders of Birmingham's black community, with total disregard for what average African Americans thought.

Yet the common black folk picked their own representatives, leaders who occasionally espoused a variant of radical Christianity. Not surprisingly, because the church formed the center of the black community, it became the seat of African American activism. Workers in the labor movement consulted ministers before going out on strike, and union organizers operated out of neighborhood churches. During the Great Depression, some Communist operatives were also lay leaders. Though scholars debate whether activists attempted to combine Communist ideology with radical Christianity, it is apparent that church culture and religious conviction informed Communist propaganda and gave some CP members an inner resolve that enabled them to persevere under adverse circumstances.[38]

When not at a party function, Hosea Hudson spent his free time with the Smithfield Vocal Singers, one of several gospel-oriented groups performing in black churches throughout the Birmingham district in the 1930s and 1940s. Typical of the new jubilee and gospel quartet music was a 1926 recording, entitled "Birmingham Boys," by the Birmingham Jubilee Singers. The song expressed the transition from the rural to the urban South with all its hope concerning the "perpetual promise." Sung a cappella and scored for four or more equal voices in complex harmony, the indigenous music incorporated religious fervor with the daily struggle of existence. Black workers naturally adapted the lyrics to fit the goals of unionization during the CIO drives in the 1930s. As a result of this choral heritage, Birmingham became a center of gospel music in the postwar period.[39]

In the main, since Reconstruction the black church had focused on otherworldly concerns; nevertheless, among a small number of churches there existed an activist tradition of radical Christianity. Although little evidence suggests that the civil rights movement in Birmingham directly tapped that rich source, it nonetheless derived cultural strength from it as evidenced by the influence of gospel music on the ACMHR. Unlike the community-based struggles in other cities such as Montgomery and Albany where participants sang Negro spirituals and hymns in a congregational style, members of the Birmingham movement expressed themselves through the "powerful, driving sound of gospel choir music." Under the direction of Carlton Reese, the Alabama Christian Movement Choir combined freedom songs with gospel hits to produce a charismatic style of music unique in the civil rights struggle. Historian and civil rights veteran Bernice Johnson Reagon recognized the distinctive music that emanated from Birmingham.[40]

Intensely personal, gospel music differed from more traditional forms in that soloists presented individualistic testimonials instead of expressions of communal suffering. The recordings of Birmingham gospel soprano Cleo Kennedy and the a cappella performance of Mississippi activist Fannie Lou Hamer on the album *Voices of the Civil Rights Movement* demonstrate the contrast between the two styles. Whereas Hamer's traditional singing of "Walk With Me, Lord" could have occurred in any rural southern community, Kennedy's gospel interpretation of "City Called Heaven" suggested an atomized urban experience transcended by a modern Christian ideology. Indeed, transcendence best describes the distinctive quality of the Birmingham movement, for members in the ACMHR, unlike many other civil rights participants, exhibited a Christian fanaticism that enabled them to face the vigilantes and power structure determined to maintain white supremacy in Birmingham.[41]

In addition to Shuttlesworth, other members of the ACMHR harnessed a radical interpretation of Christianity to power the movement's militancy. As opposed to mass meetings in Montgomery and Tuskegee, the Birmingham services resembled "typical religious prayer meetings" and attracted "regular worshippers." Overwhelmingly Baptist, but with a sprinkling of Methodists, the ACMHR drew its membership—which numbered from 900 to 1,200 in 1959—from about a dozen churches in the district. As black reporter Geraldine Moore differentiated, those attracted to the ACMHR, as opposed to other Negro civil rights organizations, believed that "the cause of the Negro can best be advanced through the concerted efforts of Christian people." A *Pittsburgh Courier* reporter observed: "When one sits in their mass meetings and hears them sing and pray and lift their voices to their God, you get the feeling that here is a boundless and ever growing faith in God that will not let these people lose their hope and their faith." Joined by their belief in a God actively empowering them to confront the evils of segregation, fanatical ACMHR members re-created community through the movement by dedicating themselves individually to a religious whole capable of sustaining the local struggle. As a result, the militant Christianity practiced by the ACMHR unified and strengthened its small membership while limiting its appeal to other African Americans in Birmingham. The use of direct action also diminished the ACMHR's attractiveness among some segments of the black community.[42]

THE LOCAL MOVEMENT

As Little Rock, Arkansas, reached a crisis over the integration of Central High School in the summer of 1957, Shuttlesworth decided to confront Birmingham's failure to desegregate its school system. With eight other black families, he petitioned the board of education to admit their children to three white schools in an August 22, 1957, registered letter to school superintendent Dr. Frazier Banks. The minister requested a reply by the September 4 registration date. Banks notified Shuttlesworth that he would discuss the issue at a September board meeting. Asa E. Carter's Klansmen responded to Shuttlesworth's challenge by picking up at random and wantonly emasculating an African American.[43]

Shuttlesworth ignored the vigilante's warning. At the September 6 meeting, the Birmingham Board of Education authorized Superintendent Banks to handle the request by the black parents according to Alabama's Pupil Placement Act. Passed in 1955 as the state's cornerstone of massive resistance, the legislation gave officials broad powers to determine which schools students would attend. Banks stalled by investigating the matter before taking action. Tired of waiting for the implementation of the *Brown* decision, an impatient Shuttlesworth decided to confront the issue of integration by registering four black students in Birmingham's largest all-white high school.[44]

At mid-morning on September 9, 1957, Shuttlesworth rode up Seventh Avenue North to the limestone-trimmed brick edifice of Phillips High School. Adjoined by the Central City Housing Project for Whites, the school attracted about 1,850 students from across the city. Shuttlesworth notified the local television station of his plans and also informed—by telegram—the police department and board of education. The minister's wife accompanied him, as did his trusted friend and assistant, the Reverend J. S. Phifer. Four students—Ruby Fredricka Shuttlesworth, 12, Patricia Ann Shuttlesworth, 14, Nathaniel Lee, 17, and Walter Wilson, 12—intended to transfer into the school. Shuttlesworth wanted the best education possible for his children and hence sought integration into the better supported and funded white high school.[45]

After Shuttlesworth left his car, he saw three clusters of eight to ten white men each coming toward him from either side of the school and from across the street. As they descended on him, he turned to run, only to encounter a different group of men wielding clubs. Shouting "Let's kill him," the mob charged, beating him to the ground with repeated blows from brass knuckles and bicycle chains. Having stumbled, and struggling to stay conscious, Shuttlesworth believed that he heard God's voice tell him: "You can't die here. Get up. I got a job for you to do." As if with superhuman strength, he regained his footing and stood up. By this point, several policemen had arrived at the scene. As the officers entered the melee, Shuttlesworth broke free and raced back to his automobile. Before he escaped, members of the mob smashed the windows and bashed the body of the vehicle. One vigilante, clutching a chain, reached into the backseat and attempted to pull out a passenger. Another man stabbed Mrs. Shuttlesworth in the hip. As Reverend Phifer drove away, the car door slammed shut on Ruby Fredricka's foot. Shuttlesworth's survival of the mob scene at Phillips High School became another example to ACMHR members and the activist himself of God's direct intervention on behalf of the civil rights struggle in Birmingham.[46]

Taken to University Hospital's emergency room following the attack, Shuttlesworth refused to be admitted so he could attend the mass meeting that night. Standing in the pulpit with his head bandaged and his arm in a sling, Shuttlesworth testified, "God is showing the world that there are some Negroes in Birmingham who are not afraid." During the service, a patrol car quickly drove past armed guards of the ACMHR stationed outside the church. A reporter noted, "Negroes, while speaking calmly, seemed prepared to meet any effort of whites to create any disturbance." Movement watchmen viewed vigilantes and policemen with the same jaundiced eyes. Despite knowing about the dangerous integration attempt at Phillips High School, the city dispatched only a handful of police officers, probably because Bull Connor had returned to power as public safety commissioner. The informal cooperation between the vigilantes and the police department increased under Connor's administration. At first arresting three men in connection with the beating of Shuttlesworth, officers later failed to identify them as the suspects, forcing the grand jury to drop the charges.[47]

In 1958 vigilantes resumed their bombings in Birmingham. A bad fuse prevented the destruction of Temple Beth-El when it extinguished before reaching fifty-four sticks of dynamite stuffed into a satchel and stashed near the foundation of the Jewish synagogue on Highland Avenue. A subsequent investigation linked the April 28 Birmingham attempt to bombings in Nashville and Jacksonville where anti-Semitic white supremacists targeted synagogues in an unmistaken belief that many southern Jews supported integration. When Shuttlesworth presented an ACMHR petition to the city commission on June 2 renewing the appeal for Negro policemen, Bull Connor responded by asking that the minister be given a lie detector

141

test to clear up "rumors" about the Christmas 1956 bombing of his house and church. Shuttlesworth readily agreed, stipulating that Connor should do likewise, but the police commissioner refused. By the end of June 1958, vigilantes struck again at Shuttlesworth's church. The chance return of a waitress early that Sunday morning prevented the blast from damaging Bethel Baptist Church, for she spotted a suspicious "fire" and notified the volunteer guard on duty. Will Hall, the sixty-two-year-old watchman, grabbed the paint can stuffed with fifteen to twenty sticks of dynamite and carried it into the street where, one minute after he set it down and ran away, it exploded, blasting a hole two feet deep into the ground, shattering the stained glass windows that had replaced those broken in 1956, and cracking the plaster in the church's ceiling. Shuttlesworth held services in the damaged sanctuary and told his congregation, "We're going to have to suffer longer, but we'll hold up our heads."[48]

In July vigilantes targeted formerly white-owned houses bought by African Americans in the neighborhood known as Dynamite Hill. This time, a black home owner who had been firebombed two months before foiled the attempt. Ernest Coppin watched three white men open the gate to his yard and light the fuse to a bomb before he called out, startling the Klansmen who fled, dropping the dynamite as they ran. After the explosion, which was immediately followed by another one near the black-owned house of William Blackwell, a large group of African Americans chased down the bombers. Although police arrived to break up the black crowd, they were forced to arrest the Klansmen. For the first time in Birmingham's history, the city captured suspected bombers. Nevertheless, the *Birmingham News* in effect condoned the act of terrorism by describing the bombings as "harmless explosions" that black people themselves probably set and asserting that the police should be more concerned with the "Negroes who ganged" up on the white men. As evidenced by the *News*, the white community continued to sanction vigilante violence, a clear message received by the Ku Klux Klan, which staged a massive show of strength by lighting eighteen crosses—fourteen near white schools—on August 30, 1958, the anniversary of Shuttlesworth's desegregation attempt at Phillips High School.[49]

That fall, the case of the twenty-one African Americans arrested for challenging segregated seating on Birmingham's buses in December 1956 reached federal court. Aware that the judge would rule the ordinance "invalid in view of past federal court decisions" and that to keep the law would only "be hurtful to the cause of segregation," the city commission repealed the discriminatory ordinance in a surprise move and substituted a new law that authorized the Birmingham Transit Company to determine the seating of bus passengers. Company president John S. Jemison Jr. announced the "new" policy of having blacks sit from the rear and whites from the front of the bus. Outraged, Shuttlesworth fired off a telegram to the transit company demanding that it desist with segregated seating. At a special mass meeting at Bethel Baptist Church on October 16, 1958, he proposed a resolution, which the ACMHR adopted, stating that Negroes would "henceforth ride in any seat available with the dignity which becomes American citizens." Bull Connor urged Birmingham's black community to ignore the integrationist leader.[50]

A group of thirty African American integrationists met Shuttlesworth at a Negro loan office on the morning of October 20, 1958, as the ACMHR prepared to mount its second confrontation with white officials over segregated seating on city buses. After briefing the volunteers on nonviolent tactics of integration, Shuttlesworth led the group outside, down Nineteenth Street to Second Avenue North. There they divided and then boarded the Ensley and Pratt City lines. Several of the activists sat in the white section and read devotional books. A crowd quickly formed to watch the direct action campaign. When the drivers comprehended the challenge, they quit accepting fares and notified the police. Twenty minutes later patrolmen arrived to escort the buses back to the company car barn. Once there, officers arrested thirteen of the hymn-singing integrationists and hauled them off to jail. At first police did not arrest Shuttlesworth, although he rode the bus, but they later charged him with inciting to violate the new ordinance. "Mr. Connor has long expressed his desire that I should be in jail," Shuttlesworth explained to a reporter, "I don't suppose I could do anything to make Mr. Connor happy except commit suicide."[51]

The heavy-handed way in which Birmingham's legal establishment conducted the bus case demonstrated the lack of justice African Americans could expect from the court system. City recorder William C. Conway found the fourteen protesters guilty at their Thursday night trial and remanded them back to jail without bond to await sentencing on the following Monday night. In an effort to circumvent the unlawful detention, ACMHR attorneys Arthur Shores and Orzell Billingsley requested a habeas corpus hearing, which circuit judge George Lewis Bailes denied. Billingsley then filed writs of mandamus that required Conway to show just cause in the refusal to set bail. Bailes ordered the hearing for Tuesday. At Monday night's sentencing, Conway gave Shuttlesworth 90 days and the Reverend J. S. Phifer 60 days plus fines for the integration attempt. The other twelve received 180-day suspended sentences and the warning that they had "better stay out of trouble." He then sent all fourteen back to jail to await Tuesday's hearing. The next day Judge Bailes rendered moot the habeas corpus request, citing the previous night's sentencing. After five days the city released the fourteen integrationists from cold jail cells that had made them sick. Shuttlesworth and Phifer appealed their convictions.[52]

In a scramble to salvage the class action suit filed by the ACMHR following the 1956 bus integration attempt, Arthur Shores petitioned to alter the original complaint by substituting the new bus seating ordinance for the repealed segregation law. On Thursday, October 30, 1958, U.S. district court judge Harlan Hobart Grooms denied the request, forcing the ACMHR to file a new court challenge to segregated seating on city buses by appealing the recent convictions of the fourteen activists. In response to Grooms's ruling, the ACMHR held a mass meeting Friday night to determine its course of action. Nearly a thousand African Americans attended the meeting, where Shuttlesworth proposed a protest boycott of Birmingham's transit system. "We believe it better to walk in dignity than to pay to ride in chains," he said, echoing the Montgomery bus boycott of two years before. As in the earlier example, an enraged black community appeared ready to bond behind the effort, but in Birmingham a different set of circumstances doomed the enterprise.[53]

The arrest of three black ministers from Montgomery on vagrancy charges by Bull Connor on October 27, 1958, unified segments of Birmingham's otherwise divided black leadership behind Shuttlesworth and the ACMHR. The Reverends S. S. Seay, H. H. Hubbard, and A. W. Wilson had arrived in the city to offer Mrs. Shuttlesworth and the ACMHR moral support during the unjust incarceration of the fourteen activists. The police detained the three MIA members under orders from Connor, who declared that he would arrest any "outside agitators coming to our city and dabbling in our affairs." The arrests so infuriated the Reverend J. L. Ware that he led his conservative organization, the Jefferson County Betterment Association, into coalition with the ACMHR. Over a hundred black ministers joined Ware in a meeting on October 28, 1958, to discuss the unlawful arrests and the integration crisis. These ministers disdained Shuttlesworth's methods, in particular his "publicity seeking," but through the Betterment Association they agreed to cooperate with the ACMHR. Nevertheless, the aroused black leadership failed to mobilize Birmingham's black community behind the boycott.[54]

The ACMHR could not have asked for a better time to strike against the

Birmingham Transit Company (BTC), for a loss of riders had seriously weakened the public transportation industry. Limited efforts at modernization failed to halt the decline in passengers as automobile ownership increased in the postwar years. John S. Jemison Jr. bought the transit company in July 1958, reorganized it, and outlined improvements that included the purchase of $2 million worth of diesel buses. The new additions arrived just as the black community—which provided 75 percent of the transit company's ridership—threatened to boycott.[55]

The white power structure moved quickly to squelch the black protest. *Birmingham News* publisher Clarence Hanson, a friend of Jemison's who served on the Citizens Transit Advisory Group, oversaw a press blackout that effectively ended all reporting on the boycott in Birmingham. When the Reverend Robert E. Hughes, the director of the city's only outlet for biracial communication, the Alabama Council on Human Relations, described the ACMHR's "limited boycott" to officials of the Southern Regional Council in Atlanta, he noted that "the press has completely ignored these developments and the white community is hardly aware of this move." Birmingham's free press deliberately kept the city's populace in the dark, a practice that left a legacy of ignorance and misinformation.[56]

Bull Connor authorized the police department to harass African Americans participating in the bus boycott. He stationed two or three officers on each street corner in the black community of the American Cast Iron Pipe Company with orders to take down "the license tags of persons giving rides to walking Negroes." Patrolmen attempted to force black schoolchildren walking to school to ride the bus. For the first time since the movement began, detectives attended ACMHR mass meetings in order to keep the department abreast of protest strategy while intimidating civil rights activists. Henceforth, officers attended every ACMHR mass meeting, and on occasion Connor sent in the fire department to interrupt the proceedings. When U.S. attorney general William P. Rogers announced that a federal grand jury would investigate the city's illegal arrest of the three Montgomery ministers, Birmingham's commissioner of public safety rejoined that he would jail "anybody else . . . who follows their foolish lead." To back up his threat, on November 17, 1958, police detained Harvey Kelly on charges of violating Alabama's antiboycott law. Kelly had been distributing leaflets that urged a citywide boycott of the BTC beginning on November 21. The county court convicted Kelly and sentenced him to the maximum six months in jail for the misdemeanor.[57]

In an attempt to suppress the boycott by silencing the preachers, police charged the Reverend Calvin W. Woods, pastor of East End Baptist Church and an ACMHR leader, with violating the state antiboycott law after he encouraged his congregation to stay off the buses. At first Woods's November 25, 1958, arrest strengthened the resolve of the city's black leadership. Twenty pastors, headed by the Reverends J. L. Ware and N. H. Smith Jr., denounced the charges against Woods as "an unwarranted and illegal invasion of the inviolability of the Christian pulpit" and promised to preach sermons the next Sunday on the sinfulness of segregated seating. Yet a majority of Birmingham's black preachers took Connor's message to heart and refused to participate in the protest, fearing that they, too, would be arrested. Although Shuttlesworth believed that bus revenues declined by nearly one-third during the boycott, the inability to organize the black community behind the effort revealed fundamental problems that the movement had to overcome in order to force the city to desegregate, the most glaring being an alienated African American population that even the churches failed to reach.[58]

After the boycott faltered, the Jefferson County Betterment Association folded when Shuttlesworth refused to merge it with the ACMHR. In December 1958 circuit court judge George Lewis Bailes upheld the recorder's court guilty verdict against the fourteen integrationists. Again, the ACMHR appealed the case, which stemmed from the October 1958 direct action challenge to bus segregation in Birmingham. Another year passed before the case reached U.S. district judge H. H. Grooms. On December 14, 1959, Grooms found as unconstitutional the city's ordinance that authorized the private company's bus drivers to enforce segregated seating. He argued that "a willful refusal to obey a request to move from the front to the rear of a bus when unaccompanied by other acts tending to disorder, *does not* constitute a breach of the peace." A joyous Shuttlesworth greeted the decision at a mass meeting in the Metropolitan Baptist Church. The ACMHR adopted a resolution that read, "We are free Now . . . to ride ANY seat available on ANY BUS." The organization distributed fliers—denounced by Connor as "dangerous"—that offered tips on integration as African Americans took to the buses a new dignity won through the struggles of Shuttlesworth and the ACMHR.[59]

The ACMHR spent most of its money financing legal challenges to segregation, an expensive undertaking paid for through the nickels and dimes of movement members. At the third annual meeting of the organization in June 1959, after special guest speaker Ella Baker addressed the audience, Shuttlesworth gave the president's report. It explained that of the approximately $53,000 raised over the past three years, the ACMHR paid nearly $40,500 in legal expenses, with $24,000 going to local Negro lawyers. Shuttlesworth believed the legal fees excessive. As he explained in a brief history of the ACMHR written the month before: "This lawyer situation is a regretful one, particularly in view of the fact that this struggle is so sacred and so encompassing. . . . They forget that they have a part also in this program to realize first-class citizenship for all Negroes." Indeed, the underhanded actions of Birmingham's black lawyers led Shuttlesworth to question which side they were on.[60]

After the city refused to consider petitions and telegrams—including one sent by Shuttlesworth while behind bars in October 1958—demanding the desegregation of the city's parks, the ACMHR prepared to file a legal challenge to the discriminatory practice. Yet the organization balked at paying the $6,000 demanded by a local Negro law firm. Instead, the ACMHR hired Ernest Jackson, a black lawyer from Florida, for $4,500. Rebuffed by Shuttlesworth, Birmingham's Negro attorneys appealed to Judge Seybourn H. Lynne—a despised segregationist—who, on February 13, 1959, signed a court order requiring all out-of-town lawyers to affiliate with a local firm in order to practice before the bench in Birmingham. The Negro attorneys had first banded together in opposition to Shuttlesworth's 1957 suit to desegregate the public schools. Under Arthur Shores's leadership, the lawyers "demanded a fee five times the amount offered," but Jackson agreed to the fee presented by the ACMHR. Responding to the petty money grubbing, Shuttlesworth referred to Shores as Calhoun, the shyster in *Amos and Andy*. When Shuttlesworth attempted to file the park desegregation case in March 1959, Jackson was handed the injunction that forced him to pay $1,500 to associate with attorney Demetrius Newton. Although the ACMHR paid the fee, Newton refused to file the suit, citing opposition from other Negro lawyers and Judge Lynne.[61]

Finally, in October 1959 the ACMHR filed the park desegregation suit in U.S. district court. Bull Connor immediately threatened to close down the recreational facilities unless Birmingham's "decent, thoughtful and good Negroes" rejected Shuttlesworth's leadership. Referring to those same "good Negroes" as the "Uncle Toms of yesteryear," the integrationist retorted that Connor's antics "gave many people the picture of a once mighty lion, now impotent because of an immovable thorn in its foot." Shuttlesworth declared that "crooks and racketeers" provided the city commission with its only link to the black community, and he called for the creation of a biracial committee to open up communication between the races. The minister stressed: "The days of frank discussion around the conference table are upon us. Negroes want to talk and be friends and brothers." Events soon to unfold made negotiations increasingly difficult as young African Americans expressed their impatience through the student movement.[62]

Shortly after four black students demanded service at Woolworth's lunch counter in Greensboro, North Carolina, on February 1, 1960, Shuttlesworth observed a similar sit-in while preaching in nearby High Point. After remaining long enough to learn more about the spontaneous student movement, Shuttlesworth telephoned the SCLC office in Atlanta and told Ella Baker, "This is the thing." With its emphasis on voter registration drives, the SCLC had resembled the NAACP, whereas the ACMHR ranked winning the vote a distant third behind dismantling segregation and integrating the schools. The sit-in movement struck a chord with Shuttlesworth, who appreciated the strategic use of direct action. The veteran civil rights activist approved of the students' forthright demand for service and their uninhibited attitude—an expression of a shared ideology of unfulfilled expectations—and he returned to Birmingham ready to promote a local sit-in campaign.[63]

Shuttlesworth discussed the rapidly spreading movement with students from the city's two black colleges. Yet Frank Dukes, the Miles College student body president, convinced those who wanted to conduct sit-ins at Birmingham lunch counters to organize a prayer vigil for voting rights instead. Dukes feared vigilante violence, so he heeded the advice of the white Reverend Robert E. Hughes of the biracial Alabama Council on Human Relations and planned the protest to coincide with a southern filibuster in Congress waged against the Civil Rights Act of 1960. At the next ACMHR mass meeting, a disappointed Shuttlesworth collected bail money in anticipation of the student protest.[64]

A handful of young demonstrators assembled in Kelly Ingram Park on March 1, 1960, to begin the "Prayer Vigil for Freedom." The students from Miles and Daniel Payne Colleges carried signs that read "The Law of God Will Be Fulfilled" and distributed leaflets that explained, "We will remain in this public place night and day, regardless of weather, as many weeks as our prayers are needed." The moral suasion failed to faze Birmingham policemen. Officers took twelve of the demonstrators to jail, where—although not charged with any crime—they were fingerprinted and photographed. That evening's edition of the *Birmingham News* included the names and addresses of the dozen protesters. Consequently, later in the month vigilantes stormed the house of Robert Jones, a sophomore at Miles College involved in the student movement, and beat him, his mother, and his sister with iron pipes, clubs, and blackjacks. Forty-five minutes after the attack, police stopped by but the assailants had fled. The next morning when two sheriff's deputies visited the mother, Mattie Mae Jones, in Bessemer General Hospital, she immediately—and horrifyingly—recognized them as having hit her the night before.[65]

On the day of Birmingham's Prayer Vigil for Freedom, a thousand African Americans silently marched up Dexter Avenue in Montgomery, sang the national anthem on the steps of the capitol, and returned to the Alabama State College campus in a demonstration against segregation. In response, Governor John Patterson and the state board of education pressured the administration at the state-supported Negro college to expel nine of the student movement leaders. In protest of the expulsions, ninety-seven white students at Birmingham-Southern College signed a petition condemning the state's "interference in the affairs of the college" as an "infringement upon academic freedom." Attention immediately turned to the white sympathizers with integration who were sheltered on the campus of the Methodist school. Birmingham-Southern president Dr. Henry King Stanford defended as freedom of speech the right of the students to express themselves. Dr. Leslie Wright, the president of the Baptist institution across town, quickly announced that no Howard College (Samford University) students had signed the protest petition. One Birmingham-Southern student, Thomas Reeves, contacted his black counterparts from Miles and Daniel Payne. Reeves, a twenty-one-year-old seminarian and part-time preacher, had previously protested the formation of the massive resistance churchmen's group, the Methodist Laymen's Union. In response to his unorthodox activities, the Ku Klux Klan threatened his life and burned a cross on the campus at Birmingham-Southern.[66]

Although not as widespread or as coordinated as demonstrations elsewhere in the region, student activism in Birmingham was far from over. Under Dukes's leadership, the student group planned another protest. On March 30, 1960, Shuttlesworth, speaking for the executive board of the ACMHR, issued a policy statement. Calling the sit-ins a "necessary tonic for a sickened democracy," he reiterated the theme of consensus gone wrong: "only when America cleans up her own house, and guarantees freedom for all her citizens, can she lead in true freedom for the world." Then, with an eerie premonition, he spoke for the ACMHR: "We deplore this new type vigilante form of law enforcement—horseback riders, firemen, and fire hoses, and even dogs—to keep Negroes from enjoying their full freedom." Shuttlesworth released the statement on the eve of the first student sit-ins conducted at lunch counters in Birmingham.[67]

Ten black college students targeted five dinettes in downtown Birmingham and split up into groups of two for the March 31, 1960, direct action challenge. After buying small items in the five-and-dime sections of the department stores, they moved to the lunch counters and requested service. Once notified of the protest, police arrested the youths for violating the city's "trespass after warning" ordinance. Bull Connor ordered officers to bring Shuttlesworth to jail. Patrolmen picked up the minister at his home, detained him on a month-old warrant, and then charged him with vagrancy. After several students confessed that they had discussed sit-ins with Shuttlesworth, officers arrested the activist again, this time on charges of conspiring to violate the city's segregation ordinances. In a preventive strike, police also arrested the Reverends Charles Billups of the ACMHR and C. Herbert Oliver of the Inter-Citizens Committee and two other students, the white Thomas Reeves of Birmingham-Southern and the black Jessie Walker of Daniel Payne. The city filed vagrancy charges against all of the residents, an act that led to an ineffective FBI investigation. The ACMHR appealed the convictions of Shuttlesworth and the students stemming from trials in recorder's court. The Ku Klux Klan responded to the student provocation by burning crosses in Birmingham.[68]

Unlike Montgomery and Little Rock, Birmingham had successfully—and amazingly—dodged the national spotlight on unsavory race relations, but with the student movement that changed. The New York Times sent Harrison E. Salisbury into Birmingham to describe racial tensions resulting from the belated student sit-ins. Under the headline "Fear and Hatred Grip Birmingham," Salisbury reported on the terroristic campaign against race reform: "Every channel of communication, every medium of mutual interest, every reasoned approach, every inch of middle ground has been fragmented by the emotional dynamite of racism, reinforced by the whip, the razor, the gun, the bomb, the torch, the club, the knife, the mob, the police and many branches of the state's apparatus." The article presented Shuttlesworth's challenge to and Bull Connor's defense of the totally segregated city. Horrific anecdotes described the actions of vigilantes and those caught in the middle of the maelstrom. Salisbury suggested that irrational and psychological forces accounted for the racism. When—in an effort to suggest libel—the Birmingham News and Post-Herald ran the articles verbatim, Birmingham citizens got the first good look at their racist community ever published in the local media. They did not like what they read.

150

Catching on to the trend that national reputation influenced economic growth, the city's chamber of commerce demanded a retraction from the *Times* "in the interest of truth, fairness and unbiased reporting." The best Turner Catledge—the managing editor and a native of Mississippi—could muster was an apology for not mentioning that the "overwhelming percentage of the citizens of Birmingham lead happy and peaceful lives in a growing and prosperous community." The response of that silent majority determined Birmingham's future, as a select group of businessmen, having ignored Harrison Salisbury's warning, moved to reform Birmingham following the national outrage after the Freedom Rides.[69]

THE LOCAL MOVEMENT

CHAPTER FIVE

Businessmen's Reform

I t was Mother's Day, May 14, 1961. A white mob milled about the Birmingham Trailways station awaiting the arrival of integrationists from the Congress of Racial Equality. After the white man, James Peck, and his black associate, Charles Person, got off the bus and approached the segregated lunch counter, several Ku Klux Klansmen intervened, six of them grabbing Peck and another five hustling Person out a side door and into an alleyway beyond the view of the public. With iron bars, lead pipes, and chains, they brutally assaulted the civil rights activists. For fifteen minutes, the vigilantes kicked and clubbed everyone suspect, leaving blood-splattered and crumpled bodies scattered about the station. Innocent black bystanders who had come to greet friends also were attacked. One witness watched the white men beat a Freedom Rider until "his face was a bloody, red pulp." *Birmingham Post-Herald* reporter Tom Langston photographed the attack on Peck. The next day's editions of the *Post-Herald* and *Birmingham News* printed the picture of the mob scene. Carried by the Associated Press across the world, the snapshot of the brutal treatment of the Freedom Riders confirmed Birmingham's national reputation as a racially intolerant

Tom Langston's famous photograph of the Freedom Ride riot in the Birmingham Trailways station on Mother's Day, May 14, 1961, helped shift white elite opinion against Bull Connor. The man whose rear protrudes to the right is Gary Thomas Rowe Jr., the Klansman who turned FBI informant. Tom Langston, *Birmingham Post-Herald.*

city. The event also revealed the relationship between the local and national movements and the growing crisis over civil rights.[1]

Outrage following the beatings convinced executives of Birmingham's nascent service-consumer sector to abandon their long-standing alliance with the leaders of the city's industrial economy. In the months that followed the Mother's Day Freedom Ride riot, a coalition of realtors, merchants, and reformers successfully challenged the industrial leaders who had controlled the political economy of Birmingham after it emerged as the New South's center of heavy industry. By 1963 the challengers had engineered a change to the city form of government, transforming it from a three-man commission system controlled by archsegregationists who acted in the interests of heavy industry to a mayor-council system dominated by racial moderates who were sympathetic to the emerging service-consumer sector of the economy. The reformers hoped the change would defuse racial tensions, rehabilitate the city's tarnished image, and foster the emergence of a diversified economy that would ultimately supersede Birmingham's obsolescing iron and steel economy and transform the city into a commercial center to rival Atlanta. Although the reformers succeeded in breaking the industrial economy's stranglehold on Birmingham politics, their efforts did little to ameliorate racial tensions or to remedy the longstanding grievances of the city's black community.[2]

THE FREEDOM RIDES originated as a direct action challenge to segregated accommodations in interstate travel conducted by the Congress of Racial Equality. Modeled on the organization's Journey of Reconciliation that challenged segregated seating in the Upper South in 1947, the Freedom Rides enlarged the confrontation to include the Jim Crow restaurants, rest rooms, and other facilities in the Deep South. James Peck participated in both protests. An upper-middle-class New Yorker who shocked fellow students and Boston society by taking a black date to the freshman dance at Harvard, Peck operated as a professional agitator, writing for the Worker Defense League before joining CORE, where he edited the *CORE-lator* 155 and, with the organization's other pacifists, opposed the draft. Peck served on the national board when it appointed the charismatic James Farmer as the first black director of CORE. The white-dominated northern group then sought a sensational protest that would thrust CORE into the forefront of civil rights organizations. Farmer endorsed the proposed Freedom Ride—an event that not only achieved CORE's objectives but also, as noted by August Meier and Elliott Rudwick, "rejuvenated the southern protest movement."[3] The Freedom Rides also precipitated a stalemate over civil rights between the local and national movements and the local, state, and federal governments.

On May 4, 1961, thirteen integrationists—six white and seven black—left Washington, D.C. headed for New Orleans. The group divided to ride both Greyhound and Trailways Bus Lines. With the exception of Farmer, the black members on the protest were under thirty and most had participated in the previous year's student sit-in movement. Many of the white people were older supporters of leftist organizations. In the Upper South, the Freedom Riders integrated segregated facilities without serious incident and experienced no difficulties in Georgia. In Anniston, Alabama, however, vigilantes bashed the windows and slashed the tires as the bus driver attempted to pull away. When a blowout forced the Greyhound onto the shoulder of the road, Klansmen tossed a firebomb through the rear

The Greyhound bus carrying an integrated group of Freedom Riders from the Congress of Racial Equality burns beside Interstate 20 outside Anniston, Alabama. Earlier, after the bus had entered the station, Klansmen slashed its tires and gave chase, firebombing the vehicle once it pulled off the road. *Birmingham News.*

window that engulfed the bus in flames. Had not a state undercover agent on board drawn his pistol and threatened the vigilantes who blocked the door, the passengers, unable to escape the vehicle, could have burned alive. Taken to the hospital, the Freedom Riders were treated by doctors for smoke inhalation. When the second bus of integrationists reached Anniston, eight Klansmen boarded it, violently forced African Americans Isaac "Ike" Reynolds and Charles Person out of the white section, and beat Jim Peck and Professor Walter Bergman when they intervened. Bergman suffered permanent brain damage. His wife, who witnessed the violence, later recalled, "I had never before heard the sound of human flesh being hit; it was terrible."[4]

For weeks Commissioner of Public Safety Bull Connor knew the Freedom Riders were coming to Birmingham that Sunday afternoon. Not only had he been informed of the protest by the FBI, but also the Reverend Fred L. Shuttlesworth, leader of the Alabama Christian Movement for Human Rights, had notified detectives at a prior mass meeting of the arrival and had sent a telegram to Connor requesting adequate protection for the civil rights activists. Unbeknownst to Shuttlesworth—although he had heard rumors to that effect—but understood by the FBI, Connor orchestrated the mob violence by arranging for local vigilantes from the Ku Klux Klan and the American States' Rights Party to attack the Freedom Riders. Klansman and FBI informant Gary Thomas Rowe Jr. explained the collusion of the Klan and the Birmingham Police Department in his exposé, *My Undercover Years with the Ku Klux Klan*. Other testimony verified Rowe's assertions. According to the plan, officers were to give the vigilantes fifteen minutes to beat the Freedom Riders and then withdraw, after which the policemen would enter the scene. A Klansman notified Howard K. Smith of CBS Television, and Smith, who was in Birmingham to interview people as a follow-up to *New York Times* reporter Harrison Salisbury's negative assessment of the year before, spent the afternoon watching "a great number of heavy-set men, wearing sport shirts, loitering around the bus terminal."[5]

When policemen learned that the Freedom Riders traveled by Trailways, they called the Klansmen gathered at the Greyhound station across from city hall and notified them of the change. Rowe described the "astounding sight" of the white gang armed with sticks, clubs, and pipes hurriedly walking the four blocks to the other terminal. A patrolman on the street stepped out of the way as the mob passed. When the men entered the depot, a bus official exclaimed, "Get the shoeshine boy out; the Klan is here." The black man tried to exit, but vigilantes struck him down and tossed him out in the traffic. Then they waited for the bus. In his office in city hall, Bull Connor waited, too.[6]

As previously arranged, the police department afforded no protection for the Freedom Riders who nonviolently received the blows of the Klansmen. Battered integrationists lay in pools of their own blood. After fifteen minutes, the mob dispersed and a few patrolmen arrived on the scene. The officers passed the vigilantes on the street as the Klansmen, charged with excitement, collected under the windows of Connor's office in Woodrow Wilson Park to regroup and discuss their act of brutality. As in the past, law enforcement officers and vigilantes worked in tandem to defend community norms in race relations. This time, however, not all of the white community sanctioned the violence. The black community responded with outrage.[7]

Reverend Shuttlesworth functioned as CORE's main contact in Birmingham. After the debacle in Anniston, he dispatched ACMHR members to pick up the stranded integrationists. In Birmingham, after Peck regained consciousness, he found Bergman and the two of them hailed a cab that took them to Shuttlesworth's house. Other Freedom Riders, such as the bruised Morehouse College student Charles Person, assembled at the minister's home. On seeing Peck, Shuttlesworth said, "You need to go to a hospital," and called an ambulance. Doctors x-rayed Peck for skull fractures and broken ribs. The cuts in his head required fifty-three stitches, and while the physician sewed up his wounds, reporters admitted to the operating room with Peck's permission asked questions about nonviolence and the Freedom Ride. Released from the hospital, Peck phoned Shuttlesworth and then stepped outside to wait for his car. A patrolman pulled up to warn him that if he "didn't get off the street," he would be arrested for vagrancy. A startled Peck turned to reenter the building only to be told by the guard that "discharged patients were not permitted in the hospital." Fortunately the minister arrived, although policemen harassed them again, stopping the activists on the ride home. With bandages nearly hiding his face, a sick and sore Peck spent what remained of the night sleeping in Shuttlesworth's bed.[8]

158

The next morning, Monday, May 15, 1961, the Freedom Riders congregated at Shuttlesworth's house and debated their plan of action. Determined to continue the journey, Peck convinced the others to return to the bus station. They decided to travel together on the three o'clock Greyhound. Shuttlesworth accompanied the integrationists to the station, but once there, they found no bus driver willing to carry them to Montgomery. As the afternoon faded a white mob formed. This time policemen protected the Freedom Riders, who sat in the white waiting room discussing the situation. Giving up on reaching Montgomery in time for a scheduled meeting, the activists decided to fly to New Orleans in order to attend a rally commemorating the *Brown* decision. Shuttlesworth and ACMHR members drove the Freedom Riders to the airport, where they bought tickets on Eastern Air Lines. Again, vigilantes assembled. Airline officials received a bomb threat that forced passengers to evacuate while they searched the plane. Finding no explosives, they nonetheless canceled the flight. A second attempt on Capital Airlines similarly failed. Shuttlesworth left to attend the weekly mass meeting of the ACMHR but kept in touch by telephone. In a show of force, the police department removed mob members from the airport and set up a blockade to prevent them from returning. At 11:00 P.M. the integrationists took off on an Eastern flight, arriving in New Orleans an hour later, ending the first Freedom Ride.[9]

The Reverend Edward Gardner began the mass meeting earlier that night by pointing an accusing finger at the white detectives seated in Kingston Baptist Church: "Our Commissioner sends them here each Monday night, but we can't find them when we need them. I tell you if the Negroes blood can flow, so can the White blood." An agitated Shuttlesworth darted in and out of the meeting, finally taking the floor after 9:00 P.M. He angrily addressed the 350 people in attendance: "This is the worse city in the world where Mr. Connor or any Commissioner of the Police Department will say 'We didn't know violence would happen.' They are a damn liar! All this trouble is caused by the Ku Klux Klan." He explained that he had warned Bull Connor by telegram when the Freedom Riders would arrive. He expected to see police protection but instead saw "broken heads, broken bones, bloody shirts and such. This is a Democracy?" Referring to Jim Peck, Shuttlesworth noted: "I saw one man with his head laid open. It took 50 stitches to sew his head up. That same man sat in my house before the TV cameras, in my bed, they knew he slept there too."[10]

Shuttlesworth moved into an account of his contact with the Kennedy administration. The negative publicity surrounding the firebombed bus in Anniston and the vigilante violence in Birmingham concerned President Kennedy because of international repercussions. According to Shuttlesworth, Attorney General Robert Kennedy called him six times on Sunday asking, "What do you think I should do?" The civil rights activist responded, "Give us some protection down here." With that he hit on the crux of the problem. Hiding behind its concept of federalism, the Kennedy administration refused to defend American citizens from civil rights violations by individuals, cities, or states, preferring that local law enforcement protect them. Burke Marshall, the assistant attorney general for civil rights, designed the Kennedy strategy that consisted largely of trying to persuade state and local officials to do their duty. Hence Shuttlesworth described his participation in Robert Kennedy's behind-the-scenes telephone calls arranged to stop the violence.[11]

Referring to the attorney general as "Bob," Shuttlesworth recounted the day's events, and detectives recorded the reconstructed dialogue. "Bob called me back again and I told him that I was at home and I was going to the Greyhound Bus Station" with the Freedom Riders to get them to Montgomery, Shuttlesworth said. Kennedy asked if he wanted police protection, and the minister responded that he did. Kennedy called back and explained: "I am sure you will get an escort. I am assured this by the Birmingham Police Department." Later the attorney general telephoned to say, "Mr. Shuttlesworth, we are concerned about your problem. Do you have my telephone number?" Grandstanding, Shuttlesworth told the audience: "Excuse me, I have a long distance call from Bob." He stepped out of the pulpit and left the church. When he returned, his comments added validity to his previous statements concerning the limited involvement of the federal government. "They got plenty of police out at the airport tonight simply because Bob talked to Bull. The police didn't bother me at the Bus Station. . . . While I was sitting there a big drunk white man came after me and said, 'There is the one I want.' About that time a big cop grabbed him and took him away. I just sat there and grinned." Then he reiterated, drawing the recitation to a close: "Bob told me, 'If you can't get me at my office, just call me at the White House.' " An uproarious cheer saluted the civil rights veteran as movement members lost their composure. Shuttlesworth had worked the emotional crowd into a state of frenzied excitement as some participants "transcended," becoming so overwhelmed by what they believed to be spirit possession by the Holy Ghost that they flailed about wildly, having to be restrained by ushers. The mass meeting broke up about the time the Freedom Riders lifted off the ground.[12]

Reflecting a shift in editorial policy, the *Birmingham News* criticized Bull Connor's handling of the Freedom Ride, emblazoning across the front page the headline: "Where Were the Police?" Only weeks before, the *News* had endorsed Connor's reelection bid. He won without a runoff, collecting a huge majority. Now the newspaper rejected the commissioner of public safety's ridiculous excuse that his officers were visiting their families for Mother's Day and hence failed to prevent the beating of the Freedom Riders. Referring to the critical coverage by Harrison Salisbury the year before, the *News* admitted, "Fear and hatred did stalk Birmingham streets yesterday." An editorial concluded: "Today many are asking 'where were the police?' The *News* asks that, too, but the *News* also asks: When will the people demand that fear and hatred be driven from the streets?" Henceforth, the paper's editorial policy shifted from tacitly condoning community-sanctioned vigilante violence in defense of segregation to actively opposing mob action while resisting race reform. In the Birmingham Chamber of Commerce, a small group of businessmen responded to the Freedom Rides in a similar fashion, wondering how to circumvent the vigilantes.[13]

The violence in Birmingham revitalized the black student movement nationally as activists protested the brutality by picketing the White House, organizing demonstrations, and initiating new Freedom Rides. Diane

Nash, the student leader of the Southern Christian Leadership Conference affiliate in Nashville, Tennessee, determined to continue the journey to Montgomery despite CORE's decision to cancel the protest. After demanding that the Department of Justice protect the Freedom Riders, she notified Shuttlesworth of her plan. The minister responded: "Young lady, do you know that the Freedom Riders were almost killed here?" She retorted, "Yes, and this is exactly why the Ride must not be stopped." Appreciating her determination, Shuttlesworth assisted the new Freedom Riders. Ten students, including original riders John Lewis and Henry Thomas, prepared for the confrontation by writing out their wills and giving Nash "sealed letters to be mailed if they were killed." The student activists explained to her that "they were afraid, but they knew that this was something that they must do because freedom was worth it." Nash herself argued, "The objective of the Freedom Ride from Birmingham was not just to point out that people cannot ride freely but to make it possible for all persons to ride and use terminal facilities without being discriminated against." Emphasizing the desire for equal access as consumers, she decried segregation: "It allows white merchants to accept the customers' money but to give them unequal service, as at the Greyhound and Trailways Bus Lines, where all customers pay the same fares but some are not free to use all the facilities in the terminals and at restaurants where rest stops are made. Fares are equal but service is not." Early Wednesday morning, May 17, 1961, eight black and two white students left Nashville for Birmingham determined to win that equal service. Nash remained behind to coordinate the protest.[14]

Outside Birmingham a detective boarded the bus, ordered the Freedom Riders to move to the back, arrested Paul Brooks and Jim Zwerg when they refused to move, and informed the rest that they would not get off in the city but would travel on to Montgomery. The driver's shift ended in Birmingham, however, and his replacement refused to carry the Freedom Riders any farther. As the integrationists sat on the bus at the Greyhound station, a white mob assembled. Police dogs kept the vigilantes at bay, but by late afternoon Chief Jamie Moore placed the students under "protective custody" because of the dangerous situation in the terminal. Treated with care by the police department in the Birmingham jail, the Freedom Riders were nonetheless unable to make contact with Diane Nash. In the middle of the night, Bull Connor roused the activists, loaded them into cars, and headed north toward Nashville. As they rode, John Lewis cracked jokes with Connor, but the police commissioner got the last laugh when he dumped the Freedom Riders on the state line in the town of Ardmore. "This is Tennessee get over there," Connor said. One of the women replied, "Mr. Bull we will see you in Birmingham about twelve." At four-thirty Friday morning the phone woke Nash with the news that they were stranded by the highway. She dispatched cars to collect them, but instead of returning to Nashville, the integrationists drove straight to Birmingham, arriving back at the bus station that afternoon.[15]

Again, no one wanted to drive the activists to Montgomery. As the Freedom Riders sat in the station, policemen protected them from the white mob that gathered. All conducted vigils lasting into the night. By dawn it appeared that the prayers of the integrationists had been answered, for they boarded a bus headed for the state capital. Having sung freedom songs to ease the tension of the night, the tired Freedom Riders—now numbering eighteen—tried to relax as the journey resumed. A handful of reporters joined them on the bus.[16]

The next forty-eight hours encapsulated the growing crisis in civil rights as intransigent state and local governments clashed with activists while a disinterested federal government resisted direct involvement in the conflict. A temporary resolution skirted the real problem facing the nation. Earlier in the week, Attorney General Robert Kennedy had called Alabama governor John Patterson to convince him to use officers to protect the protesters. Patterson had quit talking with Kennedy, requesting that because of the "sensitive nature" of the negotiations, the president should send a "personal representative." President Kennedy complied, ordering John Seigenthaler to Montgomery. By Saturday morning Seigenthaler believed that Patterson had agreed to protect the Freedom Riders, and consequently the attorney general persuaded George E. Cruit of Greyhound to provide a driver. Helicopters led a procession of state troopers that escorted the integrationists out of Birmingham and down the highway to the state capital.[17]

On the outskirts of Montgomery, the troopers drifted off and the helicopters vanished. The bus arrived at the terminal alone. Vigilantes lay in ambush. The Klansmen first attacked the assembled media, then turned on the Freedom Riders. Men and women stepped out of the white crowd of between 300 and 1,000 and began beating the black and white activists, pairing off by sex, with the women slapping and hitting the females with their purses and the men punching the males. Pointing at Jim Zwerg as he stepped off the bus, a group of women screamed, "Kill the nigger-loving son of a bitch." A handful of toughs attempted to do just that. Blood poured from the mouth of John Lewis as he received the blows of the Klansmen. Watching the melee, John Doar of the Justice Department informed his superior Burke Marshall that again white supremacists had "mobbed" the Freedom Riders.[18]

John Seigenthaler, President Kennedy's personal emissary to Montgomery, had attempted an ill-conceived plan to assist the protesters. As if undercover, the white man dressed in a sport shirt similar to that worn by the vigilantes and, driving a rented van, pulled up to the curb during the violence. Apparently to offer protection, he interjected himself between two white female students and the white mob. With no visual proof, Seigenthaler identified himself as a "federal man" and tried to get the women into the van. They ran away, leaving him to face the vigilantes. The mob beat him mercilessly and left him to die. As in Birmingham, the Klansmen ended the brutality when the police arrived. Highway patrolmen under Floyd Mann, state director of public safety, used tear gas to rout the white crowd. Mann himself stepped in and rescued one black activist by drawing his gun on the attackers. Officers left Seigenthaler, Zwerg, and the rest of the wounded where they fell, and the city's ambulance service refused to respond to calls for assistance. Once more vigilante violence had stopped the Freedom Ride.[19]

163

Having been hoodwinked by Governor Patterson, Robert Kennedy exploded. He telephoned the governor but Patterson refused the call. Ignored by state officials, the attorney general responded to the beatings by ordering four hundred U.S. marshals to Montgomery, requesting the federal courts to enjoin the Ku Klux Klan and other hate groups from further violence and petitioning the Interstate Commerce Commission to ban segregation in interstate travel.[20]

The U.S. marshals arrived in time to accompany the Reverend Dr. Martin Luther King Jr. from the airport to a protest rally at the Reverend Ralph Abernathy's First Baptist Church on Sunday night. The Freedom Riders, Shuttlesworth, and other movement members attended the mass meeting. Around 300 marshals guarded the downtown church from vigilantes and white onlookers who collected near the building. Filling the pews and standing in the aisles, 1,200 African Americans packed the sweltering structure. Dressed in their Sunday best, they shouted "Freedom" and sang songs as the white crowd outside the sanctuary grew hostile. The mob soon outnumbered the marshals. Once the vigilantes became violent, King and Shuttlesworth maintained contact with the Kennedy administration. Throwing bottles and rocks at the church, rioters overturned and ignited a car. It appeared that they would burn the building with the black people trapped inside. The mob charged and broke the marshals' ranks. Floyd Mann reinforced the defenses with troopers and notified the governor of the dangerous situation. At the last minute, Patterson announced martial law and sent in the Alabama National Guard to restore order. Surrounding the church, soldiers shot tear gas into the violent white crowd that slowly dispersed with dawn. Afraid to venture out, movement members remained in the church until after six that morning, Monday, May 22, 1961.[21]

Irritated that he had been forced to protect the civil rights activists, Governor Patterson remembered that when the attorney general telephoned the next morning he took the call and told him: "Now you got what you wanted; you got yourself a fight; and you've got the National Guard called out and martial law, and that's what you wanted. We'll take charge of it now with the troops, and you can get on out and leave it alone." With soldiers stationed at Maxwell Air Force Base, Kennedy withdrew the marshals but he demanded that the Freedom Riders receive safe passage out of Alabama. Over the next few days, he worked out a compromise with officials from Alabama and Mississippi. On Wednesday morning, a bus containing twelve integrationists rolled past rows of National Guardsmen lined up to usher it out of Montgomery. At the state line, Mississippi assumed responsibility for the Freedom Riders and the highway patrol escorted the bus into Jackson. Disembarking, the activists entered the white rest rooms and were arrested for violating city ordinances and jailed. Authorities had assured Robert Kennedy that they could maintain order, and, indeed, no violence erupted in Mississippi. The U.S. Department of Justice overlooked the continued violation of the civil rights of interstate travelers by the state. During the summer Mississippi officials jailed more than three hundred Freedom Riders, many of whom were incarcerated in Parchman State Penitentiary.[22]

As Jackson municipal court sentenced the Freedom Riders to sixty-seven days in jail for breach of the peace and violating the segregation ordinance, a triumphant Robert Kennedy addressed the world over the Voice of America: "I think the whole world, as well as all the people of our own country, are aware of what has happened in Alabama over the last two weeks." The U.S. government was "disturbed about the fact that beatings took place and about the fact that people's rights were not being protected." The attorney general identified the vigilantes as a "small group" that "certainly do not [sic] represent the attitude of the U.S. Government or the American people." He claimed that in "many areas of the United States there is no prejudice" and went on to suggest that "Negroes hold high positions in the U.S. Government. Some of our leading judges are Negroes." Kennedy quickly returned—somewhat wistfully—to the Cold War theme of the speech: "You have problems and difficulties in your areas. We have them here. Our society is set up so that everyone knows about our successes and they know about our failures." The administration feared that domestic violence might spark a foreign policy breakdown, especially in the weeks before the scheduled summit meeting in Vienna with Soviet premier Nikita Khrushchev. Ever mindful of America's image abroad, Robert Kennedy chided the vigilantes in an announcement directed at them on Wednesday: "The President is about to embark on a mission of great importance. Whatever we do in the United States at this time, which brings or causes discredit on our country, can be harmful to his mission."[23]

For a brief moment, the Freedom Rides brought into focus the stalemate between federal, state, and local governments and the local and national movements over civil rights. This would occur again at Ole Miss and Albany in 1962 and in Birmingham in 1963. In his hurry to restore order, Robert Kennedy's compromise swept aside the civil rights of the activists. Although the Montgomery mob scene tempered the defiance of Governor Patterson, his resistance marked the path taken by a more successful George C. Wallace, whose appointment of Colonel Al Lingo to replace Floyd Mann as state commissioner of public safety ended the troopers' limited cooperation with the Kennedy administration. And whereas Birmingham chief of police Jamie Moore protected the Freedom Riders from further brutality, his superior, Commissioner Connor, defended segregation in the bus terminals by repeatedly arresting the manager of the Greyhound cafeteria for serving black passengers. Taking their cue from Connor, vigilantes responded to the invasion of their community by outside agitators with massive resistance; local businessmen, however, responded by plotting to remove Connor from office.[24]

THOUGH THE VIOLENCE that accompanied the Freedom Ride riot ultimately led to political reform in Birmingham, the immediate result was a heightening of racial tensions in the Magic City. Coming in the midst of Birmingham's municipal election runoff, the hysteria and violence surrounding the episode carried racial extremists into office. Whereas city commissioner Bull Connor had received his largest majority ever in the first Democratic primary earlier that month, the second primary of May 30,

1961, pitted two moderates against archsegregationists for the remaining commission posts. Art Hanes came from behind to defeat Tom King for the position of mayor, and J. T. "Jabo" Waggoner won a close race against Earl Bruner. The lower-staus white neighborhoods of East Lake, Woodlawn, and West End and the white steelworkers of Ensley voted solidly for Waggoner and Hanes, with the latter receiving a two-to-one margin. Hanes had called Tom King the candidate of "radical labor" and "the NAACP-bloc vote," and King carried the noncraft working-class districts at the American Cast Iron Pipe Company, Stockham Valves Company, and Tennessee Coal, Iron, and Railroad Company, as well as the predominantly African American box at Legion Field.[25]

The products of white Birmingham's lower middle class, Hanes and Waggoner reflected its values. A career politician, Waggoner first had worked in the Department of Public Improvements under then Commissioner Jimmy Morgan. Bad blood between the two permeated city politics throughout the 1950s, and by the end of the decade Mayor Morgan decided not to seek a fourth term. He endorsed Hanes. A native of Birmingham, Hanes had played football at Birmingham-Southern College, attended the University of Alabama Law School, and trained as a special agent for the Federal Bureau of Investigation. During the 1950s he oversaw the security force at Hayes Aircraft Corporation and developed close ties to the Ku Klux Klan. Several union members in Birmingham industries such as steel manufacturing and aerospace engineering supported the Klan. During the commission race Hanes recruited Klan political support. Closely linked to Bull Connor, Hanes contended that the election of King "would mean the 'fall' of Birmingham as a 'segregation stronghold.'"[26]

Though not directly challenging segregation, Tom King's candidacy represented a move away from lower-status white leadership and toward race reform. The Birmingham native had worked as an administrative assistant to conservative congressman George Huddleston Jr. A group of young attorneys—Charles "Chuck" Morgan Jr., George P. Taylor, Vernon Patrick, and Abraham Berkowitz—joined to run King's campaign. They were assisted by other young attorneys who previously had organized the local Kennedy campaign: David Vann, Robert Vance, and C. H. Erskine Smith. Self-styled "leaders of tomorrow," the young lawyers subscribed to the New Frontier ideology and thus confronted not only the old political structure of Bull Connor but also the moribund economic structure of the industrialists who dominated the Birmingham Chamber of Commerce. They wanted to "create opportunity at home" so they focused on political re-

166

form, and their campaign became a "crusade for good government, led by a new generation." Eager to foster Birmingham's shift into a postwar service economy, they argued that Tom King's election "would provide vigorous leadership in attracting needed industry and business for our community's stagnating economy."[27]

Birmingham's Big Mules, the local directors of the iron and steel industry and related businesses, disliked the challenge posed by the political upstarts. In his memoir, A Time to Speak, Chuck Morgan (Charles Jr.) recalled that King's candidacy "upset many conservative business and political interests." He characterized the Big Mules as a "Consensus," and he described how these elite industrialists, bankers, and attorneys intervened in city politics ostensibly in the "best interests" of Birmingham: "At the country club, at a business lunch, over the telephone, the community leaders holding the purse strings and economic power simply make their opinions known to others." The "others" included fellow businessmen, public officials, labor leaders, the black elite, educators, club women, ministers—in short, the city's civic leadership. More often than not, the public followed the lead of the Big Mule Consensus. Morgan observed that "so long as the policies and men at City Hall did not pose a threat to Consensus interests, the membership [Big Mules] really did not give a damn whether Tweedledee or Tweedledum occupied office space in City Hall." But Tom King threatened Consensus interests with his desire for economic growth at any cost and his willingness to sacrifice segregation in order to dismantle the colonial economy with its regionally discriminatory race wage. Consequently the Big Mules backed Hanes, and he carried the votes from the affluent southside neighborhoods along Highland Avenue.[28]

King pointed to the airport as an example of the complacency of the Birmingham Chamber of Commerce. During his campaign, he told a committee of the chamber that "Birmingham had fallen behind other Southeastern communities in preparing for the jet age" as a "result of short-sighted planning . . . that . . . cramped the area's economic growth." Within hours, the reactionary chamber responded by defending the city's air transportation program and its limited growth in manufacturing. In 1931 Birmingham had constructed a municipal airport. At first, the million-dollar facility serviced commercial flights from Delta, Capital, and Eastern Airlines. In World War II the building of the Bechtel-McCone-Parsons plant increased flight traffic at the airport. Military use continued in the postwar period as Hayes Aircraft and the Alabama National Guard leased runways from the city, making Birmingham the nineteenth busiest landing field in the nation. Yet during the 1940s and 1950s the chamber left advocacy for the municipal airport to the ineffective junior chamber or Jaycees, and the city commission hesitated to spend tax dollars on a public service that benefited only a few civilians. Moreover, iron and steel were shipped by rail, and the existing airport adequately accommodated the visiting dignitaries from the U.S. Steel Corporation. But as air transportation grew in importance during the ensuing period, progressive members of the chamber of commerce attempted to wrestle control of the airport away from the city commission through the formation of an airport authority. The fight strained the relationship between the city's political leaders and its service-sector businessmen. Construction did not begin on a new terminal building until 1960.[29]

In contrast to Birmingham, Atlanta led the region in aviation. A young alderman named William B. Hartsfield championed the new transportation system. In the mid-1920s he had convinced the federal government to make Atlanta, not Birmingham, the transfer point on national flights. By the end of the decade, Hartsfield had expanded the airport and lit the field for twenty-four-hour service. As commercial flying increased, Atlanta attracted the principal routes of the airlines and used city funds to snag Delta Airlines's corporate headquarters in 1940. Through public and private efforts, Atlanta's airport continued its steady expansion after the war, becoming the fifth busiest in the nation. Soon the joke circulated in Birmingham, "If I die and go to hell, I'll have to lay over in Atlanta."[30]

After World War II advocates for economic expansion in Birmingham challenged the Big Mule Consensus. An independent movement of small businessmen who endorsed civic reform organized in 1946 as the Young Men's Business Club. It attracted entrepreneurs who felt constrained by U.S. Steel. In touch with postwar urban growth, the independent businessmen wanted to diversify the city's economic base. Many members of the YMBC rejected the nonunion policies and limited economic growth advocated by TCI and the Consensus, arguing that such practices prevented "large labor hirers from coming into Birmingham, which would inevitably raise labor salaries." A postwar rumor concerning the Ford Motor Company illustrates the public's perception that TCI dominated Birmingham. In 1945 Ford announced plans to build a major expansion on the outskirts of Atlanta in Hapeville, Georgia. In Alabama, it was rumored that Ford initially had selected Birmingham as the plant site but turned to Atlanta when U.S. Steel intimated to Ford that its TCI subsidiary would not furnish material if the automaker disrupted the city's labor market. The arrival of

168

a Ford assembly line in Birmingham would have promoted competition for workers, increased wages, and strengthened the local presence of the United Automobile Workers, a union recognized for its racial liberalism. Ford went to Atlanta, TCI provided the steel, and Birmingham remained a "one horse town." Whether true or not, the existence of the rumor underscored the concerns of the YMBC.[31]

Despite such fears, some municipal leaders had difficulty believing that TCI had deliberately hamstrung Birmingham's industrial development. When Mayor Cooper Green learned in 1949 that the Rheem Manufacturing Company closed its Birmingham operations allegedly because TCI refused to meet its steel needs, he wrote Henry Ford II inquiring whether the similar rumor that he had heard about the Ford Motor Company was true. Only months earlier, the city commission had opposed a legislative effort to annex U.S. Steel's Ensley Works into the city limits in order to tax TCI. Thus far the corporation had escaped paying municipal taxes, despite being the city's largest employer. The public relations department of TCI waged a campaign to defeat the proposed bill by mailing to its employees and others in the community intimidating literature, which graphically depicted the ax of annexation killing the goose of industry that laid the golden egg of payrolls. Many citizens absorbed the not-so-subtle message and voiced their concerns to the city commission. The failure of the annexation movement reflected the Consensus of the city behind the wishes of TCI.[32]

To blunt criticism directed against it by the YMBC, the chamber of commerce organized the Committee of 100 in 1950. The move was an attempt to diversify Birmingham's industrial base by fostering limited growth that did not challenge the existing political structure or the colonial economy. At the end of the decade the chamber claimed that it had brought "more than 225 new plants, warehouses, sales offices and service organizations" to Birmingham. Although the city commission initially supported the chamber's efforts to attract new industry to the district, the businessmen's disregard for the concerns of city politicians soon caused friction that was apparent to all by 1960. Real estate developers, area merchants, and other businessmen suffering from "Birmingham's economic stagnation" not only questioned TCI's control over the chamber of commerce and the city commission, they also appreciated the alternative offered by the King campaign. As leaders of the emerging service economy, they resented artificial restraints on economic growth.[33]

Real diversification came later in the 1960s with the burgeoning health industry anchored by the University of Alabama's medical school. Estab-

169

lished in Birmingham in 1944 and later combined with the University of Alabama in Birmingham (UAB), the complex grew quickly, boasting 2,500 employees in 1961 and an operating budget of $10 million. By 1963 UAB had surpassed Hayes Aircraft as Birmingham's second largest employer behind TCI. A related health industry sprang up around the southside campus of the medical center. The Southern Research Institute (SRI) became a leader in the field of cancer research and chemotherapy through the work of Howard Skipper and Charles F. Kettering. But this development was an "unexpected" outcome of the institute's mission. Thomas W. Martin, president of the Alabama Power Company, financed Southern Research "to assist industry in the region and to help bring new industry to the South." Yet the emphasis on cancer research created a "perplexing situation" for Martin and the other Big Mules on the board of trustees at SRI. As custodians of the colonial economy, they had intended Southern Research to devote "all its efforts to *industrial* research." With the transition to the service-consumer economy, however, the trustees came to appreciate "this *different* but *wonderful* achievement."[34]

170   Birmingham's failed G.I. revolt of the late 1940s reemerged in the 1960s as the Young Men's Business Club promoted the expansion of the medical center, the airport, and other segments of the service economy. Some of its members favored a moderate approach to race relations. Indeed, the organization adopted a resolution condemning Bull Connor for the Freedom Ride riot. Both the chamber of commerce and the Jaycees considered the YMBC radical; consequently, membership in the group fluctuated between only seventy and ninety in 1961. The Kennedyesque lawyers who led the YMBC—Morgan, Taylor, and Vann—used the organization to advocate urban reforms. These politically ambitious young white men hoped to organize a liberal voting bloc composed of African Americans, white workers, and white progressives to wrestle control of city and state politics away from such racial extremists as Bull Connor, John Patterson, and George Wallace. Baptized into Birmingham's racial politics by Tom King's campaign, the reformers sought to master the electoral process. They received assistance from an unexpected quarter: a handful of disaffected members of the chamber of commerce.[35]

When the vigilantes violently greeted the Freedom Riders on Mother's Day, 1961, Birmingham realtor Sidney W. Smyer was in Tokyo representing the Magic City at a meeting of Rotary International. Also president of the chamber of commerce, Smyer spent the rest of the trip trying to salvage Birmingham's reputation. The Freedom Ride riot rudely awakened Smyer to the need for race reform. After returning to the United States, he informed the *Wall Street Journal*: "These racial incidents have given us a black eye we'll be a long time trying to forget. We're now in as bad a situation as Little Rock." He referred to the economic stagnation of the Arkansas city in the wake of racial disturbances over school integration. Since 1957 no major industrial plant had located in Little Rock. Smyer headed the Birmingham Realty Company, which controlled the downtown real estate market. Unlike other Big Mules who remained mired in the colonial economy, Smyer understood that diversified economic growth was the key to the postwar boom. By 1961 this former Dixiecrat and citizens' councillor advocated racial moderation not out of moral concerns but because, in the emerging arena of the national service economy, resistance to integration spelled economic suicide. The issue of race reform ultimately shattered the Big Mule Consensus in Birmingham when Smyer led an open rebellion against the iron and steel interests in the chamber of commerce.[36]

Two other members of the chamber echoed Smyer's conversion. William P. Engel, another leading realtor, concurred with Smyer's assessment of the economic consequences of racial violence: "You have to have a healthy climate to attract industry, and I mean more than physical health." But he mistakenly attributed Birmingham's racial problems to the vigilantes alone: "Right now we have a racial problem, and it has slowed us down. Unfortunately, it's just those people for whom we're spending time and money to bring in industry to provide work who are causing all the trouble." The chairman of the chamber's Committee of 100, James A. Head, likewise saw vigilantism as a cause rather than a symptom: "We hope we can reach the violent elements through education." The owner of a national office supply company, Head saw race reform as a moral problem. He belonged to numerous liberal groups, such as the National Conference of Christians and Jews, that taught understanding as the key to ending prejudice. He believed that "you can't change their [vigilantes'] minds with legislation or resolutions." Following the ideology of racial liberalism advocated by the northeastern establishment, the service economy executives blamed the vigilante violence on the ignorance of the white working class.[37]

A few days after the Freedom Ride riot, Smyer organized select businessmen from the Birmingham Chamber of Commerce, the Downtown Improvement Association, the Committee of 100, and the black community into a group designed to "soothe the city's racial troubles." He explained that his association of biracial businessmen "won't be a group set up just to

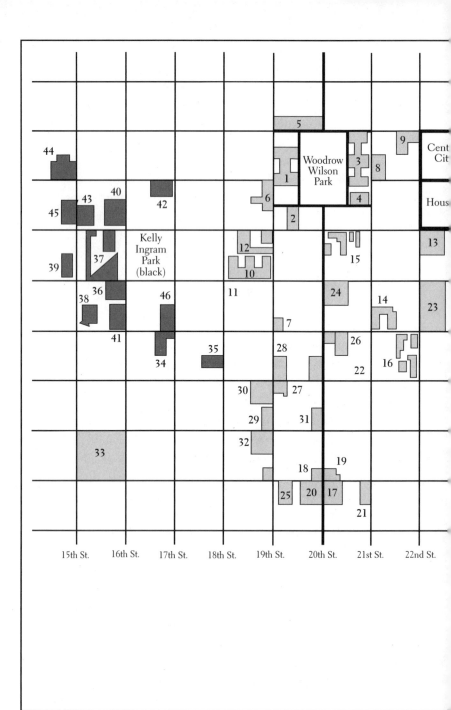

Downtown Birmingham, 1963

9th Ave. N. ——————

8th Ave. N. ——————

7th Ave. N. ——————

6th Ave. N.

5th Ave. N.

4th Ave. N.

3rd Ave. N. ——————

2nd Ave. N. ——————

1st Ave. N. ——————

Morris Ave. ——————

Phillips High School

whites

Marconi Park (white)

Central City

Housing for whites

Terminal Railroad Station

St.   24th St.   25th St.   26th St.

11 Federal Reserve Bank
12 First Methodist Church
13 First Baptist Church
14 First Presbyterian Church
15 Episcopal Church of the Advent
16 St. Paul's Catholic Church
17 First National Bank Building
18 Empire Building
19 Brown-Marx Building
20 Woodward Building
21 Protective Life Insurance
22 Title Guarantee Building
23 *News/Post-Herald*
24 Tutwiler Hotel
25 Britling Cafeteria No. 1
26 Britling Cafeteria No. 2
27 Woolworth's
28 S. H. Kress & Co.
29 J. J. Newberry's
30 Loveman's
31 Parisian
32 Pizitz
33 Sears, Roebuck and Co.
34 Carver Theater
35 Knights of Pythias
36 A. G. Gaston Building
37 A. G. Gaston Motel
38 Gaston Funeral Home
39 WENN Radio Station
40 Sixteenth Street Baptist Church
41 Metropolitan AME Zion Church
42 Seventeenth Street AOH Church of God
43 St. Paul's Methodist Church
44 St. John's AME Church
45 Sixth Avenue Zion Hill Baptist Church
46 "Colored" Masonic Building
▨ black institutions

City Hall
Chamber of Commerce
Jefferson County Courthouse
Public Library for whites
Municipal Auditorium

6 Greyhound Bus Station
7 Trailways Bus Station
8 First Christian Church
9 2121 Building (FBI office)
10 U.S. Post Office

pass resolutions either. . . . We intend to seek a solution to this problem and are prepared to back up the effort financially." Smyer's declaration that the new biracial association would do more than pass resolutions was an obvious reference to past experience. Prior limited communication between the races in Birmingham had occurred within the context of accommodation. A handful of elite white businessmen, many northern born and educated, such as banker Charles F. Zukoski, had met with a handful of elite black businessmen, such as insurance magnate A. G. Gaston, to discuss "the Negro problem" and propose moderate reforms to the city commission that did not challenge segregation. More often than not, nothing had come of the recommendations.[38]

Smyer's group signified a split in the Big Mule Consensus, for despite the leadership of important executives such as Smyer, Head, and Engel, many members of the chamber of commerce remained loyal to the interests of TCI. A struggle over the future of Birmingham's political economy slowly emerged between real estate developers, office equipment suppliers, salesmen, and ambitious lawyers acting as midwives for the service-consumer economy, on the one hand, and vigilantes, legal retainers, and mandarins of the absentee-owned corporations defending the colonial economy, on the other. The two factions divided over the issue of race reform.

The postwar effort to form a chapter of the National Urban League in Birmingham reflected the old Consensus approach to race relations. At first the initiative received support from the Big Mules. The Reverend Dr. Henry M. Edmonds, the highly respected pastor of Independent Presbyterian Church, enlisted the white power structure behind the proposal. But when investment banker Mervyn Sterne, speaking on behalf of Birmingham's iron and steel interests, informed black businessmen supporting the formation of an Urban League chapter that they could not belong to "subversive organizations" such as the NAACP and that the chapter could participate in "no controversial matters" and could not "disturb the status quo in Birmingham," the drive floundered. Sterne and the other Big Mules lost interest when they realized that they could not control a local affiliate of a national civil rights organization. Because it would have upset the status quo by challenging racial discrimination, the National Urban League initiative failed in Birmingham.[39]

The Big Mules thus saw biracial communication as a process of informing the black community of Consensus interests. Such lopsided race relations existed in part because black civic leaders acquiesced in the wishes of the white power structure. By accommodating to discrimination, the traditional Negro leadership class avoided total exclusion from the system and hence obtained some benefit from segregation. Unwilling to risk losing the influence he had with white businessmen, black businessman A. G. Gaston refused to participate in the Urban League endeavor because of its alleged radical overtones.[40] The lack of legitimate biracial communication in Birmingham proved a bone of contention for many people within the black community, yet the city's experiences with interracial cooperation demonstrated the limitations of this approach to address the real needs of race reform.

When the drive to organize an affiliate of the Urban League faltered over the issue of outside control, Birmingham's industrialists and bankers created a new biracial group, the Interracial Division of the Jefferson County Coordinating Council of Social Forces (JCCCSF), to function as a surrogate Urban League chapter. The white power structure funded the Interracial Division through the Community Chest. Board members included Big Mules such as Arthur Wiebel of TCI, Claude Lawson of Sloss-Sheffield, and Joe H. Woodward II of Woodward Iron, as well as Gaston and the city's leading black attorney, Arthur Shores. Others among the fifty members of the board included prominent clerics, bankers, and businessmen. To direct the biracial effort, the group selected Roberta Morgan, the white former head of the family services division of the Red Cross who had been instrumental in establishing Birmingham's public welfare system during the Great Depression. For several years, Bishop C. C. J. Carpenter chaired the segregated monthly meetings of the Interracial Division in his downtown Episcopal Church of the Advent.[41]

The iron and steel executives who controlled the Interracial Division channeled its energies toward issues that did not threaten segregation, such as using black policemen to patrol black neighborhoods and obtaining hospital privileges for black doctors to treat their black patients. As Florence Adams, the director of the sponsoring organization, the Community Chest, acknowledged from the outset, "segregation is strictly observed" in the Interracial Division. In 1956, at the height of massive resistance in Birmingham, white supremacists targeted the Community Chest because it funded the Interracial Division. Whereas in Atlanta white businessmen weathered a similar attack against the local affiliate of the Urban League, Birmingham's civic-minded businessmen caved in to the demands of the citizens' councils. The Community Chest disbanded the Interracial Division of the JCCCSF and acknowledged that it "had always made it clear to our Negro citizens serving on the Council that all work is within the

175

pattern of segregation." The Big Mules abandoned the one-sided biracial communication approach to race relations and substituted nothing in its place.[42]

A Birmingham industrialist living in Atlanta had laid the groundwork for biracial communication in the South. John J. Eagan, a fascinating capitalist who divined stock options from his reading of the Bible, founded the American Cast Iron Pipe Company in 1905 as an experiment in Christian industrial democracy. He established the Commission on Interracial Cooperation (CIC) in 1919 with the similar goal of using Christianity to solve social problems, for he believed that biracial communication was the best way to maintain peace between the races. Eagan authorized a survey of black Americans "to discover the real desires of the Negro" and learned that they wanted "(a) The ballot. (b) The abolition of the Jim Crow law." But rather than act on the results of his survey, Eagan did what he could to advance the welfare of African Americans except enfranchise them and end segregation because he, like other businessmen, knew that these two demands actually threatened the colonial economy. Henceforth the CIC, under the direction of the Reverend Dr. Will W. Alexander, promoted biracial communication but did not challenge segregation.[43]

In 1944 CIC leaders and other regional reformers organized the Southern Regional Council. The SRC promoted accommodationist biracial communication and did not oppose Jim Crow until 1949. The Alabama Council on Human Relations succeeded the state chapter of the CIC in 1954 as the new vehicle for biracial communication within the state. Affiliated with the SRC, the Alabama Council established chapters throughout the state. A small group of black and white racial liberals comprised the Birmingham chapter, which operated outside the mainstream of community life and hence had no real influence in the city. It did provide an avenue of biracial communication throughout the period and an important forum through which middle-class people could discuss the racial problems of the day. The white director of the Alabama Council, the Reverend Robert Hughes, reported on vigilante violence in Birmingham and the racial situation in general to the SRC office in Atlanta. He assisted such racial activists as the white seminarian Thomas Reeves, who opposed the segregationist Methodist Laymen's Union in 1959, and Miles College black student government president Frank Dukes, who organized the Prayer Vigil for Freedom in 1960. Consequently, the Ku Klux Klan burned a cross in Hughes's yard. The Klan, citizens' councils, and the Birmingham Police Department under orders of Bull Connor harassed Alabama Council members, going so far as to infiltrate the organization. A Bessemer grand jury jailed Hughes for contempt of court after he failed to divulge the Alabama Council membership list and information concerning his Spring 1960 conversation with *New York Times* reporter Harrison Salisbury, who was charged with criminal libel for his two critical articles on race relations in the Birmingham district. Chuck Morgan successfully represented the minister, but pressure by white supremacists within the United Methodist Church succeeded in Hughes's reassignment to Africa as a missionary in 1961.[44]

Hughes and his successor, the Reverend Norman C. Jimerson, were generally unsuccessful in altering race relations in Birmingham, but the reports that they filed with the Southern Regional Council recorded the herculean task that the handful of racial liberals faced in the city. A month after the Freedom Ride riot, Benjamin Muse, a director of the SRC, described a meeting with Douglas Arant, a leading corporate lawyer in Birmingham and member of the white power structure. Regarding race relations, Arant explained that elite white businessmen "were inclined to ignore or evade the issue." Yet he told Muse that if the SRC "wanted to help" ease racial tensions in Birmingham, the organization "could talk to half a dozen people outside of Alabama with possibly far reaching results." Arant identified five major corporate executives who exerted enormous influence over the city's Big Mules: Roger Blough, president of U.S. Steel; S. I. Newhouse, owner of the *Birmingham News* and WAPI television station; Harold Helm, chief executive officer (CEO) of the Chemical National New York Trust; George Champion, CEO of Chase Manhattan Bank; and Henry C. Alexander, CEO of Morgan Guaranty Trust. According to Arant, all these executives need say to their underlings in Birmingham was "that the anti-Negro business is threatening the economic stability and progress of Alabama," and the racial climate in the Magic City would begin to improve. Nothing came of Arant's suggestion despite its remarkably honest appraisal of where true power lay; but then again, these national leaders of corporate America profited by keeping Birmingham an appendage of the colonial economy.[45]

On his reconnaissance visits to Birmingham, Muse conferred with local white liberals on the racial climate in the city. He characterized the young attorneys Chuck Morgan and Dave Vann as politically savvy and about "as liberal as Roy Wilkins" of the NAACP. Muse described Charles Zukoski, an executive with First National Bank, as "one of the few upright men in an otherwise godforsaken city." The SRC director sought other racial liberals but few lived in Birmingham, and fewer still were willing to be as out-spoken in their beliefs as Morgan, Vann, and Zukoski.[46]

Having realized that to transform Birmingham economically he needed to reform it politically, Sid Smyer linked up with the ambitious attorneys. As a former state legislator and head of the Democratic Executive Committee for Jefferson County, Smyer understood the inner workings of local politics. He watched as Vann and Morgan learned the ropes during the Kennedy and King campaigns, and he recognized that they had their minds set on political careers. The Young Men's Business Club advocated reapportionment of the state legislature, hoping to foster the election of progressive representatives who would support economic growth. After Vann and fellow attorney Robert Vance filed suit for reapportionment in the name of Birmingham labor leader M. O. Sims, a three-judge federal court in Montgomery mandated a preliminary redistricting that added ten additional legislators to Jefferson County's delegation. The new legislators were to be chosen in a special election on August 28, 1962. Vann had analyzed election returns against George Wallace in the spring's guber-natorial primary, and he believed that a liberal coalition of voters could elect racial moderates if they ran for office.[47]

These reform-minded attorneys became an important weapon in Smyer's arsenal as he sought to liberate Birmingham from the dominance of the Big Mule Consensus and the three commissioners who ran city government. Smyer believed that the commission's intransigence on race reform created an obstacle to economic growth that had to be removed as quickly as possible. Not content to wait until the incumbents' terms expired in 1965, he developed a strategy for ousting Connor and the other commissioners by launching a campaign to change the structure of the city's government from the three-man commission to a mayor-council system. Smyer's resolve to remove the commissioners was bolstered in late 1961 during a crisis over the desegregation of Birmingham's public parks. This issue exposed the progressive businessmen and the city commission at loggerheads. Smyer adroitly channeled the frustrations of the service economy wing of the chamber of commerce away from Bull Connor and the iron and steel interests and toward an effort to change the form of municipal government in Birmingham. The Big Mule Consensus cracked open publicly.

On October 24, 1961, Judge H. H. Grooms of the U.S. district court ordered Birmingham to desegregate by January 15, 1962, its public recreational facilities—sixty-seven parks, thirty-eight playgrounds, eight swimming pools, and four golf courses—together with its zoo, art museum, state fair, municipal auditorium, and Legion Field stadium. The result of a court case filed in 1958 by the Reverend Fred L. Shuttlesworth and the Alabama Christian Movement for Human Rights, the ruling forced the city commission to confront segregation. Drawing the line in the dust, the commission closed the recreational facilities rather than integrate them. As Mayor Art Hanes explained to a group of taxpayers who complained about the action, "I don't think any of you want a nigger mayor or a nigger police chief . . . but I tell you that's what'll happen if we play dead on this park integration." In a state of nervous exhaustion, Hanes appeared to observers as "completely under the domination of the other two commissioners." At meetings he sounded increasingly irrational and paranoid, suggesting that communists and integrationists had taken over Washington with plans to divide the country into "ten districts" run by "autocrats." By New Year's Day 1962, the city had posted no trespassing signs, and 140 park employees had received their pink slips. Commissioners Bull Connor and Jabo Waggoner shifted the park money out of Hanes's budget to fund their own pet projects. Reactionary Birmingham fell into the spotlight again as the national media picked up the story.[48]

White racial liberals, progressive lawyers, and service economy advocates protested the closing of the parks. Representatives of the Jefferson County Board of Mental Health, Birmingham Ministerial Association, and Young Men's Business Club also voiced their opposition to the move, as did both the *Birmingham News* and the *Birmingham Post-Herald*. Even the stodgy chamber of commerce and its junior counterpart, the Jaycees, advised the commissioners to reconsider their action. But it was all to no avail. The commissioners recognized that most of the businessmen who advocated reopening the parks resided outside the city limits in bedroom communities south of Red Mountain, the so-called over-the-mountain suburbs. Thus when delegations of concerned businessmen approached the city commissioners and urged them to reconsider the closings, the officials dismissed them by curtly asking, "How many of you live in Birmingham?" The hostility of the commissioners stemmed, in part, from the white power structure's failed effort to consolidate the affluent over-the-mountain suburbs with Birmingham in 1959. Unwilling to join the city proper, the residents of these secluded white enclaves nonetheless sought to dictate municipal policy.[49]

Many members of the city's business community marshaled their forces behind the open park movement. Service economy executives from the chamber of commerce joined denominational heads from the ministerial

BUSINESSMEN'S REFORM

association and influential attorneys in preparing and circulating a petition entitled "A Plea for Courage and Common Sense." Though falling short of demanding desegregation, the petition called for a cooling-off period and a reconsideration of the park closings. Many of the twelve hundred who signed the document lived over the mountain, but more than half of the signatures came from residents of Birmingham. For the most part, the city's iron and steel interests defended the city commissioners, although Arthur V. Wiebel, president of TCI, and Thomas W. Martin, president of Alabama Power Company, signed the petition. Neither, however, actively supported the open parks initiative, and Wiebel declared, "I can't afford to get tangled up with the city commission," a rather disingenuous comment because he had not previously shown a reluctance to exert influence on city officials. On January 9, 1962, four spokesmen for the open parks movement presented the petition to the city commission: James A. Head, director of the Committee of 100; Dr. Henry King Stanford, president of Birmingham-Southern College; the Reverend David C. Wright, rector of the prestigious St. Mary on the Highlands Episcopal Church; and Barney A. Monaghan, president of Vulcan Materials Company. The commissioners rejected the petition outright. Then Bull Connor and Mayor Hanes treated the delegation to an hour-long "bombastic and abusive" discourse on desegregation, prompting Stanford to declare, "I never had such an experience in my life." The city commission's effrontery shocked the petitioners, influential members of Birmingham's white elite unaccustomed to rank insubordination.[50]

By resorting to such tactics, Connor and his fellow commissioners alienated an important segment of Birmingham's white community and played into Smyer's hands. As if toppling a third world dictator because he no longer followed the imperialist line, the Birmingham realtor engineered a corporate coup d'état that removed Bull Connor from office. As early as February 1961 chamber of commerce president Smyer had contacted Douglas Arant and other friends in the Birmingham Bar Association and suggested that the bar undertake a study on changing the city's form of government from the three-man commission to a city council system. Smyer hoped that such a reform would ameliorate race relations and woo the wealthy over-the-mountain suburbs into annexation with the city proper. The bar appointed a committee in March, and the following October it recommended a change to the mayor-council form of government. The committee presented its findings to the Birmingham Bar Association in February 1962 but did not make its report public until June. By then the Freedom Ride riot and the park crisis had occurred, emphasizing the

Mayor Art Hanes impatiently listens to a member of the white elite present a petition on December 11, 1961, calling on the city commission to desegregate rather than close Birmingham's public parks. Hanes criticized the over-the-mountain residents for supporting desegregation in Birmingham but refusing to join the city proper through annexation. Above the chamber doors reads the slogan, "Cities Are What Men Make Them." *Birmingham Post-Herald*, BPLDAM.

urgency for municipal reform to improve local race relations. Smyer and others believed that the mayor-council form of government offered the most effective method of easing racial tensions in the city. Already in contact with Dave Vann, Chuck Morgan, and Abe Berkowitz, Smyer assisted the young lawyers in organizing a "grass roots" movement in support of municipal reform under the rubric "Citizens for Progress."

To schedule a citywide referendum on altering Birmingham's form of government, the advocates needed the signatures of 7,000 residents. Smyer recommended that the lawyers create a blue-ribbon committee composed of a dozen prominent men to promote the petition drive for the municipal reform, but when the chamber of commerce and the *Birmingham News* opposed the effort, none of the bankers and industrialists contacted were willing to link their names to the Citizens for Progress. Smyer then recommended a new approach to Vann: "If you can't get 12 somebodies, get 500 nobodies." A wide variety of groups subsequently endorsed the reform movement, including the Young Men's Business Club, the Birmingham Labor Council, and the *Birmingham Post-Herald*. Virtually overnight, the Citizens for Progress had 500 members. Vann conceived the idea of soliciting signatures for a referendum petition at polling places during the August 28, 1962, election for state representatives. Citizens for Progress volunteers greeted voters as they departed the voting booth and secured the signatures of 11,000 white registered voters. That night Erskine Smith guarded the petitions with a shotgun. When Mayor Hanes refused to call the special election, Vann took the petitions to probate judge J. Paul Meeks, who ordered the referendum to be held on November 6, 1962.[51]

In addition to removing Bull Connor from office, the Citizens for Progress hoped that Homewood and Mountain Brook would elect to merge with the city proper. White liberals and moderate businessmen saw annexation of Birmingham's affluent bedroom communities as the solution to the city's woes. They believed that consolidation would bring responsible businessmen forward to lead the city on a progressive course, following the model of Atlanta, which had annexed its elite neighborhood, Buckhead, in 1952 and enjoyed phenomenal growth under the political leadership of businessmen. Atlanta emerged as the regional center of the new service-consumer economy because it used indigenous capital to build on its transportation, financial, wholesale, and manufacturing base while its civic leaders sacrificed segregation for commercial expansion. But absentee-owned corporations and the lack of indigenous capital hindered Birmingham's development; moreover, the Big Mule Consensus that controlled the city supported the status quo and thus opposed the race reforms necessary to attract outside manufacturing. Annexing the houses of bankers and industrialists would not alter the Consensus.[52]

The relationship of the Big Mules residing in Mountain Brook to their workers in the central city corresponded to the relationship of Wall Street to Birmingham. Just as the great majority of the shareholders of U.S. Steel lived outside Alabama, so too the managers of these absentee-owned corporations lived outside the Magic City. Yet both profited by the colonial relationship that exploited the material and human wealth of the city. During a previous merger campaign, Mayor Jimmy Morgan had called the over-the-mountain residents who refused to support consolidation "parasites." Many people in Birmingham shared his view. Periodically, the merger issue resurfaced, as in 1959 when Chuck Morgan and George "Peaches" Taylor campaigned for consolidation. Whereas the young attorneys hoped that the effort would result in progressive leadership for Birmingham, former governor Frank M. Dixon and state senator James A. Simpson wished that it would dilute the strength of the growing black vote. Less metropolitan-minded suburbanites carried the day, for Mountain Brook and Homewood voters rejected consolidation in May 1959. The issue of school integration defeated the proposal. No black people lived in Mountain Brook—the wealthiest city in the South and nicknamed the "tiny kingdom" by its residents. As long as it remained a separate municipality with its own school system, its residents had nothing to fear from desegregation.[53]

The failure of the 1959 consolidation movement reflected the detachment of many people living over the mountain from Birmingham. Future annexation drives suffered similar defeats. With community and civic virtue centered on a defense of property values, the affluent suburbanites related less and less to the problems of the inner city. Insulated in the thickly wooded and landscaped subdivisions of Mountain Brook, Vestavia Hills, and Homewood, they sought the comfortable and safe suburban ideal soon to be set forth by *Southern Living*, the middle-class magazine of the New South edited in Birmingham. Just as the visually rich pages of the glossy monthly would invite its readers to escape into an ordered and secure world, political independence suggested that Birmingham's suburban middle class could escape the problems of urban life. Nonetheless, while privately incorporated and politically independent of the city proper, over-the-mountain residents remained economically tied to the urban core. As Chuck Morgan recalled, "Like every other harsh, unpleasant fact concerning our city—including changes in the world that pounded at our city's ancient racial landmarks—it was much more comfortable to pretend it just didn't exist."[54]

With Vann and Erskine Smith as his front men, Smyer and his allies in Citizens for Progress ran a quiet campaign to change the form of municipal government in the weeks before the referendum. As they addressed civic club meetings around the city, proponents stressed the representational advantages of the mayor-council form without mentioning Bull Connor. Although Citizens for Progress had enlisted only white voters in the petition drive, it appealed to voters of both races to support the change to mayor-council in the upcoming referendum. The Jefferson County Voters League Progressive Democratic Conference organized leading black busi-

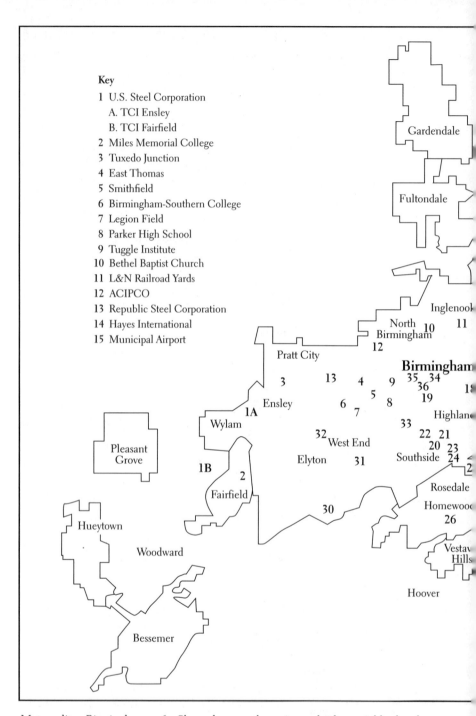

Key

1 U.S. Steel Corporation
  A. TCI Ensley
  B. TCI Fairfield
2 Miles Memorial College
3 Tuxedo Junction
4 East Thomas
5 Smithfield
6 Birmingham-Southern College
7 Legion Field
8 Parker High School
9 Tuggle Institute
10 Bethel Baptist Church
11 L&N Railroad Yards
12 ACIPCO
13 Republic Steel Corporation
14 Hayes International
15 Municipal Airport

Gardendale

Fultondale

Inglenook

North 10   11
Birmingham
12

Pratt City

Birmingham

3   13   4   9   35 34   1?
                        5   36
Ensley   6   8   19
        1A   7
Wylam   33   Highland

                32   22 21
        West End   20 23
Elyton   31   Southside 24
Pleasant
Grove   1B   2?
        2
Fairfield   Rosedale

                        30   Homewoo?
Hueytown   26

Woodward   Vesta?
                                    Hills

Bessemer   Hoover

Metropolitan Birmingham, 1963. Shown here are the various suburban neighborhoods
that surrounded the city, including the over-the-mountain middle-class communities

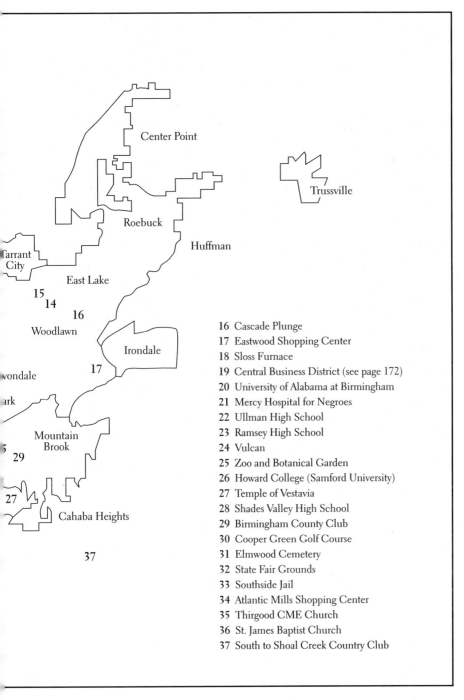

Center Point

Trussville

Roebuck

Huffman

Tarrant City

East Lake

15
14
16

Woodlawn

Irondale

vondale

17

ark

Mountain Brook

29

27

Cahaba Heights

37

16 Cascade Plunge
17 Eastwood Shopping Center
18 Sloss Furnace
19 Central Business District (see page 172)
20 University of Alabama at Birmingham
21 Mercy Hospital for Negroes
22 Ullman High School
23 Ramsey High School
24 Vulcan
25 Zoo and Botanical Garden
26 Howard College (Samford University)
27 Temple of Vestavia
28 Shades Valley High School
29 Birmingham County Club
30 Cooper Green Golf Course
31 Elmwood Cemetery
32 State Fair Grounds
33 Southside Jail
34 Atlantic Mills Shopping Center
35 Thirgood CME Church
36 St. James Baptist Church
37 South to Shoal Creek Country Club

of Homewood, Mountain Brook, and Vestavia Hills and the working-class suburbs of Tarrant City, Fultondale, Gardendale, Fairfield, and Pleasant Grove.

BUSINESSMEN'S REFORM

Bull Connor addresses an audience at West End High School on October 18, 1962, in an effort to convince area residents to retain the city commission form of government. Though he won the support of West End, he failed to convince the majority of Birmingham's citizens, who voted on November 6 to oust the commission and elect a new city council. *Birmingham Post-Herald*, BPLDAM.

nessmen in support of the change. Under the direction of A. G. Gaston and insurance executive John Drew, the organization worked with Smyer to get out the black vote. During the last two weeks of the campaign, the mayor-council advocates unleashed a media blitz that promised a better future for Birmingham through political reform. The *Birmingham News* and *Post-*

Herald assisted the campaign by contrasting an outmoded city commission with a progressive mayor-council.[55]

Bull Connor responded to the broadside attack of the reformers with the only defense he could muster: racial politics. Always a salient factor in Birmingham politics, race had become an even more volatile issue because of recent initiatives of civil rights activists. Over the previous year black students had led a boycott of white-owned businesses, and in September Martin Luther King had threatened to call for protest marches during the Southern Christian Leadership Conference's annual convention in Birmingham. To Connor and the other commissioners, the mayor-council reform was designed by the chamber of commerce to compromise segregation. Commissioner Jabo Waggoner denounced a meeting in the summer of 1962 where chamber leaders had urged the city commission to soften its resistance to integration. Waggoner recalled: "The burden of the whole meeting was that we were just going to have to change our attitude . . . [and] . . . allow blacks to become foremen and superintendents. . . . Bull and I got up and left the meeting, and told them they could do what they wanted to."[56]

187

Ever quick to resort to ad hominem tactics, Connor labeled David Vann a "communist" sent by "Hugo Black to help integrate" Birmingham. Passing out photographs depicting biracial municipal government, Connor said, "If you want Negroes on your city commission as in Nashville, vote for the city council." He identified the integrationist Birmingham chapter of the Alabama Council on Human Relations as among his opponents and noted, "any group that has the words 'human relations' is suspect." In a final appeal to unity within the lower middle class, Connor denounced the mayor-council proponents as a "bunch of over the mountain liberals" supported by area merchants. He concluded by encouraging his constituency of craftsmen, steelworkers, and shopkeepers not to "turn your city over to people who would integrate it." Connor reasoned: "It is not going to be long until they get tired of calling out the Army every time they want to put a Negro in a white school. The pressure for integration is going to let up as soon as we get the Kennedys out of the White House. So don't give up the fight for segregation too quickly." Aware that he no longer could depend on the unequivocal support of Birmingham's white power structure, Connor counted on his popularity among the lower middle class to keep himself in power.[57]

On November 8, 1962, Birmingham voted for the mayor-council form of government over the city commission and city council-manager alternatives: 19,317 to 16,916 to 943. Connor held on to his lower-status white precincts, with the commission form winning the boxes in East Lake and West End, but in his home district of Woodlawn he lost three of the four boxes. By a two-to-one margin the affluent southside neighborhoods along Highland Avenue voted for the political reform. With returns for the mayor-council over the commission and manager choices, the "Negro" boxes at Legion Field posted 693 to 35 to 14 and at Center Street, 977 to 62 to 35. The noncraft working-class boxes in East Birmingham at Stockham Valves posted 278 to 167 to 15; those in Pratt City, 428 to 299 to 15; those in North Birmingham at nonunion ACIPCO, 351 to 246 to 15; and those in the black section of Ensley at TCI, 288 to 50 to 10. The steelworkers living in the white section of Ensley and those in Wylam, as well as the railroad workers in Inglenook, supported the commission form of government.[58]

Unfortunately for Bull Connor and the other intransigent city commissioners, a majority of voters in Birmingham followed the leadership of the service economy spokesmen. Despite the best efforts of the Jefferson County Board of Registrars to the contrary, enough African Americans had successfully registered to provide the margin of difference for the mayor-council form of government. But the black vote alone did not sink the city commission, as the returns from Woodlawn suggest. Whereas in 1957 Connor had carried these lower-middle-class boxes in a tight race with the moderate incumbent commissioner Robert Lindbergh, in 1962 a slim majority of Woodlawn's voters crossed over to support the political reform. The progressive businessmen had influenced enough of the lower middle class to secure Connor's downfall.[59]

Though accepting his defeat with the comment, "that's democracy," Bull Connor questioned the legality of the referendum. In January 1963 the lower courts upheld the change in government and scheduled the election for mayor and council members in March. Yet Birmingham's iron and steel interests were unwilling to lose their influence in city hall. James A. Simpson, the TCI lawyer and former state senator, appealed to the Alabama Supreme Court in March 1963. He argued that the act authorizing the referendum was in conflict with general state law and the enabling legislation of the new government conflicted with laws that protected an official's term in office. Simpson hoped to keep Connor in power until his four-year term expired in 1965. The court sustained the legality of the referendum, but only three of the seven justices commented on Simpson's argument that the new council could not take office until the incumbents' terms expired. The other four justices ruled that the court could not consider the point

188

unless the new council brought suit. Thus the city commission legally retained power until the Alabama Supreme Court ruled on such a case.[60]

Pending the outcome of legal proceedings, the elections went ahead as scheduled in March. Although seventy-five people ran for the nine positions on the new city council, the candidates for mayor captured the interest of the electorate. Bull Connor announced his candidacy for the position of mayor, as did his fellow commissioner Jabo Waggoner. Both men ran as archsegregationists and competed for the vote of the lower middle class. Attorney Tom King, the racial liberal who had run a close campaign as a moderate against Art Hanes in the mayoral race of 1961, hoped to reverse his earlier defeat and win election as mayor. King expected to pull the vote of the electorate that had supported the mayor-council form of government in November's referendum. The white power structure had other ideas.

Having committed itself to ousting Bull Connor, Birmingham's corporate leadership—with the exception of the iron and steel interests that remained loyal to the former commissioners—searched for someone to run for mayor whose views coincided with its own. The service economy sector of the chamber of commerce found its man in mild-mannered Albert Boutwell. In 1946 Boutwell had replaced Simpson as state senator for Jefferson County, a post he held until 1958 when he assumed office as lieutenant governor. Bad health had derailed his 1962 gubernatorial campaign, and he returned to Birmingham to practice law.[61]

Throughout his legislative career Boutwell had proven himself a loyal and willing knight-errant of the corporate structure. Among his numerous achievements on Montgomery's Goat Hill, his contributions to massive resistance ranked him high in the esteem of his fellow white supremacists. He coauthored the "freedom of choice" law to circumvent the *Brown* decision and maintain segregated schools. A regular on the citizens' council circuit, the otherwise reticent Boutwell spoke as an ardent segregationist, but his racist rhetoric changed with the climate. No matter how well he conformed to the wishes of the Big Mules, Boutwell remained a perpetual outsider. Born in 1904, he grew up in Greenville, a small town in Alabama's Black Belt, and worked his way through the University of Alabama, where, in 1928, his victorious renegade candidacy for student government president broke the old-boy machine controlling the position that served as a traditional stepping stone to higher office in Alabama politics. Legalisms offered Boutwell refuge, and he used the rational approach of the lawyer to maintain social distance, appearing cold and aloof. To Birmingham's reform-minded corporate executives, he was tried and true. Responding to

189

their request and offer of support, the gray-haired, slight-of-build Boutwell stepped into the ring.[62]

As the mayoral race headed toward the March 1963 election, the campaigns of Connor and Boutwell overshadowed those of the other two candidates and the stiff competition for council seats. Both men ran as segregationists. But whereas Bull Connor promised to defy any attempt to force integration in Birmingham, Boutwell offered resistance but suggested that maintaining law and order would best stave off desegregation. A veiled reference to the Freedom Ride riot, Boutwell's pitch for orderly leadership underscored the lawlessness of the vigilante violence sanctioned by Bull Connor and focused the debate on Birmingham's uncertain future. Clearly, Connor represented a defense of the past.

Braving the tornadoes and thunderstorms that whipped through Jefferson County with foreboding force on election day, March 5, 1963, voters cast a record 44,736 ballots. Boutwell collected 17,434 votes to Connor's 13,780, King's 11,659, and Waggoner's 1,701. The former commissioner of public improvements failed to carry a single box. Reverend Shuttlesworth and others in the black community saw Boutwell as "just a dignified Bull Connor." Consequently, Tom King captured most of the black vote, winning the boxes at Legion Field, Center Street Fire Station, and the black section of Ensley. King also received support from the working class, taking the boxes at Stockham Valves, Pratt City, and ACIPCO. Steelworkers voted for the former commissioner of public safety, but Bull Connor barely carried the boxes in West End and won just over half of the boxes in East Lake and Woodlawn, losing the other half to Boutwell in close polling. The former lieutenant governor swept the field in the affluent Highland Avenue district. As Boutwell failed to receive a majority of the votes cast, he prepared to face Connor in a runoff scheduled for April 2.[63]

In the month leading up to the election, Bull Connor struck out against all of the powerful forces arrayed against him: the chamber of commerce, the daily newspapers, the white liberals, the black voters. Connor heightened his racist defiance, threatening to close the public schools in the face of an anticipated desegregation order, just as he had closed the parks the previous year. He denounced Boutwell as an integrationist and the candidate of the "Negro bloc vote." Speaking to supporters in Roebuck, Connor explained that he had resigned from "the Mountain Brook controlled Birmingham Chamber of Commerce because they tried to brainwash Ol' Bull about integration." On another occasion he told them, "stay in there and pitch . . . we've just begun to fight!" Attacking the *Birmingham News* and *Post-Herald*, he described the runoff as a "show down of whether two foreign-owned newspapers, one owned by Newhouse in New York and the other one by Scripps-Howard in Cleveland, Ohio, and the bloc vote are going to rule Birmingham or the people of Birmingham are going to rule themselves." Appealing to "the people"—the lower middle class—he emotionally implored: "Boutwell is only the image created by the newspapers and the people over the mountain. The *Birmingham News* and the image have a low opinion of you, the people of Birmingham. I think you're the finest. Birmingham doesn't need Shades Valley brains and education, it already has the finest people."[64]

Affluent whites living over the mountain in Shades Valley backed Boutwell, who repeated his call for order but otherwise took the high road as Connor resorted to smear tactics. Setting a new record with 51,278 ballots cast, the electorate heeded the advice of Birmingham's corporate executives, daily newspapers, and others in the establishment and on April 2, 1963, voted for Boutwell, who received 29,630 votes to Connor's 21,648. The lower middle class stuck with Bull to the bitter end, giving him the districts in West End, three of the five districts in East Lake, but only one of the four districts in Woodlawn, where he lost his home box. Steelworkers and craft unionists supported Connor. Choosing what appeared to be the lesser of two evils, Birmingham's black community cast its ballot for Boutwell, as did the silk stocking district of Southside.[65]

The *Birmingham News* headline read, "New Day Dawns for Birmingham," as it recounted Boutwell's victory at the polls. Yet sit-ins announcing a civil rights campaign planned by ACMHR-SCLC suggested that a different morning had arrived. To make matters worse, the legal retainers of the iron and steel industry told Connor and the other city commissioners to remain in office while they fought the legality of the new mayor-council form of government. Suddenly Birmingham had two mayors and two city governments. Smyer and the service economy wing of the chamber of commerce thought they had prevailed. The corporate coup d'état had successfully changed the form of government and removed Connor from office, but Simpson's legal maneuverings and the protests of black activists undermined this triumph. Watching their Pyrrhic victory unfold, the biracial political reformers blamed the Reverends Fred L. Shuttlesworth and Martin Luther King Jr. as the spoilers who darkened Birmingham's dawn.[66]

Responding to the Freedom Ride riot, the white businessmen had conspired to improve Birmingham's negative image. Removing Bull Connor from power might have altered outside perceptions of the city, but the political reform did not address the long-standing concerns and needs of the black community. Recognizing this, Shuttlesworth and the civil rights activists organized demonstrations that began on April 3, 1963. Indeed, a new day had dawned for Birmingham: a day of reckoning.

CHAPTER SIX

Momentum

A stalemate over race relations in Birmingham had created a crisis months before Martin Luther King
and the Southern Christian Leadership Conference arrived on the scene and exacerbated the
problem. Indeed, for years Birmingham had been
building toward just such a calamity. By the spring of 1963, the Consensus
governing Birmingham since the Great Depression had collapsed. The
industrial and financial elite split over the issue of desegregation. Most of
the Big Mules and much of the lower middle class supported the belligerent commissioner of public safety Bull Connor in his defense of racial
norms. A new renegade group oriented toward a service-consumer economy, headed by realtor Sidney W. Smyer, and tacitly supported by the
white middle class evidenced a willingness to compromise on racial matters. The change in city government from the commission to the mayor-
council system highlighted the division among the white elite. Likewise,
factionalism prevented Birmingham's black community from speaking
with one voice as the direct action against segregation waged by Fred L.
Shuttlesworth and the Alabama Christian Movement for Human Rights

competed with the ideology of accommodation practiced by the traditional Negro leadership class. Black students joined the fray by conducting a boycott of white-owned businesses. Skirmishes among the different interest groups during 1962 steadily heightened racial tensions in Birmingham. Biracial negotiations obstructed black militancy without seriously addressing the demands of the movement or compromising segregation. By involving the SCLC in the local struggle, Reverend Shuttlesworth sought to break the deadlock through an engagement with the defenders of racial discrimination.

The momentum building up to the Spring 1963 demonstrations originated in renewed student protests in Birmingham. After the short-lived Prayer Vigil for Freedom in March 1960, black students from Miles and Daniel Payne Colleges organized occasional sit-ins and, during the summer of 1961, joined the elite Jefferson County Voters League in a registration drive. Frank Dukes, the student government association president at Miles College, sought advice from Shuttlesworth; yet the students remained independent of the ACMHR as well as national civil rights organizations such as the Congress of Racial Equality and the Student Nonviolent Coordinating Committee. When the park desegregation case increased racial hostilities in the city in December 1961, the students took the initiative away from the ACMHR by proposing demonstrations. Shuttlesworth supported the students, but his acceptance of a pastorate in Cincinnati, Ohio, the previous June handicapped his Birmingham activities.[1]

Similar to student activists elsewhere in the South, the Miles College group emphasized its discontinuity with traditional black protest by expressing an impatience with the slow pace of desegregation. Seven hundred of the college's eight hundred students met on December 29, 1961, and adopted a statement entitled "This We Believe." The activists linked their struggle with that of the national student movement and announced: "We do not intend to wait complacently for those rights which are already legally and morally ours to be meted out to us one at a time. Today's youth will not sit by submissively while being denied all of the rights, privileges and joys of life." The statement listed seven "inequalities" that demanded immediate remedy, foremost among them, equal access to education and jobs. In order to "abolish these glaring practices of discrimination and injustice," the students promised "to use every legal and nonviolent mean [sic] at our disposal to secure for ourselves and our unborn children these God-given rights guaranteed by the Constitution of the United States." The name of Frank Dukes headed the list of eight student signatures.[2]

An atypical student, thirty-one-year-old Dukes had served in combat during the Korean War and worked for General Motors in Detroit before a layoff sent him back to his native Birmingham, where he enrolled in Miles College in 1959. Dukes was a regular on the dean's list and his classmates elected him president of the student body. To implement the statement, "This We Believe," he organized student leaders into the Anti-Injustice Committee in January 1962 to actively protest racial discrimination. As he explained to those gathered: "In this world you either live or die. It is time that we as black college students take the lead in our struggle against oppression." Having discussed nonviolent strategies with Shuttlesworth and representatives from SNCC and CORE, the Anti-Injustice Committee prepared "a spectacular Negro demonstration" for later that month.[3]

The president of Miles College, Dr. Lucius Holsey Pitts, feared that the students would march on city hall, precipitating a violent clash with Bull Connor and the Ku Klux Klan. He therefore attempted to deflect the growing militancy of the Anti-Injustice Committee. Pitts abhorred violence and did everything in his power to prevent civil rights confrontations. Demanding access to whites-only jobs as clerks and the desegregation of store facilities, Dukes and the Anti-Injustice Committee prepared a black boycott of white merchants in January 1962. On learning of the students' plans, Pitts immediately notified white businessmen and arranged a biracial meeting. As a result, Dukes canceled the boycott.

A newcomer, Pitts had moved to Birmingham in June 1961 from Atlanta, where he had served on the Georgia affiliate of the Southern Regional Council. He shared that organization's belief in the primacy of biracial communication as the way to effect race reform in the South, and he associated with the Birmingham chapter of the Alabama Council on Human Relations. Pitts had started out in life as one of eight children on a tenant farm in Georgia, but over time he had developed a decidedly middle-class outlook. Hard work and a bright mind had enabled him to attend Paine College in Augusta and Fisk University in Nashville. In 1955 Pitts became the secretary to the Georgia Teachers and Education Association in Atlanta. Three years later, Martin Luther King courted him for the position of executive director of the SCLC, but the black educator turned it down. Their paths would cross again.[4]

Throughout February 1962, service economy representatives such as Sid Smyer of Birmingham Realty and office supply company owner James A. Head met with Pitts, the students, and members of the traditional Negro leadership class including A. G. Gaston, John Drew, Arthur Shores,

195

Ernest W. Taggart, and the Reverend J. L. Ware to discuss the demands of the Anti-Injustice Committee. Smyer had organized this group of black businessmen after the Freedom Rides, and it accommodated his desire for cosmetic race reform in a bid to stop negative publicity about Birmingham. Indeed, the group of black businessmen consciously thought of itself as an organization with specific interests. Both Pitts and Head had prior contact with the Reverend Norman C. Jimerson and the Alabama Council on Human Relations. During the park desegregation crisis the month before, Smyer had reconvened the biracial group of businessmen and it broadened its discussions to consider the student protests. Although W. E. Shortridge, a funeral home director and treasurer of the ACMHR, attended the meetings, Reverend Shuttlesworth had been excluded. The members of the black elite assembled by the white elite had little sympathy for Shuttlesworth or his movement. Their participation in the one-sided biracial communication established by Smyer gave them an advantage in future negotiations concerning race reform in the city.[5]

196

Many people in the black community did not trust the traditional Negro leadership class. During the park desegregation crisis, Gaston had called a mass meeting for January 5, 1962, so that the black businessmen could inform the public about their contact with the white businessmen "and find out what the Negro community wanted them to do in the future." In his column in the *Birmingham World*, black editor Emory Jackson described a "resentment" expressed by many African Americans against members of the black elite "who have been unwilling to go to jail and who have never shown any interest in improving the lot of the Negro."[6]

An old liberal from the popular front days of the 1940s, Jackson had failed to make the transition to the civil rights movement of the 1960s, although he remained an ardent supporter of the ideology of integration. Jackson criticized the traditional Negro leadership class for its inactivity but nonetheless preferred its leadership to that of the "race men" who had emerged in the 1950s. He disliked Shuttlesworth, calling the activist an "up-side-downer" for trying to turn Birmingham upside down with direct action protests. Moreover, he derided demonstrations as "flash dances" for being sensational as opposed to the "constructive" voter registration drives that he promoted. In the Birmingham struggle for civil rights, Jackson endorsed the Inter-Citizens Committee (ICC), a black legalistic civil rights organization formed in 1960 and headed by the Reverends J. L. Ware and C. Herbert Oliver. The ICC did valuable work documenting cases of racial brutality in Birmingham for the U.S. Civil Rights Commission, but the organization lacked mass support. Consequently, Jackson was a civil rights gadfly who ironically missed the movement when it finally arrived in Birmingham. His years of protest work had taught him to be cautious, and he was "disagreeable and suspicious of any form of negotiation with white leaders." He also had "doubts" about Pitts.[7]

As president of Miles College, Pitts wielded influenced within the black community, but he had not won over the members of Shuttlesworth's movement to his brand of activism. When the educator addressed an ACMHR meeting on January 22, 1962, he asked, "How Christian is the Christian movement,?" adding that if the civil rights activists "truly had faith," they would emphasize voting rights. Pitts believed the ACMHR should use its money patronizing Negro businesses "instead of spending it on fines and doctor bills and court costs." In place of direct action, he encouraged the movement to trust white leaders and support negotiations. Needless to say, after the speech Shuttlesworth expressed his displeasure. Having tried negotiations for years, he and the ACMHR dismissed Pitts's pleadings. As the Reverend Edward Gardner, first vice president of the ACMHR, said at an earlier mass meeting, "these open discussions could keep right on," but the black community was "tired of the same old talk." Growing adamant, Gardner explained: "We the Negroes of the movement will tell you how we feel. We are right, our heart is right, and we have come a long way. We will not compromise. We want all the privileges that the white folks have. We will not take less." Unlike the traditional Negro leadership class, the ACMHR and the students came closer to representing the views of black Birmingham. Field secretary Benjamin Muse of the Southern Regional Council recognized this when he reported that the city's African Americans "oppose any kind of negotiation with the white community and look upon those who confer with whites with suspicion."[8]

Pitts's success in persuading Dukes and the Miles College students not to initiate a boycott against white merchants in late January 1962 derived, in part, from Shuttlesworth's incarceration. The U.S. Supreme Court, which had heard the case of the ACMHR's 1958 bus desegregation attempt on January 8, 1962, refused to overturn the convictions of Shuttlesworth and the Reverend J. S. Phifer because of a technicality. The ruling forced the men to serve their original sentences, and they surrendered to city officials on January 25. To assist Shuttlesworth, the SCLC organized preachers from regional movements to "stand-in" the pulpits of the jailed integrationists. While in jail, Shuttlesworth wrote the Reverend Wyatt Tee Walker to thank him for the SCLC's work on his behalf. He then encouraged the executive director and the conference to take "some immediate action" against segregation in Birmingham's new municipal airport by joining the ACMHR in a lawsuit against airport management. An ACMHR case pending in court concerned segregation at the Dobbs House restaurant, and Shuttlesworth wanted the SCLC to test integration at the airport motel. With typical zeal he concluded, "Let's get it all." It took a year for Shuttlesworth to convince the SCLC to join him in demonstrations in Birmingham.[9]

Subsequent appeals by William Kunstler and other lawyers representing the ACMHR resulted in the release of the two men on March 2, 1962, one week after the Supreme Court's decision outlawing segregation on public transportation. Having called his own mass meeting on March 2, 1962, to radicalize the movement, Shuttlesworth spoiled a rally Gaston had scheduled to unify the black community behind the black elite and its "conservative leadership." The Negro capitalist was "quite critical" of Shuttlesworth, who, he stressed, did "not command the loyalty of as many as 50% of the Negro citizens." With other black businessmen, Gaston had negotiated the students' demands with Smyer and progressive white businessmen. The biracial discussions achieved token reforms. Some merchants removed a few Jim Crow signs from water fountains and integrated an elevator in a downtown office building, but the white businessmen balked at wholesale desegregation, explaining that only the city commission could repeal the segregation ordinances. Tired of being stonewalled by the accommodating meetings of the black and white elite, Dukes renewed plans for a boycott.[10]

In a final warning, Dukes sent letters to two hundred merchants explaining the students' "dilemma" and requesting that they hire black clerks, establish equal promotions for black employees, desegregate store facilities, and pressure the city to offer civil service jobs to qualified African Americans. With others in the Anti-Injustice Committee including vice presidents U. W. Clemon and Rother Meridith, Dukes met with several merchants, such as Emil Hess of Parisian Department Store, Roper Dial of Sears, Roebuck, and Isadore Pizitz of Pizitz Department Store, as well as Sidney Smyer in secret meetings in the downtown Episcopal Church of the Advent. Again receiving no satisfactory answer to the demands, Dukes called the Anti-Injustice Committee into session and on March 15, 1962, it initiated a "selective buying campaign." Because an Alabama statute forbade boycotts, the students carefully worded the protest. They prepared a list of businesses that did not discriminate and circulated it in the black community with other fliers that encouraged "Negroes to spend their money wisely." The selective buying campaign caught on quickly as African Americans stopped shopping in white-owned stores.[11]

With the slogan, "Wear Your Old Clothes for Freedom," the students organized the boycott around three objectives that emphasized the movement's desire for equal employment opportunities and access as consumers: "I. Hiring of Negro clerks, salesmen, and upgrading Negro employees. II. Equal opportunity. Hiring of Negro policemen. III. Desegregation of all rest rooms and all drinking facilities in stores." The same goals would form the core of the movement's demands during the 1963 demonstrations. Handbills distributed in black neighborhoods asked, "Why spend hundreds of dollars at a store where you cannot spend twenty-five cents for a hamburger?" and "Why spend first-class money and be treated as a third-class citizen?" Several students walked downtown with sandwich boards that read, "Don't buy where you can't be a salesman."[12]

Having encouraged Dukes to conduct the boycott, Shuttlesworth and the ACMHR assisted the selective buying campaign, as did some members of the traditional Negro leadership class. Pitts promoted the boycott, and Deenie Drew, whose husband served as an adviser to Miles College, enlisted the Jefferson County Voters League to act as a support group for the students. African American society women established a car pool that transported students from campus to assignments patrolling downtown stores in an effort to discourage violators. Black customers spent anywhere from $4 million a week to $40 million a year in Birmingham stores. The students hoped to maximize the boycott's damage by targeting Easter sales geared toward African Americans. With an effectiveness of 85 to 90 percent, the withdrawal of black patronage hit merchants hard.[13]

In responding to the boycott, white Birmingham followed traditional patterns of resistance to black activism. The local press generally ignored the protest, with little coverage appearing in either the *News* or the *Post-Herald*. Some national chain stores in Birmingham, such as F. W. Woolworth, J. S. Newberry, and Sears, Roebuck, fired their black employees and terminated all contact with racial moderates. Emil Hess and other Jewish merchants from locally owned stores kept the Jim Crow signs up in support of segregation but also in fear of retaliation from Bull Connor and vigilantes.[14]

The city commission set out to suppress the protest. At its April 3, 1962, meeting, Bull Connor announced, "Last night, I am reliably informed, the Shuttlesworth crowd met and there was a lot of bragging about the boycott of our downtown stores." Shifting his weight, the commissioner of public safety continued: "I move that we cut off our appropriations to the county for our surplus-food program. A boycott can work both ways. I don't intend to sit here and take it with a smile." Mayor Art Hanes seconded the motion: "If the Negroes are going to heed the irresponsible and militant advice of the NAACP and CORE leaders, then I say let these leaders feed them." The city contributed nearly half of the $100,000 budget for the charity that distributed and stored the surplus food donated by the federal government. Black families comprised 95 percent of the 20,000 families sustained by the local program. Joining a national chorus of outraged voices over the commission's action, Roy Wilkins telegraphed that the NAACP would undertake food distribution if the city attorney assisted in lifting the injunction that prevented the charity from operating in Alabama.[15]

On April 4, 1962, Bull Connor's officers arrested Reverends Shuttlesworth and Phifer for obstructing a sidewalk outside downtown stores. Shuttlesworth explained to policemen that "he was observing the effects of the Selective Buying Campaign but he was not involved in it." The next morning's session of recorder's court found the ACMHR leaders guilty and sentenced them to 180 days in prison. Previously, the police had arrested Frank Dukes—three times—and other students for misdemeanors such as jaywalking. The commission also refused Miles College a fund-raising permit when President Pitts requested approval for the campaign to achieve accreditation.[16]

In an unusual admission of the city's racial problem, the April 5, 1962, edition of the *Birmingham News* analyzed the crisis in a front-page article, "Birmingham: Face Facts." The newspaper responded in such dramatic fashion because of the boycott's effectiveness and the resulting "unfavorable headlines throughout the nation and the world." Recounting Frank Dukes's letter to the merchants and the Anti-Injustice Committee's demands that local businesses "hire certain numbers of Negro graduates," upgrade current black employees, and desegregate facilities, the *News* criticized the students for starting the selective buying campaign. Clarence B. Hanson Jr., the paper's publisher, had participated in the previous biracial discussions. In his editorial, he returned to the need for communication: "It is time for Birmingham citizens to sit down and talk together." The *News* recognized that "Negroes seem to want an organized line of communication with white citizens and with elected city officials." The publisher refused to admit, however, that the students had found nothing to negotiate over. Instead, he confessed, "Some Negro leadership has worked hard to keep Negro students from demonstrating and from creating incidents which might lead to unpleasant conflicts in the city" and renewed biracial communication "might give moderate Negro leaders needed additional stature with their own people, thereby helping them maintain influence over the more radical Negro elements." Referring to the collapsed consensus among whites as a "tragedy" because "the community's business and political leadership" no longer stood "on common ground," Hanson recommended that the city commission cooperate with moderate businessmen by asking Mayor Hanes to convene biracial discussions. By rejecting the demands of the student activists as too radical while calling on the intransigent city commission to establish biracial communication, Hanson demonstrated his desire for cosmetic change that maintained the status quo in race relations. In the process, he joined the ranks of other black and white businessmen associated with Smyer.[17]

Frank Dukes articulated the impatience of the new ideology expressed by the black students. He told a reporter from the *New York Herald-Tribune*: "Go slow—go slow—go slow. That's what you all advise us to do. God helps those who help themselves. You pray to God but when you get off your knees, you got to go out and work if you want to eat. God will help you if you start things yourself." With the boycott, the Miles students applied nonviolent sanctions to pressure for race reform. As a consequence, Easter sales dropped 12 percent from the previous year. Feeling the squeeze applied by the young activists, Birmingham's merchants nonetheless refused to desegregate their store facilities. By June the boycott had lost steam. When three students walked downtown carrying signs in support of the selective buying campaign, police arrested them for parading without a permit. On the day of the trial, officers arrested four additional students. Bull Connor's suppression of the boycott intimidated a black community that had already begun to lose interest. Speaking before the ACMHR at its mass meeting on June 11, 1962, Frank Dukes announced that the merchants had almost surrendered in May when "the Negro started slipping back in and buying stuff." Other student leaders complained about the traditional Negro leadership class's limited support for the boycott. Yet the selective buying campaign struggled on throughout the summer.[18]

Shuttlesworth built on the momentum of the student-led boycott by asking Martin Luther King and the Southern Christian Leadership Conference to join the ACMHR in nonviolent demonstrations designed to end racial discrimination in Birmingham. While attending the May 1962 board meeting of the SCLC in Chattanooga, Tennessee, the corresponding secretary requested that the civil rights organization assist its Birmingham affiliate. Dazed by its experiences in Albany and still debating its course of action, the SCLC tabled the proposal for further consideration at the next annual convention, which, coincidentally, was slated for Birmingham in September. Brushing aside King's hesitancy, Shuttlesworth spread rumors of planned protest marches.[19]

The threat of demonstrations led by Martin Luther King and the SCLC convinced the chamber of commerce to organize an ex officio group and charge it with solving Birmingham's crisis in race relations. Formed on August 27, 1962, the eighty-nine-member Senior Citizens Committee was composed of the leading white men from the industrial, manufacturing, and service sector concerns that represented most workers in the Birmingham district. Its membership a secret, the group of seasoned chief executives severed its official ties to the chamber and acted as an independent body. In response to a request by the prominent retailer Isadore Pizitz, Birmingham's Jewish merchants were excluded from official membership for fear of a backlash if anti-Semitic extremists learned the names of the Senior Citizens. Nonetheless, the merchants played a central role during the negotiations that followed. The Senior Citizens created a subcommittee on race chaired by Sidney Smyer, and it brought together the previously organized reform-minded black and white businessmen. Because it did not meet regularly, the Senior Citizens Committee intended the subcommittee to conduct negotiations that would maintain racial peace and order. As the September date for the SCLC convention neared, an anxious Smyer convened the biracial group of businessmen in an effort to stop street protests by the ACMHR and SCLC.[20]

In addition to the Senior Citizens' biracial subcommittee on race, Smyer broadened the discussions to include white racial moderates and black activists. Members of the Alabama Council on Human Relations such as its director, the Reverend Norman C. Jimerson, and Dr. Lucius H. Pitts of Miles College moderated the meetings of the white establishment and the civil rights movement. To win the trust of Shuttlesworth, Jimerson spoke at an ACMHR mass meeting on September 10, 1962. Pitts asserted his own leadership by meeting with Burke Marshall and Robert Kennedy in early September. Although information on the secret biracial negotiations remains sketchy, it appears that Smyer met with Jimerson and Pitts on September 16, 1962. After hearing these men talk about their understanding of the movement's nonnegotiable demands for desegregation and the creation of a viable biracial committee to address concerns such as black access to whites-only jobs, Smyer correctly ascertained that Pitts, Gaston, and other traditional Negro leaders had little influence over movement activists or the black masses. Consequently, Smyer wanted direct contact with Shuttlesworth.[21]

The civil rights leader recalled that A. G. Gaston invited him downtown to meet with the "white power structure" in September 1962. Gaston explained: "I confessed to 'em that you have to talk to Fred. Fred's the man that's got the folks. I got some money, but that's all. Money don't run this thing now. He's the man with the marbles. You haveta talk to the marbles." The encounter between Shuttlesworth and Smyer occurred a few days before the SCLC arrived in Birmingham. Others in attendance included black businessmen Gaston and Drew and white merchants Roper Dial of Sears, Roebuck and Isadore Pizitz of Pizitz Department Store. The men gathered in Carpenter House, the imposing offices of the Episcopal Diocese of Alabama adjacent to the towering sandstone structure of the Church of the Advent. During the 1950s the accommodationist Interracial Division of the Jefferson County Coordinating Council of Social Forces had met in the same rich, sacred setting. The location would be used throughout the months ahead.[22]

The black minister recounted that when he entered the room of assembled white businessmen, everyone got to their feet, shook his hand, and said, "Dr. Shuttlesworth, we're glad to see you." The wiry integrationist snapped: "Well, I don't wanna be a 'doctor.' Just too bad we haven't shaken all these years. I been here now sufferin'. . . . Church been bombed twice, and nobody said nothin'. " Cutting through the feigned respect, the heavy-set Smyer, his hands shaking, got to the point: "Well, we wanna—we just wanna know how we can help (keep) Dr. King . . . outa here." Shuttlesworth reiterated the movement's goals, then, with a touch of humility, noted that the white elite "had never gotten together to bring an outcry" over his sufferings or the bombings. As a result, the independent Shuttlesworth said: "So I'm not of a mind that this morning I came to be used by you, and I'm certain I'm not your darling, and I don't propose to be. I'm nobody's darling, and if you've got some reason for calling me, what can you offer." He concluded, "That's what I'm here for, not to hold a conversation, because I don't think we're that brotherly." Smyer rejoined, "Well, ah, we—ah, we cain't—ah make promises for the merchants." Shuttlesworth stood up: "Well, I'm talkin' to the wrong crowd then. Let's go, gentlemen, . . . you wastin' my time."[23]

A heated exchange followed. Shuttlesworth turned to the "most recalcitrant" of the merchants and said: "Mr. Pizitz . . . I'll be happy to be arrested at your store. . . . Martin Luther King and Ralph [Abernathy] and I, we'll be dragged outa your store by 'Bull' Connor's efficient police." The visual image must have startled Roper Dial, for he announced, "Tell you the truth, that door to my toilet, I can just probably have my janitor paint" out the Jim Crow warning. Dial left to call Sears, Roebuck but quickly returned: "He's paintin' the door now." The other merchants fell in line, offering to remove the "whites only" signs from water fountains. On their promise that future biracial discussions would lead to the implementation of the movement's other objectives concerning black employment, Shuttlesworth called off the scheduled demonstrations. For the first time, members of the white establishment had met with a leader of the civil rights movement and granted limited concessions on desegregation. But the accord among private citizens did not hold in the public realm.[24]

The SCLC convention began on September 25, 1962, with an appearance by the baseball great Jackie Robinson, followed by New York congressman Adam Clayton Powell on Wednesday, September 26. Whenever such notable black leaders spoke in Birmingham, the community assembled in the sanctuary of Sixteenth Street Baptist Church, although its black middle-class congregation had not supported the ACMHR. On the opening night police arrested a delegate from Chicago for jaywalking. The Reverend A. D. King, the younger brother of Martin Luther King who had moved to Birmingham in March as the pastor of First Baptist Church in Ensley and had taken an active role in the ACMHR, intervened and police arrested him, too. Black attorney Orzell Billingsley posted the $50 bond that released both men, thus averting a crisis over police harassment. In a bid to squelch national coverage of the convention, Bull Connor unsuccessfully attempted to confiscate the press cards of "outside reporters." The annual convention cost the SCLC just over $3,000 to put on. The Freedom Dinner at which Robinson spoke and the public meetings held in conjunction with the convention brought in $3,000, which the SCLC and the ACMHR agreed to divide at a ratio of 6:4.[25]

On the last day of the convention, September 28, 1962, a white man attending the morning session in the L. R. Hall Auditorium of the newly completed $1.5 million A. G. Gaston Building, walked up to Martin Luther King—who spoke from the podium—and struck him. The leader of the SCLC took several blows nonviolently before others moved in and restrained the assailant. Officers arrested the white man and identified him as Roy James, a member of the American Nazi Party from Virginia. Although King refused to press charges, a city judge convicted the white supremacist that afternoon on charges of assault and Mayor Art Hanes personally banished him from Birmingham. Hanes's action reflected the pressure placed on the city commission by the Senior Citizens Committee. The businessmen wanted to maintain order and avoid racial hostilities. Connor followed through for them as he waited for King to get out of town.[26]

As soon as the SCLC adjourned, Bull Connor sent building inspectors into the downtown stores that had voluntarily desegregated before the convention. Suddenly, one merchant faced a $9,000 expenditure for elevator equipment and another confronted a total renovation costing $100,000 just to pass the fire codes. The Senior Citizens Committee had not endorsed the limited desegregation approved by the subcommittee, so without the support of the industrial and financial elite, the merchants waffled on their agreement. With the exception of the high-toned Blach's Department Store, the Jim Crow signs returned.[27]

Unable to negotiate in good faith with white leaders, black activists planned to resume the selective buying campaign during the Christmas shopping season. The Senior Citizens subcommittee continued to meet, however, in an effort to avoid protests. Someone suggested that black and white attorneys file a joint suit against the segregation ordinances that applied to stores and lunch counters. The plan called for members of the ACMHR to get arrested for a test case that would be financed by white contributions. But the integrationists rejected the proposal, asserting that the merchants should file their own desegregation suit. Responding to the renewed call for a boycott by Shuttlesworth and the determined Miles students, several members of the Senior Citizens subcommittee concluded, "you can't trust or work with Negroes." The stalemate hardened.[28]

For a second time Shuttlesworth invited Martin Luther King and the SCLC to Birmingham to assist the ACMHR with the struggling selective buying campaign and demonstrations designed to resolve the crisis in race relations. Again King put Shuttlesworth off, postponing action on the idea until after Christmas when a full assessment could be made of the problem. His assistants wanted to avoid another Albany, where King had jumped into a situation he could not control. Also, King deferred to the request of Birmingham's traditional Negro leadership class which advised against SCLC interference in local affairs, citing in this instance the campaign to change the form of government. Time and again, the "conservative militant" King heeded the advice of the black elite over the objections of Shuttlesworth.[29]

King's ties to Birmingham's traditional Negro leadership class had

MOMENTUM

clouded his understanding of the civil rights struggle in the city. Through his Baptist connections—his father, the Reverend Martin Luther King Sr., pastored Ebenezer Baptist Church, the most prestigious black Baptist church in the Deep South and one previously pastored by his maternal grandfather, the Reverend Adam Daniel Williams—King enjoyed immense influence in the region. The Reverend J. L. Ware, a rival of Shuttlesworth's, knew King through his association with the National Baptist Convention and the Baptist Ministers Conference. Two of King's acquaintances served the leading black Baptist churches in Birmingham, although neither joined the ACMHR. The Reverend John Cross headed the city's oldest and most exclusive black congregation, Sixteenth Street Baptist Church. When King's former assistant at Dexter Avenue Baptist Church in Montgomery, the Reverend John Thomas Porter, accepted a call from the largest black Baptist church in Birmingham, Sixth Avenue Baptist Church, King preached the installation service in December 1962. Inevitably, Ware introduced King when he spoke at these churches, and members of the traditional Negro leadership class sat in the audience. Yet neither church supported the weekly mass meetings of the local movement. Indeed, members of elite black congregations such as these snubbed Shuttlesworth and the ACMHR.[30]

When in Birmingham, King often stayed with his friends John and Deenie Drew. Drew was an executive for Alexander and Company, a real estate and insurance concern, and his wife promoted the interests of several Negro civic and women's clubs. The Drews lived in the area known as Dynamite Hill with other members of the black elite such as attorney Arthur Shores. In fact, Drew and Shores often traveled to Jamaica on golfing trips. When King considered joining Shuttlesworth in the boycott, Deenie Drew told him, "Mike . . . for our sake, please wait." King listened to her as she explained about the upcoming election: "It will make a difference to us psychologically. I don't think Boutwell will have any kind of feeling toward us, but we have been mistreated so badly by Bull Connor all these years that black people will feel better with him out of office. I will." Deenie Drew recalled, "If we wanted it so much, he waited." It would not be the last time King respected the wishes of his friends.[31]

Though aware of divisions within the black community, King underestimated the degree to which the traditional Negro leadership class disliked Shuttlesworth and the ACMHR. While Shuttlesworth assisted the student protesters during the first Freedom Ride in May 1961, King carried on a chatty correspondence with Deenie Drew over his addressing the elitist Alabama State Coordinating Association for Registration and Voting, which she headed with attorney Orzell Billingsley Jr. On picking the date of his speaking engagement, King suggested that the Alabama State Coordinating Association combine its drive with the Monday night mass meeting of the ACMHR. Drew responded firmly: "We have secured the 16th Street Baptist Church for our mass meeting of Wednesday, June 14. Since we had already made an engagement for Monday, June 12 we will be unable to combine our meeting with the Alabama Christian Movement for Human Rights." She had previously garnered a $500 donation from the SCLC to finance her civil rights organization, which competed with the SCLC-affiliated ACMHR. After the successful June meeting, she reminded King of her association's need for an executive director by asking him for "assistance in finding the right person[,] for this campaign must not die for want of a leader." Outside of King's original comment, no mention was made of Shuttlesworth, his successful five-year-old movement, or the apparent overlap of civil rights activities in Birmingham.[32]

In addition to his personal friendships with members of the black elite, King had financial links to A. G. Gaston. In April 1958 King sent Gaston a check for $1,000 to open a private bank account in the millionaire's Citizens Federal Savings and Loan Association, a black institution organized by Gaston and attorney Arthur Shores in 1957. John Drew served as vice president of Citizens Federal. King wrote Gaston: "This is just a little expression of the interest I have in the great work that you and your associates are doing in the area of economics." He added that a "rather large check" from the Montgomery Improvement Association would follow. Quick to take advantage of this new-found friendship, Gaston notified the "share holder, by virtue of this deposit" that he should serve on the bank's advisory board. King agreed and his name appeared on the letterhead of Citizens Federal. The bank's holdings increased from an initial $350,000 in 1957 to $1.7 million in June 1958, $3 million in July 1959, and $4 million in June 1960. The success of Citizens Federal reflected the growing prosperity of one segment of Birmingham's black community.[33]

The relationship between Shuttlesworth and King rested on polite professionalism. Following similar courses in their early careers as activists, both charismatic leaders built indigenous movements, earned stripes in the struggle against discrimination, and developed large egos commensurate with their hard-won stature. Shuttlesworth joined King and others in creating the Southern Christian Leadership Conference in 1957 as a logical response to the need to regionally coordinate the activities of autonomous civil rights groups working on the local level. The affiliate structure of the SCLC respected the independence of the local movement while acting as an umbrella organization that offered various resources to its members. Theoretically, the SCLC existed for the benefit of its affiliates such as the ACMHR. The formality with which King corresponded with Shuttlesworth underscored this respectful relationship.[34]

King admired Shuttlesworth and his work in Birmingham, and Shuttlesworth respected King. Had the two activists not gotten along, it is unlikely that the SCLC would have joined the ACMHR in the spring demonstrations of 1963. As it stood, King "went to Birmingham," the Reverend Andrew Young recalled, "because Fred Shuttlesworth pleaded with him to do it." In his memoir, Young noted, "It was the stubborn determination of Fred Shuttlesworth who insisted that either the SCLC national office join him, or he would move on alone." Shuttlesworth cited a different reason for the SCLC's decision to go to Birmingham. Since Albany, "Dr. King's image was slightly on the wane. The SCLC needed a victory." No other city offered it such an opportunity, and consequently King had little choice but to go there if he wanted to remain a nationally recognized leader of the civil rights struggle. In a letter to a friend, Wyatt Tee Walker suggested another reason for the SCLC's decision: "The truth is Wilson, that Albany nearly bankrupted SCLC and we are scrambling to get back on our feet financially. The problems posed by bail bonds are becoming insurmountable and we have not yet devised a counter-stratagem."[35]

When first assessing the Albany campaign in September 1962, Walker suggested that the Southern Christian Leadership Conference had "learned several lessons" in Albany, and he cited three of them. First and foremost, the campaign underscored the value of "the nonviolent direct mass action approach." Second, direct action worked best when combined with traditional methods of protest, such as voter registration drives. Third, the movement's use of nonviolent persuasion had "built the base for reconciliation and the beloved community." Hence Walker drew different lessons from Albany than scholars usually describe. Nowhere in his analysis of movement strategy in southwestern Georgia did he suggest that the lack of clear targets posed a problem for the SCLC. Nor did he acknowledge the public relations coup of police chief Laurie Pritchett's "passive resistance." Indeed, coming out of Albany, the SCLC remained committed to nonviolent direct action designed to persuade segregationists of the immorality of racial discrimination.[36]

During January 1963 SCLC officials gathered at the Dorchester Center in central Georgia for an opportunity to debate the future of their organization. It appears that the idea for the conference originated with a suggestion made to Walker by the Reverend Glenn E. Smiley of the Congress of Racial Equality. In late September 1962 Smiley recommended that the SCLC, SNCC, and CORE gather for a "training conference" to be held in early January 1963. Walker agreed and volunteered Dorchester as the site of the retreat. Yet instead of a training session, the SCLC decided to hold a workshop to reevaluate the organization's goals and objectives. For this purpose, King invited select members of the SCLC board of directors to the Dorchester Center on January 10 and 11, 1963. As he explained: "We have watched SCLC grow very rapidly during the past two years and now we feel that we should come together and consider our present structure and the changes which are advisable at this juncture of our program." King's memo suggests that the first Dorchester conference was yet another attempt to reevaluate the organizational structure and purpose of the Southern Christian Leadership Conference.[37]

At the Dorchester Center, Shuttlesworth again invited King and the SCLC to Birmingham. This time the invitation was accepted. As the leader of the ACMHR recalled: "The SCLC needed something and we needed something, so I said, 'Birmingham is where it's at, gentlemen. I assure you, if you come to Birmingham, we will not only gain prestige but really shake the country.'" Shuttlesworth understood that although over the years the ACMHR had "won victories" in Birmingham, it "couldn't cash in on them" because of the intransigence of the white establishment, as evidenced by the resistance of Commissioner Bull Connor to race reform. The Reverend Ralph Abernathy recalled that Shuttlesworth requested from the SCLC "precisely what everyone knew he lacked himself and needed: the ability to gather together, organize, and train large numbers of nonviolent demonstrators. He was asking us to take over and operate the movement in his own backyard. Such a willingness suggested that his ego problem might not be as big as some had told us." Nevertheless, Shuttlesworth expected to determine policy with King during the campaign. The assembled activists discussed the potential impact of protests in the city and agreed with King to accept Shuttlesworth's offer. They apparently considered plans that called for sit-ins to announce the renewal of the black boycott of white-owned businesses. Stanley Levison later said that after he had recounted a history of Bull Connor's antilabor activities in Birmingham, King startled the group by suggesting that "some of the people sitting here today will not come back alive from this campaign." On that somber note, the SCLC agreed with King to accept Shuttlesworth's invitation. Yet apparently little else concerning Birmingham was decided at the meeting.[38]

Some scholars and movement activists have identified this first Dorchester conference, in January 1963, as the meeting where the SCLC debated the "lessons of Albany" and developed the plans for "Project C," yet no evidence in the King and SCLC Papers substantiates this claim, and what little record there is actually suggests the contrary. It appears that people have confused this meeting with a second conference held at the Dorchester Center during September 5–7, 1963. It was at this meeting that the SCLC evaluated the Albany Movement in light of the Birmingham campaign. The minutes of the second meeting outlined a strategy, "How to Crack a Hard Core City," that provided a blueprint of direct action designed to manufacture "creative tension" through provocation that is usually described as "Project C."[39]

Considering that in his memoir of the event, *Why We Can't Wait*, King conflated the two Dorchester meetings, the misunderstanding becomes more apparent, yet in *Parting the Waters* Taylor Branch not only unquestioningly follows King's lead, but he also shamelessly relies on the testimony of Walker. Branch's glowing account describes Walker dominating the first Dorchester conference and distributing a blueprint of his plan for the Birmingham campaign. According to Branch, Walker named his plan "Project C" for "Confrontation" and explained that it was to unfold in four stages: first sit-ins, followed by boycotts, then mass marches, and finally Freedom Rides. Branch's account of Walker's strategy suggests how to read an occurrence backward. Subsequent events in Birmingham contradicted Branch's observation that "it was Walker's finest hour at the SCLC. Not a comma of the blueprint was altered when he finished."[40]

In *Why We Can't Wait*, King recalled that the movement's strategy centered "on the business community," because the withdrawal of the black dollar could pressure white merchants directly—and the city government indirectly—to negotiate an end to racial discrimination. The direct action aspects of the plan were secondary to the nonviolent sanctions of the selective buying campaign. As King explained, because black people in Birmingham "did not have enough votes to move the political power structure," marches on city hall would be less effective than focusing the protest on "the economic power structure." Therefore in Birmingham King bypassed the politicians, centering his strategy on the "business community." Walker concurred, but he also blamed the SCLC's inability to control the Albany Movement on competition from SNCC, CORE, and the NAACP.

He recognized that only Shuttlesworth's ACMHR and the independent student activists operated in Birmingham. Walker assisted King in the development of movement strategy in Birmingham. The two men wanted contained demonstrations, tightly focused on clearly defined, obtainable goals: desegregation of store facilities, equal employment opportunities, and the creation of viable biracial discussions with the white officials. All these reforms could be achieved in the private sector. Accepting the long-term objectives of the ACMHR, King and Walker organized the SCLC's resources behind the local movement in a campaign against Birmingham's merchants. The SCLC had returned to the simple strategy of King's initial success, the economic sanctions of the Montgomery bus boycott.[41]

After the Dorchester conference, the SCLC executive board gathered on January 23, 1963, and discussed Birmingham. The staff cited three reasons for the direct action program in the city: "The community is anxious for some kind of activity; SCLC can profit by and build on the Albany experience. (Birmingham can give a new image of the power of non-violence so much needed at this time.); Victory is possible." Still holding to the idea of moral persuasion, as evidenced by the SCLC's reliance on nonviolence, the board left open the selection of a "SPECIFIC TARGET," although it planned on some type of protest that would lead to the arrest of SCLC officials. Further details were to be worked out with Shuttlesworth and the ACMHR on February 6. King assigned Walker to the Birmingham campaign with instructions to map out movement strategy. Walker outlined his proposal as the "Tentative Schedule for Project X—Birmingham." The "X" stood for March 14, 1963, the kickoff date of the Birmingham campaign. On the advice of the Drews and other members of the traditional Negro leadership class, King decided to delay the protest until after the mayoral election of March 5 that pitted Bull Connor against Albert Boutwell and Tom King. He expected Connor to be defeated and out of office by the time the demonstrations began.[42]

Counting down to the March 14 starting date, Walker's "Project X" outlined SCLC activities designed to prepare black Birmingham for the proposed civil rights campaign. He scheduled a series of meetings in early February to "corral recruiting teams" and "get ministerial support" behind the effort. While in Birmingham, Walker met with Arthur Shores to familiarize himself with city ordinances and bail bond procedures. He also completed plans for sit-ins, selecting dinettes as the primary targets. In preparing for the protests, Walker observed the best access to the facilities and counted the seats at the lunch counters. Aware of Birmingham's successful suppression of civil rights protests in the past, he selected secondary and tertiary targets for the activists if they failed to reach the restaurants. These included the dining facilities in federal buildings and the lunch counters in the Atlantic Mills Shopping Center. Walker's plan conformed to the SCLC's desire for a limited and controlled protest against the "business community."[43]

Apparently Project X was renamed "Project C" for "Confrontation" after an outbreak of police brutality in mid-April 1963 during the Birmingham campaign. In interviews such as those included in *Eyes on the Prize*, Walker has described Project C as if it had been the SCLC's strategy from the beginning of the Birmingham campaign. Many scholars have followed this interpretation and given Walker high marks for his plan; however, extant contemporary documents do not describe a Project C until a sensationalized attack by police dogs against black bystanders two weeks into the Birmingham campaign. By failing to acknowledge Project X, scholars have misinterpreted the SCLC's original strategy in Birmingham.[44]

By the time the SCLC gathered at Dorchester Center, voters in Birmingham had abolished the office held by Bull Connor. The lame duck commissioner was fighting for his political life in running for mayor. With the odds against Connor, the SCLC had every reason to believe he would no longer be in power when Project X began. King himself thought Connor would lose on the first ballot. Indeed, to prevent a confrontation with the commissioner, the SCLC assisted Birmingham's reformers by waiting until after the municipal elections. Had King wanted violence for "creative tension," he would have launched demonstrations following Shuttlesworth's initial request in September 1962 during the SCLC's annual convention or in December 1962 in support of the ACMHR Christmas boycott. He most certainly would not have waited until the former commissioner was out of office. Instead, King postponed the starting date of Project X twice to prevent a clash with Connor. Indeed, everything about the strategy for Project X emphasized nonviolent sanctions with limited direct action that focused attention on the boycott and avoided violent confrontations with municipal authorities. Having recently been burned, the SCLC did not plan mass marches to fill the jail in Birmingham, for this had been an unobtainable goal in the Albany Movement. Instead, it anticipated arrests and collected donations to bail out protesters. Though recognizing the danger inherent in the campaign and the likelihood of vigilante violence, the SCLC thus did not set out to provoke brutality in Birmingham.

Neither did the SCLC approach Birmingham from the perspective of federal intervention for national race reform. Having cultivated a reputation as the "most segregated city in America," Birmingham epitomized southern resistance to integration. SCLC members such as Walker believed that "if we could crack that city, then we could crack any city." His comment reemphasized the SCLC's desire to achieve a local success in Birmingham that would encourage other local campaigns by persuading southern white leaders of the immorality and the futility of defending segregation. This was the essence of moral persuasion. Abernathy believed if the SCLC "beat them [white supremacists in Birmingham] on their own home grounds, we might be able to prove to the entire region that it was useless to resist desegregation." Therefore, the conference did not approach Birmingham from the perspective of national race reform.[45]

Although the Southern Christian Leadership Conference cultivated the Kennedy administration and would have welcomed federal commitment behind the movement, the civil rights record of the young president promised a less than favorable response. Despite the call to King during the 1960 campaign—a political move designed to win northern black votes—the Kennedy administration had proven itself hostile to the movement. President John F. Kennedy had abrogated his authority through the Justice Department's concept of federalism, which allowed brutality against civil rights activists, and he had steered black protest strategy toward voting rights—a conservative move accepted by a compliant King. If anything, past experience with the Kennedy administration marked it about as resistant to change as the segregationists. Indeed, King himself expressed his displeasure with the administration in the weeks leading up to the Birmingham campaign by snubbing an invitation to the White House. Nevertheless, Walker especially but also King and others in the SCLC remained enamored of Jack Kennedy and dreamed of the day the president might endorse race reform. They did not, however, base SCLC strategy in Birmingham on such hopes.[46]

Several scholars, David Garrow foremost among them, have suggested that King selected Birmingham because of the potential for state violence against nonviolent protesters. Secondary to this argument is the expected federal intervention that would follow in response to Connor's brutality. The argument fails to consider, on the one hand, that the SCLC designed its strategy with the merchants in mind and, on the other hand, that it anticipated Connor's removal from office and based its strategy on that assumption. If the violence thesis is removed, the Kennedy thesis makes less sense. Though the potential for violence always existed, the SCLC remained committed to its original teachings of nonviolence. Through Birmingham, King and his organization hoped to regain the moral imperative that had surrounded the movement coming out of Montgomery.[47]

To the surprise of the SCLC, Bull Connor placed second in the mayoral election of March 5, prompting a runoff with Boutwell scheduled for April 2, 1963. On the advice of Shuttlesworth and members of Birmingham's traditional Negro leadership class, King once again decided to postpone Project X until after the election. He selected April 3 as the starting date, although he feared that the delay would limit the selective buying campaign as it shaved off three weeks in the crucial Easter shopping season.[48]

Again put on hold, Shuttlesworth wrote King and Walker inquiring about their specific plans for Birmingham. The letter revealed the SCLC's lack of preparation for the upcoming campaign and its failure to communicate with the ACMHR. It appears that little organization went into Project X. In general, Shuttlesworth expressed his concern "that we have not clearly defined areas of action, points of emphasis, the degree of commitment, and the time and methods by which other Groups will be allowed to participate." The local leader referred to prior contact with SNCC and the Southern Conference Education Fund (SCEF), of which he was a board member. Both civil rights organizations had "made commitments for Birmingham action," but Shuttlesworth had put them off because of his agreement "to move initially with local people and SCLC." Yet unlike Walker and King, the integrationist believed that "all interested persons and Groups are free to join—subject of course to direction by ACMHR-SCLC." His identification of the Birmingham campaign as that of ACMHR-SCLC reflected his understanding that he and King together would make policy decisions.[49]

Shuttlesworth considered Bull Connor "very definitely a Contender in the Run-Off," and so he requested that the SCLC "lay low" until after the election. Acknowledging that "some few Negroes are not for D. A. [direct action] at this time," he asked that the SCLC use "April 1 and 2nd, and the night of the 2nd for intense training and stragety [sic] with the Move-Off coming April 3rd." His admission suggested that the SCLC had done little to train Birmingham activists in nonviolence. Shuttlesworth's comment, "I think Rev. Gardner, Lola [Hendricks], and others are selecting squad leaders already," apparently referred to Walker's Birmingham contacts—ACMHR members—lining up demonstrators. He also asked two specific questions: "What definite plan have we made for legal assistance? Shouldn't the Justice Dept. be notified?" Shuttlesworth concluded the letter with criticism of Walker's limited focus, suggesting that the SCLC consider "a broader scope of activities than just Lunch Counters. My feeling is that we should cover the waterfront—including Parks implementation (golf, Kiddie-Land), Roving squads to ride Taxis, Buses, ect. [*sic*]; Picketing if necessary, Marches, and even a Prayer meeting at City Hall." His final recommendation for marches and pickets demonstrated that the SCLC had not included these methods of direct action in its original strategy for the Birmingham campaign. As Garrow notes, King and Walker "stuck to their narrower focus" on sit-ins and the boycott as a result of the SCLC's negative experience in Albany. As the warnings reflected, Shuttlesworth was more experienced in civil rights activism than either King or Walker.[50]

At a meeting in New York City on March 31, 1963, a threadbare SCLC tapped the wallets of the northeastern intelligentsia to finance the upcoming Birmingham campaign. Hosted by black calypso singer Harry Belafonte, the select gathering of seventy-five supporters sat riveted in their seats as Shuttlesworth recounted his past struggles in Birmingham. The civil rights activist concluded, "You have to be prepared to die before you can begin to live." Swearing the assorted entertainers, journalists, politicians, clerics, capitalists, and professionals to secrecy, King described the upcoming Birmingham campaign. After he finished, the New Yorkers asked, "What can we do to help?" King responded, donate to the SCLC so that the movement will have bail money. Heading up a committee to collect contributions, Belafonte played a crucial role in the ensuing weeks. Two other SCLC affiliates outside the South likewise answered pleas for help. The Southern Christian Leadership Conference needed all the help it could get. Entering March 1963 with $3,673 on hand, it received donations of $14,840—for a grand monthly total of $18,513. Operating expenditures in March cost $17,959, with the organization ending the month with only $554. Tucked away in federal savings and loan banks in Atlanta, Memphis, and Nashville were deposits worth an additional $20,000 against which there was a loan of $5,700, leaving the SCLC with a potential war chest of just under $15,000 and petty cash, not much money with which to finance a major civil rights campaign. But the SCLC used it all on Birmingham, for King had decided to go for broke.[51]

As the runoff date of April 2, 1963, neared, the SCLC and the ACMHR—concerned that any suggestion of racial protest might assist Bull Connor in the upcoming election—avoided drawing attention to the movement. Outside of workshops to register voters conducted by Deenie Drew and the Jefferson County Voters League and Shuttlesworth's comment that to him

"Connor was an undignified Boutwell and Boutwell was a dignified Connor," little was said about the runoff at ACMHR mass meetings in March except to encourage members to vote. Most of Birmingham's ten thousand black voters cast ballots for Boutwell, who defeated Connor in the municipal runoff. Nevertheless, Connor refused to leave office. The bizarre events that followed left Birmingham with two municipal governments.[52]

Therefore, on the eve of demonstrations the SCLC approached Birmingham with the understanding that it entered the city on the behalf of the ACMHR with a limited strategy designed to pressure the economic power structure into accepting specific local objectives that included the desegregation of public facilities, equal employment opportunities, and the establishment of biracial communication. The SCLC neither sought a violent confrontation with Bull Connor in a bid to fill the jails nor expected the Kennedy administration to act on its behalf. It simply organized for a victory over local segregation laws and an end to racial discrimination in local employment. By winning such concessions in Birmingham, the SCLC hoped to restore its viability as an organization and salvage King's damaged reputation. It could hardly expect more. As the demonstrations unfolded, however, the SCLC broadened its scope, changed its strategy, and redefined its goals. Once the marches started, Shuttlesworth and the ACMHR had little say in the matter.

216

CHAPTER SEVEN

Another Albany?

Seven African American integrationists headed by the Reverend Abraham Woods Jr. entered Britling Cafeteria shortly after ten on the morning of April 3, 1963, sat down at the "whites only" lunch counter, and requested service. The Reverend Calvin Woods—Abraham's brother—led eight activists in a sit-in at Woolworth's. Similar demonstrations occurred at the nearby Loveman's, Pizitz, and Kress stores. The volunteers for the protest were members of the Alabama Christian Movement for Human Rights. The sit-ins marked the beginning of a major drive to force a resolution of the long-standing stalemate in local race relations.

Workers at Britling's refused to take the orders of Reverend Woods, James Armstrong, and the others who sat down in the cafeteria; instead, store officials asked the integrationists to leave and pressed charges against them when they demurred. Before noon police arrested thirteen at Britling's. The other four lunch counters responded to the sit-ins by shutting down the griddles and sending the cooks home. The five demonstrators with Calvin Woods and ACMHR choir director Carlton Reese waited at

The Reverend Calvin Woods (far right) leads the sit-in at Woolworth's lunch counter on the opening day of the Birmingham campaign, April 3, 1963. In response to the protest, management posted a sign that read "counter closed" as white observers harassed the integrationists. Several hours later the black activists left Woolworth's and sat in at Britling Cafeteria, where they were arrested. *Birmingham Post-Herald*, BPLDAM.

Woolworth's until two in the afternoon before walking down to the lunch counter still open at Britling's. They entered the diner, sat down for service, and refused to leave when asked to do so. Describing the event a few nights later, Calvin Woods said that white men came up to him as he sat at the lunch counter: "When I looked around one of them spit in my face. I looked at him and smiled." The twenty-one-year-old Reverend James L. Harris assisted seventy-one-year-old George Harris in the protest. Several Miles College students supplemented the ACMHR members arrested, for a total of twenty charged with trespassing after warning. No fanfare announced the Birmingham campaign of the Southern Christian Leadership Conference, just the quiet dignity of African Americans demanding their civil rights.[1]

Later that day, Martin Luther King and Ralph Abernathy flew into Birmingham and discovered that the SCLC had not adequately prepared for

ANOTHER ALBANY?

the civil rights demonstrations. As they disembarked at the airport, Fred Shuttlesworth and three of his assistants met the SCLC officers. King asked, "Where's Ware?" expecting the Reverend J. L. Ware to be waiting for him in a show of black Baptist unity. His absence indicated trouble for the SCLC. Shuttlesworth responded, "He's holding a meeting of the [local Baptist] Ministers Conference. . . . The others are probably there too." After the men climbed into Shuttlesworth's car, King suggested that they go to Ware's meeting: "If I can speak to the whole group today maybe we can get them to pledge their support." As the civil rights trio entered the sanctuary, Ware stopped speaking mid-sentence and those in attendance turned to see who had interrupted the proceedings. Abernathy recalled "no burst of applause and no ripple of friendly smiles. Most of the faces were grave and enigmatic." King approached Ware and requested permission to speak. Ware asked the approval of the Baptist Ministers Conference first before allowing the president of the SCLC to address the gathering. King reasoned with the ministers on behalf of the SCLC's mission in Birmingham. But despite "scattered Amens," he failed to garner the support of Birmingham's leading organization of black Baptists.[2]

The integrationists left the meeting and "drove in silence" to the A. G. Gaston Motel, where the SCLC had set up its headquarters. Located at Fifth Avenue North near Kelly Ingram Park, the motel was the only one in the city open to African Americans. Gaston gave King his best suite—Room 30, but the SCLC paid for the use of the facilities. For the rest of the afternoon, King assessed black opposition to his campaign in Birmingham.[3]

The Reverend Ed Gardner warmed up the faithful gathered in St. James Baptist Church for the opening meeting of the Birmingham campaign on Wednesday night, April 3, 1963. Reminding the congregation of the ACMHR's past successes desegregating public transportation facilities and referring to the activists who had been arrested during the sit-ins that day, Gardner said: "Freedom bells will ring in Birmingham as soon as we all get together and pull together." For nearly every night over the next five weeks, Ed Gardner coordinated the mass meeting for the SCLC, opening it up around 6:00 P.M., keeping it on schedule, and closing it down after 9:00 P.M. Reflecting the Christian orientation of movement members, the meeting adopted the structure of a regular church service: prayer, hymn, collection, sermon, altar call, benediction. The mass meetings began with prayers and freedom songs and performances by the ACMHR movement choir conducted by gospel great Carlton Reese, followed by "pep talks" by activists released from jail, and the offering conducted in processional

Crowds gather outside St. James Baptist Church, the location of the first mass meeting of the Birmingham campaign, where the Reverend Ed Gardner prepared the audience for the arrival of the Reverend Martin Luther King Jr. Since 1956, St. James had been one of a handful of black churches that sponsored the Monday night mass meetings of the Alabama Christian Movement for Human Rights. *Birmingham News*.

220

style. The evening's main program, which featured information, analysis, and speeches by SCLC officials and visiting supporters, took up an hour and ended with a call for volunteers. Usually a leader in ACMHR concluded the meeting with announcements concerning future activities and the congregational singing of "We Shall Overcome" or some other civil rights anthem.[4]

Addressing the crowd that first night, Shuttlesworth put the Birmingham campaign into the perspective of the local movement. He dismissed the idea held by some people that the "Negroes are going to put on a big bluff[,] that it will soon go over"; "we are just getting started," he asserted. When a "white man who is considered to be a liberal" called the integrationist and asked him "if Negroes wanted progress or attention?" the resolute Shuttlesworth retorted, "Go over to the City Jail and ask 21 Negroes in jail what they want." The local leader declared: "Birmingham must wake up and join the rest of the world. We have been in this fight for seven long years and we don't intend to quit now."[5]

Shuttlesworth introduced Martin Luther King as a "symbol of our aid" from the SCLC and urged the assembly to "follow him to freedom." King responded: "We in Atlanta have come to the aid of Fred Shuttlesworth. He called on us and we were glad to come because of the injustice in Birmingham." The civil rights leader hoped to defuse comparison to Albany by stressing his commitment to achieving the local movement's objectives: "It might take three days and it might take three months." Regardless of "how long," King promised to remain in Birmingham until the goals were met. Then he coached the congregation on a three-step process of nonviolent resistance. King described the facts surrounding political oppression of black people in Birmingham, the need for negotiations over the demands of the oppressed, and nonviolent direct action to "create enough tension to cause attention" to the oppression. As used by Gandhi during the independence struggle in India, such a strategy pressured the consciousness of the opponent to effect reform.[6]

Abernathy followed King. He referred to the SCLC's make-it or break-it predicament: "The eyes of the world are on Birmingham tonight. Bobby Kennedy is looking here at Birmingham, the United States Congress is looking at Birmingham. The Department of Justice is looking at Birmingham. Are you ready, are you ready to make the challenge? I have come with Martin Luther King to help lead you. I am ready to go to jail, are you?" When he asked for volunteers to join the protest, about eighty answered his call. Reminding the congregation of the "all out boycott" against downtown stores, Shuttlesworth brought the meeting to a close. The first day of the Birmingham campaign had ended with an enthusiastic ACMHR mass meeting that nonetheless did little to assuage an uneasy feeling shared by the leaders of the SCLC.[7]

To prepare the black community for the civil rights campaign, Shuttlesworth and the Reverend Nelson H. Smith Jr., the secretary of the ACMHR, assisted by the SCLC staff, drafted the "Birmingham Manifesto." Activists had distributed it on April 2, 1963—the day of municipal elections that saw the defeat of former commissioner of public safety Bull Connor in his bid for mayor and the election of former state lieutenant governor Albert Boutwell and nine members of the new city council. Although it did not mention the forthcoming boycott and sit-ins, the manifesto called on "the citizenry of Birmingham, Negro and white, to join us in this witness for decency, morality, self-respect and human dignity." The document recounted the ACMHR's years of trial and tribulation in "the worst big city in race relations in the United States." Referring to the white businessmen who negotiated the desegregation of stores in the fall of 1962 to avoid a "confrontation in race relations," the manifesto noted, "Their concern for the city's image and commonweal of all its citizens did not run deep enough." Left with "broken faith and broken promises," the black community had little option except to protest in order to gain the "American Dream." On April 4 the ACMHR—speaking also for the SCLC—issued a press release similar to the Birmingham Manifesto that addressed the criticism of outside interference by describing the decisions to postpone the boycott three times during the fight to change city government. The announcement concluded that Boutwell's support for segregation and the "adamant and inflexible attitude" of Birmingham left the integrationists with "no alternative but to act now."[8]

Reflecting the desire of the integrationists for equal access as consumers and equal job opportunities, the ACMHR-SCLC–announced campaign objectives were as follows: first, the "desegregation of lunch counters and all public facilities in all downtown stores"; second, the "immediate establishment of fair hiring practices in those stores, including employment of qualified Negroes for white collar jobs"; third, "the dropping of all charges against those who have been arrested during sit-ins"; fourth, the "establishment of fair hiring practices in all city departments"; fifth, the "reopening of city parks and playgrounds, all of which now are closed to avoid desegregation"; and sixth, the "establishment of a biracial group to work out a timetable for desegregation of all Birmingham public schools." The white elite were to comply with all the conditions set forth by the movement before it would agree to call off the demonstrations. These were the demands that Shuttlesworth and the ACMHR, as well as the Miles College students, had fought for over the past seven years.[9]

Mayor-elect Boutwell dismissed the civil rights activists as "strangers" and "outsiders" who had come to Birmingham "to stir inter-racial discord." Retrenching, Boutwell warned that "demonstrations and sit-ins can accomplish absolutely nothing." Bull Connor taunted the protesters: "You can rest assured that I will fill the jail full of any persons violating the law as long as I'm at City Hall." Taking its cue from the successful resistance of white officials during the Albany campaign, the *Birmingham Post-Herald* advised the police department to show "great patience, restraint, and intelligence" and thereby win "the respect and sympathy of people all over the country." The Negro *Birmingham World* argued that "this direct action seems to be both wasteful and worthless." Chairman of the Alabama Council on Human Relations, the Reverend Dr. Albert S. Foley, spoke on behalf of Birmingham's only biracial group when he deplored the sit-ins as having "set back negotiations to improve race relations." Referring to the activities of the Reverend Norman C. Jimerson and Dr. Lucius Holsey Pitts, Foley noted that "progress was being made before the direct action tactics of extremists." Critics of the SCLC complained of the campaign's timing by suggesting that the recent change in government was a step toward solving Birmingham's racial problem and that the "outside elements" should give Boutwell and the new city council an opportunity to address the issue. From the politicians, to the press, to the racial liberals, white Birmingham denounced the civil rights demonstrations.[10]

The twenty integrationists arrested at Britling Cafeteria during Wednesday's sit-ins went to trial in municipal court on Thursday, April 4. Supporters from the ACMHR-SCLC watched the proceedings. The recorder's court judge found the twenty defendants guilty, sentenced them to 180 days in jail, and ordered them to pay a $100 fine and court costs. Black attorney Arthur Shores appealed one of the convictions and gained the activist's release, but the other nineteen were remanded back to the warden. Bull Connor put them to work "on the [prison] farm and in the jail laundry." Later that morning, the movement had to adjust its plans for sit-ins as the dinettes targeted in the Reverend Wyatt Tee Walker's original strategy again closed their lunch counters. Britling's hired three bouncers and stationed them at the front door together with the sign, "We reserve the right to refuse service to anyone." Four black youths left one drugstore after the manager declined to press charges. When four black adults asked for service at the lunch counter at Lane-Liggett Drug Store, police arrested them, bringing to an end the protest on the second day of the campaign.[11]

Reverend Gardner welcomed the five hundred people packed into St. James Baptist Church on Thursday night. He remembered his mother saying, "Son there will be a better day," and announced, "That day is here." The limited protest of the morning suggested otherwise. As Gardner ended his remarks, however, a new development in the ranks of local black support appeared when Shuttlesworth, King, Abernathy, and A. D. King accompanied the Reverend John Thomas Porter into the sanctuary to the thunderous applause of a standing ovation. Pastor of Sixth Avenue Baptist Church, the largest black congregation in the city, Porter held an influential position in the Christian community; yet he had never supported Shuttlesworth or the ACMHR. Therefore, he felt it necessary to explain his decision to join the campaign. Having watched the morning's activists get arrested, Porter concluded: "John Porter is for freedom. John Porter will stand up for freedom and his church and his family will stand up for freedom." Porter made a significant addition to the movement, and the

ACMHR and SCLC leaders accorded him a position up front; nevertheless, most of the black middle class opposed the protest.[12]

The Thursday mass meeting centered on the selective buying campaign and racial discrimination: the movement's long-standing goals of equal employment opportunities and equal access as consumers. Shuttlesworth introduced a teenaged sit-in activist, who testified that he went to jail because "he was tired of negro youth having no opportunity." Shuttlesworth responded, "This is why we will win." The white Reverend Joseph W. Ellwanger, pastor of St. Paul's Lutheran Church and a member of the Birmingham chapter of the Alabama Council on Human Relations, made some remarks on his personal support for the movement. Martin Luther King took the pulpit and stressed the "all out boycott," telling the congregation to wear "blue jeans and old clothes," cancel their charge accounts at white-owned stores, stop paying their premiums to white insurance companies, and withdraw their money from the white banks. "We must no longer spend our money with businesses that discriminate against negroes," he insisted. Abernathy described African American life in Atlanta, where "you can go to the finest, most exclusive restaurant, sit down and order yourself a steak," and where "the business and civic leaders of Atlanta will call you down to their office, shake your hand, pat you on the back." He then asked for "volunteers for the freedom army," and fifty enlisted.[13]

While police arrested ten integrationists following sit-ins at the Tutwiler and Lane-Liggett drugstores on Friday, April 5, Shuttlesworth opened a new front in the Birmingham campaign. Shortly after ten that morning, the persistent leader telegraphed Bull Connor requesting "a permit to picket peacefully against the injustices of segregation and discrimination in the general area of second third and fourth avenues on the east and west sidewalks of 19 street." Along the three-block area he identified—the heart of the retail district—sat the stores targeted by the boycott: Loveman's, Kress, Woolworth's, Newberry's, and Pizitz. Clearly, the SCLC intended to organize pickets to draw attention to the boycott while avoiding protest marches on city hall. Connor fired back to Shuttlesworth that only the full city commission could grant a permit. "I insist that you and your people do not start any picketing on the streets in Birmingham, Alabama," he tersely replied. Shuttlesworth had other ideas.[14]

At Friday night's mass meeting held in Thirgood Colored Methodist Episcopal Church, King emphasized the boycott: "We can't all go to jail, but we can keep our money in our pockets and out of the downtown merchants' pockets." Complaining of the local white press coverage—the

224

News and *Post-Herald* played down the movement by running small stories buried deep in the paper—King stated: "The white man is trying to black out our movement by not giving news coverage. Over the next few days we must make this movement 95% effective." He reiterated the SCLC's original strategy: "If we do that then the downtown business men will sit down and talk this thing out with us." A contingent of SCLC staff attended the mass meeting, including Wyatt Tee Walker, James Lawson, Bernard Lee, Andrew Young, and Dorothy Cotton. Shuttlesworth wrapped up the service with comments about the boycott and the activists in jail. Then he announced that the activists would "march on City Hall the next day" because "he wanted to drink some of that white water in the City Hall and see if it tasted any better than the colored water." Thirty-five people volunteered to join him and the Reverend Charles Billups, a longtime leader in the ACMHR, on the "freedom march" the next day.[15]

After gathering at the A. G. Gaston Motel on Saturday, April 6, the demonstrators "stepped off in pairs," forming a procession down Fifth Avenue through the black ghetto, headed toward city hall for a prayer meeting in Woodrow Wilson Park in protest of the denied permit for pickets. Shuttlesworth and Billups led the orderly group of protesters as it passed uniformed officers who blocked traffic and pedestrians from the area, allowing only reporters on the scene. At the Federal Building Bull Connor anchored a barricade. "Let's get this thing over with," the police commissioner said. "Call the wagons sergeant, I'm hungry." Using a megaphone, police chief Jamie Moore twice informed the demonstrators that they paraded without a permit. "We are taking an orderly walk," Shuttlesworth explained. "We are not parading." The police moved in to arrest the demonstrators as they dropped to their knees and prayed. Shuttlesworth lined out the hymn, "The Lord Will Help Us." The singing shifted to "We Shall Overcome" as officers crammed the twenty-nine integrationists into two paddy wagons. One vehicle became so full that it took four policemen to push the door closed. Shuttlesworth had led the first protest march of the Birmingham campaign. Yet the *New York Times* reported that "promised mass demonstrations have not been held, however, and there appeared to be a possibility tonight that the campaign might be temporarily abandoned."[16]

Four days after it began the desegregation drive, the ACMHR-SCLC had altered its strategy to include marches on city hall—a major change considering King and Walker's original opposition to such methods. The move reflected the SCLC's scramble to generate interest in the movement. The rhetoric at Saturday night's mass meeting at St. James Baptist Church shifted to the theme of going to jail. King told the small gathering of two hundred, "The white power may think that things will blow over, but we are just getting started." He promised to get arrested: "I have been in jail 12 times, and this time in Birmingham will make 13." As a newcomer to the movement, Reverend Porter said "he had never seen the inside of the jail but he was going to soon." The Reverend Nelson H. Smith confessed that "he had been in the movement for 7 years and hadn't been in jail yet but he was going tomorrow." As Sunday began Holy Week, Smith added, "there was no better time than Easter for us to go to jail for freedom." King's younger brother, the Reverend A. D. King of the ACMHR and First Baptist Church in Ensley, urged those present to meet him the next day, when he would lead them on a march to city hall. No longer following its clear plan of boycott and sit-in, the campaign strategy slipped toward another Albany.[17]

Several hundred people attended the Palm Sunday mass meeting on April 7. Hundreds more waited outside along Sixth Avenue North. Accompanied by Smith and Porter, a determined A. D. King directed the marchers out of St. Paul Methodist Church and down the street toward town singing "Hold My Hand While I Run This Race." Again Bull Connor lined up his officers along the parade route. After the procession crossed Seventeenth Street, policemen halted the black-robed ministers and arrested the demonstrators for parading without a permit. As they knelt, King led them in prayer. Officers stepped in and loaded the twenty integrationists into paddy wagons for the trip to the jail.

The black spectators disapproved of the interruption of the march, and Connor called out the police dogs for crowd control. Leroy Allen, a non-movement nineteen-year-old black male, wrestled with one dog. "Get him, get him, get him!" shouted black observers, who encouraged Allen to resist the dog. As the young man stood up, he reached into his pocket, but then policemen unleashed two more dogs on him. As a knife flashed, a German shepherd tore his arm and police knocked him to the ground and kicked him. Suddenly onlookers, officers, and other dogs rushed over the fallen man. More policemen moved in, swinging billy clubs to clear out the bystanders. Over the next fifteen minutes, snarling dogs dispersed the crowd. Police arrested seven spectators for disorderly conduct and loitering in addition to the nineteen activists already going to jail.[18]

"I've got it. I've got it," an enthusiastic Walker telephoned King, telling him about Bull Connor's use of dogs and the subsequent police brutality against nonviolent demonstrators.[19] Walker knew that the national media

A police dog lunges at a black man as officers break up a crowd of bystanders following a protest march in Birmingham. Although not active in the nonviolent movement, black bystanders contributed to the campaign by offering the appearance of widespread support for civil rights reform. Associated Press.

had inaccurately recorded a large gathering of activists, not the actual nineteen in the march, and an attack dog pinning down a civil rights worker, not the actual angered bystander. He recognized the importance of appearances as presented through sensational media coverage that misrepresented the event in support of the movement. Henceforth Walker promoted coercive nonviolence in a bid to generate creative tension that the newspapers and television cameras could record as police suppression. Project C was born.

Walker's original strategy of steady sit-ins to emphasize the selective buying campaign had lacked the spark necessary to interest the national media and thus sully Birmingham's reputation. The ACMHR-SCLC had hoped economic pressure would convince local white businessmen to end racial discrimination. Although the boycott worked, it entailed a long campaign. Moreover, the sit-ins had not generated the headlines that Walker wanted to restore King's reputation. Apparently, the SCLC had expected the very presence of Martin Luther King to draw hundreds of protesters into the movement. That had not occurred. Only a small percentage of Birmingham's black population had supported the campaign, and an even smaller proportion had volunteered for direct action protests. The limited response to King's call for demonstrators had been noted in the national press. The protesters were overwhelmingly members of the ACMHR, and, though limited in number, they harnessed a religious fanaticism that gave them the courage to face Bull Connor and the Birmingham jail. Outside of the traditional Negro leadership class, which expressed opposition to the movement, and the unorganized onlookers who demonstrated their support by cheering as the marchers passed, the black community appeared too alienated and disinterested to get involved. Given the lukewarm response to the campaign and the fact that Walker's blueprint in Project X had called for long-term economic sanctions, it appears that the SCLC had neither adequately evaluated the black community in Birmingham nor thought through its strategy. The problem centered on how to sustain the demonstrations with so few black people involved—hence Walker's desperate need to generate some interest in the campaign and his excitement over Bull Connor's use of the police dogs.[20]

Back at the A. G. Gaston Motel, James Forman, the director of the Student Nonviolent Coordinating Committee, observed a jubilant Walker jumping up and down with Dorothy Cotton and other SCLC workers saying: "We've got a movement. We've got a movement. We had some police brutality. They brought out the dogs. They brought out the dogs. We've got a movement!" A disgusted Forman found the response "very cold, cruel and calculating to be happy about police brutality coming down on innocent people, bystanders, no matter what purpose it served." Having "found the key" he needed to generate interest in the protest, Walker began calling the Birmingham campaign "Project C" for "Confrontation." The new name signaled a shift in SCLC thinking.[21]

Eager for a confrontation with Martin Luther King, newly inaugurated Governor George C. Wallace used the violence on Sunday to justify dispatching Colonel Al Lingo, state director of public safety, and one hundred of his highway patrolmen to Birmingham. Three short months before, Wallace had promised to defend segregation and he needed an opportunity to fulfill his battle cry of resistance. In Birmingham Bull Connor had the situation under control, however, and the silver helmeted state troopers left on Tuesday. Taking the advice of the *Birmingham Post-Herald*, Connor followed the lead of Albany police chief Laurie Pritchett by "nonviolently" arresting the activists. Despite the use of dogs on Sunday, officers kept them in the kennel for the next month. Surveillance reports on black "radicals" and white "reactionaries" informed Connor of developing events and the

228

potential of vigilante violence. During the five weeks of intense demonstrations in April and May 1963, no bombings occurred, an unusual circumstance considering the more than fifty unsolved dynamitings since 1947 and a fact suggesting that Connor assured the night riders that he could maintain segregation.[22]

On MONDAY MORNING, April 8, Martin Luther King met with two hundred of Birmingham's black ministers. He hoped to convince them of the need for the demonstrations. Championing the social gospel, King "suggested that only a 'dry as dust' religion prompts a minister to extol the glories of Heaven while ignoring the social conditions that cause men an earthly hell." Frustrated by the lack of support he received from the black church, he scolded the ministers: "I'm tired of preachers riding around in big cars, living in fine homes, but not willing to take their part in the fight. . . . If you can't stand up with your own people, you are not fit to be a leader!" Although he disliked Shuttlesworth and the ACMHR, the Reverend John H. Cross, pastor of Sixteenth Street Baptist Church, decided to assist the   229
SCLC in the campaign. Cross had played no leadership role in the weeks leading up to the demonstrations, but he had pestered the SCLC about paying the power bill for using Sixteenth Street during the fall convention. Unwilling to stand alone, he made a motion that the conservative ministers go on record endorsing the SCLC. J. L. Ware, who chaired the gathering, refused to recognize the motion. At last a "general resolution on the subject of the aspirations of the local Negro group" was adopted, although no one recorded the measure. Walker claimed this as a victory for the ACMHR-SCLC, but Ware maintained his opposition to the campaign.[23]

Perhaps petty jealousy provided the motivation behind Ware's actions. In his younger days after World War II, he had joined in the black veteran's protest when returning G.I.s demanded the right to vote in Birmingham. The campaign failed but Ware retained a reputation for civil rights activism. His civil rights organization, the Inter-Citizens Committee, directed by the Reverend C. Herbert Oliver, publicly opposed the movement by criticizing it for "operating in a vacuum" during the city government's confusion. Editor Emory O. Jackson considered Ware the proper leader of Birmingham's black community, as opposed to the "non-responsible, the non-attached, and the non-program 'leader'" whose role "might be to cluster around a glossy personality and share in the reflections of his limelight without the obligation of shouldering responsibility or being held accountable." The criticism stung Shuttlesworth and King, who had expected black Birmingham to rally behind them.[24]

After Cross aligned with King and the SCLC, his church, Sixteenth Street Baptist, was made available for the campaign's use for the first time since the protest began the week before. Because of its size and location, the sanctuary quickly became the point of departure for demonstrations. The church stood on the northwestern end of the "Negro" business district catercorner to Kelly Ingram Park and a few blocks from the A. G. Gaston Motel. Nevertheless, few ministers hearkened to King's pleas and sided with the SCLC. Walker later estimated that only 10 percent of Birmingham's 250 black pastors joined the campaign.[25]

The largest crowd yet gathered at the mass meeting in First Baptist Church, Ensley, on Monday night, April 8, 1963. Its pastor, A. D. King, was in jail with Reverend Shuttlesworth and ninety-four other demonstrators. Earlier that day white civil rights attorney William Kunstler arrived in Birmingham and used a criminal code dating back to Reconstruction to successfully transfer thirty-nine protesters from state to federal court. At the mass meeting Kunstler spoke about the "fight for freedom." Yet Martin Luther King and Ralph Abernathy set the tone of the evening in addressing the opposition of the traditional Negro leadership class to the campaign. King lashed out against Negro preachers, their congregations, and black businessmen "who did not support the movement." To emphasize his point, he asked those unwilling to protest to "get up and leave the church so somebody can have your seat who wants to go to jail for freedom." He added: "We are just getting started. We are going to continue demonstrations everyday until the white people of Birmingham realize that we are going to get what we want." Appealing for volunteers to submit to arrest, King promised: "We are going to fill all the jails in Birmingham. We are going to turn Birmingham up side down and right side up." The rhetoric suggested that the ACMHR-SCLC had broadened its boycott and sit-in strategy to include marches on city hall—a major revision that would require even more protesters and money to maintain the campaign's momentum.[26]

The night, however, belonged to Ralph Abernathy, who, as one reporter put it, "scathingly assailed the black 'Bourgeoisie' to the howling delight of the rafter-packed audience." Common and earthy, Abernathy had grown up on a family owned farm in rural Alabama, and he understood the unpretentious members of the audience. "We had a roomful of the elite, the Bourgeoisie, the class of Birmingham who are now living on the hill, learning to talk proper," he said, citing a prior conference. "They've got their hair tinted various colors, trying to fool somebody. Year before last they lived like us, across the railroad tracks, took baths in a tin tub, and went to an outhouse. Now they are strutting around proper. How did they get rich? We made them rich." Abernathy encouraged the activists "to talk with your doctor, your lawyer, your insuranceman and withdraw your trade from him if he is not with this movement." Admitting King's inability to win the support of the black ministers during the meeting that morning, he said: "You ought to threaten to cut the preachers' salaries if they don't stand up with you for freedom. They say this is the wrong time and yet they have had 350 years. I want to know when the devil gives the right time." Having excoriated all manner of "Uncle Toms," Abernathy asked for volunteers to join him in jail. "If you go with me President Kennedy will be looking in, Lyndon Johnson will be looking in and 'Old Bull' will be shaking in his boots." With the congregation singing "I'm On My Way To Freedom Land," the mass meeting adjourned.[27]

King and Abernathy leveled harsh criticism against the black middle class because it actively resisted the Birmingham campaign. The failure of A. G. Gaston to endorse the SCLC rankled protest leaders. The refusal of a Gaston subordinate to allow Al Hibbler, the blind black singer from New Jersey who had traveled to Birmingham in support of the campaign, to perform in the L. R. Hall Auditorium to an assembled audience of hundreds hours before the scheduled concert and civil rights rally, further alienated the Negro millionaire from the black community. Hibbler had a hard time participating in the demonstrations. Earlier on Tuesday, April 9, Bull Connor had refused to arrest the entertainer when he joined a sit-in at Loveman's Department Store, although police apprehended Carl Keith, a white man from Evanston, Illinois, who had picketed out of curiosity. The next day officers again declined to arrest Hibbler, who complained: "The police are trying to segregate me from my own people." Unable to use Gaston's auditorium, ACMHR-SCLC leaders appealed to the city's Negro fraternal organizations in a last-ditch effort to hold the concert, but they, too, denied the use of the "Colored" Masonic Temple to the protest movement. Hibbler finally received his audience in Kelly Ingram Park, where he said a few words and gave an impromptu performance of "He" unaccompanied.[28]

As members of the black community condemned Gaston as an "Uncle Tom," the Negro entrepreneur convened a meeting of one hundred members of the traditional Negro leadership class in his "ultramodern" A. G.

A frustrated Al Hibbler is turned away from the paddy wagon on April 9, 1963, as police refuse to arrest him for participating in a sit-in at Loveman's Department Store. Undeterred, the popular blind singer would march again. Police Surveillance Files, BPLDAM.

Gaston Building to allow King an opportunity to make the case for the campaign. Opening the floor to comments, the civil rights leader listened as Birmingham's Negro businessmen and professionals verbalized their hostility to the protest movement. Reiterating the standard argument against demonstrations, one man said, "We ought to give Boutwell more of a chance." Another told the group, "I think we should wait until we're better organized." Someone else suggested, "What we need is more community cooperation and fewer picket lines." After everyone had spoken, King responded: "This is the most segregated city in America and we have to stick together if we ever hope to change its ways. I and my associates in the Southern Christian Leadership Conference have come to help you to break down the walls." Over the next half hour, he carefully detailed the campaign strategy, attempting to entice the group with promises of visits by Jackie Robinson, Sammy Davis Jr., and Harry Belafonte. He ended with the assurance that the SCLC planned "to use every nonviolent tactic we know to achieve our goals. We hope that you will help us in our task." Observing the conference, William Kunstler felt a difference in the audience after it was over. He optimistically assumed, "Those who hadn't been won over were at least neutralized and the rest seemed eager to help in the work that lay ahead."[29]

In reality, however, the divisions within the black community reflected the failure of black institutions—the church, the Masonic groups, the schools, the civic and social clubs—to support the civil rights movement. Numerous social scientists have argued the merits of mobilization theory to explain the origins of the civil rights struggle. Doug McAdam has suggested that black institutions provided the "indigenous organizational strength needed to mount and sustain a social movement." And according to Aldon Morris, "preexisting institutions, leaders, and organizations were critically involved in all phases of the movement and were especially important in the beginning stages." The example of Birmingham suggests otherwise, for black institutions and the traditional Negro leadership class hindered the civil rights struggle by actively opposing the movement.[30]

To coordinate campaign policy, Shuttlesworth and King created a "Central Committee" that combined ACMHR and SCLC members with select representatives from the traditional Negro leadership class. Comprising an informal group of thirty advisers to the civil rights movement were Shuttlesworth, Gardner, N. H. Smith, A. D. King, Lola Hendricks, and W. E. Shortridge of the ACMHR; King, Abernathy, Young, Lawson, Walker, and Dorothy Cotton of the SCLC; and Gaston, Dr. L. H. Pitts, Arthur Shores, John and Deenie Drew, J. T. Porter, Harold Long, and C. Herbert Oliver of the black middle class; and others. Over time, black businessmen linked to Sidney W. Smyer and the Senior Citizens Committee agreed to assist the ACMHR-SCLC as negotiators, although they did not necessarily accept the goals of the local movement or act in the interests of the black community. While movement leaders came and went according to their involvement in the campaign, those traditional Negro leaders who had met with the white elite before—Gaston, Pitts, Shores, Shortridge, and Drew— regularly attended the negotiating sessions.[31]

The appearance of a unified black community led some observers to suggest that a similar agreement had been reached on movement objectives. The New York Times reported that black people in Birmingham closed "ranks" behind the campaign as "appeals for unity were bringing pledges of support from many quarters." Bayard Rustin, a veteran civil rights activist and adviser to Martin Luther King and the SCLC, argued that in Birmingham "the black community was welded into a classless revolt." In his June 1963 polemic, "The Great Lessons of Birmingham,"

Rustin mentioned that A. G. Gaston "finally accommodated himself, as did the others, to the mass pressure from below and joined the struggle." Likewise, King touted the "democratic phalanx" seen in the streets of Birmingham, where "doctors marched with window cleaners. Lawyers demonstrated with laundresses. Ph.D.'s and no-D's were treated with perfect equality by the registrars of the nonviolence movement." Although the idea of classless protesters made good rhetoric, it had little to do with reality in Birmingham as the campaign stumbled along.[32]

After the summit meeting of the traditional Negro leadership class, Gaston issued a statement that presented his interpretation of events. Birmingham's racist past—the unsolved bombings, segregation, and lack of biracial communication—made the "city a very attractive target for the present unhappy situation in which we now find ourselves." The comment implied that the SCLC had selected Birmingham as a "target" and thus created the "unhappy situation." Fully aware of black aspirations, Gaston said: "We want freedom and justice; and, we want to be able to live and work with dignity in all endeavors where we are qualified. We also want the privilege of access." Referring to Atlanta, he said that Birmingham faced problems that already had been satisfactorily addressed by other southern cities. He concluded by calling "upon all the citizens of Birmingham to work harmoniously and together . . . giving due recognition to the local colored leadership among us." By definition, that excluded Shuttlesworth and King, but it underscored the role of the traditional Negro leadership class. In short, the statement neither rejected nor endorsed the stated goals of the protest movement. Although he no longer actively opposed the campaign, Gaston fell far short of signing on to march in the classless procession to Southside Jail.[33]

In a perfect example of damage control, the ACMHR-SCLC rushed to present the various elements of Birmingham's black community as in agreement on the campaign. In a press release, Walker referred to critical comments in northern newspapers when he "declared today that the sharp criticisms levied against Birmingham's wealthy A. G. Gaston are based on long-distance reporting." The executive director of the SCLC lied, "Those here on the scene know that Dr. Gaston has supported the movement from its inception." Implying that Gaston had assisted the SCLC "weeks ahead of time" in preparing for the demonstrations, Walker noted: "Our suite of rooms was leased to us at [a] modest figure and Dr. Gaston supplied most of the office furniture 'gratis.'" Shuttlesworth added: "Dr. Gaston serves on the Negotiating Committee and on our larger Central Committee that handles over-all strategy. He didn't just start participating; he has been working closely with us for the last year." To the ACMHR-SCLC leaders, the appearance of a unified black community was crucial for the success of the campaign.[34]

THE SIT-INS continued Tuesday morning, April 9, as officers arrested two women and one man at Britling Cafeteria after they refused to leave when asked to do so. Later in the day, nine integrationists entered the Bohemian Bakery Cafeteria; when employees would not wait on them, they reached over and served themselves, then sat down at two tables and began to eat. Police officers arrived and arrested them. Pickets at Loveman's in the heart of the downtown retail district carried signs reading "Don't Buy Segregation" and "Don't Shop Where You Can't Eat." At the intersection of Nineteenth Street and Third Avenue North, what activists called "integration corner," police arrested eight demonstrators during the busy lunch hour as hundreds of black and white people passed by. There was no disorder. A total of twenty activists were detained on Tuesday.[35]

235

At the mass meeting that night, Shuttlesworth emphasized black unity. Bailed out of jail earlier in the day, he reported on his stay behind bars, then announced that black businessmen and professionals had "voted to endorse" the campaign. He exclaimed, "We not only have the poor Negroes in Birmingham, we have the rich Negroes in this movement now." Abernathy praised Reverend Cross for allowing the ACMHR-SCLC to meet in the Sixteenth Street Baptist Church. Then Martin Luther King spoke. "I had a dream tonight," he said, "a dream of seeing little Negro boys and girls walking to school with little white boys and girls, playing in the parks together and going swimming together." As he polished it over time, this oration came to exemplify the aspirations of movement members and immortalized King at the March on Washington. Al Hibbler sang his 1955 hit "I Forgive" and then "Nobody Knows the Trouble I've Seen" before issuing an altar call for volunteers to join him on the picket line the next day. The white detectives reported that of the thirty-four "recruits," most "had already been to jail earlier."[36]

The Senior Citizens' subcommittee on race made overtures to movement leaders to discuss the ACMHR-SCLC campaign. Using Norman Jimerson, the white director of the biracial Alabama Council on Human Relations, as a go-between, realtor Sidney W. Smyer arranged a meeting with the civil rights activists for April 9. The black and white men secretly met in the study of the Episcopal Church of the Advent. Bishop Co-Adjutor George Murray acted as moderator. Movement representatives included Fred Shuttlesworth, A. D. King, Nelson Smith, and Andrew Young from the SCLC. Air-conditioning chilled the room, recalled Charles Morgan Jr., the young white attorney who had worked to reform the city. Shuttlesworth was cold and Morgan, who liked the temperature, offered his cord sport coat to the integrationist. One of the white men grimaced at this gesture and said: "Tell me, what is it that you niggers want?" Morgan quietly responded, "Well, one thing—probably they don't want to be called niggers." The inauspicious beginning characterized the negotiations throughout the civil rights campaign. Movement leaders presented their demands in writing, and Shuttlesworth, having succeeded in bringing representatives of the white elite to the bargaining table, upped the ante to include immediate school desegregation. Unwilling to even entertain the original demands of the activists, Smyer ended the "fruitless" session but not before deciding to meet again on April 11. At that time, both groups agreed to increase the number of negotiators in an effort to become more representative, but the move opened the door to the black businessmen previously sanctioned by Smyer. Morgan remembered: "Later negotiations became formalized, each side having representatives charged with the duty of meeting, talking, and reporting the result of conferences to their groups."[37]

Eight black activists integrated the Birmingham Public Library on Wednesday, April 10, 1963. The police did not intervene, although one white patron remarked, "It stinks in here," and another asked the demonstrators, "Why don't you go home?" After thirty minutes of walking through the stacks on three of the floors and stopping to read books or magazines at their leisure, the protesters left. Meanwhile, Al Hibbler led another group of 25 pickets in front of downtown department stores; policemen arrested the activists, but they turned back the blind singer. Bull Connor asked the performer: "What can you do? Anybody who goes to jail has to earn his food." Hibbler replied, "I can sing." The 25 arrested joined 129 African Americans who had been jailed for demonstrating, although by Wednesday all but 30 had been released on $300 bonds.[38]

A small crowd attended the mass meeting on Wednesday night in St. James Baptist Church, where King again focused on the selective buying campaign: "Everyone in the movement must live a sacrificial life. Negroes that you see shopping downtown are not fit to be free. They are traitors to the Negro race." Andrew Young later recalled how protest leaders maintained the boycott: "Three times a day we would check downtown, and anytime we saw more than five black people in a store, we got concerned that the boycott was slipping." He described how preachers who declined to march nonetheless mentioned the campaign from the pulpit: "We produced about 50,000 handbills every week and over the weekend, through the churches and door-to-door leafleting, we kept the community informed and encouraged the boycott." At the mass meeting Abernathy recounted a story that he used to enforce the boycott: "One lady told me she was going to jail, but not for sitting in but for beating on the heads of some of these sorry Negro shoppers. I told her ours was a non-violent movement and not to beat anybody, but just scare hell out of them." Wyatt Tee Walker told a different story. A black woman entered Loveman's to buy her baby some shoes. The white saleswoman said: "Negro, ain't you ashamed of yourself, your people out there on the street getting put in jail and you in here spending money and I'm not going to sell you any, you'll have to go some other place." Earlier in the evening King told the 350 people assembled that he and Abernathy would march on April 12: "I can't think of a better day than Good Friday for a move for freedom." He was responding to the latest white effort to derail the campaign.[39]

On the afternoon of April 10, Commissioner Connor and Chief of Police Moore obtained a temporary injunction from state circuit court judge W. A. Jenkins that prohibited members of the civil rights movement "from engaging in, sponsoring, promoting or encouraging mass street parades, marches, picketing, sit-ins, and other actions likely to cause a breach of the peace." The court order specifically named the ACMHR and SCLC, Shuttlesworth, King, and Abernathy, and more than a hundred other "individuals who allegedly have participated in the activities." In requesting the injunction, Connor and Moore cited the "undue burden and strain" placed on the police department by the demonstrations and the possibility of "incidents of violence and bloodshed." Officers served the court order on movement leaders at the Gaston Motel early Thursday morning, April 11. That afternoon, twelve integrationists defied the injunction. Movement members hid the activists in their cars until they arrived at the target site in front of Pizitz Department Store. When the cars stopped, the protesters jumped out with signs and took positions in three locations along Nineteenth Street between Second and Fourth Avenues North. In addition to the twelve activists arrested, seven juveniles were detained by police. Officers charged them with parading without a permit and loitering but not violating the injunction.[40]

Remembering Albany and the use of a court order to fatally disrupt the desegregation drive, King announced that the ACMHR-SCLC would ignore the ruling: "We can not in all good conscience obey an injunction, which is an unjust, undemocratic and unconstitutional misuse of the legal process." He referred to SCLC attorneys who were working to have the temporary injunction lifted. "In the past we have abided by Federal injunctions out of respect for the forthright and consistent leadership that the Federal judiciary has given in establishing the principal [sic] of integration as the law of the land," King explained. "However, we are now confronted with recalcitrant forces in the Deep South that will use the courts to perpetuate the unjust and illegal system of racial separation." Again, King promised that he and Abernathy would lead a march on Friday.[41]

Shuttlesworth released a statement clarifying the local movement's rejection of the court order. Describing a tyrannical Alabama judiciary, he condemned state judges who "do not appear to respect Negroes, nor regard us as persons subject to the same rights and treatments as others." Shuttlesworth cited the struggle of civil rights activists since 1956 "who have committed no crime but that of being born black and having courage to ask for our rights. The unwritten rule in Alabama is: If the mobs don't stop Negroes, the police can; and if the police can't, then the courts will."[42]

In his effort to trump King, Connor played another card on the movement. The commissioner informed James Esdale of the Esdale Bonding Company that the local business could no longer secure the release of jailed demonstrators, for the city considered his assets insufficient to warrant the bonds. By April 10 Esdale had posted more than $20,000 in the appeal and appearance bonds of seventy-one activists. In addition, the SCLC had spent the money previously raised for cash bonds. Financially, the movement had run dry. Without money, civil rights leaders could neither bail out the activists already in jail nor promise future protesters that they would be released after five days. King telephoned Harry Belafonte and asked if new contributions were available. He also contacted Clarence Jones, the SCLC's lawyer in New York City, and inquired about possible fund-raising. Given no assurances that money would be forthcoming, King considered leaving Birmingham for a northern speaking tour to collect donations. Struggling with his decision that Maundy Thursday, he remained in Room 30 of the Gaston Motel, unsure of what to do next. King did not attend the night's mass meeting.[43]

Across town in the Sixth Avenue Baptist Church near Tittusville, a tired Fred Shuttlesworth remarked, "We have seen a lot of each other lately, we have had to meet deadlines and do without food." Rebounding, he continued, "we have got a movement going here in Birmingham that's not creating hate, but going to set all men free." Shuttlesworth introduced King's father, the Reverend M. L. King Sr., who had traveled over from Atlanta to be with the civil rights workers. Daddy King said a few words and then sat down. A belligerent Abernathy announced, "We are going to break the injunction that was issued and if they get another one, we will break it too." He assured the gathering that "I'm not going to fail tomorrow and M. L. King's not going to fail tomorrow and lots more of us are not going to fail tomorrow." Reaching out to the congregation, Abernathy concluded: "We ain't afraid of white folks anymore. We are going to march tomorrow. We are going to a higher judge than Judge Jenkins. Fred Shuttlesworth and I are marching Good Friday." The charge of excitement that ran through the church as Abernathy spoke failed to reach Martin Luther King, who pondered his response to the injunction.[44]

As dawn broke in Birmingham on April 12, a weary King awaited the arrival of two dozen members of the Central Committee who would break his sleepless night with an early morning meeting in Room 30 of the Gaston Motel. As their low voices mingled in the moments before King spoke, they confronted their own crisis in Birmingham. Explaining the movement's bail bond situation, King offered two choices: he could leave Birmingham temporarily for a fund-raising trip up North, or he could get arrested for violating the injunction and hope for the best. In weighing his decision, he contrasted his promise to the jailed activists that the movement would bail them out with his promise of the past week to march on Good Friday. "A sense of doom began to pervade the room," King recalled, as a "feeling of hopelessness" overwhelmed the ACMHR-SCLC leaders.[45]

After several minutes, a thin voice cracked the uneasy silence: "Martin, this means you can't go to jail. We need money. We need a lot of money. We need it now. You are the only one who has the contacts to get it. If you go to jail, we are lost." Others spoke up. The members of the Central Committee from the traditional Negro leadership class "asked us not to continue the march in defiance of the injunction. They cited the need to obey the law and their own belief that things might get out of hand, that perhaps we needed a cooling off period, that it would be improper to violate the sanctity of the Easter season by acts of civil disobedience that might provoke violence." Identifying Gaston and Pitts as among the most vocal calling for the cessation of marches, Abernathy believed that "They had been influenced by those white men they regarded as their friends, who were merely using them to prevent us from doing what was necessary to bring the city to its knees." Soon the discussion shifted to the problems with the Birmingham campaign. Things had not gone as planned. Increasingly it appeared as if the SCLC was headed toward another Albany, another defeat.[46]

If King obeyed the court order, the movement would stall out as it did in Albany. In addition, all protests would fall prey to the delaying tactics of the courts, an outcome that would stop dead nonviolent movements that depended on momentum. Yet a deliberate violation of the law signaled a revolutionary shift for King, who had always subscribed to the NAACP's view of respecting the judicial system. The lack of bond money presented an obstacle but one the movement could overcome. As King understood, a well-publicized unjust arrest could raise money for the SCLC.

The Christian symbolism of Passion Week fit the SCLC's dilemma in Birmingham. As King confronted his own mortality, he considered the path before him. If he declined to march, he would forever be a failure. As he later observed, "What would be the verdict of the country about a man who had encouraged hundreds of people to make a stunning sacrifice and then excused himself?" Feeling the "deepest quiet" he had ever experienced, King looked out at the expressions of those gathered in the motel suite and came "face to face with himself." He felt "alone in that crowded room." In despair, King broke away to pray for an answer. As he "stood in the center of the floor" in the adjoining chamber, he recalled, "I think I was standing also in the center of all that my life had brought me to be." It was a defining moment. King had decided to violate the injunction. He changed into a new pair of dungarees and stepped back into the suite, announcing, "The path is clear to me. I've got to march." Daddy King tried to dissuade his son by emphasizing the seriousness of breaking the court order, but King responded: "If we obey it, then we are out of business." Unlike in Albany, where he had bailed out of jail rather than stay until Christmas, in Birmingham King opted for incarceration. As Andrew Young would observe, "That, I think, was the beginning of his true leadership."[47]

A small group of volunteers patiently waited for King in the Sixth Avenue Zion Hill Baptist Church near Fifteenth Street North on Good Friday, April 12, 1963. Nearly a thousand black bystanders lined the avenue toward town to watch the event. It was after noon—the hours of the Tenebrae— when Shuttlesworth, Abernathy, and King, all dressed in gray shirts and blue jeans to highlight the boycott, emerged from the sanctuary at the head of the march of fifty activists. A sense of foreboding clouded King's countenance. A smiling Abernathy tried to dispel his friend's doubts, while Shut-

240

The Reverends Fred L. Shuttlesworth, Ralph David Abernathy, and Martin Luther King Jr. violate a state court injunction by marching along Sixth Avenue North on April 12, 1963. King hoped his arrest would spark support for the campaign. During his incarceration he wrote "Letter from Birmingham Jail," the clearest statement of non-violent protest to come out of the civil rights struggle. Police Surveillance Files, BPLDAM.

tlesworth strolled along with easy assurance. As they passed, some specta-tors fell to their knees, others waited, then joined the march at a safe distance behind the first column. After a short walk, Shuttlesworth dropped back to stay out of jail so he could direct the campaign. Singing freedom songs, the procession traveled two blocks before confronting Bull Connor, who had cordoned off the turn north to city hall. In a surprise move, the integrationists turned south and then back east on Fifth Avenue. "Stop them," Connor hollered. "Don't let them go any farther." Two patrolmen on motorcycles took off and cut in front of the procession. The activists knelt in prayer near the Federal Building as the paddy wagons drove up. Grabbing them by the back of their shirts, officers tossed King and Aberna-thy into the vehicles. Police detained 54 and arrested 46, including Dr. Robert B. Fulton, a white professor at Miles College, and, to his delight, Al Hibbler. Afterward, officers also charged Shuttlesworth with contempt of court and parading without a permit. As the wagons left for jail, 35 patrol-men forced a crowd of 500 black spectators into Kelly Ingram Park.[48]

Once they were in jail, the warden quickly separated King and Aber-nathy from the others. Each placed in solitary confinement—ostensibly "for their own safety"—King, Abernathy, and later Shuttlesworth were held incommunicado. Guards had removed the mattress and linens, leaving a cold metal slat bed. A small window high in the concrete wall enabled a fraction of sunlight to briefly enter the bare cell. "Those were the longest, most frustrating and bewildering hours I have lived," King recalled. "Hav-ing no contact of any kind, I was besieged with worry. How was the move-ment faring?"[49]

Despite the arrests that afternoon, only 308 supporters assembled for Friday night's mass meeting in the Sixteenth Street Baptist Church. The Reverend Ed Gardner recruited several people to drive over to the jail and collect the activists just released, and Andrew Young led the singing of some freedom songs before the Reverend James Bevel addressed the con-gregation. Having heard about the city, Bull Connor, and Alabama's Ku Klux Klan all of his life, the Itta Bena, Mississippi, native on observing everything firsthand concluded that "Birmingham is sick." Bevel added that some people, black and white, "are so sick that they can't see what segregation has done to them." Preaching to believers, the former SNCC worker told a Christmas story of traveling through Alabama and stopping at a motel where the white owner, a Baptist deacon, "told me I could not get a room for my wife and myself, and she was pregnant just like Mary. That's why I want to be free." Energy passed through the charismatic Bevel and into the awakened crowd. "Doesn't the stupid white man know that Martin Luther King is a disciple of God. Fred Shuttlesworth does not lead this movement. God leads this movement." He steadily built a wave of emotion that began to crest. "God has the whole world in his hands. Police go around turning mad dogs loose on folks. They don't have sense enough to know that God is our leader." The enthusiastic gathering reached a cre-scendo, pushing Bevel over the top in a frenzied garble. The Christian fanatics transcended. "You can put me in jail," Bevel raved, "but you can't stop us. When the Holy Ghost gets to a man, nothing can stop him." Taking hold of himself, Bevel asked: "Aren't you tired of being walked on by white trash," directing the comment at the detectives in the audience. "Don't you want to be able to go downtown with your head up high," he asked the black audience. Walker stood up and appealed to the young people to join the protest: "Some of these students say they have got to go to school, but they will get more education in five days in the City Jail than they will get in five months in a segregated school." Gardner stepped in to close the service by asking people to march. Only seventeen volunteered.[50]

The jingle of the jailor's keys alerted Abernathy to the approach of a guard. The civil rights leader thought the movement had bailed him out. As the heavy iron door swung open, a warden said: "It's time for you to get some exercise." Abernathy followed him down the cement stairs and onto a rooftop prison yard enclosed by chain link and barbed wire. Behind him another door opened and out stepped a grinning King: "Hello, Ralph." The guard called for silence. As the two best friends paced the plain square, snatches of conversation passed between them. "You in a cell alone?" King asked. "You talked to anyone from the staff?" Abernathy replied. Later Saturday afternoon, April 13, attorneys made contact with King and Abernathy, yet the jailors hindered King's access to a telephone. In response, Walker encouraged Coretta Scott King to telephone the president and attorney general. On Easter King's wife called the White House but failed to reach anyone, so the operator connected her to Pierre Salinger, the president's press secretary, who was vacationing with the Kennedys in Florida. She gave him a message for the president expressing her concern over the safety of her husband. Within the hour Attorney General Robert Kennedy telephoned back promising to make inquiries into Birmingham jail.[51]

Also on Saturday, while Walker met with students to plan kneel-ins on Easter at prominent white churches downtown, six activists picketed the suburban Atlantic Mills Shopping Center on the northside of town. When they staged a stand-in at a fast-food window, officers arrested them for "trespass after warning." Police picked up six other black youths near city hall who said that they were from Ohio. Already the movement had resorted to the secondary and tertiary targets, an unexpected response that resulted from the closing of lunch counters by the department stores. The fact that Walker had not foreseen such a move reflected a weakness in his strategy.[52]

Buried in the back of Saturday morning's *Post-Herald* was an article about a statement by eight influential clergymen calling the ACMHR-SCLC campaign "unwise and untimely." As leaders of Birmingham's Judaeo-Christian community, the clerics thought of themselves as moderates, having issued a statement in January responding to Governor Wallace's inflammatory inaugural address by appealing to "law and order and common sense." The clergymen—Episcopal bishops C. C. J. Carpenter and George M. Murray, Rabbi Milton L. Grafman, Catholic bishop Joseph A. Durick, Methodist bishops Paul Hardin and Nolan B. Harmon, Presbyterian moderator Edward V. Ramage, and the Reverend Earl Stallings of First Baptist Church—headed their respective denominations in the state and spoke for thousands of white Christians in the area.[53]

The statement bemoaned the "series of demonstrations by some of our Negro citizens directed and led in part by outsiders." It pointed out that "such actions as incite to hatred and violence, however technically peaceful actions may be, have not contributed to the resolution of our local problems." After commending local law enforcement, the statement urged the black community "to withdraw support from these demonstrations, and to unite locally in working peacefully for a better Birmingham. When rights are consistently denied, a cause should be pressed in the courts and in negotiations among local leaders." For the white community, the clergymen legitimated the traditional Negro leadership class: "We agree rather with certain local Negro leadership which has called for honest and open negotiations of racial issues in our area. And we believe this kind of facing of issues can best be accomplished by citizens of our town metropolitan area, white and Negro, meeting with their knowledge and experience of the local situation." With this clarion call for negotiations, the white "moderates" set the parameters of debate by refusing to meet with civil rights "outsiders."[54]

At some point over the weekend, King received the published opinion of the eight clergymen and began to draft a reply by writing on the margins of the newspaper. His notes spilled over onto toilet tissue and then scraps of paper provided by a black trusty. During the week of his imprisonment, movement lawyers took early versions out for typing and editing and left him a legal pad on which to compose. In the tradition of Emile Zola's "J'Accuse," King's public letter stands in modern literature as a beautifully crafted statement on the obligation of all moral men to support the rights of the oppressed.[55]

Cast in the form of a Pauline epistle, King used religious metaphor to confront and then refute the arguments of the eight clergymen while addressing a larger audience. By comparing himself to Saint Paul, King dismissed the criticism of "outside agitator," adopting instead the message of the missionary. Then, as at the mass meeting on the first night of the campaign, he recounted the four steps of nonviolence—proof of injustice, negotiation, self-purification, and direct action—while regretting that the movement had no alternative but to take the struggle to the streets. With subtlety, he turned the argument on the clergymen as he justified direct action. Citing Saint Augustine, Saint Thomas Aquinas, and Judaeo-Christian tradition, King argued that all men had a moral obligation to violate unjust laws. He expressed his disappointment with the leaders of the white church, whom he believed to be the movement's natural allies, for failing to "see the justice of our cause and, with deep moral concern . . . serve as the channel through which our just grievances could reach the power structure." Having put the eight clergymen on the defensive, he then suggested that they were as bad as, if not worse than, the "rabid segregationist." King said he had "almost reached the regrettable conclusion that the Negro's great stumbling block in his stride toward freedom is not the White Citizen's Counciler or the Ku Klux Klanner, but the white moderate, who is more devoted to 'order' than to justice." For three centuries the Negro had waited for justice, but "this 'Wait' has almost always meant 'Never.'" As Shuttlesworth's experiences in Birmingham had proven that "privileged groups seldom give up their privileges voluntarily," the movement had little alternative but "to create such a crisis and foster such a tension [so] that a community which has constantly refused to negotiate is forced to confront the issue." That issue—racial discrimination— prevented black people from experiencing the American Dream.[56]

Tightly woven and rhetorically appealing, the "Letter" operated on several levels as it addressed not only the critics of the Birmingham campaign but the nation's consciousness as well. Logically sound, King's sermon refuted the position of the eight clergymen and demanded that they—and the lay reader—act on the truths he presented. With the "Letter from Birmingham Jail," King justified nonviolent direct action while expressing the righteousness of the civil rights movement. Released to the press on April 18, 1963, the initial publication of the letter made little impression and was not received by the eight clergymen in the spirit in which it was intended. On reading it, Episcopal bishop Carpenter said: "This is what you get when you try to do something. You get it from both sides." Feeling victimized by King's response, Rabbi Grafman remarked, "These eight men were put in a position of looking like bigots" when "they were all moderates or liberals."[57]

A dark-suited Reverend Andrew Young and four brightly dressed and bonneted black women attended Easter services on April 14 at the white First Baptist Church downtown. Unlike at kneel-ins held elsewhere in Birmingham that morning, ushers allowed the integrationists to enter the sanctuary and sit halfway down the aisle in a specially reserved pew. However, church officials refused to shake hands or accept a contribution offered by Young. Worshipping with the white congregation, the black activists sang "Christ the Lord Is Risen Today." After the service several church members warmly greeted the African Americans, as did the pastor, Dr. Earl Stallings, one of the eight clergymen who issued the statement calling the demonstrations "untimely." Shortly after the *Brown* decision in 1954, First Baptist had adopted a policy that "no one would be denied the privilege of worship because of race, color, or national origin." When the kneel-in occurred in 1963, Deacon Ollie Blan recalled, "They [the black activists] wanted to make their showing . . . they weren't interested in becoming members. They just wanted to do that for publicity. We all knew that." A regular since 1959, Blan had never seen a black person attempt to worship at First Baptist before. Kneel-ins also occurred at First Presbyterian Church, where two black women sat in the front row and found it a "lovely service"; but at Sixth Avenue Presbyterian, First Christian, and Central Church of Christ, ushers denied entrance to the integrationists.[58]

A sympathy march in support of the jailed trio—King, Abernathy, and Shuttlesworth—ended in violence Sunday afternoon. At first, it appeared to be a civil rights variation of the Easter parade with black people celebrating the resurrection and the coming of freedom. Movement music spilled out of Thirgood CME Church, moving the crowd of five hundred outside the building to clap their hands and sway to the rhythm. Infectious joy filled the air. Singing "We Shall Overcome," a black robed vanguard—led by A. D. King, Nelson H. Smith, and John Thomas Porter—emerged from the church. Frank Dukes, the former Miles College student, joined them at the head of the procession as it traveled down Eleventh Street toward Southside Jail, where the city held the integrationists. To intercept the marchers Bull Connor had blocked Fifth Avenue, but to avoid arrest the procession turned into an alley that let onto Sixth Avenue. Police reserves arrived and stopped the demonstration. A delay prevented the paddy wagons from pulling up to the scene, enabling the black onlookers—now numbering from 1,500 to 2,000—to congregate around the officers and arrested activists. Angered by the interference with the march, bystanders shouted at police and, once the wagons left the area, hurled rocks at the patrolmen, smashing the windshield of a motorcycle. People overflowed the surrounding sidewalks, and when officers attempted to arrest a screaming black woman, the crowd threw more objects. With raised billy clubs, policemen turned on the nonmovement participants in the protest. A black youth tried to run away, but officers clubbed him to the street. Other policemen waded into the mob, swinging night sticks in the drive to break up the gathering. The black bystanders dispersed when officers arrested three more people, bringing the total for the day to twenty-six. Bull Connor had deployed a force of about fifty patrolmen. The police dogs were in the area on standby, but he declined to call out the infamous canine corps. In its coverage of the incident, the *New York Times* emphasized the black violence.[59]

Birmingham acquired two municipal governments on Monday, April 15, 1963, when probate judge J. Paul Meeks swore in Mayor Albert Boutwell and nine city council members on the east steps of city hall. Four hundred spectators—including a sprinkling of ACMHR-SCLC activists—watched the ceremony. Addressing his comments to King and Shuttlesworth, Boutwell stated: "Whatever our short-comings may be, they are our own local problems and we shall resolve them by local effort and local unity." Though refusing to "submit to the intimidations of pressure or to the dictates of interference," he acknowledged the "magnitude" of the city's problems. In an admission of the damaging negative publicity created by the ACMHR-SCLC campaign, Boutwell promised to project a "true and positive picture" of Birmingham to the rest of the nation.[60]

Upstairs in city hall, Mayor Art Hanes and Commissioners Jabo Waggoner and Bull Connor refused to leave office, claiming the right to fulfill their original terms until they expired in 1965. A case filed on behalf of the commissioners by the law firm of former state senator James A. Simpson challenged the legality of the enabling legislation adopted by referendum with the new government in November 1962. Boutwell petitioned state circuit court to remove the city commissioners. Judge J. Edgar Bowron set a hearing for Tuesday week, and both sides anticipated an appeal to the Alabama Supreme Court. After an initial disagreement over meeting times in the city hall conference room, Hanes and Boutwell worked out a solution that enabled both governments to operate in the meantime. Following custom, the commission held its meeting at ten on Tuesday morning, and after it adjourned the new mayor convened the city council. Through the operations of the civil service, both municipal governments approved the same business down to signing the same checks.[61]

As Boutwell gave his inaugural address, King and more than fifty activists were arraigned in recorder's court for parading without a permit. Later in the day, police arrested nine integrationists when they conducted sit-ins in two downtown stores. In addition, Justice Department officials appealed to movement leaders to postpone further demonstrations until after Boutwell and the city council held office uncontested. In Hartford, Connecticut, about fifty college students and ministers stood on the capitol lawn in a prayer vigil "to show resentment against the absence of justice in Birmingham." The national outrage over events in the city had just begun.[62]

Late Monday afternoon, President Kennedy responded to Coretta Scott King's entreaties. From the family compound in Palm Beach, he telephoned her to explain that he had sent FBI agents to the Birmingham jail to check on the condition of her husband. He also mentioned that King would soon contact her. Under similar circumstances in 1960, Kennedy had telephoned her and consequently received black political support. Forty minutes after Kennedy hung up, King called from jail. On learning that the president had personally telephoned his wife, he told her to "let Wyatt know" so the ACMHR-SCLC could capitalize on Kennedy's concern. After their initial conversation about health and well-being, the Kings discussed the limited press coverage received by the Birmingham campaign.[63]

President Kennedy's concern about King neither signified his administration's support for the present campaign nor promised future action on behalf of the civil rights movement, yet ACMHR-SCLC staff members allowed the call to influence their actions. Enamored with the youthful chief executive and his administration, Wyatt Tee Walker shifted the focus of the movement to appeal to the interests of the Justice Department. He thus announced the "second phase" of the campaign: a voter registration drive. At Monday night's mass meeting, Walker asked all "non-registered voters to stand up and come forward." Staffers took down the names, addresses, and telephone numbers of one hundred people. Walker asked them to report to a meeting where they would be instructed on how to fill out the proper forms and answer anticipated oral questions in preparation of a march on the registrar's office. At the time, only 11,000 to 12,000 African Americans out of a black population of nearly 150,000 could vote in Jefferson County. Although the ACMHR-SCLC apparently believed that the Justice Department would intervene on behalf of African Americans denied the vote, the return to voting rights signified the desperation of the strategists.[64]

The selective buying campaign was failing. Two nights before, Andrew Young had complained to the people in the mass meeting: "We have to talk more whatever happens. We must call 10 people each and tell them what is going to happen tomorrow (referring to Sunday)." Young described his Friday survey of five downtown department stores where he saw nine black shoppers. "Today [Saturday, April 13, 1963] there were more. I want all of you to get on the phone and tell your people the campaign is still on."

Walker added that during his survey of nine stores at Atlantic Mills on Saturday, he saw sixty-six black people shopping. Wednesday's edition of the Negro *Birmingham World* described the boycott as "meeting with less success." The paper noted, "Integrationists sent out spotters Saturday afternoon to see how the 'selective buying' campaign was proceeding, and got back word it apparently was proving unsuccessful."[65]

Approximately 150 black people attended a voter registration clinic in the basement of Sixteenth Street Baptist Church on Wednesday, April 17, 1963. Entering the building, police chief Jamie Moore interrupted the lesson: "I don't have anything against your registering to vote. You know that. But if you march out of here as a parade you will be in violation of a city ordinance and we will take necessary action to keep you from violating the law." Earlier in the morning, Shuttlesworth had sent Moore and Mayor Hanes telegrams requesting "police protection" for the group as it marched to the Jefferson County Courthouse to register to vote. Shortly after Moore left, the Reverend Henry Crawford headed a procession of 29 demonstrators out of the church. Ten turned back after walking a block. Officers moved in and arrested Crawford, two black men, and 14 black women for parading without a permit before a crowd of 400 in Kelly Ingram Park. Later in the day, patrolmen picked up 8 activists for trespassing when they picketed the local offices of the Department of Justice in the 2121 Building. The shift to voter registration occurred because "this is the only way we can get the Justice Department in on this thing," according to Andrew Young. He added, "If we get tangled up in this, they can step in." The change in strategy revealed the movement's fluidity, but it also showed that the ACMHR-SCLC had drifted away from its original program.[66]

Lawyers for the ACMHR-SCLC campaign filed suit in federal court seeking a temporary restraining order prohibiting Bull Connor and other city officials from arresting the demonstrators. The court action would enjoin the police from "pursuing and continuing to pursue a policy" of "denying to Negro citizens the right to peacefully protest state-enforced racial segregation in the city of Birmingham." Filed by local black attorneys Arthur Shores and Orzell Billingsley and NAACP New York lawyers Jack Greenberg, Norman C. Amaker, and Leroy Clark, the suit based its petition on violations of the First, Fourteenth, and Fifteenth Amendments to the U.S. Constitution. Earlier, Amaker with Shores, Billingsley, and the SCLC's New York attorney Clarence Jones attempted to transfer 37 integrationists from recorder's court to federal district court following a prior move by William Kunstler. With more than 300 activists in jail or released

249

on $300 bonds, the court costs of the campaign had increased considerably. The legal arm of the SCLC, the Gandhi Society, could no longer financially support the movement, and consequently, the NAACP Legal Defense Fund, Inc., had offered its assistance. Moments before ACMHR-SCLC attorneys filed the suit, Walker announced that the civil rights movement would bail King and Abernathy out on Saturday.[67]

The campaign had sputtered along during the week King and Abernathy sat in jail, and their arrests had not galvanized the black community behind the movement as expected. The dedication of the Christian fanatics in the ACMHR who willingly submitted to arrest and the angry response of black spectators that made sensational type for the media had so far prevented the protest from collapsing. Indeed, staff workers struggled to keep the campaign alive. The "slackening of demonstrations" reported in the *New York Times* and the decision of some store managers not to press charges during sit-ins underscored the dwindling interest in the campaign. The voter registration drive almost threatened to put the fire out.[68]

The white community recognized the movement's difficulties. The *Post-Herald* observed that "for the agitators, things are going awry." Quoting an editorial, which originally ran in the *Memphis Commercial Appeal*, comparing the Birmingham campaign with simultaneous demonstrations in Greenwood, Mississippi, the newspaper noted: "The failure of the marchers to incite rioting by white opponents has weakened their own cause. This time national publicity has not helped them."[69]

While leaving the defense of segregation up to Bull Connor, white Birmingham responded to the ACMHR-SCLC campaign in different ways. Over-the-mountain housewives avoided shopping downtown out of fear of the demonstrations, a consequence that unintentionally increased the damage of the boycott. White office workers acted as if nothing out of the ordinary was happening. At Boutwell's inauguration, white supremacists boasting buttons printed with "I like Art, Bull and Jabo" distributed handbills that blamed "New York Communist Jews" for masterminding the demonstrations. In a letter to the editor Thomas T. Coley, a turbo operator at TCI's Ensley Steel Works, wrote: "Can't the local Negroes understand that all they have to do is wait a little longer? Then certain white businessmen, politicians and clergymen with the help of our daily local newspapers, will hand them, on a silver platter, more than could ever be gained by marches, sit-ins and kneel-ins." In a hearing over a fatal stabbing during a fight by black gang members, county judge Elias C. Watson lectured his black audience: "It would be well for the people who are here trying to uplift the colored people of this area to have been there that night to see the spectacle that took place." He continued: "Your lives are as dear as you want to make them. . . . If you think it's worth about 15 cents it makes other people feel life is that cheap, too." Despite vocal and printed criticism, white people—especially Birmingham's vigilantes—did not take action against the ACMHR-SCLC campaign. Boutwell recognized and commended this fact: "The white community, which in other places and times, have [sic] reacted in open violence to the things we have experienced here, has demonstrated a public and private restraint that I am proud of."[70]

Aware of the continuing troubles confronted by the movement and in order to invigorate the campaign, King and Abernathy decided to leave Birmingham jail on Saturday, April 20. "Lest you think we have joined the Castro brigade," Abernathy quipped to reporters, stroking his eight-day-old beard, "they took our shaving equipment from us and only brought it back this morning when they urged us to shave." King explained that the ACMHR-SCLC posted bond so he and Abernathy "could consult over the weekend with members of the Strategy Committee." Movement leaders wanted King to direct "the strategy for future actions in face of the possible arrest of many leaders next week on contempt of court citations." They depended on him to keep the campaign from stalling out.[71]

Juveniles joined the demonstrations designed to greet the Saturday release of King and Abernathy. Outside Pizitz, policemen detained seven pickets who, citing the U.S. Constitution, refused to give their names. Officers picked up fifty protesters but arrested only fifteen, transferring those under eighteen from the jail to the juvenile detention home. When waitresses again refused to serve African Americans at Britling Cafeteria, nine integrationists sat on the floor in protest and were charged with "blocking an aisle." After placards appeared at Atlantic Mills Shopping Center and Tillman-Levenson, officers detained eleven additional people. Law enforcement agents refused to release information on the youths held in custody, but the movement's increased reliance on young people signified not only the depletion of ACMHR resources but also the important cultivation of local black students by staff members. In response to King's appeal from jail, sympathy protests occurred against national chain stores with segregated branches in Birmingham on Saturday as the Congress of Racial Equality and other civil rights organizations in New York City and elsewhere across the country mobilized thousands of volunteers to picket S. H. Kress, H. L. Green, J. J. Newberry, and F. W. Woolworth.[72]

Released on bond, King and Abernathy tried to hold a press conference in the street near Southside Jail before leaving the city to preach in their Atlanta churches on Sunday. When officers intervened, the two moved to the A. G. Gaston Building, where King described his imprisonment and called his jailors "courteous." He then "decried reports of disunity within the black community." Referring to the limited biracial negotiations, Abernathy said the movement was "not at all satisfied with the communications that are going on at this time." While the two sat in solitary, Sidney Smyer had broken off negotiations after a meeting on April 16 because of the confusion surrounding Birmingham's municipal government. Unwilling to grant any of the movement's demands—especially considering the nonviolent coercion of the demonstrations—the white progressive businessmen used Connor's control over the city as an excuse to cancel the discussions.[73]

"We also are not satisfied with the coverage that is being given us in the local press," Abernathy added. "They never have printed what it is that we are demanding." Indeed, the *Birmingham News* and *Post-Herald* ran short stories hidden in the back pages. Whereas the *Post-Herald*'s coverage tended to be more factual, the *News* initially ran the Associated Press wire rather than cover the event, and when reporters were assigned, they usually wrote defensive articles. The *Birmingham World* remained hostile to the civil rights campaign, and its editor, Emory O. Jackson, routinely offered alternatives to the leadership of Shuttlesworth and King. As a result of the local newspapers' reportage, Birmingham residents remained sadly misinformed about the campaign.[74]

Monday morning, April 22, 1963, began a week spent working in the courts as the leaders of the ACMHR-SCLC appeared before state circuit court judge William A. Jenkins, who had issued the temporary restraining order prohibiting demonstrations. Initiating proceedings against King, Shuttlesworth, and thirteen other ministers, Jenkins postponed the cases of thirty-eight individuals and the ACMHR and SCLC until May 6. He then overruled the legal maneuverings made on behalf of civil rights by Arthur Shores and NAACP lawyers Amaker, Greenberg, Clark, and Constance Baker Motley. Earlier, the movement's attorneys had listed 103 witnesses for the defense, including Governor Wallace, former governor John Patterson, the city commissioners, and every judge in Jefferson County.[75]

Judge Jenkins identified two questions before the court: first, did the defendants receive the injunction, and, second, "did they willfully and knowingly violate the April 10 order banning racial parades, kneel-ins, sit-ins and similar activities?" Citing the vigilante violence during the Freedom Rides in 1961, the city defended its request for the injunction by claim-

252

ing that the demonstrations had created a dangerous climate in which "racial clashes would have occurred." The prosecution presented a *Post-Herald* reporter brained by a rock during the near-riot Easter afternoon. Another witness, state investigator Willie B. Painter, testified that Walker and Bernard Lee of the SCLC had bragged that the civil rights movement had enough supporters to "create a revolution." On cross-examination, Walker explained that he did not mean "revolution" as violent overthrow. As legal demands tied up ACMHR-SCLC leaders, the campaign saw only three women and two men protesting segregation on Monday. Arrested at Atlantic Mills Shopping Center, they joined the more than three hundred other black activists jailed over the past three weeks.[76]

Courtroom action on Tuesday, April 23, influenced the movement on three fronts. Judge J. Edgar Bowron found Boutwell and the nine-member city council the legitimate government of Birmingham and ordered the commissioners to desist their "usurpation" of power. Refusing to give up, Bull Connor and his supporters among the Big Mules appealed the decision to the Alabama Supreme Court. In U.S. district court, Judge Clarence W. Allgood—a Kennedy appointee—delivered a defeat to movement attorneys when he refused to transfer 286 cases from city recorder's court to federal court, as petitioned by William Kunstler and Arthur Shores. Late Monday, Kunstler had filed a motion requesting that the court rule unconstitutional the five ordinances under which police had arrested the integrationists. Kunstler made the move to justify his request for the caseload transfer to federal court, arguing that the defendants could not receive a fair trial under the present laws and in the local courts. Rejecting the movement's request that he enjoin the city commission from arresting demonstrators, Allgood dismissed the motions and, explaining that he could "breathe no life" into the federal criminal code from Reconstruction cited by Kunstler, remanded the defendants back to recorder's court so the cases could be "settled here and now." Expressing his "extreme confidence" in the legal system, Allgood stated that the black defendants would receive "a fair trial." In circuit court, Judge W. A. Jenkins convened a second day of testimony on the contempt-of-court hearing against King, Shuttlesworth, and nine other ministers. Movement lawyers persuaded the court to drop charges against four defendants for lack of evidence linking them to a violation of the injunction. An effort to likewise dismiss proceedings against four others failed. The legal efforts showed ACMHR-SCLC leaders trying to evade conviction after deliberately violating the injunction—a contradictory action considering King's moral high ground of accepting punishment for breaking unjust laws. Although upholding city objections to questions concerning ordinances on parades, Judge Jenkins allowed movement attorney Jack Greenberg to read into the record that despite Shuttlesworth's telegram to Connor, the city commission had never granted the movement a parade permit. That morning policemen had halted two separate demonstrations and detained thirteen activists, eight of whom were arrested for parading without a permit. That night, vigilantes near Attalla, Alabama, shot to death William L. Moore, a white postman from Baltimore, Maryland, who was making a lone trek to Mississippi to encourage integration.[77]

Jenkins heard closing arguments in the contempt-of-court trial late on Wednesday, April 24, 1963. Movement leaders reiterated their defense as one of freedom of speech and assembly. "The respondents are saying that they are protesting Alabama and Birmingham's policy of segregation," Constance Baker Motley claimed. "They are not openly defying this court." Assistant city attorney Early McBee argued otherwise, saying that the movement deliberately violated the law and that "obedience to the law is a must." Taking the case under advisement, Jenkins adjourned court until Friday morning.[78]

During the mass meeting following Wednesday's day in court, a capacity crowed packed St. James Baptist Church. Fire chief Aaron Rosenfeld made civil rights officials clear people out of the aisles. The three policemen sent by Bull Connor to spy on the movement stepped outside to confer with the fire marshal. When they returned, activists had taken their seats. Shuttlesworth chortled: "Mr. Detective, I don't know where you going to sit; but if you going to stand, then I'm going to call all these other people back." The congregation laughed as the detectives took positions just beyond the front door.[79]

For several days, SCLC staff members James Bevel, Bernard Lee, and Ike Reynolds had worked with students to involve them in the movement. They had recruited Andrew Marrisett and James Orange from Birmingham's streets. Dorothy Cotton and Andrew Young helped coordinate after-school rallies such as the one scheduled for 4:30 P.M. on Thursday in Sixth Avenue Baptist Church, where they, as Marrisett recalled, conducted workshops to help the students understand "what they were marching for" and "why." Some junior and high school principals—members of the traditional Negro leadership class—suspended the young people who participated in the demonstrations. One activist suggested that the movement "picket the high school." Staff members increasingly turned to youngsters in their search for volunteers.[80]

ANOTHER ALBANY?

The campaign appeared to be on the verge of collapse. Detectives reported that King and Calvin Woods "asked and begged for about 40 minutes trying to get volunteers to go to jail. They finally got about 20. Some were as young as eight or nine years old." People began to go home before the leaders adjourned the mass meeting, angering Abernathy, who jumped to his feet and snapped: "I don't want another person to get up to leave. We are going to operate this meeting right." Attorney Kunstler recalled: "The demonstrations, which had begun to flag a week earlier, reached rock bottom. At a mass meeting a few nights later, I watched in dismay as both King and Ralph Abernathy exhorted a packed church for almost an hour in order to persuade a dozen people to volunteer to go to jail."[81]

Demonstrations continued but seemed to lose their punch. On Wednesday a handful of integrationists—including a white female student from Birmingham-Southern College—had conducted a sit-in at Woolworth's. Since the beginning of the campaign, the local manager of the national chain had kept the lunch counter closed rather than integrate it, so when the activists entered the store, they sat down in an empty dinette. Many other stores also closed their lunch counters and ignored the protesters. Managers did not even bother to call the police. Officers did step in and arrest pickets who paraded without permits because no violation of the segregation ordinances occurred. Nevertheless, the steady trickle of integrationists willing to go to jail remained just that, a trickle, despite the best efforts of King and other movement leaders.[82]

Whether the SCLC realized it or not, the movement faced a tactical contradiction. After the press found the original boycott too boring to cover, the ACMHR-SCLC leaders altered their campaign strategy to include marches and other forms of direct action. Once King had committed the campaign to sensational protests staged to interest the media, the new events rapidly depleted its resources; this made it harder to sustain a war of attrition against the merchants. In effect, the movement had tried to have it both ways. Unfortunately, local resources—human and financial—were limited. Or so it seemed.

Several different meetings occurred on Thursday, April 25, that had significance for racial problems in Birmingham. Attorney General Robert Kennedy traveled to Montgomery to appraise Governor Wallace's resistance to the upcoming federal attempt to desegregate the University of Alabama. Burke Marshall attended the tense session that also briefly touched on the ACMHR-SCLC campaign. Complaining that his hard work attracting new industry to the state benefited black people too, Wallace criticized civil rights leaders for not having "industrial development committees" and the federal government for dismantling the race wage: "All this agitation, and all this business of this Martin Luther King, who is a phoney and a fraud, marching and going to jail and all that. . . . It is a commercial venture. Why don't they organize an industrial development committee . . . But we don't get a bit of help from them." Kennedy chipped in: "You know, we made a statement about the disturbances at Birmingham, Alabama, and that didn't stop them." Wallace counseled: "If you as Attorney General say this Martin Luther King is doing things he should not do, and is advocating lawlessness, and you call upon him to obey the law like anyone else, and be emphatic about it, but don't make an easy little statement, and then the President talks to Mrs. King over the telephone, and all those kind of things." The icily polite exchange, set up to avoid another Ole Miss, left at loggerheads state and federal policies on civil rights. In Birmingham, Sid Smyer, accompanied by the young white lawyers Dave Vann and Erskine Smith, approached the black businessmen about renewing negotiations. King met with his white clerical critics, two of whom relentlessly denounced the outsiders. "We have to be patient with them," King said later at a mass meeting, "they are all pitiful. They think we outsiders are communists."[83]

256

In a surprise development on Friday morning, April 26, Judge Jenkins handed down light sentences to the eleven black ministers charged with contempt of court for violating the injunction against demonstrations. The bench criticized the use of the church "to encourage and incite others" and admonished the "defendants to consider carefully their course of conduct in the future." Issuing a twenty-day stay, Jenkins allowed the civil rights leaders to remain free on bond pending appeal. Pleased by the turn of events, Greenberg commended Jenkins for conducting the hearing in a fair and impartial manner. He then announced that the movement would appeal to the Alabama Supreme Court and, if necessary, to the U.S. Supreme Court. King, Shuttlesworth, and the other integrationists received sentences of five days in jail and $50 fines.[84]

Although "just itching to go to jail," Shuttlesworth said he had been turned "aloose" because "Judge Jenkins was afraid to put them in jail." Had he done so, "there would have been a big march." From the looks of the nearly vacant balcony and empty spillover seats in the next door auditorium at Sixth Avenue Baptist Church, Shuttlesworth's exhortation was hot air. Nevertheless, he warmed up the faithful. "Glad to see the crushed spirits lifted," he said. A wistful King informed the gathering, "We are at the point now where the power structure realizes we are serious." He mentioned the meetings with white people and the national protests held in sympathy with the Birmingham campaign. "If we put on the brakes now, we will disappoint everyone everywhere." Abernathy reminded the young people of the Saturday morning rally but admitted, "We are not going to walk tomorrow." Instead, "We will close Ullman and Parker and the rest of the [Negro] high schools" one day next week. His promise sounded like an idle threat.[85]

CHAPTER EIGHT

The Children's Crusade

Just as the spring demonstrations appeared to collapse for want of volunteers, civil rights activists discovered an untapped resource with potential to tip the scale on behalf of the movement. For five weeks the Alabama Christian Movement for Human Rights and the Southern Christian Leadership Conference had waged a joint campaign against racial discrimination in an attempt to force a resolution of Birmingham's long-standing crisis in race relations. During April 1963 more than three hundred integrationists from the ACMHR and black student associations had faced arrest after participating in sit-ins at downtown lunch counters, picketing in department stores, and marching in illegal parades. Yet the local movement had given all it had and could offer little more. The image of Martin Luther King had failed to attract the needed new blood to keep the campaign in the public's eye. A divided black community further complicated matters as the traditional Negro leadership class publicly repudiated the authority of King and Fred Shuttlesworth. Nearly everything pointed to another Albany, another failure. As interest in Birmingham waned, ACMHR-SCLC staff struggled to keep the movement alive.

Birmingham's traditional Negro leadership class organized an accommodationist movement to counter the ACMHR-SCLC. On Sunday, April 28, 1963, while civil rights activists conducted kneel-ins at thirty-nine metropolitan churches,[1] the black elite gathered to pay tribute to the Reverend J. L. Ware. At the afternoon service in the Metropolitan African Methodist Episcopal Zion Church, the Reverend G. W. McMurray—the same pastor who, in June 1956, spoke out against the organization of the ACMHR— recognized the work of Ware, attorney W. L. Williams Jr., and Bernice C. Johnson. Ware and Williams had lost runoff elections in early 1963 as candidates for the city council. Johnson, an associate of Deenie Drew's in the Jefferson County Voters League, operated registration seminars. Billed as a "mass meeting" to compete with the ACMHR-SCLC campaign, the program concluded a two-day conference of the Alabama State Coordinating Association for Registration and Voting, an organization headed by former NAACP chapter president W. C. Patton and attorney Orzell Billingsley Jr. Bourgeois in orientation, the group held a "get-the-ballot rally" in the Colored Masonic Temple and black YMCA, facilities that were unavailable to the civil rights movement.[2]

Throughout April the city's black newspaper, the *Birmingham World*, consistently ignored the ACMHR-SCLC campaign and projected Ware as an alternative black leader to Reverend Shuttlesworth. An old champion of returning black veterans, Ware had long since lost his radicalism. Nonetheless, he promoted civic responsibility among African Americans through his position as head of the local Baptist Ministers Conference and as a leader in the National Baptist Convention—the organization that had previously fought with Martin Luther King. Editor Emory O. Jackson criticized Shuttlesworth and King for not having "contributed anything to the mass voter-registration campaign which was already under way when the march-for-freedom personalities came to Birmingham. The successful campaign for new voters . . . has been on the scene for approximately seven years or more stimulating voter-registration. The local voter-registration leadership has not promoted parades, marches and propaganda handouts." As Jackson explained to his friend Anne G. Rutledge, "The upside-downers are in the city and I have had to try to keep up with their activities both day and night. I am doing only a little writing but lots of observing. This is a hard struggle." Jackson confessed: "It seems that I have always been in need of an inspiration and somehow managed to find it—working in the NAACP, the struggle for civil rights and a single friendship. NAACP is no longer active and I am no longer involved in civil rights. In a way I am no longer either." Sparse coverage in the *World* verified his sad comment. Although many middle-class Negroes refused to associate with integrationists, some black professionals signed newspaper ads calling on the city to create a biracial committee and adopt other reforms that mirrored the ACMHR objectives. Practicing the politics of accommodation, the traditional Negro leadership class pitched its Uncle Tomish appeal to the white power structure in an effort to win recognition as the "legitimate" leaders of black Birmingham.[3]

On Monday, April 29, King convened an emergency meeting of the ACMHR-SCLC Central Committee to discuss the impending collapse of the Birmingham campaign. Two deficiencies—the lack of volunteers and the lack of sensation—suggested that the movement had about run its course. King centered his concern on publicity: "You know, we've got to get something going. The press is leaving, we've got to get going." The Reverend John Thomas Porter recalled, "I couldn't believe my ears to hear him say that we need the press." King repeated, "We've got to pick up everything, because the press is leaving." Indeed, the media had lost interest as the dwindling demonstrations dragged on. Nothing on the Birmingham movement had appeared on the front page of the *New York Times* in two weeks. A consensus quickly emerged among the ACMHR-SCLC staff: something must be done to breathe new life into the campaign.[4]

Solving the problem of recruits was the first step toward saving the campaign. The nine black students arrested on Saturday, April 27, had been the last volunteers to go to jail. As the SCLC executive director and strategist for the campaign, the Reverend Wyatt Tee Walker, impersonally recalled: "We needed more troops. We had run out of troops. We had scraped the bottom of the barrel of adults who could go [to jail]." If the ACMHR-SCLC staff found new volunteers, it could stage spectacular demonstrations to attract the media. James Bevel and Ike Reynolds encouraged the campaign to recruit schoolchildren. Increasingly, juveniles had participated in the campaign as pickets and in sit-ins. Yet King had rejected their wholesale adoption into the ranks of the civil rights movement. Members of the ACMHR-SCLC Central Committee such as Negro entrepreneur A. G. Gaston angrily opposed the idea of schoolchildren marching against the police force of Public Safety Commissioner Bull Connor. Nevertheless, Bevel and Reynolds persisted. Though not endorsing a march by schoolchildren, King agreed that the staff could hold a student meeting at noon on Thursday.[5]

Over the past week, the ACMHR-SCLC staff had mobilized a large force of black high school students willing to demonstrate. Walker later attributed the success of the effort to the charismatic Bevel, who understood the youths instinctively. Credit should also go to Dorothy Cotton, Bernard Lee, Andrew Young, and Reynolds. Bevel recognized that the recruitment problems derived from the alienation experienced by adults in the urban setting. Consequently, he enlisted prom queens and athletic stars to campaign for the movement. As he explained, "The black community as a whole did not have that kind of cohesion or camaraderie. But the students, they had a community they'd been in since elementary school, so they had bonded quite well." Bevel figured that the arrest of one would directly affect another because of their relationships as classmates. He also noted that unlike their parents, students had no financial obligations and no jobs to go to. The schoolchildren offered the movement enthusiastic volunteers.[6]

In a make-it-or-break-it gamble, leaders banked the ACMHR-SCLC campaign on the proposed Thursday march of youngsters. By Monday afternoon, April 29, staffers had blanketed Ullman, Parker, and other black high schools with hundreds of leaflets urging students to appear at Sixteenth Street Baptist Church by noon on Thursday regardless of opposition by teachers, principals, or parents. Yet at the mass meeting on Monday night, nothing was reported about youth participation except plans for two student rallies after school the next day.[7]

Addressing the crowd assembled in St. Luke's African Methodist Episcopal Church for the mass meeting on Monday night, King reaffirmed the SCLC's reasons for supporting the Alabama Christian Movement for Human Rights in the campaign: "I am committed to Birmingham. When I came here 27 days ago I made it clear that I would be with you until we gained our victory." He noted that he could not make a scheduled appearance in Houston because "what's happening in Birmingham is the most important and decisive thing in the world today." King returned to the theme of commitment: "We will be here to help and assist you." Mentioning his meeting the week before with white clergymen, he said: "I told them that when the lunch counters and rest rooms were integrated downtown and Negro clerks were hired in the department stores and when the parks were open, then we would leave." He added, "this would make

Birmingham a magic city, instead of a tragic city." Hitting the boycott, King reminded the faithful: "We got to keep it up and not go back to town until they treat us like a person with dignity. We intend to put justice in business. We have got to bring pressure to bear on the economic structure of Birmingham." He ended on a note of nonviolence: "Now leave those blades at home." The next day King left town; he planned to attend the newly integrated Metropolitan Opera in Atlanta and then travel on to Memphis for the SCLC board meeting.[8]

Working with their contacts in the high schools, Bevel, Reynolds, Cotton, and Young spent the next two days preparing for the Thursday march. At separate meetings on Tuesday morning, April 30, the city commission and the city council denied the ACMHR-SCLC request for a parade permit and police protection for the proposed march to city hall. Mayor Boutwell said that allowing the parade would be a "dereliction of duty." Bevel leaked details of the student protest at Tuesday night's mass meeting. Calling the event "D-Day," he explained that the staff had worked "on four high schools and two colleges" collecting recruits. He hoped that simultaneous demonstrations would occur elsewhere in the city. "It will be our town that day," Bevel said. "The only way to get what we want is for everybody to get together and go tell Boutwell what we want." Earlier that day Bevel's wife, Freedom Rider Diane Nash, had joined an integrated column of SNCC and CORE volunteers near Attalla on a march to Birmingham to trace the steps of the martyred postman William Moore. State troopers arrested her and seven comrades the next day.[9]

Returning to Birmingham from the two-day SCLC board meeting in Memphis, the Reverends King, Shuttlesworth, Walker, and Ralph D. Abernathy arrived in time to attend Wednesday night's mass meeting, May 1, 1963, in St. Paul's AME Church, where William "Meatball" Dothard—a veteran of two arrests over the past month of protests—spoke about the student march. "We are going to break Birmingham wide open," he declared, promising "to land where they least expect us." The movement was "going to give the employees of the Negro schools a holiday tomorrow because the students are going to march." Schoolchildren were to gather in the morning at the Sixteenth Street church and listen to Bevel for a few hours before moving "out into the city." Shuttlesworth told the parents in the audience, "Don't worry about your children. They're in good hands." He added that he did not believe the Birmingham Board of Education would expel black students who participated in the protests. In a surprise move, however, Shuttlesworth said "they might not march tomorrow," an

263

announcement that reflected the indecisiveness of King. The activist explained that the ACMHR-SCLC would hold "a summit meeting" of local advisers before deciding what to do.[10]

As King met with the Central Committee in Room 30 of the Gaston Motel on Thursday morning, May 2, thousands of black students skipped school to attend the session at Sixteenth Street Baptist Church. The efforts of Parker High School principal R. C. Johnson and other educators to detain the teenagers by locking the gates of the school yard failed miserably as the students bounded over the walls. While Bevel and other staff members worked the youngsters into a frenzy, King confronted angry members of the black middle class who opposed the use of schoolchildren by the movement. Having consistently advised King to call off the campaign, they now condemned him outright. The civil rights leader sat in his suite unable to decide what to do.[11]

When the noon deadline for the beginning of the prayer march passed without an appearance by King, Bevel and Walker decided to send a group of schoolchildren out the doors of Sixteenth Street Baptist Church. As they emerged from under the orange brick romanesque arches filling the air with freedom songs, the youngsters raised picket signs, walked down the cement steps, and headed toward town. Orderly groups of ten to fifty students attempted to reach different targets: the city hall or the downtown shopping district. Laughing and clapping, the young activists numbered in the hundreds as they peacefully surrendered to policemen. Linked by walkie-talkie, ACMHR-SCLC members coordinated the campaign. Down on Fourth Avenue at Metropolitan AME Zion Church, students received the signal to march in one direction as a group at the Apostolic Overcoming Holiness (AOH) Church of God on Seventeenth Street took off on another route. Simultaneously, ten groups headed to city hall. Hand in hand the boys and girls, some as young as six, announced "We Shall Overcome." From the crowd of cheering onlookers, one woman shouted: "Sing, children, sing!" Some teachers joined their pupils in the protest. Other youngsters dropped their signs in fright and ran away on seeing the uniformed officers. Elsewhere in Birmingham, pickets appeared as ACMHR members conducted supplementary demonstrations. In charge of the affair, Walker deftly directed the operation with military precision.[12]

A perplexed Bull Connor watched the black children stream out of the churches and wondered how to respond. For weeks he had kept his cool, "nonviolently" arresting demonstrators, keeping the vigilantes at bay. As the police surveillance reports informed him, the movement had "run out of niggers." But with the schoolchildren, Connor began to crack. Officer Jack Warren recalled: "You could see Bull moving, looking, concerned, fidgety. He was just desperate. 'What the hell do I do?' " At first, patrolmen packed the youngsters in squad cars for the trip to Southside Jail. Soon paddy wagons arrived, followed by school buses. Ordering all policemen to the eight-block area between Kelly Ingram Park and downtown, officials alerted the Jefferson County Sheriff's Department to be on standby. When two large groups of students slipped past the hastily erected police lines about an hour into the demonstration, Connor ordered fire engines to the intersection of Fourth Avenue and Seventeenth Street to block their path. For the first time in the campaign, firemen took up positions at crucial corners of the area in an attempt to contain the demonstrations in this black section of town. Although they rolled out the high-pressure hoses, they did not turn on the water and the canine corps remained caged and away.[13]

By the afternoon, policemen had arrested hundreds of juveniles. Two dozen students left the Greyhound station to crash city hall across the street. Officers stopped them before they reached the Nineteenth Street entrance to the building. Dropping to their knees, they prayed, then broke out singing freedom songs while waiting for the paddy wagons. Police arrested only a handful of adults, among them the Reverend A. D. King. The schoolchildren filled the movement's ranks with volunteers, as the number of arrested topped one thousand. With the success of the "children's crusade," as *Newsweek* labeled it, the ACMHR-SCLC leaders had broadened the campaign to include the final tactic King and Walker originally intended to avoid: filling the jail.[14]

Unlike the week before, no vacant seat remained in Sixth Avenue Baptist Church for the mass meeting on Thursday night, May 2, 1963, as two thousand people celebrated the march of the schoolchildren that had resuscitated the movement. "I have been inspired and moved today. I have never seen anything like it," said the charismatic King, expressing the feelings of the congregation. "If they think today is the end of this, they will be badly mistaken." Again he promised to stay in Birmingham "until this problem is solved." Although he never gave the go-ahead, the successful protest convinced him of the expediency of using schoolchildren in the demonstrations. An overjoyed Fred Shuttlesworth interrupted throughout the service to praise "our little folks," to remind the assembly about the boycott and about keeping the students out of school. Yet James Bevel upstaged them all. He exuberantly declared: "There ain't going to be no meeting Monday night because every Negro is going to be in jail by Sunday night. If you don't want your kids to get put in jail and help in this movement, keep them at home, don't let them go to school." His sermon evolved into song as the congregation lifted its voice, the music drawn out of the essence of the three hundred or so Christian fanatics, the core ACMHR regulars who transcended, waving their arms ever higher, standing up and stomping their feet, screaming as their spirits ascended, marching around the inside of the sanctuary as the others looked on.[15]

Mayor Albert Boutwell and members of Birmingham's white community recoiled in horror at the movement's use of schoolchildren: "When people who are not residents of this city, and who will not have to live with fearful consequences, come to the point of using innocent children as their tools . . . then the time has come for every responsible white and colored parent in this city to demand a halt." He added: "I cannot condone and you cannot condone the use of children to these ends." Attorney General Robert Kennedy likewise criticized the move: "School children participating in street demonstrations is a dangerous business. An injured, maimed or dead child is a price that none of us can afford to pay." He again called the campaign ill-timed. From Harlem, Malcolm X denounced the use of young students: "Real men don't put their children on the firing line." Shuttlesworth and King held a joint press conference for the ACMHR and SCLC. Though not directly commenting on the young recruits, they assured reporters that the demonstrations would increase in intensity and that they would not relax pressure until the movement's demands were met. "We are ready to negotiate," King announced. "But we intend to negotiate from strength. If the white power structure of this city will meet some of our minimum demands then we will consider calling off the demonstrations, but we want promises, plus action." To reopen dialogue, realtor Sidney W. Smyer contacted the black businessmen.[16]

Bull Connor would not tolerate a repeat of the day before. Yet despite the warnings, he had not anticipated such massive displays of civil unrest. On Friday morning, May 3, he deployed his troops on the eastern edge of elm-shaded Kelly Ingram Park and positioned fire trucks at key intersections leading out of the area. Officers erected barricades, and firemen unpacked the hoses and swivel mounts. Still reeling from the overwhelming number of students previously involved, the commissioner of public safety and his men anxiously awaited the day's event.[17]

Two thousand schoolchildren listened impatiently as King informed them: "If you take part in the marches today you are going to jail but for a good cause." Around one o'clock the double oak doors opened wide

266

Unable to control the hundreds of black students who comprised the children's crusade of May 1963, Bull Connor ordered the Birmingham Fire Department to turn its hoses on the nonviolent protesters. Images such as this exceptional photograph by Charles Moore were carried across the world, prompting the president to send his envoy to negotiate a truce. Charles Moore.

and out poured the boys and girls. "We're going to walk, walk, walk," they chanted. "Freedom . . . freedom . . . freedom." The students sauntered across Kelly Ingram Park to the police roadblock. "Here they come," pointed Mayor Art Hanes. With a wave of his porkpie hat, Bull Connor pushed back one hundred white onlookers and ordered his patrolmen to the front. Separate groups of activists sporadically left the church headed in different directions. During the first hour officers arrested almost seventy teenagers with no apparent end in sight. The previous day had nearly filled the jail, and officials frantically searched for available space in which to imprison the youngsters. An effort to commandeer Legion Field failed because of a previously scheduled track meet. At the moment unable to think of an alternative, Connor decided to forcibly end the demonstrations rather than arrest the activists. To bottle up the students inside the churches, he turned on the hoses.[18]

Police captain Glenn V. Evans, commander of the department's uniform patrol division, confronted a group of sixty teenagers with the fire hoses. Through a loudspeaker Evans ordered, "Disperse or you'll get wet." Most kept marching. With the first blast of water, the students, aged thirteen to sixteen, covered their heads with their hands but held their ground. As the pressure increased, they dropped to their knees, then grasped each other, bonding bodies with souls to withstand the force. As the firemen trained the stream on the lead youth, his shirt peeled away. A second group—mostly teenage girls—came into sight. The firemen turned hoses on them, the water lifting several off the ground and over a parked car. One girl received cuts around her eyes and one woman a bloody nose when struck by the blast. For the next two hours the fire hoses repulsed non-violent protesters and angry black bystanders. The day before, a peer told Captain Evans: "Ten or fifteen years from now, we will look back on this and we will say, 'How stupid can you be?'" At the time, Evans later recalled, he thought like the other civil servants in law enforcement and fire protection: "I was still under the control of my chief of police and my commissioner of public safety and the other political leaders of the community, and I was still under the influence of the community to maintain the status quo." Indeed, no mutiny broke out against Connor's brutality.[19]

The unorganized African American spectators had observed each major march, but because they were apathetic, irreligious, and alienated, they had refused to join the nonviolent movement. Yet they participated in other ways that expressed the rebellion of black Birmingham. When the firemen increased the pressure to one hundred pounds so that the water sent students spinning down the street, dreadfully skinning exposed flesh, the heretofore cheering observers changed into a wrathful mob. A barrage of bricks and bottles descended on the firemen. As glass shattered nearby, Bull Connor deployed his squad of six German shepherds for crowd control. Not since Palm Sunday had police dogs lunged at onlookers. An officer sicced a dog on fifteen-year-old Walter Gadsden for crossing Sixteenth Street. Although not a member of the movement, Gadsden was arrested for parading without a permit. The teeth of one dog tore a gash in twenty-three-year-old Milton Payne. Two German shepherds attacked Henry Lee Shambry, ripping his trousers off and lacerating his leg. Other spectators resisted. Bricks pried up from the park sidewalk became painful missiles that bombarded the canine corps. One struck and dazed a dog. Another smacked fire chief L. H. Kirk squarely on the back, and two hit Officer D. B. McCleaky on the leg and foot. Cursing, the crowd pelted the police with rocks as firemen turned on the water. The ugly scene ended as officers swept through Kelly Ingram Park, dispersing the violent protesters.[20]

Movement leaders called off the demonstration around 3:00 P.M. after Chief Inspector William Haley warned them that the black mob outside had become dangerous. With the staged event over for the day, demonstrators trapped on the inside of Sixteenth Street Baptist Church quietly filed out as firemen rolled up the hoses and policemen took down the barricades, opening the area to automobiles and relieving traffic snarls elsewhere in the city. An unusual sense of cooperation developed as the adversaries struck the sets in this strange street drama.[21]

International condemnation of the racial violence in Birmingham greatly concerned the Kennedy administration, which sent its point man, Burke Marshall, to Birmingham to urge the integrationists to end the demonstrations. Born in Plainfield, New Jersey, the timid and bookish Marshall had attended the exclusive Phillips Exeter Academy before specializing in corporate law and antitrust at Yale. He had been appointed assistant attorney general for civil rights a few weeks before the Freedom Rides, although sickness had prevented him from becoming involved in that event. Nonetheless, Marshall soon established strong contacts in Birmingham, speaking frequently with his old college friend Douglas Arant, a Birmingham corporate lawyer; New Frontierman Charles Morgan Jr.; and *Birmingham News* editor Vincent Townsend. Periodic reports on local race relations from the Reverend Norman C. Jimerson of the biracial Alabama Council on Human Relations crossed his desk. For Marshall, Friday morning, May 3, 1963, began with an urgent call from Townsend, followed by a conference on the racial crisis in Birmingham with Robert Kennedy. Immediately after leaving the meeting he tried to telephone Martin Luther King at the Gaston Motel, but without success. Marshall reached David Vann, one of the young white progressive attorneys and later talked with Arant. At lunch, he discussed the administration's take-no-official-stand-on-Birmingham policy with Justice Department representatives John Doar and Louis Martin. Late in the afternoon, after the demonstrations had ended, King returned his call; then Marshall immediately went up to the attorney general's office. "Do you think you should go down there?" Kennedy asked Marshall. "I think I should," he replied. An hour later, after brief contact with Townsend and Gaston, Marshall arranged his travel plans. The next morning he boarded a plane for Birmingham.[22]

On Friday night Sid Smyer assembled white and black negotiating teams in a back room of Birmingham Realty Company. The biracial businessmen formed the core of the group summoned to the secret meeting, the first since the aborted conferences in the Episcopal Church of the Advent in April. The Reverends Fred Shuttlesworth and Ed Gardner were present, but Gaston, attorney Arthur Shores, businessman John Drew, college president Lucius H. Pitts, and the SCLC's Andrew Young came to dominate the black negotiating team. Suffering from the boycott, Birmingham's merchants led by Roper Dial of Sears, Roebuck had contacted Dave Vann about representing their interests in the negotiations. A native of Birmingham, Vann had cultivated a friendship with Gaston, and he served as legal counsel for several of the merchants. He agreed provided that the merchants gave him "enough leeway to work with." Vann attended the May 3 session, as did fellow attorney Abraham "Abe" Berkowitz, Townsend, and Smyer. Mayor Boutwell unofficially sent his aide W. C. "Billy" Hamilton. Representatives from the iron and steel industries and the city commissioners were deliberately excluded. Most of the men present knew each other and, as Vann recalled: "From the beginning we all conscientiously sought to see how could we work this problem out."[23]

Representing only a fraction of the white power structure, the men outlined several problems, the most troublesome of which seemed to be the undetermined outcome of Bull Connor's appeal before the Alabama Supreme Court—a group of justices elected statewide on segregationist platforms. In addition, if Boutwell assumed power, he would lack control over certain committees appointed by the old city commission such as the school board, which threatened to expel the marching students. From the outset, then, the white businessmen convinced the black negotiating committee that because they "couldn't make commitments from government," they had to work out the "entire negotiations [from] within a formula of commitment that could be made and carried out in the private sector." The Negro negotiators, who could have demanded guarantees from a Boutwell government, accepted the limited parameters of debate outlined by the white businessmen. At the May 3 mass meeting, after movement leaders had deplored the police brutality of the dogs and hoses, King, who had centered campaign strategy on pressuring merchants to get the white establishment to the bargaining table, began to back away from demands for the desegregation of parks and schools and for other municipal reforms.[24]

Vigilantes hung King in effigy outside St. Paul's Roman Catholic Cathedral early Saturday morning, May 4, as Birmingham braced for another day of massive street demonstrations. At noon Walker implemented a new nonviolent strategy by sending the activists from the Sixteenth Street Baptist and Seventeenth Street AOH Churches two-by-two without picket signs in the hope that the activists could regroup north of city hall and then march on the building. Undisturbed, a group of activists—most of whom were in their teens, although some were as young as ten—gathered around a black girl who held up a previously hidden banner: "Love God and Thy Neighbor." Twenty-five strong, they proceeded toward city hall. At that moment, Connor left his office and stumbled over the schoolchildren. He ordered their arrest. Cameramen filmed the smiling faces as the youngsters followed policemen down a ramp to a holding pen in the basement of the building. A woman and a young girl nonchalantly walking by suddenly stopped and knelt in prayer on the steps of city hall. They were detained. Two teenage girls formed the next team of civil rights kamikazes. To stop the steady flow of small yet structured protests, police arrested all suspicious-looking African Americans near city hall. In addition, Connor blocked the doors to movement churches to prevent any more children from demonstrating.[25]

Violence erupted when police turned their attention away from the activists and toward the crowd of unorganized African Americans watching the event unfold. Again Connor had stationed the brunt of his fire hose defense at the intersection of Seventeenth Street and Fifth Avenue North in an effort to close access to the downtown business community and contain the black people in Kelly Ingram Park. By preventing the schoolchildren from leaving the churches, Connor ended the demonstration by default. When no marches transpired, the spectators, who had come for the show, began taunting the police. Approximately three thousand people overran the grassy block by mid-afternoon. Angry black men mockingly danced about the elms and waved their arms, daring the defenders of white supremacy to sic the dogs and shoot the water. Connor's troops obliged as the hoses opened at full force. After an hour, many black bystanders left, but a riotous remnant hurled rocks and shards at the white officials. Again the police dogs appeared, and again people on nearby rooftops rained down bricks and bottles. Afraid that the spectator violence would hurt the nonviolent movement, Bevel and the Reverend William Greer worked with city officials to break up the stragglers. "Will you please go home?" Greer pleaded through a policeman's megaphone, "Your leaders have asked you all to go home. Please do not cause trouble."[26]

After ACMHR-SCLC staffers ended the day's event, the negotiations began in earnest. Late Saturday afternoon, Mayor Art Hanes slipped into the A. L. Smith Building for "an impromptu" meeting with Walker and the Reverend Charles Billups of the ACMHR. Caught by a reporter, Hanes confessed: "I told them I would talk to anybody anytime, but that I would not talk or negotiate as long as the demonstrations were continuing."[27]

The attorney general had canceled a scheduled address at the University of Virginia in order to remain in Washington and monitor events through the assistance of his Justice Department representatives: Burke Marshall and Joseph F. Dolan. On his arrival in Birmingham, Marshall conferred with Jefferson County sheriff Melvin Bailey to get an appraisal of the situation. Bailey told Marshall that "law enforcement was containing the situation. For how long we don't know. There's a possibility it could get out of hand." After setting up a meeting with Martin Luther King for later that afternoon, Marshall touched base with his local sources. Emphasizing the need for biracial communication, he began shuffling among the interest groups, acting as a moderator to advance negotiations. As he recalled: "The pattern from the moment I got there, was first I had a meeting with the merchants and then I'd have a meeting with some Negro leaders and then it was arranged so that some Negro, local Negroes, would meet with a very small group of whites, and then I'd go and meet with King in the middle of the night. And we'd start that over again and try to get issues clarified and see if any agreement or consensus could be reached on the issues." Believing only in face-to-face conferences with the white opposition, Shuttlesworth opposed Marshall's involvement but nonetheless acquiesced to King's wishes and supported the negotiations.[28]

Increasingly the civil rights campaign appeared surreal. Reflecting the white community's desire to ignore the movement, the Sunday *Birmingham News* featured a picture of an elderly black woman who held an umbrella and casually walked on the edge of Kelly Ingram Park. In the distance, mist from fire hoses rose above a rowdy black crowd. "Just another showery day for Negro stroller. . . . She appears undisturbed by disturbances in Ingram Park," read the caption, as if the protests had not ripped asunder the very fabric of the city. Speaking on the "so-called Battle of Ingram Park," Walker recalled the perverse confrontation: "the blacks were waiting for something to happen; they started teasing the firemen; they [the firemen] started putting water on them. It was a game. . . . They [the blacks] were trying to see who could stand up against the fire hoses. . . . It wasn't any damn battle, it was a Roman holiday." "If you're not going to respect policemen, you're not going to be in the movement," SCLC staffer James Bevel told brick throwers. Bevel later recalled: "It's strange, I guess, for them: I'm with the police talking through the bullhorn and giving orders and everybody was obeying the orders. It was like, wow." Wow, indeed, as leaders organized, designed, and controlled the demonstrations for optimum media coverage, ending the protest if the nonmovement observers turned violent or in time for the film to make the six o'clock news. All the action began to center on the image projected from Birmingham: appearances replaced reality. King boasted at Friday's mass meeting, "After you saw the Huntley-Brinkley report tonight, you saw some of the action that took place today," as if the people in the audience had not been there. Reporters described horrific brutality that appeared worse than it actually was, yet symbolized the historical brutality behind race relations in the city. Nevertheless, the campaign began to blur and seem unreal. Chuck Morgan simply concluded, "It was not a rational movement."[29]

No arrests occurred on Sunday, May 5, when activists conducted kneel-ins and participated in the largest protest march to date. Whereas ushers in four white churches admitted the integrationists, nine others declined to do so; yet the thirteen attempts fell far short of the fifty-seven projected at Saturday's mass meeting. The white Ministerial Association of Greater Birmingham prayed for "God's leading hand and peace in our city." Following the ACMHR-SCLC scheduled afternoon service at New Pilgrim Baptist Church, Charles Billups, a longtime leader in the local civil rights movement, James Bevel, and Barnard Lee headed the congregation of nearly 1,500 as it left the church to conduct a prayer meeting at Southside Jail. Clothed in their Sunday best, the marchers reached the intersection of Sixth Avenue South and Fifth Street before squads of patrolmen on motorcycles blocked their path. Pumper trucks pulled up and firemen aimed six high-pressure water nozzles at the nonviolent demonstrators. Captain Glenn V. Evans asked the group to turn around and march back to the church. Several civil rights leaders conferred with police as the marchers knelt in prayer. Billups reportedly stood up and called out, "Turn on your water, turn loose your dogs, we will stand here till we die." The followers began to chant as officers held their ground. After several tense minutes, Billups led the marchers into the "Negro" Memorial Park, where he conducted a prayer meeting until dusk. Connor had banned white people from the area in a bid to minimize media coverage of the campaign. In the process, he arrested white folksingers Guy and Candie Carawan.[30]

The negotiations continued apace on Sunday as the movement reiterated its position and the progressive white businessmen considered the demands. Preaching in Atlanta, an optimistic Martin Luther King informed his congregation at Ebenezer Baptist Church: "The power structure of Birmingham is disturbed and in a few days we will have everything we are asking and maybe more." Emphasizing the goals of the local movement, he said: "If we can crack Birmingham, I am convinced we can crack the South. Birmingham is a symbol of segregation for the entire South." An insider had accurately informed King that "the white business structure was weakening under the adverse publicity, the pressure of our boycott, and a parallel falling-off of white buying." The war of attrition was working as the merchants—hurt by the boycott—reconsidered their refusal to desegregate.[31]

Burke Marshall scurried back and forth between black and white teams as he assisted the negotiators and encouraged movement leaders to compromise. After meeting with Marshall, Arthur Shores said that "nothing of real substance was discussed, just the general situation." The black attorney added, "He is here trying to bring about a meeting of minds between the two groups." Marshall held a two-hour conference with the Reverend A. D. King and apparently met with Boutwell aides and others as well. Martin Luther King later commended Marshall's "invaluable job" in opening a dialogue with the white power structure. Chuck Morgan praised the reticent Marshall: "Rarely did he inject himself into the settlement of the community's problem. But he was there and the presence of the United States coupled with his quiet skill helped bring forth Birmingham's abstainers, its business community."[32]

274

Sid Smyer and Dave Vann arranged a meeting between the merchants and the black negotiating committee for Sunday night. After sitting down, the opening discourse involved "a free interchange of counter accusations of bad faith," according to one participant. Unwilling to recognize Shuttlesworth or the SCLC, the white negotiators demanded that a member of the traditional Negro leadership class, such as the Reverend J. L. Ware, step forward to represent the interests of the black community. Over time, Shores, Lucius Pitts, and A. G. Gaston assumed this role. At this meeting, Gaston distributed the movement's "Points for Progress," which listed four principal demands: the "desegregation of all store facilities, Lunch Counters, Rest Rooms, Fitting Rooms"; the "immediate up-grading of employment opportunities available for Negroes, and the beginning of a non-discriminatory hiring policy"; that the "merchants request the City Government to drop all charges against those persons arrested while exercising their Constitutionally guaranteed right to peaceful protest"; and that the "merchants request the City Government to establish a Bi-racial Committee to deal with future problems of the community and to develop specific plans for: hiring Negroes to the police force, alleviation of obstacles in voter registration, school desegregation, re-opening all municipal facilities on a desegregated basis, desegregation of movies and hotels." The merchants agreed to discuss the first two demands—indeed, some claimed to have taken steps in that direction—but dismissed outright the other two objectives involving appeals to the city government. As one participant recalled, the merchants "absolutely refused to deal in any way with matters before the courts, or prerogatives of city government." Again the negotiations stalled.[33]

Hundreds of students skipped school to participate in Monday's march. One black educator reported that only 87 of 1,339 pupils attended class. Movement organizers blanketed the area with fliers that advised the children to "fight for freedom first then go to school." Encouraging them to "join the thousands in jail," the leaflet said: "It's up to you to free our teachers, our parents, yourself and our country." By noon, thousands of youngsters packed Sixteenth Street Baptist Church. "Everybody wants Freedom," read the sign held by black comedian Dick Gregory as he led a column of 19 children out of the church. They carried toothbrushes in anticipation of their arrest. "Don't mind walking, 'cause I want my freedom now," sang the little ones in his charge as officers warned them to disperse. They were the first of 1,000 detained that day.[34]

Returning to his prior policy of "nonviolence," Bull Connor watched the orderly schoolchildren singing "Freedom . . . Freedom . . . Freedom" as they ran into the arms of waiting patrolmen. "Boy, if that's religion, I don't want any," he scoffed, confusing the students with the Christian fanatics he had read about in the police surveillance reports on the ACMHR meetings. Two hours after the arrests began, violence erupted. As if a thunderstorm had finally broken the steady buildup of barometric pressure that muggy spring day, a black spectator threw a coke bottle that struck like lightning at the foot of an officer. Immediately patrolmen stepped into the crowd. Notified of the action, ACMHR-SCLC staffers ushered movement members back into the sanctuary. Police reinforcements arrived to supplement the three fire trucks and power hoses already stationed around the park. The officers had just about cleared the sidewalks when a movement leader burst into the street, declaring: "It's all over. It's all over for today." The city had arrested so many demonstrators that officials had lost count, but they estimated the number to be around 2,425. Hundreds of protesters packed spaces designed for dozens. Although Bull Connor denied it, the movement had "filled the jail."[35]

Burke Marshall's influence on negotiations that Monday, May 6, left the movement considering a cooling-off period in exchange for concessions on some demands by merchants. For most of the morning, Marshall met with Martin Luther King at John and Deenie Drew's house on Dynamite Hill. During these private conferences, Marshall unobtrusively worked the dis-

275

course around getting King to call off the demonstrations. He used several approaches, such as following the argument of the attorney general that the demonstrations were untimely and the movement should wait until after Boutwell took office to press for reform, or the merchants' claim that they could not negotiate under the pressure of the marches. King resisted Marshall's rhetoric, and an observer described the session as "largely fruitless."[36]

After discussing the situation with Gaston and Pitts, however, Marshall learned that King and Shuttlesworth spoke for the black community and any agreement by the traditional Negro leadership class with the white power structure had to receive the imprimatur of the movement. Informed of this, Smyer's subcommittee on race, which had met twice with black businessmen on Sunday, apparently reported back to members of the Senior Citizens Committee. By late Monday night, Smyer and the merchants appealed to King through the black businessmen's intermediaries to halt the marches in return for desegregation of area department stores and lunch counters. Movement leaders rejected the compromise as "too little and too late." In disgust, one black leader complained to a reporter that "in fact, they [the negotiations] never really got started." In Washington, members of the Kennedy administration including the president and the attorney general telephoned select members of Birmingham's white power structure to convince them to negotiate a truce.[37]

Thousands of African Americans attended Monday night's mass meeting as ACMHR-SCLC leaders reported on the successful protest and promised more of the same. So many people filled St. James Baptist that staffers sent the overflow to Thirgood CME and St. Luke's AME Churches. Concerned parents waited for word on the safety and whereabouts of their jailed children. It had begun to rain. James Forman of SNCC visited the schoolchildren who were temporarily housed in the open stockyards at the state fair grounds. Many crouched under coats trying to stay dry. Enraged, Forman went to the mass meeting and described the cold and wet conditions at the compound. Several parents got up to take blankets to their sons and daughters, but Billups convinced them to wait and see what King said to do. The civil rights leader advised against Forman's strategy to publicize the terrible conditions in order to anger the parents into supporting the movement. King feared that if the black community learned of the exposed youngsters, no parents would allow their children to demonstrate the next day. Nevertheless, he agreed to see the holding pen firsthand. When Forman, King, Billups, and Bevel arrived at the fair grounds, they found Bull Connor checking on the wet children. As Bevel debated with Connor,

King threatened to call Marshall. Forman advised King "that constant calls to the Justice Department lessened the militancy of the people," but King called anyway. Back at the mass meeting, King informed the parents that he had contacted Marshall about the situation—although he did not mention the students squatting in the rain. He added, "it was the City of Birmingham's duty to shelter these prisoners, to feed them, and give them a place to sleep, since they had arrested them."[38]

Planning the demonstrations for Tuesday, May 7, 1963, Forman and Dorothy Cotton decided to do something different. Instead of marching the schoolchildren into the arms of policemen, they planned to send them in every direction with orders to converge on the downtown business district from all sides at noon. Walker authorized assistants to file false alarms to distract fire fighters. Having filled the jail, the movement determined to shut down Birmingham.[39]

Marshall met with Smyer, the merchants, and attorneys Vann and Erskine Smith Tuesday morning to discuss the status of negotiations. The merchants remembered how, after desegregating store facilities in September 1962, the establishment refused to support them when Connor enforced the Jim Crow laws; thus they were hesitant to agree to any black demands without the full support of the industrial and financial elite. Although willing to upgrade token black workers to positions as clerks and to link the desegregation of lunch counters, fitting rooms, and other public facilities to scheduled school desegregation that fall, the merchants refused to discuss the other Points for Progress, in particular the establishment of a biracial committee charged with solving a host of long-standing racial problems that included the hiring of Negro policemen, voter registration, and the desegregation of schools, parks, and cinemas. Marshall recalled that the merchants "wouldn't do anything unless they had the backing of what they considered to be, and they all talked about power structure, or the big mules, or some phrases like that about very powerful businessmen in a really remarkable way—remarkable how much these people didn't have a mind of their own." As a result of the merchants' firm stand on wanting the endorsement of the industrial and financial elite, Smyer agreed to call the Senior Citizens Committee into emergency session later that day. The merchants broke for lunch and discovered bedlam in the streets.[40]

Only moments before, a surprise demonstration scattered the sandwiches and cold drinks being consumed by the city officials stationed around Kelly Ingram Park. Like the Children of Israel at the Battle of Jericho, a line of several hundred students exited the church and marched completely around the park, down Sixth Avenue and Seventeenth Street, across Fifth Avenue, and up Sixteenth Street, arriving back at the church as if the pounding of their feet would tumble the walls of segregation. The doors of the Sixteenth Street Baptist Church suddenly swung wide and out swept hundreds of schoolchildren. They took off in several directions but with a common destination. One group of students approached a policeman and announced, "We want to go to jail." Pointing to the southside (and the commercial center of town), he replied: "Jail's that way." The youngsters broke into a run across the park: "We're going to jail!" The spectators lining the sidewalks joined in the surge of black humanity as it overran the traffic barricades and once-formidable firemen and headed, unabated, toward the downtown business district several blocks away. Like clockwork, nonviolent activists carried out movement strategy to shut down the center of Birmingham during the lunch-hour rush. At least three thousand demonstrators milled about on Twentieth and surrounding streets, grinding traffic to a halt for half an hour. Emboldened by their strength in numbers, African Americans entered department stores and other offices they normally avoided in the retail district. Like a ribbon, Forman wove one group in and out of the shops as the activists sang freedom songs. While the students sat-in and picketed, old-line ACMHR members stopped in the middle of the sidewalk and knelt in prayer. A black crowd of several hundred encircled two officers immediately after they roughed up a black man. Movement leaders stepped in and "freed" the officers. Powerless to act, policemen stood by helplessly as civil order collapsed in the heart of the city in the early afternoon of Tuesday, May 7.[41]

As the Senior Citizens gathered in the paneled conference room of the chamber of commerce that Tuesday, it became apparent to all that a turning point had been reached. Something had to be done to resolve the stalemate in race relations. Burke Marshall watched these eighty-nine elite white men of Birmingham—presidents of banks, industries, major businesses, and utilities, editors of newspapers, and partners in prestigious law firms—grimly greet each other with reserved familiarity. Many of them belonged to the same private clubs, and through their service on municipal boards and in area churches, they wielded enormous influence in the community, in addition to their control of over 80 percent of the city's employment. Leaning over to Vann, Marshall said: "I don't think I'll ever see a city sit down with itself like I'm seeing today." Former mayor W. Cooper Green, now a vice president of the Alabama Power Company, rapped the emergency meeting to order.[42]

An elder statesman rose to speak. A World War I veteran, Dixiecrat, and former governor, Frank M. Dixon held the respect of everyone in the room. In no uncertain terms he advised Birmingham's Big Mules "that they should immediately, right then and there, call the governor and get martial law declared and send in the troops and suppress the whole business." Like the other retainers of the iron and steel interests, Dixon defended the neo-Bourbon system that he himself had helped to construct. Smyer quickly shifted the rhetoric away from Dixon's defiance to suggest that compromise on segregation was the only sane way to put down the insurrection. He understood the new reality of race relations: "If we're going to have a good business in Birmingham, we better change our way of living." Smyer pleaded with the businessmen: "Gentlemen, we've got to get this thing straight." Then he turned to Marshall. The soft-spoken assistant attorney general explained the situation as he understood it and told them "as I think nobody had told them before, that they had a solution in their hands, and the solution was to endorse certain things if done by the downtown merchants." Many of those contacted by the Kennedy administration announced their support for Marshall's negotiations. An exasperated Sheriff Mel Bailey stressed the inability of law enforcement officers to control the protests. With the jails full, city officials were considering erecting a barbed wire fence in Legion Field to house the arrested demonstrators—another negative image for the city. Bailey dared not estimate how long before Bull Connor snapped, and he warned that martial law might be necessary. Afraid of such a step, Boutwell said Birmingham should "act honorably in the situation" by finding a resolution. Others, such as attorney Joseph Johnston, echoed Smyer's sentiments. The wail of the fire engines racing by under the windows offered an eerily harmonious descant.[43]

Breaking the deadlock, the Senior Citizens agreed to token reforms that signified the dismantling of racial discrimination in the Birmingham district. As the tense afternoon wore on, negotiators hammered out the position of the white power structure. Marshall maintained telephone contact with black leaders to discuss the movement's demands. Joseph Dolan of the Justice Department called the White House, where a futile three-hour meeting transpired to debate the proper role of the federal government in the crisis. Trying to shield the merchants from vigilante retribution, Vann appealed to bankers, realtors, and other nonretail elite to announce their decision to negotiate. Speaking for the Senior Citizens, *Birmingham Post-Herald* editor James Mills said: "We have high hopes that something constructive will come within the next 24 or 48 hours." Appearing on local television, Boutwell concurred: "When we are in undisputed authority we will give immediate and determined attention to resolving the difficulties that face us." Having decided to endorse the resolution, the Senior Citizens left it up to Smyer and the subcommittee on race to work out the unpleasant details. No more than three dissents were heard as the Big Mules debated Birmingham's new consensus on race. Nevertheless, no one wanted to go on record, and the Senior Citizens expressed their concern about what would appear in the newspapers. After the meeting, an excited Marshall telephoned Washington and informed the president that "the meeting had worked and that I thought we were going to have a solution the next day." The assistant attorney general had succeeded in constructing a resolution within the strictures of federalism. The Kennedy administration had not promised the movement anything.[44]

Tuesday afternoon, May 7, while the Senior Citizens were ending the stalemate with a private agreement, Bull Connor's tank rumbled through the public streets looking for demonstrators; but most black people had already returned to the church unmolested by police. As officers restored civil order, activists celebrated their successful assault against segregation. Singing freedom songs, movement members spilled out of the Sixteenth Street Baptist Church and over the steps as onlookers packed the park and jammed nearby sidewalks. Connor swept the stragglers back into the ghetto with blasts from the fire hoses and sealed off the black district from the rest of the city to prevent a repeat of the morning's protest. Inside the church, Bevel, Young, and Shuttlesworth prepared the youngsters for a gratuitous march on the business district. Explaining the earlier spontaneous demonstration as a "beautiful fluke," Forman appealed to the ACMHR-SCLC leaders not to send the schoolchildren out to face the brutal repression prepared by Bull Connor. Unable to convince them of the callousness of their plans, Forman went to the Gaston Motel to plead with Martin Luther King, who had missed the morning's event. Dressed in his robe and pajamas, King opened the door of Room 30 and, while talking on the telephone, motioned the SNCC activist to enter and wait. It was after two o'clock and room service had just delivered a steak, completing the image of "De Lawd" lounging about while "his people" suffered in the streets. Forman left in disgust.[45]

By the time schoolchildren marched out of the sanctuary late Tuesday afternoon, skirmishes had broken out between municipal authorities and African American spectators. Water "skeeted" over the heads of the crowd as black members hurled rocks and brickbats at the white men in uniform.

As the civil rights demonstrations spin out of control, black bystanders taunt Birmingham policemen in Kelly Ingram Park. Used for crowd control and not sicced on civil rights activists, the police dogs nevertheless provided a lasting image of brutality in Birmingham. *Birmingham News*.

Soon a pitched battle erupted. "Bring on the dogs," shouted angry bystanders, "bring on the water." The temperature had soared to 87 degrees. For an hour police chased people into alleyways, beating them with billy clubs. Officers arrested only a score or two as the jail was full. Dodging in and out of the surrounding slum, the nonmovement participants charged police lines at several points in the struggle for control of the park. Pushing people out of its way, Connor's white armored car wheeled up and down Sixteenth Street. At the intersections on the other side of Kelly Ingram, firemen operated the powerful swivel mounted monitors that combined the force of two two-and-a-half-inch hoses into a knife of water that pared away bark from elm trees. Blasting the bystanders, one stream picked up a man and sent him tumbling through the park like windblown trash. Water overflowed nearby gutters. Out of control, Connor screamed for his men to get the "niggers." To supplement the hoses, he called out the five police dogs. Sheriff Bailey ordered fifty helmeted deputies to assist Connor's force of one hundred. Policemen from Leeds, Midfield, Bessemer, Libscomb, and Fairfield joined in the fight, as did an armed posse of irregulars headed by Dallas County sheriff Jim Clark. State troopers arrived and squads of officers began to brutally beat back the riotous mob. Fifteen patrolmen scattered a group of stone throwers maneuvering near a row of tenements. Similar assaults would disperse the crowd by dusk.[46]

As the state violently suppressed the racial disturbances, civil rights leaders urged black protesters to leave. "You're not helping our cause," the Reverend A. D. King announced over an officer's megaphone. Walking with Captain George Wall down Sixteenth Street, two preachers encouraged people to stop milling about and go home. ACMHR-SCLC leaders had gathered movement members back into the church for safety; after the violence subsided, they quietly slipped out the door and away. With the demonstration over and the riot quelled, Shuttlesworth left the sanctuary, but as he walked down the street, firemen opened up their hoses and the water knocked him off his feet and slammed him against the bricks of the church. Suffering chest wounds, he was taken to the new Holy Family Hospital for Negroes. Connor arrived on the scene and as the ambulance departed said, "I waited a week to see Shuttlesworth get hit with a hose. I'm sorry I missed it." As an afterthought, the commissioner remarked: "I wish they'd carried him away in a hearse." Having watched Shuttlesworth get injured, Captain Glenn V. Evans recalled wondering: "What does this accomplish? What do we *hope* to do here by doing these kinds of things?" Afterward, firemen pumped out the flooded basement of Sixteenth Street Baptist Church, adding to the surreal nature of the civil rights campaign.[47]

Speaking before the opening session of the state legislature that morning, Governor George C. Wallace had said he was "tired of the lawlessness in Birmingham and whatever it takes will be done to break it up." He sent 250 state highway patrolmen into the city to help local authorities maintain law and order. State public safety director Al Lingo increased the number to nearly 600, while explaining that the men took orders only from the governor and would not assume complete control in Birmingham unless the situation required it. Lingo armed the ill-trained state troopers with submachine guns, sawed-off shotguns, carbines, and tear gas. Brigadier General Henry V. Graham surveyed the city for the Alabama National Guard. During the Freedom Rides, Graham had enforced martial law when the riot occurred in Montgomery. In Washington, Attorney General Robert Kennedy contacted another veteran of that earlier conflict, former state public safety director Floyd Mann, and asked for his assistance. The attorney general also notified the commander of the Second Infantry Division at Fort Benning, Georgia, that the government might require its services in Birmingham.[48]

Tuesday's violence heightened local and national response to the civil rights campaign. Clarence B. Hanson Jr., the publisher of the *Birmingham News*, telegraphed the president to complain about the administration's inaction in maintaining law and order. He criticized Kennedy's past contact with Martin Luther King and blamed the president for the crisis. Hanson's telegram reflected the unwillingness of the white elite to admit responsibility for Birmingham's racial troubles. Roy Wilkins directed NAACP chapters across the country to stage sympathy protests in support of the Birmingham movement. The executive secretary recommended that activists picket city halls and state houses "to inform local communities of the outrage of your citizens over barbarity in Alabama." Jackie Robinson organized a fund-raiser in New York City for the ACMHR-SCLC. He also wired President Kennedy, "The revolution that is taking place in this country cannot be squelched by police dogs or power hoses."[49]

Nineteen rabbis joined the revolution in a "testimony in behalf of the human rights and dignity" of African Americans by boarding a plane and heading to Birmingham. They equated silence on segregation with the atrocities of the Nazi Holocaust. Local Jewry failed to make the same connection. Angered by the unannounced visit of the national leaders of the conservative Rabbinical Assembly, local Jewish leaders such as William P. Engel and Abe Berkowitz pleaded with the New Yorkers to leave. Although they failed to persuade their coreligionists, they did succeed in keeping news of the visit out of the press. Only rumors of the rabbis spread around. Many of Birmingham's four thousand Jews feared a backlash from the city's faction of anti-Semitic white supremacists. But movement leaders welcomed the rabbis, picking them up at the airport, sheltering them at the Gaston Motel, and inviting them to the mass meeting.[50]

With nightfall, a tense peace enveloped ravaged Birmingham. Movement supporters filled three churches as civil rights leaders conducted mass meetings. At Sixteenth Street, the Reverend Ed Gardner told concerned parents: "Perhaps some mothers don't want freedom but our children want freedom." He assured them, "We are near where we are going," but "if our parents betray, our children will never be forgiven." Gardner recommended prayer to relieve worry. He reported on the condition of the hospitalized Shuttlesworth. The Reverend Dr. William Sloane Coffin, chaplain of Yale University, addressed the congregation. After reporting charges of police brutality against jailed comedian Dick Gregory, Martin Luther King lectured on nonviolence.[51]

Also on Tuesday evening the black and white negotiating teams met in the downtown offices of a leading insurance executive to work out an agreement. Smyer, Vann, Edward Norton of Royal Crown Cola, and Roper Dial of Sears, Roebuck represented the white power structure and merchants. Billy Hamilton attended for Boutwell, Shores, Pitts, and Drew of the traditional Negro leadership class, and Young of the ACMHR-SCLC represented the black community. Burke Marshall observed the proceedings. Andrew Young took charge by proposing a general settlement that the white power structure could agree with. It called for facilitating "immediate 'token' employment of Negroes," setting dates for the desegregation of public accommodations, and establishing a timetable for black employment that increased from 2 percent in the first three months, to 4 percent in six months, to 10 percent by the end of the year. Other concerns such as dropping charges against demonstrators and removing segregation ordinances would be implemented when the city council took charge. Agreeing to form a biracial committee to discuss other objectives, the white negotiators accepted the first two demands, discussed the promises of the third, but had problems with dropping the charges against the jailed demonstrators. After three hours, the meeting adjourned until morning with that question still unresolved. Nonetheless, everyone felt that a settlement was near. As one white negotiator informed reporter Michael Dorman, "I think we've got a deal. If we can get everyone to agree, perhaps the worst of this is over."[52]

The black team, Burke Marshall, and a few local whites continued their discussions at John Drew's ranch-style house on Dynamite Hill. At Drew's request, Sid Smyer opened the session with a prayer. The biracial businessmen then rolled up their sleeves, loosened their ties, and picked up the discussion of the movement's demands. Debate centered on two issues: first, how to word the biracial agreement so as not to embarrass the white negotiators while convincing the black community that it had achieved something; and second, how to deal with the thousands of arrested schoolchildren if the city refused to drop the charges. The businessmen considered raising the more than $250,000 in bail money needed. The informal gathering broke up at three in the morning with the white businessmen in general accepting the watered-down demands of the movement.[53]

On Wednesday morning, May 8, the ACMHR-SCLC Central Committee assembled in the Gaston Motel to hear the report of the black negotiators. Shuttlesworth, confined to a hospital bed, was absent. In a typed memo Lucius Pitts presented his impressions of the discussion in Drew's home the night before. As a moderate member of the black elite and president of Miles College, Pitts epitomized Birmingham's traditional Negro leadership class. Like the more conservative Gaston, Pitts had opposed the ACMHR-SCLC demonstrations. His previous experiences with the biracial Alabama Council on Human Relations had taught him to trust negotiations. Therefore, he willingly discussed the movement's demands with the white power structure. Although he represented the movement, Pitts did not express a deep commitment to its objectives. He began the memo by noting that the white men spoke "in good faith" because of the "pressure" created by the ACMHR-SCLC campaign. "To say that they are frightened is an *understatement*; to say that we have completely won is an *overstatement*."[54]

Pitts recommended that the movement make further compromises on the Points for Progress. On the first demand he suggested that the desegregation of stores and lunch counters be linked to either legal recognition of the new city government or desegregation of the schools, whichever occurred first. Also, the merchants could immediately upgrade black employees, as stated in the second demand. On the unresolved third issue, Pitts believed "there could be some tacit agreement (if only verbal) between our leaders and representatives of the city government that the charges against persons arrested during the demonstrations at the order of the Commissioners would be withdrawn," and the merchants could "agree to withdraw their charges." The final point—the creation of a biracial committee to work out the hiring of Negro policemen, voter registration, and the desegregation of schools, parks, and other public accommodations— served as a catchall for the long-standing demands of the ACMHR. Pitts advised that "some firm commitments announced or unannounced from the new city government [be made] that immediately upon their taking office legally a Community Relations Commission could be appointed with a stated and promised purpose-agenda including all of the points under our fourth point and adding other items to it." Having compromised the four Points for Progress, Pitts concluded: "It is my candid opinion that if a truce is called with the above beginnings of change and with a definite time schedule on desegregating of all store facilities and upgrading of employment practices that we could be in a good position to effect continual change in the community." At the beginning of the ACMHR-SCLC campaign, the movement's demands were nonnegotiable; Pitts and the traditional Negro leadership class wanted to end the demonstrations on the vague verbal promises of white businessmen and impotent politicians. All they needed was King's approval.[55]

Pitts's memo circulated among the civil rights leaders and black elite as they discussed compromising the Points for Progress while canceling the massive street protests. For days, Marshall had counseled King to do just that. Echoing the merchants, Gaston advised movement leaders to accept the moratorium on marches and then achieve the settlement. Ralph Abernathy recalled that the traditional Negro leaders had recommended "a cessation of demonstrations in exchange for a discussion of very specific demands, such as immediate integration of all facilities, including lunch counters, as soon as Albert Boutwell's regime was certified as the legal city government." Critics pointed out the move from demanding action to accepting future discussions. Others warned of the uncertainty of the courts. As the debate raged, King quietly turned to Abernathy: "What do you think, Ralph?" Believing the national press would interpret the decision as a sign of good faith, Abernathy whispered: "Let's let them have their day's truce." A few minutes later, King closed the debate by supporting the moratorium on demonstrations. A handful opposed the decision in the vote that followed. As Andrew Young remembered it, King handed movement authority over to the traditional Negro leaders: "By and large, the leadership fell right back into the hands of the middle-class, and had they not been involved at all through the process, they wouldn't have been prepared to bring leadership in the period of reconciliation that followed. So, it was very important to have them involved in the thinking and planning, and it created a very interesting tension."[56]

The pins fell quickly Wednesday morning as word of the moratorium spread. After the white power structure held a formal meeting to endorse the proposed agreement, it sent David Vann to meet with Martin Luther King at Drew's house. The stocky white lawyer and future mayor of Birmingham stood before the huge picture window overlooking the city as King commended the brave businessmen for making their "tough decision." King said: "We would live to see the day when Birmingham would be the symbol of some of the best race relations in America," Vann recalled.[57] Burke Marshall and John Doar arrived and made preparations for a joint Kennedy-King press conference announcing the end of protest marches by schoolchildren. The Justice Department officials delighted in the triumph of federalism.

Not everyone was happy with the moratorium. James Forman recognized the decision as "merely an agreement to negotiate with the city." He understood that "Burke Marshall and Bobby Kennedy had influenced Dr. King to call off the demonstrations because of the violent resistance actions. People had become too militant for the government's liking and Dr.

286

THE CHILDREN'S CRUSADE

King's image." Black activist Vincent Harding reported that one national Negro leader "was sadly convinced that the Justice Department and the Attorney General's office were far more concerned with ending demonstrations than in working toward a real solution in Birmingham."[58]

When he learned of the moratorium on demonstrations, Fred Shuttlesworth checked himself out of the hospital in order to confront King. He feared that Marshall and Doar had "sold King on the idea that the merchants cain't negotiate with demonstrations going on." Events had vindicated his distrust of the Kennedy administration.[59]

Shuttlesworth burst into the living room of Drew's house enraged by King's betrayal. Still on medication, he was emotionally upset and personally hurt by King's failure to visit him in the hospital. "Did I hear you right?" Shuttlesworth recalled asking the civil rights leader on his arrival. King repeated, "We have decided to call off the demonstrations." Shuttlesworth responded, "Well, Martin, *who* decided?" To which King answered, "Well, we just decided that we can't have negotiations with all this going on." Growing angrier, Shuttlesworth said, "Well, Martin, it's hard for me to see . . . how anybody could decide that without me. . . . We're not calling anything off." King interrupted, "Well, uh—," but Shuttlesworth continued: "Well, Martin, you know they *said* in Albany that you come in, get people excited and started, and you leave town. But I live here, the people trust me, and I have the responsibility after SCLC is gone, and I'm telling you it will not be called off." He reminded the civil rights leader: "When you came into Birmingham, you didn't ask President Kennedy. Burke Marshall and John Doar wasn't nowhere around. There were some people here who had confidence in me 'cause they knew I wasn't gon' lie and wasn't gon' let 'em down." Shuttlesworth persisted: "You and I promised that we would *not* stop demonstrating until we *had* the victory. Now, that's it. That's it. And if you call it off . . . with the last little ounce of strength I got, I'm gonna get back out and lead."[60]

Abernathy intervened with "soothing and grieving words" to soften Shuttlesworth's resolve: "Fred, you know we went to school together. . . ." But the local leader would have none of it. Someone broke in to prepare King for his scheduled announcement with Kennedy. Shuttlesworth remarked, "Oh, you've got a press conference? I thought we were to make joint statements. Well, I'll tell you what to do: you go ahead, I'm going home." An attempt by Deenie Drew to calm him failed. The leader of the ACMHR squared off with the president of the SCLC: "Now Martin, you're mister big but you're soon to be mister nothing. You're going to fall from up

287

here to down here, and you're dead . . . let me make it plain to you . . . I'm going back home . . . I'm going to wait until I see it on TV and hear it on the radio that you've called it off."[61]

Marshall interrupted, "Well, I made promises to these people," to which Shuttlesworth demanded, "Burke, who gave you the authority to make any promises to any people without clearing it? But if you made promises, you can go back now and tell 'em that the demonstrations 'll be on 'cause you can't call 'em off, President Kennedy cain't call 'em off, and there's Martin Luther King—he cain't call 'em off." In the adjoining room, John Doar maintained contact with the White House in preparation for the Kennedy-King press conference, and Shuttlesworth overheard him saying, "We hit a snag—the frail one. The frail one is hanging up. Looks like it won't go through." King looked at Marshall and said, "We got to have unity, Burke. We've just got to have unity." Shuttlesworth turned to King and declared, "I'll be damned if you'll have it like this. You're mister big, but you're going to be mister S-H-I-T. I'm sorry, but I cannot compromise my principles and the principles that we established." Turning his back on King, Shuttlesworth left the room.[62]

In agreeing to the moratorium on marches at the insistence of the Kennedy administration, King had joined sides with the traditional Negro leadership class—which had opposed the Birmingham movement all along. A member of this class himself, he had never strayed far from its accommodationist methods. He thus struck a deal instead of holding his ground, and therein lay the conflict between the local and national movements. Whereas a difference in aims evolved during the demonstrations, a difference in methods existed throughout the campaign. The bitter scene between Shuttlesworth and King underscored the separate approaches to race reform. As a race man, Shuttlesworth unflinchingly faced the establishment and demanded Negro civil rights. As a member of the traditional Negro leadership class, King accommodated empty biracial negotiations that granted him prestige.

Shuttlesworth had mistakenly believed that King stood with him and hence decried the about-face. In Shuttlesworth's mind, calling off the demonstrations before the white power structure had publicly accepted the ACMHR-SCLC demands and ended racial discrimination was tantamount to giving up. For seven long years he had risked his life as head of the indigenous movement, and he recognized the culmination of that effort in the ACMHR-SCLC Birmingham campaign. How well he understood the ability of the white power structure to renege on vague promises of race reform. Indeed, the momentum building up to the spring demonstrations evolved out of a broken agreement in September 1962. Now his friend, his compatriot, King had sold out and left him holding sand. Observing the turn of events, James Forman described King's "betrayal in Birmingham."[63]

Although King canceled his joint statement with the president, he announced the moratorium on marches and his hope that a settlement would be reached over the next twenty-four hours. In Washington, Kennedy repeated the fact that the movement had suspended demonstrations and praised the biracial businessmen's efforts to negotiate a solution. He said the racial strife was "damaging the reputation of both Birmingham and the country," and he encouraged "the local leaders of Birmingham, both white and Negro, to continue their constructive and cooperative efforts." As the president spoke, the biracial businessmen discussed the details of the agreement while maintaining the moratorium on marches. An hour later, segregationists attempted to scuttle the negotiations.[64]

King, Abernathy, and twenty-five other integrationists sat in recorder's court on Wednesday afternoon, May 8, while on trial for the month-old charge of parading without a permit in cases remanded back from federal court. Judge Charles H. Brown found the defendants guilty and sentenced them to pay $300 fines and serve 180 days in jail. Unlike in the other cases, where he set the appeal bond at $300, the judge ordered King and Abernathy to pay $2,500 each if they wanted to post bond. Unwilling to accept the exorbitant figure, the two leaders elected to go to jail. Immediately, Walker announced: "We can only interpret this as an act of bad faith." As A. D. King prepared to renew the protests, Walker added: "If necessary, we will pull out all the stops tomorrow." Unwilling to wait, Shuttlesworth declared the moratorium over, and, wearing his "marching shoes," left the suite to join the schoolchildren in the church. Nearby a "sullen" crowd of more than a thousand onlookers milled about the park. Before Shuttlesworth had left the Gaston Motel, Joe Dolan of the Justice Department stopped him. Dolan arranged for the local leader to talk with the attorney general, and apparently Kennedy convinced Shuttlesworth to delay the resumption of marches while others attempted to get King and Abernathy released. Young referred to the near 90-degree temperature, the heated emotions of the African American spectators, and the cancellation of protests: "It's too hot. We couldn't have controlled this crowd." State troopers and law enforcement officers stood on every street corner as hundreds of activists filed out of the church and headed for home.[65]

Movement leaders notified civil rights lawyer William Kunstler of the arrests, and he contacted friends in New York City for help. Assisted by Harry Belafonte, Kunstler collected the necessary cash, but before leaving for Birmingham he received a call from Walker that A. G. Gaston had posted the appeal bonds. The Negro millionaire explained that "the moment was too crucial for both of them to be in jail." By posting bond, he hoped to maintain the moratorium and get King out of town. Shaken but relieved to be out of jail, King and Abernathy held a press conference late Wednesday. Although still upset, Shuttlesworth joined them, having convinced King to threaten new demonstrations if the white power structure failed to accept the movement's demands by Thursday morning. "We held off on massive demonstrations today as a demonstration of good faith to give the negotiators a chance to work in a calm atmosphere," King said. "But we made it clear that we would continue if the settlement is not worked out by tomorrow at 11 A.M." The biracial negotiations continued.[66]

Earlier in the day, Judge Talbot Ellis had released more than five hundred schoolchildren into their parents' custody instead of requiring the $500 cash bond. In one courtroom exchange, fifteen-year-old Grosbeck Preer Parham responded to the judge's admonition that "there is no freedom without restraint," observing: "You can say that about freedom because you've got your freedom. The Constitution says we're all equal, but Negroes aren't equal." The boy's mother, Aileen Parham, added: "I don't approve of street violence either. But after a civil rights meeting we did try to get in touch with city officials and they wouldn't see us. And I know this, Judge—these younger people are not going to take what we took." She wanted equal access, and in response to Judge Ellis's query on Booker T. Washington, she reiterated that "his day is past. The younger people won't take what we did." She recognized the new generation with its new way of thinking—something that Ellis and other white people failed to see. The concluding remarks reflected the distance between the parties: The judge paternalistically encouraged Grosbeck to return to class; the mother concurred with "thank you, judge," whereas the young man muttered under his breath, "Thanks for nothing."[67]

More than two thousand people packed Sixth Avenue Baptist Church for the mass meeting on Wednesday night. The heat of the long afternoon never dissipated, as the excitement of the congregation inched the mercury up to a steamy 88 degrees that felt more like 110. The crowd waved fans decorated with the smiling visage of Booker T. Washington, courtesy of Gaston's insurance company, in an effort to stir the stifling air and dry the beads of sweat that dotted black brows and brown lips. Reverend Gardner sent the students to New Pilgrim Baptist Church, then commented on King's release: "When you try to close one door, God opens up another door." The nineteen rabbis entered the sanctuary and sat on the platform in the front. Several of them spoke, including Richard Rubenstein, who compared Bull Connor's actions to police repression in East Berlin. The rabbis taught the congregation a song in Hebrew: "Behold how good and how pleasant it is for brethren to dwell together in unity." To the chagrin of the white detectives present, the audience arose, linked arm-in-arm, and sang it again with the black people on either side really giving the policemen "the treatment." The mass meeting adjourned as the activists exited the church singing "black and white together, we shall overcome, some day."[68]

King canceled the 11 o'clock press conference on Thursday morning, May 9, to give the biracial committee more time to complete their negotiations. The discussions centered on the release of the schoolchildren, with one black member offering to ask Nelson Rockefeller for financial assistance and another suggesting that President Kennedy raise the funds, as when he ransomed the Cuban prisoners. By noon the movement had assurances from northern unions such as the United Auto Workers that the bond money would be posted and the more than one thousand schoolchildren still in jail released.[69]

King's failure to renew demonstrations after the deadline passed convinced Shuttlesworth of the idleness of King's threats. Moreover, the leader of the SCLC postponed the press conference three times on Thursday. When at last he held it, only Abernathy joined him. King explained that Shuttlesworth remained in bed convalescing from his injuries, but reporters knew "the missing leader was not happy over the peace terms under consideration." As Abernathy recalled: "Shuttlesworth was bitterly angry during these tense hours, because he felt that outsiders had come in and taken the movement away from him though, in reality, without us there would have been no movement in Birmingham at all."[70]

During the press conference, King appeared ready to end the campaign by compromising further on the demands of the movement. He announced that the black community would accept desegregation of lunch counters and other public facilities at an unspecified "certain time" in the future as well as the "gradual" upgrading of Negro employees. On the arrested schoolchildren, King said: "The only thing that we can ask of the merchants is that they recommend in a very strong manner that the charges be dropped." On the catchall point of a biracial committee to discuss long-standing grievances in the black community, he said that the white power structure need only appoint the group but not concern itself with additional timetables for the implementation of school, park, and cinema desegregation, voter registration, the hiring of Negro policemen, and other demands.[71]

King's willingness to settle for less than the movement's original objectives and his refusal to resume protest marches suggests that he viewed *his* victory as won. The interests of the local activists no longer concerned the national civil rights leader, who apparently saw an opportunity to claim success while bailing out of Birmingham. A year later, Burke Marshall reflected on King's motives in Birmingham: "As far as King is concerned, I think that he wanted a success himself. He wanted success for himself and he wanted success for his people. It was partly cynical, and it was partly sincere." Marshall explained: "Partly cynical in the sense he wanted it for himself. He, King, as a Negro leader, wanted to be *the* Negro leader who had a success. In part he was just trying to accomplish something." The assistant attorney general added that King neither sought the intervention of federal troops in Birmingham nor anticipated federal legislation because "he wasn't thinking that far ahead. He was reacting like most people were, he was reacting to a situation." King reacted by disengaging from the campaign, leaving the local movement far short of its goals and in the hands of a hostile traditional Negro leadership class. It was not the first time he had done so.[72]

By late Thursday night, the negotiators had reached an accord. They now concerned themselves with the wording of the statement announcing the truce. The white progressive attorney Chuck Morgan worked with black activist Vincent Harding and two others, probably Arthur Shores and Andrew Young, in drafting the movement's official acceptance of the negotiated accord. Morgan recalled that no one in the white power structure wanted "to speak for the business community," and therefore the negotiators determined to "let the Negroes do it." Yet the white businessmen wanted King's statement "to be properly worded," so Morgan penned the opening lines of the accord.[73]

Neither municipal government endorsed the negotiations. A defiant Mayor Art Hanes lashed out at the white businessmen: "If they would stand firm, we would run King and that bunch of race agitators out of town." Referring to the Senior Citizens Committee, Hanes asked: "Why are they ashamed to release the names of those on the negotiating committee? Is it because they're ashamed of the fact that they are selling the white folks down the river?" He added angrily: "They call themselves negotiators. I call them a bunch of quisling, gutless traitors!" A muted Mayor Albert Boutwell showed less emotion but equal resistance: "I'm unwilling to make decisions virtually at gunpoint or as the result of agitation." Explaining his refusal to support the negotiations, Boutwell said, "I regard it as an unwarranted presumption for anyone to infer or suggest that there has been a 'truce' with any who have violated the law."[74]

National and international condemnation of police brutality in Birmingham had increased throughout the week. In many foreign newspapers events in the city competed with Haiti for top billing. A group of Africans picketed in New York City, denouncing the "hypocrisy" of American democracy and demanding that the United Nations intervene to protect black people in Birmingham. Expressing solidarity with the "American Negro freedom fighters," Jomo Kenyatta of the Kenya African National Union criticized President Kennedy for allowing racial oppression in the South: "It is ironic that a country such as the United States, which claims to be a home of democracy, should show itself as a state where oppression and discrimination are rife." Kenyatta warned: "If the United States wishes to maintain the respect and goodwill of the people of Africa, it must stand firmly by the fundamental principles of freedom and equality enshrined in its Constitution." In Congress, Representative Emanuel Celler of Brooklyn dismissed Kennedy's policy of federalism by recognizing: "There is ample basis for Federal intervention in the 13th and 14th and 15th Amendments to the Constitution." Senator Jacob K. Javits of New York recommended sweeping legislation to remove racial discrimination. He interpreted the Birmingham crisis as a tocsin that the United States appeared "close to a national emergency on civil rights."[75]

Movement leaders announced the resolution of the stalemate in Birmingham's race relations. Jailors released hundreds of schoolchildren to relieved parents, who understood that the students would be allowed back in class on Monday, while civil rights leaders faced flashbulbs as cameras recorded the historic moment on Friday afternoon, May 10, 1963. Fred Shuttlesworth sat between Martin Luther King and Ralph Abernathy at a table on the patio of the Gaston Motel as reporters gathered around to question the trio. In a final stroke of irony, Shuttlesworth—who with frustration had watched his seven years of hard work culminate in this moment—insisted on reading the prepared statement that accepted far less than he had demanded: "The city of Birmingham has reached an accord with its conscience. The acceptance of responsibility by local white and Negro

The Reverends Martin Luther King Jr., Fred L. Shuttlesworth, and Ralph David Abernathy announce the negotiated truce that ended the Birmingham campaign on May 10,
1963. Shortly after the press conference held on the patio of the A. G. Gaston Motel,
Shuttlesworth collapsed from emotional and physical exhaustion. *Birmingham News.*

leadership offers an example of a free people uniting to meet and solve
their problems." The language echoed the policy of federalism, a tribute to
Marshall, who acknowledged: "The important thing is that the settlement
was reached by the people down there."[76]

Shuttlesworth read out the compromises made on the four Points for
Progress: first, the "desegregation of lunch counters, rest rooms, fitting
rooms and drinking fountains in large downtown department and variety
stores within the next 90 days"; second, the "promotion and hiring of Negroes on a nondiscriminatory basis in stores and industries, hiring of Negro
clerks and salesmen within 60 days by the stores and appointment of a
private fair employment committee"; third, the "release of jailed Negro
demonstrators on bond or on their personal recognizance"; and fourth, the
"establishment of a biracial committee within two weeks." The local movement had failed to achieve a single one of its original objectives. As soon as
he finished reading the prepared statement, the physically and emotionally

exhausted founder of the Alabama Christian Movement for Human Rights collapsed.[77]

As the ambulance took the once formidable leader to the segregated Holy Family Hospital, King moralized: "We must not see the present development as a victory for the Negro. It is rather a victory for democracy and the whole citizenry of Birmingham—Negro and white!" Turning his attention to the black community, he lectured: "As we stand on the verge of using public facilities heretofore closed to us, we must not be overbearing and haughty in spirit. We must be loving enough to turn an enemy into a friend." King explained to reporters that he would be in Birmingham over the next two weeks and that after ninety days the civil rights leaders would evaluate the local situation. King stressed, "We must now move from protest to reconciliation."[78]

In a separate statement released later in the day, Sidney Smyer endorsed the negotiated accord for the white power structure. "It is important that the public understand, the steps we have taken were necessary to avoid a dangerous and imminent explosion." Explaining that the Senior Citizens Committee represented businesses and industries that employed most of the workforce in Birmingham, Smyer said the white businessmen were "proud to have been in a position to be of service to our city, though we share the bitterness which every citizen must feel about these demonstrations and their timing." He was the only white man willing to lend his name to the accord. Ignoring the long-standing struggle waged by Shuttlesworth and the ACMHR, Smyer thanked "God for a chance to re-establish racial peace." Disingenuously he added that the white power structure had intended all along to desegregate Birmingham and hence made no promises in the negotiations that were "inconsistent with plans which already were in the making before these disturbances." Referring to the collapse of civil order on Tuesday, May 7, he acknowledged: "We were caught in an emergency and forced to act upon the frightening information from our law enforcement agencies that the situation had been created which could erupt in a holocaust should a spark be struck." Smyer addressed the people of Birmingham in his conclusion: "But now that peace has returned to our community, it is up to all to help preserve it by doing nothing which would destroy it." In response to Bull Connor's failure to maintain segregation, however, vigilantes would attempt to disrupt the accord, using dynamite to shatter the fragile truce in an effort to ignite the feared holocaust.[79]

The ambiguous resolution revealed a fundamental conflict between the local and national movements. When he asked King into Birmingham, Shuttlesworth believed that the SCLC joined the ACMHR in a local campaign to achieve the nonnegotiable demand for an end to racial discrimination in the district. Whatever regional or national repercussions derived from the campaign were purely secondary to the local movement. On several occasions, King gave Shuttlesworth assurances that this was so. But once the Kennedy administration intervened, King altered his position. Following the dictates of the traditional Negro leadership class, he accommodated the desires of the establishment while compromising the demands of the movement. In a bitter confrontation, Shuttlesworth denounced King's betrayal. Nonetheless, the move enabled King to claim a personal success. The recognition he received from the Birmingham campaign reflected the victory of the national movement. The lack of concrete local reforms suggested that Shuttlesworth and the ACMHR had lost an opportunity for change. Indeed, King's placement of a hostile traditional Negro leadership class in a position of authority over the local movement and black community hindered the reform drive. Hence the conflicting aims and approaches to reform of the local and national movements influenced the outcome of events.

The stalwart ACMHR members and black college students who kept the Birmingham campaign alive during the long month of April 1963 embodied the civil rights struggle in its purest form. Here was the indigenous movement created by charismatic ministers in the aftermath of the Montgomery bus boycott. And here were the young African Americans whose rising expectations and demands on life had led them to reject the racist ideology of the past and to seek immediate access to the system. For seven years the ACMHR had protested Birmingham's segregation laws and racial discrimination in employment. With the sit-ins, black students joined the ACMHR in the direct action struggle. After a yearlong boycott, the local movement marshaled its resources in a campaign to force a resolution of Birmingham's racial stalemate. Through the SCLC, the national movement assisted the campaign but the volunteers remained local individuals.

Statistics from the Warden's Docket show that a grand total of 339 protesters were arrested for civil rights violations between April 3 and April 27, with no more arrests until the children's crusade began on May 2. With the arrest of 274 black teenagers on that day alone, the dynamics of the campaign changed as the movement began to fill the jail. Heretofore, most of the people arrested were charged with violating municipal code 1159, parading without a permit, or code 1663F, trespassing after warning. A few demonstrators were held for blocking the aisles, just as a handful of black bystanders were detained for loitering. Juveniles and others detained but not charged with violating city ordinances were not listed on the docket. Of the 339 arrested, the majority, 181, were black males. Only 156 of the total were black females, which suggests that not only did the men lead the movement but they also risked arrest in greater numbers than the women. Two white men were also arrested for civil rights protests at this time. In contrast to the rural South where women often organized the movement, in the urban South the men led, organized, and participated.[80]

Although students played a central role in the campaign—increasing in number as it progressed—most of the activists arrested were black people over age twenty-one. Probably 163 of the 339 total were students, with 152 of them giving their ages as twenty-one or younger and 11 giving no age at all. Most of the people arrested were released after posting a $300 bond. Several bonding companies provided this service, including the Esdale Bonding Company, Aces Bond Company, Reliable Bail Bond, and Sweet Conley's Bail Bond. Once the SCLC had depleted its war chest and could no longer hire Esdale and the other companies to post bond for movement members, black citizens filled the void by putting up their savings as cash bonds. People such as Lola Hendricks, M. W. Pipper, Dr. James T. Montgomery, Joseph H. Bowman, Willie J. Griggs, John Broadnax, John J. Drew, George Pruitt, Ada Ammons, and James R. Revis paid the fees. Hindricks and some of the others were actually members of the ACMHR. Thus a core group of activists had made the difference. Compared to the overall black population in the city, they were only a handful of individuals, but in the end they made it all possible.[81]

297

But for Birmingham

J ust as the children's crusade broke the stalemate in local race relations, so too it broke the stalemate on the national level as it forced the president and Congress to draft legislation that ended legal racial discrimination. Likewise, the Birmingham campaign transformed the Southern Christian Leadership Conference into a financially successful organization with a powerful strategy for social change and an internationally renown leader. At first it appeared that the ambiguous resolution had been achieved within the confines of federalism, but in the tumultuous months following Birmingham, as civil rights protests rocked cities across America, it became clear to the Kennedy administration that legislation was necessary to achieve desegregation in the South. Consequently, the victory in Birmingham evolved into the Civil Rights Act of 1964, which opened the system to African Americans even in recalcitrant places such as the steel city. The SCLC rode the wave of international outrage over Birmingham, increasing its revenues tenfold and honing a new strategy of nonviolent coersion. The March on Washington was simply a celebration of the victory in Birmingham. The Reverend Dr. Martin

Luther King's selection for the Nobel Peace Prize was an endorsement of nonviolence in the anticolonial struggle in Alabama and elsewhere in the world. Whereas realtor Sidney W. Smyer and the service economy faction agreed to the negotiations in Birmingham, iron and steel executives opposed the reforms. Both municipal governments denounced the biracial agreement. Despite continued white resistance, Birmingham's defense of white supremacy had failed. In time, the city desegregated public accommodations, the black middle class gained access as consumers and workers, and African Americans enjoyed political empowerment. Yet immediately after the negotiated accord, vigilantes—no longer held in check by Public Safety Commissioner Bull Connor—struck to stop the race reform.

As in the past, the Ku Klux Klan organized to defend racial norms. More than 2,500 Klansmen gathered in a field near Bessemer, thirteen miles south of Birmingham, on Saturday night, May 11, 1963, to hear Grand Dragon Robert Shelton castigate the white businessmen involved in the accord. Flames reached heavenward as the robed knights flared two twenty-foot crosses. Klansmen carried weapons and wore illegal hoods. Uniformed policemen stood about in a show of support. Surrounded by American and Confederate flags, Shelton spoke from a flatbed truck: "These stores that want the Negro trade so much, these people who are selling out the whites, they don't need our business." He threatened: "The Klan has been busy . . . working undercover and . . . we know who these white men are who have sold out our community." Later that night, as bombs set off riots in black neighborhoods, three white men were seen throwing bricks through five plate glass windows at the Parisian Department Store, owned by Emil Hess, one of the Jewish merchants who had supported the negotiated accord. In addition to the merchants, vigilantes marked civil rights leaders for reprisals.[1]

After the Klan meeting, would-be assassins dynamited two separate sites in an attempt to kill Martin Luther King. At 10:45 P.M. vigilantes bombed the house of his brother, the Reverend A. D. King. The explosion demolished the front of the brick structure, leaving a gaping hole in the cement steps and bent wrought iron dangling from the roof. The angry African Americans who quickly formed a crowd around the Ensley residence foretold of the violence to come. With knives and ice picks, they punctured the tires of police cars and fire trucks responding to the attack. At midnight the discharge of dynamite at the A. G. Gaston Motel triggered a full-scale riot. Witnesses saw four white men with their faces painted black toss the bomb from a car as it sped past the motel on Fifth Avenue North. The bundle of explosives missed its goal—Room 30—and landed between the building and three house trailers. Like a tornado, the blast twisted the prefabricated structures, knocked out the wall to a downstairs room, shattered glass windows, and damaged the motel office. The dynamite injured four people. Both bombs targeted King, who had left that afternoon in order to preach the next morning in his church in Atlanta. An anonymous caller had tipped off the motel, and an employee had notified the police department and the Federal Bureau of Investigation. Law enforcement officers told management "not to worry about it." At the sound of the explosion hundreds of African Americans left nearby homes, stores, and bars and descended on the area around the motel.[2]

The arrival of the white squad cars sent the black crowd into a rage. Now the former bystanders hurled bricks and bottles at the officers. Members of the mob shouted "Kill 'em! Kill 'em!" at the policemen, who, waiting for reinforcements, moved back. They did little for nearly an hour. Violent protesters ransacked the twenty-eight-block area around the motel. Smashing the windows of patrol cars and fire trucks, the mob vented its pent-up frustration. Innocent travelers caught in the area attracted rocks thrown from the crowd and suffered most of the white injuries. One police officer received several stab wounds. Captain James Lay, a black civil defense worker, saved the life of a white cabbie, W. A. Bowman, who inadvertently drove into the riot and was knifed by black men. They torched his taxi after turning it over. The flickering orange and red flames of the gasoline brightly contrasted with the thick black clouds that billowed above the car. Several Italian-owned grocery stores went up in smoke as rioters attempted to burn all white-owned property in the neighborhood. But the sparks knew no race and quickly spread the fire to black-owned houses. Soon the hot night sky blazed with the intensity of a blast furnace. In addition to the exploitative ghetto groceries, the African Americans looted liquor stores and other businesses. At the height of the riot, some 2,500 black people participated in the violence.[3]

Leading the offensive, Bull Connor's armored car arrived shortly before 1:00 A.M. and wheeled about Kelly Ingram Park. Behind the white "tank," Colonel Al Lingo led hundreds of state highway patrolmen ordered by Governor George C. Wallace to shoot in self-defense. Wielding carbines as clubs, the steel-helmeted troopers stormed into the mob beating rioters with impunity. Some officers ran up on front porches and into tenement houses, attacking innocent occupants. They were as incendiary as the dynamite. Birmingham police chief Jamie Moore pleaded with Lingo and

The first urban riot of the 1960s occurred in Birmingham on May 10, 1963, when African Americans responded to the dynamiting of the A. G. Gaston Motel by burning groceries, shops, and black rental property in the area between the motel and the Sixteenth Street Baptist Church. Bull Connor's white tank patrols Seventeenth Street during the disturbances. Associated Press.

302

his associate, Dallas County sheriff Jim Clark, to leave: "We don't need any guns down here. You all might get somebody killed." "You're damn right it'll kill somebody," Lingo said, slapping his automatic shotgun. When officers brought out three German shepherds, black rioters pelted them with gravel. Someone shouted, "You'd better get those dogs out of here!" Blaring its siren and routing rioters, the armored car rolled down the sidewalk with an officer inside announcing over the loudspeaker: "Everybody get off the streets now. We cannot get ambulances in here to help your people unless you clear the streets." Together, the police and rioters had injured at least fifty people.[4]

As the mob prevented firemen from reaching the flames that devoured slum properties and as ambulances screamed down the street loaded with black and white victims, civil rights leaders joined police in an effort to stop the violence. The Reverend Wyatt Tee Walker left the Gaston Motel with a megaphone and, waving his arm to attract attention, called out: "Please do not throw any bricks anymore. Ladies and gentlemen, will you cooperate by going to your homes?" In response, someone heaved a brick at him. Others shouted, "They started it! They started it!" Only moments before,

Walker had narrowly escaped severe injury. A state trooper had whacked Walker's wife over the head with a gun stock. Lunging to retaliate, the civil rights activist was tackled by reporter Bob Gordon, of Mississippi, who understood the repercussions of a black man striking a white officer. A. D. King had better luck convincing the mob that milled about his damaged house to go home. Afterward, A. D. King joined other movement personnel in the shattered office of the motel. He attempted to telephone the president at the White House but could only reach the FBI. "You've got to do something, the whole town has gone berserk," King shouted into the receiver, ". . . the Negroes are up in arms." Joining those outside, King drew three hundred African Americans into a nearby parking lot. Standing on the hood of a Cadillac, he lectured: "We're not mad at anyone. We're saying: 'Father, forgive them for they know not what they do.'" He condemned violence as "the tactic of the white man." The unnatural light cast shadows against the scarred wall of the motel as the activists sang freedom songs in the strange setting. By dawn the riot had burned out.[5]

Parts of Birmingham looked like a war zone as the sun rose on Mother's Day, May 12, 1963, two years after a very different riot at the Trailways station, where white vigilantes had attacked the Freedom Riders. And like that earlier incident, this one also provoked the federal government into taking preliminary action. President John F. Kennedy ordered more than three thousand army troops into Alabama. Ten C-47 transports from Fort Bragg, North Carolina, landed at Maxwell Air Force Base in Montgomery, and convoys carried soldiers from Fort Benning, Georgia, to Fort McClellan, Anniston, as the Eighty-second Airborne and Second Infantry Divisions mobilized for domestic service. With the army on standby, Kennedy prepared to federalize the Alabama National Guard if necessary, and he sent Assistant Attorney General for Civil Rights Burke Marshall back to Birmingham.[6]

The president wanted to deploy troops and establish martial law. Issuing a statement that outlined his response to the riot, he warned, "There must be no repetition of last night's incidents by any group." His brother, Attorney General Robert Kennedy, had called Sid Smyer to find out what was going on. Smyer reported back that Birmingham "didn't need any massive federal help," referring to troops. He was asked to go to Washington. The president feared a "race riot" and asked Smyer, "Can you handle the situation?" Smyer assured him: "We're working it out. We're gonna work it out. Don't you worry." The former head of the chamber of commerce and leader of the white power structure's Senior Citizens subcommittee on race opposed federal intervention, for as he told segregationists in Birmingham who favored such a step: "When martial law takes over, local civil authority, local courts are abolished. The community is under the heel of the military. No longer can we solve anything ourselves. Answers are provided for us." Mayor Albert Boutwell seconded Smyer's concerns: "We neither need nor want Birmingham run by Pentagon brass or by remote control from the White House." That very threat presented Wallace with an opportunity to challenge federal authority.[7]

Defending his deployment of Lingo and the state troopers in Birmingham, Wallace declared that he would do "whatever it takes" to stop the black violence except tolerate the use of federal troops. Blaming the bombings on "communist . . . outside subversives," he snidely remarked: "This is what Martin Luther King calls non-violence and passive resistance." But the cocky governor decried Kennedy's stationing of troops on Alabama soil. Having vowed to disobey federal orders to desegregate schools, Wallace chafed under the loss of state sovereignty represented by a federal occupation. "Under what authority would you send federal troops into this state?" he curtly telegraphed the president.[8]

With the negative international press and the new black threat to white-owned property, President Kennedy took an active role in the Birmingham crisis; nonetheless, it conformed to his limited policy of federalism. To justify the troop movements he cited Title 10, Section 333, of the U.S. Code, which authorized him to suppress insurrections. While sparring over Birmingham, the president and the governor were preparing for the future showdown at the schoolhouse door. For months Justice Department officials had planned the integration of the University of Alabama. The attorney general's unpleasant visit with the governor in April had failed to assure a smooth transition, yet it had clarified Kennedy's course of action.[9]

The president's staff compiled an "Alabama Notebook" that listed 375 large corporations operating in the state together with executives and boards of directors in an effort to appeal to these businessmen for racial tolerance. In addition to revealing Birmingham's interlocking directorates that actually controlled the city's political economy, the notebook gave the Kennedy administration the names of Alabama's industrial and financial elite in a handy reference that showed the widespread influence of a few white men. During the Birmingham crisis, Kennedy's staff had telephoned the white elite to promote the negotiations of Burke Marshall. The notebook facilitated a similar effort during the integration of the university. This clear example of Washington recognizing the locus of power in Alabama—the local heads of national corporations—seconded the conclusion simultaneously reached by Smyer and the white progressives working with the Senior Citizens and the civil rights activists who had targeted the same white power structure. Through Marshall's return to Birmingham, Kennedy hoped to salvage the negotiated accord despite the bombings and riots.[10]

Arriving in the city late Sunday night, Marshall found Sid Smyer and Martin Luther King eager to maintain the negotiated accord. After commending local law enforcement officers for doing a "most remarkable job under the circumstances," Smyer described things as "smoother now." He blamed the vigilantes: "I believe the community and the country are shocked that, after trying to work this matter out peacefully, a bunch of hoodlums came in here and stirred up more hate." Hurrying back to Birmingham from Atlanta, King had surveyed the riot damage and said: "I do not feel the events of last night nullified the agreement at all." The integrationist concurred with Smyer: "I do not think the bombings were perpetrated or even sanctioned by the majority of the white people in Birmingham." Satisfied, Marshall returned to Washington and reported back to the president that the truce held. Attorney General Robert Kennedy issued a statement that reiterated the policy of federalism: "We hope and expect that the problems of Birmingham will be resolved and handled by the people of Birmingham and that no further steps will have to be taken by the Federal Government."[11]

As he toured pool halls on Monday, May 13, King preached nonviolence while disarming African Americans. He passed a hat to collect knives, blackjacks, and other weapons as he moved among the juke joints with a crowd in tow. State troopers patrolling the area ordered King back to the Gaston Motel. Ever a presence, Wallace's highway patrolmen stood guard. Elsewhere black and white youths held knife fights. Grown men of both races exchanged insults on street corners.[12]

At a rally that afternoon in the Sixth Avenue Baptist Church, former baseball player Jackie Robinson and former heavyweight boxing champion Floyd Patterson praised the Birmingham movement for inspiring oppressed people everywhere. King reiterated their comments: "Birmingham is known all over the world today." To maintain the momentum of the movement, King renewed the voter registration drive. Though not a pressing subject of local interest, the move curried favor with the Kennedys. King ended with an appeal for nonviolence: "There may be more blood to flow on the streets of Birmingham before we get our freedom, but let it be our blood instead of the blood of our white brother. The agreements that

305

have been made will be met. There will be integration in Birmingham in the next few weeks." He concluded: "How long will we have to suffer? . . . I can only answer, not long." Future events would temper King's optimism.[13]

Speaking for the Senior Citizens Committee in an interview Monday, Smyer affirmed the negotiated accord and acknowledged that the present crisis derived from the black effort to remove racial discrimination in the marketplace: "We are trying to work out a climate in this community in which all people have an opportunity for a job that are willing and able to hold a job." The accord accepted by the businessmen differed slightly from the one announced by movement leaders on May 10. The ambiguity of the resolution became apparent to all when—beginning to backpedal—Smyer referred to the upgrading of Negro employees as "one Negro sales person will be employed in one store." Civil rights leaders fired off a letter to Smyer over the "mis-understanding" they thought had been clarified at the insistence of the Reverend Fred L. Shuttlesworth. They believed the merchants would promote "at least one clerk in each of the major stores," but Smyer's contradictory statement concerned them: "This we do not feel is a significant indication of good faith leading toward a policy on non-discriminatory hiring." Although Smyer reaffirmed the accord, other members of the Senior Citizens expressed their displeasure. Some, such as William J. Rushton of Protective Life Insurance Company, resigned and thereby repudiated the agreement. Not until Wednesday did the Senior Citizens Committee release the names of the industrial and financial elite that composed its membership. It never identified the people who served with Smyer on the special subcommittee on race.[14]

The resignation of Rushton revealed the division among the Big Mules. Several executives of the iron, steel, and related industries had opposed the businessmen's work for race reform. Winton M. Blount, president of a multinational construction corporation in Montgomery and head of the state chamber of commerce, gave the Justice Department the names of several members of the white power structure in Birmingham who rejected the accord. Blount believed that Lewis Jeffers, president of Hayes International Corporation, had resigned. At Hayes, a nearly all-white workforce manufactured weapons under government contract. Management there had long tolerated the Ku Klux Klan and other white supremacy groups. The name of Arthur V. Wiebel, president of the Tennessee Coal, Iron, and Railroad Company, joined those of Rushton and Jeffers on the list of Senior Citizens released to the press. Wiebel had resisted race reform even though the Kennedy administration had contacted his superior, Roger Blough, chairman of the board of the U.S. Steel Corporation, and asked him to intervene on behalf of black people in Birmingham and end the racial disturbances. Losing the fight with the president over increases in the price of steel just the year before had probably disinclined Blough to assist in the negotiations. In response to the administration's request, Blough disingenuously said: "We have fulfilled our responsibility in the Birmingham area." Of course, since 1907 U.S. Steel through its subsidiary TCI had dominated affairs in the Birmingham district by establishing the local consensus on labor and race relations. Consequently, it opposed changing the status quo. The influence of U.S. Steel hindered the formation of a new consensus on race, yet the defection of the service-consumer economy spokesmen from the Big Mules demonstrated a split in the white power structure.[15]

Several service-consumer economy executives actively supported the accord. Milton Andrews, chairman of the Bank for Savings and Trust, resisted extreme pressure by Wallace to repudiate the Senior Citizens. The governor had appointed Andrews—a strong Wallace supporter—to the plum position of chairman of the state Liquor Control Agency; yet because of his understanding of the service economy, the banker defended race reform. The president of the Birmingham Chamber of Commerce, William Spencer III of Owens-Richard Company and Orco Welding Supplies, Inc., also endorsed the inevitable. He recognized that the negative image of Birmingham in the national media had hurt local business as companies canceled orders and industries located elsewhere. "One thing that large corporations shy away from," Spencer stated, "is the lack of coordination between the political and business leaders of the community." He understood the need to attract new industries and expand old ones. Since the beginning of the decade, Birmingham had suffered economic stagnation and had compiled a terrible record of decline compared to other southeastern cities. Outside opinion of Birmingham greatly concerned Spencer: "We know it's not a true picture of us." Like many white people, Spencer previously had experienced no disorder, especially among the landscaped lawns over the mountain where he lived. An optimistic Smyer believed, "If we come out of this with a good image we're going to grow like never before." The mandarins of the service-consumer economy struggled to transform the white power structure despite the resistance of some Big Mules. Offering a new "perpetual promise," these prophets of commercial growth guaranteed to solve the ills of society. They focused on Smyer's perceptive understanding of postmodern race relations: the need to present an image of reform. They did little else.[16]

Dealing in images of defiance, Wallace kept Lingo and the state troopers in Birmingham as a direct challenge to President Kennedy. The black community saw it as brutal provocation. "The Governor is trying to sabotage the agreement," Shuttlesworth said. "He wants to provoke incidents by Negroes. We'll guarantee against violence from Negroes if the troopers leave. We want the city to return to normalcy." Referring to Smyer and the Senior Citizens, he noted: "We believe the businessmen can grant Negroes freedom without more demonstrations or martial law or troops." Yet he warned, "If they don't there will be more demonstrations and I will lead them personally." Working in tandem with Lingo, Bull Connor's men put up police barricades around the Sixteenth Street Baptist Church to dissuade people from attending the mass meeting. The action signified the commissioner's refusal to surrender his defense of segregation.[17]

Municipal leaders attempted to undermine the accord. Following the riots a vituperative Mayor Art Hanes spewed: "Martin Luther King is a revolutionary. The nigger King ought to be investigated by the Attorney General." Indeed, the government was spying on the integrationist. But Hanes reserved his hatred for Robert Kennedy: "I hope that every drop of blood that's spilled he tastes in his throat, and I hope he chokes on it." Although Hanes did little more than denounce the events, segregationist school board members appointed by the city commission attempted to jeopardize the "uneasy quiet" that marked the fragile peace.[18]

In an inflammatory act on Monday, May 20, 1963, the Birmingham Board of Education expelled over 1,000 black schoolchildren who had participated in the massive street protests earlier in the month. With only a week left before graduation, the seniors would have to attend summer school to receive their diplomas. On May 6, at the height of campaign-inspired truancy, fewer than 900 of the almost 7,500 African American students in the district had attended class. With the help of Negro teachers and administrators, Superintendent Theo Wright targeted the more than 1,000 children for the disciplinary action. On behalf of the students and the movement, the NAACP filed suit in U.S. district court to stop the proceedings. But Judge Clarence W. Allgood, a Kennedy appointee, sided with the school board: "This court was shocked to see hundreds of school children, ranging from six to sixteen, running loose, and without direction over the streets of Birmingham and in the business establishments." That afternoon, movement lawyers filed a motion in the Fifth Circuit Court of Appeals in Atlanta for a restraining order. Chief Judge Elbert Tuttle, an Eisenhower appointee, reversed Allgood's decision and sent the students back to the classroom.[19]

As the federal courts thwarted the massive resistance of the school board, the state courts resolved the question of municipal government in Birmingham. On May 21, 1963, the Alabama Supreme Court ruled in favor of Boutwell and the council and ordered the three commissioners to vacate city hall. His unceremonious dismissal ended Bull Connor's brutal tenure in Birmingham politics. To keep him out of local affairs, the Big Mules helped him get elected to a post on the Public Service Commission—a job he held until his death in 1973—where he consistently voted to raise utility rates.[20]

A different school yard provided the setting for the final showdown between Wallace and Kennedy. The events in Birmingham loomed behind the staged confrontation, for as Burke Marshall recalled about the Kennedy administration, "the threads ran through" the events in Birmingham and Tuscaloosa. Elected governor in 1962 on the campaign promise to "stand in the schoolhouse door" to prevent the desegregation of the University of Alabama, Wallace had carefully orchestrated his clash with President Kennedy in the context of states' rights in order to carry massive resistance to its logical conclusion: federal intervention by force on behalf of race reform. The futility of the political gesture paid handsome dividends in popular support. The governor's actions in Birmingham—ordering in Lingo and the state troopers despite the opposition of local law enforcement, filing suit before the U.S. Supreme Court demanding that Kennedy withdraw the troops from Alabama, and tersely informing the president at a meeting in Muscle Shoals that he would not back down—all heightened tensions in the days before the June 11 registration deadline for summer school.[21]

Annoyed by Wallace and wary of another Oxford, Mississippi, where white violence against federal marshals had made a fiasco of the desegregation effort, the Kennedy administration prepared for the worst. The president kept the troopers on standby near Birmingham. Rhetorically, the administration condemned Wallace's defiance. During a press conference for Voice of America on June 4, the attorney general criticized the international press for heavily reporting the disorders in Oxford and Birmingham but ignoring the successes such as desegregation in Atlanta. Describing race relations as "the most difficult problem we have had in the United States," Kennedy went on to encourage southerners "to accept their moral responsibility, not because the federal government comes in and says with a law, or with a soldier, or with a United States marshal that, 'This is what you must do,' but that they understand and realize that this is what you have to do morally." To him, desegregation was "the moral and right thing to do." He proposed federal laws to achieve race reform. Wallace would provide the president with an opportunity to expound on the attorney general's comments.[22]

President Kennedy's televised speech following Wallace's stand in the schoolhouse door on June 11, 1963, marked a turning point in the administration's public policy on race. The drama of the morning—Wallace's physical refusal to allow Deputy Attorney General Nicholas Katzenbach to register two black students, forcing Kennedy to federalize the Alabama National Guard in order to desegregate the university—played out in the bright summer sun as the governor bested the president in the eyes of many Alabamians while acting on the national stage. Both men claimed victory. At 8:00 P.M. Kennedy went on the air with an incomplete text written by Theodore Sorensen. The president recounted the events on campus and asked all Americans to examine their conscience in regard to race relations: "We are confronted primarily with a moral issue." Having closely monitored coverage of Birmingham abroad, he recognized that the international community viewed American democracy as hypocritical because of racism, a grave liability in the Cold War struggle over Third World labor and raw materials. Hence the president could ask: "Are we to say to the world—and more importantly to each other—that this is the land of the free, except for the Negroes? . . ." and answer: "Now the time has come for this nation to fulfill its promise."[23]

The direct action of the Birmingham campaign had forced the president to confront race reform: "The events in Birmingham and elsewhere have so increased the cries for equality that no city or state or legislative body can prudently choose to ignore them." Indeed, the more than 700 demonstrations in nearly 200 American cities producing almost 15,000 arrests since May pointed to the crisis in race relations. In a prescient phrase, Kennedy reminded the public of the racial turmoil that spring: "The fires of frustration and discord are burning in every city, North and South. Where legal remedies are not at hand, redress is sought in the streets in demonstrations, parades and protests, which create tensions and threaten violence—and threaten lives." Since the sit-ins in 1960 and the Freedom Rides in 1961, pressure had mounted steadily for some type of federal response to guarantee the rights of all American citizens. Through its policy of federalism, the

310

Kennedy administration had encouraged local law enforcement to obey court orders on desegregation, but that effort had met with stiff opposition. As the resistance of George Wallace and Bull Connor countered the increased demands of Fred Shuttlesworth and Martin Luther King, Kennedy searched for a sweeping solution to end the "repressive police action" while forcing the demonstrators off the streets and into the courts. "Next week I shall ask the Congress of the United States to act, to make a commitment it has not made in this century to the proposition that race has no place in American life or law." A week later the president proposed the Civil Rights Act of 1964.[24]

The decision to press for legislation that would outlaw racial discrimination was made during the civil rights struggle in Birmingham. Interviewed a year later by *New York Times* reporter Anthony Lewis, Burke Marshall recalled that after his return to Washington from having successfully negotiated the accord, "Everybody's mind was turned to the future and they thought this pattern of Birmingham had been established, that it would recur in many other places, and it did that summer." Heretofore the administration had not considered legislation as a solution to the racial crisis. Yet black and white people nationally and internationally pressured the president to respond. Marshall remembered, "Everyone concluded that the president had to act and . . . not only face this himself, but somehow bring the country to face this problem and resolve it."[25]

After deciding to draft legislation, Kennedy and his staff conducted numerous meetings with businessmen. Discussing the proposals with Marshall, the president expressed his desire that the bill be "comprehensive in that it didn't deal with pieces of the problem but it dealt with all parts of the problem that could be dealt with by law." Marshall recalled that the most difficult question "was in connection with employment rather than public accommodations," but the latter issue initially proved more controversial. Over the course of the "very frantic month" of May 1963, Marshall met with Robert Kennedy and immediately reached an understanding that the "law could be written, would be constitutional . . . and could be justified under the commerce clause." Because Kennedy proposed the desegregation of public (parks and schools) as well as private (motels and restaurants) accommodations, he decided not to cite the Fourteenth Amendment, in part because the 1883 U.S. Supreme Court had ruled unconstitutional the 1875 Civil Rights Act which had used similar reasoning for its defense. Instead, the administration referred to the Interstate Commerce Clause of the Constitution because, since 1937, the Supreme Court had let stand under this ruling the regulatory functions of the New Deal. On June 20, 1963, New York congressman Emanuel Celler introduced the bill in the House of Representatives. It had eight provisions that promoted voting rights and school desegregation, prohibited discrimination in public accommodations and federally assisted programs, extended the life of the Civil Rights Commission, and proposed equal employment opportunities. The omnibus bill tackled racial discrimination on several fronts but faced a difficult fight in the Congress.[26]

The climax of the civil rights movement thus occurred in Birmingham as the ACMHR-SCLC campaign and hundreds of simultaneous national demonstrations forced a reluctant Kennedy administration to propose sweeping civil rights legislation. Passed by Congress through the efforts of President Lyndon B. Johnson as a tribute to the martyred president, the Civil Rights Act of 1964 marked a watershed in American race relations as it opened the system to African Americans. Kennedy identified Birmingham as the turning point when he invited national civil rights leaders to the White House on June 22 and joked: "I don't think you should all be totally harsh on Bull Connor. After all he has done more for civil rights than almost anybody else." Shuttlesworth heard the president say something different: "But for Birmingham, we would not be here today." Indeed, the response of the federal government convinced national civil rights leaders of the success of the Birmingham campaign. In celebration they planned a national demonstration for later that summer. Integrationists designed the March on Washington to express the hope for the future that filled their hearts.[27]

Paradoxically, the national victory won in the streets of Birmingham did little for many black folk back home. In part, this resulted from the narrowness of the original goals of the civil rights movement: the struggle for access to public accommodations and equal job opportunities. By demanding incorporation into the existing inherently unequal system, as opposed to radically transforming the system to make it more equitable, civil rights activists greatly limited the opportunity for change. The sit-in movement and other militant black protests nonetheless revealed middle-class aspirations and conservative aims. The inability of integrationists to achieve anything "bigger than a hamburger" reflected the focus on individual civic rights rather than broad-based community empowerment. Having no capital to begin with did not change once African Americans gained full access as consumers. The commodity riot after the bombings suggested what many nonmovement black people thought about living in a consumer

312

society without wherewithal: given the chance they would take what they could. Movement members, however, expressed faith in the system. At a mass meeting the Reverend James Bevel recalled with humor "the students marching down the street and they didn't have 15 cents in their pockets to buy a hamburger." His optimism underscored the belief that once having won the seat at the lunch counter, then with formerly "whites only" jobs, African Americans would earn the money. In Birmingham, the movement struggled to implement the ambiguous resolution and get the seat.[28]

The white community resisted implementation of the negotiated accord. Mayor Boutwell, who had made private assurances but never publicly endorsed the agreement, failed to uphold his end of the bargain. He had ample opportunities to do so. E. L. "Red" Holland, the editorial editor of the *Birmingham News*, accused Boutwell and the city council of deliberately "delaying" implementation of the agreed-upon reforms, a heady charge considering Boutwell's determination to act with "honor." A month after the demonstrations, Boutwell had yet to appoint a biracial committee and hence recognize Birmingham's racial problems. City councilman Dr. E. C. Overton concurred with the mayor when he addressed the West End Chamber of Commerce and "flatly denied that there would be any biracial committee." Good faith efforts by the city council had not been forthcoming, for it refused to reopen parks and golf courses on a desegregated basis, and it had yet to rescind segregation ordinances. In addition, the Senior Citizens Committee backed away from its agreement. Holland believed that "nothing within the commercial community is being done to take action on the Negro-White agreements." He pessimistically concluded, "and unless I misjudge my community, the atmosphere here is of no follow-through by the whites." Holland was an astute observer of Birmingham.[29]

In the aftermath of the riot and demonstrations, the police department attempted to return to the status quo in race relations. Police chief Jamie Moore responded to the civil disorders by purchasing "100 riot type (military) 12 gauge pump shotguns" so he could arm his men in a fashion similar to that of Lingo and the state troopers. During June and July 1963, officers reexerted their control over the black community. Yet the brutal response to the protest marches compromised the authority of the police. Through force, policemen kept the poor and desperate elements of the community in line. For black people in Birmingham this force often meant "justifiable homicide." On June 28, a policeman killed Blaine Gordon Jr., a seventeen-year-old black male. On July 6, a detective shot, but did not kill, thirty-three-year-old Johnny Patterson, also black. On August 4, an officer killed

313

James Scott Jr., age thirty-five, another black male. The ease with which policemen shot and killed black men reflected a pathology within Birmingham's law enforcement that contributed to future racial crises. It also demonstrated how police brutality addressed the ambiguities of the negotiated accord. While indigenous black leaders renewed local demands for Negro policemen in an effort to gain civil service jobs and lessen legal violence, the national movement spent the summer absorbing the popular response to and recuperating from the spring demonstrations.[30]

THE APPARENT SUCCESS of the Birmingham campaign astounded the Southern Christian Leadership Conference. "We believe that Birmingham will prove to be a watershed in the history of the nonviolent revolution in America," wrote Wyatt Tee Walker in early June. A week later he boasted: "Incertitude, I do not possess concerning the Birmingham Movement. I feel very keenly that our ultimate goal which is genuine integration, will be fully achieved in that city, and all over the South." In a letter at the end of July, Walker wrote: "The volume of Dr. King's mail is staggering. I am sure you are sympathetic to the intense schedules most of us have had to respect in light of the accelerated activity in civil rights since Birmingham." And with the letters came donations.[31]

Within a month of the ambiguous resolution, the SCLC took in more money than it had seen in the previous calendar year. Among the contributions, excluding those from direct mail sources, were donations collected in the North by sympathetic organizations and at freedom rallies staged in support of the movement. The SCLC received checks totaling $2,500 from twenty-two district groups in the Kings County Democratic Executive Committee of New York. The letter, dated May 14, 1963, typified those that arrived with contributions: "It was good news for all of us to know that you got some real concession in Birmingham." Uptown at the headquarters of the Congress of Racial Equality, a second bundle of checks totaling $239.90 was sent to Shuttlesworth with the note that these were the "follow-up of monies" previously mentioned. Members of the Yale Divinity School sent $381.47 with the message, "We are sure that the money will be well spent." An NAACP chapter in Washington, D.C., mailed $689.55 to the SCLC on May 24. A demonstration of 1,200 black and white people in White Plains, New York, collected $824.05 for the SCLC to use "for Bail Bonds and any other purpose." The donations arrived daily.[32]

The big money, however, came from freedom rallies. A mass meeting in early July 1963 hosted by the Detroit Council for Human Rights collected $27,604 for the SCLC. A rally at Wrigley Field in Los Angeles netted $57,750, in part because Hollywood stars such as Frank Sinatra and Sammy Davis Jr. performed. In all, the SCLC took in $159,856 from rallies conducted in response to the Birmingham campaign. Such funding was a far cry from the $2,529 the SCLC received in the last week of March just before the demonstrations began. After Birmingham, the SCLC was a big-budget operation. By 1964 treasurer Ralph David Abernathy could muffle his concern and report to the executive board, "With your excellent cooperation both individually and collectively we were able to realize revenues of $626,758.72, our expenses amounted to $677,381.31, thusly exceeding our revenues in the amount of $50,622.59." The kicker came when Abernathy noted, "In order to pursue the several intertwining missions of this organization, we are in dire need of additional funds."[33]

Having made the SCLC a financial success, the Birmingham campaign also gave the organization the strategy it followed with mixed results in other civil rights conflicts. While directing protest marches in the streets of Birmingham, Reverend Walker discovered the value of nonviolent coercion when protests that provoked police suppression were conducted before an interested national media. Thus at the Dorchester Conference later in the summer of 1963, Walker outlined a strategy he called "How to Crack a Hard Core City." This blueprint for direct action, designed to manufacture "creative tension" through provocation, was used by the SCLC in St. Augustine in 1964, Selma in 1965, and Chicago in 1966.[34]

The Birmingham campaign generated thousands of dollars for the national civil rights movement, yet the dispersal of the money demonstrated the unimportance of the local movement and revealed Shuttlesworth's new role as intermediary between the two. Some ACMHR members, such as treasurer W. E. Shortridge and the Reverends Edward Gardner and Charles Billups, wanted a greater share of the proceeds for the local movement. Shortridge kept suggesting that the SCLC contribute $50,000 to the Alabama Christian Movement for Human Rights. "As president of ACMHR, as secretary of SCLC and as a leader of an accelerated National Movement to free Negroes," Shuttlesworth curtly responded to the criticisms. He accepted the SCLC's policy of paying the bills incurred by the campaign—including $17,000 worth of legal fees—but to be clear he added, "personally SCLC does not owe us one cent." Basking in his own national success, Shuttlesworth no longer stood at odds with the SCLC. Although still active in the local movement, he increasingly operated on the national level. Recently he had been elected president of the Southern Conference Educational Fund—a civil rights pressure group—and he remained secretary of the SCLC. "I think it would be silly at this point to go back to the old pattern in Birmingham of Negro Organizations squabbling over money. ACMHR is a local organization, and irrespective of anybody's feelings is not supposed to match the statue [sic] or do the work of SCLC." The reprimand Shuttlesworth gave his lieutenants sounded like one he might have received himself. Yet now the indigenous leader saw himself in a new light. At a mass meeting Shuttlesworth said: "Birmingham Negroes have set an example all over the country. In some places the Negro is telling the white man if he don't get us what we want we will call Shuttlesworth, King and Abernathy; and they say, 'Please don't do that.' The trouble is not all in the South; I think we need to go up North and start some trouble up there because the Negro is taking too much stuff up there." Although Shuttlesworth had made his peace with Martin Luther King, other SCLC leaders "never quite forgave him" for his confrontation in May.[35]

316

"THE SUMMER OF 1963 was a tough summer," recalled David Vann, who worked to implement the ambiguous resolution. The first steps toward that end were taken in July, when Mayor Boutwell appointed 153 citizens to serve on the Community Affairs Committee (CAC). He divided them into three groups: 45 "senior citizens" representing the industrial and financial elite, 80 "organizational members" from college to Optimist Club presidents, and 28 "colored members" comprising the traditional Negro leadership class. The organization of the CAC called for the creation of a steering committee to oversee ten working committees. The mayor assigned a different working committee to ten major problems faced by Birmingham, including the need for economic expansion, improved public relations, increased revenues, merger with affluent suburbs, better public health, education and infrastructure, training and retaining young workers, and solving the crisis in race relations. Having separated the "colored members," Boutwell kept them segregated by neglecting to appoint any of them to the key committees. Dr. Lucius H. Pitts, the Miles College president who had helped the traditional Negro leadership class negotiate the accord, telegraphed Boutwell that he was "greatly disturbed and disappointed" that no one from the black community had been appointed to the steering committee. Conscious of status and willing to accept appearances, Pitts followed the dictates of the traditional Negro leaders by proposing token representation. To the black members, he wrote of his "strong conviction that at every level in the Community Affairs Committee there ought to be Negro representation." Pitts's request went unanswered. When Boutwell convened the "biracial" committee, industrialists and bankers, black and white businessmen, civic club presidents, and church leaders from all over the city attended the opening meeting. Picketing white supremacists with protest signs packed the hall outside the city council chambers. Vann recalled: "These leaders of Birmingham walked through the lines of the Ku Klux Klan demonstrators and held their meeting; they refused to be intimidated and I believe that was one of those very critical times again as we went forward in that summer."[36]

During July the city council worked to desegregate public accommodations. At one session it repealed all the segregation ordinances. The next week Vann coordinated the actual integration of lunch counters with the Reverend Calvin Woods, who directed teams from the ACMHR as Chief Jamie Moore provided police protection. On July 31, 1963, seven teams of two lunched at previously all-white restaurants in novelty stores around Birmingham. Perhaps remembering being spat on four months earlier, Woods happily reported: "There were no incidents. The waitresses were very cordial, while the cooks looked on with quiet amazement." Over the next two weeks, Woods filed similar reports as most of the volunteers found the experience "real nice." Police officers stood watch, as did black "spotters" who observed the event. But Pizitz Department Store at first refused to serve Negro patrons and then sat them behind a post in the back of the dining room so they felt "the same as being segregated." At Woolworth's the waitress ran away when the black testers sat down. Someone called out that they must be "kin to the Kennedys." A white man who had ordered food left when a teenage boy told the cook to serve them blackbird soup. When the integrationists received their food, it was "most terrible." At Kresge's in Roebuck, the waitress brought the black women iced tea in paper cups, whereas the white patrons drank from glasses. By the end of the week, the recalcitrant stores had improved as Birmingham joined scores of other cities around the nation responding to civil rights pressure and the president.[37]

The March on Washington commemorated the victory of Birmingham. Organized by labor leader A. Philip Randolph and longtime activist and SCLC adviser Bayard Rustin, the initial protest developed into a celebration of the recent civil rights campaign as nearly 250,000 white and black moderates joined together at the foot of the Lincoln Memorial. Activists from the Student Nonviolent Coordinating Committee and Congress of Racial Equality had wanted to occupy the capitol building and shut down the city to emphasize the urgency of race reform, but civil rights leaders advised by the Kennedy administration quickly suppressed such radical talk. So completely did the Kennedys control the event that the attorney general censored prepared remarks by SNCC chairman John Lewis. Yet even Lewis got carried away by the infectious joy over Birmingham. By right, the moment should have belonged to Fred Shuttlesworth, but the indigenous leader, soon destined to fall into obscurity, simply joined the other speakers in the affirmation of the American Dream: "We came here because we love our country, because our country needs us and because we need our country." No one sounded that theme better than Martin Luther King.[38]

Before an integrated audience and the millions of people watching by television, a resplendent King gave a stirring address. With rolling cadences, his "I Have A Dream" speech epitomized the desire of many African Americans for assimilation. Remembering that August day in 1963, Coretta Scott King witnessed the sanctification of King: "At that moment it seemed as if the Kingdom of God appeared." Thereafter, the mythmakers constructed an icon of the black leader, a symbol of triumphant nonviolence. The civil rights triptych of Connor, King, and Kennedy symbolized to American moderates race relations as a regional morality play, or perhaps a Greek tragedy. Images of Birmingham became frozen in time with the fire hoses and police dogs, just as the martyred president became known as an advocate of race reform. Most dramatic was the co-optation of Martin Luther King. The new year of 1964 opened with King as *Time* magazine's "Man of the Year" and closed with his winning the Nobel Peace Prize. Overwhelmed by his transfiguration, King accepted his newfound glory with wonder. But the changes had serious consequences for the future as an increasingly radical King spent the last years of his life trying to break the symbol of moderation so carefully constructed by others.[39]

The bombing of the Sixteenth Street Baptist Church in September 1963 shattered the promising spirit of Birmingham shared at the March on Washington. It also revealed how little had actually changed in the city. Court-ordered school desegregation provoked the act of vigilante violence. Instead of complying with federal court orders, Governor Wallace mobilized state troopers to prevent the desegregation of public schools in four Alabama cities. On Wednesday, September 4, school officials at Graymont Elementary—the neighborhood school of the now "Negro" area known as

318

White students protest the federal court–ordered desegregation of Phillips High School by calling for a boycott in September 1963. Six years before, white vigilantes savagely beat the Reverend Fred L. Shuttlesworth when he attempted to register black students here. *Birmingham News.*

Dynamite Hill—registered two black children. State troopers arrived and the governor's actions prompted the closure of the schools. Later that day, vigilantes dynamited the house of black attorney Arthur Shores for the second time in two weeks. Rioting broke out. The handful of white people still living in the Graymont neighborhood had opposed the desegregation of the school. State representative J. Paul Meeks, Ku Klux Klansman Robert Chambliss, and around 150 others attended one gathering led by the Reverend Ferrell Griswold. On September 9, Alabama's five federal district court judges issued an injunction against the state troopers impeding school desegregation by ordering the governor to desist. Within hours, Wallace had called out the Alabama National Guard and stationed troops around the schools. The next day Kennedy responded by federalizing the guard, which allowed token school desegregation to occur in Birmingham. White supremacists protested. To his niece, Chambliss warned: "You just wait until after Sunday morning. And they will beg us to let them segregate."[40]

With a roar like thunder the dynamite explosion shattered the peace of worship services across Birmingham on Sunday morning, September 15, 1963. The bomb blew a hole in the basement of the Sixteenth Street Baptist Church and took the lives of four black girls who were preparing for Bible lessons: Addie Mae Collins, Denise McNair, Carole Robertson, and Cyn-

320

Steel-helmeted state troopers surround Sixteenth Street Baptist Church after a bomb exploded, killing four black girls, wounding dozens, and damaging the structure. In the weeks preceding the blast, Governor George C. Wallace had encouraged the massive resistance against school desegregation that culminated in the dynamiting by white supremacists. *Birmingham News.*

thia Wesley. As parishioners and police pulled the bodies of the innocent children from the rubble, an angry crowd of black bystanders formed around the scene. Again rioting broke out. The mob hurled rocks at police officers and cars driven by white people and burned vacant houses and one store in the area. Municipal authorities responded to the bombing by brutally suppressing the civil strife. Chief Jamie Moore wired Wallace requesting that Colonel Al Lingo and the state troopers be returned to Birmingham.[41]

After the bombing, a group of white teenagers in an old Ford painted with Confederate symbols and the admonition "Negroes Go Back To Africa" had further enraged the black youths milling about the edge of downtown. When policemen scattered a group of African Americans throwing rocks back at the car of taunting whites, Officer Jack Parker fired a shotgun loaded with birdshot at sixteen-year-old Johnny Robinson and hit him in the back as he ran down an alleyway. The black youth was dead on arrival at Hillman Hospital. Across town, two sixteen-year-old white Eagle Scouts, Michael Lee Farley and Larry Joe Sims, had just finished listening to Reverend Griswold at a segregationist rally in Midfield and were riding down the road on a motor scooter decorated with battle flags when they approached two black boys of similar age on a bicycle. Sims pulled out a pistol and fired. Thirteen-year-old Virgil Ware took two bullets in his head and chest and died. The police brutality and senseless murder by young racial extremists reflected a sick desire within the white community to defend racial norms by any means necessary.[42]

Speaking before the Young Men's Business Club, Charles Morgan Jr. announced the city's collective guilt. He blamed everyone for the bombing, although singling out the lower middle class that had resisted desegregation. Leveling his harshest criticism against the Big Mules and other members of the white power structure who had opposed progressive reform, Morgan nonetheless absolved them of responsibility by suggesting they were powerless, for they had failed to take leadership positions in Birmingham. Of course, the opposite of this elitist argument was true. Morgan's stand on racial issues had dimmed his political aspirations. With fellow attorneys David Vann and Erskine Smith, Morgan had gambled that racially moderate politicians could attract a new liberal coalition with the potential to dominate local and state politics, as they had in Atlanta and Georgia generally. Instead of bringing the populace in line with national norms, however, a reactionary Wallace had bullied it back to the age of the Dixiecrats. Socially ostracized for his impassioned speech, harassed by

321

threatening telephone calls from abusive vigilantes, and admitting that his usefulness had come to an end, Morgan with his family left Birmingham. He found the bombing of Sixteenth Street Baptist Church "absolutely unthinkable, and the reaction to it was stunned endorsement." Indeed, the actions of the police department underscored the community-sanctioned vigilante violence expressed by the relative silence of white Birmingham.[43]

In the wake of Sixteenth Street, responsible elements in the white community roundly condemned the bombing, but municipal authorities and law enforcement officials did little to solve the crime. Mayor Boutwell denounced the "vile perpetrators of this dastardly deed" and Chief Moore swore to capture "the guilty party or parties." Such promises had been made before in this city, where more than fifty racial bombings had occurred since 1947. Not one had been solved. Birmingham Police Department detectives and state investigators did little as the FBI took over the case and ignored fruitful leads in order to follow dead scents. Yet by the end of the month, agents investigating Klansmen apparently got too close for a skittish Lingo, who arrested three men on September 30 for possessing dynamite in a move to keep the defendants in state courts. Those charged— Robert Edward Chambliss, John Wesley Hall, and Charles Cagle—were prime suspects in the FBI investigation, which nevertheless ended in 1968 with no indictments. Not until 1970, when newly elected state attorney general William J. Baxley reopened the case, would a genuine effort be made to solve the crime, one that culminated in the 1977 trial and conviction of Chambliss.[44]

After the bombing Fred Shuttlesworth demanded that Kennedy take over the city: "There is a breakdown of law and order in Birmingham and we need Federal troops." Arriving from Atlanta, King seconded Shuttlesworth's request. Terrorized black families living on Dynamite Hill had formed an extralegal security force to protect themselves. Several white ministers joined in demanding the intervention of the army "to relieve the Negroes' fear of the bombers and the police." Black leaders raised again the cry for Negro policemen and biracial communication as they "charged that the agreement for hiring and upgrading of Negro employees has not been fairly implemented." Yet instead of stationing soldiers in Birmingham to establish martial law, the president sent in two old veterans on a fact-finding mission to analyze local race relations: Earl "Red" Blaik, former coach of the U.S. Military Academy football team, and Kenneth Royall, former secretary of the army. The retired military officers concluded that "Birmingham will solve its own problems and does not want outside help."

Kennedy had no plans to provide any, as demonstrated by the West Pointers' lack of initiative.[45]

In the frustrating weeks following the church bombing, civil rights leaders honored promises not to resume protest marches as the problems of the black community festered. Traveling between Birmingham and his church in Cincinnati, Ohio, Shuttlesworth remained active in local reform efforts, although his stature had diminished with official recognition by the white power structure of the traditional Negro leadership class and its conservative representatives A. G. Gaston, J. L. Ware, and Lucius Pitts. Nevertheless, the president of the ACMHR continued to act with authority. He informed General Royall and Colonel Blaik that the merchants had defaulted on their guarantee to promote black employees to white jobs. Shuttlesworth warned, "There must be some definite and substantial racial progress and soon in order to hold off a situation in which holocaust would result and chaos would reign." Little change was forthcoming.[46]

Several civic organizations of the traditional Negro leadership class attempted to fill the void in Birmingham created by an absent Shuttlesworth and King. Attorney Orzell Billingsley Jr. of the Jefferson County Progressive Democratic Council appeared before Boutwell and the city council on October 1, 1963, and presented a list of demands suspiciously similar to those made by the ACMHR-SCLC at the onset of the Spring 1963 Birmingham campaign. Claiming to be "the major political organization of the city and county representing the members of the Negro race," the elite group demanded equal employment opportunities and access to public accommodations, Negro policemen and an end to police brutality, desegregation of parks and other facilities, and the appointment of African Americans to municipal boards. A different group of would-be Negro leaders, the Inter-Citizens Committee headed by the Reverends J. L. Ware and C. Herbert Oliver, petitioned Boutwell and the city council the next week over the same issues: the hiring of black people as policemen, firemen, and city clerks; the desegregation of municipal facilities; and an end to police brutality. Over the previous year the Inter-Citizens Committee had documented and notarized numerous cases of legal violence in the state. Oliver presented the reports at the meetings of the Alabama Advisory Committee of the U.S. Civil Rights Commission on which he sat as a member. With the failure of the merchants to promote black clerks, Oliver assisted in occasional picketing outside downtown stores. Yet despite the efforts of the traditional Negro leadership class, these civic organizations lacked the grassroots following of the ACMHR-SCLC.[47]

An attempt by Gaston and Shores to rebuke the leadership of Shuttlesworth and King backfired. Nonetheless, it underscored the difficulty the ACMHR-SCLC faced when considering a resumption of protests outwardly opposed by the only Negro leadership recognized by the white community. Two weeks after the bombing of Sixteenth Street Baptist Church, King had warned the white power structure that "when negotiations are unproductive, we have no alternative but to demonstrate." Perhaps recognizing the futility of negotiations, the local media interpreted King's statement to mean a resumption of demonstrations. On learning of the misunderstanding, Gaston and Shores released a statement to the local press expressing their relief that no protests would begin. Though giving "full support" to King, Shuttlesworth, and the ACMHR-SCLC and accepting "their guiding principles and commitment, that the Negro community should see some results within a reasonable time to ease the tension and oppression we suffer," Gaston and Shores called on black Birmingham to give fact finders Royall and Blaik "a fair chance to produce results." In a conclusion that echoed the Albany Movement, they dismissed Shuttlesworth and King as outsiders available on call: "If we are not able to solve our problems through negotiations, we are glad to know that the resources of Dr. King and his organization are available, as well as other reputable organizations dedicated to the task of advancing civil rights and providing first-class citizenship for all." Unfortunately for Birmingham's traditional Negro leadership class, getting rid of Shuttlesworth would not be that easy.[48]

In early October 1963 Shuttlesworth requested an audience with Boutwell to discuss the racial crisis in Birmingham. Over the next few weeks he attempted to consolidate his power in Birmingham through a showdown with the traditional Negro leadership class. On October 20 all of Birmingham's black leaders—from the business and civic elite to the ministers in the ACMHR—signed a petition printed in the *Birmingham News* expressing their support for Shuttlesworth and King. The accompanying statement declared that the city's black community had lost faith in local law enforcement because of the brutality and unsolved bombings and suggested that the hiring of Negro policemen would "make a great difference to us." It also mentioned other concerns such as the "removal of racial signs on city-owned premises; employment of Negroes in all tax-supported municipal offices; desegregation of all public facilities, including hospitals; and desegregation of those private facilities serving the public." Neither Reverends Ware nor Oliver signed the petition, but Gaston and Shores did, and the statement included the sentence: "We affirm that Dr. King and Rev. Shuttlesworth are our leaders; their goals are ours, our struggle is theirs." The rhetoric suggested a strained but unified black front.[49]

Speaking for the black community, Shuttlesworth and King issued an ultimatum that Birmingham hire Negro policemen or face renewed street demonstrations by the end of October. To a thousand activists attending a mass meeting in St. James Baptist Church on October 21, Shuttlesworth announced: "The decision of whether we march or not is with the Mayor." He gave the city until October 29 to hire Negro policemen. Petitions with more than 6,500 signatures supporting Shuttlesworth and King and demanding "prompt city action on the rights of Negro citizens" were presented to Boutwell. Behind the scenes, however, both the movement and the city worked "to effect a disengagement so that neither side will be totally committed." Within hours Shuttlesworth and King backed down. They withdrew the deadline without gaining any clear concessions from Boutwell. Apparently King could not face a resumption of marches in Birmingham. Renewed protests would entail an admission that the spring campaign had been less than successful.[50]

The city government temporarily created a biracial committee that helped alleviate racial tensions in Birmingham. The *Birmingham Post-Herald* captured white sentiment when it applauded the end to the threats and observed, "Thus the city has more time to work out its problems with the local Negro leadership without a gun at its head." Boutwell reactivated the biracial Committee on Group Relations of the Community Affairs Committee. Chaired by Episcopal bishop C. C. J. Carpenter, this group of fourteen white and nine black leaders discussed the city's racial problems and reported back to the city council. Pitts headed the delegation from the traditional Negro leadership class that included Ware and Dr. E. W. Taggart. For the first time since the spring demonstrations, black and white people sat down together under the apparent authority of the mayor's office; yet Boutwell convened the committee only when absolutely necessary, he gave it no powers other than advisory, and he chose not to seek its advice. With token black representation coming from Negro conservatives and not grassroots leaders, Birmingham's black community remained relatively voiceless. Moreover, the committee met hostility, not from vigilantes, but from the white power structure. Either Boutwell or *Birmingham News* vice president Vincent Townsend regularly recorded the meetings. In 1964 the ineffective Committee on Group Relations disbanded. Not until rioting provoked by an egregious example of police brutality in 1969 did the

325

white power structure consciously create a biracial forum that worked: the Community Affairs Committee of Operation New Birmingham.[51]

White resistance hindered change over the decade as the black community slowly implemented the "Points for Progress." All store facilities in Birmingham did not desegregate until forced to comply with the Civil Rights Act of 1964. Indeed, Ollie's Barbecue waged and lost a landmark U.S. Supreme Court battle that challenged the public accommodations section of the legislation. In another celebrated example, all-white Elmwood Cemetery fought to prevent the burial of Bill Terry, a black soldier killed in Vietnam. Department stores resisted the advancement of African Americans to sales positions. As a result, the pickets reappeared in 1964 and remained until each of the five major downtown department stores had hired at least one black clerk. Activists used direct action against the Liberty Grocery Store chain in 1966 for refusing to hire Negroes. Municipal authorities refused to promote black employees to jobs beyond manual labor. After street demonstrations in 1966, the city finally hired four Negro policemen, nearly two decades after Atlanta had made a similar move. Slowly black people gained access to other "whites only" municipal jobs, but the victory proved smaller than expected.[52]

Birmingham's political economy was changing. With foreign competition, an end to the industrial race wage, and Environmental Protection Agency (EPA) reforms, the Tennessee Coal, Iron, and Railroad Company no longer manufactured steel at cheaper prices than elsewhere in the country, so the U.S. Steel Corporation downsized its operations in Birmingham. Management had resisted race reform through a legal battle over its seniority system. Nonetheless, during the civil rights upheavals of 1962 and 1963, TCI began the process of integrating its workforce. National union policies and the 1964 Civil Rights Act completed the transition, as U.S. Steel dismantled the segregated lines of promotion that had kept black workers in semiskilled positions. In the 1970s the courts decided cases against TCI and other Birmingham companies. Pollution controls instituted by the EPA and inexpensive steel from abroad limited the profitability of TCI. Competition and the loss of a natural market for steel in the region lessened demand. Black workers had gained access to the better paying, formerly "whites only" jobs just as the industry shut down the plants. A service-consumer economy slowly replaced the obsolescing heavy industries.[53]

The fight for the franchise almost made Birmingham, instead of Selma, the center of the SCLC's voter registration drive in 1965. After the end of

African Americans line up in the Jefferson County Courthouse to register to vote in January 1966 after President Lyndon B. Johnson selected Birmingham for federal enforcement of the 1965 Voting Rights Act. During the year, 50,000 new black voters were added to the rolls. *Birmingham Post-Herald*, BPLDAM.

that campaign, SCLC officials joined demonstrations in Birmingham in December 1965 for the first time since the spring campaign of 1963. Enforcing the recently passed Voting Rights Act, President Johnson sent federal registrars into Birmingham. Only 22,000 out of approximately 120,000 eligible black voters had managed to register; but with federal help during 1966, an additional 50,000 African Americans were added to the voting list. In 1967 Mayor George Seibels appointed Arthur Shores to fill an unexpired term, and Shores won election as the first black member of the city council in 1968. The franchise changed the racial composition of the city council, but black leaders quickly learned to compromise with the white power structure. The shift to voting rights had signified an unstated belief that through the political system the movement could resolve the ambiguities of the resolution. It also underscored a frustration over amorphous intangibles loosely defined as political freedom. Nonetheless, the movement had achieved its original objectives of gaining access and was a success.[54]

The frequent recurrence of white resistance and police brutality against African Americans in Birmingham exaggerated the significance of the limited reforms. The shooting of a robbery suspect in July 1967 triggered a riot. The assassination of Martin Luther King in 1968 saw Birmingham once more in flames. The violent beating of a black man and two black women during an arrest in March 1969 led to riots and demonstrations that resulted in the first genuine effort at biracial communication. Police brutality would become a campaign issue for Dr. Richard Arrington, who won a seat on the city council in 1971. The zoology professor had been teaching at Miles College during the spring demonstrations of 1963 although he had not participated in the movement. As councilman, Arrington began an investigation into the Birmingham Police Department that gained strength after the legal lynching of Willis "Bugs" Chambers Jr. in 1972. The brutal shooting of twenty-year-old Bonita Carter by Officer George W. Sands—a veteran of previous charges of unnecessary and excessive force—triggered rioting in the city and ultimately brought down Mayor David Vann, who, by refusing to fire Sands, attempted to placate the white vote in a municipal campaign where the black vote counted most. In 1979 Arrington defeated Vann and became Birmingham's first black mayor.[55]

Arrington's successful campaign reflected the growth of the city's black population and white flight to the suburbs. In 1960 Birmingham had 135,113 black and 205,620 white residents; in 1970, 126,388 black and 173,911 white residents; and in 1980, 158,224 black and 124,729 white residents. With the decline in the number of white people in the city and a majority black populace, Birmingham elected Arrington mayor. Even achieving black political power did not solve the problems of many people within Birmingham's black community. Although the white political leadership promoted economic growth and law and order as the solutions to society's ills, the white-legitimated traditional Negro leadership class had not changed, for it remained in power and concerned itself with token entitlements.[56]

Some black people thrived in the new service-consumer economy. In 1974 *Time* magazine featured the family of a Negro attorney in Birmingham. Describing the expensive home of J. Mason Davis and his cars and potential income, the article presented an example of the assimilated black middle class in America. Thereafter, assimilation continued apace. Yet desegregation exacerbated the decline of the black business district. With the erosion of its economic base, the symbolic importance of the traditional Negro leadership class dwindled as community disappeared.[57]

The black inner-city poor floundered in the wake of the civic reforms. A study in 1970 identified the inner-city disadvantaged as 90 percent black. Females headed half of the families of the hard-core jobless, and 60 percent earned incomes below the poverty level. By determining the characteristics of Birmingham's truly disadvantaged, the study hoped to alleviate the problem. Indeed, Great Society reformers organized the Jefferson County Committee for Economic Opportunity (JCCEO) to work within the system and help the urban black poor. Minority contracts and affirmative action followed the same logic and assisted a handful of people. Still, the black disadvantaged fell into deeper despair.[58]

As some black middle-class lives improved, other black bystanders were left behind, shut out of the system either by choice or by force. The upscale requirements of the burgeoning service economy that replaced the steel industry presented many African Americans with unexpected obstacles. Given an advantage through traditionally "whites only" jobs and massive resistance, white people more readily adapted to the new system while many black people remained mired in the old. A paternalistic federal government created black dependency through welfare for the indigent and working poor and affirmative action for the middle class. As the number of middle-income African Americans increased at an unprecedented rate, the benefits of the civil rights movement became evident. Yet the residents of the inner city experienced the unintentional fruits of the civil rights struggle: the decline of public resources and services resulting from white flight and an eroded tax base, the demise of industrial jobs, and the collapse of community.[59]

By 1980 the Birmingham district completed the transition into the service-consumer economy. The census reported that less than 20 percent of people employed in the metropolitan area worked in manufacturing. Finance, trade, public administration, and the services accounted for 60 percent of the metropolitan workforce. In the urbanized area of Jefferson County, white people dominated the better paying jobs. Only 15 percent of all managers and professionals were African Americans and most of them were schoolteachers. Black people held 20 percent of the technical, sales, and administrative jobs but were concentrated in the supportive positions of secretary, mail clerk, and stock boy. Likewise, 56 percent of the low-wage service occupation workers and 49 percent of the operators and laborers were African American. Managerial and technical positions claimed 60 percent of the jobs in Jefferson County, and white people held 85 and 81 percent of these positions, respectively, demonstrating the extent to which black people had failed to enter the service-consumer economy.[60]

In 1980 one-third of all black persons in Birmingham lived below the poverty level, compared to one out of ten white persons. The black poor concentrated in the inner city. On the southside in Census Tract 45, 38.9 percent of the families earned below the poverty level and many lived in the Southtown Housing Project. Nearly three-fourths of the almost 2,000 residents were African American. In nearby Census Tract 46, all but 5 of the 673 residents were black and 53.8 percent made family incomes below the poverty level. In Census Tract 27, which included the Central City Housing Project, two-thirds of the 3,056 residents were black and 60 percent of the families earned poverty wages. The black ghetto around Kelly Ingram Park—Census Tracts 28.01 and 28.02—housed 1,000 people, of which 65.4 and 42.6 percent lived on poverty family income. Some 2,000 African Americans lived on the northern edge of downtown near North Birmingham Homes—Census Tracts 26.01 and 26.02—and of the families there, 53.2 and 46 percent earned incomes below the poverty level. In the old industrial area of North Birmingham near the American Cast Iron Pipe Company, Census Tract 8, black people numbered 6,222 of the 6,585 total. One-third of the families lived in poverty. In adjacent Census Tract 9, one-half of the 3,253 African Americans lived in poverty. In these examples, most of the residents held jobs in the supporting services and as operators and laborers. They were the working poor. Scattered about the city in pockets of poverty that housed generations of families, black people remained the truly disadvantaged in Birmingham. Over the years, little had changed to improve their lives.[61]

Of the 651,525 people reported in Jefferson County by the 1990 census, 228,521 were African Americans. Most lived in Birmingham, which registered a black population of 168,277 out of 265,968 residents. Only 35 percent of the county's population was black, compared to 63 percent of the city's population. Three cities in Jefferson County characterized the distribution of wealth in the New South of the 1990s. Mountain Brook remained the private enclave of affluence, with household incomes listed between $62,509 and $68,516. Of the 19,810 residents in the over-the-mountain suburb, 38 were African Americans. Unemployment registered at 1.9 percent, and only 1.4 percent of the families in Mountain Brook earned incomes below the family poverty level of $12,674. White steelworkers settled the West Jefferson County suburb of Pleasant Grove. Though the steel industry had gone, just 2.6 percent were unemployed. Of the community's 8,458 residents, a handful—152—were African Americans. Median income for households in Pleasant Grove averaged between $36,017 and $41,632. Only 3 percent of the families earned incomes below the poverty level. In contrast, one-fifth of all families in Birmingham—20.9 percent—lived below the poverty line. Nearly one out of ten—9.3 percent—were unemployed. Household incomes averaged between $18,775 and $19,450. As demonstrated by the census data, the system had changed while leaving average African Americans behind.[62]

Clearly the victories of the civil rights movement failed to solve the problems experienced by many black people. The movement had gained access for a few while never challenging the structure of the system. The limited success of the struggle resulted from its conservative goals and the persistent white resistance that had helped narrow these objectives. The Student Nonviolent Coordinating Committee and black separatist groups had tried unsuccessfully to alter the reform movement. The Poor People's Campaign attempted to bring into the system those left behind, but it died with Martin Luther King in 1968. The defeat of these efforts restricted the victory of the civil rights struggle to that won in the streets of Birmingham.

Ambiguous Resolution

In 1990 skyrocketing homicide rates among African Americans in Birmingham set new records for violent deaths in a city known for brutality. Outside the system and abandoned by black and white, inner-city residents faced insurmountable problems: unemployment, drug addiction, teen pregnancy, gang warfare, AIDS, and grinding poverty. After two decades of work by the Jefferson County Committee for Economic Opportunity, scandals revealed that it had done little more than line the pockets of its minority directors. The corruption spilled over to the Birmingham Housing Authority, which was so poorly managed that the U.S. Department of Housing and Urban Development—itself a troubled agency—had to intervene. Meanwhile, public housing projects resembled war zones as drug lords and gang members fought over the units of the Collegeville and North Birmingham Homes. With drugs and gangs came an increase in violence and black-on-black homicides. Although the white power structure joined the black city government in efforts to reclaim the downtown area by containing the violence, both largely ignored the inner-city poor.[1]

Extremism characterized the desperation of the decade as nihilistic black youths shot each other over tennis shoes while elderly civil rights heroes concerned themselves with gaining access to private country clubs. No wonder, then, that almost all African Americans believed their leadership had lost touch with reality and the problems average black people faced. By the 1990s the old civil rights institutions were bankrupt, plagued by scandals of their own making. Yet the old protests strangely continued, as when Mayor Richard Arrington wrapped himself in chains, marched on the courthouse, and sat in jail claiming racism when arrested for contempt of court for failing to respond to charges of political corruption. Similarly, confused black separatists marched on Washington in order to chastise black men for allegedly fulfilling white stereotypes while issuing vague demands for access to a system they renounced. Thirty years after the movement, such civil rights protests would have appeared farcical were it not for the tragedy of it all. Many black people had no hope for the future, a legacy of the narrow focus of civil rights reform.[2]

A broadly conceived, mass-based, biracial reform movement had attempted to restructure the system during the 1930s and 1940s. The economic collapse of the Great Depression provoked the dismantling of industrial paternalism in the Birmingham district and introduced the opportunity for fundamental change. To replace the old political economy, labor organizers and liberal politicians promoted biracial unions and a politicized working class. At first the New Deal supported the move for structural change, yet the postwar transition from economic liberalism to racial liberalism killed the broad movement and left behind an abstract concern over black civic rights. The Big Mules responded to the collapse of industrial paternalism and the subsequent biracial challenge by reforming the Bourbon system. Reinforcing the race wage that buttressed the colonial economy, neo-Bourbons won white working-class support and strengthened segregation. They attempted to restore racial and political orthodoxy through the states' rights movement of 1948, but an increasingly hostile federal government shifted this internal fight to an external one as the Dixiecrats became the leaders of massive resistance. The citizens councils joined vigilantes and the Ku Klux Klan in a defense of racial norms. Over time, white resistance protected access to the new jobs as white people made the transition into the service-consumer economy built on the foundation of the neo-Bourbon system. New leadership by progressive businessmen slowly modified the structure of the city's political economy.

The traditional Negro leadership class of the postwar period continued to practice the old politics of accommodation in order to protect its interests.

334

Negro civic organizations headed by the black elite requested Jim Crow public services from a white power structure that belatedly responded with "separate but equal" facilities in an effort to maintain segregation. A crisis in housing forced the black middle class to reluctantly challenge the color line by buying lots in fringe areas zoned white. Vigilantes responded by dynamiting the structures. The failure of the police department to solve the bombings underscored the white-community-sanctioned vigilante violence in defense of racial norms.

Birmingham's white lower middle class dominated day-to-day affairs by controlling local politics. With the white middle class living in suburban municipalities and most black people and the white unskilled disfranchised, the white lower middle class dominated the electorate, and it returned to office candidates pledged to defend segregation such as Bull Connor. Advantaged by the race wage, these white people defended "whites only" jobs from black competition and viewed desegregation as destroying schools, neighborhoods, and communities. Postwar changes threatened their privileged positions. Hence the lower middle class joined the upper class in resistance to race reform. Both classes benefited as a **335** white-dominated service-consumer sector slowly replaced the obsolescing industrial economy.

Marking a clear departure from past accommodation, the civil rights movement used nonviolent direct action to demand black access as consumers and job opportunities in the new political economy. Opposed by the traditional Negro leadership class, the integrationists in the Alabama Christian Movement for Human Rights under the direction of the Reverend Fred L. Shuttlesworth challenged racial discrimination in Birmingham. Unwilling to tolerate segregation in any form, the handful of movement activists confronted the white power structure and refused to compromise on the demand for incorporation into the American system. Drawing on a deep faith in a righteous God, the African American Christian fanatics defied brutal white resistance. Religious beliefs sustained the local movement, but its tactics alienated the black middle class. While movement members expressed bourgeois values, they were not of the black bourgeoisie. In Birmingham, unlike in other cities where the movement functioned as an umbrella organization of civic and ministerial groups, the ACMHR stood alone. It also had more in common with the aims and methods of the black student movement and Freedom Riders than with the NAACP and the Southern Christian Leadership Conference. Shuttlesworth and the ACMHR wanted immediate access to the system and

willingly told white people so. Martin Luther King and the SCLC negotiated on race reform and sought voting rights.

National outrage following the brutal beating of the Freedom Riders in
Birmingham in May 1961 convinced executives from the service-consumer
sector to break away from the leadership of the iron and steel interests and
promote political reforms in an effort to ameliorate local race relations. In a
bid to catch up with other southern cities that had moderated race relations
in the early postwar years, such as Atlanta, realtor Sidney W. Smyer arranged a corporate coup d'état to remove Bull Connor from office and
institute progressive municipal leadership. A split developed in the Big
Mule consensus between Smyer's businessmen who accepted desegregation and the iron and steel executives who joined Connor and the lower
middle class in defending racial discrimination in the marketplace. The
progressive businessmen succeeded in removing Connor, but the white
power structure remained divided over racial policy. Not until the creation
of Operation New Birmingham in 1969 did the industrial and financial
elite unify behind a new consensus on race.

336   African American student protests in the spring of 1962 provided the
momentum leading up to the racial demonstrations the following year as
local integrationists forced the crisis in race relations. Through ineffective
biracial negotiations, an accommodationist traditional Negro leadership
class attempted to compromise student demands. In contrast, Shuttlesworth and the ACMHR joined the student boycott against merchants to
gain access to public accommodations and new job opportunities. White
resistance prevented the protest from being successful. Shuttlesworth appealed to King and the SCLC to assist its Birmingham affiliate in the
struggle for local race reform. The local leader hoped that King's prestige
would prompt the black masses to support the movement and provide the
numbers needed to force a resolution of the racial stalemate. Badly burned
by Albany, King needed a success to restore his reputation as a national
civil rights leader, and Birmingham offered his best opportunity.

In preparation for the campaign, King and the Reverend Wyatt Tee
Walker designed a limited strategy of sit-ins and pickets to pressure the
local business community into dismantling racial discrimination. In hind-
sight, movement activists and scholars have suggested that the strategy
called for violent confrontations with Bull Connor that would fill the jail
and thus force the Kennedy administration to intervene on behalf of the
movement. Although this is what happened, it was not the original strategy
of the SCLC. Instead, the stated goals of the national movement coalesced

with the objectives of the local movement. Once the demonstrations began, however, the local movement had little say in the matter as the national movement spoke for both.

Sit-ins announced the protests of the ACMHR-SCLC on April 3, 1963. Poor planning, open hostility by the traditional Negro leadership class, an apathetic black community, and "nonviolent resistance" by Bull Connor and the white power structure appeared to set the Birmingham campaign on the road to Albany. The limited protest attracted little attention in the national media and led movement organizers to alter their strategy in an effort to generate "creative tension." Indeed, the ease with which the campaign changed direction reflects the fluidity of the movement. Broadening its targets, the ACMHR-SCLC drained local resources. King's decision to go to jail marked a turning point in his life as a leader but did little to increase local backing of the campaign. Although African American spectators gave the appearance of mass support, most people in the black community remained apathetic to the movement. The traditional Negro leadership class attempted to undermine the campaign by accommodating the white power structure. Bull Connor successfully led the white resistance to the drive. After a month of demonstrations it appeared that the Birmingham stalemate would end in another defeat for the civil rights movement.

Schoolchildren provided the volunteers needed by the movement to generate creative tension and push the white power structure into negotiations on racial discrimination in the Birmingham district. At first arresting the hundreds of nonviolent youngsters, Connor quickly filled the jail. He then used fire hoses and police dogs to disperse them. As a consequence, near riots by black bystanders presented an unorganized force for change. The negative images carried by the media persuaded a disinterested Kennedy administration to respond. Through its policy of federalism, the government sent Assistant Attorney General for Civil Rights Burke Marshall to assist local negotiations. Two years before, federal intervention during the Freedom Rides had resulted in support for local law and order in segregationist Mississippi. In Birmingham, Marshall succeeded in fashioning a similar resolution by persuading Martin Luther King to call off the protests without winning any concessions from the white power structure.

Shuttlesworth bitterly denounced King's betrayal. Originally appearing in agreement, the local and national movements conflicted over different approaches to achieve different objectives. Shuttlesworth demanded equal access and job opportunities and refused to compromise. King followed the politics of accommodation and compromised the goals of the movement through biracial negotiations. Having salvaged his reputation, he abandoned the local goals of the movement and left Shuttlesworth with nothing concrete to show from the campaign. He also left in place a hostile traditional Negro leadership class that, as a result of the SCLC's efforts, was now recognized by the white power structure as the legitimate head of the black community. Henceforth the black middle class wielded its power over the black masses through the authority of the movement.

The aftermath of national protest, international pressure, and inner-city riot convinced a reluctant Kennedy administration to propose sweeping legislation that, once passed as the Civil Rights Act of 1964, marked a watershed in race relations and opened the system to African Americans even in recalcitrant cities such as Birmingham. The administration responded to the national protests over Birmingham and the international condemnation of American racism by drafting legislation that outlawed racial discrimination in the marketplace. The civil rights movement thus achieved its goals of gaining access to public accommodations and equal employment opportunities. Hence the climax of the civil rights struggle occurred in Birmingham. The moderate approach to reform never challenged the structure of the system. Integrationists only asked for inclusion. White resistance exaggerated the significance of the limited race reforms as vigilantes contested the token desegregation. The bombing of the Sixteenth Street Baptist Church, like the bombing of the A. G. Gaston Motel, provoked inner-city riots and police brutality but little else.

Birmingham desegregated with the Civil Rights Act of 1964. Through court cases, black activists received "whites only" jobs in the district and freedom as consumers. Implementation of the Voting Rights Act of 1965 succeeded in registering Birmingham's black population. The appointment of Arthur Shores to the city council in 1968 and the election of Dr. Richard Arrington as mayor in 1979 symbolized black political empowerment. By then, however, the transition to the service-consumer economy was complete. A growing black middle class joined many white people within the system. Yet many African Americans remained outside the system. As a result, not all black people have benefited from black political empowerment, equal access as consumers, and equal employment opportunities.

THE INTEGRATION of Birmingham's Shoal Creek County Club in 1990 underscored the ambiguities of the civil rights struggle. As in 1963, the traditional Negro leadership class continued to accommodate the wishes of the white power structure while movement veterans demanded access. The "victory" at Shoal Creek reflected the "victory" of the civil rights movement while demonstrating the legacy of bourgeois reform.

Tractor king Hall W. Thompson built the secure residential haven of Shoal Creek and enabled only the wealthiest Alabamians to buy lots on the landscaped acreage surrounding the Jack Nicklaus golf course. A Williamsburg motif covered everything, including the eagle-topped iron and gilt security gates of the patrolled compound deep in the woods of adjacent Shelby County, a half hour south of Birmingham. Wrapped in Americana, the occupants of Shoal Creek sought safety and seclusion from an increasingly hostile and dangerous world. Thompson's vanity invited that world into Shoal Creek by having the club host the Professional Golf Association (PGA) tournament in the summer of 1990. A controversy then arose over the city of Birmingham spending money to sponsor an event at a facility that openly discriminated against black people. When Thompson learned of black city councilman William Bell's objections, he told reporter Joan M. Mazzolini of the *Birmingham Post-Herald*: "Bringing up this issue will just polarize the community . . . but it can't pressure us." He went on to explain: "I think we've said that we don't discriminate in every other area except the blacks." Bell, Birmingham state representative and attorney Demetrius Newton, and the Reverend Abraham Woods, head of the local chapter of the Southern Christian Leadership Conference, demanded that Shoal Creek admit a Negro member. Thompson apologized that his comments had been "taken out of context" but said little else.[3]

Deploring the incident, Mayor Arrington balanced an insulted black community with an angered white power structure as he attempted to defuse the controversy before the tournament. But in July the issue boiled over as Woods planned protest marches on the manicured lawn unless a Negro be allowed to enter the clubhouse as a member. The idea of balding and gray civil rights activists throwing themselves in front of golf carts and television cameras, and otherwise disturbing decorum at the match, concerned PGA officials and corporate sponsors who feared a consumer backlash for promoting an "integrated" event such as golf at a "racist" country club such as Shoal Creek. By the end of July, Anheuser-Busch, Delta Airlines, IBM, and Toyota had pulled their commercials from ABC Sports. The white power structure and the *Birmingham News* attempted to convince the black community that having the PGA in the area was a "major plus" for Birmingham and that, through short-term growth, it would pour money into the coffers of hotel and fast-food franchises that benefited the city's low-wage black and white service-consumer economy workers. Ever compliant with the new "Big Mules," Arrington accommodated several plans proposed by Thompson to end the crisis, but he could not placate Woods.[4]

Finally, less than a week before the beginning of the PGA, Thompson agreed to accept Louis Willie Jr., the CEO of A. G. Gaston's various enterprises, as a token black member. Woods canceled the demonstrations. Ironically, all three men had participated in the 1963 negotiations, Thompson as a senior citizen, Willie as a traditional Negro leader, and Woods as a movement activist. The reluctant integrationist Willie—who did not play golf—joined Shoal Creek out of a deep sense of community service. His action symbolized the desegregation of country clubs by multinational corporate pressure. In the months that followed private facilities desegregated their membership in order to host major sporting events in the future. Again Birmingham's image came under national scrutiny, although unlike in 1963 the furor quickly passed, perhaps in tribute to the jaded and cynical postmodern world of the day when little moral outrage existed, or perhaps a consequence of the absurdity of the entire affair.[5]

In an age of inner-city genocide, images of "moralistic" civil rights activists demanding that a black millionaire be admitted to the most exclusive country club in the state bespoke of misplaced values. Yet old movement leaders could hardly do otherwise, for they followed the logic of civil rights reform. Cast in an individualistic paradigm, civil rights advocates struggled for access, first as consumers and commodified labor, then as associates in professional organizations, and finally as members of private clubs. The very bourgeois logic that had propelled the movement on the limited path of civil rights narrowed the goals each step of the way.

Throughout it all, the traditional Negro leadership class held on to power. It had deflected a challenge from below by co-opting civil rights activists, and it took advantage of federal race reforms to strengthen its hold over the black masses. The white power structure had adapted to the new political economy, yet the traditional Negro leadership class remained mired in the old, struggling to gain symbolic access that proved meaningless for most black people. Protected by massive resistance, many white workers made the transition into the top end of the new service-consumer sector, but many black people were left at the bottom or shut out all together. In Birmingham and elsewhere, the "perpetual promise" remained unfulfilled.[6]

Abbreviations

ADAH	Alabama Department of Archives and History
ASRA	National [American] States' Rights Association
BN	*Birmingham News*
BP-H	*Birmingham Post-Herald*
BPLDAM	Birmingham Public Library, Department of Archives and Manuscripts, Birmingham, Ala.
BW	*Birmingham World*
JFK Library	John F. Kennedy Library, Boston
JFK Papers	John F. Kennedy Papers, JFK Library
King Center	Martin Luther King Jr. Center for Nonviolent Social Change, Inc., Archives, Atlanta, Ga.
King Papers, ATL	Martin Luther King Jr. Papers, King Center
King Papers, BU	Martin Luther King Jr. Papers, Boston University
Marshall Papers	Burke Marshall Papers, JFK Library
NAACP	National Association for the Advancement of Colored People
NYT	*New York Times*
RFK Papers	Robert F. Kennedy Papers, JFK Library
SCLC Papers	Southern Christian Leadership Conference Papers, King Center
SRC	Southern Regional Council
Walker, "SCLC"	Eugene Pierce Walker, "A History of the Southern Christian Leadership Conference, 1955–1965: The Evolution of a Southern Strategy for Social Change"
WSJ	*Wall Street Journal*

Introduction

1. The background for this and the following paragraphs appears in the accounts of the Spring 1963 demonstrations of the *Birmingham News*, *Birmingham Post-Herald*, and *Birmingham World*, *New York Times*, *Time*, *Newsweek*, and *U.S. News and World Reports*, and the *Nation* and *New Republic* for April and May 1963. Contemporary books by reporters and participants that describe the period include Dorman, *We Shall Overcome*; Raines, *My Soul Is Rested*; Kunstler, *Deep in My*

Heart; and King, *Why We Can't Wait*. For historical accounts of the movement see Branch, *Parting The Waters*; Fairclough, *To Redeem the Soul*; Garrow, *Bearing The Cross*; and Morris, *Origins*. On the local movement see Garrow, *Birmingham*.

2. Seeger, *We Shall Overcome*, band 4.

3. *Time*, May 10, 1963.

4. Ibid.

5. Garrow, *Birmingham*, pp. 76, 89 (quotation).

6. U.S. Bureau of the Census, *Eighteenth Census*, vol. 1, Characteristics of the Population, Alabama, pt. 2.

7. Maids earned approximately $750 a year. U.S. Bureau of the Census, *Population and Housing*, Census Tracts, Birmingham, Report PHC (1)-17, and *Eighteenth Census*, Detailed Characteristics, table 121. In 1960, 12,114 people lived on Southside, Census Tracts 43–46; 8,858 in Tittusville, Census Tract 51; and 3,168 in Graymont, Census Tract 13. On the Negro vote and Precinct 9, Box 1, see *BP-H*, November 3, 1965, and Giddens, "The Happy-Go-Lucky Harlem of the South," pp. 40–44.

8. U.S. Bureau of the Census, *Population and Housing*, Census Tracts, Birmingham, Report PHC (1)-17. Census Tract 8 in North Birmingham had 4,809 white and 3,288 black residents; the black community of Tuxedo Junction and the Italian community in Census Tract 12 had 3,984 white and 4,686 black residents. ACIPCO returns appeared in Precinct 42, Box 1, and Italian and black Ensley returns appeared in Precinct 45, Box 1.

9. Ibid.; white Ensley, Census Tracts 31 and 37, voted in Precinct 45, Boxes 3–5, and white East Lake, Census Tracts 1–2 and 21, voted in Precinct 10, Boxes 2–5.

10. U.S. Bureau of the Census, *Population and Housing*, Census Tracts, Birmingham, Report PHC (1)-17, and *Eighteenth Census*, vol. 1, Characteristics of the Population, Alabama, pt. 2, table 72, pp. S-157–58. A majority in the communities of Highland and Forest Parks in Census Tract 47, Homewood in Census Tract A-107, Mountain Brook in Census Tract A-108, and Vestavia Hills in Census Tracts C-144 and C-129 voted for Dwight Eisenhower in 1952, although Adlai Stevenson's running mate was Alabama senator John Sparkman. See *BN*, November 5, 1952. Highland and Forest Parks voters cast ballots in Precinct 21, Boxes 1–4; the over-the-mountain electorate voted in Precinct 25.

11. Morgan, *A Time To Speak*, pp. 53–60, 88–89.

12. Wright, *Old South, New South*, esp. pp. 67–70; Woodward, *Origins of the New South*; Norrell, *James Bowron*, esp. pp. xx–xxi; Frank, *Dependent Accumulation and Underdevelopment*; Harris, *Political Power*. Harris wrote the work to question the conclusions of Floyd Hunter and Robert H. Dahl. Harris, Hunter, and Dahl debated the theories of C. Wright Mills best presented in *The Power Elite*. For an analysis of the relationship between public and private power in Birmingham see LaMonte, *Politics and Welfare*.

13. Leighton, "Birmingham, Alabama: The City of Perpetual Promise" (which Leighton published in *Five Cities*, pp. 100–139); Woodward, *Origins of the New South*, pp. 300–301.

14. *BP-H*, May 5, 1961 (quotes the county registrar identifying 80,000 registered voters); Havard, *The Changing Politics of the South*, p. 443; Strong, *Registration of Voters in Alabama*, pp. 56–57; Breedlove, "Progressivism and Nativism"; Brownell, "Birmingham"; Flynt, "Religion in the Urban South"; Snell, "The Ku Klux Klan in Jefferson County"; Norton, *Birmingham's First Magic Century*; Harris, *Political Power*, pp. 189–98. The election of East Lake's Dr. Nathaniel A. Barrett over George Ward in 1917 symbolized the triumph of the lower middle class in day-to-day civic affairs in Birmingham. See Eskew, "Demagoguery in Birmingham."

15. *Time*, December 15, 1958. See also McKiven, *Iron and Steel*.

16. Rice, "If Dixie Were Atlanta." See also the introduction to this study; Martin, *Hartsfield*; Allen and Hemphill, *Mayor*; and Kuhn, Joye, and West, *Living Atlanta*. On Atlanta's power elite see Hunter, *Community Power Structure* and *Community Power Succession*; Stone, *Regime Politics*; Hornsby, "A City That Was Too Busy To Hate"; and Garrow, *Atlanta, Georgia*.

17. Studies that analyze the collapse of the old order and the birth of the new from the perspective of political economy include Bartley, *The Rise of Massive Resistance* and *The New South*; Wright, *Old South, New South*; and Bloom, *Class, Race*.

342

18. Top-down studies either focus on King and the SCLC—such as David L. Lewis, *King*; Garrow, *Bearing The Cross*; Fairclough, *To Redeem the Soul*; and Branch, *Parting The Waters*—or they look at civil rights institutions—such as Carson, *In Struggle*, and Meier and Rudwick, *CORE*. Bottom-up studies focus on the local community, such as Chafe, *Civilities and Civil Rights*, and Norrell, *Reaping The Whirlwind*. Recent studies have expanded the bottom-up approach but emphasize continuity such as John Dittmer, *Local People*; Fairclough, *Race and Democracy*; and Payne, *I've Got The Light of Freedom*. But this is an old thesis argued by many scholars including Morris (*Origins*) and Goldfield (*Black, White, and Southern*). Novel approaches that look at white people were taken by Eagles (*Outside Agitator*) and Chappell (*Inside Agitators*).

19. Several scholars have argued for discontinuity in black protest, including Meier and Rudwick ("The Origins of Nonviolent Direct Action"). See also the contemporaneous "New Currents in the Civil Rights Movement," reprinted in Meier, *A White Scholar and the Black Community*, pp. 161–87, as well as Marable, *Race, Reform, and Rebellion*; Zinn, *SNCC*; Bloom, *Class, Race*; and Bartley, *The New South*.

20. On "race men" see Thompson, *The Negro Leadership Class*, pp. 70–78; on "New Negroes" see Bloom, *Class, Race*, pp. 7, 120–21. King quoted in Morris, *Origins*, pp. 105–6.

21. Morris, *Origins*, pp. 40–76. With his use of the concept "local movement center," Morris characterizes the indigenous movement and its dynamic of social change. Fairclough notes the emergence of new indigenous leaders in his seminal essay, "The Preachers and the People."

22. There has yet to be a comprehensive study of the southern NAACP during this period. The major works on the organization include Tushnet, *The NAACP's Legal Strategy against Segregated Education*; McNeil, *Groundwork: Charles Hamilton Houston*; Kluger, *Simple Justice: The History of Brown*; and Bracey and Meier, "The NAACP as a Reform Movement." See also Wilkins with Mathews, *Standing Fast*.

23. On the elitism of the NAACP see Marable, *Race, Reform, and Rebellion*, pp. 22.–25; Kelley, *Hammer and Hoe*, pp. 212–13, passim; Painter, *Narrative of Hosea Hudson*, pp. 255–81, passim; and Rolinson, "The Universal Negro Improvement Association."

24. Frazier, *Black Bourgeoisie*; Lomax, *The Negro Revolt*; Thompson, *The Negro Leadership Class*. One notable exception was Marable, *Race, Reform, and Rebellion*.

Chapter 1

1. Morris, *Origins*, pp. 17–25.

2. For the best treatment of the Montgomery bus boycott see Garrow, *The Walking City*, and in particular Thornton's perceptive essay, "Challenge and Response."

3. Robinson, *The Montgomery Bus Boycott and the Women Who Started It*; Durr, *Outside the Magic Circle*, pp. 282–83.

4. Walton, "The Walking City."

5. David L. Lewis, *King*, 72; Rustin, *Down The Line*, pp. 55–61; Morris, *Origins*, 62–68, 159–62.

6. *BN*, February 4, 7, 29 (quotation), 1956; *BP-H*, June 2, 1956; *BN*, January 28, 1965.

7. Thornton, "First Among Equals."

8. *Time*, January 7, 1957; McLuhan, *Understanding Media*, esp. pp. 308–37. For an analysis of the national media during the civil rights movement see Lentz, *Symbols*.

9. Morris, *Origins*, pp. 40–50; Lomax, *The Negro Revolt*, pp. 217–20.

10. Fairclough, *To Redeem the Soul*, pp. 23–34, passim; Garrow, *Bearing The Cross*, pp. 66–73.

11. Walker, "SCLC," pp. 29–33; Fairclough, *To Redeem the Soul*, 30–32, 38–39; Garrow, *Bearing The Cross*, pp. 73, 105. Rustin ghosted King's first essay ever published. On Rustin see Raines, *My Soul Is Rested*, pp. 44–51; on Baker see Payne, *I've Got the Light of Freedom*, pp. 77–102; on Levison see Garrow, *The FBI and . . . King*, pp. 21–77, and Morris, *Origins*, p. 83.

12. Walker interviewed Rustin, Baker, and Levison, and all agreed to this interpretation of events. See Walker, "SCLC," p. 32; Fairclough, *To Redeem the Soul*, pp. 31–32; and Morris, *Origins*, p. 83. Baker recalled, "I don't think that the leadership in Montgomery was prepared to capitalize . . . on [what] . . . had come out of the Montgomery situation." She noted that "There

were no plans for any follow-up and the movement was on the verge of withering away"; Giddings, *When and Where I Enter*, p. 268. So through In Friendship Baker, Rustin, and Levison attempted to "capitalize" on Montgomery by promoting a new national umbrella organization.

13. "Working Papers," box 32, file 6, SCLC Papers; Garrow, *Bearing The Cross*, pp. 85–87; Walker, "SCLC," pp. 32–33.

14. "Working Papers," box 32, file 4, SCLC Papers; Garrow, *Bearing The Cross*, pp. 90–91, 97; Walker, "SCLC," pp. 33–34.

15. Garrow, *Bearing The Cross*, pp. 71–72, 91; Fairclough, *To Redeem the Soul*, p. 45; Lomax, *The Negro Revolt*, pp. 112–32.

16. Walker, "SCLC," pp. 37–38; Fairclough, *To Redeem the Soul*, pp. 39–40; Garrow, *Bearing The Cross*, pp. 92–93. Shuttlesworth's address at the May 17, 1957, event is in box 4, Shuttlesworth Papers, King Center.

17. Walker, "SCLC," p. 44; Martin, *Atlanta and Environs* 3:288; Garrow, *Birmingham*, pp. 24–28.

18. Garrow, *Bearing The Cross*, pp. 97–98, 100–101; King to SCLC Executive Board, October 18, 1957, box 48, file VI 153, King Papers, BU.

19. "Meeting of the Administrative Committee," December 19, 1957, box 32, file 5, SCLC Papers; Morris, *Origins*, pp. 102–3; Garrow, *Bearing The Cross*, pp. 97–98, 102–3; Payne, *I've Got the Light of Freedom*, pp. 93–94.

20. "Meeting of the Administrative Committee," December 19, 1957, box 32, file 5, SCLC Papers; Morris, *Origins*, pp. 108–11; King to Adam C. Powell, February 7, 1958, box 32, file 7, SCLC Papers; Walker, "SCLC," p. 47; Garrow, *Bearing The Cross*, pp. 103–4; Ella J. Baker to Edwin R. Edmons, April 16, 1958, box 32, file 7, SCLC Papers; Baker to King, May 19, 1958, box 121, file 24, King Papers, BU.

21. "SCLC Administrative Committee, 1958," box 48, file VI 152, King Papers, BU. This gathering was hailed as the "best meeting yet." See "Minutes of the Meeting," May 29, 1958, box 48, file VI 153, ibid. On Mississippi and the NAACP see Dittmer, *Local People*, pp. 77–79.

22. Box 48, file VI 152, King Papers, BU (King's telegram); Walker, "SCLC," pp. 53–54.

23. "SCLC Executive Board Minutes," October 18, 1957, box 48, file VI 153, King Papers, BU; John L. Tilley to Heber Ladner of Mississippi, June 24, 1958, to Bruce Bennett of Arkansas, June 25, 1958, to Wade O. Martin of Louisiana, July 1, 1958, box 32, file 1, and Tilley to Ella Baker, June 24, 1958, box 32, file 7, SCLC Papers; Tilley to "Dear Sir," June 30, 1958, box 48, file VI 153, and Tilley to King, October 17, 1958, box 121, file 24, King Papers, BU; Fairclough, *To Redeem the Soul*, p. 48; Walker, "SCLC," pp. 50–51, 60–63; Garrow, *Bearing The Cross*, pp. 104–5, 111.

24. "Mobilizing and Utilizing Our Resources for Full Citizenship," Fall 1958, box 48, file VI 152, and W. L. Hamilton to Friend of Civil Rights, October 24, 1958, box 48, file VI 153, King Papers, BU.

25. John L. Tilley to "Dear Reverend," October 29, 1958, King to Tilley, January 6, 1959, Tilley to William A. Fordham, March 19, 1959, and Tilley to Hubert H. Bryant, March 20, 1959, box 32, file 1; Ella Baker to Tilley, March 4, 1959, box 32, file 8, SCLC Papers; Fairclough, *Race and Democracy*, p. 228. Fairclough (*To Redeem the Soul*, p. 48) suggests that Tilley was unduly criticized. See Garrow, *Bearing The Cross*, pp. 111–16. Garrow (p. 113) notes Levison's request for more activity by SCLC in order to generate needed financial support.

26. Fairclough, *To Redeem the Soul*, p. 50.

27. For an analysis of King's childhood and college years that establish his class background and offer examples of his writings see Carson, *Papers of . . . King*, vol. 1, *Called To Serve*, and vol. 2, *Rediscovering Precious Values*, esp. Carson's informative introductions, and Meier, "The Conservative Militant."

28. Garrow, *Bearing The Cross*, pp. 116, 118; Fred L. Shuttlesworth to King, April 24, June 15, 1959, box 9, King Papers, BU.

29. Report of the Executive Director, May 16–September 29, 1959, box 48, file VI 153, King Papers, BU; Garrow, *Bearing The Cross*, pp. 120–21, 149, 151, 161; Baker's "MEMORANDUM," July 2, 1959, box 32, file 39, SCLC Papers.

30. Report of the Executive Director, May 16–September 29, 1959, box 48, file VI 153, King Papers, BU.

31. King's handwritten recommendations, September 29, 30, October 1, 1959, box 48, file VI 153, King Papers, BU.

32. Ibid.; "Recommendations Adopted at Fall Meeting of SCLC," October 1, 1959, box 32, file 5, SCLC Papers.

33. Baker, "SCLC as a Crusade," box 48, file VI 153, King Papers, BU.

34. King's "Recommendations," October 27, 1959, box 48, file VI 153, ibid.; Baker to A. G. Gaston, October 29, November 6, 1959, box 32, file 8, SCLC Papers.

35. King's "Recommendations," October 27, 1959, box 48, file VI 153, King Papers, BU; Baker to SCLC Board Members, January 12, 1960, box 32, file 16, SCLC Papers.

36. Chafe, *Civilities and Civil Rights*, pp. 98–141.

37. Shuttlesworth and Baker are quoted in Morris, *Origins*, p. 201; see also p. 202.

38. Baker, "Memorandum," March 23, 1960, box 32, file 39, and Baker to S. G. Dunston, March 22, 1960, box 32, file 9 (see also the materials in box 32, file 10), SCLC Papers; Carson, *In Struggle*, pp. 19–30.

39. Ella J. Baker to Fred L. Shuttlesworth, June 14, 1960, Baker to Glenn Smiley, June 20, 1960, Smiley to Baker, June 17, 1960, "Information on Persons for Workshops on Nonviolence," July 6, 1960, all in box 32, file 38, and Baker to S. G. Dunston, March 22, 1960, box 32, file 9, SCLC Papers; Garrow, *Bearing The Cross*, pp. 132–34, 141; "SCLC's Future Program," May 10–11, 1960, box 5, file I 31, King Papers, BU.

40. Morris, *Origins*, pp. 183–88 (Walker's quotation, p. 184); Garrow, *Bearing The Cross*, pp. 136–37; Walker, "SCLC," p. 84.

41. Walker's "Report of the Director to the Executive Board," October 11, 1960, box 121, file XVI 27, King Papers, BU. In negotiating over the position, Walker wanted to make sure that he "would be *the* chief of SCLC's staff—and not anyone in New York" (Walker's emphasis). Quoted in Garrow, *Bearing The Cross*, p. 136.

42. Walker's "Report of the Director to the Executive Board," October 11, 1960, box 121, file XVI 27, King Papers, BU; Garrow, *Bearing The Cross*, p. 143 (King's quotation).

43. Walker's "Report of the Director to the Executive Board," October 11, 1960, box 121, file XVI 27, King Papers, BU; Fairclough, *To Redeem the Soul*, p. 66.

44. For donation notebooks see box 63, files 1–2, SCLC Papers. See also John L. Tilley to Ella J. Baker, June 24, 1958, box 32, file 7, ibid.; *Jet*, October 22, 1959; Garrow, *Bearing The Cross*, p. 121. Prior to Walker, SCLC had an annual budget of $65,000 according to Lomax, *The Negro Revolt*, p. 107.

45. Garrow, *Bearing The Cross*, pp. 130–31, 135, 162; Fairclough, *To Redeem the Soul*, pp. 66, 70. The figures are from Branch, *Parting The Waters*, pp. 574–75.

46. James R. Wood to John H. Bustamante, November 3, 1960, and "Shreveport Conference—Freedom Rally," October 20, 1960, box 63, file 2, SCLC Papers.

47. "Monthly Budget Summaries" and "Monthly Statements of Accounting," box 63, file 4, and weekly "Statement of Income and Disbursements" for 1962, box 63, file 9, SCLC Papers; Fairclough, *To Redeem the Soul*, p. 70. The November 1960–April 1961 figures are cited in Walker, "SCLC," p. 86.

48. Fairclough, *To Redeem the Soul*, pp. 68–69, 95–96; Branch, *Parting The Waters*, pp. 575–79; Garrow, *Bearing The Cross*, pp. 149–51, 153.

49. Fairclough, *To Redeem the Soul*, pp. 95–96; Branch, *Parting The Waters*, p. 578; Garrow, *Bearing The Cross*, pp. 161–64.

50. Police Report, May 11, 1961, box 9, file 24, Connor Papers, BPLDAM; Garrow, *Bearing The Cross*, p. 157.

51. Brauer, *John F. Kennedy*, pp. 98–125.

52. Walker accused Wood of criticizing SCLC and its leadership. In response, Wood told King: "I thought of all the things that have been said to me about SCLC and the men who lead it. Things I have not chosen to repeat nor even accepted as truth. . . . As I listened to the things I was charged with saying I recognized them as things I've heard many times in many places here in Atlanta, Petersburg, and others." Quoted in Garrow, *Bearing The Cross*, p. 165; see also pp. 159–61, 163,

165–66. The January and February 1961 budgets are from box 63, file 4, SCLC Papers (which also contain other examples); the figures have been rounded off to the nearest dollar.

53. The best studies on the Albany Movement include Ricks, "'De Lawd' Descends"; Carson, *In Struggle*, pp. 56–65; Watters, *Down To Now*; Zinn, *SNCC*, pp. 123–46; and Anderson, "Reflections," pp. 4–5. In his two essays, "'The Way Out May Lead In'" and "Rev. Samuel B. Wells," Michael Chalfen looks at race relations in Albany before and after what he calls the "classic" period of 1961–62 in order to argue for continuity in black protest and to posit the thesis that it is wrong to consider the Albany Movement a "failure." Instead, Chalfen agrees with Fred Powledge and numerous veterans of the movement who argue that Albany represented a "A Failed Success." See Powledge, *Free At Last?*, pp. 400–420. The general conclusion of many observers remains that King and the Albany Movement failed to win their objectives during the civil rights campaign. Perhaps A. C. Searles, the editor of the black newspaper, the *Southwest Georgian*, answered the question best when he told Watters: "What did we win? We won self-respect." Watters, *Down To Now*, p. 158.

54. Carson, *In Struggle*, pp. 58–60; Zinn, *SNCC*, pp. 128–30; Anderson, "Reflections," p. 8.

55. Anderson, "Reflections," pp. 8–9. The Albany Movement also invited the NAACP, which sent its regional director Ruby Hurley and field secretary Vernon Jordan to Albany. Instead of offering help and getting involved, Hurley observed the protest and later concluded that the Albany Movement was successful if the objective was "to go to jail." David L. Lewis, *King*, p. 169.

56. Ricks, "'De Lawd' Descends," p. 5; Zinn, *SNCC*, p. 131 (King's sermon). Anderson ("Reflections," p. 11) admitted that he "tricked" King into joining the Albany Movement, a charge made by Young and Walker.

57. Walker added: "So it [Albany] was a natural place for him [King] to be. But without having organizational input and control it was a very difficult campaign for him." Hampton and Fayer, *Voices Of Freedom*, p. 105.

58. Lomax, *The Negro Revolt*, pp. 107–8; Carson, *In Struggle*, p. 60; David L. Lewis, *King*, pp. 151–55 ("De Lawd" and next two quotations); Zinn, *SNCC*, p. 131 (last quotation; also reported in Lewis, *King*, p. 151).

59. Garrow, *Bearing The Cross*, p. 185 (quotations), 186–87; Fairclough, *To Redeem the Soul*, p. 90.

60. David L. Lewis, *King*, p. 154. Ricks ("'De Lawd' Descends," p. 6) echoes Lewis's thesis of a black conspiracy.

61. Fairclough, *To Redeem the Soul*, pp. 90–91 (Walker); Branch, *Parting The Waters*, p. 558. The *Eyes on the Prize* segment on Albany, "No Easy Walk, 1961–1963," skirts the issue by blurring the December release with the July release.

62. Fairclough, *To Redeem the Soul*, p. 90; Branch, *Parting The Waters*, p. 552; Walker, "SCLC," p. 115; Anderson, "Reflections," pp. 12–13; Garrow, *Bearing The Cross*, pp. 184–87, 210, 665 n36. On Marion Page see also Watters, *Down To Now*, pp. 147–50, and Ricks, "'De Lawd' Descends," p. 13.

63. Young quoted in Hampton and Fayer, *Voices Of Freedom*, p. 104.

64. Lomax, *The Negro Revolt*, p. 110; Lentz, *Symbols*, pp. 62–63; David L. Lewis, *King*, p. 154. *Time* made the comparison of Albany to Montgomery in its August 3, 1962, issue.

65. Lomax, *The Negro Revolt*, pp. 110–11.

66. Zinn, *SNCC*, pp. 132–33; Ricks, "'De Lawd' Descends," p. 22.

67. Watters states that Young said, "We couldn't see any handles to anything," and that Walker agreed with his assessment that SCLC should not resume the protest in July but that King and Abernathy felt otherwise. Watters, *Down To Now*, p. 175; Garrow, *Bearing The Cross*, pp. 201–3; Ricks, "'De Lawd' Descends," p. 9.

68. *NYT*, July 13, 1962; Garrow, *Bearing The Cross*, pp. 203–4. Ricks ("'De Lawd' Descends," p. 8) identifies Kelley's law partner, the white B. C. Gardner, as being the "well-dressed Negro man" who paid the bond.

69. Garrow, *Bearing The Cross*, pp. 206–7. Pritchett quoted in *NYT*, August 1962. The Kennedy administration encouraged dialogue, noting that the disturbances were beginning to have international implications. See Brauer, *John F. Kennedy*, pp. 170–71.

70. Garrow, *Bearing The Cross*, pp. 209–11.

71. Lomax, *The Negro Revolt*, pp. 108–9; Garrow, *Bearing The Cross*, p. 185.

72. *Time*, August 10, 1962 (quotation); Brauer, *John F. Kennedy*, pp. 171–79.

73. Ricks, " 'De Lawd' Descends," p. 11; Garrow, *Bearing The Cross*, p. 215.

74. For the final tallies see Ricks, " 'De Lawd' Descends," p. 12.

75. In some ways it appears that the money was drying up. Garrow notes that SCLC had trouble funding its Gandhi Society and poor bookkeeping compromised the VEP funds. See *Bearing The Cross*, pp. 222–23, 233; Ricks, " 'De Lawd' Descends," p. 12; and Walker, "MEMO, Albany, Georgia, Expenditures, July 12–August 15," and weekly budgets, box 63, file 9, SCLC Papers.

76. Walker, "Report of Director," October–September 1962, box 36, file 12, SCLC Papers. See also Walker's newspaper column "THE CONGO, USA," dated August 29, 1962, and his March 1963 speech, "The American Dilemma In Miniature: Albany, Georgia," both in box 37, file 8, SCLC Papers. The latter reference was revised and published as "Albany: Failure or First Step?" in *New South*.

77. *Time*, August 3, 10, 1962; Lentz, *Symbols*, p. 70. Likewise, the *New York Times* (August 4, 1962) complimented "the remarkable restraint of Albany's segregationists and the deft handling by the police of racial protests"; also quoted in Garrow, *Bearing The Cross*, p. 213.

Chapter 2

1. There is lacking in the literature a thorough examination of the racially motivated residential bombings in the postwar South and their relationship to the civil rights movement. For an overview of southern cities and their varied responses to race reform in the period see Jacoway and Colburn, *Southern Businessmen and Desegregation*. In Dallas, a series of residential bombings in the early 1950s and the subsequent progressive action of white businessmen ushered in a sustained period of racial harmony; see Thometz, *The Decision-Makers*, and Schutze, *The Accommodation*. Likewise in Nashville, the bombing of a school in 1957 encouraged white support for desegregation; see Doyle, *Nashville since the 1920s*, pp. 238–43. When the white activists Ann and Carl Braden bought a house in a white suburb of Louisville for a black man, it was dynamited; see Braden, *The Wall Between*. With the exception of one early residential bombing and the Jewish temple bombing of 1958, Atlanta was spared the dynamite blasts that irregularly rocked other southern cities, in part because the white leadership worked with the black leadership to provide adequate—but segregated—housing for the black middle class; see Martin, *Atlanta and Environs*, 3:286–88, and Stone, *Regime Politics*, pp. 25–50. Silver and Moeser (*The Separate City*, p. 10) observe that "changing community characteristics in turn contributed to a redirection in racial politics during this crucial prelude to the full-fledged civil rights movement. It is one of our key assumptions that the emergence of the 'separate city' contributed directly to the increased political activism of African Americans in the post-Depression urban South." This chapter explores that "redirection in racial politics" by analyzing changes in black protest in postwar Birmingham.

2. Leavy, "Zoning Ordinances," pp. 7–10; Meyer, " 'Doing the Master's Business' "; Harris, *Political Power*, pp. 188, 215–16; White, *Downtown Birmingham*, pp. 57, 111–15; "Report of the Birmingham Zoning Commission," June 21, 1926, and John H. Adams, chairman, zoning commission, to T. F. Weiss, June 14, 1933 (quotation), box 7, file 9, Jones Papers, BPLDAM. The zoning commission revised its code after the war in response to black demands. See John H. Adams to James W. Morgan, August 21, 1946, box 9, file 17, Green Papers, BPLDAM. In *Buchanan v. Warley* (1917), the U.S. Supreme Court ruled the racial zoning ordinances of Louisville, Kentucky, unconstitutional.

3. Zoning map of North Smithfield, box 6, file 4B, Police Surveillance Papers, BPLDAM; Leavy, "Zoning Ordinances," pp. 26–28. For an analysis of how residential segregation in Birmingham promoted the growth of institutions within the black community see Feldman, "A Sense of Place."

4. E. B. Lewis to Chief C. Floyd Eddins, August 20, 1947, box 7, file 24, Police Surveillance Papers.

5. *BN*, August 1, 1947; *BW*, August 22, 1947; *Birmingham Age-Herald*, August 20, 1947 (quotation), condemning the nighttime work of "culprits, vandals and other sneakers"; statement of Willie Lee Patterson, September 6, 1947, and "State Bureau of Investigation and Identification" Report of W. H. Lee, September 25, 1947, box 7, file 24, Police Surveillance Papers. See also *Matthews v. City of Birmingham*, No. 28-6046, N.D. Ala. 1947.

6. Report of W. H. Lee, September 25, 1947, box 7, file 24, Police Surveillance Papers; Leavy, "Zoning Ordinances," p. 32.

7. Davis, *Autobiography*, pp. 77–78, 95–96. Davis's mother was a schoolteacher and her father owned a gas station in the black business district two blocks from the Sixteenth Street Baptist Church.

8. Statements of John J. Gould, April 7, 1949, and Detective P. E. McMahan et al. to Chief C. F. Eddins, report on "Bombing of Three Unoccupied Dwellings," March 26, 1949, box 6, file 4A, Police Surveillance Papers.

9. Statements of Mrs. W. A. Thomas, July 5, 1949, and Bishop S. L. Green, July 2, 1949, box 6, file 4A, ibid. Several black organizations protested the bombings. See Emory O. Jackson, Omega Psi Phi Fraternity, to Cooper Green, April 4, Mrs. M. E. Haney, Emanuel Grand Court Heroines of Jericho, to Green, March 30, and telegram of Mrs. A. O. Ward, Birmingham Metropolitan Council of Negro Women, to Green, March 29, 1949, box 10, Green Papers.

10. Statements of H. G. Hicks and his wife, April 21, 1949, J. E. Monteith, April 7, 1949, John J. Gould, April 7, 1949, and Sam L. Chesnut, April 21, 1949, box 6, file 4A, Police Surveillance Papers.

11. Statements of Sam L. Chesnut, April 21, 1949, Watchmen T. J. Dusenberry Jr., Joseph F. Bass, May 29, 1949, and Supervisor C. A. Bingham, July 19, 1949, of the Alabama Power Co., and C. E. Henderson, April 18, 1949, box 6, file 4A, ibid.

12. Statements of Mary Atkins and Annie Sims, April 7, 1949, George Smith, April 14, 1949, and Rev. O. C. Bickerstaff, July 5, 1949, box 6, file 4A; Report of Paul E. McMahan to Chief C. F. Eddins, May 21, 1949, box 6, file 4B, all in ibid.

13. *Birmingham Age-Herald*, May 2, 1949; statement of Robert E. Chambliss, May 23, 1949, box 6, file 4A, Police Surveillance Papers; Leavy, "Zoning Ordinances," 36; Sikora, *Until Justice Rolls Down*, pp. 153–54.

14. E. O. Jackson to W. Cooper Green, May 7, and Green to Jackson, May 9, 1949, box 9, file 19, Green Papers; Leavy, "Zoning Ordinances," pp. 37–40; Statement of Rev. Milton Curry, June 9, 1949, box 6, file 4A, Police Surveillance Papers; NAACP statement in support of Curry, June 3, 1949, box 4, file 26, Green Papers.

15. Statement of Arthur D. Shores, August 9, 1949, box 6, file 4A, Police Surveillance Files, BPLDAM (police corroborated the FBI's actions by calling agent Payton Norvell); Leavy, "Zoning Ordinances," p. 37.

16. Cochran, "Arthur Davis Shores"; *BN*, September 18, 1977; Norrell, "Labor at the Ballot Box," pp. 224–25; Raines, *My Soul Is Rested*, pp. 384–87. For a critical view of Shores see Painter, *Narrative of Hosea Hudson*, pp. 276–80, and *Steele v. Louisville and Nashville Railroad*. A. P. Tureaud waged a similar fight over the same years in New Orleans; see Fairclough, *Race and Democracy*.

17. *BW*, August 12, 1949; copy of August 9, 1949 ordinance, box 6, file 4B, Police Surveillance Papers.

18. James H. Willis to James A. Simpson, August 16, and Simpson to Willis, August 18, 1949, box 9, file 24, Green Papers.

19. *BN*, August 9, 1949. The new ordinance, No.709-F, joined ordinances 1604 and 1605 in the *General Code of . . . Birmingham*, pp. 639–41.

20. *BN*, August 9, 1949; *BW*, August 12, 1949.

21. U.S. Bureau of the Census, *Sixteenth Census*, Housing, 2:9–23, and *Seventeenth Census*, Housing, Birmingham, Characteristics of the Population by Census Tracts, pp. 7–26.

22. Thompson, Lewis, and McEntire, "Atlanta and Birmingham," pp. 53–55 (see also map on p. 52 showing black neighborhoods); Leighton, "Birmingham," pp. 235–36; Bobby M. Wilson,

"Black Housing Opportunities," pp. 52, 57 n13. For a discussion of shotgun dwellings and other forms of worker housing in Birmingham see White and Hudgins, *Village Creek*, pp. 66–82.

23. White and Hudgins, *Village Creek*, p. 71; Ellen Dorsey to "To Whom It May Concern," October 12, 1951, box 26, file 1, James W. Morgan Papers, BPLDAM; U.S. Bureau of the Census, *Seventeenth Census*, Characteristics of Dwelling Units by Census Tracts, pp. 23, 25.

24. *BN*, September 26, October 12, 14, 1951; Julia Simmons to "Dear Sir," October 11, 1951, box 26, file 1, Morgan Papers. For background on the Tuxedo project see Annual Reports, Housing Authority of the Birmingham District, 1952, 1957. The NAACP aided black home owners in their often futile struggle to keep their property; see Ruby Hurley to Morgan, December 15, 1953, and other documents in box 25, file 20, Morgan Papers.

25. For background on public housing in the city see Ninth Annual Report, Housing Authority of the Birmingham District, 1948; on federal housing and segregation see Goering, *Housing Desegregation and Federal Policy*, pp. 75–82.

26. Charles P. Marks Village for whites opened in May, and Joseph H. Loveman's Village for Negroes opened in October 1952; White and Hudgins, *Village Creek*, pp. 66, 71. The vacancy rate in public housing can be determined in two ways: by comparing the number of forced removals by race and by comparing the number of vacancies by race. Whites consistently showed a higher turnover rate. For example, in 1950 more than one out of three whites left the projects as opposed to one out of five blacks. And whereas during 1948 and 1949 public housing enabled black residents to save enough to buy a home, by 1951 and 1952 few left for this reason. By checking tenant placement figures one can also see the mobility of white public housing residents. Between 1949 and 1952 one out of every two whites who applied received housing as opposed to one out of every four blacks. Because the possible number of units remained constant, the variable depended on the number of vacancies. See Annual Reports, Housing Authority of the Birmingham District, 1948–52, box 14, Morgan Papers.

27. Annual Report, Housing Authority of the Birmingham District, 1952; *BN*, October 24, 1951; press release, Housing and Home Finance Agency, November 25, 1953, box 25, file 20, Morgan Papers.

28. Bobby M. Wilson, "Black Housing Opportunities," pp. 49–57; Thompson, Lewis, and McEntire, "Atlanta and Birmingham," pp. 57–58, 62. For a contemporary black discussion of housing in Birmingham see Geraldine Moore, *Behind the Ebony Mask*, pp. 34–38, and Leavy, "Zoning Ordinances," pp. 73–82. Mayor Green commissioned a pamphlet on race relations in 1946 that purported to demonstrate how Birmingham had addressed the needs of its black citizens. Instead, the brochure documented discrimination in street lighting, paving, public housing, education, and health care. See boxes 10 (for pamphlet) and 9 (for flooding), file 18, Green Papers.

29. In contrast to Birmingham, Atlanta worked out a biracial solution to its housing crisis. African Americans made up one-third of the population but lived on one-ninth of the land in 1945. By 1956, through negotiated settlements that maintained Jim Crow, black housing stock had increased by 8,500 units. The traditional Negro leadership class in Atlanta "made no frontal assault on the idea of racially exclusive neighborhoods, but instead pursued a policy of improved housing opportunities for blacks within the system of segregation." Stone, *Regime Politics*, p. 33 (this quotation); *BN*, August 9, 1949; Leavy, "Zoning Ordinances," p. 54.

30. For a helpful discussion on race relations during the transition of a neighborhood from white to black see Myrdal, *An American Dilemma*, pp. 622–27. For a historical account that explores the unscrupulous and exploitative potential of residential racial change and that considers the human stories involved see Orser, *Blockbusting In Baltimore*.

31. Statements of Rev. E. B. DeYampert, August 16, B. W. Henderson, August 22, John J. Gould, August 15, Johnnie Brooks, August 17, Rev. J. H. Coleman, August 23, H. V. Early to Chief C. F. Eddins, August 13, demolition expert D. Petrig, August 16, 1949, and DeYampert, box 6, file 4A, Police Surveillance Papers. On DeYampert's extended family see Lynne Barbara Feldman, "A Sense of Place."

32. Davis, *Autobiography*, pp. 78–79. DeYampert had moved onto the "white" side of Center Street next door to the Monteiths.

349

33. J. J. Green of the NAACP to Cooper Green, August 13, 1949, James W. Morgan's Press Release, August 13, box 4, file 26, and the August 17 resolutions, box 10, file 9, Green Papers. The flier "Negroes' Homes Bombed Again!!" listed the following black sponsors: the Birmingham Business League, Property Owners Protective Association, Progressive Democratic Association, Interdenominational Ministerial Alliance, Birmingham-Jefferson County Housewives League, Birmingham Emancipation Association, and Social Workers Council; box 6, file 4B, Police Surveillance Papers.

34. August 17, 1949, "Resolution," box 10, file 9, Green Papers; Thompson, *The Negro Leadership Class*. Thompson argued that three different types of black leaders existed: Uncle Toms, who petitioned white leaders for services within the rubric of separate but equal; racial diplomats, who proposed biracial negotiations to achieve concessions within a segregated framework; and race men, who rejected compromises that maintained segregation. Lomax, *The Negro Revolt*, described only two types of Negro leaders: those who worked within the system and those who rejected outright segregation. As Lomax noted, "The sit-ins marked the end of the great era of the traditional Negro leadership class, a half century of fiercely guarded glory" (pp. 138–39). The subtle distinctions Thompson drew between Uncle Toms and racial diplomats are collapsed in this analysis of Birmingham to conform to Lomax's description of a traditional Negro leadership class challenged by the new race men.

35. Pettiford, "How to Help the Negro to Help Himself"; Birmingfind [Robert J. Norrell], *The Other Side*; Parker, *A Dream That Came True*; Harris, "Stability and Change in Discrimination," pp. 396, 403–4. On the ideology of the traditional Negro leadership class see the classic Meier, *Negro Thought in America*; see also Dailey, "Neither 'Uncle Tom' Nor 'Accommodationist,'" pp. 20–33.

36. The size of the black middle class in a city influenced local race relations, as demonstrated by Norrell, *Reaping The Whirlwind*, and Chafe, *Civilities and Civil Rights*, but, as Chafe recognized, the traditional Negro leadership class participated in civilities without gaining civil rights for the larger black community. The sociologist E. Franklin Frazier (*Black Bourgeoisie*) identified this elite group of African Americans as the "black bourgeoisie" and in his writings described its ideology. Frazier's work supports Lomax's view of a traditional Negro leadership class. For another view of the black elite see Myrdal, *An American Dilemma*, pp. 645–48, 689–93, 727–33. On Birmingham's black middle class see Geraldine Moore, *Behind the Ebony Mask*, pp. 52–54, 63–66, 114–23.

37. The seminal work on Communist Party activities in Birmingham is Kelley, *Hammer and Hoe*; see esp. pp. 78–91, 134. Kelley's analysis of protest from the black masses is extended in *Race Rebels*. The standard account of the Scottsboro Boys remains Carter, *Scottsboro*, but see also Goodman, *Stories of Scottsboro*, and Painter, *Narrative of Hosea Hudson*, pp. 271–72.

38. *Chicago Defender*, February 2, 1946; *BW*, February 5, 22, 1946; Richards, "The Southern Negro Youth Congress"; SNYC programs of the 1940 and 1948 All-Southern Negro Youth Conferences held in Birmingham, private collection of James and Esther Jackson, New York City, copies in author's possession.

39. Emory O. Jackson to Gloster B. Current, June 12, NAACP Papers, BPLDAM. Current approved the idea. See Current to Jackson, September 17, 1951, ibid.; *Pittsburgh Courier*, September 27, 1975, file 70.1.3.1.4, and Jackson to Lerone Bennett, n.d., file 70.1.1.1.1, Jackson Papers, BPLDAM; and Edward A. Jones, *A Candle in the Dark*, p. 291. Because the *Birmingham World* was a subsidiary of the *Atlanta Daily World* newspaper chain, its final editorial policy resided in the hands of the general manager and editor C. A. Scott of Atlanta, but he generally allowed Jackson free reign. Jackson belonged to the NAACP, ACMHR, YMCA, Omega Psi Phi, Jefferson County Progressive Democratic Council, and Sardis Baptist Church.

40. *BW*, February 12, 15, 22, March 3, 1946. For an analysis of the southern popular front see Sullivan, *Days of Hope*.

41. On NAACP membership statistics see Gloster B. Current to L. Pearl Mitchell, March 14, 1952, W. C. Patton to "NAACP Leader," May 29, 1951, Emory O. Jackson to Current, February 11, 1952, NAACP Papers. For an analysis of the Alabama NAACP that notes a decline in the postwar

350

activism of the Birmingham chapter see Autrey, "The National Association for the Advancement of Colored People in Alabama."

42. Emory O. Jackson to W. E. Shortridge, April 8, Jackson to Rev. R. L. Alford, April 11, 1952, NAACP Papers. Jackson apparently returned to office only to resign again in October. See Jackson to Dr. J. King Chandler III, October 4, 1952, ibid.; *BP-H*, April 24, 1952, and *BW*, March 21, 1952.

43. Emory O. Jackson to Anne G. Rutledge, February 23, 1956, Jackson Papers.

44. The national NAACP office had selected Birmingham as its southeastern headquarters and stationed Mrs. Ruby Hurley in the city as regional secretary. On the branch's membership problems see Hurley's "Report to the Executive Board," April 27, 1953, NAACP Papers. At one point Patton resigned as president. See W. C. Patton to Officers and Members, June 10, 1953, ibid., to which Gloster B. Current commented to Walter White in a confidential memo dated July 16, 1953, that Patton's resignation would "do no great harm," but Patton returned to office by the end of the year; see "Ballot of the Birmingham Branch," December 13, 1953, ibid.; *BW*, February 24, 1953; *BP-H*, June 16, 1955.

45. Emory O. Jackson to W. D. Kendrick, president of the Jefferson County Commission, March 26, 1951, and J. King Chandler III to Rev. R. L. Alford, February 26, 1951, NAACP Papers; *BP-H*, January 15, 1953; *BN*, July 24, 1953. For an analysis of the federal policy and the NAACP's defense of black property see Scribner, "The Housing Act of 1949."

46. "The American Heritage Program: A Plan to Raise the Level of Active Citizenship in Our Country," telegrams of Thomas D'A. Brophy to W. Cooper Green, December 16, Green to Brophy, December 17, 1947, Hayes King [a black man] to Green, n.d., Green to King, December 17, 1947, with the note "Your people have endorsed this plan," NAACP's "Citizens Committee Statement," box 7, file 15, Green Papers. Earlier in life Dr. Ernest W. Taggart had taken a more radical stand on race relations by heading a local faction of the NAACP that briefly supported the ILD. See Taggart to J. C. DeHoll, May 4, and DeHoll to Taggart, May 6, 1936, box 5, file 2, Jones Papers; Kelley, *Hammer and Hoe*, pp. 87, 89, 124–25; and Painter, *Narrative of Hosea Hudson*, p. 280 (Hudson's quotation in text). Langston Hughes used the Birmingham situation for the subject of the poem "Freedom Train"; Hughes, *Selected Poems*, p. 276.

47. A. G. Gaston to W. Cooper Green, October 22, Green to Gaston, October 23, 1947, box 6, file 24, Green Papers; Leslie L. Gwaltney to James W. Morgan, June 8, Morgan to Gwaltney, June 15, 1955, box 2, file 29, Morgan Papers; Gaston to Eugene Connor, August 5, 1946, box 6, file 23, Green Papers. In recognition of Gaston's work representing his race, the city named a park and a swimming pool after him; see Gaston to Morgan, August 25, 1961, box 19, files 17–35, Morgan Papers. For a description of the Tuggle School see Davis, *Autobiography*, pp. 87–92. By 1972 Gaston had changed little, still urging black activists to "take it slow." See Franklin, *Back To Birmingham*, 103–4; Gaston, *Green Power*; *BN*, July 4, 1992; *Atlanta Journal-Constitution*, January 20, 1996.

48. Dr. E. W. Taggart to James Downey Jr., February 11, Green to Taggart, February 12, King Sparks Jr., superintendent of parks, to Green, February 15, and Green to Charles W. Hall, February 28, 1952 (quotation), box 10, file 10, Green Papers; Green to Sparks, April 17, Sparks to Green, May 27, and Emory O. Jackson to Sparks, August 16, 1952, box 19, file 22, Morgan Papers. Jackson investigated the behind-the-scenes negotiating after learning of Gaston and Rev. John W. Goodgame Jr.'s effort to prevent a protest of the Jim Crow facility; Sparks later resigned after charges of mismanagement and malfeasance surfaced concerning his running of the parks department. Atlanta desegregated its golf courses in 1955. See *BN*, December 23, 1955.

49. Cooper, *Metropolitan County*, pp. 70–76; LaMonte, *Ward*, p. 16; Olmstead report, box 11, file 7, Green Papers; Harris, *Political Power*, p. 167. The city commission asked the corporate structure to assist in the construction of parks. When Birmingham planned a new Negro park, it approached the Tennessee Coal, Iron, and Railroad Company about giving a few acres of land for that purpose, but TCI declined and offered to sell the area at a high price, which the city refused; see J. W. Brooks to W. Cooper Green, September 9, 1942, box 11, file 12, Green Papers. About the only thing the U.S. Steel Corporation ever gave Birmingham was the small area of land under the statue of Vulcan on top of Red Mountain. When African Americans began using the park, the city

removed the tables; see J. W. Morgan to Mrs. D. P. Newby, September 1, 1954, box 19, file 24, Morgan Papers. Other companies proved more willing to work with the city than TCI. The American Cast Iron Pipe Company constructed the white ACIPCO–Clayton Park and leased it to the city to operate as well as the facility at Slossfield; see Green to C. O. Hodges, vice president of ACIPCO, May 12, 1952, box 19, file 22, Morgan Papers. Regardless of whether they helped finance the public parks, corporations used the facilities for company functions, as when the U.S. Pipe Company hosted a picnic for its employees at the Colored Memorial Park; see C. E. Cole to Bob Shelton, July 9, 1956, box 19, file 26, Morgan Papers, and *BP-H*, August 27, 1952.

50. Interdenominational Recreational Council petitions (box 11, file 12, Green Papers), also signed by members of the traditional Negro leadership class including Gaston, Jackson, and Taggart. The civic leagues coordinated their efforts through the Alabama State Federation of Colored Civic Leagues. See "Declaration of Incorporation," January 19, 1933, box 4, file 3, Jones Papers; Rufus Jones to W. Cooper Green, May 31, 1943, box 11, file 12, Green Papers; J. J. Ryles to J. W. Morgan, April 27, 1953, box 19, file 23, C. L. Burns to Morgan, January 21, 1952, box 20, file 24, Morgan Papers. Black middle-class organizations petitioned the city commission for public awards, as when the Imperial Club asked Mayor Morgan to acknowledge John T. "Fess" Whatley's contributions to Birmingham as band director at Parker High School, where he trained many of the country's great jazz musicians; see Imperial Club to Morgan, February 25, 1956, box 7, file 17, Morgan Papers.

51. Program, "First Annual Celebration of the Colored Memorial Park," May 31, 1943, Emory O. Jackson to W. Cooper Green, July 22, Jackson to R. S. Marshall, September 2, Green to Jackson, September 11, 1942, box 11, file 12, Green Papers. As an example of increased Jim Crow services that were less discriminatory than in the past, Birmingham built swimming pools during the 1950s, having completed four for whites and three—with one more under construction—for blacks. See *BN*, November 23, 1952, May 13, 1954, James W. Morgan to Sarah Sanks, June 3, 1960, box 19, file 28, Morgan Papers. Kelly Ingram Park was originally a "white" park. See also R. S. Burgins to T. R. Broom, October 10, 1957, and King Sparks Jr. to Burgins, January 3, 1958, box 19, file 27, Morgan Papers.

52. Cooper, *Metropolitan County*, pp. 77–82; LaMonte, *Ward*, p. 44; Harris, *Political Power*, p. 167; R. Paul Huffstutler, president library board, to W. Cooper Green, September 19, 1952, box 6, file 22, Morgan Papers.

53. For a description of library services for African Americans and the building of the new Negro branch see Davis, *Autobiography*, p. 97; Paul R. Huffstutler to the City Commission, September 17, 1953, box 6, file 22 (first quotation), Rev. Luke Beard to Emily Miller Danton, director of the library, March 28, 1952, box 5, file 5, "Preliminary Committee" (undated list of black library advisers), E. A. Carter to Morgan, October 7, November 18, 1953 (second quotation), D. Scurlark, Ensley Civic League president, to Morgan and Morgan to Scurlark, November 20, 1954, box 5, file 6, Morgan Papers. Also on the conversion of "white" parks to "Negro," see Jessie M. Saffoe to Jabbo Waggoner, August 24, 1956, box 19, file 26, and R. S. Burgins to T. R. Broom, October 10, 1957, box 19, file 27, Morgan Papers.

54. Martin, *Hartsfield*, pp. 68, 99–101; L. B. Cooper, chairman, Jefferson County Board of Registrars, to state senator James A. Simpson, May 14, 1935, Simpson Papers, ADAH (black voting statistics for 1935). While conducting research for Gunnar Myrdal, Ralph J. Bunche estimated the number of registered black voters in Jefferson County: 419 in 1928, 549 in 1936, and 712 in 1938; Bunche, *Political Status of the Negro*, pp. 266 (statistics), 253–70 (registration in Jefferson County in general), 258–62 (Right to Vote Club). Hosea Hudson quoted Emory Jackson as saying that less than 500 black people could vote when the Right To Vote Club organized at the instigation of Joseph Gelders in 1938; Painter, *Narrative of Hosea Hudson*, pp. 268, 381 n4.

55. Painter, *Narrative of Hosea Hudson*, p. 264 (quotation); Bunche, *Political Status of the Negro*, pp. 478–80.

56. Estimates vary on the number of registered black voters in Jefferson County. Whereas Arthur Shores claimed that 2,000 Negroes were added to the rolls in 1939, Bunche believed that only 166 were registered between 1938 and 1940. The SRC stated that 7,200 African Americans voted in

1952 but the number declined by 1954, whereas Emory Jackson maintained that the number of registered black voters increased to 7,000 by 1954. The *Birmingham News* of May 20, 1956, suggested that 7,000 African Americans voted in 1956. The steady increase in registered black voters appears accurate. Bunche, *Political Status of the Negro*, p. 266; "Registration of Negro Voters in Alabama in 1954," file 41.1.6.2.31, SRC Papers, BPLDAM; *BW*, April 13, 1954; Strong, *Registration of Voters in Alabama*, pp. 57–58. As Strong demonstrated, Birmingham's white lower middle class jealously guarded the franchise by allowing only a few people to vote; see also his essay "Alabama: Transition and Alienation," in which he estimated that the number of black voters in the state increased from 6,000 in 1947 to 25,000 in 1952, to 50,000 in 1954, to 66,000 in 1960, to 113,000 in 1966, and to 250,000 in 1968. Repealing the cumulative feature enfranchised a total of 200,000 voters in Alabama, one-eighth of whom were black; Franklin, *Back To Birmingham*, p. 36.

57. Bunche, *Political Status of the Negro*, pp. 253–58; Geraldine Moore, *Behind the Ebony Mask*, pp. 202–3 (quotation); MacNair, "Social Distance," pp. 101–3. Shores at one time headed an organization called the Alabama Progressive Democratic Association, which endorsed Robert Lindbergh in 1953 for the position of police commissioner; see "Open Letter of the Alabama Progressive Democratic Association," box 11, file 27, Morgan Papers.

58. Statement of Mary Means Monk, January 8, 1951, box 7, file 35, Police Surveillance Papers.

59. James H. Willis to James A. Simpson, August 16, 1949, J. R. Gardner Jr. to W. Cooper Green, November 2, 1949, and Green to Gardner, November 12, 1949, box 9, file 20, Green Papers. An angry Green responded to Gardner: "All efforts on my part to 'hold the line' for my College Hill–Graymont friends, appear not to be appreciated by at least two of your members who have been my critics at every meeting . . . for ten years I have fought their battle and I feel like I am due an apology." See also Leavy, "Zoning Ordinances," pp. 43–46.

60. Horace C. Wilkinson to James H. Willis, November 14, 1949, box 9, file 24, Green Papers; see also Feldman, *From Demagogue to Dixiecrat*, p. 165. A contemporary example of Birmingham's parsimony was the building of the new city hall, completed in 1950 at a cost of $4 million paid for in cash; see "Outlines on New City Hall," box 8, file 23, and James W. Morgan to Wm. S. Foster, September 13, 1950, box 8, file 24, Morgan Papers. The mayor was less than optimistic: "All I can say is that I hope for a victory"; Green to J. R. Gardner, November 12, 1949, box 9, file 20, Morgan Papers.

61. Horace C. Wilkinson to James H. Willis, December 28, 1949, box 9, file 24, George B. Alexander to W. Cooper Green, December 14, and Mrs. R. D. DeLaure to Green, December 15, 1949, box 9, file 20, Green Papers; Leavy, "Zoning Ordinances," pp. 45–47.

62. George R. Byrum Jr., chairman, zoning board of adjustment, to James W. Morgan, November 19, and Sidney W. Smyer to Cooper Green, November 16, 1948, box 4, file 26, Green Papers.

63. *Birmingham Post*, April 14, 1950.

64. United Press wire service newspaper clipping, April 22, 1950, with note attached: "This looks bad your honor. The whole USA saw this"; box 4, file 26, Green Papers; *Birmingham Age-Herald*, April 24, 1950.

65. *BN*, August 23, 1949, April 15, 1950; *Birmingham Age-Herald*, April 25, 1950 (see also editorial cartoon on April 15); *Birmingham Post*, April 24, 1950. Foreign newspapers also reported the racial bombings; see undated and unidentified British clipping "This Is Dynamite Town!," box 4, file 26, Green Papers.

66. "Button Gwinnett Says: Disgrace in Smithfield," *Shades Valley Sun*, May 4, 1950.

67. Zukoski, "A Life Story," pp. 190–92, 330–32. Zukoski wrote on many subjects in addition to race. The best of his columns are reprinted in his *Voice in the Storm*.

68. *Birmingham Post*, April 24, 1950, and undated and unidentified clipping, "Man Is Freed After Quiz in Bomb Probe," box 4, file 26, Green Papers.

69. Horace C. Wilkinson to Cooper Green, October 18, 1950, box 9, file 24, Green Papers; *City of Birmingham v. Monk*. The Supreme Court denied Wilkinson's final appeal on January 25, 1951.

70. Statements of Mary Means Monk, January 10, and Monroe Monk, January 11, Birmingham Police Department preliminary investigation report, January 10, 1951, box 7, file 35, Police Surveillance Papers.

71. Leavy, "Zoning Ordinances," p. 48; Davis, *Autobiography*, 95. Leavy concludes that Connor and the police were involved in the bombings, a charge confirmed by the testimony of Detective Henry Darnell in *BN*, January 28, 1953. Later, Angela Davis became the center of a cause célèbre in 1970 and then went on to become a theorist on the class struggle and black feminism.

Chapter 3

1. U.S. Bureau of the Census, *Seventeenth Census*, vol. 2, General Characteristics of the Population, Alabama, pt. 2, Detailed Characteristics, tables 77, 87.

2. Ibid., table 78. For an analysis of segregation and job security among the white working class see McKiven, *Iron and Steel*.

3. Strong, *Registration of Voters in Alabama*, pp. 48–74; U.S. Bureau of the Census, *Seventeenth Census*, vol. 2, General Characteristics, table 33; *BP-H*, October 13, 1953. The *Post-Herald* (November 30, 1964) reports that the number of qualified voters in Birmingham had increased to 90,000; the State Legislators' Recapitulation Sheet for the Democratic Primary Election, May 5, 1953, recorded 22,064 votes for president of the city commission and 44,427, with electors casting two ballots each, for associate commissioners. From this one can estimate that approximately 22,000 people voted in the election. Estimated number of black voters from *BW*, April 13, 1954; Beiman, "Birmingham," p. 121.

4. Strong, "The Jefferson County Story," in his *Registration of Voters in Alabama*, pp. 48–63. For a similar view of the Jefferson County Board of Registrars, see Bunche, *Political Status of the Negro*, pp. 253–70.

5. State Legislators, Recapitulation Sheet, Democratic Primary Election Runoff, June 4, 1957, with returns posted as Precinct 10, Districts 1–5 for East Lake, Precinct 10, Districts 7–10 for Woodlawn, and Precinct 9, Districts 5–6, 10 for West End; U.S. Bureau of the Census, *Seventeenth Census*, Characteristics of the Population by Census Tracts, pp. 7–10. East Lake comprised Tracts 1–2, 19–22; Woodlawn comprised Tracts 3, 5, 18, 23; and West End comprised Tract 40.

6. Birmingfind [Robert J. Norrell], *Elyton-West End*.

7. Ibid. In general, all of Birmingham's distinctive neighborhoods suffered decline as community disintegrated during the postwar years. This was also revealed through the transformation of politics from the precinct and box system scattered about the neighborhoods to a few machines in select locations. Disintegration occurred not only in residential areas (see Birmingfind [Robert J. Norrell], "The Best People in the World Live in Wylam," and Acton, *The Pierian Club of Birmingham*) but also within ethnic communities as members assimilated into the white mainstream. Silver (*Twentieth-Century Richmond*, pp. 98–99) also describes discernible neighborhoods that retained their distinctiveness into the 1940s. Birmingham followed a typical pattern of southern suburban growth after 1900. For a discussion on the phenomenon see Abbott, *The New Urban America*, 11–12, 79–87; Atkins, "Growing Up around Edgewood Lake"; and Barefield, *A History of Mountain Brook*. On the role of the automobile in the transformation of the city see Brownell, "Birmingham."

8. Statistical information for this and the next three paragraphs was collected from the U.S. Bureau of the Census, *Sixteenth Census*, Statistics for Census Tracts, Birmingham, pp. 12–34; *Seventeenth Census*, Housing, Birmingham, Block Statistics, pp. 3–50, and Statistics for Census Tracts, Birmingham, 7–26; *Eighteenth Census*, Census Tracts, Birmingham, SMSA, pp. 15–71; *Nineteenth Census*, Census Tracts, Birmingham, SMSA, P2–P59, H1–H21; and *Twentieth Census*, Census Tracts, Birmingham, SMSA.

9. Nunnelley, *Bull Connor*, pp. 13–23; Beiman, "Birmingham," p. 117. Connor later explained, "I really had no interest in politics, I just wanted to see how many friends I had made as a baseball announcer"; *BN*, May 3, 1961. With the election of Sidney W. Smyer to the state house in place of Connor in 1938, a somewhat different yet mutual relationship developed with Simpson: they coordinated their legislative efforts without the obsequiousness; see James L. Davidson to J. A. Simpson, May 9, 1945, and Joel E. Johnson to Smyer, May 9, 1945, Simpson Papers, ADAH.

10. Simpson, "Recollections"; Foreman, "Decade of Hope," p. 141; *Birmingham Age-Herald*, May 19, 1937; *Birmingham Post*, November 1, 1937; *Alabama: The News Magazine of the Deep*

South, December 14, 1936, May 17, 1937; Atkins, "Simpson and Birmingham Politics"; Nunnelley, *Bull Connor*, pp. 22–23, 30–31; *Birmingham Post*, January 15, July 17, 1935, September 3, 1945; *BN*, September 4, 1977; Powell, "Simpson and His Civil Service Law," Samford University Archives, Birmingham; Beiman, "Birmingham," pp. 117–18.

11. Clifford J. Durr and Virginia Foster Durr, oral interview for the Lyndon B. Johnson Presidential Library, 1975, copy in Virginia Durr Papers, Schlesinger Library, Cambridge. The Durrs identified Connor's replacement at TCI as "Crack Hanna," a man listed as James B. Hann, policeman at TCI, in the *Birmingham City Directory* of 1941.

12. *BN*, January 21, March 22, 1941, April 13, 1951. For a thought-provoking discussion of the lower middle class see Lasch, *The True and Only Heaven*. The *Birmingham News*'s editorial for September 24, 1948, stated that "Birmingham's morals are being watched by the city's Department of Public Safety" but warned: "Arbitrary control by one man over the reading matter of a community is both unwise and dangerous, no matter how well-intentioned that person may be." Among other cities, Chicago banned movies and New Orleans comic books. The *Birmingham Post* questioned if Connor wanted "thought police next?" January 17, 20, 1941 (quotation), September 24, 1948; *BP-H*, May 18, 1951; N. H. Waters to Bull Connor, February 4, 1946, box 6, file 23, Green Papers, BPLDAM.

13. *BP-H*, June 15, 1953; *BN*, July 3, 1953; A. Berkowitz to Judge O. B. Hall, July 21, 1952, box 23, file 14, Morgan Papers, BPLDAM.

14. *BP-H* and *BW*, July 17, 1951; *BN*, March 16, 1951. See also correspondence in the NAACP Papers, BPLDAM.

15. *BP-H*, October 10, 1951.

16. Wilkinson's letter is printed in *BN*, October 4, 1951. On spastics see *BN*, February 22, 1952; on juveniles see *BN*, October 3, 1951; on women see *BN*, January 13, 1952, and *BP-H*, July 24, 1952, also for charges dropped.

17. *BP-H* and *BN*, June 15, 1953.

18. *BP-H*, November 1, 1951. For a different case of illegal detention concerning a black woman see Louis Silberman to Cooper Green, December 8, and C. Floyd to Bull Connor, December 9, 1949, box 9, file 20, Green Papers; concerning a white man, see *BN*, October 5, 1951; and concerning a white woman, see *BN*, October 4, 1951, the latter involving vagrancy charges after she refused to have sexual intercourse with the patrolman.

19. Ward to Bull Connor and "Statement by Bessie B. Ammons," both dated January 24, 1951, box 14, file 22, Morgan Papers; "Birmingham Jail," lyrics by James Tarlton, sung to the tune of "Down in the Valley," copy in Tutwiler Collection, Birmingham Public Library. In his letter to Connor, N. C. Ward, the manager at Smithfield Court, expressed his outrage over the police treatment of Ammons, whom he described as neither a "prevaricator" nor an "alarmist"; hence he accepted her testimony and the reconstructed dialogue as fact. He added that the experience left her "upset emotionally" and "bewildered." Similar treatment of black people by police occurred in other southern cities; see Kuhn, Joye, and West, *Living Atlanta*, pp. 337–40. On the condition of the city jail see Jim Esdale to Connor, August 14, 1944, box 8, file 14, and Dave Birmingham to Green, January 11, 1952, and telephone log of Gladys Calvin's undated phone call [1952] requesting an outside investigation of the "sweat box" in the city jail, box 9, file 23, Green Papers; *BN*, February 6, 1952. Conditions in the jail improved under the administration of Commissioner Robert Lindbergh (see jail inspection reports, box 16, file 1) and worsened when Connor returned to office in 1957 (see Morgan to W. Morgan Baker, February 26, 1958, box 4, file 9), Morgan Papers.

20. Charles White McGehee to Mrs. [W. Cooper] Green, October 3, W. Cooper Green to McGehee, October 5, L. O. McKeehan to Bull Connor, Green to McKeehan, October 10, John P. O'Hare to Green, October 1, John M. Bradley to Green, October 10, and Mrs. Pauline E. Hutchens to Green, October 11, 1951, all in box 21, file 11, Morgan Papers; *BN*, September 29, October 1, 3, 1951; *BP-H*, October 5, 1951.

21. *BP-H*, March 21, 28, 1951; *BN*, October 1, 1951 (quotation). Korea influenced the number of resignations; Paul L. Singer to J. King Chandler III, May 6, 1954, box 18, file 39, memo of Cooper Green on increased employment of policemen (from 246 in 1940 to 413 in 1952), box 22, file 6, and Program of the March 1951 Graduating Class, box 21, file 9, Morgan Papers.

22. Acting Chief E. H. Brown to Bull Connor, June 8, 9, 1953, box 21, file 18, Morgan Papers.

23. Nunnelley, *Bull Connor*, pp. 48–49; "A Friend" to Cooper Green, undated [1952], box 22, file 1, Morgan Papers; *BP-H*, October 14, 26–28; *BN*, October 17, 25, November 29, 1953.

24. *BN*, December 14–16, 20, 1951, January 28, 1953, and June 9, 1954 (Ward's conviction for operating a bawdy house and aiding and abetting prostitution). Nunnelley (*Bull Connor*) glances over the Tutwiler incident and subsequent police department scandals in his treatment of the police commissioner. Other cities suffered from police scandals during the period, with perhaps New Orleans's situation being the most similar; Haas, *DeLesseps S. Morrison and the Image of Reform*.

25. *BN*, November 25, December 22, 26–27, 1951, January 6, 7, 1952.

26. *BN*, January 6–7, 1952.

27. *Montgomery Advertiser*, January 8, 1952; *BP-H*, January 24–25, 1952, *BN*, January 15, 24, 1952; C. E. Armstrong to Cooper Green, January 25, 1952, and a copy of the "Odum Report," box 21, file 17, Morgan Papers.

28. *BN*, January 16 (quotation), January 17–20, February 7, 1952. The attorney who filed the recall petition had his office ransacked, and policemen parked in front of his house day and night. *BN*, January 20, 1952; Green's undated [January 1952] notes on a statement about the investigation, box 22, file 5, Morgan to Green, January 16, and Morgan Press Release, January 9, 1952, box 22, file 1, Morgan Papers. For Morgan's personal and negative view of Connor see Morgan to his nephew W. Morgan Baker, January 11, 1952, box 4, file 8, Morgan Papers.

29. *BN*, January 12, 15, 21, February 8, 1952.

30. "Report of the Citizens' Committee on the Birmingham Police Department," February 19, 1952, Tutwiler Collection; *BN*, February 20–21, 1952.

31. *BN*, November 25, December 10, 1951, March 11, 23, 27, April 4, 21, 25, 30, May 1, July 27, 29, October 3, 6, 8, December 18, 1952, January 26, 1953; *BP-H*, January 19, October 3, 22, November 26, 1952; Morgan to W. Morgan Baker, October 10, 1952, box 4, file 8, Morgan Papers.

32. *BN*, January 10, 16, 26–27, 1953; *BP-H*, January 30, 1953; George A. Palmer to Chief of Police, February 28, 1953, box 22, file 8, Morgan Papers.

33. As Beiman noted, what passed for Birmingham's G.I. revolt was the decision of six of the city's eight legislative delegates not to seek reelection following the unpopular adoption of a bill against federal low-cost housing—the two that did run for reelection in 1945 were defeated; see Beiman "Birmingham," p. 119. On G.I. revolts see Abbott, *The New Urban America*, pp. 119–42; R. E. Lindbergh to Personnel Board, November 3, and Ray Mullins to Lindbergh, November 5, 1953, box 21, file 19, Morgan Papers; *BP-H*, November 16, December 12, 15, 25, 1953, January 6; *BN*, March 1, 6, December 10, 15, 1953. On the press see *BP-H*, March 20–21, 1951, and *BN*, April 8, 1954. On exams see *BP-H*, January 6, 14, 26, 1954. On pep talks see *BP-H*, February 10, 1954. On democratic reforms see *BN*, March 28, 1954, and *BP-H*, March 31, 1954. On training see *BN*, May 13, October 21, 1954, and Col. Paul E. Singer, "Final Report," November 4, 1954, box 21, file 20, Morgan Papers.

34. J. W. Morgan to J. King Chandler III, May 4, and Paul L. Singer to Chandler, May 6, 1954, box 18, file 39, Morgan Papers.

35. *BN*, January 5, 1955; Mrs. J. W. Siniard to J. W. Morgan, January 5, 1955, box 21, file 24, Morgan Papers.

36. Mrs. A. S. Davis to J. W. Morgan, January 5, Mrs. J. E. Hall to Morgan, January 1, Robert H. Loeb of YMBC to Morgan, January 27, 1955, all in box 21, file 24, and Jerome A. Cooper to R. E. Lindbergh, December 30, 1954, box 21, file 23, Morgan Papers. To Morgan and Wade Bradley, December 30, 1954, "A Tax Payer" wrote, "you *two* made it more obvious that the Police Department is made up of crooks and bums"; see box 21, file 23, Morgan Papers; *BN*, January 5, 1955, adding as if to distinguish acceptable brutality, "This was no beating that resulted from resisting arrest."

37. "Resolution of the NAACP Sponsored Mass Meeting," January 16, 1955, box 21, file 24, Morgan Papers; *BW*, January 22, 1952; *BN*, February 17–19, 1952; *BP-H*, January 15, 1953; W. I. Pittman memo to JCCCSF, October 2, 1952, with "Pamphlet on Negro Police," box 21, file 13, Morgan Papers. The department also debated hiring women; see *BN*, September 7, 12, 1953,

December 2, 1954, and J. W. Morgan to Leo Bashinsky, M.D., November 9, 1956, box 21, file 24, Morgan Papers.

38. *BN*, September 17, 1953, 60; *BP-H*, September 18, 1953 (quotation), March 23, 1954. The ordinance made it "unlawful for a Negro and a white person to play together or in company with each other in any game of cards, dice, dominoes, checkers, baseball, soft ball, football or basketball." *General Code of . . . Birmingham*, sec. 597, p. 201. See also Fullerton, "Striking Out Jim Crow."

39. Morgan explained the commission's action to a critical Thomas Woodman of Home Federal Savings and Loan: "Birmingham happens to be practically alone in the entire South forbidding professional teams to play where negro players are involved, all of which has given us very bad publicity in the press throughout the nation." Morgan to Woodman, February 6, 1954. See also Wallace G. Howell Jr., YMBC secretary, to Morgan, February 24, 1954; Rev. L. Wilkie Collins to Morgan, February 22, 1954; Birmingham Baptist Association News Letter 5, no. 7 (February 23, 1954); clipping, *Dallas News*, June 2, 1954; Morgan to Willis interoffice correspondence, June 4, 1954—all in box 19, file 16, Morgan Papers. The measure passed 19,640 to 6,685.

40. Bartley, *The Rise of Massive Resistance*, pp. 77–78, 108–16; *BN*, May 21, 23, August 8, 1954; Stewart, "Birmingham's Reaction," pp. 18–19.

41. *BN* and *BP-H*, May 18, 1954; *BW*, May 21, 28, 1954; Stewart, "Birmingham's Reaction," pp. 35–62, 68, 73, 95–99.

42. Grafton and Permaloff, *Big Mules and Branchheads*, pp. 185–211; Bartley, *The Rise of Massive Resistance*, pp. 280–87 (Boutwell quoted on p. 284 n62). On Boutwell's "freedom of choice" plan, see *BP-H*, June 23, September 9, 1954; *BN*, October 11, 22, 1954; Bartley and Graham, *Southern Politics and the Second Reconstruction*, pp. 67–68; Carter, *Politics of Rage*, p. 96 (Wallace quotation).

43. *BN*, November 21, 1954; Bartley, *The Rise of Massive Resistance*, pp. 87–88. For information on the ASRA, see the misnamed National States' Rights Association Papers, BPLDAM. The *Birmingham World* (April 6, 1954) published a list of 44 members of the ASRA.

44. *BN*, November 21, 1955, January 10, February 17, March 4, 1956; *BP-H*, January 14, 17, February 17, 21, 27, 1956; *Christian Science Monitor*, May 16, 1956.

45. *BN*, April 5, 1956, p. 7; Kundahl, "Organized Labor in Alabama," pp. 46–48, 68–69. On Hayes see *BP-H*, April 6, 1956, August 20, 1958; *BN*, February 26, October 10, 1956. At its height in 1957, Hayes employed nearly 10,000 workers in Birmingham. The president was Lewis F. Jeffers, and the directors included attorneys William J. Cabaniss and Joseph F. Johnston, *BN* publisher Clarence B. Hanson, and financier Mervyn H. Sterne. See also "This Is Hayes" [1956], Hayes Vertical File, BPLDAM.

46. *BN*, January 10, February 21, 1956; Nunnelley, *Bull Connor*, pp. 52–53.

47. *BN*, December 12, 15, 1954; *BP-H*, December 17, 21, 1954, May 6, 1955.

48. *BN*, May 5, 1938, December 8, 12, 1954; *BP-H*, December 15, 1954.

49. *WSJ*, May 23, 1963; *BN*, August 2, 1940, March 22, 1970, August 16, 1985; *Birmingham Age-Herald*, May 27, 1942; Harris, *Political Power*, pp. 107–8; Eskew, "Demagoguery in Birmingham."

50. *WSJ*, May 23, 1963; *Birmingham Post*, January 26, 1934; *Alabama: The News Magazine of the Deep South*, October 3, 1938.

51. *BP-H*, May 26, 1967; *BN*, May 26, August 17, 1967, March 22, 1970, May 28, 1971, December 14, 1972.

52. Brochure, "Highlands Methodist Church, 1956, Birmingham, Alabama," and church newsletter *Highlands Piper* 1, no. 11, Methodist Churches Vertical File, BPLDAM; *BP-H*, December 17, 21, 1954; May 6, 13, 1955; *BN*, May 12, 1955.

53. United Methodist Church, *Discipline*; *BN*, June 3, 1956, September 17, 1958.

54. Methodist Laymen's Union, *A Pronouncement*; *BP-H*, March 20, May 27, July 17, August 12, 1959; *NYT*, July 7, 1959; Prestwood, "Social Ideas of Methodist Ministers," pp. 365–83.

55. Carter campaign material from 1957, box 11, file 16, Morgan Papers; *Atlanta Journal-Constitution*, October 27, 1991.

56. Chalmers, *Hooded Americanism*, pp. 344–45; *NYT*, October 4, 1991; *BP-H*, April 13, 17, 1956; *Tuscaloosa News*, September 2, November 14, 1956.

57. *BP-H*, September 7, October 30–31, November 1, 6, 8, December 4–5, 1957, February 11, 18, 21, 1958, December 2, 1960; *BN*, September 9, October 31, November 1, 6–7, 1957, February 19, 1958, March 12, 1959, December 22, 1960; *Montgomery Advertiser*, October 8, November 5, 1957. The four convicted were Joe B. Pritchett, Bart A. Floyd, Jesse W. Mabry, and Grover McCullough. Two others—William J. Miller and John N. Griffin—received suspended sentences for testifying for the state. On Wallace see Raines, *My Soul Is Rested*, 187.

58. *The Southerner* 1, no. 7 (September–October 1956), located in 169.7.19.3.19, Anti-Defamation League Papers, BPLDAM. Among the lower-middle-class establishments buying ad space were Pierson Grocery, Sax Grocery, Calera Cafe, Hemphill Plumbing and Heating Co., Alex's Central Park Gulf Service, Midfield Drug and Apothecary, Chicken in the South Drive In, Bowden's Economy Store, Sunbright Cleaners, Curt's Motor Service, and Dick Webb Insurance Agency. See also the material in the ASRA Papers.

59. *Alabama Official and Statistical Register*, 1959, pp. 570–71, and 1971, pp. 423–25; *NYT*, October 4, 1991. Carter received 15,441 votes of the million cast.

60. *NYT*, August 5, 1975, August 26, 1976; *BN*, July 4, 1979; *Contemporary Authors*, 107:79; Vinson and Kirkpatrick, *Twentieth Century Western Writers*; see also Dan Carter's essay, *NYT*, October 3, 1991; *Atlanta Journal-Constitution*, October 27, 1991. A recent reprinting of the *Education of Little Tree* has been a surprise best-seller.

61. Bartley, *The Rise of Massive Resistance*, p. 105; *BN*, March 4, 10, April 9, May 11, 16, 1956; *BP-H*, March 13, April 9, 20, May 11, 1956; *Tuscaloosa News*, March 10, 16, 1956; *Montgomery Advertiser*, April 15, May 10, July 13, 1956. By July 1956 Engelhardt had organized fourteen councils in Birmingham.

62. *Montgomery Advertiser*, May 21, June 8, July 13, September 13, 17, 1956, March 13, 1957; *BN*, March 12, 15, 1957; *BP-H*, March 5, 16, 1957; Chalmers, *Hooded Americanism*, pp. 345–47; Bartley, *The Rise of Massive Resistance*, pp. 340–45.

63. Ace Carter campaign material, box 11, file 16, Morgan Papers. Of the other candidates, former commissioner of public improvements Wade Bradley won 2,515 and Joseph E. Captain Jr. 602 votes; State Legislators, Recapitulation Sheet, Democratic Primary Election, May 7, 1957.

64. Nunnelley, *Bull Connor*, pp. 49, 51, 56–59; *BN*, June 2–5, 1957.

65. With the vote tabulated for Connor to Lindbergh, the lower-status white neighborhoods reported: East Lake, Precinct 10, Box 1A with 381 to 232, 2A with 256 to 209, 2B with 316 to 221, 3A with 316 to 198, 3B with 284 to 231, and 4A with 332 to 130; Woodlawn, Precinct 10, Box 7A with 265 to 208, 8A with 198 to 186, 9A with 253 to 96, 9B with 257 to 88, and 10A with 318 to 257; and West End, Precinct 9, Box 5A with 291 to 146, 5B with 278 to 149, 5C with 278 to 144, and 10A with 287 to 186. State Legislators, Recapitulation Sheet, Democratic Primary Runoff, June 4, 1957. The Highland Avenue district was Precinct 21, Boxes 1A, 2A, 2B, and 3A. Lindbergh's anti-union stand during the South Central Bell strike should have disqualified him as the candidate of labor; see the union telegrams to James W. Morgan, April 9–10, 1955, box 22, file 30, Morgan Papers. The *Birmingham News* (June 3, 1960) identifies the Graymont Armory box and notes that only 4 of the 800 votes cast in 1960 were by white voters. Some Lindbergh supporters believed that Connor stole the election.

Chapter 4

1. Clipping, *Pittsburgh Courier*, February 14, 1959, box 3, Shuttlesworth Papers, King Center; Lewis W. Jones, "Shuttlesworth," pp. 115–19.

2. Ibid.

3. Manis, "Religious Experience," pp. 143–54; Lewis W. Jones, "Shuttlesworth," pp. 127–31. Manis is working on a full-length biography of Shuttlesworth that should illuminate the minister's theological roots.

4. Manis, "Religious Experience," pp. 143–54; Lewis W. Jones, "Shuttlesworth," pp. 127–31.

5. Manis, *Southern Civil Religions in Conflict*, p. 62; Lewis W. Jones, "Shuttlesworth," pp. 132–33; Shuttlesworth, "An Account of the ACMHR," p. 134; Stewart, "Birmingham's Reaction."

6. Lewis W. Jones, "Shuttlesworth," pp. 132–33; J. W. Morgan to Mrs. A. J. Bowron, April 9, 1957, box 6, file 7, and Jefferson County Coordinating Council of Social Forces pamphlet on Negro policemen, October 2, 1952, box 21, file 13, Morgan Papers, BPLDAM; *BN*, June 23, September 30, 1955; "Petition" of 77 black ministers to city commission, July 25, 1955, box 12, file 43, Boutwell Papers, BPLDAM; Shuttlesworth, "Alabama Christian Movement for Human Rights," p. 135; Whitfield, *A Death in the Delta*.

7. Lewis W. Jones, "Shuttlesworth," p. 134; *Pittsburgh Courier*, February 14, 1959. No mention of Shuttlesworth's 1956 address was made in the *Birmingham World*, but the event had attracted other important speakers including Aubrey Williams, a southern liberal and racial egalitarian from Montgomery in 1954; Rev. T. J. Jemison, leader of the Baton Rouge bus boycott in 1955; and Rev. Dr. Martin Luther King Jr., leader of the Montgomery bus boycott in 1956. Shuttlesworth, "Alabama Christian Movement for Human Rights," p. 136; Braden, "The History That We Made," pp. 48–54.

8. Braden, "The History That We Made," pp. 50–51.

9. Ibid.; Shuttlesworth, "Alabama Christian Movement for Human Rights," pp. 136–39.

10. *BN*, June 6, 1956; *New Orleans Times-Picayune*, June 7, 1956. Danny Lyon's (*Memories*, p. 94) photographs of Shuttlesworth capture the minister's charisma.

11. *BW*, June 8, 1956; *BN*, June 6, 1956; Shuttlesworth, "Alabama Christian Movement for Human Rights," p. 140.

12. *BW*, June 5, 1956; Morris, *Origins*, p. 45; Shuttlesworth, "Alabama Christian Movement for Human Rights," pp. 146–47. On class conflict within the black community, Shuttlesworth explained: "Our professional people need to understand that the gap between the class and the masses must be closed. The classes evolved up from the masses and where would you go and what would you do without the masses?" See speech before the Fair Share Organization of Gary, Indiana, September 25, 1958, box 4, Shuttlesworth Papers; Clarke, *These Rights They Seek*, p. 66. Pastor of Trinity Baptist Church, Ware also headed the prestigious Greater Birmingham Emancipation Association; Robey served as assistant secretary in the ACMHR.

13. Clarke, "Goals and Techniques," app. D, pp. 102, 163–73; Shuttlesworth, speech before the Fair Share Organization, September 25, 1958, Gary, Indiana, box 4, Shuttlesworth Papers.

14. Shuttlesworth, "Alabama Christian Movement for Human Rights," pp. 146–47. Hence the ACMHR, unlike as argued by Morris, was not an "organization of organizations." Morris, *Origins*, p. 45 (see also p. 69); Robinson, *The Montgomery Bus Boycott and the Women Who Started It*, pp. 27–40.

15. For a discussion of the process of commodification—or proletarianization—of out groups see Wallerstein, *The Capitalist World-Economy*; Eskew, "The Alabama Christian Movement for Human Rights," 22–23; *BN*, July 10, 1956; *BW*, July 26, August 1, 1956; Fred L. Shuttlesworth to Directors of Transit Co., July 7, 1956, Shuttlesworth to City Commission, July 16, 26, 1956, and "Statement of the City Commission," July 10, 1956, box 24, files 33B, 33C; L. E. Newman, Eastern Section Citizens' Council, to City Commission, July 18, 1956, box 2, file 21; and F. M. Jessup, Alabama Citizens Councils to J. W. Morgan, June 26, 1956, box 24, file 33, Morgan Papers.

16. The ACMHR viewed school desegregation as an important step toward gaining a marketable education. On Negro policemen see "Petition," July 25, 1955, box 12, file 43, Boutwell Papers; Shuttlesworth to Directors of Transit Co., July 7, 1956, box 24, file 33B, Morgan Papers. The city dropped the "whites only" clause and the ACMHR sued to prove discrimination; see *BN*, July 5, 1958.

17. *BN*, August 20, 22, 27, 1956; Corley, "The Quest for Racial Harmony," pp. 73–77; Shuttlesworth, "Alabama Christian Movement for Human Rights," pp. 148–49.

18. Garrow, *The Walking City*; see esp. Walton's narrative, "The Walking City."

19. *BN*, December 20–21, 1956; *BW*, December 26, 29, 1956; Eskew, "The Alabama Christian Movement for Human Rights," pp. 23–24; Shuttlesworth, "Alabama Christian Movement for Human Rights," p. 149.

20. Harris, *Political Power*, p. 188; "Amendment to Section 6002," box 5, file 7, Jones Papers, BPLDAM; Bull Connor to C. L. Harris, June 29, 1944, Birmingham Electric Co., "Report Involving Race Question," March, April 1944, and Charles E. Oakes to W. Cooper Green, June 29, 1944,

359

box 10, file 13, Green Papers, BPLDAM. Shootings apparently occurred in 1942, 1944, and 1949. For a creative analysis of this record see Kelley, *Race Rebels*, pp. 55–76, and Connor to Maj. Gen. Edward H. Brooks, February 14, and Brooks to Green, February 19, 1946, box 6, file 24, Green Papers.

21. *BN*, December 22, 1956; *BW*, December 26, 1956.

22. Garrow, *Bearing The Cross*, p. 81; *BN*, December 25, 1956.

23. *BN*, December 26, 1956; *BW*, December 29, 1956; Eskew, "The Alabama Christian Movement for Human Rights," pp. 25–26.

24. Eskew, "The Alabama Christian Movement for Human Rights," pp. 25–26.

25. *BN*, December 26, 1956; Morris, *Origins*, p. 70.

26. "No Easy Walk, 1961–1963," *Eyes on the Prize*.

27. Earl Newman to J. W. Morgan, June 23, and F. M. Jessup to Morgan, June 26, 1956, box 24, file 32, Morgan Papers. Asa Carter proposed creating vigilante "Minute Men" who, in response to a white woman's call, would board a bus and beat up black passengers sitting in the white section. See Walton, "The Walking City," p. 43; *BN*, December 26, 1956.

28. *BN*, December 26, 1956; *BW*, December 29, 1956; Rosa Walker quoted in "People In Motion," undated pamphlet on the Birmingham movement published by the ACMHR and the Southern Conference Educational Fund, Inc., box 1, Shuttlesworth Papers.

29. Eskew, "The Alabama Christian Movement for Human Rights," pp. 27–28. Demonstrating the dangers of depending on oral interviews as sources, Shuttlesworth, as quoted in "No Easy Walk, 1961–1963," *Eyes on the Prize*, gives inaccurate information. The city arrested only 21 people, not all of the 250 who participated in the bus challenge.

30. Shuttlesworth fit the description of the "race man" presented in Thompson, *The Negro Leadership Class*, as well as the new Negro leadership class as argued by Lomax, *The Negro Revolt*. On the student ideology of the sit-ins, see Meier and Rudwick, *CORE*, pp. 101–31. The argument presented here, one of discontinuity in black leadership, builds on an earlier essay by Meier and Rudwick, "The Origins of Nonviolent Direct Action." Not only the methods differed but also the objectives, a reflection of a changing ideology among black people. For a theoretical discussion of transitions in ideology and cultural hegemony see Forgacs, *An Antonio Gramsci Reader*.

31. Eskew, "The Alabama Christian Movement for Human Rights," pp. 25, 28; Walton, "The Walking City," p. 40; *BW*, December 26, 1956.

32. *BN*, December 22, 1956; *BW*, December 26, 1956.

33. *BW*, March 9, 1957, July 17–21, 1991 (on Weaver); *Birmingham Mirror*, March 6, 9, 1957; Eskew, "The Alabama Christian Movement for Human Rights," p. 30.

34. *BN*, 12, 18, 21, 1957.

35. ACMHR anniversary program for 1957, box 1, Shuttlesworth Papers; Garrow, *Bearing The Cross*, p. 90. Steele and Shuttlesworth served as officers in the SCLC.

36. *Chicago Daily Defender*, February 21, 1957; *The Militant*, February 18, 1957; text of Shuttlesworth's speech at the Prayer Pilgrimage, May 17, 1957, and "Meeting and Matching the Challenge of This Hour," Shuttlesworth address before the NAACP in Akron, Ohio, November 24, 1957—all in box 4, Shuttlesworth Papers.

37. Shuttlesworth, "Alabama Christian Movement for Human Rights," p. 137; Fairclough, *To Redeem the Soul*, p. 13.

38. McKiven, "Class, Race, and Community," p. 248. Neither Painter (*Narrative of Hosea Hudson*) nor Kelley (*Hammer and Hoe*) analyze the CP's use of religion by working people to challenge capitalist ideology. Kelley (pp. 107–8) questions the effort to combine the beliefs.

39. Painter, *Narrative of Hosea Hudson*, pp. 23–25, 269–71; McCallum, "Songs of Work and Songs of Worship." See also the recording, *"Birmingham Boys": Jubilee Gospel Quartets from Jefferson County*.

40. Several black congregations had assisted the Southern Conference for Human Welfare by signing petitions for the FEPC in 1945. Some, such as St. John AME, Thirgood CME, and St. Paul Methodist, would be centers of civil rights activism in the 1960s. See file 19-A-B-1 (4) in the Southern Conference for Human Welfare Papers, Woodruff Library, Emory University, and "History of the Alabama Christian Movement Choir," box 1, Shuttlesworth Papers; Reagon, "Songs of

the Civil Rights Movement," pp. 146–48, 178, and *Voice of the Civil Rights Movement* (quotation from p. 19 of liner notes).

41. Reagon, *Voices of the Civil Rights Movement*.

42. Marx, "Religion," pp. 362–75; Clarke, *These Rights They Seek*, pp. 60–63, and "Goals and Techniques," app. D, pp. 163–73; Geraldine Moore, *Behind the Ebony Mask*, p. 201; clipping, *Pittsburgh Courier*, February 7, 1959, box 4, Shuttlesworth Papers.

43. BN, August 29, 1957; Corley, "The Quest for Racial Harmony," pp. 133–37.

44. Eskew, "The Alabama Christian Movement for Human Rights," p. 32. The black parents had asked to send their children to Graymont Elementary and Woodlawn and Phillips High Schools, the case became *Shuttlesworth v. Birmingham*, and in 1958 the U.S. Supreme Court upheld Alabama's Pupil Placement Act, which "legitimized a tightly controlled tokenism." See Bartley, *The Rise of Massive Resistance*, pp. 291–92; BN, December 6, 1958, February 12, 1959. In *United States v. Jefferson County Board of Education*, the court ordered compulsory integration to achieve a racially nondiscriminatory school system.

45. BN, September 9, 1957; *Christian Science Monitor*, September 10, 1957.

46. BN, September 9, 1957; *Christian Science Monitor*, September 10, 1957; Corley, "The Quest for Racial Harmony," pp. 138–39; Manis, "Religious Experience," pp. 148–49.

47. BN and *Christian Science Monitor*, September 10, 1957. Shuttlesworth's actions typified those of a charismatic leader.

48. BN, April 28, May 1, 1958; Lawrence E. Walsh, Department of Justice, to Representative Emanuel Celler, April 30, 1958, and J. W. Morgan telegram, May 1, 1958, Morgan Papers. The attacks led Senators Jacob K. Javits and Kenneth B. Keating to propose federal antidynamiting legislation, and they toured Birmingham in this regard in November 1958; see Morgan's notes and guest list, November 7, 1958, box 6, file 21, Morgan Papers. Birmingham's Jewish community generally opposed desegregation and any attempts by northern Jews to influence the local civil rights movement; see Elovitz, *A Century of Jewish Life in Dixie*, pp. 166–75. In May 1957 the ACMHR joined other Negro groups in calling for a federal investigation of the unsolved bombings; see BN and BP-H, May 8, 1957. The ACMHR's June 2, 1958, petition is in box 12, file 43, Boutwell Papers. Noting a grave discrepancy, Rev. Dr. R. D. Bedinger, a Presbyterian, said that churches in Birmingham "should protest just as vigorously as they did when Temple Beth-El was almost bombed." Reflecting the community-sanctioned vigilante violence, most white churches remained silent, although the Birmingham district of Methodist ministers deplored the bombing. BN, June 3, 30, July 1, 1958; *Montgomery Advertiser*, July 5, 1958; *Greensboro [North Carolina] Daily News*, June 30, 1958. The inconsistency in white outrage over the dynamiting was not lost on Martin Luther King, who echoed Bedinger's sentiments; see King to Morgan, July 15, 1958, box 6, file 21, Morgan Papers.

49. BN, July 18–20, August 6, 31, December 3, 1958. Police arrested Ellis Lee, 42, Cranford Neal, 28, and Herbert Eugene Wilcutt, 23; Robert E. Hughes to Frank W. Baldan, September 15, 1958, and Hughes, "Special Program Report: Birmingham High School Mob Scene, September 1958," file 41.1.1.1.15, SRC Papers, BPLDAM.

50. BN, October 14, 17, 1958; Eskew, "The Alabama Christian Movement for Human Rights," pp. 36–37.

51. BN, October 20–21, 1958; *Nashville Tennessean*, October 21, 1958; *Montgomery Advertiser*, October 21–22, 1958.

52. During the trial black and white spectators packed the courtroom, with an additional thousand African Americans assembled on the lawn outside in silent prayer. Robert E. Hughes to Fred Routh, October 29, 1958, file 41.2.16.3.41, SRC Papers; *Montgomery Advertiser*, October 24, 28, 1958; BN, October 24, 26, 28, 1958.

53. BN, October 26, 29–30, 1958; H. H. Grooms "Segregation, Desegregation, Integration, Resegregation," pp. 37–41. An exacting judge who followed the letter of the law and as a result handed down important rulings in support of the civil rights struggle, Grooms accounted for his involvement in several Birmingham cases in his dispassionate memoir. See also *Nashville Tennessean* and *Nashville Banner*, November 1, 1958.

54. BN, October 27–28, 1958; *Montgomery Advertiser*, October 29, 1958; *Nashville Banner*,

November 1, 1958; MacNair, "Social Distance," pp. 101, 138–39; Robert E. Hughes to Fred Routh, October 29, 1958, file 41.1.1.1.15, SRC Papers. In a confidential letter seized during an unlawful search of his hotel room by police, Rev. Glenn Smiley characterized Shuttlesworth as "willing to do almost anything to keep the spotlight on himself," yet Smiley, a civil rights activist from the Fellowship of Reconciliation who had assisted King and the MIA and who was in Birmingham to help the ACMHR, added that Shuttlesworth's "group is the only one that is moving, and he cannot be boxed in." *BN*, December 22, 1958.

55. On the transit system's troubles see *BN*, May 24, 1951, and October 14, 1952. For an insightful study of bus desegregation see Barnes, *Journey from Jim Crow*. On the BTC operating in the red see N. H. Hawkins to William P. Engel, August 1, 1952 (box 5, file 11), on the sale to John S. Jemison Jr. see Morgan to Doug Walker, January 17, 1958, Jemison to Grady Fullerton, city comptroller, July 1, December 31, 1958 (box 5, file 11), and for "The Story of Birmingham Transit" [1958] (box 5, file 12), all in Morgan Papers. John S. Jemison Jr., the brother of real estate developer Robert Jemison Jr., retained the family interests in public transportation. Questions of financial improprieties, such as paying large salaries, bonuses, and stock dividends when the company operated at a loss, continued to plague the reputation of the BTC; see "Complaint and Petition" before the Public Service Commission, 1954, box 5, file 13, Bull Connor to Jemison, September 29 (box 5, file 17), and Jemison to Citizens Transit Advisory Committee, October 6, 1961, file 17, Morgan Papers.

56. Robert E. Hughes to Fred Routh, October 29, Hughes to Jack Anderson, November 12, and Hughes memo of November 6, 1958, to "Leadership Personnel," file 41.1.1.1.15, SRC Papers.

57. Robert E. Hughes to Jack Anderson, November 12, 1958, file 41.1.1.1.15, SRC Papers; *Washington Post*, November 14, 1958; *Montgomery Advertiser*, November 14, 18, 1958; *BN*, November 18, 25, 1958; Shuttlesworth to City Commission, December 1, 1958, box 1, Shuttlesworth Papers. The ACMHR financed Kelly's appeal. See also "President's Annual Report" [1959], box 1, Shuttlesworth Papers.

58. *Nashville Tennessean*, March 27, 1959; *BN*, December 13, 1958; Shuttlesworth, "Alabama Christian Movement for Human Rights," p. 142. Several female members of Woods's church complained that he told them not to ride the buses but to get their employers to give them rides. After his arrest, other members of the congregation barred the informants from the church.

59. MacNair, "Social Distance," pp. 100–101; *BN*, November 13, December 2, 1958, November 23, December 21, 1959; integration fliers and ACMHR resolution of December 14, 1959, box 1, Shuttlesworth Papers.

60. "Program of the Third Annual Meeting" and "President's Annual Report," June 5, 1959, box 1, Shuttlesworth Papers; Shuttlesworth, "Alabama Christian Movement for Human Rights," p. 153.

61. Shuttlesworth also opposed the lawyer's practice of requiring one-half down and one-half at motion to dismiss because "cases are thus paid for in full long before the merits are argued"; quoted in "President's Annual Report," June 5, 1959, box 1, Shuttlesworth Papers; MacNair, "Social Distance," pp. 138, 166 n51; Police Report on ACMHR, March 8, 1961, box 9, file 24, Connor Papers, BPLDAM. Hosea Hudson also had problems with Shores and suggested that he was overly concerned with money; Painter, *Narrative of Hosea Hudson*, pp. 272–80.

62. *BN*, October 20, 1959; F. L. Shuttlesworth to Eugene Connor, October 26, 1959, box 3, Shuttlesworth Papers. District court judge H. H. Grooms decided the case on October 24, 1961, and gave the city until January 15, 1962, to desegregate the parks.

63. Garrow, *Bearing The Cross*, pp. 116–20; Morris, *Origins*, p. 201 (quotation); Clarke, *These Rights They Seek*, pp. 43, 75.

64. Morris, *Origins*, p. 201; Robert E. Hughes to Harold Fleming, March 1, 1960, file 41.1.1.1.19, SRC Papers. In his letter Hughes expressed a faith in moral reform by idealistically explaining that the protest would set off spontaneous prayer vigils across the South that could lead to international demonstrations in support of the proposed legislation: "the amount of impatience generated against fillabusters because thousands of people across the South or nation are standing in freezing weather, rain, etc., night and day. . . ."

65. Robert E. Hughes to Harold Fleming, March 1, 1960, "Vigil for Freedom" leaflet, file

41.1.1.1.19, SRC Papers; *BN*, March 1, 13, 1960. In April a white woman claimed that Bessemer deputies beat her for dating black men; see *BN*, April 4, 1960.

66. *Nashville Banner*, March 1, 1960; *BN*, March 4, 1960. A staunch segregationist, Patterson had "out-niggered" George C. Wallace to get elected governor in 1958. Refusing to expel Birmingham-Southern students involved in the protest, Stanford lost support among the college's trustees and his position hurt the school financially. Eskew interview with Henry King Stanford; *NYT*, April 12, 1960.

67. "Press Release," March 30, 1960, box 1, Shuttlesworth Papers.

68. *BN*, April 1, 10, 28, 1960. In the sporadic protests, students selected Kress, Loveman's, Newberry's, Woolworth's, and Pizitz, and apparently after the March action nothing occurred until August, when the students again conducted sit-ins, seemingly in response to similar actions in Atlanta and Montgomery; see *BN*, August 15, 1960. Reporter Harrison Salisbury accurately claimed: "By Birmingham custom, persons charged with vagrancy are not admitted to bail. They are held incommunicado for three days. In actual practice, such a prisoner is sometimes permitted to make one telephone call. But not always. A person arrested on a vagrancy warrant simply disappears for three days. His friends and family may not know what has happened to him." This was a "favorite technique" of Bull Connor. *NYT*, April 12, 1960. After the Jefferson County Betterment Association folded, Rev. Ware organized the Inter-Citizen's Committee to continue to counter the ACMHR. Oliver, Ware's assistant, had pastored the church that hosted the Southern Negro Youth Congress in 1948 when Connor arrested the Progressive Party vice presidential candidate, Senator Glen Taylor. F. L. Shuttlesworth. "Statement to the United States Civil Rights Commission," Spring 1961, box 4, file 2, Shuttlesworth Papers; *Washington Post*, May 15, 1960.

69. *NYT*, April 12, May 4 1960. Other than the December 15, 1958, piece in *Time*, "Birmingham: Integration's Hottest Crucible," little appeared in the national media about racial problems in the city, suggesting the lack of interest in the subject. Robert E. Hughes to Paul Rilling, July 22, 1960 (file 41.1.1.1.19, SRC Papers) included the observation that the articles "aroused a great deal of antagonism, of course, but nevertheless they were informed and practically everything there was true. *BN*, April 20–21, 1960. In March 1960 Shuttlesworth signed an ad in defense of King that ran in the *New York Times* and prompted the Montgomery police commissioner to sue for libel. Birmingham officials impounded Shuttlesworth's car in February 1961 as a result of state court judgments, but he was ultimately vindicated by the landmark U.S. Supreme Court decision in *New York Times v. Sullivan*, which ruled that public officials had no right to damages in libel cases unless they could demonstrate a reckless disregard for facts or malice aforethought.

Chapter 5

1. Peck, *Freedom Ride*, pp. 114–32; *Washington Post*, June 12, 1961; Rowe, *My Undercover Years*, pp. 38–50; Howard K. Smith, "Who Speaks For Birmingham?," BPLDAM (quotation, p. 30); Nunnelley, *Bull Connor*, pp. 97–98 (Langston interview and photograph). Rowe claimed that Connor devised the Klan attack, a charge challenged by Nunnelley in his apologia for Connor. On the Freedom Ride see Meier and Rudwick, *CORE*, pp. 34–39, 130–31, 135–37, and Carson, *In Struggle*, pp. 31–34.

2. The Freedom Ride riot marked a turning point in Birmingham, for it forced progressive white businessmen to seek municipal reforms designed to ameliorate race relations in the city. Had such a resolve existed before May 1961, Connor would have faced corporate opposition in his reelection bid instead of weak opposition and the endorsement of local newspapers. Historians differ over the centrality of the Freedom Ride. Thornton ("Municipal Politics") emphasizes that prior efforts at reform stressed continuity in racial progress in Birmingham, a progress hindered by the Freedom Ride and the Spring 1963 demonstrations. A similar analysis that highlights the attempts of businessmen to solve Birmingham's racial problems can be found in Corley, "The Quest for Racial Harmony" and his essay "In Search of Racial Harmony." Likewise, a series of events culminated in white efforts at race reform according to LaMonte, *Politics and Welfare*, pp. 164–71. Scribner

("Federal Funding") identifies federal incentives as triggering the white move toward race reform in Birmingham; this argument neglects the conflict within Birmingham's white civic leadership during the period, for it was the Freedom Ride riot that broke the Big Mule Consensus behind segregation. Established through elite corporate reform in 1911, the Birmingham city commission consisted of three members who shared legislative and executive responsibilities for city government. In the 1961–63 period, the commission consisted of Arthur T. Hanes, mayor; Jabo Waggoner, commissioner of public improvements; and Bull Connor, commissioner of public safety. For historical background on the commission see Harris, *Political Power*, pp. 81–84, 183–84.

3. Meier and Rudwick, *CORE*, pp. 34–39, 130–31, 135–37 (quotation, p. 135); Peck, *Freedom Ride*, pp. 38–42. The Journey of Reconciliation followed *Morgan v. Virginia* (1946), and the Freedom Ride followed *Boynton v. Commonwealth of Virginia* (1960).

4. Meier and Rudwick, *CORE*, pp. 137–38; Carson, *In Struggle*, pp. 31–34; Patterson interview; Peck, *Freedom Ride*, p. 127 (quotation).

5. Rowe, *My Undercover Years*, pp. 38–44; Smith, "Who Speaks for Birmingham?," p. 29. Despite Nunnelley's (*Bull Connor*, pp. 104–10) apologia for Connor, the evidence suggests that the commissioner of public safety arranged the beating of the Freedom Riders. As Kennedy complained: "Information came to the FBI and Department of Justice a week ago Sunday that there would be violence in Birmingham, Alabama. The Birmingham police and local authorities were informed"; draft of speech, May 22, 1961, General Correspondence, Civil Rights, Alabama, May 22, 1961, JFK Papers. Although exaggerated, other sources confirm the outline presented in Rowe. See Corley, "The Quest for Racial Harmony," pp. 216–17, and "Birmingham Police Department Inter-Office Communication" on ACMHR meeting, May 11, 1961, box 9, file 24, Connor Papers, BPLDAM. CBS fired Smith over his proposed conclusion to the program: "The basic question soon may well be, do we deserve to win the cold war?"; *BN*, November 9, 1961.

6. Rowe, *My Undercover Years*, p. 42 (quotations); Smith, "Who Speaks for Birmingham?," p. 29.

7. Smith, "Who Speaks for Birmingham?," p. 30; Rowe, *My Undercover Years*, pp. 43–44.

8. SCLC Newsletter, August 1961, p. 1, box 58, II, 44B, King Papers, BU; Peck, *Freedom Ride*, pp. 129 (first quotation), 130 (remaining quotations).

9. Peck, *Freedom Ride*, pp. 131–32.

10. "Birmingham Police Department Inter-Office Communication" on ACMHR meeting, May 16, 1961, box 9, file 24, Connor Papers.

11. Ibid. According to the attorney general's telephone logs, Shuttlesworth exaggerated the number of calls Robert Kennedy made to him on that Sunday and Monday; nonetheless, the records demonstrate contact between the two. See General Correspondence, 1960–64, Civil Rights, Alabama, May 23–25, 1961, box 10, RFK Papers. For a discussion of the Kennedy administration's strategy, see Marshall, *Federalism and Civil Rights*, and Belknap, *Federal Law and Southern Order*, chap. 4, "Crisis Management in the Kennedy Administration," pp. 70–105; and Marshall interview by Eskew. Presidents hid behind federalism when it suited their political needs, for section 1 of the Fourteenth and Fifteenth Amendments to the Constitution provide the president with adequate justification for enforcing the law of the land.

12. Police Report on ACMHR meeting, May 16, 1961, box 9, file 24, Connor Papers. According to the telephone log, Kennedy called Shuttlesworth at 3:40 P.M. and George E. Cruit, the local representative of Greyhound, at 5:10 P.M. A typescript of his call to Cruit reveals the attorney general's limited understanding of the situation and his frustration over his inability to solve the problem: "Well, Hell, you can look for one [a driver] can't you? After all these people have tickets and are entitled to transportation to continue the trip or project to Montgomery. We have gone to a lot of trouble to see that they get to this trip and I am most concerned to see that it is accomplished." Cruit: "Yes, but drivers refuse to drive. . . ." Kennedy: "Well, can't you get some Negro school bus driver to drive the bus to Montgomery or this sixty or more miles?" Cruit: "I don't condone what happened yesterday but drivers refuse to drive." . . . Kennedy: "Well, Mr. Cruit, I think you should—had better be getting in touch with Mr. Greyhound or whoever Greyhound is and somebody better give us an answer to this question. I am—the Government—is going to be very much upset if this group does not get to continue their trip." Typescript in General Correspondence, 1960–64, Civil Rights, Alabama, May 23–25, 1961, box 10, RFK Papers.

13. *BN*, May 15, 1961. On the election see *BP-H*, May 3, 1961.

14. Carson, *In Struggle*, pp. 31–44; Zinn, *SNCC*, pp. 44–45; Morris, *Origins*, pp. 231–36 (Shuttlesworth and Nash exchange, p. 232); Nash, "Inside the Sit-Ins and Freedom Rides," pp. 42–60 (other quotations, pp. 53, 49). Nash (p. 57) explains the initiative behind the movement: "The Negro is seeking to take advantage of the opportunities that society offers; the same opportunities that others take for granted, such as a cup of coffee at Woolworth's, a good job, an evening at the movies, and dignity."

15. Office memo of Shuttlesworth's and Floyd Mann's May 17 telephone calls to Robert Kennedy, General Correspondence, Civil Rights, Alabama, May 15–May 20, 1961, box 10, RFK Papers; Nash, "Inside the Sit-Ins and Freedom Rides," p. 54; Nunnelley, *Bull Connor*, pp. 102–3. Shuttlesworth gives the exchange between Connor and the female during the mass meeting; see Police Report on ACMHR meeting, May 24, 1961, box 9, file 24, Connor Papers.

16. Nunnelley, *Bull Connor*, p. 103.

17. Zinn, *SNCC*, pp. 45–47; Telephone log, General Correspondence, Civil Rights, Alabama, May 23–May 25, 1961, box 10, RFK Papers; Guthman, *We Band of Brothers*, pp. 170–71. Guthman claims that twenty-one Freedom Riders were on the bus.

18. Zinn, *SNCC*, pp. 47–49; Patterson interview (quotations, p. 33); Carson, *In Struggle*, p. 36 (Doar's quotation).

19. The beating of Seigenthaler reflected the bungled response of the Kennedy administration. The governor was especially critical of Seigenthaler's actions. See Patterson interview, p. 34, and Guthman, *We Band of Brothers*, p. 171. The only thing Kennedy remembered about the Freedom Rides in his interview with Anthony Lewis was the beating of Seigenthaler. Throughout the interview Burke Marshall prompted Kennedy to say yes and then went on to explain what occurred. See Robert F. Kennedy interview, p. 370.

20. Zinn, *SNCC*, p. 49. According to Guthman (*We Band of Brothers*, p. 172), the Justice Department's hastily created force was composed of "marshals, boarder patrolmen, prison guards, and revenue agents." On the use and effectiveness of the marshals see Belknap, *Federal Law and Southern Order*, pp. 73, 81–85. U.S. district judge Frank M. Johnson issued the temporary restraining order against vigilante violence; see Yarbrough, *Judge Frank Johnson and Human Rights*, pp. 81–83. Some cities in the Deep South ignored the *Morgan* and *Boynton* rulings desegregating interstate travel. The Interstate Commerce Commission banned segregation on November 1, 1961, reinforcing the Kennedy administration's strategy of using interstate commerce to achieve desegregation in the South. For a discussion of this see Barnes, *Journey from Jim Crow*, pp. 168–73.

21. Zinn, *SNCC*, pp. 50–51; Telephone log, General Correspondence, Civil Rights, Alabama, May 23–May 25, 1961, box 10, RFK Papers; Stewart interview with Patterson, p. 35; Guthman, *We Band of Brothers*, pp. 173–75. Vincent Harding (*Hope And History*, p. 194) notes that Shuttlesworth "courageously, foolhardily, push[ed] his way from the outside, through the mob and the police, clearing the path for himself and James Farmer to join the beleaguered folks on the inside."

22. Patterson interview, p. 36; Holloway, "Travel Notes." Barnes (*Journey From Jim Crow*, p. 167) observes: "Though dissatisfied with the mass arrests in Mississippi, Kennedy and Marshall thought the preservation of order by local officials took precedence over desegregation, especially when the Freedom Riders could vindicate their right to integrated travel by appealing their convictions through the courts."

23. "Excerpts of Voice of America Broadcast by Attorney General Robert F. Kennedy," May 26, 1961, in Attorney General Speeches, 1961–64, and "Statement by the Honorable Robert F. Kennedy," May 24, 1961, General Correspondence, Alabama, box 10, RFK Papers; Holloway, "Travel Notes," pp. 6–7. In an earlier draft of the VOA broadcast, Kennedy wrote: "The whole world is aware of the problems and difficulties in one section of our country last week. This is basically the difference between our system and the Communist system. . . . the Soviet Union will make mistakes against some of its citizens, the Moslems of Kazakistan, or destroy the religion of the people of Soviet Central Asia; the Chinese Communists can allow millions of their citizens to starve, nobody has the information." Responding to criticism that the federal government failed to stop the vigilante violence, Kennedy callously cited federalism as his excuse: "Now maybe it's going to take a decade; and maybe a lot of people are going to be killed in the mean time; and I

think that's unfortunate, . . . But in the long run I think it's for the health of the country and the stability of this system; and it's the best way to proceed"; quoted in Belknap, *Federal Law and Southern Order*, p. 73. At the Birmingham mass meeting, Rev. Edward Gardner noticed a contradiction in federal policy: President Kennedy "sent one hundred men to Laos. Alabama is much closer. He can send more to Alabama much quicker and cheaper and keep them here much easier." Gardner mistakenly thought that the president would use federal force to protect American citizens. Police Report on ACMHR meeting, May 24, 1961, box 9, file 24, Connor Papers. But the attorney general offered this clarification: "We feel strongly that these matters are essentially ones of local law enforcement and that the Marshals should not remain in Alabama a minute longer than was necessary." "Statement," May 25, 1961, General Correspondence, Civil Rights, Alabama, May 23–25, 1961, RFK Papers.

24. Former governor James "Big Jim" Folsom called Kennedy to encourage the use of marshals to protect the activists; see transcript of Folsom's telephone call, May 22, 1961, General Correspondence, Civil Rights, Alabama, box 10, RFK Papers. On Connor's enforcement see *BN*, November 9, 11, December 5, 1961.

25. The *Birmingham Post-Herald* published returns on May 3, with runoff returns printed on May 31, 1961. Hanes and Waggoner carried East Lake, Precinct 10, Boxes 1–5; Woodlawn, Precinct 10, Boxes 7–10; West End, Precinct 9, Boxes 5–6, 10; and Ensley, Precinct 45, Box 3. King won the unskilled and semiskilled working-class votes at ACIPCO, Precinct 42, Box 1; Stockham Valves, Precinct 10, Box 12; and Ensley, Precinct 45, Boxes 1–2 as well as the black vote registered at Legion Field, Precinct 9, Box 1.

26. On the feud known as the "Merrill Case," see Morgan's letter firing Waggoner, February 2, 1952, box 20, file 32, Morgan Papers, BPLDAM. Hanes accused King of wanting "to make Birmingham into another Atlanta"; Morgan, *A Time To Speak*, pp. 90–91. Second only to TCI, Hayes

employed 11,000 craftsmen with a payroll of $48 million in 1958; *BN*, November 12, 1958. The Klan campaigned for Hanes; Rowe, *My Undercover Years*, p. 38. High-ranking Klansmen were in unions—e.g., Robert Creel, the grand dragon of Alabama and president of a local in Fairfield. Two of the three Klansmen who killed the white volunteer Viola Liuzzo were steelworkers. See Kundahl, "Organized Labor in Alabama State Politics," pp. 46–48, 68–69, 431–32; see also Draper, *Conflict of Interests*, pp. 24–25. After leaving office Hanes defended several Klansmen in court, including Robert Chambliss for the bombing of the Sixteenth Street Baptist Church and James Earl Ray for the assassination of Martin Luther King. On Hanes and the Ku Klux Klan see *BN*, January 22, 1979.

27. Morgan, *A Time To Speak*, pp. 66, 87, 89–90. Blaming the Freedom Ride for King's defeat, Morgan titled a chapter in the book "The Freedom Bus Struck a Pedestrian." Vann also attributes King's defeat to the Freedom Riders; Vann interview; Benjamin Muse, "Memorandum," September 30, 1960, SRC Papers, BPLDAM.

28. Morgan, *A Time To Speak*, pp. 88–91. On the Big Mule Consensus behind segregation see Corley, "The Quest for Racial Harmony," pp. 152–55. Hanes to King returns in Precinct 21, Box 1, showed 270 to 197, Box 2 showed 566 to 325, Box 3 showed 557 to 278, and Box 4 showed 546 to 353; *BP-H*, May 31, 1961.

29. King quoted in Morgan, *A Time To Speak*, p. 91. The Birmingham-Atlanta rivalry is one of the more interesting stories of the twentieth-century urban South. Although Atlanta had clearly taken the lead, the rivalry continued into the postwar period. On September 9, 1940, Mayor J. W. Morgan complained to Congressman William B. Bankhead that Atlanta had hijacked more airplane routes from Birmingham; see also "Airport Facts," n.d., "Chamber Advocates Establishment of Airport Authority," press release and responding "Statement by J. W. Morgan," both June 10, 1958, and Amzi G. Barber to Morgan, July 1, 1958, all in box 1, files 5, 24, Morgan Papers. Not until 1956 did the Birmingham Planning Commission propose a comprehensive plan for expanding the airport; see "Agenda," March 7, 1956, and other documents, box 20, file 32, Morgan Papers.

30. Underwood, "A Progressive History," pp. 1–27. Although the rumor is probably apocryphal, it is not as far-fetched as it may seem. Executives from U.S. Steel and the Ford Motor Co. coordinated production for the war effort. They could have easily discussed postwar development. After the war there was a projected shortage of steel. Oddly enough, once it formalized plans to expand in the

South, Ford considered only sites in Georgia, some 140 in all, despite Alabama's superior industrial labor force. And in selecting Atlanta, Ford chose a metropolitan area that had a labor shortage with two jobs for every one worker available. See *Atlanta Constitution*, May 21, 27, 1945; "Workers Seeking Jobs, Jobs Seeking Workers," 1945 bulletin, bound minutes, Atlanta Chamber of Commerce Records. Vann heard a similar rumor about General Motors, and he believed that TCI opposed the plant to limit the strength of unions in Birmingham. Vann interview.

31. W. Cooper Green to Henry Ford II, August 17, 1949, box 9, file 19, and D. W. LaRue to Green, August 25, 1949, box 3, file 21, Green Papers, BPLDAM. LaRue, who managed Ford's property department, explained to Green: "Atlanta was chosen as the assembly plant site because Ford had maintained operations there in the past and was entirely satisfied with the location," and TCI "had no bearing on our decision." The city commission received numerous letters opposed to annexation, including the ones from the Ensley Civitan Club, O. R. McIllhenny, Pauline Berthon of Berthon's Cleaners, Ellis Jewelry, and Optical Co., April 27–28, 1949, all in box 8, file 19, Morgan Papers, which also includes E. D. LeMay of TCI to Morgan, May 6, 1949, on TCI's flier.

32. Morgan to the Harnishchfeger Corp., January 31, 1952; Morgan to Clarence B. Hanson Jr., May 12, 1952; Morgan to Publicity Department, Birmingham Chamber of Commerce, August 10, 1960; Doris Dodds Starnes to Morgan, August 12, 1960—all in box 4, file 23, Morgan Papers; Underwood, "A Progressive History," p. 39. In contrast to Birmingham, Atlanta in 1960 boasted five skyscrapers under construction or projected and eight more in the planning stages; Martin, *Atlanta and Environs*, p. 316. Not until 1968 were plans announced for the first postwar skyscraper to be built in Birmingham.

33. By 1971 UAB had grown to 6,000 employees and a budget of $55 million, of which some $38 million comprised the payroll. On UAB see Volker, *The University and the City*, pp. 6, 25 (UAB president Volker gave this essay as an address before the Alabama dinner of the Newcomen Society on November 3, 1971); Holmes, *History of the University of Alabama Hospitals*; *Washington Post*, April 12, 1963, p. A6; Alsobrook, "Mobile v. Birmingham." Howard L. Holley, "Medical Education in Alabama," gives the history behind Birmingham's fight for the medical center. On the founding of Southern Research Institute, see William M. Murray, *Martin*, pp. 119–29. The growth of the health industry in Birmingham can almost be tracked through the successes of SRI director Kettering in [Southern Research Institute], *In Memoriam*, and Graves, *History of Southern Research Institute*.

34. Martin, *Hartsfield*, pp. 12–15, 79, 109–11, 119, 138–39; Martin, *Atlanta and Environs*, 3:6, 24, 91, 138, 258; Morgan, *A Time To Speak*, p. 91 (quotation). Atlanta built a modern terminal in 1958; Lewis and Newton, *Delta*, pp. 73–79. On the rivalry in the postwar period see Hartsfield to Ken Turner, October 30, 1945, box 3, file 20, Hartsfield Papers, Woodruff Library, Atlanta. The joke in Atlanta went, "if you are going to heaven or hell, you have to go by way of Atlanta."

35. On the efforts of returning veterans to reform municipal politics in the postwar period see Abbott, *The New Urban America*, pp. 123–45. On the aborted G.I. revolt in Birmingham see Beiman, "Birmingham," pp. 119–20; Underwood, "A Progressive History," pp. 45, 56–57, 78, resolution in app. K; Nichols, " 'Cities Are What Men Make Them,' " pp. 221–23.

36. *BN*, December 13, 1953, May 17, 1963; *BP-H*, May 26, 1967; *Alabama: The News Magazine of the Deep South*, October 3, 1938; *WSJ*, May 26, 1961. For a character sketch see *WSJ*, May 23, 1963, which quoted Smyer responding to the demonstrations that spring: "Sure, what I'm doing is of more interest to our stockholders than anything else I could do for them. . . . Every dime of our assets is in Birmingham, but 30% of our property is vacant and unproductive. We've got to have growth if we want to develop it and you can't have it in a city of hate and violence." Smyer joined the ranks of other regional executives who compromised segregation for pecuniary gain; see Bartley, *The Rise of Massive Resistance*, pp. 340–45. Former mayor Vann recalled that many "people trusted him [Smyer] to deal with problems like this [race] where they wouldn't have trusted other people"; Vann interview. For a contemporary analysis that realized the influence of the new service economy and the role of corporations within it see Helen Hill Miller, "Private Business and Public Education in the South," pp. 75–88. Miller acknowledged: "The South has a new economy. Its output is pleasant, but some of its implications are not only violently opposed to old ways but opposed to the point of creating violence." For copies of the essay circulated in

Birmingham, see Benjamin Muse, "Memorandum," December 14, 1960, file 41.1.3.2.5, SRC Papers.

37. *WSJ*, May 26, 1961. Engel headed a real estate conglomerate called the Engel Companies. The service economy spokesmen often communicated their concerns to one another; see William P. Engel to James A. Head, September 12, October 4, 1961, Head Papers, BPLDAM. A supporter of President Kennedy, Head followed the civil rights movement closely after the Freedom Ride. See also *Washington Post*, June 14, 1961. As a result of their racial liberalism, Engel and Head faced criticism from Big Mules such as Allen Rushton Jr., an associate with Lange, Simpson, Robinson, and Summerville, whose family owned the Birmingham Ice and Cold Storage Co. and the Protective Life Insurance Co. Rushton accused the businessmen of placing "the quest for an extra dollar from an extra industry above our principles"; *BP-H*, September 17, 1961.

38. Smyer quoted in *WSJ*, May 26, 1961. This group formed the basis of what would become the Senior Citizens Committee, the elite businessmen who negotiated the truce with civil rights activists in the spring of 1963. Zukoski and Gaston served on the Interracial Division of the JCCCSF. On Zukoski see *Voice in the Storm*; see also Gaston, *Green Power*.

39. Sterne quoted in Nelson C. Jackson to Lester B. Granger, February 28, 1950, National Urban League Papers, BPLDAM. This letter provides the background on the Urban League in Birmingham, an effort that began in 1925 and concluded in 1967, when a chapter finally formed. In 1932 interested National Urban League officials found Edmonds using the Commission on Interracial Cooperation affiliate to combat communism in the city through recreational programs for African Americans. Parris and Brooks, *Blacks in the City*, pp. 225–26. See also Charles F. Zukoski to Lloyd K. Garrison, July 2, 1948, National Urban League Papers; Corley, "The Quest for Racial Harmony," pp. 43–61; and Edmonds, *A Parson's Notebook*, pp. 266–83. For a brief biographical sketch of Sterne, see LaMonte, *Ward*, pp. 1–5.

368

40. As Benjamin Muse noted in his "Memorandum," September 30, 1960, SRC Papers: "Those Negroes who cheerfully accept the servant-master relationship get along relatively well materially. Some are wealthy. White businessmen more or less surreptitiously seek the favor of A. G. Gaston." On Gaston see Corley, "The Quest for Racial Harmony," p. 51.

41. Jefferson County Coordinating Council of Social Forces Papers and Roberta Morgan Papers, BPLDAM. Minutes of JCCCSF general meetings are also in box 8, file 17, Green Papers. On the Interracial Division see box 19, file 23, Roberta Morgan Papers. For an account of the Interracial Division see LaMonte, *Politics and Welfare*, pp. 151–57, and Bass, "Bishop C. C. J. Carpenter." In March 1955 the JCCCSF held an integrated Institute on Race Relations at Birmingham-Southern College attended by 800 people.

42. Adams quoted in Corley, "The Quest for Racial Harmony," pp. 62–63. For the JCCCSF "Pamphlet on Negro Police" see box 21, file 13, James W. Morgan Papers, BPLDAM. Not until 1966 did Birmingham hire a black policeman. In contrast, the issue spurred the Atlanta Chamber of Commerce to advocate limited race reforms in 1943. Atlanta hired its first black policeman in 1948 to patrol the black community. See minutes, May 3, 1943, January 31, 1944, October 29, 1947, Atlanta Chamber of Commerce Records, and Martin, *Hartsfield*, p. 51. To practice in Birmingham, doctors had to associate with the Jefferson County Medical Society, an all-white organization that resisted integration by supporting a movement to Jim Crow black doctors in a new "Negro Hospital." Under the direction of textile magnate Donald Comer, the white elite and city commission supported the charity drive in order to maintain segregation. As Comer explained to Green: "You and I know that the only satisfactory way for negroes and whites to live together is on the basis of segregation. To be allowed to work out our own problem, we are going to have to be mindful of the Supreme Court's decisions and we are going to have to make reasonable progress in providing separate but equal facilities. This hospital matter is a real test of whether we mean it when we say we can handle our own problem." Comer to Green, June 29, 1950, box 10, file 11, Green Papers. The Holy Family Hospital was built as a black facility; a similar policy existed in Atlanta, where a Negro wing at Grady Hospital was dedicated in 1950. Most of Atlanta's hospitals remained segregated in 1963. See Martin, *Atlanta and Environs*, pp. 162, 366, and LaMonte, *Politics and Welfare*, p. 155.

43. Speer, *Eagan*, pp. 74–108; Rebecca L. Thomas, "Eagan and Industrial Democracy at Acipco"; Tindal, *Emergence of the New South*, pp. 177–83; Ellis, "The Commission of Interracial

Cooperation"; Dykeman and Stokely, *Seeds of Southern Change*. Conservatives viewed this attempt at biracial communication as radical, yet it did not solve the problem of racial discrimination as demonstrated by Chafe, *Civilities and Civil Rights*.

44. Atlanta welcomed the CIC and the SRC. Tindal, *Emergence of the New South*, pp. 718–21; Sosna, *In Search of the Silent South*, p. 163. According to the local council director, moderates in the white power structure considered the Alabama Council on Human Relations "a group of crackpots and radicals," and at one point Birmingham attorneys drafted a bill to submit to the state legislature calling for an Alabama Un-American Activities Committee to hound the biracial group. See Norman C. Jimerson to Paul Rilling, January 5, 1962, file 41.2.1.3.9, Jimerson to Burke Marshall, October 19, 1962, and Benjamin Muse, "Confidential Memorandum," September 30, 1960, SRC Papers; Jan Gregory Thompson, "History of the Alabama Council of Human Relations," *BP-H*, July 27, 1959; and Morgan, *A Time To Speak* (on Reeves see pp. 63–65, 175; on Hughes see pp. 68–85, 174).

45. Benjamin Muse, "Confidential Memorandum," July 13, 1961, SRC Papers.

46. On Vann, see ibid.; on Morgan, see Benjamin Muse, "Memorandum," December 14, 1960, file 41.1.3.2.5; on reference to Wilkins see Muse, "Memorandum," December 12, 1960. Morgan, Vann, and Zukoski assisted the ACHR; see Norman C. Jimerson to Paul Rilling, January 5, 1962, SRC Papers. During the 1950s Zukoski published his racially liberal views in the *Shades Valley Sun* under the pseudonym Button Gwinnett, several of which were reprinted in *Voices in the Storm*.

47. Vann interview. On the initial decision of the federal court see *Sims v. Frink* (1962); Nichols, "Cities Are What Men Make Them," p. 220; Morgan, *A Time To Speak*, pp. 26, 61. Vann recognized "an unconscious coalition of voters of middle class, upper class [whites] and blacks voting for the same candidates"; Vann, "Speech," Duard LeGrand Conference, p. 15. Such a coalition elected moderate businessman Ivan Allen over archsegregationist Lester Maddox in Atlanta in 1961; Allen and Hemphill, *Mayor*, pp. 43–63.

48. The ruling, 202 F.Supp. 59, declared several city segregation ordinances unconstitutional, including No. 597, which forbade blacks and whites to play sports together. See *General Code of . . . Birmingham*, p. 201. According to H. H. Grooms ("Segregation, Desegregation, Integration, Resegregation," pp. 27–29), "The closing of the facilities became a political 'must' for the Commissioners, or at least they thought so." On Hanes see Norman C. Jimerson to Paul Rilling, January 5, 1962, file 41.2.1.3.9, and Benjamin Muse, "Confidential Memorandum," January 11, 1962, file 41.1.3.2.8, SRC Papers. The Birmingham Parks and Recreation Board, which included former Mayor Jimmy Morgan, resisted the commissioner's order, prompting Hanes to excoriate them, calling the reluctant members "integrationists"; "That's What'll Happen," *Time*, December 22, 1961.

49. Vann recalled that after Grooms had ordered the integration of the parks: "our young lawyers got up a resolution to the [Birmingham] Bar Association urging the city to obey the law. The members [iron and steel interests] sort of panicked that the bar association might actually pass such a thing. They got all the house counsel from the big companies to come to the meeting. I'm still not sure they had the right to vote even, but they packed it, but they only won by six votes." Vann interview. The commissioners accused Vann of living outside Birmingham, but in fact his house was just inside the city limits bordering Mountain Brook. Vann, "Speech," Duard LeGrand Conference, pp. 12–13; Norman C. Jimerson to Paul Rilling, December 27, 1961, file 41.1.1.1.23, and Benjamin Muse, "Confidential Memorandum," January 11, 1962, file 41.1.3.2.8, SRC Papers.

50. The ad appeared in *BN*, January 10, 1962. Sid Smyer, Douglas Arant, Mervyn Sterne, Chuck Morgan, and David Vann directed the open parks movement, but Charles F. Zukoski, possibly fearing for his job at First National Bank, remained silent on the issue; soon he would be forced to take early retirement. Zukoski recalled: "The pressures which had been building up at the Bank because of my public stands on the race and other social questions came to a head in April of 1962. . . . General [John Persons] and John [Hand] told me that criticisms of my outside conduct had reached a point whereby the Bank's Board felt that my services should be terminated. . . . They said no criticism of my services in directing and developing the Trust Department through the years had been voiced or were currently felt,—that the reason for asking my resignation was only

my outside attitudes and conduct." Zukoski, "A Life Story," pp. 330–31. Also refusing to get involved was the president of Hayes Aircraft Corp., Lewis L. Jeffries, whose industry profited from the race wage. See Benjamin Muse, "Confidential Memorandum," January 11, 1962, file 41.1.3.2.8, SRC Papers. For the park crisis in the national media see *Business Week*, May 12, 1962.

51. Smyer quoted in Nichols, "Cities Are What Men Make Them," p. 222. Ironically, it was Smyer's uncle, E. J. Smyer, who had advocated the Greater Birmingham movement of 1910 that led to the creation of the city commission in 1911. In 1953 Jefferson County state senator Hugh Kaul sponsored the enabling legislation to change the form of government from the commission to the city council–manager form. In response, Mayor Morgan convinced the legislature to adopt a third alternative, the mayor-council form, with the stipulation that if the matter ever came to a vote, all three alternatives would be offered. He hoped to force a runoff and thus keep the city commission in power. Efforts in 1957 and 1959 to change the form of government in order to persuade affluent suburbs south of Birmingham to merge with the central city failed in part because white vigilantes stole the referendum petitions. A copy of the Birmingham Bar Association's report that details the chronology of events is in box 25, file 43, Vann Papers, BPLDAM; see also file 34 for correspondence concerning the bar's committee and file 38 for the referendum petitions; Vann, "Speech," Duard LeGrand Conference, pp. 4–5; *Saturday Evening Post*, March 3, 1963; LaMonte, *Politics and Welfare*, pp. 164–71. Smyer believed that the removal of the city commission was necessary "to avoid even more serious conflict." As quoted in Harrison, "A Change in the Government," p. 18 and passim.

52. Vick, "Survey of the Governing Body." On Atlanta see Hunter, *Community Power Structure* and *Community Power Succession*; Rice, "If Dixie Were Atlanta." Chuck Morgan suggested that the failure of consolidation and the lack of middle-class leadership in city government created the crisis of 1963, an argument somewhat echoed by LaMonte and Corley.

370 53. "Statement of James W. Morgan," August 25, 1948, box 8, file 18, Morgan Papers; Connerly, " 'One Great City,' " BPLDAM; Morgan, *A Time To Speak*, pp. 54–60.

54. Morgan, *A Time To Speak*, p. 60. The literature on the relationship among urban centers, suburbs, and exurbs has grown extensively. As the case of Atlanta suggests, annexation is not the solution to urban decay. With the 1959 failure of annexation, the city commission considered using an occupational tax to compensate for lost revenues as a result of moves to the suburbs; see R. W. McBride to J. W. Morgan and Morgan to McBride, May 13, 1959, box 19, file 15, Morgan Papers. Mayor Richard Arrington used this method to raise revenues. Old money, new money, and the Jewish community tended to live in Mountain Brook; Vestavia attracted similar but less ostentatious folk, as did Homewood, where the old middle class, comfortably well-off but not wealthy, resided. All three served as havens for northern corporate transplants sent South to manage absentee-owned industries. As Huie (*Mud on the Stars*, p. 141) describes it, "Over the Mountain—out of the smoke zone and into the ozone—stood the Houses of Have and the Houses of pretenders to the Houses of Have." On *Southern Living* see the entry by John Shelton Reed in Wilson and Ferris, *Encyclopedia of Southern Culture*, pp. 973–74; on the attitude of Birmingham's affluent suburbanites see the psychoanalytic critique of Birmingham sponsored by the chamber of commerce in 1958. The Southern Institute of Management from Louisville, Ky., combined four reports into the *Birmingham Metropolitan Audit* (1960), now located in the Tutwiler Collection, Birmingham Public Library. Report 2 noted "a sense of inferiority" among residents, who were "marked by a tendency to be negative and defensive." The *Audit* criticized the over-the-mountain elite as self-centered and lacking civic humanism.

55. Vann, "Speech," Duard LeGrand Conference, pp. 22–23; Nichols, "Cities Are What Men Make Them," pp. 225–28; MacNair, "Social Distance," pp. 97–98. The *Birmingham News* had actively resisted the petition drive, but once the election was set, its editorial policy shifted in support of the change in city government.

56. LaMonte, *Politics and Welfare*, pp. 171–76; Eskew, "The Alabama Christian Movement for Human Rights," pp. 66–72; Nunnelley, *Bull Connor*, p. 136 (quotation).

57. Connor's televised address of November 1, 1962, is quoted in Nichols, "Cities Are What Men Make Them," p. 226. Vann had clerked for Justice Black and had heard the U.S. Supreme Court deliver its landmark *Brown* decision in 1954; Vann interview.

58. State Legislators, Recapitulation Sheet, Referendum, November 6, 1962. The commission form carried—precinct:box—West End 9:5, 9:6, 9:10; East Lake 10:1, 10:2, 10:3, 10:4; and Woodlawn, 10:9. But it failed to win in Connor's home box at 10:10, where returns posted 453 to 403 to 92. Connor never again won his home box, possibly as a result of criticism by racial moderates such as his pastor, Rev. John Rutland of Woodlawn Methodist Church, who supported the Alabama Council on Human Relations. The mayor-council form carried—precinct:box—Legion Field 9:1, Center Street 9:4, East Birmingham 10:12, Pratt City 29:1, North Birmingham 42:1, and Ensley 45:1. Steelworker and craft unionist returns included 45:3, 45:4, 45:5 in Ensley; 52:1 in Wylam; and 10:13 in Inglenook. *BP-H*, November 8, 1962.

59. Strong, "Alabama," pp. 443–45. Strong identifies 11,900 black voters in Jefferson County in 1960.

60. In *Reid v. City of Birmingham* (1963), Jim Simpson questioned the legality of the change in government. As head of the Big Mule law firm of Lange, Simpson, Robinson, and Somerville, he had filed the defense of Connor out of friendship and a desire to protect the race wage. See *BN*, September 4, 1977, p. 2A, and Nunnelley, *Bull Connor*, pp. 134, 138, 161–62. Responding to Simpson's resistance, the city council filed suit. In the May 23, 1963, decision *Connor v. State*, the Alabama Supreme Court ordered the commissioners to vacate city hall immediately. TCI defended racial discrimination in employment to the bitter end, refusing to dismantle segregated lines of promotion that kept black workers in semiskilled positions until forced to do so by the federal courts. *BN*, May 2, June 24, August 13, 1973.

61. "I understand that there are a lot of behind the scenes discussions trying to encourage high caliber men to run for the office of mayor and the city council," Norman C. Jimerson wrote Paul Rilling, November 19, 1962, SRC Papers; LaMonte, *Politics and Welfare*, pp. 173–75; Nichols, "Cities Are What Men Make Them," p. 228.

62. *Atlanta Journal*, May 20, 1960; *NYT*, April 17, 1963, p. 22; Grafton and Permaloff, *Big Mules and Branchheads*, pp. 8, 165–67, 189–90; *Alabama Official and Statistical Register*, 1951, pp. 223–24.

63. Shuttlesworth quoted in King, *Why We Can't Wait*, p. 59. Pollsters expected between 35,000 and 40,000 people to vote in the election. See *BN*, March 4, 1963, and State Legislators, Recapitulation Sheet, Special Municipal Election, March 5, 1963. With precinct:box results listed for Boutwell, Connor, King, and Waggoner, Legion Field at 9:1 reported 231, 6, 915, and 10; Center Street at 9:4 reported 274, 6, 934, and 9; Ensley at 45:1 reported 57, 36, 457, and 4; Stockham at 10:12 reported 123, 165, 318, and 12; Pratt City at 29:1 reported 140, 236, 648, and 44; ACIPCO at 42:1 reported 175, 211, 447, and 14. Bull Connor posted strong support among steelworkers in Ensley at 45:3, 45:4, 45:5; Wylam at 52:1 and in the L and N Railroad neighborhood of Inglenook at 10:13. The southside neighborhoods along Highland Avenue at 21:1 through 21:4 voted for Boutwell. *BP-H*, March 6, 1963.

64. Corley, "The Quest for Racial Harmony," pp. 247–48; Nunnelley, *Bull Connor*, p. 136; *BP-H*, March 6, 1963; Nichols, "Cities Are What Men Make Them," p. 233.

65. Connor won precinct:box 9:5, 9:6, 9:7, 9:10 in West End; 10:1, 10:3, 10:4 in East Lake; 45:3, 45:4, 45:5 in Ensley; 10:13 in Inglenook; and 52:1 in Wylam. The black vote for Boutwell to Connor in 9:1 registered 1,273 to 3 and in 9:4 1,679 to 2. Candidates of the white power structure won seats on the city council. The nine members elected were Dr. John E. Bryan, the former vice president of the chamber of commerce and superintendent of public schools in Jefferson County; M. Edwin Wiggins, a retired treasurer of Alabama Power Co.; Don A. Hawkins, an industrial salesman; George A. Seibels and Alan T. Drennen Jr., both insurance men from "old families" in Birmingham; Tom W. Woods, a Woodlawn merchant; E. C. Overton, an optician; and attorneys John T. Golden and Nina Miglionico. Of the original seventy-five candidates for the council, three were white women and two black men, including W. L. Williams, who garnered 8,829 votes in the runoff, a figure that roughly suggests the voting strength of Birmingham's black community. Only the woman Miglionico won. *BN*, April 3, 1963 (election returns); *BP-H*, April 3, 1963. On dirty politics see Nunnelley, *Bull Connor*, p. 136.

66. *BN*, April 3, 1963; Nunnelley, *Bull Connor*, p. 138. Smyer, Vann, and Gaston considered the demonstrations ill-timed because of the recent change in city government, a thesis echoed by

LaMonte, Corley, and Thornton. Vann recalled that the black leaders "had worked very hard to get a new government put in, and they had some pretty strong promises from Albert Boutwell. . . . and they saw King simply coming in to pick up the—they had loaded the table with chips and King was going to come in and pick up their chips and take credit for it and they were going to get no credit for what they had done"; Vann interview.

Chapter 6

1. Norman C. Jimerson to Paul Rilling, December 27, 1961, file 41.1.1.1.23, Jimerson to Rilling, January 5, 1962, file 41.2.1.3.9, and Benjamin Muse, "Confidential Memorandum," January 11, 1962, file 41.1.3.2.8, SRC Papers, BPLDAM. Jimerson's report describes the police intimidation of a field secretary for CORE who had attempted to open an office in Birmingham. Muse identifies the students as the "most coherent Negro group" who avoided CORE and SNCC for fear of being labeled "outside agitators." Alarmist in nature, the reports of Jimerson and Rilling must be read with caution; MacNair, "Social Distance," pp. 97–100. Adene "Deenie" Drew, the wife of John Drew, an insurance executive for Alexander and Co., headed the housewives in the Jefferson County Voters League.

2. The student manifesto "This We Believe" can be found in Benjamin Muse, "Confidential Memorandum," January 11, 1962, file 41.1.3.2.8, SRC Papers. Here again, one sees discontinuity in black protest.

3. Osborne, "Boycott in Birmingham"; Nichols, "'Cities Are What Men Make Them,'" p. 156 (Dukes); Corley, "The Quest for Racial Harmony," p. 231; Benjamin Muse, "Confidential Memorandum," January 11, 1962, file 41.1.3.2.8, SRC Papers (the proposed "demonstration"). Dukes described having applied for and passed five civil service examinations between 1961 and 1963 although he never got a municipal job because of his race. For ACMHR meeting of March 11 see Police Report, March 12, 1963, box 13, Connor Papers, BPLDAM.

4. Pitts served as a Negro contact for Jimerson, Muse, and other moderates from the SRC. For a biographical sketch of Pitts in which he suggests that the radicals were right see Egerton, *A Mind To Stay Here*, pp. 107–20.

5. PR to LWD [Paul Rilling to Leslie W. Dunbar], March 5, 1962, file 41.1.1.1.24, and Benjamin Muse, "Confidential Memorandum," January 11, 1962, file 41.1.3.2.8, SRC Papers; MacNair, "Social Distance," pp. 101–3. MacNair notes that during the period of the Interracial Committee of the Jefferson County Coordinating Council of Social Forces in the 1950s, there was created "a consciousness among the black businessmen of their potential influence over whites through common identity as businessmen." *WSJ*, May 26, 1961, p. 1; March 12, 1962, p. 10.

6. Norman C. Jimerson to Paul Rilling, January 5, 1962, and Benjamin Muse field report, "Dangerous Situation in Birmingham," January 11, 1962, file 41.1.3.2.8, SRC Papers.

7. Emory Jackson to Anne Rutledge, April 12, 1963 ("up-side-downer"), Jackson Papers, BPLDAM; for the character of Jackson see his papers generally. In 1965, with the return of the NAACP and Oliver's move to New York City, the ICC disbanded; see MacNair, "Social Distance," p. 104. For copies of the ICC reports on police brutality see box 45, Student Nonviolent Coordinating Committee Papers, King Center.

8. Police Report on ACMHR meeting, January 24, 1962, box 12, file 17 (Pitts), and Police Report on ACMHR meeting, December 20, 1961, box 9, file 25 (Gardner), Connor Papers. Pitts prefaced his talk: "They said I wouldn't come to the Alabama Christian Movement to make some statements, and I must confess I wasn't too anxious to come." During the January meeting Gardner cracked macabre jokes about the "wrong churches being bombed" by vigilantes who mistakenly believed they had targeted movement churches, demonstrating the white community's monolithic view of the black community. For more on the bombings of three Negro churches see *BN*, January 17, 1962, which explains that, although the attacks occurred early that morning on the heels of a Ku Klux Klan meeting, Bull Connor and his police suspected that a young black man set the dynamite.

9. "News Release from SCLC," January 31, 1962, and Martin Luther King to "Dear Doctor,"

February 6, 1962, box 1, file 6, King Papers, ATL; Shuttlesworth to Walker, February 12, 1962, box 36, file 8, SCLC Papers.

10. Released on bail, Shuttlesworth and Phifer waited two years before the courts overturned their convictions. Helping to finance the legal fees, the SCLC issued an appeal on behalf of Shuttlesworth and Phifer that raised several thousand dollars. See box 22, files 15–19, SCLC Papers. On the case see also Kunstler, *Deep in My Heart*, pp. 82–85, and Corley, "The Quest for Racial Harmony," pp. 232–33.

11. Norman C. Jimerson to Paul Rilling, March 22, 1962, and Jimerson, "Confidential," April 5, 1962, file 41.1.1.1.24, SRC Papers; MacNair, "Social Distance," pp. 98–100; Nichols, "'Cities Are What Men Make Them," pp. 159–60. For a sketch of U. W. Clemon see Egerton, *A Mind To Stay Here*, pp. 120–27. Bishop Coadjutor George M. Murray moderated the meetings held in the downtown church and acted as a contact of the SRC.

12. *Nation*, May 5, 1962, pp. 397–401; Nichols, "'Cities Are What Men Make Them,'" p. 161.

13. *Nation*, May 5, 1962, p. 398; MacNair, "Social Distance," pp. 98–99; Corley, "The Quest for Racial Harmony," pp. 233–34. During March 1962 Burke Marshall, assistant attorney general for civil rights in the Kennedy administration, investigated the racial situation in Birmingham, focusing on voting rights abuses; see Norman Jimerson, "Confidential," April 5, 1962, file 41.1.1.1.24, SRC Papers.

14. *BN* and *BP-H*, March 1962; Nichols, "'Cities Are What Men Make Them,'" pp. 162–74.

15. *Nation*, May 5, 1962, p. 401 (quotations); Corley, "The Quest for Racial Harmony," p. 234; undated clipping on the NAACP [*BP-H*, April 1962], box 2, and "People in Motion" (pamphlet published by the ACMHR in late 1966), box 1, Shuttlesworth Papers, King Center. The pamphlet refers to integrated meetings held in Birmingham sponsored by SNCC, SCEF, and ACMHR.

16. Norman C. Jimerson, "Confidential," April 5, 1962, file 41.1.1.1.24, SRC Papers; *Nation*, May 5, 1962, p. 401; Nichols, "'Cities Are What Men Make Them," pp. 169–71.

17. *BN*, April 5, 1962, clipping in box 2, Shuttlesworth Papers.

18. *BN*, April 16, 1962 (first Dukes quotation—reflecting the shift in policy at the *News*, it published the syndicated article from the *Herald-Tribune*); *Business Week*, May 12, 1962; "Selective Buying: Right of Protest," undated flier, box 1, Shuttlesworth Papers; Police Report on ACMHR meeting, June 13, 1962, box 12, file 18, Connor Papers (second Dukes quotation). During June Miles students joined with the Alabama Council on Human Relations in a "Workshop on Equal Employment Opportunities" for Birmingham; see Norman C. Jimerson to State Directors, July 3, 1962, SRC Papers. On August 13, 1962, Dukes and other members of the Anti-Injustice Committee approached the city commission with a petition signed by more than 800 people requesting desegregation. The commissioners laughed at the request. Having graduated from Miles, Dukes no longer served as president of the student body and hence lost some influence among the students, although Pitts kept him as director of the office of development. *BW*, May 4, 1963.

19. Wyatt T. Walker memo to Board Member on SCLC meeting, May 15–16, 1962, box 1, file 11, SCLC Papers; King, *Why We Can't Wait*, pp. 52–53; Garrow, *Bearing The Cross*, pp. 198–99.

20. Mystery still surrounds the Senior Citizens Committee and its subcommittee that conducted negotiations in 1962 and 1963. The chamber of commerce has consistently refused to release any materials on the committee and its work, but scattered news accounts shed some light. The *Birmingham News* (May 16, 1963) lists 77 of the 89 members, all of whom were white, suggesting that the missing 12 were black (or Jewish) members. Except for Smyer, the names of those on the subcommittee and those who initially agreed to the negotiations were never released. The paper claimed that the first issue to be addressed was school desegregation. See *BN*, May 11, 1963; LaMonte, "Politics and Welfare in Birmingham," pp. 312–14; and Corley, "The Quest for Racial Harmony," pp. 235–36. Although she acknowledges that Pizitz demurred from serving as a Senior Citizen, Nossel suggests that the "exclusion" was possibly "in accordance with an official or unofficial anti-Semitic policy" that reflected "the power structure's anti-Jewish bias"; Nossel, "Weathering The Storm," pp. 118–22 (quotation, p. 120). David Vann, who represented several Jewish merchants, made sure that his clients' names were not associated with the Senior Citizens.

21. Corley, "The Quest for Racial Harmony," p. 236; Garrow, *Bearing The Cross*, p. 220; Police Report on ACMHR meeting, September 12, 1962, box 12, file 18, Connor Papers. As a result of his

work, Jimerson received threats, as when someone called his office and said, "I'm coming up there and kill you all!" Other white moderates in Birmingham shared similar experiences. See J. J. Brewbaker to Leslie W. Dunbar, August 23, 1962, SRC Papers, and L. H. Pitts telegram to Burke Marshall, September 17, 1962, box 1, file 1, Marshall Papers, BPLDAM.

22. Raines, *My Soul Is Rested*, Shuttlesworth quoting Gaston, p. 168. Shuttlesworth said that five or six merchants attended the meeting.

23. Ibid., p. 169. Shuttlesworth re-created the dialogue as he remembered it for Raines.

24. Ibid., pp. 169–70 (quotations); Corley, "The Quest for Racial Harmony," p. 237. Pizitz Department Store was a large, locally owned business that many black people patronized. Concerning the merchant's reputation, Birmingham's leading rabbi, Dr. Milton Grafman, recalled: "It really upset me that the first store boycotted was Pizitz. Louis Pizitz [the late founder] really tried to help the Negro; he aided the negro hospital, and gave them credit when they didn't have any money. He was wonderful to them." Quoted in Nichols, " 'Cities Are What Men Make Them,' " p. 164. See also Nossel, "Weathering The Storm," pp. 124–25. The Ku Klux Klan picketed Sears, Roebuck; J. J. Brewbaker to Leslie W. Dunbar, August 23, 1963, SRC Papers.

25. Martin Luther King to W. E. Shortridge, September 4, 1962, box 1, file 6, King Papers, ATL; Police Report on ACMHR meeting, September 19, 1962, box 12, file 18, Connor Papers; Norman C. Jimerson to Paul Rilling, September 27, 1962, SRC Papers; Underwood, "A Progressive History," pp. 94–95; King, *Why We Can't Wait*, p. 53; "Sixth Annual Convention, Preliminary Report —Divisible Funds," and "Expenses for Annual Convention, September 25–28, 1962," box 63, file 13, SCLC Papers.

26. For an eyewitness account of the attack on King see the description appended to the letter of Robert Brank Fulton, a white faculty member at Miles College, to King, October 4, 1962, box 33, file 15, SCLC Papers; see also Garrow, *Bearing The Cross*, p. 221, and John J. Brewbaker to Leslie W. Dunbar, October 29, 1962, file 41.1.1.1.25, SRC Papers. Fund-raising presented a possible area of conflict between the SCLC and its affiliates such as the ACMHR, as demonstrated by an incident following the Birmingham convention. ACMHR treasurer W. E. Shortridge wrote Walker asking why a $500 donation he made for an undertaker's association was not divided between the two groups. Walker explained that King and Shuttlesworth "had agreed tentatively to a 60–40 division of funds raised in connection with the National Convention. The usual arrangement is 2/3–1/3, but the prior sharing was suggested because of ACMHR's tremendous burdens financially." Walker made no offer to share the donation that he considered to be unrelated to the convention. See Shortridge to Walker, October 6, and Walker to Shortridge, October 10, 1962, box 33, file 15, SCLC Papers.

27. In form letters, King reflected on the Birmingham convention: "There is no telling how great an impact it will have on race relations. Already Fred Shuttlesworth tells me there are some hopeful signs"; King to William Stuart Nelson, October 2, 1962, box 1, file 11, SCLC Papers. See also Nichols, " 'Cities Are What Men Make Them,' " pp. 176–77; Raines, *My Soul Is Rested*, pp. 169–70; and Norman C. Jimerson to Paul Rilling, November 19, 1962, file 41.2.1.3.9, SRC Papers.

28. "A Statement of Facts," undated flier [post–SCLC convention, 1962], box 1, Shuttlesworth Papers. A flier distributed by the "Students and Adult Citizens Committee" explained: "Our leaders were told by the 'downtown' leaders that certain things would be done in the very next week following the SCLC meeting. In fact, some signs came down—only to be later put back. Our leaders kept their end of the bargain. The 'downtown' leaders were not able to deliver." See also King, *Why We Can't Wait*, p. 53; Norman C. Jimerson to Burke Marshall, October 19, file 41.2.1.3.9, Jimerson to Paul Rilling, October 25, file 41.1.1.1.25, and November 19, 1962, file 41.2.1.3.9, SRC Papers. Reflecting on the negotiations, Jimerson agreed with the opinion of the Senior Citizens. After the renewal of the boycott, vigilantes dynamited Shuttlesworth's old church in Birmingham, Bethel Baptist Church, on December 14, 1962. King wired a demand to Kennedy that the president stop the "reign of terror" in Birmingham; King telegram to Kennedy, December 14, 1962, box 27, file 8, SCLC Papers.

29. Although King talked of leading massive protests in Alabama in the near future, no plans had been set; *Montgomery Advertiser*, September 21, 1962. August Meier coined the phrase "conservative militant" to describe King; see Meier, "The Conservative Militant."

30. On King's background see Branch, *Parting The Waters*, pp. 27–68; King Sr., with Riley, *Daddy King*; and Coretta Scott King, *My Life with Martin Luther King*. On the installation see John Thomas Porter to Martin Luther King Jr., October 15, 1962, box 1, file 7, King Papers, ATL; on King at Sixteenth Street see W. E. Shortridge to King, February 8, 1962, box 36A, V, 26, and on the black middle class attending his speeches, see the program to the Men's Day Celebration at New Pilgrim Baptist Church on March 6, 1960, box 48, VI, 155, King Papers, BU. On the lack of support for the ACMHR by Sixteenth Street and Sixth Avenue Baptist Churches, see Eskew, "The Alabama Christian Movement for Human Rights," p. 78.

31. Garrow, *Bearing The Cross*, pp. 256–57, 602–3, 669 n4 (quotations); Abernathy, *And the Walls Came Tumbling Down*, p. 233. Abernathy recalled that the golfing trips of the two black businessmen drove "whites wild with envy."

32. Eskew, "The Alabama Christian Movement for Human Rights," p. 79; Mrs. John J. Drew to Martin Luther King, May 12, 1961; King to Drew, May 17; Drew to King, May 19, 31; Dora E. McDonald to Drew, June 2; Drew to King, June 19; and King to Drew, June 29, 1961, box 36A, V, 26, King Papers, BU. Vigilantes attacked the Freedom Riders in Birmingham on May 14, 1961. On SCLC contact with the Alabama State Coordinating Association for Registration and Voting see W. C. Patton to King, July 28, 1957, box 71A, IX, 9A 2 of 4; Minutes of the SCLC executive board, October 18, 1957, box 48, VI, 153; and Department of the Director, May 15, 1959, box 47A, VI, 151, King Papers, BU. Working behind the scenes on voting rights, the association had accomplished little by 1961; nevertheless, the SCLC sent it $500. Whereas King corresponded with Drew, Walker wrote Shuttlesworth, "I know you have been busy as have we," and, referring to an enclosed check, he added, "We really wish we could do more, but this we hope will help some"; Walker to Shuttlesworth, July 11, 1961, box 58, II, 44A, 2 of 3, King Papers, BU. In early 1963 W. E. Shortridge, the treasurer of ACMHR and a Negro businessman, sent letters to "select citizens," identified as "practically all of the Negro doctors, lawyers, and funeral homes in Birmingham," **375** asking for donations to the movement. Attorneys Orzell Billingsley and Arthur Shores each sent $25 and a few doctors made contributions, but no one else did. See Police Report, February 7, 1963, on ACMHR meeting of February 4. The next week Shortridge said, "Many [black] Businessmen should give $200 or $300 a year"; Police Report, February 13, 1963, on ACMHR meeting of February 11. Always one to stress self-help and racial solidarity, Shortridge encouraged ACMHR members to patronize black businesses that supported the movement. See Police Reports, March 20, 27, and also "Notice: For Burial Protection Call Shortridge"—all in box 1, Shuttlesworth Papers.

33. Martin Luther King to A. G. Gaston, April 30, 1958, and Gaston to King, May 5, 1958, July 31, 1959, June 15, 1960, box 1, I, 3, King Papers, BU; Gaston, *Green Power*, pp. 112–14. Other bank directors included Secretary-Treasurer L. J. Willie, Afton M. Lee Sr., B. M. Montgomery, and John W. Nixon, DDS.

34. On the professional relationship between King and Shuttlesworth see Shuttlesworth to King, April 22, 1960, and King to Shuttlesworth, May 5, 1960, box 71A, IX, 9B, King Papers, BU. In his seminal work, the sociologist Aldon Morris analyzes the movement from many perspectives; although he considers the conflicts between such groups as the SCLC, NAACP, CORE, and SNCC, he assumes that the objectives of the SCLC and its affiliates coalesced. But they often did not. See Morris, *Origins*, esp. pp. 88–99, 279–86.

35. Garrow, *Bearing The Cross*, p. 229 (first Young quotation); Young, *A Way Out of No Way*, pp. 74–75 (second Young quotation); Hampton and Fayer, *Voices Of Freedom*, p. 125; Wyatt Tee Walker to Wilson W. Lee, October 9, 1962, box 33, file 14, SCLC Papers. In a telegram dated April 14, 1960, King told Shuttlesworth after the latter's arrest during Birmingham's first sit-ins, "We are always deeply inspired by your courageous witness, and your willingness to suffer in this righteous cause"; box 71A, IX, 9B, King Papers, BU.

36. Walker, "Report of Director," October–September 1962, box 36, file 12, SCLC Papers. In his correspondence Walker offers a slightly different analysis of Albany; as he explained to one friend, "your letter came while I was in Albany and I didn't have time to answer from there, things were so hot." Walker to Douglas Gale, October 10, 1962, box 33, file 13, SCLC Papers. On Pritchett and "passive resistance" see *U.S. News and World Reports*, September 3, 1962, pp. 43–46.

37. Glenn E. Smiley to Wyatt Tee Walker, September 27, 1962, and Walker to Smiley, October 8, 1962, box 33, file 14, SCLC Papers; King memo, December 24, 1962, box 60, file 6, SCLC Papers; King, *Why We Can't Wait*, pp. 54–55. King notified L. D. Reddick, Joseph Lowery, Kelly M. Smith, Shuttlesworth, C. K. Steele, Abernathy, Walker, Dorothy Cotton, and Andrew Young of the meeting. Branch (*Parting The Waters*, pp. 688–92) identifies those in attendance at Dorchester as Shuttlesworth, King, Walker, Abernathy, Young, Lowery, Cotton, Clarence Jones, Jack O'Dell, Stanley Levison, and James Lawson.

38. Hampton and Fayer, *Voices of Freedom*, p. 125 (Shuttlesworth); Abernathy, *And the Walls Came Tumbling Down*, pp. 232–33; Garrow, *The FBI and . . . King*, p. 58 (Levison). Apparently no written records exist of this first Dorchester conference.

39. See "Minutes of Staff Conference at Dorchester, September 5–7, 1963," box 153, file 21, SCLC Papers. See also Wyatt Tee Walker to James Lawson, August 27, 1963, notifying him of "an urgent and special meeting of the staff at Dorchester Center"; box 33, file 20, SCLC Papers.

40. At the time of the second Dorchester meeting, King was completing *Why We Can't Wait*; drafts of the work are in box 88A, King Papers, BU. Branch uncritically cites two interviews with Walker; see *Parting The Waters*, pp. 688–691, 983. No contemporary record of this master plan is in the SCLC or King Papers. Indeed, the "Project C file" that King described (*Why We Can't Wait*) does not exist at the King Center. The inventory to the SCLC Papers recognizes that "Although he [Walker] was instrumental in the organization of the Birmingham demonstrations during 1963, little documentation of his efforts is found in the SCLC Papers, and few records from 1963 exist at all. In the Department of Affiliates, all of the files of the directors are missing."

41. King, *Why We Can't Wait*, pp. 54–55; Garrow, *Bearing The Cross*, pp. 226–27. Ironically, the black vote in Birmingham had played a crucial role in recent elections although politicians considered African American support a dangerous endorsement.

42. "Executive Staff Meeting on Birmingham," January 23, 1963, box 36, file 15, SCLC Papers; "Tentative Schedule for Project X—Birmingham," box 1, file 7, King Papers, ATL; Garrow, *Bearing The Cross*, p. 231; King, *Why We Can't Wait*, pp. 55–56. The "Tentative Schedule" makes no mention of a "Project C." For a different view of King's nonviolence and moral persuasion as strategy see Fairclough, *To Redeem the Soul*, pp. 51–52.

43. "Tentative Schedule for Project X—Birmingham," box 1, file 7, King Papers, ATL; Garrow, *Bearing The Cross*, pp. 229, 234; Hampton and Fayer, *Voices of Freedom*, pp. 125–26. The SCLC scheduled a meeting in Birmingham on February 12, 1963, at New Hope Baptist Church, according to Police Report on ACMHR meeting, February 13, 1963, box 13, Connor Papers. The date is confirmed by the SCLC telephone log, which lists Walker's registration at A. G. Gaston's motel for February 12; see Telephone Log Incoming Calls, 1963, box 101 XIII, King Papers, BU. Fairclough (*To Redeem the Soul*, p. 116) cites Walker organizing various committees to sustain the campaign. Instead of this being something Walker created, it appears that he used the ACMHR resources already in place; see Shuttlesworth to Wyatt [Walker] and Martin [King], March 15, 1963, box 22, file 11, King Papers, ATL. SCLC itineraries list Walker in Birmingham only on March 3–4, 1963 (box 60, file 6), the same days King was to attend a Mens Day Program at New Pilgrim Baptist Church (Daily Reminder 1963, box 29), SCLC Papers.

44. See " 'Project C' Memo to King and Abernathy from WTW," box 1, file 8, and " 'Project C' General Format-Mass Meeting" and " 'Project C' List of Volunteers," box 1, file 7, King Papers, ATL. All three documents appear to have been typed at the same time, and all three are undated, although it can be established that the memo was written on April 18, 1963, the Thursday of King's week in the Birmingham jail. For scholars who have accepted the existence of Project C from the beginning without question, see Morris, *Origins*, pp. 260–61, and Branch, *Parting The Waters*, pp. 689–91.

45. Many scholars cite the Kennedy intervention thesis as the basis of the SCLC strategy in Birmingham. Yet if the violence thesis is removed, the Kennedy thesis makes less sense. See Sitkoff, *The Struggle for Black Equality*, pp. 128–29; Morris, *Origins*, pp. 250–51; and Fairclough, *To Redeem the Soul*, p. 114. See also Abernathy, *And the Walls Came Tumbling Down*, p. 234.

46. Brauer, *John F. Kennedy*, pp. 205–29. On the White House invitation see Branch, *Parting The Waters*, pp. 693–99.

NOTES TO PAGES 209–13

47. For the violence thesis see Garrow, *Protest At Selma*, pp. 212–36, esp. pp. 220–23, and Garrow, *Bearing The Cross*, pp. 227–30. For a different view that stresses the economic boycott see Morris, *Origins*, pp. 257–58, and pp. 321–22 n94. Garrow (*Bearing The Cross*, p. 228) quotes King as saying that "the key to everything is federal commitment," which, of course, turned out to be true but not the crux of Project X. While at Dorchester, activists discussed the damage done to the movement by Chief Pritchett when he made segregation appear "nonviolent." They realized the need to change public perceptions of racial discrimination—wrong-headed perceptions endorsed by the Kennedy administration. Yet SCLC could not depend on the Kennedy administration to act at all.

48. King, *Why We Can't Wait*, pp. 56–57; Garrow, *Bearing The Cross*, pp. 234–35, 669 n4.

49. Fred [Shuttlesworth] to Wyatt [Walker] and Martin [King], March 15, 1963, box 22, file 11, King Papers, ATL.

50. Ibid. Shuttlesworth also quoted in Garrow, *Bearing The Cross*, p. 234.

51. King, *Why We Can't Wait*, pp. 57–58; Garrow, *Bearing The Cross*, p. 669 n5. For "Summary of Bank Balances, March 1–8, 11–15, 18–22, and 25–29, 1963," and "Summary of Bank Balances for March 30, 1963," see box 63, file 13, SCLC Papers. The SCLC figures have been rounded off to the nearest dollar amount.

52. Police Reports on ACMHR meetings, March 12, 20, 27, 1963, box 13, Connor Papers; *BN*, April 3, 1963 (election returns).

Chapter 7

1. Warden's Docket, April 3, 1963, BPLDAM; *BP-H*, April 4, 1963, p. 5; Police Report, April 10, 1963, on ACMHR meeting of April 8 (quotation), box 13, Connor Papers, BPLDAM. The ACMHR claimed that twenty-one were arrested. See Police Report, April 5, 1963, on ACMHR meeting of April 3. See also Armstrong Papers, King Center. On Woods see Raines, *My Soul Is Rested*, pp. 161–65. In his recollection of the campaign, Andrew Young ("And Birmingham," p. 24) said that the elder Harris participated because "he had lived his life, and that he was ready to give his life in order that young people might have a better life." According to R. L. Polk and Co., *Birmingham City Directory*, 1963 (pp. 167–68), Britling Cafeteria operated in several locations, including downtown, although local newspaper reporters identified the disturbances as occurring at Brits.

2. Young (*A Way Out of No Way*, p. 75) recalled that Walker was responsible for enlisting the Baptist Ministers Conference behind the campaign. The failure of the most powerful black religious institution in Birmingham to support the movement calls into question the role of black institutions in the struggle. The quotations are from Abernathy, *And the Walls Came Tumbling Down*, pp. 238–39.

3. As the demonstrations progressed, the SCLC revised its strategy during discussions held in the suite; see Abernathy, *And the Walls Came Tumbling Down*, pp. 239–40. Abernathy [the SCLC treasurer] said the organization paid for the rooms, although Gaston suggested otherwise; Hampton and Fayer, *Voices Of Freedom*, p. 129. The movement press release of April 1963 (in box 50, file 26, SCLC Papers) supports Abernathy's claim.

4. When Bull Connor returned to office as commissioner of public safety in 1957, he sent detectives to the ACMHR mass meetings to observe the movement and report back to him. Although the detectives were often racist, they strived for accuracy because of the importance of the surveillance. The police bugged the services, with other officers listening to the transmissions in squad cars parked outside the church, getting word-for-word quotations from the speakers. Shuttlesworth complained about the "doohickey" listening device that, ironically, left an unsurpassed record of the civil rights struggle in Birmingham. Housed in the Connor Papers, the police reports should be used with caution. See Police Report, April 5, 1956, on ACMHR meeting of April 3, box 13, file 4, Connor Papers. On the structure of mass meetings see "PROJECT C, General Format—Mass Meeting," box 1, file 7, King Papers, ATL. The police reports in the Connor Papers generally confirm this structure of the meeting. On Gardner see Raines, *My Soul Is Rested*, pp. 148–57.

5. Police Report, April 5, 1963, on ACMHR meeting of April 3, box 13, file 4, Connor Papers.

6. Ibid.

7. Ibid.

8. "Birmingham Manifesto" and "News, Alabama Christian Movement," April 4, 1963, box 13, file 2, Connor Papers; *BW*, April 6, 1963. Walker's "Tentative Schedule for Project X—Birmingham, Alabama" (box 1, file 7, King Papers, ATL) called for the writing on March 1, 1963, of the "Birmingham Manifesto—Broken Faith." *BW* of April 6, 1963, p. 2, printed the Birmingham Manifesto.

9. *NYT*, April 5, 1963, p. 16. Similar demands were printed in the *Washington Post*, April 5, 1963, p. A2.

10. *BP-H*, April 5, 1963, pp. 1, 4, 14; *BP-H*, April 8, 1963, p. 10 (Foley); *BW*, April 10, 1963, p. 6; *Washington Post*, April 6, 1963, p. A4. The *Post* echoed the view of "ill-timed" demonstrations by mentioning that Boutwell "had hoped to take office April 15 in an era of calm and get on with the job of establishing Birmingham's new image." The Young Men's Business Club adopted a resolution that made this argument; see *BP-H*, April 9, 1963. The progressive white attorney David Vann said the same thing in Hampton and Fayer, *Voices Of Freedom*, p. 128; see also Gaston's comments on p. 129. For the SCLC's answer to the criticism see King, *Why We Can't Wait*, pp. 65–66. Vincent Townsend, vice president of the *Birmingham News*, made the argument to Burke Marshall, convincing the assistant attorney general for civil rights to telephone King to call off the demonstrations. After placing the call, Marshall realized that the city and the newspaper had King's telephone tapped, a "fact that was a great asset afterwards to me, I mean, I think in connection with my good faith with the whites down there." Quoted in Marshall interview by Anthony Lewis, p. 101, and the telephone logs in Marshall Papers, JFK Library. See also Garrow, *Bearing The Cross*, pp. 238–39.

11. *BP-H*, April 5, p. 4, April 6, 1963, p. 2; *NYT*, April 5, 1963, p. 16. Critical of King and the SCLC, the *Times* described the campaign as "much less than the 'full-scale assault' that had been promised." It mentioned "mass demonstrations" that "failed to materialize," evidence that King and the SCLC expected larger protests by more local people. As revealed by this inside reportage, the SCLC had cultivated the *Times* as a favored source in advance of the campaign. Shuttlesworth said that five were arrested; see Police Report, April 5, 1963, on ACMHR meeting of April 4, box 13, Connor Papers.

12. Police Report, April 5, 1963, on ACMHR meeting of April 4, box 13, Connor Papers. For the next two nights Porter joined Shuttlesworth, King, Abernathy, and others in a leadership role. Porter did not get along with Shuttlesworth, and he saw the ACMHR as "a one man show. It was Fred all the way. He made decisions . . . he was just a dictator. That was his style." Porter recalled that Shuttlesworth said: "Porter, this is *my* movement. You get in line or get out." Quoted in Garrow, *Bearing The Cross*, p. 238.

13. Police Report, April 5, 1963, on ACMHR meeting of April 4, box 13, Connor Papers; Garrow, *Bearing The Cross*, pp. 237–38. Ellwanger served as the only white member of the ACMHR-SCLC Central Committee; see "Central Committee Members," box 137, file 7, SCLC Papers.

14. Shuttlesworth telegram to Connor, April 5, 1963, Connor telegram to Shuttlesworth, April 5, 1963, box 13, file 2, Connor Papers. Most of the thirty-four arrested appear to have been members of the ACMHR; see *BP-H*, April 6, 1963, p. 2. For a description of the retail district see White, *Downtown Birmingham*, pp. 46–51.

15. Police Report, April 10, 1963, on ACMHR meeting of April 5, box 13, Connor Papers. Journalist Pat Watters's memoir (*Down To Now*, pp. 233–43) of the movement contains an excellent account of a sermon by Shuttlesworth that includes the water anecdote as well as other characteristics of the charismatic minister.

16. *BW*, April 10, 1963; *Washington Post*, April 7, 1963, p. A2; King, *Why We Can't Wait*, pp. 68–69; *NYT*, April 7, 1963, p. 55.

17. Police Report, April 10, 1963, on ACMHR meeting of April 6, box 13, Connor Papers.

18. Warden's Docket, April 7, 1963; *BP-H*, April 8, 1963, p. 2; clipping, *Cleveland Call and Post*, April 13, 1963, box 2, Shuttlesworth Papers, King Center; Forman, *The Making of Black Revolutionaries*, p. 311. The use of police dogs for crowd control had become common in the civil rights

struggle, as the simultaneous protest in Greenwood, Miss., demonstrated; yet Bull Connor's brutal application of dogs made Birmingham distinctive. Only the year before Connor had threatened that if the Freedom Riders returned to Birmingham, "he would bring out the dogs and yell 'Sic 'em!'"; *Nation*, May 5, 1962, p. 399. For an analysis of the "onlookers" that interprets their participation in and contributions to the movement, see Kelley, "Resistance, Survival," pp. 55–59.

19. Walker quoted in Garrow, *Bearing The Cross*, p. 239. In the police report of April 10, 1963, on the ACMHR meeting of April 8 (box 13, Connor Papers), Walker referred to the "five police dogs [that] had to subdue this man and he said that it was a sin and a shame that the police had to sic dogs on these non-violent Negroes. 'It might be tomorrow or Wednesday but that the dogs would be put on someone else.'"

20. Bennett, *What Manner of Man*, the chapter on King as "Symbol," pp. 111–67; Lentz, *Symbols*; *NYT*, April 5, p. 16, April 7, 1963, p. 55. The news weeklies did not cover the demonstrations until late April.

21. Forman, *The Making of Black Revolutionaries*, p. 312; Garrow, *Bearing The Cross*, pp. 239–40.

22. Bill Jones, *The Wallace Story*, p. 70 (Wallace's quotation); *BW*, April 10, 1963, p. 1; *BP-H*, April 9, 1963, p. 2; "Bulletin No. One" on expected arrival of American Nazi Party members from Florida, "Bulletin No. Two" on expected arrival of CORE members from Louisiana, April 9, 1963, box 13, Connor Papers; Nichols, "Cities Are What Men Make Them,'" pp. 282–84. The next time that Birmingham officers used police dogs was on May 3, 1963.

23. *BW*, April 13, 1963, p. 2; King, *Why We Can't Wait*, p. 67 (first quotation); Fairclough, *To Redeem The Soul*, p. 119; Morris, *Origins*, p. 263 (second quotation); John H. Cross to Rev. G. [*sic*] W. Gardner, October 29, 1962, box 33, file 15, SCLC Papers. No civil rights activists were arrested on April 8, see Warden's Docket.

24. *NYT*, April 9, 1963, p. 53; *BW*, April 17, 1963, p. 2. Jackson later commended as a proper Christian leader the Congregationalist minister and friend of Andrew Young's, Rev. Harold D. Long, a black member of the Alabama Council on Human Relations; see *BW*, April 20, 1963, p. 8. Late in April Ware issued the statement: "We are against segregation in all phases, but we haven't taken a specific stand as such. . . . There is quite a bit of dissension, but we would not do anything to handicap the Movement"; quoted in David L. Lewis, *King*, p. 179.

25. Police Report, April 10, 1963, on ACMHR meeting of April 8, box 13, Connor Papers. Young ("And Birmingham," p. 23) inaccurately suggests that Cross had supported the movement all along. Leaders announced that the meeting of Tuesday, April 9, would take place at Sixteenth Street Baptist Church, the first such meeting at the church according to other police reports. The advertisement on voter registration campaigns being held at movement churches in the *Birmingham World* (April 24, 1963. p. 5), demonstrates the limited number of black churches involved in the movement.

26. Police Report, April 10, 1963, on ACMHR meeting of April 8, box 13, Connor Papers. Rev. J. S. Phifer, who had moved to New York, also spoke at the meeting. From behind bars Shuttlesworth informed the press that Attorney General Robert Kennedy had asked him to cancel the demonstrations. He was released the next day. See *BP-H*, April 9, 1963, p. 2; *NYT*, April 10, 1963, p. 29.

27. Clipping, *Cleveland Call and Post*, April 13, 1963, box 2, Shuttlesworth Papers. The reporter quoted Walker, who explained the class conflict: "Dissention is nothing new. We are just strong enough now, and mature enough, and confident enough, so that we don't mind the white man knowing about our differences." Police Report, April 10, 1963, on ACMHR meeting of April 8, box 13, Connor Papers. On Abernathy's background see his autobiography, *And the Walls Came Tumbling Down*, pp. 1–31.

28. The *New York Times* (April 6, 1963, p. 20) reported that "many prominent members of the Birmingham Negro community are known to have opposed a direct action campaign at this time." See also *NYT*, April 10, p. 29, April 11, 1963, p. 21 (Hibbler quotation); Carl Keith Jr. to Martin Luther King Jr., May 1, 1963, box 1, file 9, King Papers, ATL; *Cleveland Call and Post*, April 13, 1963; and Gaston, *Green Power*, pp. 124–25. Walker later explained: "in all fairness, it must be said that the Hibbler affair was partially due to a misunderstanding of the mechanics of securing the L. R. Hall Auditorium"; News Release, n.d. [April 1963], box 50, file 26, SCLC Papers.

29. Gaston, *Green Power*, p. 125; Kunstler, *Deep in My Heart*, pp. 182–84. King addressed these

379

criticisms in his "Letter from Birmingham Jail." As Young ("And Birmingham," p. 23) described it: "Birmingham had its militants, it had its middle class comfortable constituents, and it had its people that we called 'Uncle Toms'—people who were still living on a survival ethic and were only willing to protect themselves. The Negro middle-class had adopted almost an education ethic that if you were educated you could protect yourself and you could make it in the white man's world by imitating and assimilating his education and his culture."

30. McAdam, *Political Process*, p. 231; Morris, *Origins*, pp. 277–78.

31. "News Release," n.d [April 1963], box 50, file 26, and list of "Central Committee Members," box 139, file 7, SCLC Papers.

32. *NYT*, April 11, 1963, p. 21; Rustin, "The Great Lessons of Birmingham," p. 308; King, *Why We Can't Wait*, p. 39. After the massive street protests and violent retaliation by black bystanders in May, Malcolm X offered a different "lesson of Birmingham": "Negroes have lost their fear of the white man's reprisals and will react today with vi000lence, if provoked. This could happen anywhere in the country today"; *NYT*, May 11, 1963, p. 9.

33. *NYT*, April 10, 1963 (quotations). Of Gaston, the *Birmingham World* (April 13, 1963, p. 8) observed: "That one of the steady voices of our community has seen fit to rally the hometown leadership to its duty, responsibility and a new sense of solution is encouraging." The *Birmingham Post-Herald* (April 10, 1963, p. 3) identified Gaston as "long a leader in the city's Negro community." According to the *New York Times* (April 10, 1963, p. 29), the statement "reflected the ambivalent attitude of so many Negro leaders in the dispute."

34. "News Release," n.d. [April 1963], box 50, file 26, SCLC Papers. For examples of negative reporting on Gaston see *Cleveland Call and Post*, April 6, 1963, and *NYT*, April 13, 1963.

35. *NYT*, April 10, 1963, p. 29; Kunstler, *Deep in My Heart*, p. 184.

36. Police Report, April 11, 1963, on ACMHR meeting of April 9, box 13, Connor Papers. Father Foley of the Alabama Council on Human Relations also attended the mass meeting. Although saying that he "didn't approve of the statement" Foley had issued opposing the campaign, King invited the white racial moderate to the front. As the Jesuit priest passed by, the two detectives heard him whisper, "How did I get myself in this mess?" Welcoming Foley and Jeremiah X, the local leader of the Black Muslims, King stood in the middle and embraced the two: "We don't love what Brother X advocates, black supremacy, we don't love white supremacy, but we love our white brother and we love integration."

37. Corley, "The Quest for Racial Harmony," pp. 254–55; Raines, *My Soul Is Rested*, pp. 196–97 (first quotation, p. 197); Morgan, *A Time To Speak*, pp. 153–54. The *New York Times* (May 11, 1963) gives a brief retrospective of the biracial negotiations.

38. Warden's Docket, April 10, 1963; *BW*, April 13, 1963, p. 8; "Bondsmen Who Have Made Appeal & Appearance Bonds on Sit In Cases," April 10, 1963, box 13, file 4, Connor Papers. Other reports state that 111 were arrested; *NYT*, April 11, 1963, p. 21. Hibbler performed in a bowling alley the next evening. See *NYT*, April 12, 1963, p. 1. His treatment by police was similar to that of the black comedian Dick Gregory, who tried unsuccessfully to get arrested in Greenville, Miss.

39. Police Report, April 12, 1963, on ACMHR meetings of April 10–11, box 13, file 4, Connor Papers; Young, "And Birmingham," p. 25. For an example of the leaflets, see box 1, Shuttlesworth Papers.

40. *Washington Post*, p. A6, and *NYT*, p. 1, April 12, 1963. The *Birmingham Post-Herald* (April 12, 1963, p. 4), reported that 156 people had been arrested since the demonstrations began, although the Warden's Docket lists only 140 people charged with violating city ordinances in regard to civil rights protests. Detained juveniles were not registered on the Warden's Docket unless they refused to give their age. Hence there is a discrepancy in the record.

41. King quoted in *Washington Post*, April 12, 1963, p. A6.

42. "Statement by Rev. F. L. Shuttlesworth, April 14, 1963," box 1, Shuttlesworth Papers.

43. Warden's Docket, April 10, 1963; "Bondsmen Who Made Appeal & Appearance Bonds on Sit In Cases," April 10, 1963, box 13, file 4, Connor Papers; King, *Why We Can't Wait*, pp. 71–72; Garrow, *Bearing The Cross*, p. 241.

44. Police Report, April 12, 1963, on ACMHR meeting of April 11, box 13, Connor Papers. Movement leaders asked members to sign property bonds to get others out of jail. Critics have

assailed Abernathy's memoir, *And the Walls Came Tumbling Down*, as grossly inaccurate; see *NYT*, p. 8, and *Atlanta Constitution*, p. 1, October 13, 1989. Like other forms of remembrance, sections of the book are fraught with errors or exaggerate his role, yet overall, the material he presents on his personal experience with the movement in Birmingham appears to be accurate. For example, Abernathy recounts the April 11 mass meeting and describes the "doohickey" [detective's bug] in detail (p. 247). The police report of April 12 on the ACMHR meeting of April 11 in the Connor Papers—a source he would not have consulted in writing his autobiography—presents a similar account. His book offers an anecdotal narrative of the SCLC different from King's own polemics and should be regarded as an important source on the movement.

45. King, *Why We Can't Wait*, pp. 71–72; Garrow, *Bearing The Cross*, pp. 241–42.

46. King, *Why We Can't Wait*, p. 72 (first quotation); Abernathy, *And the Walls Came Tumbling Down*, p. 248 (second and third quotations).

47. King, *Why We Can't Wait*, p. 72; Garrow, *Bearing The Cross*, p. 242; Hampton and Fayer, *Voices Of Freedom*, p. 130 (Young's quotation).

48. According to the Warden's Docket, King's arrest brought the total for the campaign to 186. The *Birmingham Post-Herald* (April 13, 1963, p. 10) claimed that 213 had been placed behind bars; on the same day the *Washington Post* (p. A5,) and the *New York Times* (p. 1) described the event as "the most spectacular of many demonstrations held." Abernathy (*And the Walls Came Tumbling Down*, p. 252) overheard Connor calling him and King the "Gold Dust Twins." He remembered Connor say: "Let's see if they can get along without one another for a change. Put them in solitary," to which King replied, "he's a smart old cracker." Although his name is not on the Warden's Docket, there is a picture of Hibbler's arrest in box 4, Police Surveillance Papers, BPLDAM.

49. King, *Why We Can't Wait*, p. 74. Walker telegraphed the president and attorney general identifying the jailed activists as "political prisoners"; *NYT*, April 15, 1963. Abernathy (*And the Walls Came Tumbling Down*, p. 253) recalled that while no one could get in to see them, "It never occurred to us that we might be entitled to call a lawyer ourselves."

50. Police Report, April 18, 1963, on ACMHR meeting of April 12, box 13, Connor Papers. The press also confirmed the accuracy of the police report; see *BP-H*, April 23, 1963, p. 20. Bevel had married Diane Nash of the Freedom Rides, and he often got carried away at mass meetings; see Police Report, April 30, on ACMHR meeting of April 27, box 13, Connor Papers. A similar quotation by Walker appears in the *Washington Post*, April 14, 1963, p. A2.

51. Abernathy, *And the Walls Came Tumbling Down*, pp. 253–54; *NYT*, April 14, 1963, p. 46; King, *Why We Can't Wait*, p. 74; Garrow, *Bearing The Cross*, pp. 243–44; *Washington Post*, April 14, 1963, p. A2. The *Post* quoted Burke Marshall as saying: "The Federal Government has no authority to take legal action to intervene in Birmingham as the situation now stands." Marshall then described his policy of federalism. The *Post* also reported that the movement considered bailing King and Abernathy out to lead Easter demonstrations.

52. The Warden's Docket identifies the six arrested as local black youths, four of whom refused to give their ages. The six from Ohio were apparently released; see *NYT*, April 14, 1963, p. 1.

53. *BP-H*, April 13, 1963, p. 10. An editorial on April 15, p. 10, repeated the theme of the clergymen's letter, with the headline "Send the Trouble-Makers Away!" The *Birmingham News* printed the statement on April 13, 1963; see also Bass, "Bishop C. C. J. Carpenter." An overlooked statement by the local interracial group of nine clerics—among them, Rev. Joseph W. Ellwanger of St. Paul Lutheran—expressed a different sentiment: "At stake is the freedom of human beings to associate and to act without fear, as conscience dictates." Recognizing the constitutional right to protest, this statement affirmed "the rightness of the aims of all who seek equal employment opportunities and equal access to all public facilities regardless of color or creed." *BW*, April 17, 1963, p. 1.

54. *BP-H*, April 13, 1963, p. 10. Billy Graham likewise responded, advising King and the black activists that "they ought to put the breaks on a little bit" because "great progress was being made" in Birmingham; *NYT*, April 18, 1963, p. 21.

55. The Sunday *New York Times* (April 14, 1963, p. 46) reported: "It is understood they are drawing up an answer to white churchmen's appeal, the gist of which will be that the time for

compromise has passed, that the Negro is going to insist on the start toward desegregation now." Because the paper went to press late Saturday night, it appears that someone on the outside of the jail must have decided that the movement would respond to the statement.

56. The full text of the "Letter" is reprinted in King, *Why We Can't Wait*, pp. 76–95. For an essay that appreciates the beauty of King's argument see Fulkerson, "The Public Letter as a Rhetorical Form"; and for an enlightened analysis of the religious metaphor see Snow, "Martin Luther King's 'Letter From Birmingham Jail' as Pauline Epistle."

57. Branch, *Parting The Waters*, p. 745 (Carpenter); Nossel, "Weathering The Storm," pp. 133–35 (Grafman). Shuttlesworth felt that all of the movement leaders should have been listed as the authors of "Letter from Birmingham Jail"; Shuttlesworth interview, December 21, 1987.

58. *BP-H*, p. 6, and *NYT*, p. 1, April 15, 1963. At Sixth Avenue Presbyterian, ushers said, "This church was built by white people and white people worship here"; *BW*, April 17, 1963, p. 1. McGinnis, "The Controversy and Division of First Baptist Church," p. 34 With the integration of the neighborhood and Central City Housing Project in 1968, First Baptist would confront a changing parish. Despite a tradition of open membership, the congregation voted in 1970 to reject the application of two black women. Immediately, the pastor denounced the "racist church" and resigned. First Baptist split apart, with those favoring integration forming a new congregation. The old church closed its downtown sanctuary rather than operate in an integrated environment and moved its Christian stained glass to a new building over the mountain.

59. Warden's Docket, April 14, 1963; *NYT*, p. 1, and *BP-H*, p. 6, April 15, 1963.

60. A trio of civil servants—city clerk Judson P. Hodges, city attorney J. M. Breckenridge, and city comptroller Grady Fullerton—coordinated city affairs. African Americans comprised one-fourth of the crowd. See *BP-H*, April 16, 1963, p. 1.

61. *BP-H*, April 17, 1963, p. 3; *NYT*, April 16, p. 1; April 17, 1963, p. 22.

62. Warden's Docket, April 15, 1963; *NYT*, April 16, 17 (p. 22), 1963.

63. *NYT*, April 16–17, 1963; text of King's conversation with his wife, April 15, 1963, box 13, file 3, Connor Papers. Police chief Jamie Moore denied that Kennedy's concern influenced the jail's treatment of King. Of Kennedy's involvement, King said: "I think it will make a very good statement" and "I think this gives it a new dimension." On Monday morning Burke Marshall called Arthur Shores, Orzell Billingsley, Wyatt Tee Walker, and Andrew Young to express the Kennedy administration's concern. See Telephone log for April 15, 1963, Marshall Papers, JFK Library. The *Birmingham Post-Herald* (April 17, 1963, p. 6) criticized the president and the "special consideration" that King received.

64. "Project C" memo, box 1, file 8, King Papers, ATL; Garrow, *Bearing The Cross*, p. 246; Police Report, April 17, 1963, on ACMHR meeting of April 15, box 13, Connor Papers; *NYT*, April 17, 1963, p. 22. The *Birmingham News* (April 14, 1963) contacted Burke Marshall, who "made it clear . . . the federal government is not going to intervene in the Birmingham racial situation unless some federal law is violated." Skeptical of the president's intentions, Shuttlesworth called Marshall on Thursday morning "to straighten out stories of who called who" during King's incarceration. That afternoon Walker telephoned to get Shuttlesworth an appointment with Marshall. On Friday morning the assistant attorney general met with Shuttlesworth and Walter Fauntroy of the SCLC, but again the assistant attorney general hid behind the policy of federalism. The meeting increased Shuttlesworth's suspicions of the Kennedy administration. See Telephone log for April 18–19, 1963, Marshall Papers, JFK Library. To confuse Connor's spies, Walker gave staffers nicknames that revealed his fascination with the Kennedy administration—for example, he became RFK and King became JFK; see Branch, *Parting The Waters*, p. 690.

65. Police Report, April 15, 1963, on ACMHR meeting of April 13, box 13, file 3, Connor Papers; *BW*, April 17, 1963. Women comprised a majority of the foot soldiers in the movement and played a crucial role informing members of activities. The ACMHR created a "telephone tree," generally operated by women, that spread news throughout Birmingham within minutes. Shuttlesworth interview, December 21, 1987. Young also criticized the Birmingham newspapers for "playing the movement down." A. D. King said that the *News* had refused to sell advertising space to the movement to enable it to publicize the boycott. Before the boycott, African Americans comprised 75 percent of the shoppers at Atlantic Mills and 50 percent of those at Pizitz; see *NYT*, May 11, 1963, p. 9.

66. Undated ACMHR-SCLC press release on the arrest of 16 people trying to register to vote, box 1, file 8, King Papers, ATL. According to the Warden's Docket, a total of 33 people were arrested on April 17 for civil rights protests. Seven African Americans filled out applications without incident; see BW, April 20, 1963, p. 1. Officers also arrested 4 pickets in front of Sears, Roebuck and 5 at Britling Cafeteria. Newspapers listed the total arrested since April 3 as 310 (see NYT, p. 21, and BP-H, p. 7, April 18, 1963), although the April 17 Warden's Docket listed only 272 arrests.

67. NYT, April 20, 1963 p. 12. The *Birmingham Post-Herald* (April 13, 1963, p. 10) reported that movement lawyers had filed petitions to transfer 61 cases to federal court the week before; see also BP-H, April 18, p. 7, and Kunstler, *Deep In My Heart*, p. 188. The Good Friday arrests of King and Abernathy resulted in the U.S. Supreme Court's divided decision in *Walker v. City of Birmingham* (1967) determining that injunctions against protests were to be challenged in the courts and not defied in the streets. With the ruling, five justices diminished greatly the constitutional protection afforded protesters under the Bill of Rights. The ruling stifled student protests as it ushered in a new era of law and order.

68. NYT, April 17, 1963, p. 22.

69. BP-H, April 18, 1963, p. 14. A similar editorial from the *Charleston News and Courier* ran in the *Post-Herald* on April 19, 1963, p. 14.

70. BP-H, April 16, 18 (Coley), 19 (Watson, p. 7), 20 (Boutwell, p. 3), 1963. Time and again, movement leaders appealed to local street toughs for nonviolence. During recruitment drives staffers disarmed the black volunteers in a process Abernathy (*And the Walls Came Tumbling Down*, p. 249) called "work-shopping them."

71. BN and NYT, April 21, 1963; *Montgomery Advertiser*, April 20, 1963.

72. Warden's Docket, April 20, 1963; NYT (p. 70) and *Montgomery Advertiser*, April 21, 1963. The *Birmingham News* (April 21, 1963) reported that 29 (not 15) were arrested on Saturday. There were no arrests on Sunday, April 21.

73. NYT, April 21, 1963, p. 70 (quotations); Corley, "The Quest for Racial Harmony," pp. 254–55. King (*Why We Can't Wait*, p. 96) claimed that he had bailed out for two reasons: first, "it was necessary for me to regain communication with the S.C.L.C. officers and our lawyers in order to map the strategy for the contempt cases," and second, "I had decided to put into operation a new phase of our campaign [the use of schoolchildren], which I felt would speed victory." The first reason is demonstrable, the second is unsubstantiated.

74. Abernathy quoted in NYT, April 21, 1963, p. 70. Rev. Abraham Woods opened one mass meeting holding a copy of the newspaper and saying, "This ain't so and that ain't so." Police Report, April 19, 1963, on ACMHR meeting of April 18, box 13, Connor Papers. On the *News*, see the article by Washington correspondent James Free on April 15 and the article by staff writer Edward P. Badger on April 23. Unfortunately, a 1988 *News* retrospective twenty-five years later, "Reality in Black and White: Then & Now," did little to clear up those misconceptions.

75. BP-H, p. 20, and NYT, April 23, 1963. The Warden's Docket lists five arrests on April 22. The thirteen ministers were Abernathy, Walker, Young, Bevel, A. D. King, Gardner, C. Woods, A. Woods, J. L. Palmer, J. W. Hayes, N. H. Smith, J. T. Porter, and T. L. Fisher; see BP-H, April 16, 20 (p. 13), 1963.

76. The Warden's Docket lists only 307 arrests up to this time, although newspapers put the figure at 350. See NYT, April 23, 1963, and BP-H, April 23, 1963, pp. 2, 20.

77. Warden's Docket, April 23, 1963; BP-H, April 24, p. 1, May 2, 1963; BN, April 23–24, 1963. Jenkins dropped the charges against Gardner, C. Woods, A. Woods, and J. Palmer. On Moore see NYT, April 25, 1963, p. 20. Shuttlesworth and the ACMHR-SCLC failed to properly apply for the permit. According to sec. 1159, the ordinance specifically states that applications for parade permits had to be made to the entire commission, as Connor claimed in his telegram back to Shuttlesworth. Furthermore, it required "written application setting forth the probable number of persons, vehicles and animals . . . the purpose for which it is to be held . . . and the streets or other public ways . . . desired." The commission retained the right to grant the application "unless in its judgment the public welfare, peace, safety, health, decency, good order, morals, or convenience require that it be refused." Had the movement filed a completed application, the commission

383

probably would have rejected the application on the latter grounds. *General Code of . . . Birmingham*, p. 424. Lola Hendricks testified that she petitioned Connor on the first day of the campaign and he responded: "You will not get a permit in Birmingham, Ala., to picket: I'll picket you over to city jail." See *BN*, April 23, 1963. Shuttlesworth filed suit against the city for refusing to grant the permit. In *Shuttlesworth v. Birmingham* (1969) the U.S. Supreme Court ruled that ordinances such as Birmingham's unconstitutionally restricted freedom of speech.

78. *NYT*, April 25, 1963, p. 20; *Montgomery Advertiser*, April 25, 1963. Orzell Billingsley filed suit in the Fifth Circuit Court of Appeals, claiming that the city ordinances denied them their constitutional rights; see *BP-H*, April 25, 1963, p. 2. A neo-Nazi attempted to travel to Birmingham to attend the trial, according to police surveillance reports; see memo to Chief Moore, April 24, 1963, box 13, Connor Papers. Shuttlesworth criticized McBee, saying that King and Abernathy had not lied. "Shouldn't anyone say anything bad about Ralph," he said, adding that Walker was "the brains of this Movement," and that what whites heard as "revolution" was really "evolution." Police Surveillance Report, April 29, 1963, on ACMHR meeting of April 25, box 13, Connor Papers.

79. Police Surveillance Report, April 26, 1963, on ACMHR meeting of April 24, box 13, Connor Papers.

80. Raines, *My Soul Is Rested*, pp. 157–59.

81. Police Surveillance Report, April 26, 1963, on ACMHR meeting of April 24, box 13, Connor Papers; Kunstler, *Deep in My Heart*, p. 189.

82. Three white students at Southern attended the mass meeting on April 23. The students, Barbara Jo McBride, Minnie Martha Turnipseed, and Samuel Curtis Shirah Jr., were all natives of Alabama and children of Methodist ministers. Turnipseed volunteered for the sit-in at Woolworth's. When informed by detectives of their subversive students, faculty members at Southern, unlike under the tenure of President Henry King Stanford, promised disciplinary action. See memo on "Birmingham- Southern College Students," April 24, 1963, and Police Surveillance Report, April 25, 1963, on ACMHR meeting of April 23, box 13, Connor Papers. Although Turnipseed demonstrated and was detained by police, she was not arrested, as were six African Americans; Warden's Docket, April 24, 1963.

83. *BN*, April 25, 1963; Transcript of Kennedy-Wallace conversation, Attorney General Personal Correspondence, Civil Rights Miscellaneous File, RFK Papers; Garrow, *Bearing The Cross*, p. 246; Police Surveillance Report, April 30, 1963, on ACMHR meeting of April 26, box 13, Connor Papers. The meeting convinced Kennedy of the need for federal troops when desegregation at the university occurred; see *NYT*, April 27, 1963, p. 9. For a full account of Wallace during Birmingham's racial crisis and the months that followed see Carter, *The Politics of Rage*, pp. 110–94; see also Frady, *Wallace*, pp. 150–69. In Birmingham, five activists were arrested; see Warden's Docket, April 25, 1963.

84. The eleven ministers were Martin Luther King, Abernathy, Shuttlesworth, Young, Walker, Bevel, A. D. King, Hayes, Smith Jr., Fisher, and Porter. See *NYT*, p. 9, and *BP-H*, p. 5, April 27, 1963; *BN*, April 26, 1963. See also *Walker v. City of Birmingham*. The court dismissed the charges against Gardner, C. Woods, A. Woods, and Palmer.

85. Police Surveillance Report, April 30, 1963, on ACMHR meeting of April 26, box 13, Connor Papers. Only four demonstrators were arrested; Warden's Docket, April 26, 1963.

Chapter 8

1. Only nine congregations accepted the black worshipers. In a typical response to the threat of kneel-ins, over-the-mountain Trinity Methodist adopted a policy to bar black people from services by first turning them away vocally and then, if necessary, having ushers "clasp hands across the entrance." No confrontation occurred, although an associate minister removed the sign "Let Us Enter Into His Gates With Thanksgiving" that hung above the segregationist statement posted in the vestibule. Wheeler, *Trinity United Methodist Church*.

2. *BW*, April 20, 24, 27, 1963.

3. *BW*, April 24, 1963; Emory O. Jackson to Anne G. Rutledge, April 12 (first quotation) and

April 5 (second quotation) 1963, Jackson Papers, BPLDAM. The *Birmingham News* (April 12, 1963) carried an ad signed by black businessmen A. G. Gaston, Louis J. Willie, John J. Drew; attorneys Billingsley, Arthur D. Shores, Peter A. Hall, Oscar W. Adams Jr.; Dr. James T. Montgomery; dentist John W. Nixon; prominent pastors John H. Cross and Harold D. Long; civic reformers Bernice C. Johnson and Deenie Drew; and activists Frank Dukes and Rev. Edward Gardner. Perhaps suffering from the withdrawal of patronage of nonmovement black professionals, Negro dentists and doctors published an ad in support of the campaign in the *Post-Herald* (April 23, 1963).

4. Garrow, *Bearing The Cross*, p. 247. Porter remembered King saying "We cannot wait until the afternoon. We must march in the morning—the press is here." Porter yelled back: "I want God with us not the press. We must win by righteousness"; quoted in Nichols, "Cities Are What Men Make Them," p. 282. Yet as Porter soon learned, King and Walker staged events in the morning so the press could get the footage on the evening news.

5. Warden's Docket, April 27–May 2, 1963, BPLDAM; Garrow, *Bearing The Cross*, p. 247 (quotation). Gaston (*Green Power*, p. 125) later spoke on the issue: "If wanting to spare children, save lives, bring peace was Uncle Tomism, then I wanted to be a Super Uncle Tom."

6. Hampton and Fayer, *Voices of Freedom*, pp. 131–32. Bevel recognized that the last to get involved were the black males because "the brunt of the violence in the South was directed toward the black male. The females had not experienced that kind of negative violence, so they didn't have the kind of immediate fear of, say, white policemen, as the young men did." At the height of the protests on Monday, when officers arrested one thousand schoolchildren, nearly two to one were female; see *NYT*, May 9, 1963.

7. Memo of Lieutenant M. H. House to Chief Jamie Moore, April 30, 1963, and Police Report, box 13, April 30, 1963, on ACMHR meeting of April 29, Connor Papers, BPLDAM. Dorothy Cotton played a crucial role in organizing the students, yet nothing in the files of the Citizenship Education Program, which she directed, mentions her activities in Birmingham; see box 153, file 9, SCLC Papers. James Forman (*The Making of Black Revolutionaries*, p. 312) recalled that the "organizing committee of the students wanted to affiliate openly with SNCC," a dubious claim considering that the Miles students had previously rejected overtures by CORE and SNCC.

8. Police Report, April 30, 1963, on ACMHR meeting of April 29. On King at the opera see House memo to Moore, April 30; on the SCLC convention in Memphis see police memo of May 1—both in Connor Papers. With an air of moral self-righteousness, the Metropolitan Opera refused to perform in cities that forbade integrated seating and with that justification struck Birmingham from its touring list and made much political hay from the matter. In fact, it had threatened to drop the city for years because it lost money there.

9. According to the *Birmingham Post-Herald* (May 1, 1963, p. 2), "included in the denial was (1) failure to specify the number involved in parade, (2) not in the public's welfare, (3) failure to give appropriate time period and (4) did not specify the exact location at City Hall." See also Garrow, *Bearing The Cross*, p. 248; Police Report, May 2, 1963, on ACMHR meeting of April 30, Connor Papers; *B P-H*, April 30 (p. 3), May 2, 1963.

10. Police Memo, May 1, 1963, and Police Report, May 2, 1963, on ACMHR meeting of May 1, Connor Papers. According to the Warden's Docket, Dothard was arrested on April 3 and 13. Twenty-five visitors from Gadsden observed the meeting. Although integrationists on the Moore march were arrested in Etowah County, demonstrations would break out there in August 1963. The next day a group of twenty-five were arrested when they marched on city hall. See *Newsweek*, May 13, 1963; Kunstler, *Deep in My Heart*, p. 190.

11. Garrow, *Bearing The Cross*, p. 248. According to Garrow (p. 671 n21), Kunstler said: "Martin was about the most indecisive man I've ever seen. He really had trouble being decisive"; see also Kunstler, *Deep in My Heart*, p. 190. The *Birmingham Post-Herald* (May 3, 1963, p. 3) reported that teachers called roll twice, having "been alerted to the demonstration plans"; in addition, "persons distributing literature had been evicted from school property for several days before the demonstrations."

12. *Newsweek*, May 13, 1963, p. 27; *BP-H*, May 3, 1963, p. 3; Garrow, *Bearing The Cross*, p. 248. Walker bragged about the success of the protest to the *Birmingham News*, May 3, 1963.

13. *Newsweek*, May 13, 1963; Nunnelley, *Bull Connor*, p. 147. According to Nunnelley, Warren

said that "you could see the tension . . . he [Connor] was beginning to see that this was so damn big, he wasn't sure what the hell to do." Though not as reactionary as Connor, Sheriff Melvin Bailey of Jefferson County promised "to offer any assistance we can, and will co-operate in every way with Birmingham officials"; *BP-H*, May 4, 1963, p. 2. See also May 3, p. 3; *BN* and *NYT*, May 3, 1963.

14. *BP-H*, May 3, 1963, p. 3; *Newsweek*, May 13, 1963. The *Birmingham News* (May 3) reported 700 arrests, of which 319 children—some 240 of them female—were placed in the Detention Home, with the males going to the Bessemer and county jails.

15. Police Report, May 3, 1963, on ACMHR meeting of May 2, Connor Papers. Shuttlesworth recounted a conversation with one officer, who asked him: "'Hey, Fred, how many more have you got' and I said at least 1,000 more; and the policeman said 'god Amighty.'" James Farmer of CORE also spoke at the mass meeting.

16. *BP-H*, May 4, 1963, p. 2 (Boutwell); *NYT*, May 4, p. 8 (Kennedy and King). See also *NYT*, May 11, 1963.

17. *BP-H*, May 4, 1963, p. 2.

18. Ibid.; *Newsweek*, May 13, 1963; Corley, "The Quest for Racial Harmony," p. 259.

19. *NYT*, p. 8, and *BP-H*, p. 2, May 4, 1963; Raines, *My Soul Is Rested*, pp. 187–88. The schoolchildren failed to behave as well as the day before, according to reports that said one group refused to obey an officer. When a group of elementary schoolchildren approached, the firemen shut down the hoses and ushered them into a school bus for the ride to jail; at one point a vigilante attempted to drive his car into a line of activists, but he was arrested. The *Birmingham News* (May 3, 1963) reported that Evans gave the order to "sprinkle them with water."

20. *NYT*, May 4, 1963, p. 8; *BP-H*, May 4, 1963, p. 2; Inter-Citizens Committee, "Documents on Human Rights in Alabama," June 3, 1963, box 1, file 7, King Papers, ATL. *Life* magazine photographer Charles Moore was also injured. His exceptional photographs of the demonstration can be seen in his *Powerful Days*, pp. 90–119.

21. Officers arrested 200, bringing the total arrested to 1,300, about 900 of them schoolchildren; see *NYT*, May 4, 1963.

22. Marshall interview by Eskew; Corley, "The Quest for Racial Harmony," pp. 262–63; Telephone log for May 3, 1963, Marshall Papers, JFK Library. On Marshall's background and the policy of federalism, see Marshall, *Federalism and Civil Rights*; Belknap, *Federal Law and Southern Order*; Brauer, *John F. Kennedy*, pp. 93–94; *NYT*, May 10, 1963; and Marshall interview by Lewis. In the interview, Marshall explained that he went to Birmingham "to do something" within the confines of federalism but that the administration did not anticipate "legislation" as in the civil rights bill of 1963.

23. Vann, "Speech," Duard LeGrand Conference, pp. 30–32. Marshall also contacted Vann about representing the merchants in negotiations; see Marshall interview by Lewis, p. 97.

24. Vann, "Speech," Duard LeGrand Conference, pp. 31–32; Police Reports, May 7, 3, 1963, on ACMHR meetings of May 6 and May 3, respectively, Connor Papers.

25. About 225 were arrested that day, 111 of whom were under sixteen years of age, for a total of 1,600 arrested since April 3. See *BP-H*, May 6, 1963; police memo of May 4, 1963, Connor Papers; *NYT* (p. 82) and *Montgomery Advertiser*, May 5, 1963.

26. *NYT* and *Montgomery Advertiser*, May 5, 1963.

27. *BP-H*, May 6, 1963; *Montgomery Advertiser*, May 5, 1963. Billups referred to the meeting that night; see Police Report, May 7, 1963, on ACMHR meeting of May 6, Connor Papers.

28. *Montgomery Advertiser*, May 5, 1963; Marshall interview by Lewis, p. 99. Shuttlesworth recalled: "I never did agree, and only . . . because I respected Martin Luther King did I agree to allow Burke Marshall, who was assistant attorney general, and John Doar to talk to us on one side and then go talk to the white folks on the other side. I did not believe in that. I thought we should have gotten together face-to-face, 'cause its never a true negotiation when that's being done." Quoted in Raines, *My Soul Is Rested*, p. 171.

29. *BN*, May 5, 1963; Bains, "Birmingham 1963," p. 271 n86 (Walker); Hampton and Fayer, *Voices of Freedom*, p. 134 (Bevel); Police Report, May 7, 1963, on ACMHR meeting of May 3, Connor Papers; Raines, *My Soul Is Rested*, p. 197 (Morgan).

30. Police Reports, May 6–7, 1963, on ACMHR meetings of May 4–5, Connor Papers. The Billups march has gained mythic proportions in civil rights lore; see Young, "And Birmingham," p. 27. The *Post-Herald* (May 6, 1963, pp. 2–3) suggested that a compromise was reached to hold the prayer meeting in the park rather than at the jail. King (*Why We Can't Wait*, p. 101) claimed that Connor said, "Dammit. Turn on the hoses," and the firemen proved unable to do it. Forman (*The Making of Black Revolutionaries*, p. 312) reported that after Billups explained the march to authorities, "they were waved on through." Billups told Forman, "the police officer had given orders to the firemen to turn the hoses on the people but the all-white firemen had 'frozen,' . . . they just couldn't do it."

31. *NYT*, May 6, 1963, p. 59; Morris, *Origins*, p. 269. "Sales of Birmingham's downtown stores dropped 10% when Negroes began boycotts and picketing, fell another 15% when the city brought out the firehoses and police dogs. Birmingham's pass-through tourist trade is off 40%"; unidentified clipping [*Business Week*, June 1963], box 1, file 11, Marshall Papers, JFK Library. Figures comparing the decline of 1963 to sales in 1962 neglect to mention the black student boycott of that year when sales declined 11 percent, suggesting a greater loss of trade to the merchants than reported in the press.

32. *NYT*, May 6, 1963, pp. 1, 59, and May 7; King, *Why We Can't Wait*, p. 103. On Marshall see also *NYT*, May 11, 1963, p. 8; Morgan, *A Time To Speak*, pp. 154–55.

33. "Points for Progress," box 1, file 7, King Papers, ATL; Garrow, *Bearing The Cross*, p. 252 (quotation of unnamed participant); Abernathy, *And the Walls Came Tumbling Down*, p. 265. Figures in this paragraph have been rounded off to the nearest dollar amount.

34. *NYT*, May 7, 1963, p. 33; Abernathy, *And the Walls Came Tumbling Down*, p. 266; Gregory and Lipsyte, *Nigger: An Autobiography*, pp. 178–80. Jailed until May 9, Gregory claimed police brutality; see *NYT*, May 10, 1963, p. 14.

35. *NYT* (p. 33) and *BP-H* (p. 2), May 7, 1963.

36. *NYT*, May 7, 1963; Marshall interview by Lewis, pp. 97–98; Raines, *My Soul Is Rested*, p. 171.

37. Abernathy, *And the Walls Came Tumbling Down*, p. 265; Garrow, *Bearing The Cross*, p. 253; *NYT*, May 7, 1963, p. 33; Marshall interview by Lewis, pp. 100–101.

38. Police Report, May 7, 1963, on ACMHR meeting of May 6, Connor Papers; Forman, *The Making of Black Revolutionaries*, p. 313. On conditions in the jail see *NYT*, May 8 (p. 29), 9 (p. 17); *BP-H*, May 7, 1963, p. 2.

39. Forman, *The Making of Black Revolutionaries*, p. 314.

40. Garrow, *Bearing The Cross*, p. 253; "Points for Progress," box 1, file 7, King Papers, ATL; Marshall interview by Lewis, p. 100. Marshall identified several Big Mules including the executives of U.S. Steel, Hayes International, and South Central Bell and the directors of Birmingham's two leading banks, First National and Birmingham Trust.

41. *BP-H*, p. 2; Forman, *The Making of Black Revolutionaries*, p. 314; *Time*, May 17, 1963, p. 24. The *New York Times* (May 8, 1963) reported that "2,500 to 3,000 persons rampaged through the business district."

42. Marshall interview by Lewis, p. 100; Vann, "Speech," Duard LeGrand Conference, pp. 32–33.

43. Marshall interview by Lewis, pp. 101–2; Raines, *My Soul Is Rested*, pp. 179–80 (Smyer); Vann "Speech," Duard LeGrand Conference, p. 33; *BP-H*, May 8, 1963, p. 2. As Dixon's comments suggest, when considered in light of the governor's exchange with Robert Kennedy, the racist Wallace had no trouble working with Alabama's corporate structure.

44. *NYT* (pp. 1, 28) and *BP-H* (p. 2), May 8, 1963; Marshall interview by Lewis, pp. 98, 102; Vann, "Speech," Duard LeGrand Conference, p. 33. Theodore C. Sorensen, Lee C. White, Nicholas de B. Katzenbach, John Doar, Berl I. Bernhard, and Louis E. Martin, all advisers to the president, met in a "think session" for five hours, "and they ended up with nothing. I mean there was nothing to do," according to Marshall; notes on meeting, Attorney General, General Correspondence, Civil Rights, Birmingham, May 1963, RFK Papers.

45. Forman, *The Making of Black Revolutionaries*, p. 314.

46. *BP-H*, May 8, 1963, p. 2; Harding, "A Beginning in Birmingham," p. 16. For "skeeted" see

Hampton and Fayer, *Voices of Freedom*, p. 134. Several hundred white people watched from Eighteenth Street. The *New York Times* (May 8, 1963, p. 28) described the event as a riot, as did Forman (*The Making of Black Revolutionaries*, p. 315).

47. *BP-H*, May 8, 1963; Raines, *My Soul Is Rested*, pp. 190–91 (Evans's quotation). Eight policemen and at least four bystanders were injured.

48. *BP-H* and *NYT*, May 8, 1963. Kennedy also called Claude Sitton of the *New York Times*; see "List of Phone Numbers Called by Attorney General," May 7, 1963, General Correspondence, Civil Rights, Birmingham, May 1963, RFK Papers.

49. *NYT*, May 8, 1963, pp. 1, 28–29.

50. Ibid., pp. 1, 28–29; Elovitz, *A Century of Jewish Life in Dixie*, pp. 169–75. For a more nuanced analysis of Birmingham's Jewish community during the desegregation crisis see Nossel, "Weathering The Storm," 140–46 and passim.

51. Police Report, May 9, 1963, on ACMHR meeting of May 7, Connor Papers.

52. Harding, "A Beginning in Birmingham," p. 16; Garrow, *Bearing The Cross*, p. 255; Young, "Prospective Negotiation Procedure with Merchants," box 1, file 7, King Papers, ATL; Dorman, *We Shall Overcome*, p. 157.

53. *NYT*, May 11, 1963, p. 9; Harding, "A Beginning in Birmingham," pp. 16–17; Dorman, *We Shall Overcome*, p. 157. Other negotiators included white attorney Erskine Smith and Negroes A. G. Gaston and Rev. Harold Long. Occasionally Young was joined by Abernathy and other movement leaders. Although Smyer refused to recognize him, he might have met King at some point as King was staying in Drew's house. Rev. Abraham Woods recalled attending negotiations with Smyer: "And I had never seen an old white man cry, but at one of the meetings . . . he actually broke down and cried"; quoted in Raines, *My Soul Is Rested*, p. 163.

54. Untitled typed notes of negotiations, box 139, file 7, SCLC Papers. Garrow (*Bearing The Cross*, p. 672 n29) identifies Pitts as the author. On the original "Points for Progress," see box 1, file 7, King Papers, ATL.

55. Untitled typed notes of negotiations, box 139, file 7, SCLC Papers.

56. Abernathy, *And the Walls Came Tumbling Down*, pp. 267–68; Young, "And Birmingham," p. 23.

57. Vann, "Speech," Duard LeGrand Conference, pp. 34–35. Drew's house sat near Interstate 59 where it now intersects with Arkadelphia Road.

58. Forman, *The Making of Black Revolutionaries*, p. 315; Harding, "A Beginning in Birmingham," p. 17. Forman recalled feeling "that the masses of young people who were the backbone of the protest in Birmingham and throughout the South had been cheated once more. The mighty leader had proven to have heavy feet of clay."

59. Raines, *My Soul Is Rested*, p. 171.

60. Ibid., pp. 172–74; Garrow, *Bearing The Cross*, pp. 256–57. Emphasis Shuttlesworth's.

61. Raines, *My Soul Is Rested*, pp. 172–74; Garrow, *Bearing The Cross*, pp. 256–57. Abernathy (*And the Walls Came Tumbling Down*, p. 268) recalled that Shuttlesworth "lit into Martin, calling him a coward and a double-crosser."

62. Raines, *My Soul Is Rested*, pp. 172–74; Garrow, *Bearing The Cross*, pp. 256–57. The exchange between Shuttlesworth and King is also recalled in an interview Shuttlesworth gave to Blackside, Inc.; see Hampton and Fayer, *Voices of Freedom*, pp. 136–37.

63. In *The Making of Black Revolutionaries*, Forman titled the chapter on the demonstrations, "Betrayal in Birmingham"; see pp. 311–16.

64. *NYT*, May 9, 1963; Dorman, *We Shall Overcome*, p. 157.

65. *BP-H*, May 9, 1963; *NYT*, May 9, 1963, p. 17; Dorman, *We Shall Overcome*, pp. 158–59; *BN*, May 10, 1963. White professor Robert B. Fulton of Miles College also had to pay the higher appeal bond.

66. *BN*, May 10, 1963; *NYT*, May 9, 1963, p. 17; Kunstler, *Deep in My Heart*, pp. 192–93; Harding, "A Beginning in Birmingham," p. 17. Years later when Shuttlesworth remembered his "compromise" with King "to announce limited demonstrations," he said that the conflict between the two had also caused King to "agonize." As he stated, " 'I don't think that the man was a liar, I

really don't. I have seen him talk in ways to make people think that he might would [*sic*] have done it another way, but I do not think that Martin Luther King, Jr., was a liar. I don't think that." Quoted in Raines, *My Soul Is Rested*, p. 174.

67. *BP-H*, May 8, 1963, p. 2; *NYT*, May 9, 1963. Many white people failed to recognize the simple demands of black people. Young ("And Birmingham," p. 24) recalled: "the white community didn't understand. . . . No one in the white community ever thought it was a major issue for a black person to go to the bathroom in a department store."

68. Dorman, *We Shall Overcome*, pp. 158–60; Police Memo, May 8, 1963, and Police Report, May 9, 1963, on ACMHR meeting of May 8, Connor Papers. The visit of the rabbis underscored the support for segregation by Birmingham's Jewish community; Elovitz, *A Century of Jewish Life in Dixie*, pp. 169–75.

69. *NYT*, May 10, 1963, pp. 1, 14; Garrow, *Bearing The Cross*, p. 258; Harding, "A Beginning In Birmingham," p. 17.

70. *NYT*, May 10, 1963, pp. 1, 14; Abernathy, *And the Walls Came Tumbling Down*, p. 268.

71. *NYT*, May 10, 1963. The lead sentence reported that "negotiators reached full agreement tonight on terms for settling this city's racial crisis after Negroes had scaled down their demands." King "accepted promises of progress from white business and civic leaders in lieu of immediate action. . . . There was speculation among observers that, despite the apparent sincerity of the negotiators the situation might deteriorate into the pattern set in a similar dispute in Albany."

72. Marshall interview by Lewis, pp. 98–99. King's action signified a conflict between the local and national movements. In *The Politics of Nonviolent Action*, Gene Sharp details four major factors that influence nonviolent movements: the social structure, the opponent group, third parties, and nonviolent activists. One must also consider the complex relationship among the activists, for local and national movements may espouse similar goals and their efforts may coalesce at times, but their objectives may not remain the same.

73. Harding, "A Beginning in Birmingham," p. 17; Morgan, *A Time To Speak*, p. 154.

74. *NYT*, May 10, 1963, p. 14. Speaking on events in Birmingham, Malcolm X recognized that "white southerners were more forthright and courageous in their opposition to desegregation and integration than the 'hypocritical liberal whites in the North.'" He explained: "The northern liberals publicly advocate desegregation but flee to the suburbs when the Negroes approach."

75. *NYT*, May 10, 1963, p. 14.

76. *BP-H* and *BN*, May 11, 1963; Raines, *My Soul Is Rested*, p. 174; *NYT*, May 11, 1963, pp. 8, 9. Shuttlesworth told reporters: "I am satisfied that they [the whites] are dealing in good faith. . . . I wouldn't double-cross my people; they know that."

77. *NYT*, May 11, 1963. While marking the first time the white power structure publicly announced the need for race reform—an admission never made before—the businessmen only conceded vague promises of future action. Both municipal governments denounced the accord.

78. Ibid.

79. Ibid. In an editorial, the *Birmingham News* (May 11, 1963) abdicated responsibility for the negotiations when it described the official version of events: "Birmingham was in a vacuum. Into this vacuum outside Negroes came and organized demonstrations." When the protests upset civil order, white businessmen "of the non-official Senior Citizens Committee" met with black leaders as individuals speaking "*only* for themselves . . . they knew they could not agree with Negroes *for* you-the-citizen to do *anything*. They knew they could not do so for *any* elected city official." The *News* added, "Negroes obviously accepted that basis for the discussion. They obviously knew nothing that anyone 'agreed upon' was binding. They knew anything would represent *only* the conclusion and possibly the hopes of that particular white group. Negroes judged this, however, limited as it was, adequate."

80. Warden's Docket, April 3–May 2, 1963. Payne (*I've Got the Light of Freedom*) called the movement in the Mississippi Delta "a woman's war"; see also his essay, "Men Led, But Women Organized," pp. 1–12.

81. Warden's Docket, April 3–May 2, 1963.

389

1. *BW*, May 15, 1963, p. 1; Minutes of the May 22, 1963, Alabama Advisory Committee meeting of the U.S. Civil Rights Commission, box 1, file 10, Marshall Papers, BPLDAM. Like the Klan, Bull Connor had urged defiance, telling white people to boycott stores that agreed to the negotiations. See *NYT*, May 12, 1963, p. 53. One study concludes that "the Jewish merchants felt imprisoned by the competing demands of the black boycotters and the white commercial leaders. After a settlement was reached, the department stores became the first public institutions in Birmingham to be officially integrated. The merchants received support from neither the Senior Citizens nor the black community as they bore the brunt of the anti-Semitic hostility, violence, and economic reprisals that followed the truce. By this time, the Jewish community's attitudes and leadership structure had undergone significant alteration." Nossel, "Weathering The Storm," p. 167.

2. *NYT*, May 13, 1963, p. 1. A Klan informant also told Officer Ben Allen of the planned bombing, and Allen informed Col. Al Lingo with the request that state troopers remain in the city through the weekend; but Lingo withdrew the highway patrolmen, commenting that he could handle the Klan. His troopers returned to the city within minutes of the blast, suggesting that Lingo was directly involved in the bombing and that the state worked in tandem with the vigilantes. See Raines, *My Soul Is Rested*, p. 195.

3. *Montgomery Advertiser*, May 13, 1963; *BN*, May 15, 1963; *NYT*, May 13, 1963, p. 24. Arguing that the black civil defense workers had the situation under control, Lay said the intervention of state troopers provoked the riot. King claimed it would not have occurred had Birmingham hired Negro policemen; see *Montgomery Advertiser*, May 14, 1963. The local press (*BN* and *BP-H*, May 14, 1963) reported that the rioting African Americans were "drinking heavily," a charge reiterated by movement leaders. See King, *Why We Can't Wait*, p. 106; see also Police Report, May 14, 1963, on ACMHR meeting of May 13, Connor Papers, BPLDAM. Some conservative Negroes blamed the black Muslims; see Alabama Advisory Committee minutes, May 22, 1963, box 1, file 10, Marshall Papers, BPLDAM. Rev. Abraham Woods recalled: "That was a terrible night, when blacks went wild. I knew then that we were not going to be able to long hold this element in check"; quoted in Raines, *My Soul Is Rested*, p. 165. The area of the riot encompassed First to Eighth Avenues North and Fourteenth to Eighteenth Streets. Three of the Italian groceries were owned by Jerome Ippolito, Mike Capri, and Vincent Capri. Capri told the *Birmingham News* (May 13, 1963): "It probably wasn't anybody who lived around here. I don't believe it was my customers." See also *NYT*, May 14, 1963, p. 27. On looting see *BP-H*, May 14, 1963. For an interesting discussion of urban riots see Capeci and Wilkerson, *Layered Violence*.

4. *NYT*, May 12–13, 1963.

5. Silberman, *Crisis in Black and White*, p. 67; *NYT*, May 13, 1963, p. 24; *BW*, May 15, 1963; Hampton and Fayer, *Voices of Freedom*, pp. 137–38; *Montgomery Advertiser*, May 13, 1963; *Newsweek*, May 20, 1963. Rev. Abraham Woods recalled: "What I saw at the motel was the forerunner of what happened. Later it was 'Burn, baby, burn and Carmichael. That came later and I saw it coming"; Quoted in Raines, *My Soul Is Rested*, p. 165.

6. *NYT*, May 13, 1963; *BP-H*, May 14, 1963; *BW*, May 15, 1963. See also the reference to state forces arrayed under Lingo and the message: "Tell Mr. Kennedy go to Birmingham on stand-by," in "Notes of Floyd Mann to A. G.," May 1963, General Correspondence, Civil Rights, Birmingham, RFK Papers.

7. General Correspondence, Civil Rights, Birmingham, May 9–12, 1963, RFK Papers (the president's statement of May 12, 1963); Raines, *My Soul Is Rested*, pp. 176–79, and *NYT*, May 12, 1963, p. 53 (Smyer); *BN*, May 13, 1963 (Boutwell).

8. *BN*, May 13, 1963.

9. Malcolm X argued that a black rebellion forced Kennedy to respond. In "Message to the Grass Roots," he said: "Birmingham had exploded, and the Negroes in Birmingham—remember, they also exploded. They began to stab the crackers in the back and bust them up 'side their head—yes, they did. That's when Kennedy sent in the troops, down in Birmingham. After that, Kennedy got on the television and said 'this is a moral issue.' That's when he said he was going to put out a civil-rights bill. And when he mentioned civil-rights bill and the Southern crackers started talking

390

about how they were going to boycott or filibuster it, then the Negroes started talking—about what? That they were going to march on Washington." Quoted in Carson, *The Eyes on the Prize Civil Rights Reader*, p. 258; see also Cotman, *Birmingham, JFK*, pp. 69–95, and *NYT*, May 14, 1963, p. 26. President George Washington established the precedent during the Whiskey Rebellion of 1794. Following Eisenhower at Little Rock in 1957, Kennedy cited the code during the Freedom Ride riot at Montgomery in 1961 and at Ole Miss in 1962.

10. "Alabama Notebook," box 11, Personal Correspondence, RFK Papers. Winton M. Blount gave Kennedy the names of 375 corporate heads in Alabama; see Brauer, *John F. Kennedy*, p. 256. For example, in 1963 the directors and officers of First National Bank included John C. Persons, CEO; Thomas W. Martin, CEO Alabama Power; Crawford Johnson Jr., CEO of Coca-Cola; C. Pratt Rather, CEO of Southern National Gas; Clarence P. Hanson Jr., publisher of the *Birmingham News*; Edward L. Norton, CEO of Royal Crown Cola; Donald Comer Jr., and Hugh M. Comer, owners of Avondale Mills; Charles W. Ireland of Vulcan Materials; Paschal G. Shook and Alfred M. Shook III of Shook and Fletcher Supply; David Roberts Jr., CEO of Brilliant Coal Co.; William M. Spencer III of Owen-Richards, Co.; Allen Rushton, CEO of Birmingham Ice and Cold Storage and attorney in Lange, Simpson and Somerville; William J. Rushton of Protective Life Insurance; William French Jr., CEO of Moore-Handley Hardware; Joseph H. Woodward II, CEO of Woodward Iron; Hugh Kaul, CEO of Kaul Lumber; Robert E. Garrett, CEO of U.S. Pipe and Foundry; and attorneys William J. Cabaniss and Forney Johnston. Of the sixteen directors in the late 1930s, ten men still served as principal directors in 1963. Woodward Iron and U.S. Pipe had replaced TCI, and cotton interests had declined in influence. William J. Rushton demonstrated the interlocking directorates, as he served on the boards of Protective Life, Moore-Handley, and Alabama Power and as a trustee of Southern Research Institute. Five other directors at Protective Life headed companies with direct links to the board at First National. In a June 6, 1963, memo to Robert Kennedy, William H. Orrid Jr. reported that 108 of the 375 corporations had been contacted and 80 CEOs said they would request that Wallace not stand in the schoolhouse door; see box 2, file 1, Marshall Papers, BPLDAM.

11. *NYT*, May 14–15, 1963. Marshall returned to Washington on May 17. See "Civil Rights Release," May 18, 1963, General Correspondence, Civil Rights, Birmingham, RFK Papers.

12. *BN* and *BP-H*, May 14, 1963.

13. *NYT*, May 14, 1963. During the mass meeting, officers ticketed parked cars outside the church; see Police Report, May 14, 1963, on ACMHR meeting of May 13, box 13, Connor Papers.

14. *BN*, May 14, 1963; Smyer statement on the accord, box 1, file 10, Marshall Papers, BPLDAM; "Memorandum," May 17, 1963, to Smyer, David Vann, W. C. Hamilton, and Marshall from Shuttlesworth, King, and Abernathy, box 1, file 10, on Rushton's resignation see "Notes of Winton M. Blount," box 2, file 1, Marshall Papers. Later Smyer said, "I'm still a segregationist but I hope I'm not a damn fool"; *BN*, May 17, 1963. For the names of the Senior Citizens see *BN*, May 16, 1963.

15. "Notes of Winton M. Blount," including the names of key industrial Wallace supporters, box 3, file 1, and "Memorandum" of John Martin to Burke Marshall, December 2, 1963, box 2, file 7 (on discriminated black labor at TCI and Hayes), Marshall Papers, BPLDAM; King, *Why We Can't Wait*, p. 113 (quotation). The Kennedy administration contacted Roger Blough; see Marshall interview by Lewis. The celebrated incident defined Kennedy's relationship with corporate America. Having received wage concessions from labor, Kennedy appealed to capital for price controls in an effort to check inflation. While appearing to support the administration, Blough increased steel prices in April 1962. U.S. Steel led the industry, and it seemed that other companies would follow suit. A week later, Blough backed down and Kennedy claimed victory. In some circles, the episode led to a loss of respect for the young chief executive, who was reported to have called businessmen "sons-of-bitches" and "bastards." See Schlesinger, *A Thousand Days*, pp. 634–40.

16. *BP-H*, May 31, 1963 (Spencer); *BN*, May 17, 1963 (Smyer). According to Blount, many of Birmingham's corporate elite had supported Wallace, including Elton B. Stephens of EBSCO Industries, Craig Smith of Avondale Mills, Hugh Daniel of Daniels Construction, and R. B. Garrett of U.S. Pipe. For a good analysis of Alabama during some of the Wallace years see Bass and DeVries, *The Transformation of Southern Politics*, pp. 57–86.

17. *NYT*, May 15, 1963, p. 1.

391

18. Hanes quoted in *NYT*, May 13, 1963, p. 24. The *Birmingham News* of May 17, 1963, described an "uneasy quiet." For an account of the unconstitutional federal surveillance of King see Garrow, *The FBI and . . . King*.

19. *BN*, May 16, 1963; *Montgomery Advertiser*, May 17, 1963; Telephone log, May 17, 1963, box 1, file 10, Marshall Papers, JFK Library; Kunstler, *Deep in My Heart*, pp. 193–94; *Time*, May 31, 1963 (quotation); *BN*, May 20, 1963. Further appeals to the board failed. A "Students" flier (in Connor Papers) called for a boycott of the schools on May 21, 1963. When David Vann learned of this, he contacted Andrew Young of the SCLC and complained that the movement had violated the accord. Young notified King, who returned to Birmingham and defused the situation at a mass meeting, where he asked all students to report to school as usual and those expelled to "stay home and study." See Police Report, May 21, 1963, on ACMHR meeting of May 20, Connor Papers.

20. The state supreme court ruled on May 23, 1963, in *Connor v. Boutwell, Southern Reporter* 153, 2d series, pp. 787–94. The law firm of former state senator James A. Simpson represented Connor in the appeal. While on the Public Service Commission, Connor suffered a stroke and former city commissioner James T. "Jabo" Waggoner acted on his behalf. See *BN*, January 12, 1965, December 7, 1966, and Raines, *My Soul Is Rested*, p. 181.

21. Marshall interview by Lewis, p. 107; *Newsweek*, May 27, 1963, p. 27; *BN*, May 26, 1963. Kennedy had traveled to Muscle Shoals for the thirtieth anniversary of the Tennessee Valley Authority, and he briefly met with Wallace on board a helicopter. Reflecting his paternalism and lack of comprehension regarding the race wage, the president asked the governor: if Alabamians could have Negroes serve them at their tables at home, why not let them serve white people in the stores? Wallace accurately observed that despite King, most Birmingham Negroes "behaved theirselves [*sic*] very well during the recent trouble"; *BN*, May 19, 1963, *BP-H*, May 17, 1963. See also Brauer, *John F. Kennedy*, p. 255.

22. "Press Conference USA," Voice of America, June 4, 1963, Attorney General Speeches, 1961–64, RFK Papers. The president had no idea what Wallace would do; see Marshall interview by Lewis, p. 107. At the time of Robert Kennedy's speech, the administration was busily drafting new civil rights legislation.

23. Frady, *Wallace*, pp. 169–71; Brauer, *John F. Kennedy*, pp. 257–64; *Montgomery Advertiser*, June 11–12, 1963; Levy, *Let Freedom Ring*, pp. 117–19 (the text of Kennedy's speech). On the president's speech see Marshall interview by Lewis, pp. 109–10. The two students who integrated the university six years after the aborted attempt by Autherine Lucy were Vivian Malone and James Hood. On the event see Carter, *The Politics of Rage*, pp. 133–55. For examples of the Kennedy administration's surveillance of the foreign press see "Reaction to Racial Tensions in Birmingham, Alabama," May 9–10, 15, 1963, collected by the U.S. Information Agency and located in Attorney General's General Correspondence, Civil Rights, Birmingham, box 10, RFK Papers.

24. Levy, *Let Freedom Ring*, pp. 117–19. Robert Kennedy argued that prior to Birmingham, race relations were of little concern to the majority of people: "Everybody looks back on it and thinks that everybody was aroused about this for the last three years, but what aroused people generally in the country and aroused the press was the Birmingham riots in May of 1963"; Kennedy interview by Martin. An analysis by the Associated Press in August said the same thing: "Birmingham triggered . . . [the] . . . administration's drive for new civil rights legislation." It quoted a White House official saying "This hasn't been the same kind of world since May." *BN*, August 18, 1963. Box 31 of the Marshall Papers (in JFK Library) is full of accounts describing demonstrations around the country. Morris, *Origins*, p. 274, lists 758 demonstrations in 186 cities resulting in 14,733 arrests. No sooner had Kennedy finished his speech than Byron de La Beckwith assassinated civil rights leader Medger Evers in Jackson, Miss.

25. Marshall interview by Lewis, pp. 102 (first quotation), 98 (second quotation); Graham, *The Civil Rights Era*, pp. 75–76.

26. Marshall interview by Lewis, pp. 103–5; Graham, *The Civil Rights Era*, p. 79; Whalen and Whalen, *The Longest Debate*. Robert Kennedy said the civil rights bill was designed to end demonstrations by providing a legal means for black protest. He emphasized, "I believe all laws

and court orders should be obeyed." "Answers to Questions on Civil Rights," Attorney General Speeches, 1961–64, RFK Papers.

27. Fairclough, *To Redeem the Soul*, pp. 133–35; Garrow, *Protest At Selma*, p. 144. Fairclough is correct in taking issue with Garrow's assumption that "there was no widespread national outcry, no vocal reaction by the nation's clergy, and no immediate move by the administration to propose salutary legislation." Indeed, there was a "national outcry" and Kennedy responded with "salutary legislation." Garrow's tight focus on the Congress is misleading but understandable considering his attention to Selma, an argument similarly followed by Colburn (*Racial Change and Community Crisis*) in regard to movement pressure for the Civil Rights Act of 1964. The key here is the historical context of race reform. Kennedy's civil rights bill—even as proposed legislation—signified a turning point in the governmental policy of the executive branch. It also opened the system to women. See Graham, *The Civil Rights Era*, pp. 74–83. Kennedy arranged the meeting to stop the March on Washington; see Schlesinger, *A Thousand Days*, p. 971. Raines (*My Soul Is Rested*, pp. 175–76) quotes Shuttlesworth and adds: "'But for Birmingham,' I think that oughta be remembered. That's a good title."

28. Police Report, May 21, 1963, on ACMHR meeting of May 19, Connor Papers.

29. "Memo" of E. L. Holland to Burke Marshall, June 19, 1963, box 1, file 5, Marshall Papers. Boutwell was not too busy, for he had found time to thank the president of San-O-Rent for furnishing the city with rental Port-O-Johns for policemen to use during the disturbances; see Boutwell to Luke Whittle, June 20, 1963, box 31, file 4, Boutwell Papers, BPLDAM.

30. Jamie Moore to Commanding Officer, Defense Surplus Sales Office, June 4, 1963, box 31, file 5, Boutwell Papers; Birmingham Police Department memos on Gordon (June 28), Patterson (July 6), and Scott (August 4), 1963. Although officers brutalized white people—as when they shot but did not kill sixteen-year-old Jessie J. Carroll on October 11, 1963—such actions were unusual and resulted in detailed explanations, as when the detective concluded in the above incident that "in the opinion of the witnesses, the officers did all they could to subdue the defendant before they were forced to shoot him"; box 31, file 4, Boutwell Papers. Black people did not warrant as thorough an investigation. Few white people were ever shot by policemen.

31. Walker to Michael Potoker, June 7, and Walker to Beatrice Kinne, June 18, box 33, file 18, Walker to Alfred N. Willie, July 29, 1963, box 33, file 19, SCLC Papers. With the letters, Walker or King enclosed a copy of the "Letter from Birmingham Jail." On donations see also L. H. Pitts to Shuttlesworth, June 11, 1963, box 1, file 13, SCLC Papers.

32. Thomas Kilgore Jr. to Martin Luther King (May 14, 1963), Gladys Harrington to Fred L. Shuttlesworth (May 25, 1963), and Joel Williams to King (May 17, 1963), file 19; Edward A. Hailes to King (May 24, 1963) and James E. Cook Jr. to King (May 29, 1963), file 15—all in box 63, SCLC Papers.

33. Thomas G. Neusom to Martin Luther King, June 1, 1963, file 19, and Ralph David Abernathy to Executive Board of SCLC, file 20, box 63, SCLC Papers.

34. "Minutes of Staff Conference at Dorchester," September 5–7, 1963, box 153, file 21, SCLC Papers.

35. Shuttlesworth to W. E. Shortridge, June 1, 1963, box 3, Shuttlesworth Papers, King Center; Shuttlesworth interview, November 9, 1989; Police Report, May 17, 1963, on ACMHR meeting of May 14, Connor Papers; Raines, *My Soul Is Rested*, p. 175.

36. Vann, "Speech," Duard LeGrand Conference, pp. 36–37; Boutwell to "My Fellow Citizens" (July 16, 1963) and "Report of the Council Committee on Community Affairs" (May 28, 1963), box 1, file 13, Marshall Papers, BPLDAM (for a list of the members on the CAC see box 2, file 5); L. H. Pitts to "Negro Membership of the Community Affairs Committee," July 25, 1963, box 1, file 9, King Papers, ATL. The CAC viewed economic growth as key to solving social problems, but it acted defensively, charging the public relations committee to "present a fair and undistorted picture of our city" and calling the city's racial problems "distorted and exaggerated because of a lack of communication and incomplete information." It referred positively to the former paternalistic race relations yet suggested that the committee's "constant goal must be to reduce both the immediate and the underlying problems in order that all citizens of the city may have fair

393

opportunities, equal treatment before the law, and a fair enjoyment of municipal facilities and services." With public schools, it hoped to "devise alternative recommendations" to prevent school desegregation, and it recognized "the problems of chronic unemployment" and the need for "immediate and long range training programs to reduce our unemployment and relief rolls and to guarantee that we will always have a trained pool of skilled and semi-skilled craftsmen necessary to maintain healthy industrial growth." In short, the CAC presented the most comprehensive evaluation of Birmingham's problems in years, but the civic leadership failed to seriously undertake the recommended reforms.

37. Birmingham repealed its segregation ordinances on July 23, 1963. Vann, "Speech," Duard LeGrand Conference, pp. 37–38. Vann recalled, "As we went through the program, we had calls from Eastwood Mall and Five Points West asking: 'Please integrate us too, while we can do it as part of a supervised program.'" Reports of Calvin W. Woods, July 31, August 1, 8, 1963, box 1, file 9, King Papers, ATL. Local managers informed national headquarters of the transition; see Ira C. Kepford to Burke Marshall, August 12, 1963, box 1, file 6, Marshall Papers, BPLDAM. Brauer (*John F. Kennedy*, p. 277) cites Justice Department figures that found 177 cities in the South and border states showing some racial progress, with 22 more on the way.

38. Carson, *In Struggle*, pp. 91–95; Coretta Scott King, *My Life with Martin Luther King*, p. 238 (quotation); Garrow, *Bearing The Cross*, pp. 280–86. Progressive elements of the corporate structure supported the March, including Currier, who gave nearly $1 million to the foundation established to direct the event. Malcolm X called the event the "farce on Washington"; quoted in Marable, *Race, Reform, and Rebellion*, p. 81.

39. The text of "I Have A Dream" and Coretta Scott King's quotation are in Washington, *A Testament of Hope*, pp. 217–20. On Martin Luther King as an image see Lentz, *Symbols*. As Birmingham native Diane McWhorter noted, henceforth Birmingham became "the national warehouse for the white man's burden"; quoted in *Nation*, October 8, 1990, p. 379.

40. Desegregation occurred on September 3 in several cities around the South, including Memphis, Charleston, and Baton Rouge. Only in Alabama did the nation find such defiance. On Wallace's intervention in Tuskegee see Norrell, *Reaping The Whirlwind*. The other cities were Mobile and Huntsville. Vigilantes bombed Shores's house on August 21 and September 4, 1963, and they firebombed A. G. Gaston's house on September 8; see box 9, file 10, Police Surveillance Papers, BPLDAM. Although many white people opposed school desegregation, others—such as Rev. Dr. Denson N. Franklin of First Methodist and Councilwoman Nina Miglionico—rejected the governor's defiance and worked to keep the schools open; see *BN*, August 9, 1963. In protest of school desegregation, parades of white people with children marched; see the preliminary Royall-Blaik report, box 3, file 1, Marshall Papers, BPLDAM. On the Klan see file 169-7-5-3-5, Anti-Defamation League Papers, BPLDAM; "Meeting of the Jefferson County Citizens' Council" (September 7, 1963), "Memorandum" (November 5, 1963), and "Citizens Council Meeting" (November 2, 1963), box 4, file 8, Police Surveillance Papers. Already 144 school districts across the South had peacefully desegregated. See Brauer, *John F. Kennedy*, pp. 293–97; see also *United States v. Jefferson County Board of Education*, which clarified *Brown* by ordering compulsory integration to achieve school desegregation, hence ruling unconstitutional resistance plans such as Boutwell's freedom of choice amendment. The Supreme Court upheld compulsory integration in *Green v. School Board of New Kent County, Virginia*. Chambliss quoted in Sikora, *Until Justice Rolls Down*, p. 140; the niece at that time was Elizabeth Cobbs, but later she underwent a sex change and became known as "Pete" Smith. *Atlanta Constitution*, November 8, 1994. See also the memoir by Petric Justice Smith, *Long Time Coming*.

41. On the bombing see Sikora, *Until Justice Rolls Down*. The bombing temporarily united black leadership as Gaston, Pitts, and Ware joined King and Shuttlesworth in requesting a meeting with Robert Kennedy to discuss the "tragedy" and the "extreme tension that grips the city." As companies canceled the insurance on black churches, schools, and houses after the bombing, the SCLC initiated a fund-raising campaign to rebuild Sixteenth Street. The church reopened in 1964 with a beautiful stained glass window of a crucified black Christ donated by the people of Wales. See September 16 telegram and John J. Drew to Burke Marshall, September 20, 1963, box 1, file 6,

Marshall Papers, BPLDAM; John H. Cross to M. L. King, October 14, 1963, box 1, file 10, King Papers, ATL; and King to Cross, December 20, 1963, box 3, file 28, SCLC Papers. Unfortunately, the graves of three of the bombing victims fell into serious disrepair for a number of years until new headstones were placed in 1990; see BW, July 18–22, 1990, and BN and Atlanta Constitution, September 16, 1990. By 1995 the graveyard was again in a state of neglect; see Atlanta Journal Constitution, September 29, 1995. Twenty-two people were injured by the blast, and the Birmingham News (September 10, 1988) carried a story on some of the survivors. Jamie Moore to Wallace, September 15, 1963, box 31, file 4, Boutwell Papers.

42. Police department memo on shooting of Johnny Robinson, September 15, 1963, box 8, file 40, Police Surveillance Papers; Washington Evening Star, September 21, 1963; Newsweek, September 30, 1963.

43. Morgan, A Time To Speak. Some white residents blamed the Young Men's Business Club—a liberal forum directed by the young progressives—for the secret negotiations that had ended the demonstrations; see BP-H, June 11, 1963. Most scholars of Birmingham during this period follow the same logic; see Corley, "The Quest for Racial Harmony," and LaMonte, "Politics and Welfare in Birmingham." Because of his moderate racial views, Vann was forced to resign from his law firm (see NYT, September 22, 1963), but he was elected mayor in 1975. Tragically, Smith died young after a stroke in 1973; BP-H, July 26, 1973. Morgan took a position with the American Civil Liberties Union. See Raines, My Soul Is Rested, pp. 198–202; Morgan stated (p. 200): "I was of the belief then and I am of the belief now that that bombing was as natural an event in the history of that city . . . as any other event in American history."

44. Morgan, A Times To Speak, p. 2 (quotations). Information on the bombing may be found in box 9, file 12, Police Surveillance Papers. At one time Bull Connor had kept Chambliss on the city payroll but was forced to dismiss him after his arrest for flogging integrationists. By 1963 Chambliss lived in a formerly all-white neighborhood mostly occupied by African Americans; see Sikora, Until Justice Rolls Down, pp. 26–27, 78, 80, 114, and Brauer, John F. Kennedy, pp. 296–97; see also Rowe, My Undercover Years, pp. 100–101. Chambliss maintained his innocence; see BN, April 18, 1978.   395

45. Shuttlesworth also denounced the biracial committee as a "fraud" and called for a massive march on Montgomery; see Newsweek, September 30, 1963, p. 23, and Montgomery Advertiser, September 17–18, 1963; NYT, September 18, 1963; ministers' memo to Robert F. Kennedy, September 19, 1963, box 1, file 11, Marshall Papers, BPLDAM; Brauer, John F. Kennedy, pp. 295–99; copies of preliminary Royall-Blaik reports and other related materials, in box 3, file 1, Marshall Papers, BPLDAM. See also Blaik interview, which explains why Robert Kennedy initially wanted Gen. Douglas MacArthur to head the investigation.

46. Shuttlesworth statement to Royall and Blaik, October 2, 1963, box 50, file 27, SCLC Papers.

47. Other members of the Jefferson County Progressive Democratic Council included attorneys Arthur Shores and Peter A. Hall and editor Emory O. Jackson. Orzell Billingsley Jr. to Robert Kennedy, October 5, 1963, with October 1 "Statement Addressed to the Mayor," and Burke Marshall to Billingsley, October 9, 1963, box 1, file 7, Marshall Papers, BPLDAM. A similar bourgeois group with many of the same members headed by W. C. Patton—the Alabama State Coordinating Association for Registration and Voting—sought federal assistance to force entrance into the political system in its effort to desegregate the Democratic Party. See "Agenda of the ASCARV," n.d. [1963], box 1, file 10, Marshall Papers, BPLDAM. Several members of the traditional Negro leadership class worried about matters other than Birmingham's racial turmoil. Shores and Billingsley were concerned with collecting $15,000 from the SCLC for legal services rendered during the demonstrations. See Shores to Shuttlesworth, October 18, 1963, box 3, Shuttlesworth Papers. Gaston, Pitts, and Shores would soon capitalize a new "nondiscriminatory" bank—the American National Bank—in an effort to lure federal deposits away from white banks that discriminated. See "Script for Voice of America," April 15, 1964, box 1, file 8, and L. S. Gaillard to Robert F. Kennedy (May 21, 1964), Oscar Hyde to Michael Monroney (July 22, 1964), and Monroney to Hyde (July 27, 1964), box 1, file 9, Marshall Papers, BPLDAM; J. L. Ware to Boutwell, September 28, 1963, box 1, file 9, King Papers, ATL. On Oliver see minutes, Alabama

Advisory Committee, May 22, 1963, box 1, file 10, Marshall Papers, BPLDAM. Also on Ware see *BN*, August 28, 1972. On the Inter-Citizens Committee see MacNair, "Social Distance," p. 149; and "Document No. 11," box 1, file 5, and "Documents No. 33–40," box 1, file 7, King Papers, ATL.

48. "Statement of King" and "Statement of Gaston and Shores," September 30, 1963, box 3, Shuttlesworth Papers.

49. Shuttlesworth to Boutwell, October 4, 1963, ibid.; *BN*, October 20, 1963. Other members of the black elite who signed included Dr. and Mrs. J. T. Montgomery, Bishop E. P. Murchison, John J. and Addine Drew, W. C. Patton, Bernice Johnson, attorneys Shores, Billingsley, Peter A. Hall, and Demetrius C. Newton, and Reverends Harold D. Long and John H. Cross. From the movement were Reverends Abraham Woods Jr., Edward Gardner, Joseph Ellwanger (a white Lutheran), Calvin Woods, and N. H. Smith, and civic leaders Frank Dukes, Thomas E. Wrenn, and James Armstrong.

50. *BP-H*, October 22, 24, 1963; petitions, box 12, file 43, Boutwell Papers; Abe Berkowitz to Burke Marshall, October 22, 1963, box 1, file 7, Marshall Papers, BPLDAM. A preliminary Royall-Blaik report referred to the ACMHR-SCLC ultimatum and similar threats of September 27, October 8, 18, 22, 1963, and noted that the city council and white power structure refused to act under such conditions; box 3, file 1, Marshall Papers, BPLDAM. Alabama attorney general Richmond Flowers issued a stern warning to King and Shuttlesworth in response to "constant threats and attempted coercion of the City Council to meet immediate demands of some publicity-seeking, money-raising outside agitators working with a few local trouble makers who seek to continue unrest in Birmingham so that the proper officials and responsible and respected local Negro leadership cannot work out their differences in order for Birmingham to prosper in peace and harmony and grow under law and order"; *BN*, October 24, 1963. See King, *Why We Can't Wait*, pp. 112–15.

51. *BP-H*, October 24, 1963; *BN*, July 7, 1964; Royall and Blaik "Preliminary Report," n.d. [1963], box 3, file 1, Boutwell to Pitts, April 24, 1964, box 1, file 8, and Marshall to Lou Oberdorfer (comments on bug by committee member Rabbi Milton Grafman), October 28, 1963, box 1, file 11, Marshall Papers, BPLDAM; LaMonte, "Politics and Welfare in Birmingham," pp. 326–30; Jim Murray, "Interracial Communication in Birmingham." Townsend later suggested that the "moral decay" in America began in Birmingham in 1963, when the movement "led to certain people believing they could take the law in their own hands when they chose . . . that they could knock a policeman in the head . . . that they could break windows, loot and steal and nothing would be done about it." Quoted in coverage of Townsend's speech before the FBI, vol. 8, p. 51, Civil Rights Scrapbooks, BPLDAM.

52. The Supreme Court ruled that Ollie's Barbecue was in violation of the Civil Rights Act of 1964 by refusing to serve black people in *Katzenbach v. McClung*, a case combined with *Heart of Atlanta Motel, Inc. v. United States* to enforce the public accommodations section of the legislation. On Shuttlesworth's attempts to renew demonstrations see Shuttlesworth to King (November 7, 1963), Shuttlesworth to Pitts and Shuttlesworth to Ware (December 11, 1963), and Shuttlesworth to King (December 12, 1963), box 22, file 11, King Papers, ATL. See also David Vann to Louis Oberdorfer, December 11, 1963, box 1, file 8, and "Memorandum," December 17, 1963, box 1, file 11, Marshall Papers, BPLDAM; "Points for Progress," box 1, file 7, King Papers, ATL. On the 1964 act see *BN*, July 4, 1964; on Ollie's see *BP-H*, September 24, October 1, 1964, and *BN*, August 20, September 1, December 17, 1964. The October 27 *BN* said the Exchange Security Bank headed the defense fund drive for Ollie's, a reflection of the Big Mules defense of segregation, for directors of the bank included industrialist Alfred M. Shook, Judge Seybourn H. Lynne, and attorneys R. H. Lange and former state senator James A. Simpson of the old-guard law firm of Lange, Simpson, Robinson, and Somerville. Like the futile Mary Monk case of 1950, the Ollie's case went down to defeat. When the law went into effect, Boutwell announced: "However distasteful the Act is to many who are affected by it, and who regard it as unjust and unconstitutional, nonetheless the testing of its provisions, without significant disorder thus far, demonstrates clearly the common sense and dedication to law and order of our citizens, white and Negro." "Statement," July 3, 1964, box 39, file 25, Boutwell Papers. According to the *Birmingham News* (January 5, 1970), one of the

396

last wishes of the black soldier, Bill Terry, was to "be buried in the [white] cemetery across the street from his boyhood home." His estate won the legal battle in federal court. A thousand people attended his funeral, where the priest said, "When he had done his best for his country and had no more to give, his country was doing its worst for him." The event is fictionalized in John Logue's novel, *Boats Across the Current*. See also "People in Motion," box 1, Shuttlesworth Papers. On the resumption of demonstrations by the ACMHR see *BN*, March 20, 1964, Shuttlesworth to Pitts (May 20, 1964), Pitts to Shuttlesworth (May 21, 1964), and Shuttlesworth to King (May 29, 1964), box 22, file 12, King Papers, ATL; Kuhn, Joye, and West, *Living Atlanta*, pp. 341–45. Birmingham hired its first black policeman, Leroy Stover, in March 1966, ten years after the city had hired women police officers.

53. Denying discrimination in its mills, U.S. Steel fought every inch of the way during the class action suits filed by black lawyers against the Fairfield works. See *BP-H*, February 15, 1967, and *BN*, December 16, 1970, June 18, July 9, October 12, December 9, 1972. U.S. District Court judge Sam Pointer ruled against U.S. Steel on May 2, 1973. On other industries in Birmingham forced to comply see *BN*, June 24, August 13, 1973; on the EPA and U.S. Steel, see *BP-H*, June 18, 1976, *BN*, July 1, 1976, March 30, 1978, and Slogan, "The Day They Shut Down Birmingham"; on U.S. Steel's plant closings, see *BN*, August 15, 19, 1979, May 17, 1980, and *BP-H*, September 19, November 28, 1979, June 11, 1980; on the regional labor market and race wage see Wright, *Old South, New South*, and Stein, "Southern Workers in National Unions," pp. 201–22. Stein notes that not until 1964 did TCI end the race wage.

54. "For Immediate Release," January 3, 1965, box 1, file 5, King Papers, ATL; "People In Motion," box 1, Shuttlesworth Papers; Richard H. King, *Civil Rights and the Idea of Freedom*.

55. As King explained, "a riot is the language of the unheard." On the 1979 killing of Carter and Arrington's early political career see Franklin, *Back To Birmingham*.

56. U.S. Bureau of the Census, *Eighteenth Census*, General Characteristics of the Population, p. 15; *Nineteenth Census*, Race by Sex, for Areas and Places, table 23, p. 2–60; *Twentieth Census*, Persons by Race, table 15, p. 2–12. The inverse occurred in Jefferson County (Birmingham's SMSA) as the population increased from 415,035 white and 219,542 black residents in 1960 to 520,636 white and 217,447 black residents in 1970 and 603,890 white and 239,673 black residents in 1980.

57. "Birmingham," *Black Enterprise*, pp. 40–42; "Middle Class Blacks: Making It in America," *Time*, June 17, 1974. A member of the state and county Democratic executive committees, Davis, CEO of the Protective Industrial Insurance Co., worried about his political potential: "When you come from a middle-class bag, it's not easy to convince the masses that you're an all-right dude." On the decline of the black business district see Franklin D. Wilson, "The Ecology of a Black Business District," pp. 353–75.

58. The JCCEO formed in 1965. Holley, "Employment Practices Relating to the Hard-Core Jobless," statistics from pp. 21–22.

59. Wright, "Economic Consequences of the Southern Protest Movement," pp. 178–81; Kelley, *Race Rebels*, pp. 77–100.

60. U.S. Bureau of the Census, *Twentieth Census*, vol. 1, Characteristics of the Population, Alabama, pt. 2, tables 15, pp. 121–22, 135.

61. Ibid., tables 131, 137; Population by Census Tracts, tables P-7, P-11. The statistics are even more striking when listed by "persons," on average raising the figure by three to five percentage points.

62. U.S. Bureau of the Census, *Twenty-first Census*, Population and Housing, Summary, Social, Economic, and Housing Characteristics, Alabama, tables 5, 9, 19; General Population Characteristics, Alabama, table 6. Statistics on employment and census tracts are not yet available; the number of poor whites in metropolitan Birmingham increased during the 1980s. The white union stronghold of Gardendale registered unemployment figures of 20.5 percent. Bessemer, with 11.3 percent unemployment and 26 percent of all families living below the poverty level, Brighton, with 15.2 percent unemployment and 21 percent of families living below the poverty level, and Libscomb, with 12.7 percent unemployment and 16.4 percent of families living below the poverty

level demonstrated the lasting effects of the collapse of the steel industry in the district. Reinhart, "Racial Separation during the 1970s," pp. 1255–62. The authors concluded, "Birmingham's blacks were more separated from whites in 1977 than they were in 1970."

Epilogue

1. Birmingham had held the distinction of murder capital of the country in 1931, and it appeared headed that way again by the end of 1990. The city's homicide rate conservatively estimated by the FBI had climbed for the second year in a row with 125 murders, an increase of 25 percent. In general, violent crime in Birmingham rose 13.7 percent. See *BP-H*, March 26, 1991. On the JCCEO scandal see *BN*, September 11, 13, 16, October 4, 10, 15, 1990; on public housing, October 21, 1990; on gangs, November 20, 1990; and on the white power structure and its "Birmingham Plan," July 29–31, 1990. For a similar analysis of the inner-city black poor see the reports of the Southern Center for Studies in Public Policy edited by Bob Holmes, *The Status of Black Atlanta* and *The Status of Black Atlanta 1994* (Atlanta, Ga.: Clark Atlanta University, 1993, 1994).

2. On nihilism among black youth see *Atlanta Constitution*, April 10, 1993, "Why Are Kids Killing Kids?" In one poll more than 94 percent of the black respondents suggested that the NAACP and SCLC had "lost touch with problems blacks face"; see *Atlanta Journal*, February 24, 1992. The scandals in both organizations during the 1990s underscore the point. On Arrington's theatrics see *Time*, February 3, 1992.

3. Hall Thompson headed Thompson Tractor Co.; a few years earlier he had waged an unsuccessful fight to prevent the desegregation of Rotary Club. Initiation fees at Shoal Creek were $35,000. See Diane McWhorter, "The White Man's Last Stand," *Nation*, October 8, 1990, pp. 379–90; *BN*, July 1, 1990; *BP-H*, June 20–22, 29, 1990. In its coverage, the *Post-Herald* accurately presented the Shoal Creek incident, whereas the *News* first ignored and then played down the affair. When awarding Pulitzer Prizes in 1991, the committee overlooked Mazzolini's investigative reporting that created the Shoal Creek incident and instead recognized the editorial writers of the *Birmingham News* for a series on "What They Won't Tell You About Your Taxes" that ran on August 26–September 2, 1990. What the *News* did not tell its readers was that for years its own editorial policies had defended "Alabama's unfair, inadequate and growth-stifling tax system," as publisher Victor H. Hanson II accurately described it in an introduction to a booklet by the same title published by the *News*. A concurrent art exhibit in the main branch of the Birmingham Public Library illustrated the point of Shoal Creek in a different way. The work of two middle-class white women—members of the over-the-mountain Bluff Park Arts League—displayed their paintings. Through brightly colored still lifes, one artist captured the rich warmth of brocade fabrics and plush rugs, golden objets d'art, and expensive decor, painted settings as seen in *Southern Accents* or *Architectural Digest*, wealth confined and to be envied, secure and introverted. The other woman approached the 1980s from the opposite perspective. Her work featured lean black wolves with eyes glaring, stalking empty identifiable city streets in packs.

4. *BN*, July 1, 25–27, 1990. The vicious criticism of the white power structure and the need for black political unity led Arrington into a game of racial politics that Bull Connor would have recognized. Like other black mayors, he had his troubles. After a bitter reelection campaign in 1991, Arrington, like the Bourbon Democrats a century before, swiftly moved to restore black political orthodoxy through the building of a Civil Rights Institute and other memorials to the movement.

5. *BP-H*, August 1, 1990; *Birmingham Times*, August 9, 1990. The Augusta National, one of the most exclusive clubs in the world, which counted among its members the chairmen of many leading blue-chip corporations such as IBM, quickly and quietly desegregated following Shoal Creek. On Willie a year later see *Atlanta Journal-Constitution*, November 27, 1994.

6. Black and Black, *Politics and Society in the South*, pp. 75–171. The Blacks follow this logic by describing African American assaults on the "outer color line," the "intermediate color line," and the "innermost color line" where people experience interracial "intimacy." The irony of the "perpetual promise" was apparently lost on the *Birmingham News* (July 29, 1990), which used the phrase to title a series on economic growth as the cure to social ills.

398

Manuscript and Archival Material

Alabama
Birmingham
  Birmingham Public Library
    Department of Archives and Manuscripts
      Anti-Defamation League Papers
      Albert Boutwell Papers
      Civil Rights Scrapbooks
      T. Eugene "Bull" Connor Papers
      W. Cooper Green Papers
      James A. Head Papers
      Emory O. Jackson Papers
      Jefferson County Coordinating Council of Social Forces Papers
      James W. "Jimmie" Jones Papers
      Burke Marshall Papers (copies; originals in JFK Library)
      James W. "Jimmy" Morgan Papers
      Roberta Morgan Papers
      NAACP Papers (Birmingham Branch file; microfilm)
      National [American] States' Rights Association Papers
      National Urban League Papers (Birmingham Branch file; microfilm)
      Police Surveillance Papers
      Southern Regional Council Papers (copies; originals in Atlanta)
      David Vann Papers
      Warden's Docket, Avenue F Prison
      Zukoski Committee Papers
    Tutwiler Collection of Southern History
      "Citizen's Councils" Vertical Files
      "Elections: Birmingham" Vertical File
      "Employment of Minorities in Birmingham" Vertical File
      "Gaston, Arthur George" Vertical File
      "Hayes International Aircraft Corporation" Vertical File
      "Ku Klux Klan" Vertical File

"Ku Klux Klan Mahem Case of 1957" Vertical File
"Methodist Churches, Birmingham, Highlands" Vertical File
"National Association for the Advancement of Colored People" Vertical File
"Pitts, Lucius Holsey" Vertical File
Report of the Citizens' Committee on the Birmingham Police Department, February 19, 1952
"Simpson, James Alexander" Vertical File
Smith, Howard K. "Who Speaks for Birmingham?" Transcript of *CBS Reports* broadcast, May 18, 1961
"Smyer, Sidney W., Sr." Vertical File
Southern Institute of Management, comp., *Birmingham Metropolitan Audit*, 1960
Tarlton, James. "Birmingham Jail." Lyrics.
"United States Steel Corporation" Vertical File
Samford University Archives
William David Powell, "James Alexander Simpson and His Civil Service Law," n.d.
Montgomery
Alabama Department of Archives and History
Frank Murry Dixon Papers
James Alexander Simpson Papers

Georgia
Atlanta
Atlanta Chamber of Commerce Records, Chamber Office
Martin Luther King Jr. Center for Nonviolent Social Change, Inc., Archives
James Armstrong Sr. Papers
Martin Luther King Jr. Papers
Fred L. Shuttlesworth Papers
Southern Christian Leadership Conference Papers
Student Nonviolent Coordinating Committee Papers
Robert W. Woodruff Library, Emory University
William Berry Hartsfield Papers

Massachusetts
Boston
John Fitzgerald Kennedy Library
John F. Kennedy Papers
Robert F. Kennedy Papers
Burke Marshall Papers
Special Collections Department, Mugar Library, Boston University
Martin Luther King Jr. Papers
Cambridge
Schlesinger Library, Radcliffe College, Harvard University
Virginia Foster Durr Papers

Government Documents

Alabama Official and Statistical Register. Montgomery: State of Alabama Department of Archives and History, 1927, 1935, 1943, 1947, 1951, 1959.
The General Code of the City of Birmingham, Alabama. Charlottesville, Va.: The Michie Co., 1944.
National Emergency Council. *The Report to the President on the Economic Conditions of the South*. Washington, D.C.: GPO, 1938.

State Legislators, Recapitulation Sheet. Democratic Primary Election, June 2, 1942. Jefferson County Courthouse, Office of Probate Court.
——. Democratic Primary Election, May 5, 1953. City Clerk's Office, City Hall, Birmingham.
——. Democratic Primary Election, May 7, 1957. City Clerk's Office, City Hall, Birmingham.
——. Democratic Primary Election Runoff, June 4, 1957. City Clerk's Office, City Hall, Birmingham.
——. Referendum, November 6, 1962. City Clerk's Office, City Hall, Birmingham.
——. Special Municipal Election, March 5, 1963. City Clerk's Office, City Hall, Birmingham.
U.S. Bureau of the Census. *Fifteenth Census of the United States*, 1930.
——. *Sixteenth Census of the United States*, 1940.
——. *Seventeenth Census of the United States*, 1950.
——. *Eighteenth Census of the United States*, 1960.
——. *Nineteenth Census of the United States*, 1970.
——. *Twentieth Census of the United States*, 1980.
——. *Twenty-first Census of the United States*, 1990.

Court Cases

Boynton v. Commonwealth of Virginia, 364 U.S. 454 (1960)
Brown v. Board of Education, 347 U.S. 483 (1954)
Brown v. Board of Education, 349 U.S. 294 (1955)
Buchanan v. Warley, 245 U.S. 60 (1917)
City of Birmingham v. Monk, 185 F2d 859, 341 U.S. 940 (1950)
Connor v. State. 153 So. 2d 787 (1963)
Green v. School Board of New Kent County, Virginia, 391 U.S. 490 (1968)
Heart of Atlanta Motel, Inc. v. United States, 397 U.S. 241 (1964)
Katzenbach v. McClung, 379 U.S. 294 (1964)
Matthews v. City of Birmingham, no. 28-6046, N.D. Ala. (1947)
Morgan v. Virginia, 328 U.S. 373 (1946)
New York Times v. Sullivan, 376 U.S. 254 (1964)
Reid v. City of Birmingham, 274 Ala. 629 (1963)
Shuttlesworth v. Birmingham, 394 U.S. 147 (1969)
Sims v. Frink, 208 F. Supp. 431 (1962)
Steele v. Louisville and Nashville Railroad Company et al., 323 U.S. 192 (1944)
United States v. Jefferson County Board of Education, 372 F2d 836 (5th Cir, 1966)
Walker v. City of Birmingham, 388 U.S. 307 (1967)

Memoirs

Abernathy, Ralph David. *And the Walls Came Tumbling Down: An Autobiography*. New York: Harper and Row, 1989.
Allen, Ivan, Jr., and Paul Hemphill. *Mayor: Notes on the Sixties*. New York: Simon and Schuster, 1971.
Anderson, William G. "Reflections on the Origins of the Albany Movement." *Journal of Southwest Georgia History* 9 (Fall 1994): 1–14.
Cooper, Jerome A. " 'Segregating Together': Memories of a Birmingham Labor Lawyer." Edited by C. Roger Nance. Manuscript, Birmingham Public Library, Department of Archives and History.
Dorman, Michael. *We Shall Overcome*. New York: Delacorte Press, 1964.
Durr, Virginia Foster. *Outside the Magic Circle: The Autobiography of Virginia Foster Durr*. Edited by Hollinger F. Barnard. Tuscaloosa: University of Alabama Press, 1986.
Edmonds, Henry M. *A Parson's Notebook*. Birmingham: Birmingham Publishing Co., 1961.

Gaston, A. G. *Green Power: The Successful Way of A. G. Gaston.* Birmingham: Southern University Press, 1968.

Gregory, Dick, and Robert Lipsyte. *Nigger: An Autobiography.* New York: Pocket Books, Inc., 1965.

Grooms, H. H. "Segregation, Desegregation, Integration, Resegregation." 1979. Tutwiler Collection of Southern History, Birmingham Public Library, Department of Archives and History.

Guthman, Edwin. *We Band of Brothers.* New York: Harper and Row, 1964.

Herndon, Angelo. *Let Me Live.* New York: Random House, 1937.

Hudson, Hosea. *Black Worker in the Deep South.* New York: 1972.

King, Coretta Scott. *My Life with Martin Luther King, Jr.* New York: Holt, Rinehart and Winston, 1969.

King, Martin Luther, Jr. *Stride Toward Freedom: The Montgomery Story.* New York: Harper and Row, 1958.

——. *Why We Can't Wait.* New York: Signet Books, 1964.

King, Martin Luther, Sr., with Clayton Riley. *Daddy King: An Autobiography.* New York: Morrow, 1980.

Kunstler, William. *Deep in My Heart.* New York: Morrow, 1966.

Lyon, Danny. *Memories of the Southern Civil Rights Movement.* Chapel Hill: University of North Carolina Press, 1992.

Marshall, Burke. *Federalism and Civil Rights.* New York: Columbia University Press, 1964.

Moore, Charles. *Powerful Days: The Civil Rights Photography of Charles Moore.* New York: Stewart, Tabori, Chang, 1991.

Morgan, Charles, Jr. *A Time To Speak.* New York: Harper and Row, 1964.

Nash, Diane. "Inside the Sit-Ins and Freedom Rides: Testimony of a Southern Student." In *The New Negro,* edited by Mathew H. Ahmann. Notre Dame, Ind.: Fides Publishers, 1961.

Parker, Arthur Harold. *A Dream That Came True: The Autobiography of Arthur Harold Parker.* Birmingham: 1932.

Peck, James. *Freedom Ride.* New York: Simon and Schuster, 1962.

Robinson, Jo Ann Gibson. *The Montgomery Bus Boycott and the Women Who Started It.* Edited by David J. Garrow. Knoxville: University of Tennessee Press, 1987.

Rowe, Gary Thomas, Jr. *My Undercover Years with the Ku Klux Klan.* New York: Bantam Books, 1976.

Rustin, Bayard. "The Great Lessons of Birmingham." In *Negro Protest Thought in the Twentieth Century,* edited by Francis L. Broderick and August Meier. Indianapolis: Bobbs-Merrill, 1965.

——. *Down The Line: The Collected Writings of Bayard Rustin.* Chicago: Quadrangle Books, 1971.

Simpson, James A. "Recollections of Life in Ruskin Colony." December 28, 1963. In possession of James E. Simpson, Birmingham.

Shuttlesworth, Fred L. "An Account of the Alabama Christian Movement for Human Rights." In App. B of "Goals and Techniques in Three Civil Rights Organizations in Alabama" by Jacquelyne Johnson Clarke. Ph.D. diss., Ohio State University, 1960.

Smith, Petric Justice [Elizabeth H. Cobbs]. *Long Time Coming: An Insider's Story of the Birmingham Church Bombing That Rocked the World.* Birmingham: Crane, 1994.

Vann, David. "Speech Delivered by Mayor David Vann." Duard LeGrand Conference, November 15, 1978. Tutwiler Collection of Southern History, Birmingham Public Library, Department of Archives and History.

Volker, Joseph F. *The University and the City.* New York: Princeton University Press, 1971.

Walker, Wyatt Tee. "Albany: Failure or First Step?" *New South.* 18, no. 6 (June 1963): 3–8.

Watters, Pat. *Down To Now: Reflections on the Southern Civil Rights Movement.* 1971. Reprint. Athens: University of Georgia Press, 1993.

Wilkins, Roy, with Tom Mathews. *Standing Fast: The Autobiography of Roy Wilkins.* New York: Viking Press, 1982.

Wiebel, A. V. *Biography of a Business.* Birmingham: United States Steel Corp., 1960.

Young, Andrew. "And Birmingham." *Drum Major* 1, no. 2 (Winter 1971).

——. *A Way Out of No Way: The Spiritual Memoirs of Andrew Young.* Nashville, Tenn.: Thomas Nelson Publishers, 1994.

Zukoski, Charles Frederick, Jr. "A Life Story." Manuscript, Birmingham Public Library, Department of Archives and History.

——. *Voice in the Storm: The Button Gwinnett Columns Written during the Civil Rights Struggles and Other Writings.* Edited by Lyn Safford Brown. Birmingham: Birmingham Public Library Press, 1990.

Newspapers and Periodicals

Alabama: The News Magazine of the Deep South
Atlanta Journal-Constitution
Birmingham Age-Herald
Birmingham News
Birmingham Post
Birmingham Post-Herald
Birmingham World
Business Week
Chicago Defender
Christian Science Monitor
Cleveland Call and Post
Montgomery Advertiser
Nashville Banner
Nashville Tennessean
Nation
New Orleans Times-Picayune
New Republic
Newsweek
New York Times
Pittsburgh Courier
Saturday Evening Post
Shades Valley Sun
Southern Living
Time
U.S. News and World Reports
Wall Street Journal
Washington Evening Star
Washington Post

Interviews, Transcripts, Films, and Recordings

"Birmingham Boys": Jubilee Gospel Quartets from Jefferson County, Alabama. Alabama Traditions, 101.

Blaik, Colonel Earl H. Oral interview by Charles T. Morrissey, December 2, 1964. JFK Library.

Kennedy, Robert F. Interview by John Barlow Martin, March 1, 1964. JFK Library.

——. Oral interview by Anthony Lewis, December 4, 1964. JFK Library.

Marshall, Burke. Oral interview by Anthony Lewis, June 20, 1964. JFK Library.

——. Oral interview by Glenn T. Eskew, New Haven, Conn., October 11, 1991. In author's possession.

"No Easy Walk, 1961–1963." *Eyes on the Prize.* Boston: Blackside, Inc., 1986.

Patterson, Governor John. Oral interview by John Stewart Montgomery, May 26, 1967. John F. Kennedy Library, Boston.

Reagon, Bernice Johnson. *Voices of the Civil Rights Movement: Black American Freedom Songs, 1960–1966*. Washington, D.C.: Smithsonian Institution, 1980.

Shuttlesworth, Fred L. Oral interviews by Glenn T. Eskew, Cincinnati, Ohio, December 1987, November 9, 1989. In author's possession.

Seeger, Pete. *We Shall Overcome*. Recorded Live at Carnegie Hall, June 8, 1963.

Stanford, Henry King. Oral interview by Glenn T. Eskew, Athens, Ga., June 1987. In author's possession.

Vann, David J. Oral interview by Glenn T. Eskew, Birmingham, December 20, 1994. In author's possession.

Books

Abbott, Carl. *The New Urban America: Growth and Politics in Sunbelt Cities*. 1981. Reprint. Chapel Hill: University of North Carolina Press, 1987.

Acton, Hul-Cee Marcus. *The Pierian Club of Birmingham: With Biographies of Members and Memories of East Lake*. Birmingham: Banner Press, 1962.

Ahmann, Mathew H., ed. *The New Negro*. 1961. Reprint. New York: Bilbo and Tanen, 1969.

Allen, Robert S., ed. *Our Fair City*. New York: Vanguard Press, 1947.

Armes, Ethel. *The Story of Coal and Iron in Alabama*. Cambridge, Mass.: The University Press, 1910.

Atkins, Leah Rawls. *The Valleys and the Hills: An Illustrated History of Birmingham and Jefferson County*. Woodland Hills, Calif.: Windsor Publications, 1981.

Auerbach, Jerold S. *Labor and Liberty: The La Follette Committee and the New Deal*. Indianapolis: Bobbs-Merrill, 1966.

Barefield, Marilyn Davis. *A History of Mountain Brook, Alabama, and Incidentally of Shades Valley*. Birmingham: Southern University Press, 1989.

Barnard, William D. *Dixiecrats and Democrats: Alabama Politics, 1942–1950*. 1974. Reprint. Tuscaloosa: University of Alabama Press, reprint 1985.

Barnes, Catherine A. *Journey from Jim Crow: The Desegregation of Southern Transit*. New York: Columbia University Press, 1983.

Bartley, Numan V. *The Rise of Massive Resistance: Race and Politics in the South during the 1950's*. Baton Rouge: Louisiana State University Press, 1969.

——. *The Creation of Modern Georgia: Second Edition*. Athens: University of Georgia Press, 1990.

——. *The New South*. Baton Rouge: Louisiana State University Press, 1995.

Bartley, Numan V., and Hugh D. Graham. *Southern Politics and the Second Reconstruction*. Baltimore: The Johns Hopkins University Press, 1975.

——. *Southern Elections: County and Precinct Data, 1950–1972*. Baton Rouge: Louisiana State University Press, 1978.

Bass, Jack, and Walter DeVries. *The Transformation of Southern Politics: Social Change and Political Consequences since 1945*. New York: Meridian Books, 1976.

Belknap, Michal R. *Federal Law and Southern Order: Racial Violence and Constitutional Conflict in the Post–Brown South*. Athens: University of Georgia Press, 1987.

Bennett, Lerone, Jr. *What Manner of Man: A Biography of Martin Luther King, Jr*. 1964. Reprint. Chicago: Johnson Publishing Co., 1968.

Bernard, Richard M., and Bradley R. Rice, eds. *Sunbelt Cities: Politics and Growth since World War II*. Austin: University of Texas Press, 1983.

Biles, Roger. *Memphis in the Great Depression*. Knoxville: University of Tennessee Press, 1986.

Birmingham Chamber of Commerce. *Industrial Birmingham*. 1929, 1938.

Bloom, Jack M. *Class, Race, and the Civil Rights Movement*. Bloomington: Indiana University Press, 1987.

Bond, Horace Mann. *Negro Education in Alabama: A Study in Cotton and Steel*. Washington, D.C.: Associated Publishers, 1939.

404

Braden, Ann. *The Wall Between*. New York: Monthly Review Press, 1958.

Branch, Taylor. *Parting The Waters: America in the King Years, 1954–63*. New York: Simon and Schuster, 1988.

Brauer, Carl M. *John F. Kennedy and the Second Reconstruction*. New York: Columbia University Press, 1977.

Broderick, Francis L., and August Meier, eds. *Negro Protest Thought in the Twentieth Century*. Indianapolis: Bobbs-Merrill, 1965.

Brooks, Bessie A. *A Half Century of Progress in Family Welfare Work in Jefferson County*. Birmingham: Roberts and Son, 1936.

Brownell, Blaine A. *The Urban Ethos in the South, 1920–1930*. Baton Rouge: Louisiana State University Press, 1975.

Bunche, Ralph J. *The Political Status of the Negro in the Age of FDR*. Edited by Dewey W. Grantham. 1940. Reprint. Chicago: University of Chicago Press, 1973.

Capeci, Dominic J., Jr., and Martha Wilkerson. *Layered Violence: The Detroit Rioters of 1943*. Jackson: University Press of Mississippi, 1991.

Carson, Clayborne. *In Struggle: SNCC and the Black Awakening of the 1960s*. Cambridge: Harvard University Press, 1981.

——. *The Eyes on the Prize Civil Rights Reader*. New York: Penguin Books, 1991.

——, gen. ed. *The Papers of Martin Luther King, Jr*. Vol. 1, *Called To Serve*. Berkeley: University of California Press, 1992.

——. *The Papers of Martin Luther King, Jr*. Vol. 2, *Rediscovering Precious Values*. Berkeley: University of California Press, 1994.

Carter, Dan T. *Scottsboro: A Tragedy of the American South*. Baton Rouge: Louisiana State University Press, 1979.

——. *The Politics of Rage: George Wallace, The Origins of the New Conservatism, and the Transformation of American Politics*. New York: Simon and Schuster, 1995.

Caudill, Harry M. *Theirs Be the Power: The Moguls of Eastern Kentucky*. Urbana: University of Illinois Press, 1983.

Chafe, William H. *Civilities and Civil Rights: Greensboro, North Carolina, and the Black Struggle for Freedom*. New York: Oxford University Press, 1980.

Chalmers, David M. *Hooded Americanism: The First Century of the Ku Klux Klan, 1865–1965*. New York: Doubleday, 1965.

Chappell, David L. *Inside Agitators: White Southerners in the Civil Rights Movement*. Baltimore: Johns Hopkins University Press, 1994.

Charlton, Louise O. *Official Proceedings of the Southern Conference for Human Welfare*. Birmingham: N.p., 1939.

Childers, James Saxon. *A Novel About a White Man and a Black Man in the Deep South*. 1936. Reprint. Tuscaloosa: University of Alabama Press, 1988.

——. *Erskine Ramsey: His Life and Achievements*. New York: Cartwright and Ewing, Publishers, 1942.

Clarke, Jacquelyne Johnson. *These Rights They Seek: A Comparison of the Goals and Techniques of Local Civil Rights Organizations*. Washington, D.C.: Public Affairs Press, 1962.

Clayton, Horace R., and George S. Mitchell. *Black Workers and the New Unions*. Chapel Hill: University of North Carolina Press, 1939.

Cobb, James C. *The Selling of the South: The Southern Crusade for Industrial Development*. Baton Rouge: Louisiana State University Press, 1982.

——. *Industrialization and Southern Society, 1877–1984*. Lexington: University Press of Kentucky, 1984.

——. *The Most Southern Place on Earth: The Mississippi Delta and the Roots of Regional Identity*. New York: Oxford University Press, 1992.

Cobb, James C., and Michael V. Namorato. *The New Deal and the South*. Jackson: University Press of Mississippi, 1984.

Cobb, James C., and Charles R. Wilson, eds. *Perspectives on the American South, Volume 3*. New York: Gordon and Breach, 1985.

405

Colburn, David R. *Racial Change and Community Crisis: St. Augustine, Florida, 1877–1980.* 1985. Reprint. Gainesville: University of Florida Press, 1991.

Cooper, Robert Weldon. *Metropolitan County: A Survey of Government in the Birmingham Area.* Birmingham: Birmingham Publishing Co., 1949.

Cotman, John Walton. *Birmingham, JFK, and the Civil Rights Act of 1963.* New York: Peter Lang, 1989.

Cowett, Mark. *Birmingham's Rabbi: Morris Newfield and Alabama, 1895–1940.* Tuscaloosa: University of Alabama Press, 1986.

Crawford, Vicki L., Jacqueline Anne Rouse, and Barbara Woods, eds. *Women in the Civil Rights Movement: Trailblazers and Torchbearers, 1941–1965.* Brooklyn, N.Y.: Carlson Publishing, 1990.

Culp, D. W., ed. *Twentieth-Century Negro Literature: Or a Cyclopedia of Thought.* Atlanta: J. L. Nichols and Co., 1902.

Daniel, Pete. *Breaking the Land: The Transformation of Cotton, Tobacco, and Rice Cultures since 1880.* Urbana: University of Illinois Press, 1985.

Daniels, Jonathan. *A Southerner Discovers the South.* New York: MacMillan, 1943.

Davis, Angela Y. *Women, Race, & Class.* New York: Vintage Books, 1983.

——. *An Autobiography.* 1974. Reprint. New York: International Publishers, 1988.

——. *Women, Culture, & Politics.* 1984. Reprint. New York: Vintage Books, 1990.

Dittmer, John. *Local People: The Struggle for Civil Rights in Mississippi.* Urbana: University of Illinois Press, 1994.

Dodd, Donald B., and Wynelle S. Dodd. *Historical Statistics of the South, 1790–1970.* Tuscaloosa: University of Alabama Press, 1973.

Doyle, Don H. *Nashville since the 1920s.* Knoxville: University of Tennessee Press, 1985.

Draper, Alan. *Conflict of Interests: Organized Labor and the Civil Rights Movement in the South, 1954–1968.* Ithaca, N.Y.: ILR Press, 1994.

DuBose, John Witherspoon. *Jefferson County and Birmingham, Alabama: Historical and Biographical.* 1887. Reprint. Easley, S.C.: Southern Historical Press, n.d.

Dykeman, Wilma, and James Stokely. *Seeds of Southern Change: The Life of Will Alexander.* Chicago: University of Chicago Press, 1962.

Eagles, Charles W. *Outside Agitator: Jon Daniels and the Civil Rights Movement in Alabama.* Chapel Hill: University of North Carolina Press, 1993.

——, ed. *The Civil Rights Movement in America.* Jackson: University Press of Mississippi, 1986.

Edwards, Charles W., ed. *Report of the Alabama Policy Conference on Industrial Planning for Alabama.* Birmingham: Alabama Policy Bulletin No. 3, 1937.

Egerton, John. *A Mind To Stay Here: Profiles from the South.* London: Macmillan, 1970.

Elovitz, Mark H. *A Century of Jewish Life in Dixie: The Birmingham Experience.* Tuscaloosa: University of Alabama Press, 1974.

Fairclough, Adam. *To Redeem the Soul of America: The Southern Christian Leadership Conference and Martin Luther King, Jr.* Athens: University of Georgia Press, 1987.

——. *Race and Democracy: The Civil Rights Struggle in Louisiana, 1915–1972.* Athens: University of Georgia Press, 1995.

Feldman, Glenn. *From Demagogue to Dixiecrat: Horace Wilkinson and the Politics of Race.* Lanham, Md.: University Press of America, 1995.

Fite, Gilbert C. *Cotton Fields No More: Southern Agriculture, 1865–1980.* Lexington: University of Kentucky Press, 1984.

Flynt, Wayne. *Poor But Proud: Alabama's Poor Whites.* Tuscaloosa: University of Alabama Press, 1989.

Forgacs, David, ed. *An Antonio Gramsci Reader: Selected Writings, 1916–1935.* New York: Schocken Books, 1988.

Forman, James. *The Making of Black Revolutionaries: A Personal Account.* New York: MacMillan, 1972.

Frady, Marshall. *Wallace.* New York: Meridian Books, 1970.

Frank, Andre Gunder. *Dependent Accumulation and Underdevelopment*. New York: Monthly Review Press, 1979.

Franklin, Jimmie Lewis. *Back To Birmingham: Richard Arrington, Jr., and His Times*. Tuscaloosa: University of Alabama Press, 1989.

Frazier, E. Franklin. *Black Bourgeoisie: The Rise of a New Middle Class in the United States*. 1957. Reprint. New York: Collier Books, 1962.

Frazier, E. Franklin, and C. Eric Lincoln. *The Black Church in America* and *The Black Church since Frazier*. New York: Schocken Books, 1974.

Garrow, David J. *Protest At Selma: Martin Luther King, Jr., and the Voting Rights Act of 1965*. New Haven: Yale University Press, 1978.

——. *The FBI and Martin Luther King, Jr.: From 'Solo' to Memphis*. New York: Norton, 1981.

——. *Bearing The Cross: Martin Luther King, Jr., and the Southern Christian Leadership Conference*. New York: Morrow, 1986.

——, ed. *Atlanta, Georgia, 1960–1961: Sit-ins and Student Activism*. Brooklyn, N.Y.: Carlson Publishing, 1989.

——, ed. *Birmingham, Alabama, 1956–1963: The Black Struggle for Civil Rights*. Brooklyn, N.Y.: Carlson Publishing, 1989.

——, ed. *Martin Luther King, Jr.: Civil Rights Leader, Theologian, Orator*. Brooklyn, N.Y.: Carlson Publishing, 1989.

——, ed. *The Walking City: The Montgomery Bus Boycott, 1955–1956*. Brooklyn, N.Y.: Carlson Publishing, 1989.

——, ed. *We Shall Overcome: The Civil Rights Movement in the United States in the 1950's and 1960's*. Vol. 3. Brooklyn, N.Y.: Carlson Publishing, 1989.

Giddings, Paula. *When and Where I Enter: The Impact of Black Women on Race and Sex in America*. New York: Morrow, 1984.

Goering, John M., ed. *Housing Desegregation and Federal Policy*. Chapel Hill: University of North Carolina Press, 1986.

Going, Allen Johnston. *Bourbon Democracy in Alabama, 1874–1890*. Tuscaloosa: University of Alabama Press, 1951.

Goldfield, David R. *Cotton Fields and Skyscrapers: Southern City and Region, 1607–1980*. Baton Rouge: Louisiana State University Press, 1982.

——. *Black, White, and Southern: Race Relations and Southern Culture, 1940 to the Present*. Baton Rouge: Louisiana State University Press, 1990.

Goodman, James. *Stories of Scottsboro: The Rape Case That Shocked 1930's America and Revived the Struggle for Equality*. New York: Pantheon Books, 1994.

Gorman, Ethel Miller. *Red Acres*. Birmingham: Vulcan Press, 1956.

Grafton, Carl, and Anne Permaloff. *Big Mules and Branchheads: James E. Folsom and Political Power in Alabama*. Athens: University of Georgia Press, 1985.

Graham, Hugh Davis. *The Civil Rights Era: Origins and Development of National Policy*. New York: Oxford University Press, 1990.

Graves, John Temple. *The Fighting South*. New York: Putnam, 1943.

——. *History of Southern Research Institute*. Birmingham: Birmingham Publishing Co., 1955.

Griffith, Barbara S. *The Crisis of American Labor: Operation Dixie and the Defeat of the CIO*. Philadelphia: Temple University Press, 1988.

Hall, Jacquelyn Dowd, et al., eds. *Like A Family: The Making of a Southern Cotton Mill World*. Chapel Hill: University of North Carolina Press, 1987.

Hamilton, Virginia Van der Veer. *Hugo Black: The Alabama Years*. Baton Rouge: Louisiana State University Press, 1972.

——. *Lister Hill: Statesman from the South*. Chapel Hill: University of North Carolina Press, 1987.

Hampton, Henry, and Steve Fayer. *Voices Of Freedom: An Oral History of the Civil Rights Movement from the 1950s through the 1980s*. New York: Bantam Books, 1990.

Harding, Vincent. *There Is a River: The Black Struggle for Freedom in America*. New York: Vintage Books, 1981.

407

BIBLIOGRAPHY

———. *Hope And History: Why We Must Share the Story of the Movement*. Maryknoll, N.Y.: Orbis Books, 1991.

Harris, Carl V. *Political Power in Birmingham, 1871–1921*. Knoxville: University of Tennessee Press, 1977.

Hass, Edward F. *DeLesseps S. Morrison and the Image of Reform: New Orleans Politics, 1946–1961*. 1974. Reprint. Baton Rouge: Louisiana State University Press, 1986.

Havard, William C., ed. *The Changing Politics of the South*. Baton Rouge: Louisiana State University Press, 1972.

Hoff, Nelson P. *Alabama Blue Book and Social Register, 1929*. Birmingham: Blue Book Publishing Co., 1929.

Holmes, Jack D. L., Sir. *A History of the University of Alabama Hospitals*. Birmingham: Birmingham Print Shop, 1974.

Hornady, John R. *The Book of Birmingham*. New York: Dodd, Mead, 1921.

Hughes, Langston. *Selected Poems of Langston Hughes*. 1959. Reprint. New York: Knopf, 1983.

Huie, William Bradford. *Mud on the Stars*. New York: L. B. Fischer, 1942.

Hunter, Floyd. *Community Power Structure: A Study of Decision Makers*. Chapel Hill: University of North Carolina Press, 1953.

———. *Community Power Succession: Policy-Makers Atlanta's Revisited*. Chapel Hill: University of North Carolina Press, 1980.

Inscoe, John C., ed. *Georgia in Black and White: Explorations in the Race Relations of a Southern State, 1865–1950*. Athens: University of Georgia Press, 1994.

Jacoway, Elizabeth, and David R. Colburn, eds. *Southern Businessmen and Desegregation*. Baton Rouge: Louisiana State University Press, 1982.

Jones, Bill. *The Wallace Story*. Northport, Ala.: American Southern Publishing Co., 1966.

Jones, Edward A. *A Candle in the Dark: A History of Morehouse College*. Valley Forge, Pa.: Judson Press, 1967.

Kelley, Robin D. G. *Hammer And Hoe: Alabama Communists during the Great Depression*. Chapel Hill: University of North Carolina Press, 1990.

———. *Race Rebels: Culture, Politics, and the Black Working Class*. New York: Free Press, 1994.

Key, V. O. *Southern Politics in State and Nation*. New York: Vintage Books: 1949.

King, Richard H. *Civil Rights and the Idea of Freedom*. New York: Oxford University Press, 1992.

Kirby, Jack Temple. *Rural Worlds Lost: The American South, 1920–1960*. Baton Rouge: Louisiana State University Press, 1987.

Kluger, Richard. *Simple Justice: The History of Brown v. Board of Education and Black America's Struggle for Equality*. New York: Vintage Books, 1977.

Krueger, Thomas A. *And Promises to Keep: The Southern Conference for Human Welfare*. Nashville: Vanderbilt University Press, 1967.

Kuhn, Clifford M., Harlon E. Joye, and E. Bernard West. *Living Atlanta: An Oral History of the City, 1914–1948*. Athens: University of Georgia Press, 1990.

LaMonte, Edward Shannon. *George B. Ward: Birmingham's Urban Statesman*. Birmingham: Oxmoor Press, 1974.

———. *Politics and Welfare in Birmingham, 1900–1975*. Tuscaloosa: University of Alabama Press, 1995.

Lasch, Christopher. *The True and Only Heaven: Progress and Its Critics*. New York: Norton, 1991.

Lawson, Steven F. *Black Ballots: Voting Rights in the South, 1944–1969*. New York: Columbia University Press, 1976.

Leighton, George R. *Five Cities: The Stories of Their Youth and Old Age*. New York: Harper and Brothers, 1939.

Lentz, Richard. *Symbols, the News Magazines, and Martin Luther King*. Baton Rouge: Louisiana State University Press, 1990.

Levy, Peter B. *Let Freedom Ring: A Documentary History of the Modern Civil Rights Movement*. New York: Praeger Press, 1992.

Lewis, David L. *King: A Critical Biography*. New York: Praeger Publishers, 1970.

Lewis, Ronald L. *Black Coal Miners in America: Race, Class, and Community Conflict, 1780–1980*. Lexington: University Press of Kentucky, 1987.

Lewis, W. David. *Sloss Furnaces and the Rise of the Birmingham District*. Tuscaloosa: University of Alabama Press, 1994.

Lewis, W. David, and Wesley Phillips Newton. *Delta: The History of an Airline*. Athens: University of Georgia Press, 1979.

Lincoln, C. Eric, ed. *Martin Luther King, Jr.: A Profile*. 1970. Reprint. New York: Hill and Wang, 1986.

Logue, John. *Boats Against the Current*. Boston: Little, Brown, 1987.

Lomax, Louis E. *The Negro Revolt*. New York: Signet Books, 1963.

McAdam, Doug. *Political Process and the Development of Black Insurgency, 1930–1970*. Chicago: University of Chicago Press, 1982.

McKiven, Henry M., Jr. *Iron And Steel: Class, Race, and Community in Birmingham, Alabama, 1875–1920*. Chapel Hill: University of North Carolina Press, 1995.

McLuhan, Marshall. *Understanding Media: The Extensions of Man*. New York: McGraw-Hill, 1964.

McMillan, Malcolm Cook. *Constitutional Development in Alabama, 1798–1901: A Study in Politics, the Negro, and Sectionalism*. Spartanburg, S.C.: Reprint Co., 1978.

McNeil, Genna Rae. *Groundwork: Charles Hamilton Houston and the Struggle for Civil Rights*. Philadelphia: University of Pennsylvania Press, 1983.

Manis, Andrew Michael. *Southern Civil Religions in Conflict: Black and White Baptist and Civil Rights, 1947–1957*. Athens: University of Georgia Press, 1987.

Marable, Manning. *Race, Reform, and Rebellion: The Second Reconstruction in Black America, 1945–1982*. 1984. Reprint. Jackson: University Press of Mississippi, 1989.

Martin, Harold H. *William Berry Hartsfield: Mayor of Atlanta*. Athens: University of Georgia Press, 1978.

——. *Atlanta and Environs: A Chronicle of Its People and Events*. Vol. 3. Athens: University of Georgia Press, 1987.

Meier, August. *Negro Thought in America, 1880–1915*. Ann Arbor: University of Michigan Press, 1966.

——. *A White Scholar and the Black Community, 1945–1965*. Amherst: University of Massachusetts Press, 1992.

Meier, August, and Elliott Rudwick. *CORE: A Study in the Civil Rights Movement*. Urbana: University of Illinois Press, 1975.

——, eds. *The Making of Black America*. Vol. 2, *The Black Community in Modern America*. New York: Atheneum, 1969.

Methodist Laymen's Union. *A Pronouncement*. Birmingham: 1959. Copy in Samford University Archives.

Miller, Marc S. *Working Lives: The Southern Exposure History of Labor in the South*. New York: Pantheon Books, 1980.

Miller, Randall M., and George E. Pozzetta, eds. *Shades of the Sunbelt: Essays on Ethnicity, Race, and the Urban South*. Westport, Conn.: Greenwood Press, 1988.

Mills, C. Wright. *The Power Elite*. New York: Oxford University Press, 1956.

Mohl, Raymond A., ed. *Searching for the Sunbelt: Historical Perspectives on a Region*. Knoxville: University of Tennessee Press, 1990.

Mohl, Raymond A., et al., eds. *Essays on Sunbelt Cities and Recent Urban America*. College Station: Texas A & M University Press, 1990.

Moore, Charles. *Powerful Days: The Civil Rights Photography of Charles Moore*. New York: Stewart, Tabori, Chang, 1991.

Moore, Geraldine. *Behind the Ebony Mask*. Birmingham: Southern University Press, 1961.

Moore, Winfred B., Jr., Joseph F. Tripp, and Lyon G. Tyler Jr., eds. *Developing Dixie: Modernization in a Traditional Society*. Westport, Conn.: Greenwood Press, 1988.

Morris, Aldon D. *The Origins of the Civil Rights Movement: Black Communities Organizing for Change*. New York: Free Press, 1984.

Murray, William M., Jr. *Thomas W. Martin—A Biography*. Birmingham: Oxmoor Press, 1978.

Myrdal, Gunnar. *An American Dilemma: The Negro Problem and Modern Democracy*. New York: Harper and Brothers, 1944.

Nixon, H. C. *Lower Piedmont Country: The Uplands of the Deep South*. 1946. Reprint. Tuscaloosa: University of Alabama Press, 1984.

Norrell, Robert J. *Reaping The Whirlwind: The Civil Rights Movement in Tuskegee*. New York: Knopf, 1985.

——. *James Bowron: The Autobiography of a New South Industrialist*. Chapel Hill: University of North Carolina Press, 1991.

[Norrell, Robert J.]. *"The Best People in the World Live in Wylam."* [Birmingham: N.p., n.d.]

——. *Birmingham's Lebanese: "The Earth Turned to Gold."* [Birmingham: N.p., n.d.]

——. *Elyton—West End: Birmingham's First Neighborhood*. [Birmingham: N.p., n.d.]

——. *The Italians: From Bisacquino to Birmingham*. [Birmingham: N.p, n.d.]

——. *The New Patrida: The Story of Birmingham's Greeks*. [Birmingham: N.p., n.d.]

——. *The Other Side: The Story of Birmingham's Black Community*. [Birmingham: N.p., n.d.]

Norton, Bertha Bendall. *Birmingham's First Magic Century: Were You There?* Birmingham: Lakeshore Press, 1970.

Nunnelley, William A. *Bull Connor*. Tuscaloosa: University of Alabama Press, 1991.

Orser, W. Edward. *Blockbusting In Baltimore: The Edmondson Village Story*. Lexington: University Press of Kentucky, 1994.

Painter, Nell Irvin. *The Narrative of Hosea Hudson: His Life as a Negro Communist in the South*. Cambridge: Harvard University Press, 1979.

Parris, Guichard, and Lester Brooks. *Blacks in the City: A History of the National Urban League*. Boston: Little, Brown, 1971.

Payne, Charles M. *I've Got the Light of Freedom: The Organizing Tradition and the Mississippi Freedom Struggle*. Berkeley: University of California Press, 1995.

Peake, Thomas R. *Keeping the Dream Alive: A History of the SCLC from King to the Nineteen-Eighties*. New York: Peter Lang, 1987.

Perry, Charles R. *Collective Bargaining and the Decline of the United Mine Workers*. Philadelphia: University of Pennsylvania Press, 1984.

Pierce, Neal R. *The Deep South States of America*. New York: Norton, 1974.

R. L. Polk and Co. *Polk's Birmingham City Directory, 1963*. Richmond, Va.: R. L. Polk and Co., 1963.

Powledge, Fred. *Free At Last?: The Civil Rights Movement and the People Who Made It*. New York: HarperCollins, 1991.

Pratt, Robert A. *The Color of Their Skin: Education and Race in Richmond, Virginia, 1954–89*. Charlottesville: University Press of Virginia, 1992.

Rabinowitz, Howard N. *Race Relations in the Urban South, 1865–1890*. Urbana: University of Illinois Press, 1980.

Raines, Howell. *My Soul Is Rested: Movement Days in the Deep South Remembered*. Reprint. New York: Bantam Books, 1978.

Reed, Merl E. *Seedtime for the Modern Civil Rights Movement: The President's Committee on Fair Employment Practice, 1941–1946*. Baton Rouge: Louisiana State University Press, 1991.

Robinson, Armstead L., and Patricia Sullivan, eds. *New Directions in Civil Rights Studies*. Charlottesville: University Press of Virginia, 1991.

Schlesinger, Arthur M., Jr. *A Thousand Days: John F. Kennedy in the White House*. Boston: Houghton Mifflin, 1965.

Schutze, Jim. *The Accommodation: The Politics of Race in an American City*. Secaucus, N.J.: Citadel Press, 1986.

Sharp, Gene. *The Politics of Nonviolent Action*. 3 vols. Boston: Extending Horizons Books, 1973.

Shouse, Sarah Newman. *Hillbilly Realist: Herman Clarence Nixon of Possum Trot*. Tuscaloosa: University of Alabama Press, 1986.

Sikora, Frank. *Until Justice Rolls Down: The Birmingham Church Bombing Case*. Tuscaloosa: University of Alabama Press, 1991.

Silberman, Charles E. *Crisis in Black and White*. New York: Random House, 1964.

Silver, Christopher. *Twentieth-Century Richmond: Planning, Politics, and Race*. Knoxville: University of Tennessee Press, 1984.

Silver, Christopher, and John V. Moeser. *The Separate City: Black Communities in the Urban South, 1940–1968*. Lexington: University Press of Kentucky, 1995.

Sims, George E. *The Little Man's Big Friend: James E. Folsom in Alabama Politics, 1946–1958*. Tuscaloosa: University of Alabama Press, 1985.

Sitkoff, Harvard. *The Struggle for Black Equality, 1954–1980*. New York: Hill and Wang, 1981.

Smith, Douglas L. *The New Deal in the Urban South*. Baton Rouge: Louisiana State University Press, 1988.

Sosna, Morton. *In Search of the Silent South: Southern Liberals and the Race Issue*. New York: Columbia University Press, 1977.

[Southern Research Institute]. *In Memoriam: Charles F. Kettering*. Birmingham: Southern Research Institute, n.d.

Speer, Robert E. *John J. Eagan: A Memoir of an Adventurer for the Kingdom of God on Earth*. Birmingham: Privately printed, 1939.

Spence, Ruth S. *Bibliography of Birmingham, Alabama, 1872–1972*. Birmingham: Oxmoor Press, 1973.

Stocking, George W. *Basing Point Pricing and Regional Development: A Case Study of the Iron and Steel Industry*. Chapel Hill: University of North Carolina Press, 1954.

Stone, Clarence N. *Regime Politics: Governing Atlanta, 1946–1988*. Lawrence: University Press of Kansas, 1989.

Strong, Donald S. *Registration of Voters in Alabama*. Tuscaloosa: University of Alabama Press, 1956.

Sullivan, Patricia. *Days of Hope: Race and Democracy in the New Deal Era*. Chapel Hill: University of North Carolina Press, 1995.

Taft, Philip. *Organizing Dixie: Alabama Workers in the Industrial Era*. Westport, Conn.: Greenwood Press, 1981.

Thomas, Mary Martha. *Riveting and Rationing in Dixie: Alabama Women and the Second World War*. Tuscaloosa: University of Alabama Press, 1987.

Thometz, Carol Estes. *The Decision-Makers: The Power Structure of Dallas*. Dallas: Southern Methodist University Press, 1963.

Thompson, Daniel C. *The Negro Leadership Class*. Englewood Cliffs, N.J.: Prentice-Hall, 1963.

Tindal, George. *Emergence of the New South*. Baton Rouge: Louisiana State University Press, 1967.

Tushnet, Mark V. *The NAACP's Legal Strategy against Segregated Education, 1925–1950*. Chapel Hill: University of North Carolina Press, 1987.

United Methodist Church. *Discipline*. N.p., 1956.

Vinson, James, and D. L. Kirkpatrick. *Twentieth Century Western Writers*. Detroit, Mich.: Gale Research, 1982.

Walker, Alyce B. *It's Nice To Live in Birmingham Because. . . .* Birmingham: Birmingham News Publishing Co., 1963.

Wallerstein, Immanuel. *Historical Capitalism*. London: Verso, 1987.

———. *The Capitalist World-Economy*. 1979. Reprint. New York: Cambridge University Press, 1989.

Ward, Brian, and Tony Badger. *The Making of Martin Luther King, Jr., and the Civil Rights Movement*. New York: New York University Press, 1996.

Washington, James Melvin, ed. *A Testament of Hope: The Essential Writings of Martin Luther King, Jr*. New York: Harper and Row, 1986.

Weiner, Jonathan M. *Social Origins of the New South: Alabama, 1860–1885*. Baton Rouge: Louisiana State University Press, 1978.

Weisbrot, Robert. *Freedom Bound: A History of America's Civil Rights Movement*. New York: Norton, 1990.

Whalen, Charles, and Barbara Whalen. *The Longest Debate: A Legislative History of the 1964 Civil Rights Act*. New York: Mentor Books, 1985.

Wheeler, Annie Ford. *Trinity United Methodist Church, 1889–1989*. Homewood: Trinity United
Methodist Church, 1989.
White, Marjorie Longenecker. *Downtown Birmingham: Architectural and Historical Walking
Tour Guide*. Birmingham: Birmingham Publishing Co., 1980.
——. *The Birmingham District: An Industrial History and Guide*. Birmingham: Birmingham His-
torical Society, 1981.
White, Marjorie L., and Carter L. Hudgins. *Village Creek: An Architectural and Historical Re-
sources Survey of Ensley, East Birmingham, and East Lake*. Birmingham: Birmingham Histor-
ical Society, 1985.
Whitfield, Stephen J. *A Death in the Delta: The Story of Emmett Till*. Baltimore: Johns Hopkins
University Press, 1991.
Wiggins, Sarah Woolfolk, ed. *From Civil War to Civil Rights: Alabama, 1860–1960*. Tuscaloosa:
University of Alabama Press, 1987.
Wilson, Charles Reagan, and William Ferris, eds. *Encyclopedia of Southern Culture*. Chapel
Hill: University of North Carolina Press, 1989.
Wood, Clement. *Nigger: A Novel*. New York: Dutton, 1922.
Woodward, C. Vann. *Reunion and Reaction: The Compromise of 1877 and the End of Reconstruc-
tion*. New York: Doubleday, 1956.
——. *The Strange Career of Jim Crow*. 1955. Reprint. New York: Oxford University Press, 1966.
——. *Origins of the New South*. 1951. Reprint. Baton Rouge: Louisiana State University Press,
1971.
Woofter, T. J., Jr. *A Study of the Economic Status of the Negro, Volume One*. Chapel Hill: Univer-
sity of North Carolina Press, 1930.
Wright, Gavin. *Old South, New South: Revolutions in the Southern Economy since the Civil War*.
New York: Basic Books, 1986.
Yarbrough, Tinsley E. *Judge Frank Johnson and Human Rights in Alabama*. Tuscaloosa: Univer-
sity of Alabama Press, 1981.
Zieger, Robert H., ed. *Organized Labor in the Twentieth-Century South*. Knoxville: University of
Tennessee Press, 1991.
Zinn, Howard. *SNCC: The New Abolitionists*. Boston: Beacon Press, 1965.

Articles

Alsobrook, David E. "Mobile v. Birmingham: The Alabama Medical College Controversy, 1912–
1920." *Alabama Review* 36, no. 1 (January 1983): 37–56.
Atkins, Leah Rawls. "Senator James A. Simpson and Birmingham Politics of the 1930s: His Fight
against the Spoilsmen and Pie-Men." *Alabama Review* 41, no. 1 (January 1988): 3–29.
——. "Growing Up around Edgewood Lake." *Alabama Review* 44, no. 2 (April 1991): 83–100.
Bains, Lee E., Jr. "Birmingham 1963: Confrontation over Civil Rights." In *Birmingham, Ala-
bama, 1956–1963: The Black Struggle for Civil Rights*, edited by David J. Garrow, pp. 151–289.
Brooklyn, N.Y.: Carlson Publishing, 1989.
Bartley, Numan V. "Writing about the Post-World War II South." *Georgia Historical Quarterly*
68, no. 1 (Spring 1984): 1–18.
——. "The Southern Conference and the Shaping of the Post-World War II Southern Politics."
In *Developing Dixie: Modernization in a Traditional Society*, edited by Winfred B. Moore, Jr.,
Joseph F. Tripp, and Lyon G. Tyler Jr. Westport, Conn.: Greenwood Press, 1988.
Bass, S. Jonathan. "Bishop C. C. J. Carpenter: From Segregation to Integration." *Alabama Re-
view* 45, no. 3 (July 1992), 184–215.
Beiman, Irving. "Birmingham: Steel Giant with a Glass Jaw." In *Our Fair City*, edited by
Robert S. Allen. New York: Vanguard Press, 1947.
Bracey, John H., Jr., and August Meier. "Allies Or Adversaries?: The NAACP, A. Philip Ran-
dolph, and the 1941 March on Washington." *Georgia Historical Quarterly* 75, no. 1 (Spring
1991): 1–17.

——. "The NAACP as a Reform Movement, 1909–1965: 'To Reach the Conscience of America.'" *Journal of Southern History* 59, no. 1 (February 1993): 3–30.

Braden, Anne. "The History That We Made: Birmingham, 1956–1979." *Southern Exposure* 7, no. 2 (Summer 1979): 48–54.

Breedlove, Michael A. "Progressivism and Nativism: The Race for the Presidency of the City Commission of Birmingham, Alabama in 1917." *Journal of the Birmingham Historical Society* 4 (July 1980).

Brownell, Blaine A. "Birmingham, Alabama: New South City in the 1920s." *Journal of Southern History* 38, no. 1 (February 1972).

Browning, Al. "The Fertile Fields of Gospel Music." *Alabama Magazine* 53, no. 5 (September–October 1989): 19–24.

Chalfen, Michael. "Rev. Samuel B. Wells and Black Protest in Albany, 1945–1965." *Journal of Southwest Georgia History* 9 (Fall 1994): 37–64.

——. "'The Way Out May Lead In': The Albany Movement beyond Martin Luther King, Jr." *Georgia Historical Quarterly* 79, no. 3 (Fall 1995): 560–98.

Corley, Robert Gaines. "In Search of Racial Harmony: Birmingham Business Leaders and Desegregation, 1950–1963." In *Southern Businessmen and Desegregation*, edited by Elizabeth Jacoway and David R. Colburn, pp. 170–90. Baton Rouge: Louisiana State University Press, 1982.

Couch, W. T. "Southerners Inspect the South." *New Republic* 97 (December 14, 1938): 168–69.

Dailey, Maceo Crenshaw, Jr. "Neither 'Uncle Tom' nor 'Accommodationist': Booker T. Washington, Emmett Jay Scott, and Constructionalism." *Atlanta History* 38, no. 4 (Winter 1995): 20–33.

Eskew, Glenn T. "Demagoguery in Birmingham and the Building of Vestavia." *Alabama Review* 42, no. 3 (July 1989): 192–217.

——. "The Alabama Christian Movement for Human Rights and the Birmingham Struggle for Civil Rights, 1956–1963." In *Birmingham, Alabama, 1956–1963: The Black Struggle for Civil Rights*, edited by David J. Garrow, pp. 3–114. Brooklyn, N.Y.: Carlson Publishing, 1989.

Fairclough, Adam. "The Preachers and the People: The Origins and Early Years of the Southern Christian Leadership Conference, 1955–1959." *Journal of Southern History* 52, no. 3 (August 1986): 403–40.

Fell, Charles A. "The Crash and the Moratorium." *Journal of the Birmingham Historical Society* 1, no. 1 (January 1960): 7–10.

Flynt, Wayne. "Religion in the Urban South: The Divided Religious Mind of Birmingham, 1900–1930." *Alabama Review* 30, no. 2 (April 1977): 108–34.

Foreman, Clark. "Decade of Hope." *Phylon* 12, no. 2 (1951): 138–42.

Fulkerson, Richard P. "The Public Letter as a Rhetorical Form: Structure, Logic, and Style in King's 'Letter From Birmingham Jail.'" In *Martin Luther King, Jr.: Civil Rights Leader, Theologian, Orator*, edited by David J. Garrow. Brooklyn, N.Y.: Carlson Publishing, 1989.

Giddens, Lucia. "The Happy-Go-Lucky Harlem of the South." *Travel* 53, no. 3 (July 1929): 40–44.

Harding, Vincent. "A Beginning in Birmingham." *Reporter*, June 6, 1963.

Harris, Carl V. "Stability and Change in Discrimination against Black Public Schools: Birmingham, Alabama, 1871–1931." *Journal of Southern History* 51, no. 3 (August 1985): 375–416.

Holley, Howard L. "Medical Education in Alabama." *Alabama Review* 7, no. 4 (October 1954): 245–64.

Holloway, Frank. "Travel Notes from a Deep South Tourist." *New South* 17, no. 7 (July–August 1961): 5–8.

Hornsby, Alton. "A City That Was Too Busy To Hate." In *Southern Businessmen and Desegregation*, edited by Elizabeth Jacoway and David R. Colburn, pp. 120–36. Baton Rouge: Louisiana State University Press, 1982.

Huntley, Horace. "The Rise and Fall of Mine Mill in Alabama: The Status Quo against Industrial Unionism, 1933–1949." *Journal of the Birmingham Historical Society* 6, no. 1 (January 1979): 5–13.

Ingalls, Robert P. "Antiradical Violence in Birmingham in the 1930s." *Journal of Southern History* 47, no. 4 (November 1981).

413

Jones, Lewis W. "Fred L. Shuttlesworth: Indigenous Leader." In *Birmingham, Alabama, 1956–1963: The Black Struggle for Civil Rights*, edited by David J. Garrow, pp. 115–50. Brooklyn, N.Y.: Carlson Publishing, 1989.

Lankford, Frank E. Foreword to *Journal of the Birmingham Historical Society* 1, no. 1 (January 1960): 1.

Leighton, George R. "Birmingham, Alabama: The City of Perpetual Promise." *Harper's Magazine*, August 1937.

McCallum, Brenda. "Songs of Work and Songs of Worship: Sanctifying Black Unionism in the Southern City of Steel." *New York Folklore* 14, nos. 1–2 (1988).

Manis, Andrew Michael. "Religious Experience, Religious Authority, and Civil Rights Leadership: The Case of Birmingham's Reverend Fred Shuttlesworth." In *Cultural Perspectives on the American South, Volume 5*, edited by Charles Reagan Wilson. New York: Gordon and Breach, 1991.

Martin, Charles H. "The Rise and Fall of Popular Front Liberalism in the South: The Southern Conference for Human Welfare." In *Perspectives on the American South, Volume 3*, edited by James C. Cobb and Charles R. Wilson. New York: Gordon and Breach, 1985.

Marx, Gary T. "Religion: Opiate or Inspiration of Civil Rights Militancy among Negroes?" In *The Making of Black America*, vol. 2, *The Black Community in Modern America*, edited by August Meier and Elliott Rudwick, pp. 362–75. New York: Atheneum, 1969.

Meier, August, "The Conservative Militant." In *Martin Luther King, Jr.: A Profile*, edited by C. Eric Lincoln, pp. 144–56. 1970. Reprint. New York: Hill and Wang, 1986.

Meier, August, and Elliott Rudwick. "The Origins of Nonviolent Direct Action in Afro-American Protest: A Note on Historical Discontinuities." In *We Shall Overcome: The Civil Rights Movement in the United States in the 1950's and 1960's*, edited by David J. Garrow. Brooklyn, N.Y.: Carlson Publishing, 1989.

Miller, Helen Hill. "Private Business and Public Education in the South." *Harvard Business Review* 38, no. 4 (July–August 1960): 75–88.

Mitch, William. "Labor's Depression Recovery." *Journal of the Birmingham Historical Society* 1, no. 1 (January 1960): 18–19.

Morgan, Roberta. "Social Implications and the Human Side." *Journal of the Birmingham Historical Society* 1, no. 1 (January 1960): 11–17.

Norrell, Robert J. "Caste in Steel: Jim Crow Careers in Birmingham, Alabama." *Journal of American History* 73, no. 3 (December 1986): 669–94.

——. "Labor at the Ballot Box: Alabama Politics from the New Deal to the Dixiecrat Movement." *Journal of Southern History* 57, no. 2 (May 1991): 201–34.

Osborne, George R. "Boycott in Birmingham." *Nation* (May 5, 1962): 397–401.

Painter, Nell Irvin. "Hosea Hudson and the Progressive Party in Birmingham." In *Perspectives on the American South, Volume 1*, edited by Merle Black and John Shelton Reed. New York: Gordon and Breach, 1981.

Payne, Charles M. "Men Led, But Women Organized." In *Women in the Civil Rights Movement: Trailblazers and Torchbearers, 1941–1965*, edited by Vicki L. Crawford et al. Brooklyn, N.Y.: Carlson Publishing, 1990.

Pettiford, W. R. "How to Help the Negro to Help Himself." In *Twentieth-Century Negro Literature: Or a Cyclopedia of Thought*, edited by D. W. Culp, pp. 468–72. Atlanta: J. L. Nichols and Co., 1902.

Reinhart, George R. "Racial Separation during the 1970s: The Case of Birmingham." *Social Forces* 58, no. 4 (June 1980): 1255–62.

Rice, Bradley R. "If Dixie Were Atlanta." In *Sunbelt Cities: Politics and Growth since World War II*, Rice and Richard M. Bernard, pp. 31–57. Austin: University of Texas Press, 1983.

Ricks, John A. "'De Lawd' Descends and Is Crucified: Martin Luther King, Jr., in Albany, Georgia." *Journal of Southwest Georgia History* 2 (Fall 1984): 3–14.

Rolinson, Mary Gambrell. "The Universal Negro Improvement Association in Georgia: Southern Strongholds of Garveyism." In *Georgia in Black and White: Explorations in the Race Rela-*

tions of a Southern State, 1865–1950, edited by John C. Inscoe, pp. 202–24. Athens: University of Georgia Press, 1994.

Scribner, Christopher MacGregor. "Federal Funding, Urban Renewal, and Race Relations: Birmingham in Transition, 1945–1955." *Alabama Review* 48, no. 4 (October 1995): 269–95.

Slogan, Patrick J. "The Day They Shut Down Birmingham." *Washington Monthly* 4, no. 5 (May 1972): 41–51.

Snow, Malinda. "Martin Luther King's 'Letter From Birmingham Jail' as Pauline Epistle." In *Martin Luther King, Jr.: Civil Rights Leader, Theologian, Orator*, edited by David J. Garrow. Brooklyn, N.Y.: Carlson Publishing, 1989.

Starr, Barton J. "Birmingham and the 'Dixiecrat' Convention of 1948." *Alabama Historical Quarterly* 32, nos. 1–2 (Spring–Summer 1970).

Stein, Judith. "Southern Workers in National Unions: Birmingham Steelworkers, 1936–1951." In *Organized Labor in the Twentieth-Century South*, edited by Robert H. Zieger. Knoxville: University of Tennessee Press, 1991.

Stoney, George C. "Southerners Write Their Own Prescription." *Survey Graphic: Magazine for Social Interpretation* 28, no. 1 (January 1939): 42–43.

Strong, Donald S. "Alabama: Transition and Alienation." In *The Changing Politics of the South*, edited by William C. Havard, pp. 427–71. Baton Rouge: Louisiana State University Press, 1972.

Thomas, Rebecca L. "John J. Eagan and Industrial Democracy at ACIPCO." *Alabama Review* 43, no. 4 (October 1990): 270–88.

Thompson, Robert A., Hylan Lewis, and Davis McEntire. "Atlanta and Birmingham: A Comparative Study in Negro Housing." *Studies* (1960).

Thornton, J. Mills, III. "Challenge and Response in the Montgomery Bus Boycott of 1955–1956." *Alabama Review* 33, no. 3 (July 1980): 163–235. Reprinted in *The Walking City: The Montgomery Bus Boycott, 1955–1956*, edited by David J. Garrow, pp. 323–79. Brooklyn, N.Y.: Carlson Publishing, 1989.

———. "First Among Equals: The Montgomery Bus Boycott." In *The Walking City: The Montgomery Bus Boycott, 1955–1956*, edited by David J. Garrow, pp. xix–xx. Brooklyn, N.Y.: Carlson Publishing, 1989.

———. "Municipal Politics and the Course of the Movement." In *New Directions in Civil Rights Studies*, edited by Armstead L. Robinson and Patricia Sullivan. Charlottesville: University Press of Virginia, 1991.

Walton, Norman W. "The Walking City: A History of the Montgomery Bus Boycott." In *The Walking City: The Montgomery Bus Boycott, 1955–1956*, edited by David J. Garrow, pp. 3–58. Brooklyn, N.Y.: Carlson Publishing, 1989.

Webster, Becky. "The Zukoski Planning Committee of Two." *Birmingham Magazine* (November 1984): 71–76.

Wilson, Bobby M. "Black Housing Opportunities in Birmingham, Alabama." *Southeastern Geographer* 17, no. 1 (1977).

Wilson, Franklin D. "The Ecology of a Black Business District." *Review of Black Political Economy* 5, no. 4 (Summer 1975): 353–75.

Wright, Gavin. "Economic Consequences of the Southern Protest Movement." In *New Directions in Civil Rights Studies*, edited by Armstead L. Robinson and Patricia Sullivan. Charlottesville: University Press of Virginia, 1991.

Dissertations, Theses, and Papers

Autrey, Dorothy. "The National Association for the Advancement of Colored People in Alabama, 1913–1952." Ph.D. diss., University of Notre Dame, 1985.

Bevis, John David. "Frank M. Dixon: Alabama's Reform Governor." M.A. thesis, Samford University, 1968.

Breedlove, Michael A. "Donald Comer: New Southerner, New Dealer." Ph.D. diss., American University, 1990.

Clarke, Jacquelyne Johnson. "Goals and Techniques in Three Civil Rights Organizations in Alabama." Ph.D. diss., Ohio State University, 1960.

Connerly, Charles E. "'One Great City': Birmingham's Struggle for Greatness through Suburban Annexation and Consolidation, 1890 to the Present," 1991, and "Federal Urban Policy and the Birth of Democratic Planning in Birmingham, Alabama, 1949–1974," 1991.

Corley, Robert Gaines. "The Quest for Racial Harmony: Race Relations in Birmingham, Alabama, 1947–1963." Ph.D. diss., University of Virginia, 1979.

Ellis, Ann Wells. "The Commission of Interracial Cooperation, 1919–1944: Its Activities and Results." Ph.D. diss., Georgia State University, 1975.

Emspak, Frank. "The Break-up of the Congress of Industrial Organizations (CIO), 1945–1950." Ph.D. diss., University of Wisconsin, 1972.

Feldman, Lynne Barbara. "A Sense of Place: Homeownership and Community-Building among African Americans in Smithfield, 1900–1920." M.A. thesis, Florida State University, 1993.

Fullerton, Christopher Dean. "Striking Out Jim Crow: The Birmingham Black Barons." M.A. thesis, University of Mississippi, 1993.

Harrison, Mary Phyllis. "A Change in the Government of the City of Birmingham: 1962–1963." M.A. thesis, University of Montevallo, 1974.

Holley, William Henry, Jr. "Employment Practices Relating to the Hard-Core Jobless: A Study of the Metropolitan Birmingham Area." Ph.D. diss., University of Alabama, 1970.

Huntley, Horace. "Iron Ore Miners and Mine Mill in Alabama, 1933–1952." Ph.D. diss., University of Pittsburgh, 1977.

Kelley, Robin D. G. "Resistance, Survival, and the Black Poor in Birmingham, Alabama, 1929–1970." 1991. In author's possession.

King, Jere C., Jr. "The Formation of Greater Birmingham." M.A. thesis, University of Alabama, 1936.

Kundahl, George G., Jr. "Organized Labor in Alabama State Politics." Ph.D. diss., University of Alabama, 1967.

LaMonte, Edward Shannon. "Politics and Welfare in Birmingham, Alabama, 1900–1975." Ph.D. diss., University of Chicago, 1976.

Leavy, Oliver W. "Zoning Ordinances in Relation to Segregated Negro Housing in Birmingham, Alabama." M.A. thesis, Indiana University, 1951.

McGinnis, Timothy Scott. "The Controversy and Division of First Baptist Church, Birmingham, Alabama, 1968–1970." Senior honors thesis, Samford University, 1990.

McKiven, Henry M. "Class, Race, and Community: Iron and Steel Workers in Birmingham, Alabama, 1875–1920." Ph.D. diss., Vanderbilt University, 1990.

MacNair, Ray Hugh. "Social Distance among Kin Organizations: Civil Rights Networks in Cleveland and Birmingham." Ph.D. diss., University of Michigan, 1970.

Meyer, Stephen G. "'Doing the Master's Business in Alabama': Residential Segregation in Birmingham and the First Dynamite Hill Bombings, 1947–1954." Paper read at the 1993 annual meeting of the Southern Historical Association. In author's possession.

Murray, Jim. "Interracial Communication in Birmingham, Alabama, and the Creation of Operation New Birmingham's Community Affairs Committee." 1990. In author's possession.

Nichols, Michael Cooper. "'Cities Are What Men Make Them': Birmingham, Alabama, Faces the Civil Rights Movement, 1963." Senior honors thesis, Brown University, 1974.

Nossel, Suzanne F. "Weathering The Storm: The Jewish Community in Birmingham, Alabama, during the Civil Rights Revolution." B.A. honors thesis, Harvard University, 1991.

Patton, Randall L. "Southern Liberals and the Emergence of a New South, 1938–1950." Ph.D. diss., University of Georgia, 1990.

Prestwood, Charles M. "Social Ideas of Methodist Ministers in Alabama since Unification." Ph.D. diss., Boston University, 1960.

Reagon, Bernice [Johnson]. "Songs of the Civil Rights Movement, 1955–1965: A Study in Cultural History." Ph.D. diss., Howard University, 1975.

Reed, Linda. "The Southern Conference for Human Welfare and the Southern Conference Educational Fund, 1938–1963." Ph.D. diss., Indiana University, 1986.

Richards, Johnetta. "The Southern Negro Youth Congress: A History." Ph.D. diss., University of Cincinnati, 1987.

Rikard, Marlene Hunt. "An Experiment in Welfare Capitalism: The Health Care Services of the Tennessee Coal, Iron, and Railroad Company." Ph.D. diss., University of Alabama, 1983.

Scribner, Christopher MacGregor. "The Housing Act of 1949: Birmingham as a Test Case." M.A. thesis, Vanderbilt University, 1992.

Snell, William Robert. "The Ku Klux Klan in Jefferson County, Alabama, 1916–1930." M.A. thesis, Samford University, 1967.

Stewart, George R. "Birmingham's Reaction to the 1954 Desegregation Decision." M.A. thesis, Samford University, 1967.

Straw, Richard Alan. "This Is Not a Strike. It Is Simply a Revolution': Birmingham Miners Struggle for Power, 1894–1908." Ph.D. diss., University of Missouri-Columbia, 1980.

Sullivan, Patricia. "Gideon's Southern Soldiers: New Deal Politics and Civil Rights Reform, 1933–1948." Ph.D. diss., Emory University, 1983.

Thompson, Jan Gregory. "The History of the Alabama Council on Human Relations from Roots to Redirection, 1920–1968." Ph.D. diss., Auburn University, 1983.

Underwood, Anthony Paul. "A Progressive History of the Young Mens Business Club of Birmingham, Alabama, 1946–1970." M.A. thesis, Samford University, 1980.

Vick, Mary-Helen. "A Survey of the Governing Body of Birmingham, Alabama, 1910–1964." M.A. thesis, Alabama College of Montevallo, 1965.

Walker, Eugene Pierce. "A History of the Southern Christian Leadership Conference, 1955–1965: The Evolution of a Southern Strategy for Social Change." Ph.D. diss., Duke University, 1978.

417

tute, 398 (n. 4); as councilman, 328; as
mayor, 334, 338–40, 370 (n. 54)
Atlanta, Ga., 367 (nn. 31, 34); and aviation,
168; and black policemen, 104–5, 368
(n. 42); racial reforms in, 13–14; and residential segregation, 347 (n. 1), 349 (n. 29);
rivalry with Birmingham, 366 (n. 29); voter
registration drives in, 31

Bailes, George Lewis, 143
Bailey, Melvin, 279, 281, 386 (n. 13)
Baker, Ella, 24–25, 27–32, 34–35, 146, 343–44
(n. 12)
Baldwin, Carl and Alexinia, 135
Bankhead, William B., 366 (n. 29)
Banks, Frazier, 140
Baptist Ministers Conference, 124, 377 (n. 2)
Barrett, Nathaniel A., 342 (n. 14)
Baton Rouge, La., 20
Baxley, William J., 322
Beard, Luke, 76, 137
Bedinger, R. D., 361 (n. 48)
Beiman, Irving, 105
Belafonte, Harry, 27, 215, 232, 238, 290

Bell, William, 339
Berg, H. A., 99, 101
Bergman, Walter, 156
Berkowitz, Abraham, 94, 166, 270, 283
Bernhard, Berl I., 387 (n. 44)
Bethel Baptist Chruch, 132, 142
Bevel, James, 383 (n. 75); and beginning of
Birmingham campaign, 242; on Birmingham campaign, 272, 313; marriage of, 381
(n. 50); and recruitment of students, 254,
261–63; and schoolchildren's march,
265–66, 272, 280
Bickerstaff, O. C., 60
Big Mules: and Button Gwinnett columns,
81; and Connor, 90–91, 309; challenges to,
167–68; end of consensus among, 279, 306,
307, 336, 364 (n. 2); and enforcement of
segregation ordinances, 91; and Marshall,
387 (n. 40); Morgan on, 167, 321; power of,
10–13, 177; Simpson and, 90; Smyer's revolt
against, 170–71, 174–75
Billingsley, Orzell, Jr., 72, 260; and ACMHR,
127; demands for reform by, 323; financial
contributions of, 375 (n. 32); and Jefferson
County Progressive Democratic Council,
395 (n. 47); legal defenses by, 143, 204; and
negotiations, 396 (n. 49); and restraining
order on Connor, 249; suit filed by, 384
(n. 78); support of Birmingham campaign
by, 385 (n. 3)

Billups, Charles, 7, 273; arrests and jail time
of, 150; and boycott, 225; and local movement, 315; meeting with Hanes, 271; and
schoolchildren's march, 276
Biracial solutions: CAC, 316–17; coalitions,
70, 269–70, 277, 284, 313, 325, 381 (n. 53),
393–94 (n. 36); and communication, 174–
76, 195, 198, 201, 272, 369 (n. 42); Shuttlesworth on, 395 (n. 45)
Birmingham-Age Herald, 80
Birmingham Board of Education, 308
Birmingham Business League, 350 (n. 33)
Birmingham Emancipation Association, 350
(n. 33)
Birmingham Housing Authority, 333
Birmingham-Jefferson County Housewives
League, 350 (n. 33)
"Birmingham Manifesto," 221
Birmingham Methodist Ministers Association,
112
Birmingham News, 87, 90, 93, 99, 101, 104–5,
106, 112, 118, 131, 145, 150, 153, 177, 179, 181,
186, 190–91, 269, 283, 313, 324, 325, 339, 355
(n. 12); on Birmingham campaign, 272;
on bus desegregation, 131; criticism of by
Abernathy, 252; criticism of police by, 160;
ignores civil rights protests, 199, 225, 252; on
negotiations, 389 (n. 79); on petition drive,
370 (n. 55); on selective buying campaign,
200; on vigilante violence, 80, 142
Birmingham Parks and Recreation Board, 369
(n. 48)
Birmingham Police Department, 92–104;
applicants for, 95–96, 103; and black
policemen issue, 104–5, 124, 325; corruption
in, 96; criticism of, 80, 95, 160; and Freedom Rides, 157; harassment of blacks in
bus boycott, 145–46; and negotiations, 313.
See also Police brutality
Birmingham Post-Herald, 81, 97, 101, 106, 150,
153, 179, 182, 186, 191, 222, 225, 228, 250, 253,
279, 325, 339; ignores civil rights protests,
199, 243, 252
Birmingham Realty Company, 112, 171, 195,
269
Birmingham-Southern College, 8, 149, 150,
166, 180, 255, 363 (n. 66), 384 (n. 82)
Birmingham Transit Company (BTC), 145
Birmingham World, 38, 71, 92, 104, 135, 196,
249, 350 (n. 39); on bus boycott, 135; criticism of by Abernathy, 252; criticism of by
Walker, 38; on direct action, 222; on housing issues, 63; and lack of support for Birmingham campaign, 260; on NAACP, 127

Blach's Department Store, 205
Blackwell, William, 142
Blaik, Earl "Red," 322, 323, 324
Blan, Ollie, 246
Blough, Roger, 177, 307, 391 (n. 15)
Blount, Winton M., 306, 391 (n. 10)
Bombings: of houses, 53–61, 79–80, 82–83, 131–32, 300, 319, 394 (n. 40); in postwar period, 12, 53; as reaction to ruling on *Browder v. Gayle*, 23; of Sixteenth Street Baptist Church, 318, 319–20, 390 (nn. 2, 3), 394–95 (n. 41)
Boutwell, Albert, 211, 253, 378 (n. 10), 393 (n. 29); background of, 189–90; and bi-racial committee, 325; on Birmingham riots, 304; on bombing of Sixteenth Street Baptist Church, 322; and *Brown*, 117; on Civil Rights Act, 396 (n. 52); defeat of Connor by, 216; legal defenses by, 94; meetings with Shuttlesworth, 324; and negotiations, 270, 279, 293, 313; on outside agitators, 222; reaction to schoolchildren's march, 266; sworn in as mayor, 247; on vigilante violence, 251
Bowman, Joseph H., 297
Bowman, W. A., 301
Bowron, J. Edgar, 247, 253
Boycotts: bus, 20–22, 129–46; Connor on, 390 (n. 1); effects of, 227–28, 274; of schools, 392 (n. 19). *See also* Selective buying campaign
Boykin, Joel A., 79
Boynton v. Virginia, 41, 365 (n. 20)
Braden, Ann and Carl, 347 (n. 1)
Bradley, Wade, 104, 358 (n. 63)
Branch, Taylor, 45–46, 210
Breckenridge, J. M., 382 (n. 60)
Britling Cafeteria, 217, 218, 223, 235, 251
Broadnax, John, 297
Brooks, Paul, 161
Browder v. Gayle, 22–23
Brown, B. S., 57
Brown, Charles H., 289
Brown, Christina, 97
Brown, E. H., 102
Brown v. Board of Education, 17, 106–19
Bruner, Earl, 166
Bryan, John E., 371 (n. 65)
Buchanan v. Warley, 347 (n. 2)
Bunche, Ralph J., 352 (n. 54)
Burnham, Louis E., 70
"Button Gwinnett" columns. *See* Zukoski, Charles F.
Byrd, Harry F., 106

Cabaniss, William J., 357 (n. 45)
CAC. *See* Community Affairs Committee
Cagle, Charles, 322
Capri, Mike, 390 (n. 3)
Capri, Vincent, 390 (n. 3)
Captain, Joseph E., Jr., 358 (n. 63)
Carawan, Guy and Candie, 273
Carpenter, C. C. J., 175, 243, 245
Carter, Asa Earl "Ace," 107, 114–18, 140, 360 (n. 27)
Carter, Bonita, 328
Catledge, Turner, 151
Celler, Emanuel, 293, 312
Censorship, 355 (n. 12)
Central Committee (ACMHR and SCLC), 233, 239, 261, 284–85
Chafe, William H., 350 (n. 36)
Chalfen, Michael, 346 (n. 53)
Chambers, Willis "Bugs," 328
Chambliss, Robert E. "Dynamite Bob": and Connor, 395 (n. 44); convicted of Sixteenth Street Baptist Church bombing, 322; Hanes defense of, 366 (n. 26); and house bombings, 60, 81; role in school desegregation, 319; role in train desegregation incident, 135
Champion, George, 177
Chandler, J. King, III, 103
Chesnut, Sam L., 59
Christian activism, 137–39, 219. *See also* Churches; Ministers
Churches: role in civil rights movement, 15, 16, 20, 87, 137–39, 335, 384 (n. 1). *See also* Ministers
Citizens' Committee, 99–101
Citizens' councils, 108–9, 114, 117, 175, 334
Citizens Federal Savings and Loan Association, 207
Citizens for Progress, 181–82
Citizenship Education Program (CEP), 19, 33, 40
Citizens' Steering Committee, 21
Citizens Veterans' Committee, 70–71, 356 (n. 33)
City of Birmingham v. Monk, 79, 82
Civil Rights Act (1964), 17, 299, 310–12, 326, 338, 392–93 (n. 26), 393 (n. 27), 396 (n. 52)
Clark, Jim, 281, 302
Clark, Leroy, 249, 252
Clark, Septima O., 33, 40
Class distinctions: in civil rights movement, 15–17, 30, 193, 196, 359 (n. 12), 379 (n. 27). *See also* Traditional Negro leadership class
Clemon, U. W., 198

Cobbs, Elizabeth, 394 (n. 40)
Coercive nonviolence, 227, 228, 315
Coffin, William Sloane, 283
Coleman, William R., 56
Coley, Thomas T., 250
Collins, Addie Mae, 319
Comer, Donald, 368 (n. 42)
Commission on Interracial Cooperation
(CIC), 176
Communist Party (CP), 70
Community Affairs Committee (CAC),
316–17, 326, 393–94 (n. 36)
Community Chest, 175
Congress of Industrial Organizations (CIO),
86, 108
Congress of Racial Equality (CORE), 15,
209; and Freedom Rides, 41, 155; and fund-
raising, 314; and March on Washington,
318; and SNCC, 36
Connor, T. Eugene "Bull," 117, 270; adultery
of, 97–98; and arrests of schoolchildren, 6;
background of, 89–91; on bonds, 238; and
bus boycott, 145; and campaign for mayor,
189; and Chambliss, 395 (n. 44); character
of, 102; end of political tenure of, 309; on
franchise, 108–9; and Freedom Rides,
161–62, 364 (n. 5); impeachment trial of,
98–101; intimidation of black community
by, 201; and morality, 91–92; and municipal
elections, 165–66; and municipal reform,
180, 186, 188, 247; nonviolent arrests by,
228; opposition to negotiations, 308; on
parade permits, 383–84 (n. 77); and park
desegregation, 147; and politics, 354 (n. 9);
and reaction to negotiations, 390 (n. 1); and
reelection as commissioner of public safety,
118; restraining order on, 249; on selective
buying campaign, 199–200; and Shuttlesworth, 150, 224; support for, 85; use of spies
by, 254–55, 377 (n. 4); use of violence by,
4–6, 266–68, 271; and vagrancy charges,
363 (n. 68); and zoning ordinances, 62, 67,
83
Connor v. Boutwell, 392 (n. 20)
Connor v. State, 371 (n. 60)
Conway, William C., 143
Cooper, Jerome A., 91, 104
Coppin, Ernest, 142
CORE. *See* Congress of Racial Equality
Cotton, Dorothy, 225, 233, 254; and Highlander Folk School, 40; and schoolchild-
ren's march, 262, 277, 385 (n. 7); and
SCLC, 38
Crawford, Henry, 249

Creative tension, 4, 210, 221
Creel, Robert, 366 (n. 26)
Cross, John H., 206; as member of black
elite, 396 (n. 49); and SCLC, 229, 235, 379
(n. 25); support of Birmingham campaign
by, 385 (n. 3)
Cruit, George E., 162, 364 (n. 12)
Crusade for Citizenship, 27, 28
Current, Gloster B., 351 (n. 44)
Currier, Stephen R., 41, 394 (n. 38)
Curry, Milton, Jr., 60

Dahl, Robert H., 342 (n. 12)
Daniel, Hugh, 391 (n. 16)
Daniel Payne College, 69, 148–50, 194
Darnell, Henry, 97, 101
Davis, A. L., 24
Davis, Mrs. A. S., 104
Davis, Angela Y., 57, 68, 83, 348 (n. 7), 354
(n. 71)
Davis, J. Mason, 329, 397 (n. 57)
Davis, Sammy, Jr., 232, 315
DeLaure, Mrs. R. D., 79
Detroit Council for Human Rights, 315
DeYampert, E. B., 67, 349 (n. 32)
Dial, Roper, 198, 203, 270, 284
Direct action, 34, 36, 205, 214, 283, 383
(n. 70); in bus issues, 129–30, 143; in
employment issues, 129; Freedom Rides as,
155; King on, 283; reasons for in Birming-
ham, 211; rejection of by traditional Negro
leadership class, 139, 222; Shuttlesworth on,
131; in sit-in movement, 148; Walker on,
226–27
Dixon, Frank M., 111, 183, 279
Doar, John, 163, 269, 286, 386 (n. 28), 387
(n. 44)
Dobbs, John Wesley, 14
Dogs, police. *See* Police brutality: and use of
police dogs
Dolan, Joseph F., 272, 279, 289
Donald, Thad, 94
Dorchester Conference, 209, 210, 315, 376
(nn. 37, 40), 377 (n. 47)
Dorman, Michael, 284
Dorsey, Ellen, 64
Dothard, William "Meatball," 263, 385 (n. 10)
Drennen, Alan T., Jr., 371 (n. 65)
Drew, Deenie, 206–7; and Central Com-
mittee, 233; as member of black elite, 396
(n. 49); and selective buying campaign,
199; and Shuttlesworth, 287; support of Bir-
mingham campaign by, 385 (n. 3); and
voter registration drives, 215

Drew, John J., 203, 206–7, 297; and ACMHR, 127; and Central Committee, 233; as member of black elite, 195, 396 (n. 49); and municipal reform, 186; and negotiations, 269, 284; support of Birmingham campaign by, 385 (n. 3)

Dukes, Frank, 176, 246, 396 (n. 49); and Anti-Injustice Committee, 373 (n. 18); background of, 194–95; and Hughes, 148; and merchants, 198; racial discrimination against, 372 (n. 3); support of Birmingham campaign by, 385 (n. 3); and traditional Negro leadership class, 201; and voter registration drives, 148–49

Dumas, Lawrence, 112, 113, 114

Durick, Joseph A., 244

Durr, Virginia, 90

Dynamite Hill, 8, 68, 83, 275, 284, 319, 322

Eagan, John J., 176

East Lake, 9, 87, 118–19, 166, 188, 191

Eddins, C. Floyd, 81

Edmonds, Henry M., 174, 368 (n. 39)

Eisenhower administration, 26, 29–30

Elections: for city commission, 102–3, 118, 358 (n. 65), 366 (n. 25); for commissioner of public safety, 118–19; mayoral, 189–90; municipal, 371 (nn. 63, 65); for municipal reform, 182, 186–88; municipal runoff, 165–66, 214–15, 366 (n. 25); on sports ordinance, 106

Elite: black, 15–16, 32, 35, 66, 69–70, 78, 138, 396 (n. 49) (see also Traditional Negro leadership class); white, 138 (see also Big Mules)

Elliott, Robert J., 49

Ellis, Talbot, 290

Ellwanger, Joseph W., 224, 378 (n. 13), 381 (n. 53), 396 (n. 49)

Employment, racial discrimination in, 85–86, 129, 198–99

Engel, William P., 171, 283, 368 (n. 37)

Engelhardt, Sam, Jr., 107, 114, 117

Ensley, 9, 64, 76, 119, 166, 169, 190, 226, 230, 250

Environmental Protection Agency (EPA), 326

Esdale, James, 238

Evans, Glenn V., 267, 273, 282, 386 (n. 19)

Evers, Medgar, 29

Fairclough, Adam, 46, 137, 393 (n. 27)

Fanaticism: among activists, 160, 242

Farley, Michael Lee, 321

Farmer, James, 155, 365 (n. 21)

Federal Bureau of Investigation (FBI), 61, 150, 322

Federalism, policy of. See Kennedy administration: and federalism

Fellowship of Reconciliation (FOR), 15, 21, 24, 35, 362 (n. 54)

Field Foundation, 40

Fields, U. J., 21, 39

First Baptist Church, 244, 245–46, 382 (n. 58)

First Southwide Institute on Nonviolent Resistance to Segregation, 33

Fisher, T. L., 383 (n. 75)

Flowers, Richmond, 396 (n. 50)

Floyd, Bart A., 115, 358 (n. 57)

Foley, Albert S., 222, 380 (n. 36)

Folsom, James E., 22, 82, 106–7, 366 (n. 24)

Ford Motor Company, 366 (n. 29), 367 (n. 31)

Forman, James, 228, 276, 277, 280, 286, 388 (n. 58)

Foster, John, 98

Franchise. See Voting rights

Franklin, Denson N., 394 (n. 40)

Frazer, Stanley, 109

Frazier, E. Franklin, 16–17, 350 (n. 36)

Freedom rallies, 314–15

Freedom Rides, 153–65; and Birmingham Police Department, 157; and Connor, 161–62, 364 (n. 5); effects of, 41–42, 165, 335–36, 363–64 (n. 2); first, 153–58; and Kennedy administration, 162–65, 365 (n. 19); and King, 163; and Marshall, 365 (n. 19); Supreme Court on, 41; and Vann, 366 (n. 27); and vigilante violence, 41, 153–56, 161–64, 375 (n. 32)

Freedom Train incident, 73

Fullerton, Grady, 382 (n. 60)

Fulton, Robert B., 241

Fund-raising, in civil rights movement, 215, 375 (n. 32); for bail money, 238, 284, 290; from freedom rallies, 314–15; and NAACP, 41; and property bonds, 380–81 (n. 44); and SCLC, 30, 38–41, 373 (n. 10), 374 (n. 26); Shortridge on, 375 (n. 32); Shuttlesworth on need for, 127

Gadsden, Walter, 268

Gandhi Society, 250, 347 (n. 75)

Gardner, B. C., 346 (n. 68), 353 (n. 59)

Gardner, Edward, 7, 233, 242; arrests and jail time of, 383 (n. 75); and beginning of Birmingham campaign, 219, 223; on blacks' rights, 197; on federal policy, 366 (n. 23); on local movement, 315; and negotiations,

269–70, 396 (n. 49); and schoolchildren's march, 283; support of Birmingham campaign by, 385 (n. 3); on vigilante violence, 159, 372 (n. 8)

Garrett, David "Little Buddy," 93–94

Garrett, R. B., 391 (n. 16)

Garrow, David, 46, 213, 347 (n. 75)

Gaston, A. G., 195, 351 (n. 47); and attempts to rebuke leadership of King and Shuttlesworth, 324; background of, 74; and Birmingham campaign, 231, 234, 239–40, 385 (n. 3); and bond for King and Abernathy, 290; and Central Committee, 233; conservatism of, 175; and franchise, 186; house of bombed, 394 (n. 40); as member of black elite, 351 (n. 48); and negotiations, 269, 274, 388 (n. 53); and schoolchildren's march, 261, 385 (n. 5); and Shores, 207; and Shuttlesworth, 198; Smyer on, 203; and white businessmen, 368 (n. 40)

German, William, 60

Givhan, Walter C., 107, 114, 117

Golden, John T., 371 (n. 65)

Goodgame, John W., Jr., 70, 137, 351 (n. 48)

Gordon, Blaine, Jr., 313

Gordon, Bob, 303

Gould, John J., 59

Grafman, Milton L., 243, 245, 374 (n. 24)

Graham, Billy, 381 (n. 54)

Graham, Henry V., 282

Granger, Lester B., 29

Grant, Vernon, 92–93

Graves, Bibb, 111

Gray, Fred, 22

Graymont–College Hills Civic Association, 59

Green, S. L., 58

Green, W. Cooper: on Birmingham's industrial development, 169; on charges against Connor, 99; and communications with Gardner, 353 (n. 59); and Methodists, 113; and pamphlet on race relations, 349 (n. 28); and park desegregation, 74–76; and Senior Citizens Committee, 278; suspension of Connor by, 60

Greenberg, Jack, 249, 252, 254

Green v. School Board of New Kent County, Virginia, 394 (n. 40)

Greer, William, 271

Gregory, Dick, 275, 283, 380 (n. 38)

Griffin, John N., 358 (n. 57)

Griggs, Willie J., 297

Griswold, Ferrell, 319

Grooms, Harlan Hobart, 144, 146, 178, 361

(n. 53); on park desegregation, 362 (n. 62), 369 (n. 49); on sports, 369 (n. 48)

Hagood, H. E., 56, 60–61, 78

Haley, William, 268–69

Hall, Charles W., 74

Hall, Mrs. J. E., 104

Hall, John Wesley, 322

Hall, Oliver B., 93, 95

Hall, Peter A., 72, 82, 385 (n. 3), 395 (n. 47), 396 (n. 49)

Hall, Will, 142

Hamer, Fanny Lou, 139

Hamilton, W. C. "Billy," 270, 284

Hancock, Marcus, 92, 97

Hand, John, 369 (n. 50)

Hanes, Art: and banishment of James, 205; campaign for mayor, 189; defense of Chambliss, 366 (n. 26); election as mayor, 166; and elections, 366 (n. 25); on King, 308; and Klan, 366 (n. 26); meeting with Billups and Walker, 271; and municipal reform, 247; and negotiations, 292–93; on park desegregation, 179–80; on Robert Kennedy, 308; and selective buying campaign, 200

Hann, James B. "Crack Hanna," 355 (n. 11)

Hanson, Clarence B., Jr., 145, 200–201, 283, 357 (n. 45)

Hanson, Ruth Lawson, 112

Hardin, Paul, 244

Harding, Vincent, xi, 287, 292, 365 (n. 21)

Harmon, Nolan B., 244

Harris, Carl V., 342 (n. 12)

Harris, George, 218

Harris, Henry, 77

Harris, James L., 218

Hartsfield, William B., 14, 168

Hawkins, Don A., 371 (n. 65)

Hayes, J. W., 383 (n. 75)

Hayes Aircraft Corporation, 108, 357 (n. 45), 366 (n. 26)

Head, James A., 171, 180, 368 (n. 37)

Heart of Atlanta Motel, Inc. v. United States, 396 (n. 52)

Helm, Harold, 177

Henderson, B. W., 61, 67, 80

Hendricks, Lola, 233, 297, 384 (n. 77)

Henry, Aaron, 29

Hess, Emil, 199, 300

Hibbler, Al: arrests and jail time of, 241, 381 (n. 48); participation in demonstrations by, 231, 236; performances by, 235, 380 (n. 38)

Highlander Folk School, 33, 40

426

428

Nixon, E. D., 20, 21
Nixon, John W., 127, 385 (n. 3)
Nonviolence. *See* Direct action
North Smithfield, 8, 54–56, 66, 79–80, 82
Norton, Edward, 284
Nunnelley, William A., 356 (n. 24), 363 (n. 1),
  364 (n. 5)

Odum, J. Edmund, 98, 99; "Odum Report,"
  99
Oliver, C. Herbert, 150, 196, 229, 233, 322
Ollie's Barbecue, 396 (n. 52)
Orange, James, 254
Outside agitators, 24, 42, 165, 222, 244
Overton, E. C., 313

Page, Marion, 43, 46
Painter, Willie B., 253
Palmer, J. L., 383 (n. 75)
Parham, Aileen, 290
Parham, Grosbeck Preer, 290
Parisian Department Store, 198, 199, 300
Parker, Jack, 321
Parker, Ralph E., 99, 135, 136
Parker High School, 69, 257, 262, 264
Parks: desegregation of, 74–76, 147, 178–81,
  351 (n. 49), 362 (n. 62), 369 (nn. 48–50)
Parks, Rosa, 20
Parsons, James, 96
Parting the Waters (Branch), 210
Patrick, Charles, 103
Patrick, Vernon, 166
Patterson, Floyd, 305
Patterson, John, 252; and election as governor,
  363 (n. 66); and Freedom Rides, 162–63; on
  NAACP, 22; and student activists, 149; and
  Wallace, 107
Patterson, Johnny, 313
Pattie, G. L., 94
Patton, W. C., 260, 396 (n. 49); as head of
  Alabama State Coordinating Association
  for Registration and Voting, 78, 395 (n. 47);
  and lack of support for ACMHR, 127; and
  leadership of NAACP, 72; and SCLC, 29
Payne, Milton, 268
Peck, James, 153, 155
Person, Charles, 153, 156
Persons, John, 369 (n. 50)
Petersburg (Va.) Improvement Association, 37
Pettiford, William Rufus, 69
Phifer, J. S., 140, 143–44, 197, 200, 379 (n. 26)
Pierce, Charles L., 99, 101–2
Pipper, M. W., 297
Pitts, Lucius Holsey: and biracial communi-

cations, 202, 223; on CAC, 316–17; and
  Central Committee, 233; and Crusade for
  Citizenship, 28; and negotiations, 270, 274,
  284–85; opposition to Birmingham cam-
  paign, 239–40; as president of Miles Col-
  lege, 195, 197; and support for movement,
  199, 372 (nn. 4, 8)
Pizitz, Isadore, 198, 202, 203
Pizitz Department Store, 198, 203, 217, 224,
  237, 251, 317, 374 (n. 24)
Pleasant Grove, 88, 331
Plessy v. Ferguson, 15
"Points for Progress," 274–75, 277, 285–86,
  291–92, 294, 300, 323, 326
Police. *See* Birmingham Police Department
Police brutality, 356 (n. 28); against African
  Americans, 92–95, 355 (nn. 18, 19); condemnation of, 92–93, 248, 293; and Hood
  case, 71; and Patrick case, 103–4; after negotiations, 313–14, 328; and reaction to house
  bombings, 57; and schoolchildren's march,
  5–6, 281; and use of police dogs, 212, 226,
  247, 268, 281, 302, 318, 378–79 (n. 18), 379
  (n. 19); against whites, 92–93, 393 (n. 30)
Poor People's Campaign, 331
Porter, John Thomas, 206, 383 (n. 75); and
  ACMHR, 378 (n. 12); on Central Committee, 233; on jail, 226; as pastor of Sixth Avenue Baptist Church, 223–24; on press, 385
  (n. 4); and sympathy march for King, 246
Powell, Adam Clayton, 27, 204
Powledge, Fred, 346 (n. 53)
Prayer Pilgrimage for Freedom, 26–27, 137
"Prayer Vigil for Freedom," 148–49
Preachers. *See* Ministers
Press:
—local, 145, 324; A. Woods on, 383 (n. 74);
  Abernathy dissatisfaction with, 252; black,
  23–24; blackouts on protests, 38, 224–25; on
  Brown, 106; criticism of, 224–25, 382 (n. 65);
  on negotiations, 389 (n. 79); on selective
  buying campaign, 200; on vigilante violence, 80
—national, 42; on Albany Movement, 46–47,
  51–52; inaccuracy of reporting by, 226–27;
  and loss of interest in movement, 261; on
  park desegregation, 179; and role in desegregation, 23; Salisbury article, 150–51; on
  schoolchildren's march, 265; Smith article,
  157; and weekly magazines, 272, 379 (n. 20)
Pritchett, Joe B., 358 (n. 57)
Pritchett, Laurie, 43, 46, 48, 52, 208
Progressive Democratic Association, 21, 350
  (n. 33)

429

worth, 324; background of, 61–62; and Central Committee, 233; as city council member, 338; financial contributions of, 375 (n. 32); and franchise, 77; and Gaston, 207; as head of Alabama Progressive Democratic Association, 353 (n. 56); house of bombed, 319, 394 (n. 40); and housing shortages, 54, 57, 60–61, 68–69; on Interracial Division of Jefferson County Coordinating Council of Social Forces, 175; and Jefferson County Progressive Democratic Council, 395 (n. 47); legal defenses by, 143, 223, 249, 252; and meetings with service economy representatives, 195; as member of black elite, 396 (n. 49); and Monk case, 82; and negotiations, 274, 284, 292; and park desegregation, 147; on segregated seating, 136; support of Birmingham campaign by, 385 (n. 3); as voter registrar, 328

Shortridge, W. E., 233; and ACMHR, 315; on fund-raising, 374 (n. 26), 375 (n. 32); and NAACP, 72, 73, 126–27, 196

Shuttlesworth, Fred L., 4, 27; and airport protests, 198; arrests and jail time of, 143–44, 150, 200, 241–42, 256, 373 (n. 10); at Atlanta SCLC conference, 25; background of, 122–24, 378 (n. 12); and beginning of Birmingham campaign, 219–21, 224; and Central Committee, 233; on conflict within black community, 359 (n. 12); contact with Kennedy administration, 159–60, 364 (nn. 11, 12), 379 (n. 26); criticisms of, 196–97; and Doar, 386 (n. 28); exclusion of by black elite, 196; and formation of ACMHR, 24, 125–27; and Freedom Rides, 156–58; on Gaston, 234–35; on hiring black policemen, 325; and injunctions; on judiciary, 238; and King, 52, 201–2, 205–6, 208, 209, 337–38, 363 (n. 69), 375 (n. 35), 388–89 (n. 66); and lawyers, 362 (n. 61); on "Letter From Birmingham Jail," 382 (n. 57); and Marshall, 288, 386 (n. 28); meeting with Smyer, 203–4; and mobs, 365 (n. 21); and NAACP, 124–25; on need for fund-raising, 127; and negotiations, 269–70, 293–94, 294–95, 389 (n. 76); nonviolence taught by, 131; and park desegregation, 147; on participants in Birmingham campaign, 235; participation of in Prayer Pilgrimage, 137; as "race man," 32–33, 360 (n. 30); radicalism of, 27, 32–33, 205, 208; and reaction to settlement of Birmingham campaign, 287–89; reaction to Sixteenth Street Baptist Church bombing, 322; and schoolchildren's march,

263–64, 265, 280; and SCLC, 315–16; on sit-in movement, 36; support for, 324–25; on traditional Negro leadership class, 127; and train desegregation incident, 135–36; use of direct action by, 6–7; and vigilante violence, 132, 141–42, 159, 374 (n. 25); and voter registration drives, 249; on Walker, 197, 214–15, 384 (n. 78); Young on, 208

Shuttlesworth, Patricia Ann, 140

Shuttlesworth, Ruby Fredricka, 140

Shuttlesworth, Ruby Keeler, 122, 132

Shuttlesworth v. Birmingham, 361 (n. 44), 384 (n. 77)

Simmons, Julia, 65

Simpson, James A., 189, 247; background of, 90–91; on merger issues, 183, 396 (n. 52); on municipal reform, 188, 371 (n. 60); on segregation, 62

Sims, Larry Joe, 321

Sims, M. O., 178

Sinatra, Frank, 315

Singer, Paul L., 103

Siniard, J. W., 103

Sit-in movement, 217, 223, 337, 377 (n. 1); in Albany, 43–44; in Birmingham, 217–18, 235, 317; nature of, 312; in North Carolina, 36, 148; and students, 41–42, 194

Sitton, Claude, 388 (n. 48)

Sixteenth Street Baptist Church, 69, 76, 137, 229, 230, 235, 242, 249, 264, 266, 270, 275, 278, 280, 282, 283, 308, 338; joins movement, 229

—bombing of, 318–22; effect of on movement, 394–95 (n. 41); King on, 390 (n. 3); Klan informant on, 390 (n. 2)

Sixth Avenue Baptist Church, 137, 223, 238, 254, 256, 290, 305

Sixth Avenue Zion Hill Baptist Church, 240

Skipper, Howard, 170

Smiley, Glenn E., 21, 24, 209, 362 (n. 54)

Smith, C. K. Erskine, 166, 182, 256, 277, 321, 388 (n. 53), 395 (n. 43)

Smith, Craig, 391 (n. 16)

Smith, Howard K., 157

Smith, Nelson H., Jr., 383 (n. 75); and bus boycott, 130, 146; and Central Committee, 233; and draft of "Birmingham Manifesto," 221; on jail, 226; as member of black elite, 396 (n. 49); support for movement, 7, 125, 126; and sympathy march for King, 246

Smith, "Pete," 394 (n. 40)

Smithfield Court Housing Project for Negroes, 54, 65, 68

Smyer, Edgar Jones, 111, 370 (n. 51)
Smyer, Rufus Brandon, 111
Smyer, Shuford Brandon, 111
Smyer, Sidney W., 79, 198; background of, 111–12; on Birmingham riots, 303–4; on demonstrations, 367 (n. 36); and economic reform, 170–71, 174–75, 178; election of to state house, 354 (n. 9); and governmental reform, 178; meetings with civil rights leaders, 203–4, 235–36; and negotiations, 252, 256, 269–70, 270, 274, 279, 284, 295, 306, 388 (n. 53); and park desegregation, 369 (n. 50); and resistance to *Brown*, 109; role in desegregation, 13, 14
Smyer, Sidney W., Jr., 112
SNCC. *See* Student Nonviolent Coordinating Committee.
Social Workers Council, 350 (n. 33)
Sorensen, Theodore, 310
Southern Christian Leadership Conference (SCLC), 15, 229, 235, 379 (n. 25); administrative problems of, 42; advisers to, 25; and Albany Movement, 44, 50–51; in Birmingham, 4, 19–20, 37–40, 201–2, 209, 219; Birmingham campaign effect on, 314; Birmingham campaign strategy and goals of, 211–14; board meetings of, 263; comparisons with NAACP, 27, 29; critics of, 223; early days of, 27–29; formation of, 24, 26, 136, 207–8; and fund-raising, 30, 38–41, 373 (n. 10), 374 (n. 26); Norfolk meetings of, 30; objectives of, 27–29, 33, 225–26; public opinion of, 398 (n. 2); role of, 16, 17; and sit-in movement, 36; and SNCC, 36, 44–45; staff of, 30, 37–38; tactical contradictions in, 255; white response to campaign of, 250–51
Southern Conference for Human Welfare, 91, 360 (n. 40)
Southern Crafts, Inc., 108
Southern Negro Leaders' Conference on Transportation and Nonviolent Integration, 26
Southern Regional Council (SRC), 40, 77, 176, 177
Southern Research Institute (SRI), 170
Spencer, William, III, 307
Sports: desegregation of, 74–76, 105–6, 357 (n. 39), 369 (n. 48)
Stallings, Earl, 244, 246
Stanford, Henry King, 149, 180, 363 (n. 66), 384 (n. 82)
State troopers, 228, 281, 282, 289, 301, 321
Steele, C. K., 24, 25, 131

Steele v. Louisville and Nashville Railroad Company et al., 61
Stephens, Elton B., 391 (n. 16)
Sterne, Mervyn H., 99, 101, 174, 357 (n. 45), 369 (n. 50)
Stockham, Richard J., 112, 113
Stride Toward Freedom (King), 30
Strong, Donald S., 353 (n. 56)
Student Nonviolent Coordinating Committee (SNCC), 15; formation of, 36; and March on Washington, 318, 331; and tensions with SCLC, 44–45; and traditional Negro leadership class, 48; and Voter Education Project, 41
Students: and Albany Movement, 49; and Anti-Injustice Committee, 195, 198, 373 (n. 18); and Freedom Rides, 41–42, 161; Muse on, 372 (n. 1); role of in desegregation, 36, 148–50, 254, 297; and selective buying campaign, 198–201; similarities to ACMHR, 335; and sit-in movement, 41–42, 194; white, 384 (n. 82). *See also* Schoolchildren's march; Student Nonviolent Coordinating Committee
Supreme Court (Ala.), 309, 371 (n. 60)
Supreme Court (U.S.): on parade permits, 384 (n. 77); ruling in *Browder v. Gayle*, 23; on school desegregation, 394 (n. 40); on segregated seating, 130, 197; on zoning ordinances, 347 (n. 2)

Taconic Foundation, 40–41
Taggart, Ernest W., 73, 74, 196, 325, 351 (n. 46)
Tate, Greye, 99
Taylor, George P., 166, 170, 183
Taylor, Glen, 363 (n. 68)
Tennessee Coal, Iron, and Railroad Company (TCI), 10–11, 62, 90, 91, 108, 166, 168–69, 174, 175, 180, 188, 250, 306, 326. *See also* U.S. Steel Corporation
Terry, Bill, 397 (n. 52)
Thirgood Colored Methodist Episcopal Church, 224, 246, 276
Thomas, Amie, 59
Thomas, Darius A., 112
Thomas, Henry, 161
Thompson, Daniel C., 17, 350 (n. 34), 360 (n. 30)
Thompson, Hall W., 339, 398 (n. 3)
Thompson, J. J., 80
Thompson, R. Dupont, 99
Thornton, J. Mills, III, 363 (n. 2)
Tilley, John L., 30–31, 344 (n. 25)